D0204966

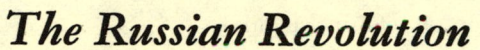

The Russian Revolution

John L. H. Keep

Professor of Russian History at the University of Toronto

The Russian
Revolution

A Study in Mass Mobilization

 *W·W·Norton & Company·Inc·* NEW YORK

Contents

Introduction

This book seeks to show how and why the Russian revolution of 1917, an elemental popular movement inspired by the most egalitarian and libertarian ideals, gave birth to the twentieth century's most durable dictatorship.

Despite all the changes wrought in Soviet life over more than half a century, the ruling Communist party still remains remarkably faithful to the basic assumptions of the Leninist era. As the world's leading exponent of 'scientific communism', it aspires to direct man's progress towards goals which it holds to be historically predetermined. These ideological pretensions have not gone unchallenged, either outside or inside the USSR. Yet, as Soviet dissidents have recently pointed out, the fact that they are put forward in all seriousness, and are backed by a powerful coercive apparatus, is a major international reality of our time.

The historian cannot but be fascinated by the circumstances in which the Soviet single-party State was born. Countless books have been written about the Russian revolution and its antecedents. However, we still lack a comprehensive account of the events of 1917. There are good reasons for this. Such a work could be written only if Soviet archives for this period were opened freely to non-Communist investigators, and only after many more preliminary studies have been made, for the literature, although vast, is uneven in scope and quality, and many of the most important questions remain obscure.

The present volume does not therefore offer a complete or definitive history of the revolution.[1] Nor does it contain a full account of the role played in that revolution by the Bolsheviks – the radical Social Democrats who proudly took the name 'Communist' a few months after they seized power. Such a work would probably be superfluous, since there is no shortage of English-language studies of Lenin and Leninism, to which one may confidently refer the reader;[2] several more monographs on the subject are in preparation. The party-political struggles in Petrograd between February and October 1917, when Russia was nominally ruled by a succession of coalition cabinets (commonly referred to as 'the Provisional Government'), have also been treated with expertise in a number of historical works.[3] Indeed, so familiar is the picture they draw, regardless of their authors' political orientation, that one can almost speak of a consensus on the reasons for that government's poor showing and the collapse of Russian democracy.

What has so far been lacking in the scholarly literature, at least in English, is a study of the 'lower depths' of Russian society in 1917, of those who were the actual makers of the revolution if not its ultimate beneficiaries. Soviet historians, to be sure, have written at length about the 'popular masses', but the value of their work is limited by the narrow ideological restrictions within which it has to be constrained. The canons of orthodoxy demand that the common people be portrayed as inherently revolutionary and devoted to the party; all too often they are reduced to mere stereotypes, and it requires an effort of will to remember that we are dealing with real individuals.

If this volume has any heroes, they are the ordinary men and women caught up in great events over which they had no control, to whom the revolution brought not only intoxicating political opportunities but also difficulties, danger, perhaps even death. These common folk have left no memoirs; their presence often goes un-documented and has to be reconstituted by an act of imagination. One may distinguish between them and those individuals who took a more active part in political life as strikers, demonstrators, rioters or rank-and-file members of some organization; and again between the latter and activists who had some party-political commitment. Such distinctions are important since they tend to become blurred in the more romantic accounts, which would have us believe that there were no intermediate strata worthy of attention between the 'grey faceless masses' and the leaders at the summit, and that the revolution was the product of their almost mystical interaction. Reality, alas, is more prosaic. And our natural concern with the exhilarating triumphs of popular creativity should not blind us to the social distress that accompanied the upheaval: to the prevalence of hunger, epidemic disease and unemployment, which brought about massive shifts of population. In these disturbed conditions the cruder forms of violence flourished. Many ordinary people in town and country, suddenly freed from customary social restraints, sought to advance their interests by whatever means came to hand. This, too, is an essential part of the narrative. Without condoning such actions, which were often unnecessarily brutal, the historian must try to understand the circumstances that caused them to be perpetrated.

Chaos and anarchy are the words which best describe the state of Russia during 1917. Yet amidst the confusion engendered by the war and the dissolution of the political, social and economic system certain processes were under way which determined the shape of the new order. It is upon these developments that our attention will primarily be focused. In particular we shall consider the role played by the mass organizations: the soviets (councils) of workers' and soldiers' deputies in the towns and their rural counterparts, together with their various offshoots, as well as other such self-constituted bodies: trade unions, factory committees and militia bands. This was where the pulse of revolution beat most strongly. At the lowest level these organs gave a modest element of structure to the inchoate and disorderly mass movement. What was more important, they brought a large segment of the population into contact with political activists, who subjected them to sustained propaganda and agitation; it was here that these more articulate elements had a chance to voice the masses' real or presumed aspirations and to project them to the outside world. These organizations were forums in which potential leaders could acquire a following, clientele or base. In the development of the revolution they performed a supremely important role as organs of mass mobilization. Without them the impact of the political parties would have been confined to the social élite, since their active membership consisted in the main of intellectuals.

All parties except those on the right of the political spectrum endeavoured to gain influence over the mass organizations. Where they were successful in bringing them under their control they could often direct them into the channels they desired without the rank-and-file members fully realizing what was afoot: namely, that their organization was losing its former autonomy and pursuing different goals, prescribed for it from without. As we shall see, in this political game Lenin's party, with its well-articulated organizational philosophy, had no equal. More than any other factor, it was the Bolsheviks' ability to capture the energies contained in the most important of these bodies that brought them victory in the struggle for power.

After October 1917 those mass organizations which opposed the Bolsheviks were eliminated from the scene, while those that survived rapidly became pillars of the new Soviet establishment. The term 'soviet' ought more properly to be enclosed within inverted commas, for the real locus of power under the new regime did not lie in the mass organizations, from which it derived an appearance of legitimacy, but in the upper echelons of the Communist party leadership; in these early years there were many central policy-making bodies inside and outside the formal government structure (headed by the Council of People's Commissars), but all of them took their cue from the leading organs of the CPSU. Several years later Stalin would refer to the mass organizations, in a celebrated phrase, as the 'transmission belts' by means of which the ruling party communicated its directives to the working people; and this essentially is the role they still play today. In the revolutionary period the future pattern of subordination was evident only in embryo. As yet the soviets, trade unions and so on preserved a certain amount of their original autonomy and their leaders had their own ideas about the nature of the social transformation under way. Yet the movement towards a single-centred structure of authority proceeded apace with relentless logic, almost as if pre-ordained.

Franz Borkenau has written of 'the law of the two-fold development of revolutions: they begin as anarchistic movements against the bureaucratic state organization, which they inevitably destroy; they continue by setting in its place another, in most cases a stronger, bureaucratic organization, which suppresses all free mass movements.'[4] Whether this process should indeed be considered a societal law, and whether there is any way whereby 'Thermidor' may be avoided, are questions best left to revolutionary theorists and to social philosophers. We are concerned here merely to examine the phenomenon as it occurred in one particular historical context.

The author of a recent monograph on Russian liberalism during the revolutionary period (which came to hand when the manuscript of this book was already complete) remarks that 'we still have much to learn about . . . the revolution as a social (as distinct from political) process, its development in the provinces, the form or composition of crucial local organizations and groups, [and] the influence of such factors as wage levels or socio-economic status on urban political affiliation.'[5] If some light has been shed on these questions in the pages that follow, this volume will have served its purpose.

Several objections may be raised to the approach taken here. First there is the view – almost general among Russian politicians in 1917, especially those of the democratic left and centre – that in a time of revolutionary flux what matters most is the articulation and dissemination of ideas. Leadership, we may be told, involves understanding the mood of the masses, appealing to their emotions by devising appropriate programmes, encapsulating these in slogan form, and broadcasting these ideas as widely as possible; in this way a successful revolutionary party may whip up immense popular enthusiasm for its policies, provided that they correspond to the fickle temper of the crowd. If this is so, should not the historian direct his attention to the rhetoric which issued forth from Petrograd in such a steady stream, compare the various viewpoints expressed, analyse the propaganda instruments available to each, and seek to discover how far these messages were relevant to the aspirations of different segments of the public?

This argument may be disposed of without much difficulty. Historians have already dealt at length with what was said in 1917. To be sure, a technical study of what Communists call *agitprop* may prove to be rewarding, and efforts have indeed recently been undertaken in this direction.[6] However, one may doubt whether this line of investigation can take us very far, and at its least successful it may simply prove the obvious: for example, that the most radicalized elements were attracted to the most extreme ideas. History has passed its own verdict on the orators of the Russian revolution. It should by now be obvious that, in order to derive lasting political benefit from the transient goodwill of a crowd, organizing ability is of the essence. The Bolsheviks for their part were in no danger of overlooking this precept. They were quick to capitalize upon any vote which went in their favour at some mass gathering by forming their supporters into a group with some measure of discipline, prepared to assume a leadership role. If they succeeded in doing this where their rivals so often failed, this was only in part due to the superior popular appeal of their propaganda; it was also the result of the emphasis they laid upon the 'organizational weapon', which they often handled to deadly effect. Thus the content, style and modes of transmission of propaganda are certainly valid subjects of research, but they are best studied in an institutional context.

A more powerful objection is one that might be made, not by a believer in the force of the written or spoken word, but by a fervent anti-revolutionary. Can we speak of regularly functioning institutions in a revolutionary situation, when destruction and anarchy are the order of the day? Even if one grants that the study of organizations is worth while, are not such bodies in the nature of things so ephemeral, so amorphous, as to render any examination of them precarious and any conclusions highly tentative? Furthermore, are not revolutionaries notorious mythologizers, who seek to envelop their activities in an aura of make-believe in order to persuade themselves and others of their legitimacy, and who present as solid popular-based bodies what are in reality but tiny sects or coteries? In taking such organizations at face value, may we not fall victim to deception?

These are indeed real difficulties, but they are not insuperable. They oblige the investigator to engage in painstaking research in order to separate fact from fiction. Anyone seeking to probe into the lower depths of Russian political life in 1917 requires a keen scalpel and an ample reserve of patience: he must dissect what seems to be a homogeneous organization into its constituent parts and locate the actual whereabouts of its directing centre; he must follow closely its evolution in time in order to discern subtle shifts in the degree of membership participation ('democracy'); he must seek out obscure organizational details hidden from the casual observer. Such problems are not, of course, unique to historians of the Russian revolution, although they are perhaps of unusual magnitude owing to the nature of the available source material.

A second point that may be made in refutation of this argument is that anarchy and disorder are dominant characteristics only of the first phase of the revolutionizing process; moreover, they are accompanied throughout by steps, hardly discernible at the time, leading to the construction of the new order. The October insurrection which brought the Bolsheviks to power is less of a watershed than is customarily supposed; it might more aptly be compared to a shifting of gears, an acceleration of tempo. As early as the spring of 1917 the mass organizations constituted an incipient 'counter-authority', an alternative power structure rivalling that headed by the weak Provisional Government. This rudimentary apparatus was then taken over by the Bolsheviks and redirected to form a governmental system under their own control. The pre- and post-October phases of this operation need to be viewed as part of a single continuum. It follows that organizations which in their infancy were inconspicuous or even artificial deserve to be taken seriously. They had considerable growth potential; and it would be wrong to apply to a developing country undergoing rapid change the criteria appropriate to a more stable and modern community.

The foregoing remarks will, it is hoped, clarify the methodological approach adopted in this book. It remains to define rather more carefully its chronological, geographical and topical scope.

Our starting-point is the fall of the monarchy in March 1917. Part I outlines the socio-economic antecedents of the revolutionary crisis; developments in town and country are then examined in turn, first during the period March to October (parts II and III) and then after October 1917 (parts IV and V). In principle the terminal date is March 1918, but this rule has not been interpreted too rigorously; in the case of rural organizations the account is continued until the end of that year, since their fate was so intimately bound up with that of the agrarian revolution still under way. The second stage in the consolidation of the dictatorship, that of full-scale civil war (spring 1918–21), deserves separate consideration.

In terms of geographical area, the focus is primarily upon the provinces of European Russia rather than Petrograd, which hitherto has received a disparate share of historians' attention. An effort has been made to give the major geographical regions their due and to avoid the common but erroneous assumption that the inhabitants of the Russian Empire formed a homogeneous or uniform mass. It must be emphasized that in the early twentieth century many Russians, especially in rural areas, still saw themselves primarily as members of some local or regional community, and that the tie to the central State authority was much weaker than it is today. To be sure, these local or regional bonds were less evident than in, say, Germany or the United States, since Russia's historical tradition had been one of autocratic centralism, not of particularism or federalism; nevertheless large distances and poor communications combined to preserve a significant degree of regional disparity. Russian public opinion of the day frequently overlooked or minimized these differences, and this bias has affected historians, too. Fortunately there are now signs of a change in this regard.

No attention, however, has been given here to developments in the national minority areas (other than the Ukraine and White Russia, and then only in the all-Russian context). This is partly because they deserve to be treated as problems in their own right, and partly for reasons of space. Happily there exists an excellent study in English of the revolution's impact upon the ethnic regions.[7] Siberia and the Far Eastern area have also had to be omitted from consideration, not without regret.

The bulk of the population in provincial Russia consisted, of course, of peasants and others who gained their livelihood from agriculture or related pursuits. This is why a good deal of attention is paid in these pages to the 'agrarian movement' (the conventional euphemism for the wave of confiscation and redistribution of landed property which occurred in 1917–18). This has some claim to be considered the main dynamic force behind the Russian revolution, for the peasants were by far the largest group in the population and their immediate demands received satisfaction in a way denied to industrial workers. If the events of 1917 are nevertheless customarily regarded from the vantage-point of the cities, this is not only a reflection of the fact that political leadership was provided from that quarter but also a product of the bias inherent in our sources, since those who have written about the revolution – whether as ideologues, journalists or memorialists – have with very few exceptions been urban residents.

As for the common belief that the October overturn was a 'proletarian revolution', this, alas, rests on insubstantial foundations. The Bolsheviks regarded themselves as 'the party of the proletariat' and as the sole political faction entitled to express the immanent interests of that social class. To make good their claim they strove to build up their support among the industrial workers, but the extent of such support was irrelevant to their determination of the class character of their regime, which depended on ideological, not social criteria. Moreover, even if one grants that by October 1917 a majority of those Russian industrial workers who were politically articulate (and the qualification in important) preferred the Bolshevik party to any other, it does not necessarily follow that the revolution was 'proletarian': for the Bolsheviks and their allies also won significant support among soldiers and sailors, peasants, artisans, tradesmen and intellectuals – in short from a broad spectrum of social and occupational groups; and it is at least arguable that many of these played a role as important as that of the industrial workers. As a *historical fact*, therefore, the 'proletarian revolution' may be consigned to the realm of revolutionary mythology; which is not to say that it is of no significance as a *concept*, for, as is now generally recognized, human conduct is powerfully affected by social myths. Ideological assumptions are of little help in elucidating what actually happened in history, and a study of the Russian revolution in particular may be thought to justify an empirical approach, for scarcely any phenomenon in modern times has suffered more from dogmatic treatment.

One may hope that no apology is needed today for considering the agricultural producer as an individual whose human and social worth is no whit less than that of the producer of manufactured goods, or for refusing to see in the 'class struggle' a motive force propelling humanity towards ultimate salvation. The ferocity of the Russian revolution may more easily be explained in terms of that country's history than of classical Marxist sociology. Where an apology may be called for is in regard to that neglected element in the revolutionary triad, the war-weary soldier. Peasants and industrial workers are treated here at some length; yet the *serye shineli*, 'the men in grey overcoats' (sailors as well as soldiers) stand in the wings, as it were, rather than in the centre of the stage. This is indeed an injustice, for at many of the most critical moments during the revolutionary year their role was decisive and they ought perhaps to be regarded as the principal actors in the drama.

Three points may be made in extenuation. First, this book is long enough already. Second, much more preliminary work needs to be done on the Russian army and navy in 1917, for it is only in recent years that extensive documentation on this topic has become available. Third, Professor Allan Wildman is at present engaged upon a monograph devoted to this subject which, when completed, will no doubt make possible a much more sophisticated analysis of the interrelationship between the various social forces involved in the Russian revolution.

This book is based almost wholly on published sources. Soviet archive holdings for the revolutionary period remain closed to foreigners whose topics of research impinge too closely upon sensitive areas. Fortunately the 'sacramentalization' of the history of the Russian revolution is less of an obstacle to independent investigation than one might suppose. Western libraries contain much material published in Soviet Russia between 1917 and the late 1920s, including works that are no longer freely available to Soviet citizens. Moreover, since 1956 a number of studies have appeared in the USSR based in part upon sources inaccessible to western historians. Such works are often of considerable value; at the very least they allow one to know that the original document exists and to cite it at second hand.[8] Furthermore, many collections of historical documents drawn from Soviet archives have been published in recent years. These volumes likewise contain a great deal of useful information, although they have to be used with caution since in almost every case the material has been closely vetted according to political and ideological criteria. The way in which this documentary evidence is presented means that some laborious source criticism may be required to establish fairly simple facts.

It is a pleasure to acknowledge the debt I owe to friends and colleagues who have ploughed this field before me: to Leonard Schapiro, for his initial encouragement and sage advice; to the late Sergey Melgunov, who was among the first participants in the Russian revolution to submit it to scholarly investigation; to Oskar Anweiler, who has pioneered the study of the soviet movement in the West; to Oliver Radkey, for the stimulus afforded by his provocative history of the Socialist-Revolutionary party; and to many others, too numerous to mention here, whose works are listed in the bibliography. None of these persons, it should be added, is in any way responsible for the views expressed in this volume, for which the author bears sole responsibility.

Particular gratitude is due to the staff of the Bibliothèque de Documentation Internationale Contemporaine, Université de Paris, who provided a most agreeable atmosphere in which to study their rich collection of sources; to the Canada Council and to the Centre for Russian and East European Studies, University of Toronto, for financial aid without which this project could not have been completed; and to the publishers for their patience. My final privilege is to thank my wife Ann, who gave more help in the preparation of this book than I had any right to expect.

Russian names have been transliterated according to the British standard system, with some minor simplifications; diacritical marks have been omitted from proper names, and wherever possible English equivalents have been used for the titles of Russian organizations (for example CEC, not VTSIK: see the full list of these abbreviations on pp. 579–80). The word 'soviet' has been capitalized only where it refers to the state order of the USSR: thus 'soviet movement' but 'Soviet government'.

Dates are given in the Old Style until 1/14 February 1918, when Russia adopted the Gregorian calendar, leaping the thirteen days that had hitherto divided her from the rest of Europe.

The following table gives the equivalents of the chief Russian weights and measures in use in 1917:

1 dessyatine (*desyatina*)	2·70 acres (1·09 hectares)
1 arshin	28 inches (71 centimetres)
1 sazhen	7 feet (2·13 metres)
1 verst	1166·4 yards (1·067 kilometres)
1 pud	36·11 pounds (16·38 kilograms)
1 funt	0·90 pounds (409·4 grams)

I Roots of Rebellion

ONE *The Legacy of Backwardness in the Countryside*

THE REVOLUTIONARY UPSURGE of 1917 derived its dynamic impetus from processes deeply rooted in Russian history, above all from the close connection forged between autocracy and serfdom. Until the middle of the nineteenth century the impressive political edifice built by the tsars rested upon the direct or indirect subjugation to the State of the vast majority of the empire's inhabitants, who were peasants in one category or another of servitude. The injustices and brutalities of serfdom provoked a number of violent revolts, which were put down with great severity and failed to alleviate the peasants' condition. As the system became entrenched, a fundamental cleavage developed between the mass of the population and the privileged élite. This division was as much psychological as social. It stemmed in large measure from the unequal impact on Russia of influences from the West. The upper classes could not fail to be attracted by an alien life-style which placed emphasis upon individual material achievement. Their dependants, however, clung by and large to the traditional Orthodox and patriarchal values of the countryside. From the Napoleonic Wars onward a growing number of enlightened public men, many of them in official positions, came to realize that, unless something were done to narrow the gulf between rulers and ruled, the autocratic political order was likely to collapse. However, their efforts to promote reform were obstructed by conservative elements at court and in the bureaucracy. The abortive revolt of December 1825 so alarmed Nicholas I and his advisers that for the next thirty years they clung to a negative policy of which the chief aim was to uphold the *status quo*, cost what it may.

Not until Russia experienced humiliating defeat in the Crimean War did the slow-moving imperial regime reluctantly embark upon measures of modernization which, for all their deficiencies, did much to refashion the country's social and political structure. During the half-century that followed the emancipation of the serfs in 1861 and the other 'great reforms' associated with this act, the economy made considerable progress and mass living standards improved. The changes were naturally most marked in the towns, but they also radiated outwards into rural areas. The expansion of the railway network, together with the spread of schooling, helped to encourage greater geographical and social mobility. Unfortunately the government sought to keep the peasants in bondage to the commune and to uphold the position of the landowning gentry, which it saw as the natural fulcrum of authority in the countryside, even though this class had always been oriented towards State service and was now clearly in decline. Towards the close of the nineteenth century its influence was challenged by a small but potentially significant stratum of intellectuals, many of whom were employees of the new elective agencies of rural self-government, the zemstvos. By the turn of the century democratic and egalitarian ideas had made a great deal of headway, even in the remoter districts. How far the popular mentality had changed was shown by the turbulent events of 1905, when in many areas the peasants joined in a nation-wide movement of protest against autocracy, which seemed to symbolize Russia's backwardness and the burdens imposed by the war with Japan.

The violent riots, strikes and disturbances which occurred throughout the empire at this time forced Nicholas II and his ministers to take some half-hearted steps along the road to constitutional government. Civil and electoral rights were extended to a sizeable segment of the population, peasants included, which had hitherto been all but excluded from political life. However, before the new order could take root Russia found herself embroiled in the First World

War, and the fragility of the bonds that held the tsarist empire together soon became all too apparent.

By and large it is probably true to say that in 1914 the outlook of most Russian peasants was either local or else universal in scope : they did not think in terms of the nation-state. The central government was a distant, abstract entity, whereas communal and regional ties mattered a great deal. The masses shared neither the cultural values nor the moral ideals treasured by the social élite; on the contrary they had an instinctive feeling that the civilized refinements on which the privileged classes prided themselves had been bought at their expense. Social antagonism was not just an artefact of the extreme left : it was a spontaneous outgrowth of ancient wrongs.

It is customary to view the bulk of the population as divided into two main categories : the industrial workers who gained their livelihood in the towns or factory settlements and the much more numerous group engaged in agriculture or related pursuits (rural crafts, fishing, forestry and so on). The distinction is partly sheer common sense, but it also owes something to the ideological controversies of the age. Russian Marxists, who set the tone on the left wing of intellectual opinion, emphasized the differences deemed to exist between workers and peasants. The Social Democratic party (RSDLP) saw itself from the start as an expressly proletarian body; among its leaders it was an article of faith that the peasantry did not form a homogeneous group, but on the contrary was becoming stratified by the process of capitalist development into mutually antagonistic classes; much of the argument between Bolsheviks and Mensheviks during the years 1905–7 revolved around the question how far this process had gone, and to what extent the proletariat (or more correctly, the party which spoke in its name) could look to the poorer segments of the peasantry as allies in the common struggle against tsarism. The Socialist-Revolutionary party (PSR), whose ideology was shaped by the 'Populism' or nativist agrarian socialism of the 1870s, had by 1905 accepted, at least implicitly, the Marxist notion of a 'proletarian vanguard', although its leaders preserved their faith in the revolutionary potential of the rural masses.

The political débâcle experienced by the SRS (as we shall for convenience call them) in 1917–18 should not lead us to assume that this necessarily disproves their sociological analysis or justifies that of their Marxist rivals. In retrospect it appears that V.M. Chernov, the leading SR theorist, and others were closer to the truth in minimizing the extent of class divisions within the peasantry and emphasizing that all working ('toiling') people in town and country shared a basically similar psychological make-up. A large proportion of Russia's industrial employees were first- or second-generation peasants, and their outlook was necessarily shaped to some extent by their rural origin or experiences. As late as 1914 a considerable number of factory workers still maintained a more than nominal link with their native village. Some owned a land allotment; others returned annually to help gather in the harvest; others again had relatives in the countryside who were dependent on them for financial support. Such ties were to enable industrial workers to withstand the privations of famine and unemployment during the civil-war years, when the relationship between town and countryside was temporarily reversed.

The most prominent feature of the Great Russian popular *Weltanschauung* was its collectivism. This was rooted in the ancient traditions of the commune (*obshchina, mir*) and the craftsmen's cooperative (*artel'*); ultimately, no doubt, it had a religious foundation in the beliefs of the Orthodox Church. One need not accept the mystical speculations of the Slavophils to recognize that the course of Russian history had been antipathetic to the growth of the individualistic ethos that one associates with nineteenth-century western free-enterprise economics. The notion that private enrichment was disadvantageous to the community, and therefore discreditable and even sinful, was widely accepted. Those who thought otherwise were popularly regarded with a mixture of scorn and envy which might or might not be justified by their activities.

This communal spirit went hand in hand with an indifference or scepticism in regard to the merits of political action. The concept of politics as a necessary means of adjusting competing interests within a framework of generally shared principles, or even as a game of skill in which outsiders could take a legitimate interest, was alien to most ordinary Russians of the day – as it was, indeed, to many of their social superiors also. The reason for this is obvious : tsarist officialdom had consistently shown the utmost reluctance to associate the broader public with the decision-making process, or even to explain what the government was attempting to do on its behalf. The vacuum created by lack of interest in politics was filled by a passion for social justice. This egalitarian sentiment likewise had deep roots in traditional Orthodox culture. In normal times it took a peaceful and benign form, fostering such virtues as charitableness and hospitality, but at moments of stress it was liable to explode into violence. On such occasions the generally submissive, pliant and good-natured *narod* ('common people') would attempt to set the world aright with a zeal unequalled elsewhere in Europe.

It is important to bear these general considerations in mind when looking at the tsarist authorities' policy, or lack of policy, on the all-important agrarian problem. The defects of the emancipation settlement are familiar; in equity, however, one might make the point that even the most generous terms would scarcely have satisfied the millennarian longings of the servile population. As the ex-proprietorial peasants saw it, once freedom (*volya*) had been granted there was no reason why large-scale landowning should continue to exist : all land, like the air men breathed, was rightfully 'God's' or 'no one's' – that is to say, the property of those who worked it with their own labour; non-'toilers' had no place in the village society. This archaic view, rooted in an attempt to rationalize the injustices of serfdom, proved to be remarkably persistent. Thus whatever steps were taken after 1861 to extend the acreage of land in peasant possession seemed not only inadequate in the eyes of the beneficiaries but probably enhanced their sense of victimization : nothing less than *all* the land would suffice.

Yet on economic grounds alone, to say nothing of the social and political implications, any Russian government was obliged to balance the claims of large-scale property against those of the peasant family farm. The former, favoured as it was by so many advantages, was far more efficient; it produced most of the marketed surplus that supplied the urban population, the armed forces and, above all, the grain exports which in the late imperial era were vital to the country's prosperity. It was virtually impossible to reconcile the demands of social justice and economic progress.

This is not to say that Russia's leaders before 1914 tried to do so, or that they had any clear policy on this issue. It was some time before officials began to give serious study to the problems of developing agricultural productivity; for many years they simply temporized and left farmers to adjust as best they could to the fluctuations of the market. An enlightened leadership might have done much more to ease the transition from serfdom to commercialized agriculture and to develop entrepreneurial skills. As it was, the government erected a number of artificial barriers which prevented the emancipated peasants from making the best use of such land as they received at the settlement: they were burdened with heavy taxes and redemption dues; educational opportunities were stunted; and last but not least they were subjected to the constraints of the commune and the bureaucratic agencies set above it.

In the post-reform period whatever social benefits the commune conferred upon its members were far outweighed by its economic disadvantages. Ownership of allotment land was vested in the commune rather than in the individual householders who comprised it, and the latter were not even free to part with their portions without the permission of their fellow-villagers. The communal and rural district (*volost'*) elders, although elected, were responsible to superior authority. As the lowest rungs in the ladder of rural administrative controls their purpose was primarily fiscal: to pump out of the village, by the device of collective responsibility of all householders for one another's obligations, the various taxes and dues owed to the State. As late as 1905 over three-quarters of Russian communes were of the 'repartitional' type, in which allotment land could be redistributed periodically among householders to ensure that their means were in rough approximation to the burdens they were expected to bear. Only in about half these communes were such repartitions actually carried out, but everywhere egalitarian pressures made themselves felt. They were strongest in the Central Agricultural region south of Moscow and in the middle Volga provinces. These were regions where arable farming was the principal source of peasant income; much of the land was fertile 'black soil' (*chernozem*), but overcrowding was a serious problem. Levelling sentiments were less in evidence in the more recently settled areas further to the south (New Russia) and in the non-black-soil provinces of the north and centre, where industrial employment and handicrafts were vital to the economic health of the farming population.

Membership of the village commune obliged the householder to adhere to an agreed timetable for the principal agricultural operations (sowing, harvesting and so on). It dissuaded him from making technical innovations or from investing additional effort in cultivating land to which his title was insecure; on the contrary it gave him every incentive to try to extract the maximum profit from it, however wasteful the means employed. Communal ownership perpetuated the ancient three-field system, whereby each household was allocated several parcels of land of varying quality, some of which might be situated far from the village. Intermingling of strips (*cherespolositsa*) provoked conflicts and hindered the use of machinery or fertilizer. The latter was in any case scarce owing to the relative shortage of livestock; this in turn was due to the enforced concentration on grain farming, which led to an inadequacy of grazing and meadow land. Pasture and woodland were held communally, and access to these facilities was another frequent source of friction. Where, as was often the case, the landowner's possessions and livestock were inter-mingled with those of the peasants, who might well be his tenants or otherwise financially dependent upon him, the scene was set for confrontation. The rights of the contending parties were seldom clearly defined in law, and in such instances the landed proprietor, as the immediate representative of an alien privileged world, was the most vulnerable target for popular wrath. The fact that he would normally leave more of his land fallow than the peasants could afford to do was an additional reason for them to cast envious eyes upon his property.

Landowners' estates were unevenly distributed throughout the country. The largest concentrations were to be found in the belt of territory running north and south from the Baltic provinces to Bessarabia; there were also a good many properties in the Ukraine and in the provinces situated immediately south and south-east of Moscow. In the north most non-peasant land belonged to the State or Crown. Even within the same province there were as a rule considerable disparities between one county and another, which would be reflected in employment opportunities and income levels. It may be supposed that peasant attitudes toward large-scale land-owning will have been appreciably affected by local socio-economic conditions, but this point has yet to be investigated.

Social tensions in the countryside were aggravated by the rapid growth of the rural population, which rose from 56 million in 1867 to 81·7 million in 1897 and to 103·2 million in 1913.[1] The increase was particularly marked in the black-soil zone stretching from Poltava province to the middle Volga. Here the amount of allotment land available per household shrank dramatically, forcing peasants to lease land from proprietors at rents higher than they could afford. Individuals and whole communities also purchased land, often with credit facilities provided by the government, but this likewise was a costly affair; in any case the additional territory thus acquired could not make up for the effects of the population increase. Russian peasants in the late nineteenth century had a high reproduction rate. Possession of a large family conferred high prestige in the community. It also held out the promise of greater prosperity, since a householder with many mouths to feed could expect due provision to be made for their needs at the next repartition. Indeed, the life of the village to a large extent revolved round the functioning of a natural biological cycle : those families with more able-bodied males were impelled to intensify their labour input and to exploit economic resources more dynamically, so attaining greater wealth and power; however, as years passed and a new generation grew up, the family unit would split and its property would be divided up, so giving other families an opportunity to compete for leadership roles within the village.[2] The pattern was one of perpetual inter-dynastic struggle mitigated by horizontal cross-relationships such as inter-family marital ties. It may be added that the social structure of the pre-revolutionary Russian village was extremely intricate and not readily intelligible to outsiders who approached it with their own preconceptions. As a self-contained community it suspected intruders, not without reason, of seeking to impose upon it alien ideas and ways of conduct.

Yet new influences were irresistibly seeping in. The large number of country-dwellers, especially in the less fertile northern and central provinces, who went off to work in industry, building or transport, were often a source of innovative ideas. The first institution to be affected by these currents was the patriarchal 'extended family' itself. The authority of the paterfamilias, and of the older members generally, was increasingly challenged by the young. Where such conflicts became acute, they might assume an expressly political form. Apart from this, men who had worked in the cities (or served in the army) might come under radical influences there and transmit to their native villages the attitudes of their new associates and mentors. This helps to account for the spread of rural unrest in 1905. However, the 'agrarian movement' of that year by and large remained within the framework of Populist ideology and was little influenced by the explicitly proletarian doctrine of Marxism. The peasants' ultimate objective was the expulsion of the 'non-toiling' proprietors and a general redistribution of the land among those who worked it with their own labour. Radical intellectuals sympathetic to their cause might refer to this goal as 'socialization' or 'nationalization', but such terminology was not used by the peasants themselves. They looked forward to a situation in which, having at last become masters of their fate, they would till the land as they thought fit as individual proprietors. They might be willing to allot some role in the future social order to the commune or to other organizations of a cooperative type, but in their view the basic unit of production was to be the small family farm.

Shocked by this massive upsurge of violence among those whom it had complacently assumed to be wholly loyal to the throne, the tsarist government embarked upon a radical change in its agrarian policy. Official support for the commune, which had been in some doubt since 1903, was abandoned. Instead every encouragement was henceforth given to those who wanted to opt out, to consolidate their holdings as individual property, and to farm on their own account. This policy had been adumbrated by Count Witte, but it became indissolubly associated with his eventual successor as prime minister from 1906 to 1911, P.A. Stolypin. The latter approached the scheme in a more overtly political frame of mind than his forerunner. Heartened by his experiences as a provincial governor, when he had successfully contained peasant disorders by forceful action, he took the view that a similar approach could produce results on a national scale. Resolute prosecution of the reform, with coercion applied where necessary, would win for the regime the support of the most responsible elements of the peasantry – those whom he referred to, in a phrase that became notorious, as 'the solid and the strong' in contrast to 'the weak and the drunken'.

Stolypin did not set out, as his left-wing critics asserted, to favour a class of richer peasants or kulaks; indeed, it was doubtful whether such a class existed (the term *kulak* literally meant 'fist' and was widely employed as a pejorative). His aim was to give a boost to agricultural productivity and rural living standards from which all sections of the agricultural community would ultimately benefit; or, in more political terms, to steal the revolutionaries' thunder by offering the peasant masses a viable alternative both to communalism and to the prospect of socialization of the land. He sought to exploit the latent contradiction between the collectivist principles professed by the socialist theoreticians (whether Marxist or Populist) and the individualistic propensities of the average peasant farmer, who could be expected to relish the prospect of security of tenure. If the government granted this, Stolypin reasoned, it would kill two birds with one stone : politically it would earn the gratitude and loyalty of the smallholders, as the immediate beneficiaries of the reform; economically it would encourage the growth of that entrepreneurial spirit which had been thwarted by perpetuation of the communal system. The progress made by the more fortunate or talented villagers would lead their fellows to emulate their example; those unable to do so would either find employment with their neighbours (at rising wage rates) or else would forsake the countryside, as they were already doing in such numbers, to seek work in the towns.

It was a bold concept, and one which raised almost as many problems as it solved. Could the inexperienced tsarist bureaucracy create the administrative apparatus necessary to carry out efficiently and humanely such a complex scheme of social engineering? Could the treasury bear the high capital cost involved in setting up so many individual farms? Would Russia's industries be able to absorb a flood of migrants from the countryside? Last but not least, would the imperial regime be granted enough time in which to reshape peasant modes of thought and action in the sense desired? Stolypin himself thought the plan needed twenty years of peace. A bare three years separated the reform's final legislative enactment (in May 1911) from the outbreak of the First World War.

Making due allowance for the impact of the war, which slowed down and eventually halted implementation of the scheme, a study of the results suggests that it was a less than adequate answer to the country's well-nigh insoluble agrarian problems. The overall statistics give a favourable impression that is somewhat misleading.[3] From November 1906 to May 1915, in forty of the forty-seven provinces in European Russia for which data are available, just under two million (1,992,387) householders had been granted title to 13·9 million dessyatines of land as their individual property. To these should be added approximately half a million householders in communes on hereditary (non-repartitional) tenure, bringing the total of land involved to 16·3 million dessyatines. About 1·7 million other farmers were converted to individual tenure automatically as a result of the law of 14 June 1910, which ruled that an entire hereditary commune could be broken up at the request of even a single member wishing to separate (whereas in a repartitional commune a two-thirds affirmative vote was required); it would be unsound to regard all these persons as genuine 'separators', as a number of historians have done. Taking the figure of separators as 2·5 million, this represents about a fifth of the peasant householders eligible, who held 14 per cent of communal allotment land (or nine per cent of *all* peasant land). In the circumstances this must be adjudged a relatively modest proportion. Moreover, not all these separators actually consolidated their holdings. By 1916 only 1·3 million independent farms had been set up, embracing about ten per cent of the rural population, and of these a mere quarter (twenty-two per cent, according to one authority) were *khutora* as distinct from *otruby*.[4] It is arguable that only the former deserve to be taken as a true criterion of the reform's success. The difference between the two categories consists in the fact that the proprietor of an *otrub*, although no longer a member of the commune (where this still existed), continued to live among his fellows in the village, whereas a *khutoryanin*, or proprietor of a *khutor*, was an independent farmer in the western sense, whose homestead stood in its own enclosure in proud isolation – a challenge and a provocation to neighbours who continued to adhere to the old way of life.

Moreover, when examining these figures several other factors need to be taken into account. In the first place, a large but uncertain number of consolidations was achieved as a result of pressure from above. One critic claimed that no less than three-quarters of separations from the commune were brought about by official coercion without the local communities' consent,[5] although this estimate is probably too high. That separations would harm the general interests of the villagers as they themselves conceived them was in the circumstances unavoidable; but all too frequently measures were taken that injured the interests of the independent smallholders as well. The latter might find that they had too little good-quality land to make the new farm an economically viable unit; they often lacked sufficient water resources or pasturage for their livestock; and the general inadequacy of rural communications was a serious handicap to men whose livelihood now depended entirely upon their ability to compete in the agricultural market. For these and many other reasons the new proprietors quickly ran into debt to the resettlement agency, to grain merchants or to commercial banks, much as the squires had done before them. Some were still dependent in fact on the community from which they had sundered themselves, which laid them open to all manner of harassment. By 1914 few beneficiaries of the Stolypin reform as yet measured up to the government's ideal of a soundly based, self-reliant yeoman farmer, the equal of those in central or western Europe.

It is also significant that those parts of the tsar's domains which bordered on the German or Austro-Hungarian empires should by and large have had the greatest success in implementing the reform. These regions had long been exposed to individualist influences from the West. Communes here tended to be of the non-repartitional type, in which the locus of power lay with the householder rather than with the assembly (*skhod*) or its elected elders. This meant that for many such peasants the reform amounted to little more than an improvement in their juridical status. In south-eastern European Russia its relative success was largely attributable to a different factor : the generous endowments of land possible in this still under-populated area. Thus in the Ukraine (right-bank) the proportion of holdings enclosed reached 12·9 per cent, in the western region 16 per cent and in New Russia 29·2 per cent – all figures considerably above the national average; on the other hand in the Moscow region enclosures accounted for only 8·3 per cent of holdings and in the Central Agricultural region 7·9 per cent.[6] The reform thus had only a modest impact in those areas where agrarian tensions were most acute, and in some respects it served to aggravate them.

Nevertheless the years between 1906 and 1914 witnessed a greater investment of money and effort in the countryside than in any previous comparable era. The Stolypin reform was a belated attempt to make up for decades of governmental neglect (indeed, at times of deliberate exploitation of rural producers for the higher purposes of the State). By the eve of the First World War a small but significant step had been taken to narrow the historic gap between town and country. Quite apart from the expenditure on the land resettlement scheme, measures were taken to improve the efficiency of Russian agriculture by increasing the use of machinery and fertilizer, diversifying the crop pattern and developing popular education. The number of agronomists graduating from Russian institutes rose impressively. Crop yields were also rising, although admittedly progress was less substantial on peasant smallholdings than on larger properties, and the general level lagged behind that of more advanced countries. Russia produced only 55 puds of wheat per dessyatine in 1913, whereas the comparable figure was 81 in Italy, 89 in Austria and France, 149 in England and 168 in Belgium; the figures for other grains and for potatoes were comparable.[7] Nevertheless the lag could be expected to diminish in so far as the programme of agricultural development was vigorously sustained.

Before the First World War Russian grain exporters benefited from a favourable turn in agricultural prices. This was reflected in increased consumption in rural areas: a more varied diet, better clothing and domestic furnishings, and the replacement of wooden roofs by iron sheeting. More than ever the *muzhik* began to expect a ready supply of city-made goods.

Another beneficial development was the continued encouragement given to peasants wishing to migrate to under-developed parts of Asiatic Russia, even though this could have only a slight effect in easing population pressure in the most overcrowded provinces.

All these measures were more than mere palliatives; nevertheless they did not add up to a comprehensive 'development strategy' commensurate with the problem of rural backwardness – which itself was the major obstacle to rapid modernization of the Russian economy. This judgement is admittedly one coloured by hindsight. Stolypin and his officials were concerned less with economic progress than with social stability, and it is arguable that, given the context in which they operated, their priorities were correct. Time, however, was not on the government's side.

What seemed in the easy-going circumstances of pre-war Russia to be a radical change in the structure of rural society would soon appear, after the revolutionary cataclysm had swept across the land, as no more than an attempt to shore up a doomed and crumbling order. In Stolypin's defence it may be said that he was the first to establish a governmental agency capable of communicating with Russian society at the village level;[8] nevertheless it was unfortunate that it embarked upon its tasks so late in Russia's history. Had a similar policy been adopted during the reform era of the 1860s the agrarian crisis would have been much less acute. Moreover, official thinking had yet to be fully emancipated from traditional bureaucratic rigidities. In these years the rural cooperative movement registered a striking growth, above all in dairy farming. This initiative was looked upon with little favour in government circles; yet this was but another manifestation of the entrepreneurial spirit that the reformers sought to foster by encouraging the development of independent peasant farms. The cooperatives met a real economic and social need and gave large numbers of agricultural producers a vested interest in stability. A more far-sighted government would have assisted this movement as a valuable additional safeguard against the threat of subversion.

TWO *The Discontents of Industrial Labour*

Although the stolypin reform had serious shortcomings, it did at least bear witness to the government's desire to strengthen its base among the rural population. So far as policy towards industrial labour is concerned, one looks in vain for evidence of any similar intention. Nicholas II and his ministers seem to have resigned themselves to the idea that the urban poor, and the factory workers in particular, were all but irretrievably lost to the cause of socialism. It is remarkable that, whereas the agrarian unrest of 1905–6 impelled the government to embark upon a consistent (if in some ways misguided) reform policy, the strikes and riots in the empire's industrial areas had no corresponding effect. Repression of violence, often unduly severe and arbitrary in its impact, was not accompanied by any bold measures designed to alleviate the social distress that had prompted the disturbances. The reason for this neglect lies partly in the *laissez-faire* climate of the age and partly in the persistence of a physiocratic tradition in Russian social thought which affected officials as well as much of the general public. Another more obvious factor is the existence, under the aegis of the ministry of Internal Affairs, of a large and influential police organization which saw its *raison d'être* in the stamping out of real or alleged subversion among industrial labour.

The statistics compiled in the ministry of Trade and Industry led contemporaries to minimize the relative weight and importance of the industrial working class. Modern Soviet historians, faced with the necessity of explaining the success of a 'proletarian revolution' in a country with far fewer proletarians than peasants, have strained the evidence in the opposite direction. Thus A.G. Rashin, a leading demographer, not content to rectify the exclusion from tsarist statistical compilations of those employed in mines or small firms not subject to the factory inspectorate, counts as 'proletarian' various groups of artisans and craftsmen working at home on contract, agricultural labourers, building and transport workers, employees of commercial establishments, domestic servants and so on, whose social status is ambiguous, to say the least.[1] We may accept Soviet estimates for 1910 of 3·1 to 3·3 million factory workers and miners, and of approximately ten million non-agricultural employees (in a total population of over 160 million),[2] so long as we bear in mind that many of these persons were predominantly countrymen in their life-style and outlook, while others, as 'white-collar' workers, regarded themselves as socially superior to men who toiled at a factory bench. In the railways, as in the civil service, ideas of hierarchical rank prevailed. The large indeterminate group best described as 'urban poor', often semi-employed or even vagrants, should not be light-heartedly categorized as proletarian in the Marxist sense of the term. Social class, as is today generally recognized, is a more complex matter than it seemed to nineteenth-century social theorists with a strong commitment to radical change. This is particularly true of a developing country such as pre-revolutionary Russia, for which we still lack the detailed sociological information which alone could raise discussion of this subject to a proper scholarly level.

This is not the place to survey the range of goods produced or the geographical location of Russian industry before 1914, but it is worth noting here the major regional differences in so far as they affected the distribution of the labour force. One of the largest groups numerically, if not in economic or political importance, comprised workers engaged in processing various agricultural products (foodstuffs, spirits, leather, tobacco and so on). They were scattered over most parts of the country, as were the hundred thousand or so persons employed in the wood-working industry. Those in engineering and metallurgical trades generally possessed higher qualifications and were better paid than other groups; they were also more heavily concentrated territorially – in the industrial areas of Russian Poland, the north-west (Riga, St Petersburg), Moscow, the Ukraine (Yekaterinoslav province, Odessa, Nikolayev) and the Urals; there were also important arms works near Tula and enterprises producing railway rolling-stock near Nizhniy Novgorod on the middle Volga. In 1913 Moscow and the area north and east of the city (Vladimir province), the principal region in the empire for the manufacture of textiles, gave employment to 519,000 workers, of whom 248,000 were located in Moscow province. A subsidiary centre of the textile industry, with about 40,000 persons, was to be found in and round St Petersburg. The capital city harboured a wide variety of enterprises engaged in food-processing, shipbuilding and so forth, and was also of course a major commercial and administrative centre. The Ukraine could claim several hundred thousand industrial employees, the most important group being the miners of the Donets valley, who were 107,000 strong. Another 75,000 workers whose livelihood depended directly or indirectly upon coal-mining were to be found in the Urals. The southern Ukraine (New Russia) and the Baltic (especially Riga) were the areas of the empire where the industrial population was growing most rapidly. Its density reached a maximum of 4·8 per cent in the Central Industrial region.[3]

Speaking very generally, it was in the west and north-west of the country, the regions most exposed to extraneous influences, that industrial workers' earning power was greatest; here, too, their way of life had more in common with that of workers in more advanced countries. They had a better opportunity than in the Central Industrial region to acquire professional skills and to develop a sense of personal dignity. It is significant that more workers in St Petersburg than in Moscow could afford to live in rented rooms or (shared) apartments, as distinct from barrack-like blocks built by their employer to house a labour force hired fresh from the village. In St Petersburg an investigation in 1908 showed that 8·7 per cent of workers (mostly single men) lived in accommodation provided by management; in Kiev the corresponding figure was 17·3 per cent.[4] A more representative survey of Moscow textile-workers carried out in the same year indicated that 43 per cent of them (more than half women) fell into this category.[5] So far as amenities were concerned, there was probably not much to choose between the two types of accommodation, but the extent of private housing may be taken as evidence of modernization. As one might expect, links with the village were weaker in the north-west than in the centre. In the former region mechanization of industrial processes had made greater headway, so that the number of hours worked tended to be less than in Moscow, where some factory proprietors were noted for their conservatism. In the Ukraine industrialization was a more recent phenomenon and capital costs were high; entrepreneurs sought to offset them by drawing on the reserves of cheap labour in the region. Although industrial conditions here were generally poor, especially in regard to housing – of Donets coal-miners in 1913, 47 per cent lived in barracks and only 14 per cent in private quarters[6] – they were at least superior to those in the Urals, which was a veritable backwater. The workers in the mines and metallurgical plants of this region had a tradition of militancy rooted in the harsh experiences of serfdom.

One factor which had a considerable bearing upon industrial workers' morale and attitudes was the size of the enterprise in which they were employed. Russia was a country of extremes where archaic cottage crafts coexisted alongside giant concerns equipped with the most up-to-date machinery. The abundant supply of cheap labour gave industrialists an incentive to establish large enterprises employing many hundreds of work-people. These concerns were particularly numerous in the metallurgical and textile industries. In the Ukraine in 1913 nine plants were responsible for 79 per cent of the pig-iron produced in that area and for 53 per cent of that produced in the whole empire.[7] According to data compiled by the factory inspectorate in 1914, no less than 41·4 per cent of the workers within its purview were in enterprises employing more than a thousand persons and 56·5 per cent in those employing more than five hundred persons.[8] The proportion was higher than in any other country; and the fact that these enterprises tended to be concentrated in certain industrial regions or cities (notably St Petersburg), some of which drew their labour force from distant regions, added to the political risks.

However modern some of these concerns were in a technical sense, few had as yet been influenced by modern notions of industrial relations. Because labour productivity was low, especially judged by international standards, employers sought to drive their men hard and to maintain strict discipline. Of some 220,000 employees in Moscow province surveyed in 1908, 92,000 worked nine hours or less, 94,000 nine to ten hours, and 33,000 over ten hours. In 1913 the average working day in Russian industry measured ten hours (including 0·3 hours of overtime). There were, however, many more public holidays than in western countries, so that only 257 days in the year were actual working days.[9] Managers and foremen felt they could afford to deal severely with employees who were disobedient or negligent, since there were plenty of fresh recruits willing to take the place of men dismissed. On the other hand workmen who managed to acquire technical proficiency could expect to command a privileged status and considerably higher earnings than their fellows. Sometimes the most complex tasks in the production process were performed by foreigners, at even higher rates of pay; this, naturally enough, was likely to add to the tensions generated on the factory floor.

There were few legal ways in which grievances could be ventilated. Workmen were permitted to establish informal associations for social or cultural purposes at the factory or shop level, such as clubs, cooperatives or *zemlyachestva* (fraternities of persons originating from the same area), but any organization with more extensive connections or broader objectives was frowned upon. Sometimes an employer might be willing to tolerate such a body but have to yield to the views of the police, who were ever alert to the possibility that mass organizations of this kind could become politicized and be manipulated to serve revolutionary ends.

A particularly close watch was kept upon trade unions. These had shown a remarkable vitality and militancy in 1905–6. Regulations of March 1906 provided for the first time a legal framework for such associations, but in the years that followed they came to be interpreted very narrowly by the local authorities. Those unions permitted to exist, notably among printers and other craftsmen, were little more than what in Anglo-Saxon parlance would be called 'branches' or 'locals'. Of these there existed a mere 114, with 34,000 members, at the end of 1913.[10] They were subjected to various forms of official harassment, so that their membership fluctuated and their general influence was slight. This restrictive policy helped to bring about the very result it was designed to avert : the political radicalization of the union movement.

Early in 1912 a massacre of striking workers in the Lena goldfields in eastern Siberia, which cost a hundred and seventy lives, led to a nation-wide wave of protest actions. The government responded tardily with two palliative measures : legalization of sick-benefit funds and an act providing for accident insurance. The sick funds were financed jointly by workers and employers on a purely local basis. However limited their scope, they did provide a forum in which representatives of the two sides in industry could meet and discuss common problems. About 2,800 funds, with a total membership of over two million persons, were functioning in 1914.[11] Insurance against accidents, a frequent occurrence in Russian industry, had been instituted in 1903, but there were many loopholes in the law which could be used by unscrupulous employers to evade its provisions. The new measure made employers wholly responsible for providing medical aid and pensions to those who suffered disabilities in the course of their work. This modest advance was designed to reinforce the paternalistic traditions in Russian industrial life.

As yet there was no question of insurance against unemployment, which from the workers' viewpoint was a major scourge. There are no reliable statistics on this matter, but as an illustration one may cite an unofficial investigation of 572 respondents in Kiev in 1910 (admittedly, a very small sample), of whom 263 had been unemployed for part of that year; of these 199 had been unemployed for a term exceeding one month.[12] Even labour exchanges were unknown. The prevalent assumption in official and business circles was that unemployed workers could return to their villages and eke out a living there until conditions improved. This might have been feasible in former times, but it had ceased to be so as links with the countryside became attenuated; moreover, the attack on the commune undermined its members' sense of charitable obligation towards members in misfortune. In this respect as in so many others the tsarist government clung to an attitude that had been rendered obsolete by changing social realities. This was all the more reprehensible in so far as these changes were the foreseeable result of a process of industrial development sponsored by the State itself.

As a result of this industrial expansion nominal wages in enterprises subject to the factory inspectorate rose thirty per cent above 1900 levels by 1913,[13] but this advance seems to have been almost wholly eaten up by climbing prices. One western authority estimates that the increase in real terms 'cannot have been very large'.[14] In 1926 the Soviet economist S.G. Strumilin reckoned that real wages rose by 8·2 per cent between 1900 and 1913.[15] Such overall national averages cannot in any case tell us much, for there were marked differentials between industries and regions. An investigation of some 35,000 workers in Moscow province in 1908 showed that in mechanical plants men earned 30·8 roubles per month, whereas men employed in spinning cotton and weaving cloth earned 20·1 (and women 15·4) roubles; adolescents aged fifteen to twenty years received 62 per cent, and juveniles aged twelve to fifteen years 39 per cent of the average adult wage.[16] Another source puts the average annual wage in 1908 for textile-workers in this area at 293 roubles, and for those in St Petersburg at 338 roubles; in the latter city, with its preponderance of metallurgical workers, the median industrial wage was 381 roubles.[17] In 1913, according to an investigation of retail prices in over two hundred major centres, the cost (in roubles) of certain basic foodstuffs was as follows :

rye flour (1 funt)	2·4
potatoes (1 funt)	4·9
cabbage (1 funt)	1·8
beef (1 funt)	37·2
milk (bottle)	4·7
eggs (piece)	1·9
refined sugar (1 funt)	15·2[18]

Corresponding figures for wage rates in 1913 are unfortunately not available; nevertheless it is clear that the average industrial worker had trouble in making ends meet.

Studies of working-class budgets indicate that a large proportion of total expenditure went on food. S.N. Prokopovich, who analysed data pertaining to 632 workers in St Petersburg in 1908, found that this item accounted for 48·7 per cent of the total expenditure of married men and 37·3 per cent of that of unmarried men – in monetary terms, respectively 8·1 and 13·9 roubles per month.[19] Whereas nearly all the married men ate at home, only 46 per cent of the bachelors did so; the others went to an inn or cooperative dining-room. In terms of calories workers were adequately fed, but their diet was unbalanced. An investigator in Kostroma province in 1911 noted that 'workers eat the minimum amount of food necessary for them to stay at work, the staple items being cheap and indigestible products of vegetable origin'; bread was 'the basis of their diet' and in lieu of hot food they drank large quantities of tea.[20] Few could afford proper clothing. In St Petersburg single men spent an average of 62 roubles a year on this item and married men 91 roubles (including some bought for their families). More than a third reported that they bought second-hand clothes.[21] In interpreting these findings some allowance must be made for imperfections in the technique of social research, then still in its infancy.

Reference has already been made to the tendency for workers to leave the crude type of shelter provided for them by the factory management as soon as they could afford to do so. Not only economic resources but also family status and general level of culture were involved in such a decision. It followed that residents of communal dwellings on or near factory premises were predominantly young and single – a state of affairs which had political as well as social implications. Of the single men covered by Prokopovich's inquiry who lived in rented accommodation, only one per cent could afford an apartment of their own; just over half either had a room to themselves or shared a room with one other person; the rest had to make do with what in the language of statistics was called 'a corner', 'a bed', or even 'half a bed' (that is to say the occupants slept in shifts). In the smaller provincial towns some workers owned their own dwellings, but for most privacy and comfort were an unattainable ideal.[22]

In these conditions it was scarcely surprising that alcoholism was rife, to say nothing of more serious diseases and afflictions. In Kiev expenditure on liquor and tobacco was equivalent to twelve per cent of the total expenditure on foodstuffs, and in St Petersburg the figure was over twenty per cent. The great majority drank spirits (vodka) in preference to beer.[23] Prokopovich recorded that nearly eighteen per cent of his informants neither smoke nor drank, a fact which presumably reflects the influence of the temperance movement, which in Russia as elsewhere in Europe on the eve of the First World War was a force to be reckoned with, although the resources at its disposal were pathetically inadequate.[24]

In addition to the temperance associations, which maintained tea-gardens and reading-rooms, a large number of public organizations struggled to provide educational and cultural facilities for Russian workers. In St Petersburg Countess Panina, a well-known philanthropist, set aside a large house for meetings, lectures and entertainments. The standard was high and they were well attended. So-called 'people's universities' flourished in several cities. In 1911–12 45,100 students were enrolled in the courses offered by the Moscow people's university; this was nearly four times as many as in 1906.

In Kharkov in 1911 the local commission for the encouragement of popular education arranged 141 lectures, which were attended by a total of 30,000 persons. Naturally enough the smaller industrial centres had less to offer; nevertheless at the Ivotskaya glass foundry, part of the large complex known as the Maltsev works near Bryansk, there was a 'people's house' at which dramatic performances and lectures were given during the winter; in summer there were sporting events and excursions into the surrounding countryside.[25] Workers tended to prefer such group activities to more individualistic ways of spending their leisure hours, which were in any case limited.

There are no reliable figures on the educational standards of Russian workers at this time. The 1897 census showed that in industry, transport and trade (excluding servants and labourers) 57·8 per cent of male and 28·4 per cent of female workers were literate. In that year the general literacy rate for both sexes in town and country was 21·1 per cent; sixteen years later it had risen to about 30 per cent.[26] Given the concentration of educational effort in urban areas after 1907, it is reasonable to assume that working-class literacy stood in a better ratio to general literacy than it had done in 1897. Some years later, in 1918, a census showed 79·2 per cent of male and 44·2 per cent of female workers as literate.[27] Bearing in mind the adverse effects of war and revolution, including the dispersion of workers from the cities, the literacy figure in 1913 may have been higher than this. In a study of some seventy thousand workers in Moscow province (1908) I.M. Kozminykh-Lanin found that 76 per cent of male and 26 per cent of female workers could read and write.[28]

In 1910 a total of 90,300 pupils were recorded as attending trade schools.[29] In addition to municipal and zemstvo schools financed out of state and local revenue some educational institutions were maintained by employers. A number of organizations offered evening courses and public libraries were well attended. Those workers who had succeeded in broadening their intellectual horizons despite the many obstacles placed in their path enjoyed high prestige among their fellows and exercised a corresponding influence. This meant that – as in the village – younger men were able to challenge the authority previously accorded as of right to their elders; where the conflict of generations acquired a political flavour all the advantages were on the side of youth. The close association between age and educational attainment, due to the relative neglect of primary schooling until the last years of the imperial regime, is strikingly brought out in the study by Kozminykh-Lanin cited above: of those aged over forty a mere 37 per cent were literate, whereas 63 per cent of those aged fifteen to twenty and 82 per cent of those between twelve and fifteen could read and write.[30]

In view of all these factors it is not surprising that discontent among Russia's industrial population should have often taken a violent form. The number of strikes declined from a peak of nearly 14,000 incidents (involving 2,863,000 persons) in 1905 to 222 (47,000 strikers) in 1910; but by 1912 it had climbed again to 2,032 (725,000 strikers).[31] The latter figures were swollen by the sympathy strikes that followed news of the Lena massacre and increased the proportion of incidents officially categorized (by somewhat arbitrary criteria) as political rather than economic. By 1914 the total number of days lost through industrial unrest had climbed to more than one million. Particularly serious was the general strike which broke out in Baku in June 1914 and spread from there to St Petersburg. Most of the capital's workers took to the streets; barricades were set up in the poorer quarters of the city and shots exchanged with police and troops. The younger men fresh from the villages were noticeably more militant. The disturbances continued until the very eve of Russia's entry into the First World War. To some activists it appeared that the outbreak of hostilities had been contrived by the government to divert attention from the troubled industrial scene. This view was, however, unfounded. The evidence points rather in the reverse direction: the tsarist authorities consistently underestimated the serious threat which industrial conflict posed to the empire's internal cohesion and clung to the naive assumption that firm police measures would suffice to contain it.

As matters stood in 1914, all but a thin segment of Russian labour was alienated from the existing political and social order. Workers could not be expected to feel that they had a stake in a system that brought them so much hardship and so little prospect of amelioration. Few would have been impressed by the argument, even had it been brought to their attention, that their tribulations were an inevitable but temporary concomitant of the process of modernizing a backward country, and that in time they could look forward to a growing share of the material rewards bound to flow from an advanced market economy. Even industrialists and business leaders did not see matters this way. Preoccupied with their own immediate concerns, not least with maintaining profit levels in a competitive world, they took little interest in broader questions such as the prospects for continued economic growth or the social implications which this would have. Nor were officials in the ministry of Trade and Industry much better endowed with foresight. They took a certain pride in the empire's expanding industrial output, as an essential constituent of its international prestige, and they were aware of the principal shortcomings (notably, in the labour field, the need for more technical education); but no sense of urgency inspired the deliberations which, from time to time, brought these civil servants into contact with the business community.[32] Subconsciously members of both groups contented themselves with the vague belief that continuing 'westernization' – that is to say, the approximation of Russia's economic system, cultural pattern and political institutions to the model of Germany, England or France – would somehow lead to an attenuation of social conflict.

Thus a class-oriented viewpoint came naturally to Russia's industrial workers. After the traumatic experience of 1905 they no longer needed the services of political agitators to explain, often in violent emotional language, the rudiments of the socialist *Weltanschauung*. They accepted as self-evident a Manichean outlook which opposed 'the proletariat' or 'the toilers' (the former term favoured by the Marxists, the latter by the Populists) to 'the bourgeoisie' (*burzhuaziya*). But what was the bourgeoisie? The word was alien to the Russian tongue, and this may conceivably have helped to foster antagonism towards Russia's incipient middle class. Labour activists were in no mood to ponder the point that Russian entrepreneurs differed from their eighteenth- or nineteenth-century French prototypes in quantity and quality, still less that Russia was actually deficient in managerial skills. Such terms as 'bourgeois' and 'capitalist' belonged to the language of revolutionary mythology; they had lost their original roots in socio-economic reality and had become negative symbols. If so many of Russia's intellectuals failed to resist the blandishments of this superficial way of thinking, impoverished and half-educated workmen can scarcely be blamed for following suit.

It is impossible to gauge accurately the impact of revolutionary ideology on industrial workers before 1914. In seeking to define their political outlook we are reduced to speculation and hypothesis. Many workers had regional and professional affiliations which were not always compatible with wider class loyalties. Intellectuals, whether moderates or radicals, tended to regard themselves as purveyors of enlightenment and 'the masses' as passive recipients of their influence. It would be more accurate to see the young or more militant workers attaining spontaneously a new awareness of their dignity as human beings, their rights as citizens or consumers, and their latent power to enforce their will. In the course of this awakening they came into contact with a whole range of modern ideas, from which they took whatever suited their temperament or condition. Even those expressly committed to one of the political parties kept their options open. They were not attracted to dogma; on the other hand, there is no gainsaying their emotional identification with the cause of progress, which it was widely assumed could best be advanced through social conflict.

For all this, in July 1914 few observers would have predicted that Russia's industrial workers would soon play such a capital role in the country's history. Those who spoke of revolution expected a more successful version of 1905, not the total cataclysm unleashed in 1917. The government was still firmly in control and the country-side was peaceful. Before the situation could change, Russia had to experience the horrific slaughter and wholesale social upheaval that ensued from its involvement in the First World War.

THREE *Rural Russia and the War*

T HE EFFECTS OF the war upon Russia's fragile social and economic structure were as catastrophic as they were in the military and political domain. Civilians in town and country found themselves caught up in a desperate struggle to meet the insatiable demands of a conflict in which prospects of victory seemed ever more remote. Defeat on the battlefield and the bitter privations of daily life combined to sap the nation's morale. Reactions to the crisis varied according to an individual's social status and his proximity to the front, but all segments of the population gradually came to share a feeling that something was profoundly wrong with the way the country's affairs were being handled. This general sense of malaise undermined the credibility of the tsarist regime. When the monarchy finally collapsed in February–March 1917 the pressures that had been building up irresistibly for two and a half years burst forth with explosive force.

In retrospect perhaps the most striking development in Russia's social history during the First World War was the growing tension between town and country. Market relationships soon became distorted from their peacetime pattern, chiefly to the disadvantage of the urban segments of society. The effects were particularly noticeable in Petrograd and other towns of the north and centre, in what significantly came to be called the 'consuming provinces' as distinct from the 'producing provinces' situated mainly in the south (in the fertile Central Agricultural region, the lower Volga and New Russia) as well as in certain regions of Asiatic Russia. The strain imposed on the transport system and the administrative confusion made it increasingly difficult to ensure a regular supply of foodstuffs, fuel and raw materials to the major industrial regions. City folk came to feel that they were bearing an undue share of the hardships which the war inflicted upon the civilian rear.

This sentiment was accompanied by a widespread belief that the peasants were benefiting materially from the emergency – even though the villages supplied the bulk of manpower for the army. It is not easy to say how much justification there was for this view, which was echoed by historians for many years thereafter and has only recently been seriously challenged. One western student of the problem has claimed that the peasants' average income exceeded the pre-war level by 19·5 per cent in 1915 and by 17·8 per cent in 1916.[1] This assessment rests upon shaky premises and is probably too high. On the other hand Anfimov, the leading Soviet authority on the subject,[2] strains the evidence to support his thesis that the peasants were becoming gravely impoverished. He does not offer any alternative estimate of their total income, and his argument misses the point that what mattered most was *relative* rather than absolute levels of prosperity or misery, and the way in which these differences were perceived by those concerned.

More money undoubtedly flowed into the village through several new channels. One of these was the allowances and pensions paid to relatives and dependants of serving soldiers, which amounted to more than 1·6 milliard roubles by the end of February 1917.[3] Against this income must be set the additional expenditure incurred by peasants in acquiring and sending comforts to their kinsmen in the army.

A second source of cash in peasant pockets came from savings accumulated as a result of the ban on the sale of alcoholic spirits. This was imposed (to the surprise of the general public) within a month of the war's outbreak. Not all the revenue lost to the treasury in rural areas automatically stayed there, since many of the heaviest drinkers were away on active service. Moreover, the less abstemious among those left behind now had to pay considerable sums to illicit distillers, whose number was legion. Nevertheless this flourishing contraband activity was also a source of profit to people closely connected with the rural economy, many of whom naturally enough were peasants.

Thirdly, those whose horses, draught animals, carts and such like were requisitioned by the military authorities were awarded financial compensation for the loss incurred, although payment was often made at a rate below the rapidly rising market value of such stock.[4]

In the fourth place, although the countryside lost the off-farm earnings of those peasants who were now in uniform, their place was sometimes taken by others (many of them women) who were either attracted by the higher wages now paid in industry, especially those branches working for the war effort, or were forced to take up factory employment from economic necessity. It appears that on balance more industrial earnings found their way to the villages than before 1914, although the evidence on this point is inconclusive.[5] The drain to the towns was particularly marked from the Central Agricultural region, where it helped to mop up some of the surplus population that had long been both a symptom and a contributory cause of peasant misery.

Fifthly, the prices which peasants could obtain on the free market for their crops and livestock rose appreciably. By the autumn of 1916 a producer of rye grain in the middle Volga region could earn 2·23 times as much as in 1909–13; the corresponding figure for spring wheat was 2·43, for barley 2·45, and for oats (which were in great demand) 6·08.[6] Corresponding data for livestock products are much scantier. In Orenburg beef fetched 2·28 times the 1913 price in 1916; in Omsk butter had more than doubled.[7] From these increases nearly everyone stood to benefit, at least indirectly, in those villages which had a surplus. It is true, as Anfimov points out, that some poorer peasants also had to purchase foodstuffs at these high prices during lean months; however, as he shows in another connection, such households contributed a considerable proportion of marketed produce.[8] It may be added here that nominal agricultural wages likewise doubled between 1909–13 and 1916.

For all these reasons it may be asserted confidently that in cash terms the peasants' overall income did indeed rise. But what was the real value of the money they received? The price index, as calculated for urban consumers, stood at 228 in 1916 (1913 : 100) (see below

p. 46). It must be borne in mind that the goods which peasants normally bought on the market were not the same as those purchased by townsmen, so that in order to measure the former's purchasing power with any degree of reliability we would need an index constructed on the basis of an entirely different 'product mix'. In the absence of such an index we may simply note that the increased free-market price for agricultural produce was roughly commensurate with the rise in urban prices.

The value of the paper rouble fell rapidly as the war dragged on, and the attractiveness of long-term interest-bearing bonds (in which State agencies sometimes made payment) likewise decreased. There is no cloud without a silver lining, and inflation did at least reduce the tax burden; however, to the countryman it was the disadvantages of inflation that naturally loomed larger. There was little satisfaction to be had from depositing one's swelling funds in savings banks (where rural depositors' holdings rose from 480 million roubles in 1913 to 638 million roubles in 1915)[9] and even less from hoarding them in some place of concealment. Cash and bonds were a poor substitute for the manufactured goods which peasants were accustomed to buy on the market : agricultural implements, textiles, footwear and such everyday items as kerosene, nails and needles. Russia's only factory capable of producing the high-grade steel used to make scythes was situated in enemy-occupied territory, and the authorities' leisurely efforts to persuade some entrepreneur in the hinterland to take its place proved to be unavailing : by 1916 output of these vital tools was only 8,200, as compared with 46,000 in 1913.[10] The production of sickles fell from two and a half million to half a million; and the figures for the principal types of agricultural machinery (of less interest to peasants than to landowners) likewise fell by about four-fifths.[11] No doubt other shortages less easy to document were felt more bitterly.

These material hardships helped to create in the countryside an ill-defined anti-urban (as distinct from the more obvious anti-government or anti-war) sentiment – an attitude, one might say, of 'what we have we hold'. This was potentially a most serious phenomenon, since it was bound to have a harmful effect upon agricultural productivity and food supplies. How was the farmer to be induced to part with the surplus of cereals, meat and dairy products which the rest of the country needed at prices it could afford? This problem, which deserves to be regarded as the *leit-motif* of twentieth-century Russian history, posed itself with increasing sharpness in 1915 and 1916. As a result of the war the efficiency of Russian agriculture, already poor by international standards, suffered a series of major setbacks.

Two of these blows may be considered here : first, the decline in the number of horses and livestock; second, the decline in available manpower. The army authorities seem to have had an insatiable appetite for horses. No fewer than 2·6 million had been bought or requisitioned by February 1917; this was over ten per cent of the total number of horses aged four years or more.[12] As a result the percentage of peasant households without horse traction, in thirteen provinces for which reliable data are available, rose from 25 per cent to 30 per cent.[13] The overall figure (for all owners in fifty provinces) showed a drop from 24·8 to 22·0 million.[14] The loss was more significant than these figures might suggest, for the beasts that remained, which even in normal times were underweight and inadequately cared for, could not cope with the heavier tasks they were now expected to perform, especially at the peaks of the agricultural cycle. Requisitions and excess slaughtering also took a high toll of cattle. In the same thirteen provinces the number of beasts in peasant ownership decreased by eleven per cent as compared with the pre-war figure, and by 1917 it is estimated that 22·8 per cent of peasant households did not possess a cow of their own.[15] This mattered a great deal to those households which had yet to enter the machine age – and these were the overwhelming majority.

Even more serious, and certainly more obvious to contemporary observers, was the lack of manpower. Russian peasant women had traditionally done much of the farm work, including tasks involving strenuous physical exertion, but there were some operations for which even they lacked sufficient fortitude. Yet it is estimated that in 1916 no less than seventy-two per cent of the agricultural labour force on peasant farms, and fifty-eight per cent of that on land-owners' estates, was female.[16] The remainder comprised old men and boys, refugees and enemy prisoners of war. The refugees who arrived from the combat zone were usually destitute and demoralized; they could hardly be expected to work with a will. Nor could the prisoners, although in some cases they might possess skills denied to their hosts. In any event the majority of the 639,000 captured enemy personnel who had been assigned to agricultural work by

1916 were sent to help out on landowners' estates.[17] The allocation and employment of these unfortunates provided yet another source of friction within the rural milieu. Some peasants complained that they were being discriminated against in the assignment of prison labour, and others that the low wages which these men were paid (about one-quarter to one-third of those earned by native hired workers) were keeping wage rates down.[18]

The landowners experienced the same problems as the mass of the peasantry. In their case the impact on living standards was of course less drastic, since most members of this class had sufficient resources to cushion themselves against major adversities. Nevertheless the war hit the private proprietors severely, depriving them of the hired labour and the income from rented land to which they were accustomed, tightening credit facilities, and making it harder than ever for them to bring large quantities of produce to the market quickly once the harvest had been gathered in. Whether any deductions can legitimately be drawn from the difficulties experienced by the two groups as to the relative efficiency of large- and small-scale farming (as was freely done by Populist writers) seems doubtful. The peasants adjusted more easily to war-time conditions than the larger proprietors, but they could not produce the additional amounts of food required to meet growing demand. Perhaps the safest conclusion is that the two types of agricultural economy were still so interdependent that each suffered from the inefficiency of the other.

There is in any case no doubt that the area under cultivation fell both on 'privately owned land' (which as defined by the census-takers in 1916 included land owned by independent peasant proprietors) and on that held by the rest of the peasants. On the former the decline appears to have been greater, at least in the second year of the war. This at any rate is the conclusion that emerges from the census data, although it should be pointed out that these understate the sown area, partly because informants deliberately gave false returns in the hope of evading requisitioning orders.[19] According to Anfimov, by 1916 the 'private owners' had 37·7 per cent less land sown to food grains (but a little more sown to fodder grains) than in 1914; the decline was from 8·4 to 6·6 million dessyatines in all. On 'peasant' land the area sown to food and fodder grains shrank by only 9·8 per cent and 11·7 per cent respectively, or from 77·3 to 69·2 million dessyatines.[20] It is estimated that the total area sown to grain and potatoes declined from 88·7 million dessyatines in 1914 to 78·3 million dessyatines in 1916, a reduction of 11·7 per cent.[21]

Fortunately both 1915 and (to a lesser extent) 1916 were favourable years climatically. Nevertheless according to the best available estimate the gross harvest of cereals fell from an average of 4,869 million puds in 1909–13 to 4,669 million puds in 1914–15; the following year registered a rise to 4,810 million puds, but in 1916–17 the figure sank again to 3,966 million puds, or 23·5 per cent below the pre-war figure.[22] So far as food grains were concerned, the decline in the harvest, as in the sown area, was considerably greater on privately owned land than on peasant farms. The most vital point is that a smaller fraction of what was harvested found its way on to the market. Unfortunately the data for 'commercialized' cereals are sadly deficient. According to one estimate, in 1916–17 this figure was 32·6 per cent below that for 1913–14, even though before the war only about one-fifth of the gross harvest had been marketed.[23] The implication seems clear : agricultural producers, deprived of the peacetime economic incentives to market their crop, were consuming more of it themselves. Some was used to distil spirits; much was evidently kept in storage, either by producers or by middlemen. Their gain was the townsman's and the soldier's loss.

The information on the livestock market during the war years is much scantier. The military authorities placed enormous orders for meat and fats (mostly of animal origin). The army's meat consumption in 1916 has been variously estimated at forty and fifty-six million puds.[24] As a result of this increased demand and other factors livestock herds may have fallen by some seven to eight million head. Higher figures are, however, also encountered.[25]

It is hard to say how far the crisis in food supply was caused by the decline of commercial production and how far by problems of transport and administrative organization. Most contemporary observers, and most historians since, have concentrated on the latter aspect of the problem, although if we accept Anfimov's figure of a 32·6 per cent fall in marketed cereals, cited above, it is possible that this emphasis is misplaced. It is even harder to suggest, in the light of later experience, how producers and dealers might best have been brought to part with their stocks. If the tsarist authorities can be indicted for excessive reliance on the market mechanism, their successors displayed an excessive faith in the merits of coercion.

In theory it would seem that the system adopted under the old regime, which combined limited state intervention with ample scope for private business enterprise, had much to commend it. However in practice the results were disappointing. There was continual tension between the central bureaucratic and military agencies on one hand and the public 'voluntary organizations', banks and commercial firms on the other.

The first important measures were taken by the government in February 1915. It allowed the ministry of Agriculture's local supply commissioners to impose embargoes on produce earmarked for the army and to fix the purchase price in the light of local conditions. Those who refused to sell at this price were liable to be issued with a requisitioning order, in which case they were paid only eighty-five per cent of the fixed price. This provision was designed to give producers an incentive to market their crop promptly. It is not known how frequently the punitive clause was invoked, but the authorities were certainly none too discriminating in their exactions. These were larger than immediate needs dictated and fell with particular severity upon farmers in provinces close to the front.

In the following months, responding to protests from several quarters, the government conceded a more significant role in the supply network to civilian 'voluntary organizations'. Representatives of the public were accorded two-thirds of the seats on the Special Council for Food Supply, which was set up in August 1915; its chairman, however, was a nominated official who was vested with quasi-dictatorial powers. Similar bodies came into being at the provincial (*guberniya*) and county (*uyezd*) levels. The result was the creation of an unwieldy bureaucratic apparatus which the central authorities could not keep under proper control. Periodically conferences were held with the provincial supply commissioners, but these meetings, instead of leading to better coordination, were used by the liberal-minded 'public men' as a platform from which to air their political grievances against the regime, as well as legitimate complaints at the central supply authorities' lack of a clear policy.

These complaints centred upon the problem of price control. Early in the war efforts had been made by some local authorities to fix ceiling prices for certain commodities, but these unsystematic ventures had proved to be totally ineffective. Most of those involved in food-supply work thought that the price of at least the most essential products should be determined by central government regulation. Their view eventually prevailed over that of the more conservative officials, who doubted whether such action was either wise or practicable. In February 1916 rules were adopted whereby supply commissioners were empowered to make the rail transport of scarce commodities dependent on possession of a permit, which they would issue only if the supplier agreed not to sell above a certain agreed price, fixed according to local conditions.[26] Some months previously the Special Council had begun to regulate the price of two key foodstuffs, sugar and flour, for which separate agencies were established under its aegis, likewise with public participation. One result was that millers throughout the country in effect became employees of the Central Flour Bureau, for they were remunerated solely by a fixed commission on each contract assigned to them by this body. Partly in protest against this, and partly for technical reasons (lack of skilled labour and breakdown of milling machinery), by the spring of 1916 their output had fallen some 20–25 per cent below normal.[27] Sugar output was less adversely affected : in 1915–16 it declined by 8·6 per cent over the previous year.[28] Thus the supply officials found themselves in a dilemma : if they intervened, they aroused the opposition of producers and traders, who were reluctant to sell at the fixed prices; if they refrained from intervention, the prices charged on the market shot up to unacceptable levels, and they themselves became more unpopular than ever. The two-price system was very difficult to operate in practice. The free-market price quickly caught up on the fixed price, which had to be reviewed; knowing this, traders gave priority to meeting orders placed on the army's behalf rather than selling to the civilian market. Even banks joined in the rush to corner stocks of produce in the expectation that they would gain by a rapid rise in the price.

Such speculative activities were seen by contemporaries as the principal cause of food shortages in the towns. This was the theme of numerous reports submitted by informants in the provinces to the grandiloquently named Commission for Combating the High Cost of Living, one of the many semi-official bodies sheltering under the wing of the Special Council for Food Supply. For example, a meeting of the supply council of Kherson province, held on 30 November 1915 with the governor in the chair, 'recognized that there was absolutely no justification for the high prices noted in his province, and that they are of a plainly speculative nature'; a similar report from Kostroma stated that 'the flour-millers and merchants, here as elsewhere, have taken advantage of existing conditions to derive the largest possible profit from sale of their stocks'.[29] Allowance ought to be made here for the anti-capitalist bias common among officials as well as intellectuals; nevertheless there is no doubt that profiteering was rife. If the government was slow to check it, this was partly because it recognized the grave problems that would arise if sole responsibility for feeding the population were to be assumed by the official supply organizations. All the odium for shortages would inevitably fall upon the latter. Yet this was precisely what happened at the end of 1916. Under pressure from the lower echelons of the supply apparatus the government decided to take upon itself the obligation to provide a specific proportion of the foodstuff needs of certain consuming areas (25–50 per cent in Moscow, 75 per cent in Petrograd and 100 per cent in Finland); the rest was to be furnished by 'voluntary organizations' and private traders. Price regulation was now extended to grain (9 September 1916) and shortly afterwards to all other foodstuffs dealt with by the authorities.[30]

These measures, adopted after harvesting had already begun, gave producers an additional incentive to withhold their crop. The officials' problem now assumed nightmare proportions. The tsar's last agricultural minister, A.A. Rittikh, added to the confusion by a scheme for a compulsory grain levy. This measure is of particular interest in that it anticipated similar policies imposed by the Bolsheviks little more than a year later. Introduced by an order of 29 November 1916, its purpose was to cover the army's estimated deficit of 772 million puds of cereals. This figure was broken down into quotas for each province, determined by its estimated harvest, stocks and consumption requirements; this provincial quota was then divided up between counties, and the latter repeated the process betwen rural districts; finally the latter were to assign an obligatory amount to each village. In this way each primary producer would bear an appropriate share of the total burden. To give him an added incentive to comply, he was required only to take the crop to the normal place of storage before claiming payment. Bonuses were promised for exceeding the norm. The scheme thus indirectly recognized that existing fixed prices were unrealistically low. It imposed upon the local supply organizations an immense new task, that of collecting the grain quotas from the peasants' barns. In the event this problem was spared them, since the revolution supervened – accelerated, perhaps, by the unpopularity of the levy among those expected to enforce it. These officials secured a reduction of about one-third in the minister's original target, and in the event only some 130–170 million puds are said to have been collected.[31]

By the winter of 1916–17, as a result of declining commercial production and the ever-worsening administrative tangle, serious shortages of bread, fats, sugar and other staple foodstuffs made themselves felt in many urban centres. They were most acute in the capital itself, which geography and history had contrived to place in a corner of the empire remote from the principal grain-growing areas. Even the army was running short, despite the high priority allocated to the satisfaction of its needs. In the last years before the war the twenty-five 'consuming' provinces had imported an average of nearly two hundred million puds of cereals from the 'producing' regions. In 1915 the former had an unusually good harvest, as a result of which their needs were halved, while the south had plenty to spare. In 1916 the harvest was down by twenty per cent in the south and by forty per cent in the north.[32] This put an impossible strain on the transport system, already overburdened by other demands. The amount of grain transported by rail fell from 1,297,000 puds in 1913 to 847,000 puds in 1915. Considering that about forty per cent of the 1913 harvest had gone for export, the 1915 one sufficed to meet the needs of both the army (235 million puds) and the deficiency areas.[33] Unfortunately no data on the composition of rail freight are available for 1916, but the general situation is fairly clear. The army consumed the equivalent of 250–265 million puds of cereals, which was roughly the same amount as the deficit of the consuming areas (256 million puds); yet the south had a theoretical surplus of only half this amount : 285 million puds. A little could be obtained from stocks or from Asiatic Russia, but these sources could not fill the gap. As for meat, it has been estimated that only one-third of the total requirements of the army and the cities (91·5 million puds) could be met from officially recognized sources.[34] But by this time the notion of 'requirements' of meat was unreal, since this had become more of a luxury than ever at the ordinary townsman's table. Even in the army the meat ration had to be reduced from 1 funt to ¾ funt per day in combat units, and to ½ funt for non-combatants, while none at all was issued on two days each week.[35]

It was only to be expected that public opinion should attribute the responsibility for these shortcomings to the government, without regard for the underlying economic factors – about which little information was in any case available. In a sense this was fortunate for agricultural producers, who for the time being avoided the odium that would otherwise surely have befallen them. Apart from a few large proprietors, these producers could not hope to influence the shaping of policy; they could only reduce the sown area or withhold their produce from the market. Theirs was in effect a campaign of passive resistance, or at least could be interpreted as such. A few months later such action (or inaction) would be given the most sinister connotation, and soldiers and townsmen would exact a fearful revenge for the wrongs which they thought they had suffered at the hands of peasant 'speculators'.

In the countryman's view his grievances were equally well-founded. In 1916 there was no one in the village to provide active leadership for the peasants, whose political attitudes were, if anything, less coherent than usual. It would be over-simple to assume (as is frequently done) that their economic dissatisfaction was automatically translated into political dissent, or even that there was any connection between the two. Less volatile and more pragmatic than the townsmen, they reacted according to a logic all their own.

At the war's outset the peasants had responded without much trouble to the order for mobilization, but their spirit was one of resignation rather than enthusiasm.[36] In 1915, as the heavy toll of casualties became known in the villages, this mood became tinged with despondency and bitterness. There were a few protests at fresh levies of recruits, but reports of military successes could still bring satisfaction. The front was far away, and military operations did not impinge directly upon village life, which went on in its proverbial isolation. The war was seen as an additional misfortune, to be borne stoically in the hope that better times would follow. Newspapers were scarce and uninformative; the arrival of batches of refugees from the front-line areas was often the first contact that peasants in the interior had with the reality of war. From time to time soldiers came home on leave, especially if they had been wounded. Another channel of communication was correspondence between men at the front and their relatives. Although such letters were censored, they may have helped to generalize the civilians' grievances and to give them a political slant. For example, a soldier named Kh. Grishin (who did not identify his unit) wrote to his wife in the village of Beguny (province not stated) that he had learned from talking to his comrades that the war was not a necessary evil sent by the Almighty, but 'the handiwork of cunning persons in power who don't know how to use it (*sic*) but instead pursue their selfish ends'.[37] In guarded language soldiers would tell of their sufferings and their hopes for a speedy peace.

In this and other ways a segment of the peasantry, the size of which cannot be determined with any confidence,[38] came to share the general distrust of the empire's political and military leaders. They were seen as incompetent and possibly even traitorous. The rumour and gossip that were the staple intellectual fare of educated persons in Petrograd and Moscow seeped down to the provincial centres, and from there in distorted form to the villages.

Some information on peasant attitudes is provided by outsiders' reports. A zemstvo employee travelling in the Volga region stated that 'everywhere people are discussing political questions and passing resolutions directed against the landowners and merchants, and cells of various organizations are being formed'.[39] An Okhrana official confirmed that political matters were in the forefront of attention in the countryside: 'rural Russia ... has lost all faith in a successful end to the war. According to insurance agents, teachers, tradesmen and other representatives of the village intelligentsia, everybody is impatiently awaiting the end of this "accursed war".'[40] Neither of these judgements can be considered wholly reliable. The first was clearly influenced by its author's liberal or Populist convictions; the second bears traces of the interdepartmental conflict to which the security services were a party. It also shows that the latter were content to obtain their information on peasant morale at second hand – a vivid illustration of the gulf that separated the tsarist bureaucracy from the lower depths of society.

Anfimov has unearthed evidence of 557 outbreaks of agrarian violence between July 1914 and December 1916.[41] However he admits that it is difficult to say how many of these deserve to be considered revolutionary. Many of the incidents recorded were part of the normal fabric of life in the Russian countryside, where collective acts of violence were by no means unusual. For example, in April 1916 the peasants of Ryzvyanka (Volhynia province) pastured their cattle on unsown arable land belonging to a proprietor named Otfinovskaya and resisted efforts to dislodge them until troops were called in.[42] Should this be categorized as an 'anti-landowner uprising' or just a routine dispute over rights to facilities left unexploited? There were cases of recruits sacking official liquor outlets before they left for the front,[43] which may or may not have been expressions of anti-war sentiment. Other protests were directed against the zeal of tax-collectors or requisitioning officers, the imposition of cartage and quartering obligations, the shortage of timber for firewood, and above all rising prices for foodstuffs or city-made goods. Some incidents developed into riots involving casualties on both sides.

It is noteworthy that these protests do not seem to have been directed overtly against the war as such. This was regarded quite properly as a weighty issue beyond the legitimate scope of popular pressure. The dissenters' aim was not to subvert the existing political or social order but to win immediate tangible concessions from it. Even though the issues involved were no longer simply local in character, the element of organization behind these protests was still very feeble, both territorially and technically; indeed, it is hardly correct to speak of organization at all.

For this reason the agrarian movement, taken in isolation, did not represent a mortal threat to the tsarist regime. It was repressed without difficulty, as it had been on so many previous occasions. Yet this was a Pyrrhic victory. There were ominous portents for the future, as well as echoes of the past, in the protesters' assumption that all 'non-toilers' – merchants, landowners or officials – were their natural enemies; that they were collectively guilty of selfish and immoral conduct; and that social justice required that they be eliminated from the rural milieu. Two and a half years of war had intensified the Russian villagers' ancient suspicion of privileged outsiders and had prepared the soil for a mighty upheaval.

FOUR *The Impact of the War on Industrial Labour*

THE URBAN POPULATION, particularly those in lower income brackets (most but not all of them working in industry), felt wartime hardships more acutely than those who gained their livelihood from the land. What was more important, they had a better opportunity as well as a more powerful incentive to convert their sense of grievance into conscious political action. This pressure made itself felt above all in the growing incidence of strikes, one of which, in Petrograd, eventually initiated the chain of events that led to the fall of the monarchy. Only a fraction of these strikes had a political motivation, but in existing conditions even those that could unhesitatingly be qualified as economic were bound to have political repercussions. The element of coordination and direction behind these industrial troubles was never very great, so that their effects could not be predicted either by revolutionaries or by the tsar's officials – still less by the general public. This helps to explain the surprise with which Russian educated society greeted the events of February 1917.

For industrial employees the war meant not only the conscription of men of military age into the armed forces (it is thought that by 1917 about four million servicemen had been drawn from the towns and about eleven million from the countryside) but also a tightening of official controls over their place and habits of work. These regulations were applied with particular stringency to those in factories fulfilling defence contracts. These concerns, 5,278 in number, had almost two million workers on their books by the spring of 1917; to them should be added a large but indeterminate proportion of those engaged in mining, transport and construction. This was a measure of the extent to which Russian industry was geared to prosecution of the war.[1]

Already on 20 July 1914 an imperial decree placed large areas of European Russia, mainly in the west but including the province of Petrograd (as St Petersburg was now called), under martial law.[2] Other areas were declared to be in a state of 'reinforced security'. This meant that in certain circumstances civilians could be tried by military courts.[3] In October 1914 the Council of Ministers installed a system of control over industrial enterprises working on contracts placed by the military or naval authorities. These supervisors were empowered 'to take all necessary steps to prevent delays in fulfilling orders from these agencies'[4] – which could be interpreted as covering any form of industrial action involving stoppage of production. One year later there were set up, under the authority of the Special Council for Defence, so-called 'factory councils' composed of officials and representatives of the local war-industries committee (a voluntary organization); their chairman could appoint production supervisors, sack directors and managers, close down inefficient factories and fix wage rates.[5] Some local military authorities, worried by what they regarded as 'laxity in the rear', uttered draconian threats which could not be enforced and undermined their own credibility. In September 1916 General Frolov in Petrograd ordered all cases involving work stoppages in enterprises on defence work to be heard by field courts-martial. So far as is known this remained a dead letter, perhaps because the ministry of Trade and Industry urged a more cautious approach; in any case strikes continued to occur in these establishments.[6] In practice officials had to show restraint in applying emergency powers, not only because they were unwilling to antagonize the more resolute elements in the labour force, but also because there was such an acute shortage of workers possessing the necessary technical skills.

More important, perhaps, as a means of enforcing industrial discipline was the policy of granting deferment of military service to those whose role in production was deemed essential. In the first weeks of the war mobilization orders were issued indiscriminately, with the result that about one-fifth of the industrial labour force found itself in uniform. However, the short-sightedness of such measures soon became apparent and a number of men were returned to factory work. Later mobilization orders were carried through more selectively and the proportion of men exempted gradually rose; by October 1916, according to general staff estimates, as much as 27 per cent of the labour force fell into this category.[7] Deferments were granted most readily to employees in the oil industry, coal-mining and mechanical trades. By 1916 25 per cent of the nation's coal-miners enjoyed such prerogatives; this compared with 12 per cent of the textile-workers.[8] In the Ukraine the proportion was considerably above the national average, for on 1 March 1917 45 per cent of the coal-miners and 39 per cent of metallurgical-workers in this region were covered by deferments.[9] Since these men were liable to be turned over to the military authorities if they lost their jobs, for whatever reason, they had a strong incentive to avoid trouble. A police official in Yekaterinoslav province reported in April 1915 that fear of dispatch to active service was a factor limiting the spread of industrial action among Donets miners; shortly afterwards, however, they did join in the strike movement and a number of them suffered this penalty.[10] The deputy head of the Petrograd police department, Kafarov, claimed in December 1915 that a general strike in the city had been averted because 'the workers are afraid of being sent to forward positions' and advised that, if this risk were to be reduced, further unrest could be expected.[11] Early in the following year a strike broke out in the naval yards at Nikolayev which lasted forty-two days before the Admiralty stepped in and applied forceful measures. Some 6,000 strikers were sent to their units; significantly, however, all but 312 of them were returned within five months.[12] Apart from the desire to maintain production, which also accounts for the Admiralty's initial leniency, it seems that the armed forces were none too anxious to have 'trouble-makers' on their hands. Sometimes they would refuse to accept parties of men consigned to them by civilian agencies. It was military officials in the rear, preoccupied with security problems, who were keenest on this solution to their dilemmas, as we have seen in the case of General Frolov.

All in all there can be no doubt that the juridical status of industrial labour deteriorated as a result of such regimentation. This was accompanied by a decline in real incomes and living standards. The statistics available on industrial earnings are of limited reliability, partly because data were not collected systematically for all areas (although price levels varied greatly), and partly because price indexes ought to be weighted in such a way as to take account of changes in purchasing habits brought about by scarcity of goods and other factors. Moreover, many workers, especially those with families, were able to purchase cheap foodstuffs up to forty per cent below local market prices in special shops run by their enterprise,[13] and the existence of such facilities was not reflected in data provided by business associations or the factory inspectorate. In July 1916 the military authorities decided (against some opposition by civilian officials and industrialists) that certain workers in defence-related industries should receive soldiers' rations from reserves earmarked for army use. Some 2·1 million employees or their dependants were to be covered by the scheme,[14] but it is uncertain how far it was implemented.

Information on wage rates published at the time is of next to no value, since no effort was made to relate wages to prices. One investigator of nominal rates of pay in the Moscow area calculated that in 1916 unskilled labourers were earning 46 per cent more than in the previous year, carpenters 45 per cent more, and fitters 67·8 per cent more (47·1 kopecks an hour in lieu of 28).[15] A serious analysis of the labour market during the war years was not attempted until the 1920s. According to calculations published by S.G. Strumilin in 1923, by the latter half of 1916 overall real wages had fallen to 85 per cent of their 1913 value (or in terms of 1913 currency from 22 to 18·7 roubles a month).[16] He reckoned that in Moscow the average monthly wage had declined from 27·1 to 24·4 roubles, while in Petrograd it had risen slightly from 34·7 to 35·2 roubles.[17] This difference was due to the varying composition of the labour force in the two cities : whereas Moscow continued to cater in considerable measure to the needs of the civilian market (especially for textiles), Petrograd had a higher proportion of workers in metallurgical and chemical industries fulfilling defence orders. The average national wage of employees in the latter two branches rose in real terms by 7·7 per cent and 21·0 per cent between 1913 and 1916, whereas those employed in the manufacture of cotton and woollen goods suffered a decline of 3·4 per cent and 16·4 per cent respectively.[18]

ANNUAL REMUNERATION OF RUSSIAN LABOUR 1913–16[19]
(in roubles)

year	Retail Price Index	data of factory inspectorate*		data of CSA census					
				nominal wage			real wage		
		nominal wage	real wage	in factories working for defence	in others	average	in factories working for defence	in others	average
1913	100	257	257	393	218	258	393	218	258
1914	108	272	252	442	222	275	408	206	255
1915	151	322	213	594	276	365	394	183	242
1916	228	(478)	210	912	417	573	400	183	251

* for all Russia except Warsaw factory inspection district; excludes state-owned works

A few years later Strumilin had a chance to revise his estimates in the light of new data on retail prices, and offered the table shown opposite.

Strumilin pointed out that the Soviet Central Statistical Administration (CSA) figures, which covered only thirty-one provinces under Soviet control in 1918 and therefore excluded the Ukraine and part of the Urals, understated the decline in wages. On the basis of another investigation carried out under the auspices of the factory inspectorate in 1917, covering over a million workers, he suggested that the general decline in wages between 1913 and 1916 amounted to seven per cent – about half his original estimate. In a study which he revised in 1956 he calculated that in terms of monthly earnings the decline was of the order of ten per cent and, if allowance were made for subsidized housing, nine per cent.[20] His final figure is thus about two-thirds of his first estimate.

Such is Strumilin's reputation that other Soviet historians have been wary of contesting his views, although in writing about the period many of them give a bleaker picture. One recent investigator who has undertaken research into the situation in the Ukraine claims that Donets coal-miners suffered a drop of 25 per cent in real wages by the spring of 1916 : although their monetary earnings had risen one and a half times, the cost of a monthly food ration for an adult male had risen from 12–13 to 23–4 roubles a month. According to the same source by February 1917 real wages were only 50–70 per cent of what they had been before the war.[21] However, these figures are derived, not from a comparison of actual income and expenditure, but from the estimated cost at current prices of a miner's normal budget in March 1914 – although this comprised many commodities which had either been priced out of his range or were simply unavailable (for instance, one jacket, three pairs of trousers and seven shirts a year).[22] Soviet statisticians have long made use of calculations based upon such 'consumption norms', overlooking the point that they necessarily have an abstract character in a period of scarcity, when the pattern of effective demand is subject to rapid change. At best they indicate the extent to which consumers were deprived of goods they had been accustomed to, and so give a rough idea of their sense of impoverishment. In plain words, if a Donets miner in 1916 had been asked how far he felt his living standards had worsened since the outbreak of war, he might well have replied that he was about a third to a half poorer.

Politically, his perception of his relative situation might matter more than the actual fall in the value of his wages. The importance of this 'subjective factor' was recognized by the police at the time. An Okhrana report of October 1916 stated that in Petrograd workers felt that prices had risen about threefold, whereas their wages had doubled at most. Only a tenth of those questioned considered that their earnings were higher than they had been before the war, and only one man in fifty expressed himself as satisfied with his material standards.[23] In January 1917 a Moscow labour exchange reported, on the basis of interviews with carpenters, mechanics and manual labourers, their impression that wages had doubled since the war, while prices had risen fourfold.[24]

Apart from declining income levels there were many other reasons for discontent. Managements and local authorities had less money than before to spend on housing or other amenities. Accommodation was more cramped than ever owing to the influx of new workers into factory settlements. There was pressure to work extra shifts and to keep production going round the clock. The wear and tear on machinery meant that more jobs had to be done by hand. Men had to learn new skills or move to other factories to replace workers who had been called up, and this, though it might lead to higher pay in some instances, disrupted routine habits and family life. Sometimes plants had to suspend production owing to shortage of fuel or raw materials, and the men suddenly found themselves laid off (which might mean a drop in wages). The incidence of illness increased, as a result of low hygienic standards, under-nourishment and fatigue. Already in the summer of 1915 more than a hundred cases of cholera were registered in the mines and factories of the Donets, and early in the following year typhus made its appearance in the same region. Medical facilities were inadequate and nearly half the cholera victims perished.[25] The rising incidence of disease strained the meagre resources of sickness-benefit funds, some of which had to reduce their scale of payments or even cease operations altogether.

Lurking behind all these immediate issues, of course, was the overriding problem of the war. It is not surprising that, once the patriotic enthusiasm of the early months had spent its force, industrial workers should have resumed their pressure for improvements in their material well-being. This agitation was almost wholly economic in nature, at least until 1916. According to data compiled by the factory inspectorate, in the last five months of 1914 less than a thousand working days were lost as a result of disputes characterized as non-economic, as against 169,000 in the economic category; in 1915 the corresponding figures were 34,000 and 1,654,000, and in 1916 673,000 and 4,076,000. However arbitrary the criteria used in classifying strikes, these figures do give a rough indication of the proportions of industrial unrest.[26]

The incidence of strikes varied not only seasonally and regionally, but also according to the composition of the labour force. As we have seen, large numbers of women entered industry; the influx of adolescents (aged fifteen to eighteen) and juveniles (under fifteen) was smaller but nevertheless significant. An investigation carried out into 700,000 war workers by the Special Council for Defence in 1917 found that 17 per cent of them were women and 12·5 per cent adolescents.[27] In manufacturing industry generally the proportion of women rose from 27·4 per cent in late 1914 to 34·2 per cent in January 1917; the corresponding figures for adolescents and juveniles (of both sexes) were 10·9 per cent and 14·0 per cent.[28] In the engineering industry female labour accounted for a mere 1·1 per cent of the total number of employees in 1913 but for 14·3 per cent in January 1917; the percentage of adolescents and juveniles rose slightly from 9·4 per cent to 11·7 per cent.[29] In the textile industry, where women had always played a very important part, their proportion now doubled, reaching 43·4 per cent. Women were even recruited for underground work in the mines, although at least not as face-workers. On the registers of the factory inspectorate there were virtually as many women and young people as there were men.[30]

From the political standpoint this change in the composition of the labour force was a stabilizing factor. Women were unlikely to be as militant as men; or, to put the point in the ideological terms favoured by Soviet historians, 'their entry into industry could not but be accompanied by a certain lowering of class consciousness among the proletarian mass'.[31] Probably the reverse was true of adolescents, whose revolutionary potential was to be revealed so strikingly in 1917.

Another factor which made for instability was the accelerated tendency for the labour force to be concentrated in large enterprises. More than half of those subject to the factory inspectorate were employed in 787 large firms, nearly all working directly for the war effort.[32] In Petrograd province alone there were 343,000 workers in concerns with more than 500 persons on their books; at their head stood the great Putilov plant, which employed over 26,000 persons. The degree of concentration also increased in the Moscow area, but to a less striking extent.[33] In the Ukraine virtually all metallurgical workers and nine-tenths of the miners were employed in such large concerns; nearly a quarter of the former toiled in enterprises proudly classed in the 'giant' category with over 10,000 work-people.[34]

This factor attained special importance in view of the fact that, as noted above, Russian industry was localized in a few well-defined centres. As the war progressed, Petrograd and the north-west emerged as the principal focus of working-class dissent. The first year was relatively quiet. The tenth anniversary of 'Bloody Sunday' in 1905 was marked by the customary brief work stoppages, but on a much more modest scale than usual: in Petrograd a mere 2,500 persons went on strike, as against 111,000 in the previous year, and there were no disorders.[35] Another anniversary fell on International Labour Day, which the vagaries of the Russian calendar caused to be celebrated on 18 April. Characteristically enough, the occasion provoked the greatest response in Russian Poland and the Baltic provinces, where internationalist traditions were strongest; even so the number of those involved was very small. In Petrograd an undercover police agent reported that discontent among workers of the Putilov plant had a patriotic motif: it was suspected that German-born elements in the board of directors were deliberately delaying work on two mine-layers under construction, and the men demanded that the culprits be dismissed.[36]

During the summer attention shifted to the Central Industrial region. In May there were riots in Moscow directed against the influence exerted in certain firms by enemy aliens. There is some evidence of police connivance in these outbreaks. More important were two incidents in which trigger-happy security forces opened fire upon striking workmen. At Kostroma on 5 June four men were killed and nine wounded. Critics of the government, basing themselves on unofficial local sources, put the number much higher, at twelve killed and forty-five wounded.[37] In the second incident, at the textile centre of Ivanovo-Voznesensk on 10 August, the number of casualties was unofficially put at thirty killed and fifty-three wounded.[38] Whatever the exact figures, the authorities' actions evoked memories of the Lena shootings three years earlier. There was no justification for such brutal acts of repression, which helped to politicize what had hitherto been a purely industrial dispute. Questions were asked in the duma and workers in several other centres, including Petrograd, withdrew their labour as a gesture of sympathy.

By the autumn of 1915 a quarter of a million working days were being lost each month, and during the first three months of 1916 the figure rose to almost half a million.[39] Nearly all these stoppages were of an economic nature. This was true even of the strike at the naval shipyard in Nikolayev, mentioned above, as is clear from letters written by the strikers. 'If only you knew how expensive things are', wrote one of them, 'three times dearer than before; this is what has made the men stop work.'[40] In December 1915 there were disturbances in Petrograd and Moscow over lack of food, especially meat, fats and white flour. A police report noted that women queuing for supplies eagerly passed on rumours about alleged irregularities in distribution. 'These days it is a rare shop in which one does not hear them threaten to "settle up" with the shopkeeper unless he satisfies all his regular customers with meat.'[41] At the Sytnyy bazaar, an open-air market in Petrograd, the police had to intervene to restrain angry shoppers who, disappointed at their failure to obtain supplies, ventilated their frustration by damaging several traders' booths.[42]

Alarmed by these disorders, the authorities arrested a number of leading activists, including the entire Bolshevik Central Committee (31 December 1915), which had met to discuss its tactics on the impending anniversary of 'Bloody Sunday'. In the event this occasion was marked by withdrawal of labour on a much more extensive scale than in the previous year : according to police figures, in the capital nearly 67,000 men in 55 enterprises were affected.[43] Many of them were engaged on war work. So too were those involved in the dispute that broke out in a shop at the Putilov plant on 4 February 1916. The strikers shut off the electricity supply, whereupon men in several other departments joined them in demanding higher pay; in consequence the plant was closed for three days. Despite the threats uttered against them, the strikers won an increase in wages.[44] The ministry of Trade and Industry estimated that three-quarters of the industrial disputes occurring at this time ended in concessions by management.[45]

These economic concessions, and the many difficulties placed in the path of activists by the regime, brought about a certain relaxation of tension during the spring and summer of 1916 – although there was a violent clash early in May at Gorlovo, in the Donets valley, between striking miners and police, in which four people lost their lives; after a seven-day stoppage the protesters won a 25 per cent increase in pay.[46] Many workers, preoccupied with the struggle to make ends meet, returned to the countryside in search of food. With the arrival of autumn, however, the breakdown of the supply mechanism made itself felt with redoubled effect among industrial wage-earners. The situation in many smaller provincial centres is exemplified by that at Lyudinovo (Kaluga province), the site of the Maltsev engineering works. Its 5,000 employees complained of lack of food and rising prices. In September they went on strike, demanding a 75 per cent increase in wages, and after two days were granted a 50 per cent rise. At the end of October, when supplies again ran short, they stopped work once more, voicing the simple but evocative slogan 'Bread! Sugar!' Another 75 per cent increase in wages followed together with an allocation of flour and sugar. Despite this mild treatment a correspondent who visited the area reported that 'all around there is grumbling and dissatisfaction; people seem to be expecting something.'[47]

Security officials sent in alarmist reports. The Moscow police chief considered that queues had an effect equal to that of 'tens of thousands of revolutionary proclamations'; such expressions as anger and indignation, he reported, were no longer adequate to describe the popular mood in the city, which was more hostile to the government than it had been in 1905–6.[48] Again one must make some allowance for the fact that such dispatches reflected attitudes prevalent in the police hierarchy.

Most serious of all was the supply situation in Petrograd. Proximity to the centre of power enabled rumours to spread more easily and encouraged the idea that popular action might have some direct influence upon events. In the latter half of October workers in a number of metallurgical enterprises, led by those in the Renault works on the 'Vyborg side' (across the Neva), came out on strike. On the 17th of the month some activists trying to extend the strike clashed with police outside barracks occupied by men of the 181st reserve infantry regiment, who were shortly due to be sent to the front and made no secret of their sympathies. Stones were thrown and shots fired at the police. Having thus crossed the Rubicon, the soldiers successfully appealed to the workers for support and urged them to intensify their protests.[49] Demonstrators chanted revolutionary songs and shouted political slogans : 'down with autocracy' and even 'down with the war'. By 28 October nearly 62,000 men were on strike, the majority of them metallurgical-workers.[50] The authorities did not take harsh reprisals, and this was correctly interpreted as an admission of weakness; nevertheless, lacking firm leadership and exhausted by the struggle, the strikers soon returned to work. The last two months of the year were relatively quiet, but discontent continued to simmer beneath the surface. This confrontation may be seen as a dress rehearsal for the events of February 1917.

The director of the police department took comfort in the fact that the revolutionary forces were fragmented and out of step with those of the moderate opposition gathered round the duma.[51] This was true, although it was not enough to save the regime.[52] Nor was the isolation of the labour movement from educated society by any means complete. The proceedings of the duma were followed with some interest in working-class circles, especially after the assembly reconvened in November 1916. Despite the censorship, typed copies were circulated of speeches delivered by radical parliamentarians, notably N.S. Chkheidze and A.F. Kerensky. Nevertheless the over-cautious tactics of the Progressive Bloc of opposition parties were not likely to inspire ordinary working men to shed their inherited suspicions of the 'bourgeoisie' or to seek guidance from the duma in their own struggles.

It was a rather different matter with the Labour Group on the Central War Industries Committee (CWIC). The CWIC was the lead-ing 'voluntary organization', devoted to mobilizing the nation's industrial resources for the war effort. The Labour Group served as a national coordinating body for all manner of 'legal' (that is to say non-clandestine) working-class organizations such as trade unions, sick-benefit funds and cooperatives, and had a network of local agencies of its own. In 1914–15 most of the few trade unions and workers' newspapers in the country had been suppressed, but in practice the local authorities were allowed a measure of autonomy in deciding how to act. Police controls were most thorough in the capital, as one would expect; in Moscow, where the situation was slightly easier, there existed several unions of local scope, notably among craftsmen or tradesmen, and a Central Bureau which maintained sporadic contact between them, whose activities were, however, closely watched.[53] In the absence of trade unions the labour groups on the provincial war-industries committees were almost the only legal channel through which aspirations for improvement could be ventilated, and for this reason, if no other, a sizeable segment of working-class opinion came to look upon their activities with favour, or at least to take an interest in them.

When the idea of labour groups was first mooted in 1915 there was a good deal of hostility to any collaboration with entrepreneurial interests. In September of that year elections were arranged in Petrograd factories as the first step in choosing delegates to serve on the committees. After agitation by Bolsheviks and others the men decided by a narrow majority (90 : 81) to boycott the proceedings on the grounds that 'it is impossible on principle for representatives of the proletariat to participate in any organization sympathetic to the war.' However, two months later this decision was reversed by a vote of 109 to 67.[54] Subsequently similar groups were chosen in twenty regions and ninety-eight localities.[55] The norm was one representative for each thousand workers employed in larger enterprises and one for each plant with more than five hundred but less than a thousand employees.

The chairman of the central Labour Group was K.A. Gvozdev, a worker who had been a Menshevik before the war and still leaned towards the moderate socialists. He established a cordial relationship with A.I. Guchkov, the industrialist A.I. Konovalov and other 'public men' in the committee, who gave their backing to many of the proposals which he and his colleagues put forward. The latter declared that they were pursuing a dual aim : to help save the country from disaster and 'to defend energetically labour's interests ... and to give the workers every assistance in organizing themselves.'[56] Their attitude was pragmatic rather than ideological, and they did not consider that there was necessarily any contradiction between national and socialist objectives.

The labour leaders utilized the war-industries committees' organizational network to communicate with their sympathizers in the provinces without much fear of censorship and even established a skeleton administration of their own. The central group set up ten commissions for such matters as food supply, establishment of labour exchanges and trade unions, mobilization of industry and labour protection; these had corresponding agencies at the local level, although naturally on a less extensive scale. Five issues of a *Bulletin* were published containing news of the labour groups' activities and publicizing their aspirations.[57] Gvozdev was eager to arrange regular meetings between labour representatives on the war-industries committees and their electors in the factories. Although Guchkov supported the idea, it was too radical for the government, which realized its potential political implications; for the same reason it turned down proposals for nation-wide workers' conferences to discuss food supply and other topical questions. Another setback was the closure by the authorities, within a few weeks of its establishment in August 1916, of a nation-wide union embracing workers in the all-important metallurgical industry.[58] Nevertheless the Labour Group did much to encourage men to organize at enterprise level and also raised political issues. At the second congress of war-industries committees in February 1916 Gvozdev read out a declaration on behalf of workers from twenty industrial centres inspired by the principles of 'revolutionary defencism' (that is to say continuing defensive military operations in order to achieve a democratic peace without annexations or contributions); this was greeted with general applause by those present.[59] In December, at a conference of regional war-industries committees, the Labour Group issued a more powerful statement in the same sense, expressing regret that the duma had refused to discuss German peace overtures and calling for 'full democratization' of the country's political life as the only alternative to defeat and chaos.[60]

This political activity clearly had much in common with the objectives of the Menshevik wing of the RSDLP, and for this reason was vigorously opposed by such Bolsheviks as were then active in Russia; this factional dispute spilled over into *émigré* polemical literature and has come to overshadow all historical writing on the subject. The rights and wrongs of the argument are irrelevant to our theme. There can be no doubt that Gvozdev and his colleagues made skilful use of the opportunities open to them to spread their ideas and to build up the nucleus of a nation-wide labour organization. Their activities exceeded the limits which the government was prepared to tolerate. It had agreed only reluctantly to the representation of labour on the war-industries committees, assuming that the revolutionary potential of these groups would be held in check by the more 'responsible' business representatives and public figures. In practice, however, the government faced an alliance between these two elements which had as its immediate objective the overthrow of the existing order.

In a belated effort to avert this threat, the military governor of Petrograd, General S.S. Khabalov, acting on the instructions of the minister of Interior, A.D. Protopopov, had most members of the central Labour Group arrested (26/27 January 1917).[61] In a situation that had by now become highly explosive, this was a provocative act. It was certainly interpreted as such by the opposition. The bureau of cwic called a meeting with sympathetic members of the legislature to discuss the matter. It was decided to circulate a report among various public organizations explaining how helpful the Labour Group's activities had been to the cause of national defence.[62] Gvozdev, who was said to be in poor health, was for a time placed under house arrest, thanks to his friend Guchkov's intercession; this enabled him surreptitiously to continue his political activities. It seemed as though the organization which he and his comrades had built up had been beheaded, but there was still some life left in its limbs and it could serve a wider purpose.

The arrests were grist to the mill of those radical elements who had all along been critical of the Labour Group for its 'defensist' leanings. At this time the Petrograd Bolsheviks were endeavouring to re-establish contact between their nuclei in various industrial centres and to form a skeleton nation-wide organization. It is probably true to say that they had more success in this than their Menshevik rivals, but their influence was limited and sporadic; it could not in any case compare with that of the Labour Group. Such strength as the radicals had lay in the factories themselves, for their urban (city-wide) committees had been debilitated by frequent arrests. Even in the great Putilov works, with its 26,000 employees, only 150 men were committed to support the Bolsheviks.[63] Extreme left-wing militants were sometimes able to address meetings or to circulate appeals for strike action – for example, during the troubles in Petrograd in October 1916 – but it is difficult to gauge the impact of this agitation. In general it may be said that it intensified existing discontents rather than instigated them. Even in Petrograd, where dissatisfaction was reaching a feverish pitch, the mass of workers took little account of party labels. Of those who did draw such distinctions many found the Bolsheviks' line too doctrinaire, since they placed a heavy emphasis upon the need to end the war by international action from below. However attractive in itself such a prospect might be, it scarcely seemed to be practical politics at the moment, when everyone was preoccupied with domestic issues : the food supply, the high cost of living and the harsh policies of the government. Others, paradoxical as this may sound, will have found the Bolshevik attitude too moderate, for their agitators warned against premature or ill-prepared local actions which might fritter away energies that needed to be husbanded for a concerted blow. In January 1917 the Bolshevik committee in the Vyborg district of Petrograd (which had replaced the city-wide committee arrested shortly before) issued a leaflet that struck a characteristically ambivalent note. While calling on the workers to 'prepare for a general assault' because 'events are moving with incredible speed', it stated that 'although it goes against the grain, we should not let ourselves be provoked into separate [that is to say uncoordinated] actions, in order to economize our forces.'[64] It would be a misreading of the situation to claim that this caution discredited the Bolsheviks or the radical elements generally among their potential supporters. The mood in the capital at this time was such that a message of this kind will probably have been construed by those who received it as an appeal to action and treated in much the same way as a more inflammatory directive. In a sense such communications from outside the factory milieu had become superfluous.

Confirmation of this judgement may be found in the fact that the Petrograd workers responded with almost equal zeal both to the radicals' call for a strike to commemorate the twelfth anniversary of 'Bloody Sunday' (9 January 1917) and to the moderates' appeal to mark the resumption of sessions of the duma on 14 February.[65] The latter manifestation was sponsored by the rump of the Labour Group, which remained faithful to the notion of collaboration with the liberals, although in the eyes of extremists this was virtual treason to the proletarian cause. Among those who went on strike that day were men from the great Putilov plant, which a few days later was to provide the signal for revolution.

The events that followed came as a surprise to labour leaders of every hue, just as they did to duma members and government officials. On 18 February a few hundred men in one shop of the

Putilov plant came out in support of a claim for higher wages and the rehiring of some fellow-workers who had been dismissed. The senior military officers in charge of the firm's administration refused to grant these demands and threatened to close down the production unit concerned unless the men returned to work at once. They refused. Men in several other sections of the plant thereupon laid down tools in sympathy. On 22 February the management, hoping to intimidate them and to prevent the strike from becoming general, closed the factory gates.[66] This was a serious tactical error. It forced out into the streets several thousand men who were deeply embittered at their treatment and were able to provide leadership for other groups of workers and the general public.

Among the latter one should note the housewives obliged to queue for hours in biting cold weather in the hope of obtaining food for their families. In Petrograd the rationing system was still in an experimental stage, and it seems that unfamiliarity with its workings, coupled with a general distrust of the supply authorities, both official and municipal (whose disagreements were public knowledge), led to a wave of panic buying. The stocks of provisions in the city were apparently no lower than they had been in previous weeks (and were certainly greater than they would be a few months later); in the next few days the authorities increased the amounts distributed in a vain and belated effort to appease the crowds.[67] Whatever the truth about the supply position, the government now had to pay the price of its short-sighted policy of restricting information on matters of legitimate public concern, which gave ample scope for rumour-mongers to ply their trade.

Another point worth stressing is that many of the protesting housewives were themselves industrial employees, especially in the textile mills; several of these firms on the Vyborg side of the city ceased work on 23 February. This happened to be International Women's Day, which provided an additional impetus to the stoppages. These attained a scope that surprised local militants, who were quick to exploit their opportunity.[68] The role of women and of young people was particularly important. It indicated that the revolutionary movement in Petrograd was a genuinely popular phenomenon which overflowed the banks of working-class resentment in the narrower sense. On the immediate practical plane it made it psychologically harder for soldiers to suppress the demonstrators by force : might not these 'trouble-makers' be the kinsfolk of their comrades-at-arms? As the Soviet historian E.N. Burdzhalov notes, working-class youths 'marched in the front rank of the demonstrators, were present at meetings, took part in clashes with the police, [and] ... acted as the scouts of the revolution, being the first to tell [adult] workers when troops and police were approaching, where demonstrators were gathering, etc.'[69] To some extent the February revolution may be seen as a generational phenomenon : the adolescents, who displayed such militancy in the initial stages, triggered off a sympathetic response among the 'fathers' in military uniform, whose intervention settled the outcome of the conflict in favour of the revolutionaries.

The decisive turning-point did not come until the night of 26/27 February. The preceding four days saw the strike spread rapidly from the Vyborg quarter to other industrial areas of Petrograd, until by the 25th it could reasonably be called general.[70] As if drawn by an unseen magnet, large crowds flocked to the centre of the city. They swept past the police and military pickets, sometimes crossing the ice of the frozen river Neva and the canals, and paraded along the Nevsky Prospekt, carrying their symbolic red banners with the by-now traditional slogans : 'Bread', 'Peace', 'Down with Autocracy'. Well-to-do citizens looked on with mixed feelings at the unfamiliar tatterdemalion throng – those 'grey masses' who had emerged from their customary seclusion to show that they had had enough of the war and the miseries it engendered. The police and military authorities, under the command of the freshly appointed Khabalov, at first reacted mildly. Cursed and taunted by the crowd, bombarded with stones, lumps of ice or whatever else came to hand, they made occasional efforts to stem the flood but when this became impossible gave up their posts and withdrew to safety. They did not make use of their firearms, which in view of the precedents (such as in 1905) was a sign of considerable restraint. However, charges were made by mounted police and cossacks with drawn swords, which caused casualties in the crowds, and some guardians of public order were badly mauled or even killed.

The situation was one of escalating violence, with the government and duma all but paralysed by their mutual war of words and the other authorities seemingly at a loss as to what to do. On the evening of the 25th the emperor, away at General Headquarters, reacted in the blunt soldierly manner that he thought was expected of him by dispatching a curt telegram to Khabalov instructing him 'to end the disorders in the capital tomorrow'. This showed lamentable lack of judgement and, coming as it did after many similar moves, helped to seal the doom of the monarchy. The immediate effect was to force Khabalov's hand. On the following afternoon, a Sunday, when the crowds surged into the city centre for the fourth successive day, they were met by salvoes of rifle fire from troops stationed at various strategic points. (The oft-repeated story that machine-guns were also employed has never been substantiated.) Casualties were heavy and makeshift ambulances raced to and fro to pick up the victims. A police report stated that preliminary warning shots were disregarded by the demonstrators and that 'only when loaded cartridges were fired into the heart of the crowd was it possible to disperse the mob, who however for the most part hid in the court-yards of nearby houses and then re-emerged into the street when the firing had ceased.'[71] Some retaliatory shots were fired by marchers who were armed, but the general reaction, not surprisingly, was to retire to the industrial suburbs. Here some labour leaders drew the conclusion that, as so often in the past, the regime had managed to survive by the massive use of force and that the popular movement had been crushed. 'One thing seems evident : the insur-rection is dissolving', noted V. Kayurov of the Bolshevik Vyborg district committee.[72]

Indeed, this might well have been the case but for the un-expected reaction of soldiers in the Petrograd garrison. That even-ing a company of the reserve battalion of the Pavlovsk guards regiment rose in mutiny. Early the following morning their example was followed by several hundred Volhynian guardsmen. Having killed one of their officers, they sallied forth from their barracks and were soon joined by men from other military units. Altogether on 27 February some 66,000 men, about a third of the troops in the city, defied their officers. Some of them simply went home; others merged into the riotous crowds, which they sometimes led in attacks on the last centres of resistance. The elementary fact that the soldiers were armed, whereas (with few exceptions) the striking workmen were not, more than made up for the disparity in numbers between the two groups. In this way what began as a workers' revolt – or more accurately as a revolt of the urban poor – became a revolution through involvement of the soldiers. The February events now entered upon their second phase, which led to the collapse of the monarchy and the assumption of power by the Provisional Government and the Petrograd soviet.

The crumbling of military discipline not only deprived the tsarist government of its most obvious source of support but also unleashed into the urban milieu a reservoir of discontented, often desperate men who were eager to shed their service obligations. Some workers obtained arms, either directly from mutinous soldiers or by pilfering weapon stores, and formed para-military bodies of their own (see below, pp. 90–5). More important was the fact that the factory could serve as a natural focus of men's loyalties in a way that the barracks, in Russian conditions a veritable symbol of servitude, could not. Workers were thus better able than soldiers to develop a sense of cohesion. No doubt there is also something in the point, much stressed by Marxist writers, that the bulk of the army consisted of peasants rather than workers, who were adjudged less receptive to socialist ideas and less amenable to organization – although this is a question that might well repay closer investigation.

We must leave out of consideration here the echo which the Petrograd events had in other cities and industrial centres of the empire. Here the February revolution generally took a more peaceable course, but was characterized by similar incidents : strikes, street demonstrations, the effective collapse of the old authorities and the formation of broadly based mass organs.[73]

Already during the first days of the revolt the demonstrating strikers had recognized the need for some centre of authority which could give shape and consistency to their movement. Once again this led to rivalry between the moderate and radical elements. The radicals urged the workers not to neglect the task of establishing action committees in the factories. The nucleus of such bodies already existed in so far as certain militant leaders had emerged who enjoyed the respect and confidence of their fellows. However, in the tumultuous excitement of the February days marching and fighting in the streets seemed a much more rewarding and honourable activity than humdrum organizational work. Thus for the moment nothing came of these ideas and the leadership fell almost naturally to the moderates. They took up again an idea that had proved to be so popular in 1905 : that of the *soviet* – a council of deputies elected directly by workers in their factories and operating on a city-wide scale. In the nature of things such a body seemed likely to have a much greater influence upon events than scattered factory committees could ever hope to exercise, even if these took a more militant line.

On 25 February some thirty to thirty-five labour leaders met in the office of the Petrograd Union of Workers' Cooperatives and resolved to set up such a soviet, which was to meet for the first time on the following day. However, that same evening half those involved were arrested in the course of a police swoop.[74] Two days later, when the tide had turned, several of the imprisoned leaders (and also some members of the Labour Group) were released from 'Kresty' jail by the crowd. They lost no time in constituting themselves as the provisional executive committee of such a soviet. An announcement was issued summoning the first meeting for that evening and inviting soldiers and workers to send deputies to attend it. Interestingly enough, it was suggested that these representatives should be chosen according to much the same procedure as had been employed for the Labour Group (one deputy per thousand workers in larger factories, and one from each factory with less that number). Thus there was an element of continuity between the labour organizations of the pre- and post-revolutionary period. The most striking innovation (also on the 1905 precedent) was that the soldiers were directly involved as well: they were to elect one representative from each unit of approximately a thousand men. This accounts for their initial predominance in the Petrograd soviet.[75]

Some 150 persons, whose credentials were in some cases of questionable validity, were present at the first meeting. The Menshevik duma deputy N.S. Chkheidze was elected chairman. A presidium was formed consisting of intellectuals from all the major socialist groups; Gvozdev was appointed one of the four secretaries.[76] This body immediately set about its self-appointed tasks, the most important of which was to bring the mutinous troops under its control. Early in the morning of the following day the presidium was expanded into an executive committee of fifteen members. It defined its aims broadly as 'to organize the people's forces and to struggle to consolidate political liberty and popular government'. On 1 March the title of the organization was amended to reflect the presence on the executive of nine representatives elected by soldiers from the garrison. The Petrograd Soviet of Workers' and Soldiers' Deputies occupied one wing of the Tauride Palace; the Provisional

Government occupied the other. The arrangement was more than symbolic : the famous 'dual power' had begun.

One important result of these developments was that the industrial workers of Petrograd, who had launched the February events, lost influence – not only to the soldiers but also to the socialist intellectuals and professional revolutionaries who directed the new soviet organization. In the first flush of enthusiasm and good feeling after the overthrow of tsarism their interests might coincide, but for how long would this continue to be the case?

II Labour on the Offensive: The Rise of the Urban Mass Organizations

March—September 1917

FIVE *The Drift to Industrial Anarchy*

THE COLLAPSE OF tsarism was the signal for militant action on a hitherto unparalleled scale by an ever-growing segment of Russia's labour force. The sudden disappearance of the old regime raised intoxicating hopes of a new golden age, or at least of a dramatic improvement in living standards. To most ordinary working people the new freedoms were meaningless unless accompanied by immediately tangible economic benefits. There was a widespread conviction that the upper classes generally, and industrialists in particular, had done well out of the war and that now wage-earners had a moral right to demand greater equality and social justice. If this demand were frustrated, the fault was assumed to lie with the egoism of the privileged groups. Arguments in favour of moderation were suspect, whether they stemmed from considerations of national interest or of economic rationality.

In this way a gulf began to yawn between the country's educated minority, whose attention was focused on political problems, and the popular masses, especially in the towns, who became increasingly preoccupied with the struggle to protect or advance their material interests. During the earlier part of 1917, at any rate, very few ordinary workmen thought about destroying the 'capitalist' social order : such abstract questions concerned only a small number of activists subject to the influence of the radical intelligentsia. Of a hundred petitions which industrial employees submitted to various central authorities in March 1917, scarcely any mentioned socialism : but 51 per cent of the petitioners demanded a reduction of working hours, 18 per cent called for higher wages, 15 per cent complained about poor hygienic conditions in their place of employment, and 12 per cent claimed rights for the committees which had sprung up spontaneously in many enterprises. The analyst of these data concludes reasonably enough that at this juncture 'the workers sought to ameliorate their condition, not to transform it.'[1] Yet the scope of their demands quickly escalated until their cumulative force amounted to a call for a new system of industrial relations, an implicit challenge to the basic principles of a free-enterprise market economy. Even prosperous and well-disposed firms faced collapse if they were to concede all the demands put forward simultaneously on behalf of their employees. What was more significant, these demands could not be wholly satisfied by any of the parties or groups active in Russian political life during 1917 : even the Bolshevik programme did not do justice to the almost apocalyptic hopes engendered among a broad segment of their clientele. These sentiments did, however, lend themselves to exploitation for other purposes.

Any account of the development of the Russian labour movement in 1917 is liable to be somewhat impressionistic. There are two main reasons for this. First, the economic breakdown, which assumed catastrophic proportions in the latter half of the year, led to a near-collapse of the statistical services. The fragmentary information collected at that time is of doubtful reliability. In the second place Soviet historical writing on the subject suffers from a strong element of ideological bias.[2] Nevertheless a few general points are clear enough. Chronologically, peaceful forms of protest gave way to more violent and aggressive actions as the year wore on; geographically, the main focal points of unrest were Petrograd and the North-west, then Moscow and the Central Industrial region; sociologically, the movement was led by workers in larger factories, who were most amenable to organization for militant ends, while those employed in transport, distribution, clerical or service occupations tended to be more modest in their demands. To some extent the distinction between skilled and unskilled men coincided with that between moderates and radicals, but this was not a golden rule. Workers in metallurgical plants fulfilling defence contracts, who were one of the best-paid groups in industry, assumed a vanguard role. The explanation for this lies in their eagerness to renounce their close involvement in what seemed to them a disastrous and senseless war.

We may consider first the actions taken by labour to press its sectional claims and then turn to the organizational structure which political leaders and activists built in an attempt to bring this largely spontaneous popular movement under their control.

The demand for an eight-hour day had an almost sacramental character for the more politicized elements. No sooner had the Petrograd strikers returned to work, in most cases within three days of the tsar's abdication, than men in several of the city's factories decided to lay down their tools at the end of each eight-hour shift. Their example was infectious. A similar development had occurred after the general strike of October 1905. At that time the employers had offered stout resistance and compelled the men to abandon their campaign. Now the situation was different. Some managers had sound economic reasons for curtailing production; others hoped that concessions on this point might demonstrate the merits of social harmony and defuse a potentially explosive situation. Accordingly on 10 March the Petrograd industrialists' association, after discussions with a delegation from the soviet led by Gvozdev, agreed to the immediate introduction of an eight-hour working day. Since the accord provided that this should not lead to any diminution of pay, this was equivalent to an automatic wage rise proportionate to the reduction in the work load. Overtime was to be regulated by agreement with the factory committees (see below, pp. 78–89), which thereby received explicit sanction. These organs were to be established in all enterprises and were entrusted with wide powers. Conciliation boards were also to be set up at various levels to settle disputes.[3] Rather more to the point was a provision in the agreement prohibiting 'the removal of foremen and other administrative officials' by arbitrary action from below. Instances of this practice had already caused alarm in entrepreneurial and government circles. Five days later the eight-hour day was introduced in munition plants operating under the control of the War Ministry's Main Artillery Department. The order was signed by Guchkov, who on succeeding to the post of War minister took a liberal line of which he evidently soon repented.[4]

The action of the Petrograd employers, however comprehensible from the standpoint of political tactics, was of dubious wisdom. It undercut the position of their colleagues in Moscow and other centres, who not unreasonably held that a matter of such importance in the country's social and economic life should be the object of legislation by the central government. These men soon found themselves under heavy pressure to make similar concessions. Since entrepreneurial associations were still but feebly developed, individual manufacturers were often obliged to capitulate to demands on this issue presented by their work-people or on their behalf. In Moscow the soviet decided to introduce the eight-hour day in all enterprises in the city by direct action as from 21 March. Some firms had already introduced it, voluntarily or under pressure, and the soviet explained that it did not want to be left behind by events.[5] By the end of April the eight-hour day had been introduced in practice, if not always with full juridical force, in large enterprises throughout the country.[6] The Soviet historian Volobuyev comments with some justice that this victory 'strengthened the workers' confidence in their strength' and helped to radicalize the attitude of many thousands of men and women who had hitherto been indifferent to politics, although one may query his assertion that it was achieved in the teeth of stiff opposition by the employers.[7]

The latter complained loudly that a shortened working day was a luxury which Russian industry could ill afford, especially so long as the war continued. Unfortunately there is no reliable way of measuring the eight-hour day's actual impact on labour productivity or company profits. However, it is plain that – along with unofficial 'go slows', absenteeism and other infractions of industrial discipline – it contributed to the difficulties which many concerns experienced in making ends meet. Within a few months a considerable number of enterprises had been forced to close and part-time working had been introduced in many others.

This was part of a larger problem : the rapid increase in the wages bill that entrepreneurs now had to pay as a consequence of inflationary settlements, many imposed on them under duress. This pressure seems to have been most intense in the first three or four months after the collapse of tsarism; from July onwards, although nominal wages continued to rise by leaps and bounds, their value in real terms sank so fast that the employers had no grounds for complaint on this particular score. Their preoccupation was now simply to keep production going at all in the face of acute shortages of fuel and the breakdown of the transport system, and to sell enough goods at rapidly inflating prices to meet current expenses. Few succeeded in doing so; the overwhelming bulk of industrial enterprises that continued to function operated at a deficit and had to draw on basic capital to survive at all.[8]

It is in the light of this situation that one has to examine the massive drive for increased wages. At first these demands were put forward in a chaotic manner at enterprise level. Sometimes the local soviet (or its 'labour department', if it had created one) took a hand in the bargaining. Curiously enough, all parties to the talks, employers included, seem to have proceeded from the assumption that unskilled workers had the strongest claim to an increase and should be awarded a minimum wage; this would then serve as a criterion in determining the rates paid to other groups. Negotiations were conducted in social rather than economic terms and at a low level of sophistication. Could a worker survive on three roubles a day or was five roubles the least amount needed to keep the wolf of hunger from the door? Should one take fixed prices or those on the free market (about which views differed widely) as a guide to living costs? Employers' representatives sometimes spoke vaguely of the impact which large increases would have upon their firm's well-being, but were reluctant to support their statements by documentary evidence – partly because up-to-date and accurate figures were seldom available, partly from a concern lest their difficulties should become known to their competitors, and partly because they thought that hard economic arguments would not be understood by the simple workmen with whom they were accustomed to deal. Paternalistic traditions were still strong among Russian industrialists. Labour leaders were quick to suspect their negotiating partners of bad faith and to threaten strike action to back their claims. Some of them were familiar with the concept of a sliding scale of wages keyed to price increases, and pressed for this to be introduced. The soviet representatives, usually Mensheviks or SRs (although some of those active in such work were moderate Bolsheviks, such as the Moscow leader V.P. Nogin), urged the merits of industry-wide wage tariff agreements. But before the necessary institutional structure could be established or procedural rules worked out the economy had collapsed and power had passed to the Bolsheviks.

In Petrograd, according to data supplied by the local employers' association, some enterprises had already by mid-March granted wage increases of 30–50 per cent over pre-February levels, although the agreement on working hours entailed increases of only 20–28 per cent.[9] According to government sources (the ministry of Trade and Industry and the Special Council for Defence) the average (nominal) pay of workers in three Petrograd metallurgical plants doubled by the beginning of June 1917 and some skilled men obtained a three-fold rise.[10] A minimum daily wage of five roubles for male labourers and four roubles for females employed in the capital was established on 24 April, when the municipal arbitration board endorsed the workers' claims; this compared with a rate for men of 3·60 roubles in January.[11] In fourteen metallurgical works subject to the Admiralty labourers were granted six roubles (21 March), while skilled fitters and mechanics received twice that amount.[12] These examples were soon emulated in other branches of industry. Petrograd textile-workers' earnings rose by 47·6 per cent between January and July.[13]

A similar situation prevailed in the Moscow region, where in May workers in certain textile mills demanded threefold to sixfold wage rises. The claim went to arbitration and the employers conceded a figure of 210 per cent.[14] The industrialists of the south offered tougher resistance. In the Donets valley miners negotiated an increase of fifty per cent from their employers, assembled in conference at Kharkov, to take effect from 1 April; a few days later proprietors of the region's metallurgical plants followed suit by offering a pay rise of thirty-five per cent. In both cases the minimum daily wage was fixed at 2·5 roubles, or half the Petrograd rate; overtime was to be paid at rates fifty per cent above the norm.[15] According to a memorandum submitted to the government by the manufacturers, the increases agreed to were significantly larger : ninety per cent for the miners and 'even more' (sic) for metal-workers; to their dismay the ink on this agreement was scarcely dry when they were faced with an unexpected demand for a four-rouble minimum daily rate. This, they calculated, would double the price of coal and iron, and (together with other rising costs) absorb ten times their gross profits.[16] Spokesmen for the Baku oil industry reckoned that wage rates increased by more than fifty per cent between February and July.[17] A figure of fifty per cent was quoted by other representatives on both sides of industry, as well as by government officials; and Volobuyev concludes that this may be taken as the average rate of increase in the country as a whole during the first three months of the period.[18]

But what was the significance of this increase in real terms? According to M.P. Kokhn's nation-wide price index, published in 1926 and used by a number of Soviet historians, prices rose by 42·8 per cent between 1 March and 1 June and by 82·8 per cent between 1 March and 1 July.[19] S.G. Strumilin, in a study published in 1919 of the price of a fixed ration (*payok*) of foodstuffs in Petrograd and Moscow, found a comparable rate of increase for the period February–May (40 per cent and 39·3 per cent respectively). His figures for the period February–June (48 per cent and 57·1 per cent) show a less drastic leap than Kokhn's; he also displays a proper caution in refusing to venture any data after June.[20] Another early statistical calculation correlated prices in Moscow with metalworkers' average earnings and found that between January and June the former had risen by 60·8 per cent whereas the latter had risen by only 44·6 per cent.[21] The former figure is a good deal higher than Strumilin's and seems to be inconsistent with another table in the same source which puts the general rise of foodstuff prices in Moscow during the same six-month period at fifty per cent.[22] Nevertheless, it is arguable that this investigator may have had a better opportunity to observe actual spending habits more closely than Strumilin, who was concerned with an increasingly abstract 'shopping basket' – and who took as his base year 1913, rather than his colleague's more realistic choice of June 1916. In the light of these data it seems clear that a wage rise of fifty per cent must have been largely eaten up by rising prices, and that only those who succeeded in winning very large awards will have felt that the revolution had significantly alleviated their material lot. Among these groups were men (and especially women) in the lowest-income brackets, the relatively well-organized printers, and workers in the metallurgical and chemical industries whose role was so crucial to the war effort.[23]

It is scarcely possible to follow the twisting wage-price spiral after July 1917. Strumilin has offered a figure for real earnings in the year 1917 as a whole, relative to 1916, indicating a drop of 8·8 per cent (9·0 per cent if rents and communal services are taken into account),[24] but this almost certainly underestimates the extent of the decline. According to the 1918 industrial census (covering thirty-one provinces at that time under Soviet control), overall nominal pay during the year 1917 was almost three times higher than it had been in 1916,[25] but estimates of price rises vary widely. Strumilin reckoned that real wages in the Moscow region fell during the latter half of the year by 37 to 46 per cent.[26] In Shuya, the important textile centre, an investigation by local entrepreneurs found that by 1 October weavers' wages had more than doubled in nominal terms (from 25 to 59 roubles a month) since the beginning of the year, whereas the price of food had gone up two to three times.[27] This seems realistic. The decline does not appear to have been so catastrophic in the more outlying areas. In Baku prices are estimated to have doubled while wages rose by one and a half times between January and October.[28] By the autumn many workers had come to realize that the chase for more paper roubles had lost its rationale and began to seek payment in food instead. Where this was not forthcoming, it was tempting to resort to direct action, such as appropriation of goods or equipment belonging to the factory for resale to anyone who could pay for them in produce.

Violence was a familiar feature of the industrial scene in 1917. The most 'normal' form of conflict was of course the strike, which might well be accompanied by coercive acts of one kind or another : destruction of property, assaults on managerial personnel or threats to the security of anyone deemed hostile to the militants' cause. The factory inspectorate was unable to keep an accurate record of the incidence of strikes, and its figure of 3,823,000 working days lost between January and September, as compared with over 4·7 million in 1916, is clearly an underestimate.[29] Of these disputes between two-thirds and three-quarters were said to be non-economic in nature. A Soviet student of the question has claimed that the monthly number of *strikers* (a less reliable indicator) rose from 35,000 in April to 175,000 in June, and then climbed to 1·1 and 1·2 million in the months of September and October respectively.[30] These calculations owe something to an ideologically inspired compulsion to present the labour movement as becoming progressively more militant and better organized (under Bolshevik leadership, of course). They do not take account of the interrelationships between strikes and other forms of protest, whether active, such as the seizure of factories — which made strikes superfluous — or passive, such as the drift of work-people from the cities to the countryside. The strike weapon lost a good deal of its appeal once it became apparent that employers had nothing more to give. Moreover, many employees who found their living standards falling rapidly could not afford to remain absent from their jobs for long.

Especially in the earlier months of the year, strikes were relatively brief. Gaponenko admits that this was because the employers were obliged to yield to pressure from below, with the result that between April and June more than four-fifths of disputes ended favourably for the strikers.[31] It was significant that employers and public authorities responsible for war production were in general readier to grant concessions to their work-people, so that an abnormally high proportion of strikers were tradesmen, artisans and workers in the consumer-goods industries.[32] The nature of the evidence is such that it is often hard to decide whether men were idle because they were on strike or because there was no work for them to do. An increasing number of factories, especially in the textile industry of the central region, was compelled to close their gates, but only in some instances were such closures due to a desire on the employers' part to counter wage demands or discipline the labour force. Radical activists at the time habitually represented such actions as 'lock-outs', and this interpretation has become traditional among Soviet historians. However, of 568 enterprises employing 104,000 persons which shut down between March and July, only 79, employing about a tenth of that number, closed because of labour disputes.[33]

The ineffectiveness of strike action enhanced the appeal of more violent measures, up to and including the forcible removal of managerial representatives and sequestration of the plant. In March and April the overwhelming majority of the industrial conflicts reported to the militia involved such disturbances. The proportion of such incidents then fell in relation to the number of strikes, but this tendency was more notable in the Central Industrial region than in the turbulent North-west, the Urals and especially the Ukraine : in the latter area fifty-five strikes and seventy-four other incidents were notified between March and October.[34] In the Urals no less than 145 managers, directors, supervisors and other administrative personnel were dismissed from forty-two enterprises in the four months March to June.[35] These actions were normally the work of militant groups which claimed that they were acting with the consent of the general body of employees. How genuine such claims were could scarcely be determined with any precision at the time, let alone in retrospect. Sometimes the mood in a factory might indeed become so inflamed that the activists could reasonably be said to have the men behind them. In other cases there were significant groups of moderates who disapproved of such actions but were intimidated into remaining silent or absenting themselves from the scene of action.

The exaggerated suspicions of management often entertained by ordinary workmen helped to win extremist agitators a hearing. In May miners at the Nikolayevsky pit in the Donets valley alleged that its proprietor had deliberately failed to repair the pumps in order to allow the water level to rise and flood the mine. This served as a pretext for the removal of the manager, who was replaced by a Bolshevik fitter and 'an elected board of workers'.[36] The local coal-owners' association complained to Petrograd that

> ... every day the workers continue to put forward the most varied and quite unfounded demands. If the firms refuse, these demands are accompanied by threats and even acts of violence, mainly the removal of managers of mines, engineers and other experienced technicians. ... There have been cases where by blackmail and threats of violence workers have managed to extort large sums of money, which they regard as back pay, even for work done in 1916. As well as presenting economic claims they offer stiff resistance to all kinds of measures designed to maintain discipline and order and to ensure safety in the pits.

This telegram was followed by one from an engineer named Deger, of the Berestovo mine, who reported that after he had refused demands for higher wages the men had locked him in his office and threatened to put him in a sack and beat him; when he pointed out that his superiors in Kharkov were responsible for such decisions, the angry crowd had released him, warning that unless he returned within four days with a favourable settlement, 'it would not go well for him'.[37] At the Rykov mine the director agreed under duress not only to a twenty per cent wage rise but also to a lump-sum payment of 100,000 roubles 'in the guise of additional compensation for last year's work'.[38] The employers in this region publicly attributed their falling productivity figures, which ranged from twenty to forty per cent below those of the previous summer, almost wholly to labour unrest.

The practice that best conveys the flavour of industrial relations in Russia during this period is that of thrusting an unpopular individual into a wheelbarrow and trundling him through the factory gates, to the jeers of the assembled crowd; if nothing worse befell him, the victim might then be ducked in a nearby stream or pond.

Several instances of this curious and archaic procedure have been recorded from different parts of the country.[39] At the Metal Pipe works in Petrograd this treatment was meted out by men in the forging shop to no less an individual than a deputy of the soviet, an SR by political affiliation, who was also a member of the factory committee set up within the enterprise; before the procession reached the river Neva, men in other departments were alerted and came to his rescue; a fist fight broke out and there were 'many victims' (none of whom seem to have been seriously hurt).[40] At Blagodat in the Urals a mining engineer named Domrachev was seized by a mixed crowd of workers and soldiers who 'carted him through the streets in a barrow and threatened to take his life'; the ministry of Labour decided to investigate the incident, but the outcome of the inquiry is not known.[41]

All in all this was mild inoffensive stuff, a kind of preliminary sparring before the match began in earnest. Outright seizures of enterprises were still very rare. Where 'workers' control' was established, as it was for instance already in March over the factories of Savva and Vikula Morozov at Orekhovo-Zuyevo, it was either with the owner's consent (as in this instance : the Morozovs were well-known for their eccentric left-wing views) or else nominal; often it was seen only as a temporary measure, provoked by the collapse of the existing management, without the revolutionary implications it was to acquire later. For this development the responsibility lay chiefly with the movement to set up enterprise or factory committees (*fabrichno-zavodskiye komitety*). Of all the *ad hoc* organizations set up by Russia's workers in 1917 these were perhaps the most significant, since they gave expression to their instinctive distrust of authority in any form and their desire to assert control over everything which might affect their conditions of employment. Although the political impact of these committees was slighter than that of the soviets, they were essential adjuncts to the latter in mobilizing popular sentiment. Above all, they were the first mass bodies in which the Bolsheviks were able to strike root.

SIX *The Factory Committees*

I T WAS NATURAL that those who organized the informal strike committees which emerged in Petrograd during the February days should seek to perpetuate their existence once the men had returned to work. The first reliable documentary evidence of the establishment of a body with such long-term aims dates from 1 March. It appeared in the Petrograd Cable Works – significantly a metallurgical firm engaged on war work under the control of the military authorities. The latter promptly accepted the men's demands that they be allowed to form an armed militia force, paid by the management, and – in less martial vein – that their committee should run the factory shop, at which foodstuffs were retailed at special prices.[1] In the following days similar committees appeared in a number of other enterprises, with metallurgical-workers in the lead. They began by presenting demands to management on wages, working hours and other matters concerning the internal life of the establishment. Above all the committees sought to win explicit recognition of their right to represent the men in all dealings with management and to control the recruitment and dismissal of personnel – that is to say to establish the principle of the 'closed shop' It was but a step from this to demands for virtual veto rights over appointments at managerial level and to naming individuals whom the committee insisted should be dismissed. As early as 5 March certain foremen at the Treugolnik plant in Petrograd were dismissed by the management after they had been accused of 'disorganizing production', apparently by insisting on overtime working to which the men objected. At another factory the committee men described their foes sweepingly as 'marauders, former servants of the old regime and persons found committing thefts or any other disloyal acts' – the loyalty in question being to the committee and its supporters, of course, rather than to the administration.[2] In four leading Petrograd metallurgical works 174 persons were expelled in this fashion, among them no less than seventy from the Treugolnik plant. The Baranovsky shell factory lost a sixth of its 150 engineers and technicians.[3] Some of the victims who had hitherto enjoyed military deferment were unceremoniously handed over to the local army authorities for despatch to the front, in a procedure reminiscent of that occasionally employed by managers under the old regime.[4]

Initially at least the army chiefs in Petrograd appear to have taken a soft line toward the workers' demands. This must have had some impact upon the readiness with which the manufacturers of the capital as a body concluded the agreement of 10 March providing for the establishment of factory committees in all enterprises. The explanation lies partly in the euphoria with which Russian society generally greeted the collapse of the old regime and partly in the military authorities' understandable desire to maintain the flow of armaments at any price. Some manufacturers may have acted in the hope that factory committees would be more tractable than trade unions, which were bound to become linked to left-wing political parties;[5] if so, they were destined to be disappointed.

It was not long before the committees took steps to coordinate their activities, in some cases displaying more energy than the emergent unions. Again it was men in State-owned or State-controlled metallurgical works who took the lead. One may suppose that their activism was prompted by a deep-seated aversion to the bureaucratic forms of management with which they were familiar as well as by a desire to make the best of their employers' relative flexibility. Already on 13 March a meeting was held of representatives of the committees in twelve works subject to the Main Artillery Administration, who set themselves up as a kind of standing conference;[6] it was on this occasion that the question of workers' control over production, which opened up such enticing perspectives, was first formally raised. In the following month they elaborated a detailed 'instruction' inspired by syndicalist ideas of industrial democracy. 'All administrative personnel, such as works directors, departmental and workshop heads, all technical officials (*klassnye chiny*) and other managerial staff are to assume their duties with the approval of the general factory committee.' The latter defined its role as 'to control the activity of the works management in an administrative-economic and technical sense'. For this purpose its representatives were to be present in all departments of the enterprise and were to have access to all documents, accounts and other official papers.[7] These ideas were rapidly taken up by workers in the private sector of industry, although this was less subject to bureaucratic regimentation and the men had fewer grounds for such extremism. Workers in the Putilov plant were rather slow to form a factory committee, partly it seems because they wanted to hold regular elections, and this took time in such a vast enterprise; however, in April they issued a call for a city-wide conference of factory committee representatives. The idea was promptly taken up by the Bolsheviks, who gave it every encouragement in the hope of winning control over what had hitherto been largely a spontaneous movement. The first factory committees in Petrograd had emerged without external direction and their leaders had no specific political affiliation. Some of them (for example, at the Obukhov arms works) called themselves Socialist-Revolutionaries, but appear to have done so simply because the name of this party seemed to harmonize with their own ideals.[8]

A glimpse into the activities of one of the more energetic factory committees may be obtained from the minutes (which happen to have been published) of the organization set up in the Petrograd works of the 1886 Electric Power Company. It met no less than forty-five times during March and April. Within a few days of its appearance on 2 March it had set up various commissions, demanded the dismissal of administrators appointed under the old regime, and introduced the eight-hour working day. Resolutions were also adopted on a variety of political questions such as punishing members of the former ruling dynasty, amnestying political offenders and ending the war. These resolutions were notable for their radicalism, and it was not surprising that in April, when the committee was re-elected on party-political lines, the Bolsheviks should have secured 673 votes out of a total poll of 1,230; the Mensheviks and SRS won 406 votes; the remainder were cast for delegates who had no party affiliation.[9]

As the factory committees became more politicized they often developed a fair-sized apparatus of their own. That in the Nevsky shipbuilding yards had a two-tier organization, with a central 'council of elders' and five subordinate commissions; the latter concerned themselves respectively with militia affairs, supply work, education and culture, wages and employment.[10] Of the militia more will be said in chapter 7. What was involved under the seemingly inoffensive heading 'supply work' may be deduced from a newspaper report that a Moscow official had discovered a stock of flour in a bakery earmarked by 'the supply committee of the workers of Presnya district', as part of an arrangement which contravened the rationing regulations.[11] 'Education and culture' was often a euphemism for political propaganda, although this activity was not invariably conducted on narrow party lines and some genuinely cultural events were arranged as a means of raising funds. The Izhorsky naval armaments works had ten such commissions, and another metallurgical enterprise no less than twenty-eight agencies employing two hundred persons.[12] In the Putilov works each of the forty-six workshops is said to have had its own committee, all of them in constant contact with the twenty-two-man central body; the latter had a Bolshevik chairman but a majority of non-affiliated members.[13] Naturally enough, the time spent in maintaining this complicated institutional structure became a matter of concern to employers, especially since meetings were often held during working hours and committee members were supposed to draw full pay.

The Provisional Government soon became alarmed at the growth of syndicalist tendencies and the disruption of industry. On 23 April it published a set of regulations based upon the 10 March accord in Petrograd, designed to confine the factory committees' activities within tolerable limits. These regulations provided that for such committees to be considered legal they must be elected on a secret ballot with a minimum participation of fifty per cent of all employees, and that general meetings should be held to endorse the 'instructions' embodying the committees' duties, procedural rules and so on. These duties were to conform to principles which were defined in the decree so vaguely as to permit very varied interpretations.[14]

In practice the loopholes in this law were of little account since it was never seriously applied. Many factory committees were permitted to operate with impunity even though their members had in fact been nominated by bodies extraneous to the factory concerned – for instance by the local soviet, which might mean the bureau of the political party that controlled the latter's executive committee – and were then confirmed in office by the men. In general the procedure followed at elections was scarcely calculated to allow free expression to minority opinions, and at open mass meetings the natural tendency was to support those candidates for office who spoke most persuasively. Thus the situation was generally one which favoured manipulation by the leadership and hindered efforts to assert control from below.

The more radical activists did not intend to allow any concern for juridical formalities to inhibit them from extending their powers as widely as possible at enterprise level or from forming local associations of factory committees. Such efforts naturally enough centred on Petrograd, where on 30 May delegates to the first 'all-city' conference of factory committees assembled amid the tarnished splendours of the Tauride Palace. Of the 568 delegates nearly half (261) were from the metallurgical industry. The proceedings began with a series of reports from the floor in which speakers described how and why they had taken over various operational or administrative functions in their enterprises. Most of them were at pains to present their activities as a form of self-defence : they claimed that shortages of fuel and raw materials, together with the inability of existing management to cope with the crisis, had given them no choice but to take action, such as sending out men to look for stocks of fuel and negotiating with officials or bankers for orders or loans. In this way, they claimed, they had assisted in maintaining discipline, slowing down the decline of industrial output, and preserving their own jobs in the face of threats of management to curtail or suspend production. However, a metallurgical-worker named Naumov sounded a more ideological note, stating that such actions had provided the men with valuable experience in preparing for 'the socialist production of the future', and another deputy called the factory committees a weapon in 'the workers' counter-attack on the bourgeoisie' which would lead to 'a capitalist retreat'.[15] There was an angry scene when the delegates decided, by 230 votes to 128, not to permit the Mensheviks to present a formal report on workers' control. The presidium, headed by Shlyapnikov, was obliged to stand down and when reconstituted had an additional member to safeguard minority rights. The incident had no immediate consequences, yet it was an ominous precedent.

The Menshevik minister of Labour in the new coalition government, M.I. Skobelev, set forth the argument that in a 'bourgeois-democratic revolution' it was inexpedient to pursue socialist ends and pleaded for restraint. But his speech had much less impact than that of Lenin, who addressed the meeting on 31 May. It was one of the Bolshevik leader's first appearances before a mass audience since his return to Russia, and he took the opportunity to hammer home his party's basic message that the moderate socialists could not be trusted. They were 'openly taking the part of the capitalists' and trying to lull the workers' vigilance by talk of State control of industry; such a system could only be a parody of genuine workers' control, which meant that 'in all responsible institutions there should be a majority of workers and that the management should render account of its actions before the most authoritative labour organizations'.[16] To his listeners this naturally suggested that the factory committees themselves were to be counted among these 'authoritative labour organizations', although his words were capable of bearing a different interpretation. The anarchists and syndicalists present could be forgiven for thinking that Lenin had been converted to their views, or at any rate that there were no serious divergences between themselves and the Bolsheviks. This helps to explain the heavy vote in favour of a resolution, drafted by Lenin and presented by Zinoviev, which was passed by 297 votes to 21 with 44 abstentions (1 June).[17]

Entitled 'On Economic Measures to Combat the Chaos', it contained a number of amendments to the Bolshevik leader's original draft. For instance, where Lenin had called for three-quarters of managerial posts to be entrusted to workers, the conference was satisfied with two-thirds; where he had called for firms' accounts to be opened to inspection by 'all large democratic and socialist parties' and by the soviets, the conference decided that this inspection should be restricted to factory committees and trade unions.[18] These differences showed that the activists were concerned to establish a system that would have a chance to work in practice rather than to score political points, and also that they wanted to keep the locus of power at the enterprise level rather than see it shifted to any political organization – still less to any organ of a future socialist state. However, these seeds of future controversy were obscured by the radical language of the resolution. This called *inter alia* for full regulation by workers of the production and distribution of goods, 'transfer into the hands of the people of a large part of the profits, income and property' of wealthy merchants, bankers and so on, direct exchange of produce between town and country, and the establishment of a workers' militia. The resolution's significance lay in its programmatic character : it demonstrated that the most militant elements in the capital were willing to follow the Bolsheviks' lead and to put their nascent organization at their service. The conference decided to set up a twenty-five-man executive, the Central Committee of Factory Committees of Petrograd (CCFCP). Its chairman, a printer named N.I. Derbyshev, was a Bolshevik and it normally followed that party's line. The CCFCP aspired to play a national role. It dispatched 'instructors' to other centres whose task it was to help set up similar organizations there.

In most provincial cities the labour movement was still less radicalized than in Petrograd. In Moscow the first conference of factory committees was not held until the end of July. Its Menshevik orientation was evident from an ambiguous resolution which called for 'general control over production to be introduced as soon as possible' and welcomed confiscation of enterprises by the existing 'bourgeois' state.[19] In Odessa the soviet concluded an agreement with the industrialists for enterprise committees to be established on a parity basis : management representatives were given an equal voice with those of workers, and the chairman was to be chosen by mutual agreement.[20] In Kharkov, by contrast, where a conference of factory committees met at the end of May, the delegates' mood was extremely militant and syndicalist tendencies were pronounced. One orator cried : 'the trade unions are bankrupt the world over. Wherever they exist they only hold us back from the struggle. When the trade unions want to subordinate the revolutionary factory committees, we say "hands off", we won't take your road.' Shiryaev, of the Helfferich-Sade metallurgical works, suggested that the movement should set up a national executive organ of its own, independent of the trade unions.[21]

By mid-summer, when the political mood was veering somewhat to the right, the Provisional Government began to take some tardy steps to assert its authority in the industrial-relations field. On 1 July, faced with the threat that one of Moscow's principal metallurgical works, familiarly called the Goujon factory, might have to close because the management could no longer meet increased costs, the Special Council on Defence decided to sequester the plant.[22] Such action was received with mixed feelings in business circles. Some directors and boards of companies, especially smaller ones, welcomed and even requested government intervention, which they saw as a lesser evil than control from below. Others considered that major breaches in the free-enterprise system should be carried out only after discussion with representatives of the interests concerned and should have a limited scope : the old boards should retain full autonomy and merely be required to submit their accounts for periodic inspection. These divisions of opinion were reflected in the regional and national employers' associations, which by this time were beginning to find their feet. On 22 July the council of the Union of United Industry, formed a few weeks earlier by Moscow textile manufacturers, advised its members in a circular letter 'to abandon the idea of running enterprises on pre-revolutionary lines' and 'to support labour organizations such as the [factory] committees organized ... within the limits of the law of 23 April', but to have as few dealings as possible with the soviets, which had no authorized status in law. In this way, it hoped, 'the principle of legality might be generally inculcated into the workers' milieu.'[23] These ideas were elaborated in a circular to its members dispatched on 22 August, after talks with local representatives of the ministry of Labour. Members of factory committees might be excused from work for a few hours each week to attend to their duties, but unauthorized absence should be punished by an appropriate deduction from pay, and after two weeks' absence such offenders should be dismissed.[24]

Earlier in the month a leading Moscow industrialist and public figure, P.P. Ryabushinsky, inaugurating the second congress of the All-Russian Union of Trade and Industry, delivered a philippic against the government ('a shadow power') and the soviets ('charlatans' and 'deceivers of the people'), and called on all those engaged in commerce and industry to rally behind a reinvigorated state power. It was on this occasion that he uttered the phrase, much quoted (usually out of context) at the time and since in left-wing circles, about 'the bony hand of hunger' which sooner or later would 'clutch by the throat ... the members of various committees and soviets, forcing them to come to their senses'.[25]

In practice, however, the employers did little to improve the climate of industrial relations, preferring rather to await a positive turn of events in the political sphere. The factory committees, naturally enough, were one of the main targets of their wrath, yet it was scarcely possible, politically or practically, to make them observe the law. There were occasional instances when employers refused them recognition, on the grounds that they were irregularly constituted or had exceeded their powers, or subjected them to petty harassment, such as denial of premises in which to meet, in the hope that this would oblige them to conduct their activities outside working hours, as in principle they were supposed to do. One employers' association carried out an inquiry among its members to discover the scale on which these bodies were being maintained at management's expense : the fourteen firms which replied stated that they had spent about 1·5 million roubles on this purpose between March and July inclusive.[26] Another inquiry in the Urals elicited a figure of 400,000 roubles.[27] Despite these costly irregularities the employers did not launch a general assault upon the factory committees, and ignored various recommendations they received to the contrary.[28]

Characteristically, perhaps, their most frequent response took the form of passive resistance : placing their enterprises on part-time working and dismissing some employees, or even closing entire plants outright. In such cases the factory committees soon found themselves on the defensive and the 'closed shop' principle loomed larger than ever in the activists' eyes. Their chief preoccupation was now the fate of those already on the firm's books. Sometimes they found themselves invited by management to help in the invidious task of selecting those to be laid off. The problem was complicated by the fact that at this time of year there was normally an efflux of workers to the countryside, and that the deteriorating food situation in the cities made many men more than usually eager to leave, especially if they had families to go back to. The evacuation from the cities was particularly marked in the textile-manufacturing settlements of the centre, most of whose employees were women. Some of those who left for the villages were activists, and this helped to disorient the movement.

Meanwhile the second coalition ministry, which came into office toward the end of July, was steering an uneasy course between enemies on the right and left. Responsibility for labour matters was shared by Skobelev and S.N. Prokopovich – the latter a professional economist, wiser and more tactful than some of his cabinet colleagues but out of his depth in industrial affairs. At the State Conference in August he was outspoken in condemning industrial anarchy but his proposals for dealing with it were feeble and irresolute.[29] A few days later, on 22 August, his colleague Skobelev issued a circular re-affirming the right of management to settle questions of employment.[30] This stated that coercive measures were henceforth to be 'regarded as liable to prosecution as criminal acts'. This circular was followed by a second specifying the conditions in which factory committees might meet, which empowered employers to make deductions from pay for time lost from production.[31] Radical critics maintained that these instructions limited the scope of the law of 23 April and were issued under pressure from the employers. However this may be, their practical effect was slight. As it happened, the second circular was issued on the very day of Kornilov's 'revolt', a development which undermined crucially both the right and centre forces in the nation's political life.

In the last two months or so before the Bolshevik takeover the factory committee movement spread more widely[32] and became thoroughly politicized. Actions at enterprise level continued but were less significant than measures taken by local leaders, through the city-wide and regional institutions they had established, to support the campaign for 'soviet power'. It was in this period that 'maximalist' elements, as they were generally called at the time, most of whom were close to the Bolshevik party if not actually members of it,[33] took over control of the enterprise-level committees from those who were of more moderate persuasion or had no definite political affiliation. In Petrograd the factory committees served the Bolsheviks as a handy base from which to launch their assault on the moderate leadership of the soviet, which after the 'July Days' moved somewhat to the right. A conference held on 7–12 August confirmed their hold on this organization. A resolution on workers' control presented by V.P. Milyutin was passed without difficulty, as was another which suggested that the factory committees should in principle be subordinated to the trade unions. The main interest of the proceedings lay in the ventilation, by N.A. Skrypnik and others, of views which were closer to anarchism than to Bolshevism. The CCFCP was now given a more formal and elaborate structure. According to one source it was to have no less than seventy-five members and a fifteen-man executive.[34] More would doubtless have been heard of this body had not the Bolsheviks soon afterwards won control of the Petrograd soviet, which the CCFCP was clearly designed to rival.

In Moscow a local Bolshevik newspaper, reviewing conferences of factory committees that took place in several districts of the city during September, claimed that 'even in those enterprises whose representatives were unificators [that is to say left-wing Mensheviks] and SRs, the masses' mood is definitely to the advantage of the Bolsheviks'. On that day elections were held in the Trekhgornaya textile mill in the Presnya district for a new committee to replace that hitherto controlled by the SRs; the Bolsheviks swept the board.[35] However, the moderates seem to have been strong enough to prevent another city-wide conference from being called, as a follow-up to that held late in July and in emulation of Petrograd.

In the capital a third city-wide conference was held from 5 to 10 September. One of the chief issues raised before the four hundred deputies (apart from the Kornilov affair) was the government's plan to evacuate industrial plants, with their work-people, to areas in the interior less exposed to enemy attack. The Bolsheviks were at pains to represent this move as a deliberate attempt to discourage working-class militancy. A protest resolution was duly adopted, along with others calling for extension of the factory committees' powers, by an all but unanimous vote.[36] This emphasis on political issues showed graphically, if proof were needed, the extent to which the Petrograd factory-committee network had become 'bolshevized'. Yet the rank-and-file delegates seem to have been animated as much by economic as by political considerations. In order to keep up employment in the capital, they sought to prevent orders from being placed with provincial firms or with provincial branches of Petrograd-based concerns. This indifference to the effects of such action upon fellow-workers elsewhere shows the extent to which their thinking was geared to the enterprise (or the region) rather than to the proletariat as a class – the abstraction that mattered so much to their political mentors. Similarly, their efforts to control raw material or fuel stocks were designed as much to satisfy the needs of their own work-people as to promote proletarian insurrection. For the time being the paths of the syndicalist-minded factory committees and the Bolshevik party ran parallel, but their latent differences of orientation were bound to come to the fore as soon as the latter seized power and attempted to implement its state socialist programme.

These differences were evident at the first All-Russian conference of factory committees, which opened in Petrograd on 17 October (preceded by a fourth city-wide conference a few days earlier). The CCFCP had throughout seen its role as to coordinate the activities of like-minded bodies all over the country, and the second of these gatherings crowned its work by setting up a nation-wide executive. Over half the 167 voting delegates were Bolsheviks; the SRs had 24 (most of them from that party's left-wing faction), the Anarcho-Syndicalists 13, and the Mensheviks a mere 7.[37] Trotsky spoke on the theme of the hour, the imperative need for power to pass to the (Bolshevik-controlled) soviets, and a resolution in this sense was adopted by 54 votes to 5 with 9 abstentions.[38] But the most interesting part of the proceedings were the reports on the action taken to maintain supplies and implement the movement's basic objective of 'workers' control'.[39] There is little doubt that the majority of delegates took this slogan in its literal sense, as meaning a real transfer of power within the enterprise to the men's chosen representatives, who were to exercise the functions of management in the interests of their electors. Needless to add, they showed no concern whatever for the effects which the full 'democratization' of industrial relations would be bound to have on productivity and the national economy as a whole. They would not have to wait long for a lesson in the realities of revolutionary power politics.

SEVEN *The Workers' Militia*

THE GROWING INTRANSIGENCE and aggressiveness displayed by the factory-committee movement enhanced the importance of the para-military formations organized under its aegis. These units are customarily referred to by the colourful name of 'Red guards', as they were christened by enthusiasts. However one should not overlook the distinction between them and the workers' militia groups from which they were derived.

The workers' militia, like the factory committees, originated in the armed clashes of February. The revolt of the soldiers in the capital led to acquisition of weapons by a number of working-class activists. From the arsenal alone the insurgents seized 40,000 rifles and 30,000 revolvers. Another 24,000 rifles and 400,000 cartridges were handed over under duress by the Provisional Government's Military Commission between 2 and 4 March.[1] When the men returned to work, some of those with arms took on the function of patrolling factory premises and maintaining order in industrial districts of the city. At first they pursued limited aims of a defensive kind : for example restraining 'hooligan elements' who were liable to get drunk and engage in actions that would discredit the new order. It was not long, however, before they began to direct their energies against suspected 'counter-revolutionaries', including of course managerial personnel. The cases of violence discussed above were as a rule perpetrated not by ordinary workmen acting on impulse but by members of these armed bands. They generally referred to themselves as 'the militia' or 'militiamen'; the word 'workers' or 'factory' was sometimes attached to distinguish them from the regular militia (civilian police), which on the morrow of the February revolution was placed under the nominal jurisdiction of the organs of local self-government (municipalities, zemstva).

In Petrograd a geographical division emerged between the industrial areas (notably Vyborg, Narva and Vasilyevsky Island districts), where workers' militia bands exercised a preponderant influence, and other districts (Moscow, Kolomna) where the city militia held control. In the Petrograd district, situated between the northern and central arms of the river Neva, a tripartite struggle occurred. This was initially won by militia groups loyal to the soviet, led by A.V. Peshekhonov, a strong-willed Populist politician, who nevertheless was obliged to recognize that 'in essence all power rested completely in the hands of the crowd'.[2] It has been estimated that by 19 March eighty-five militia centres were functioning in the city, of which twenty were under the influence or control of units formed spontaneously by workers in the factories; but these are said to have had some 10,000 to 12,000 members as against 8,000 for the regular militia.[3]

In Petrograd as elsewhere the relationship between the two formations was a complex and shifting one. Legally, only the latter had any right to exercise police powers. In practice they were obliged to share responsibility with bands of armed men acting at the behest of various unofficial organs : factory committees, trade unions or urban and city-district soviets. Sometimes they took their instructions directly from one or other of the political parties. The relationship between the municipal authorities (or 'committees of public organizations') and these unofficial bodies reproduced in microcosm the so-called 'dual power', the uneasy coexistence between the Provisional Government and the Petrograd soviet. Some more determined municipal leaders endeavoured to bring local militia groups under closer control by verifying the qualifications of those who had joined them and expelling individuals whose loyalty to the new order was in doubt. Frequently, however, such efforts were hamstrung by pressure from radical elements within the municipal board or in the soviet, so that the regular militia was obliged to tolerate the presence within its ranks of men who made no secret of their subversive intentions.

Appeals for the voluntary surrender of weapons had little or no effect, and the general political and military situation made it impossible to uncover them by force. Sometimes regular militiamen were bribed or threatened into surrendering their arms to their rivals. However, major confrontations were generally avoided. In practice the two systems of police authority contented themselves with mutual surveillance. They spent their days in routine tasks such as guarding buildings while such major problems as catching law-breakers and bringing them to justice were neglected. This opened up tempting opportunities to members of the criminal underworld, who sometimes disguised their activities by adopting political labels.

While the Mensheviks and other moderate elements in the soviets vacillated, generally seeking to effect compromises between the two forces, the Bolsheviks endeavoured to consolidate the workers' militia groups under their own control, to build up their popular support, and to give their activities a more overtly political character. Until the Kornilov affair at the end of August these tasks do not seem to have been given a very high priority by the party leadership, despite Lenin's repeated insistence on their urgency. A.G. Shlyapnikov, the senior Bolshevik in Petrograd at the time of the February revolution, disagreed with certain young hotheads who wanted to make the formation of militia groups the party's chief task and urged them to concentrate instead on propaganda among the troops, whose revolutionary potential in his view was likely to be much greater.[4] This became accepted doctrine on the subject during subsequent months. The Bolshevik Central Committee maintained a network of military organizations concerned almost exclusively with agitation among the soldiers. Furtherance of the workers' militia was in practice left to the party's local organs (especially its committees in the city districts) – or simply to the factory committees wherever these could be relied upon to follow the Bolsheviks' lead.

For such limited purposes as overawing hostile elements within the enterprise, or protecting strikers and demonstrators against possible attack, it was scarcely necessary to form an elaborate paramilitary organization. Local bands of men who possessed arms or had a taste for physical combat were simply called upon to act as the occasion arose. One must therefore beware of attaching too much credence to the high figures sometimes given for the strength of workers' militia units in these early days.[5] The fact remains that in a number of factories groups of several hundred men could be mobilized when required; and in the existing administrative vacuum they were a force to be reckoned with. Moreover, the high rate of turnover among members of these bands – in one Petrograd metal works, out of a cumulative total of 470 militiamen registered between March and July 1917, only ten served the full four months, and maximum membership at any time did not rise above 140 – helped to spread a sense of solidarity. 'Thousands of workers were exposed to political propaganda through their daily conversations and learned all sorts of practical knowledge necessary for a revolution.'[6]

The process of acquiring organizational structure was relatively rapid. In the Petrograd works of the 1886 Electric Power Company a forty-five man squad of volunteers appeared on the scene as early as 2 March. Two weeks later they acquired a chief, whom they picturesquely referred to by the medieval title of *sotnik* ('hundreds-man').[7] They wore insignia such as red armbands and carried official-looking permits issued by the factory committee. They were maintained at the expense of their enterprise, receiving a monetary allowance for their efforts in addition to their wages.[8] After a few weeks the members of this band were caught up in the movement to form a city-wide organization. On 28 April a conference was called on the initiative of a left-wing Menshevik (N. Rostov). At this gathering, attended by men from 156 enterprises, a model statute was worked out for a force to be called 'Red guards'. This move prompted the local Bolsheviks, led by Shlyapnikov, to formulate a draft statute of their own. The two documents scarcely differed. A few days later Shlyapnikov's draft was adopted by the Bolshevik-controlled soviet in the Vyborg district of the city. The new organization's tasks were defined in contradictory fashion. It was to 'struggle against the counter-revolutionary intrigues of the ruling classes [and] defend with arms in its hands all conquests of the working class', but simultaneously 'to safeguard the lives, security and property of all (*sic*) citizens without distinction of sex, age or nationality'. This ambiguity highlighted the insoluble problem faced by Social Democrats of both factions in reconciling their commitment to the class interests of the proletariat and to general democratic ideals. Membership in such a band was to be open to any working man or woman who belonged to a socialist party or a trade union and was recommended or chosen at a general meeting of his (or her) workmates. This provision was designed to ensure class purity among the members. Arms and funds were to be sought from official sources. The draft statute went on to outline a hierarchical pattern of organization. The basic nucleus was to be the squad of ten (*desyatok*); these were to combine into units of one hundred (*sotnya*); ten such companies were to form a battalion. The whole force was to depend on the district soviet (most of which were Bolshevik-controlled). All officers were to be elected by their men.[9]

Similar statutes were devised elsewhere, but they do not appear to have had much impact upon the actual operations of these bands. Seldom, if ever, did the militia forces achieve the neat hierarchical structure sketched out for them by radical politicians. Until August, at least, it could be said that the average militiaman's intellectual horizons remained bounded by his factory walls. The number of such units, however, grew apace, particularly in the provinces. For example, at the textile centre of Orekhovo-Zuyevo it was resolved in May to set up a militia unit, but to keep the decision secret; three hundred rifles and sixty thousand cartridges were obtained from soldiers stationed nearby.[10] After the July Days, an abortive effort by pro-Bolshevik troops to force the soviet leadership to take power, most militia units were obliged to lie low, and in the Petrograd area some arms caches were uncovered by troops loyal to the government.[11]

It was the 'Kornilov affair' at the end of August which transformed the situation. Overnight the militia groups became respected 'defenders of democracy', tolerated if not actively assisted by the public authorities. In Petrograd three thousand rifles (out of seven thousand originally promised) were handed over to a self-styled 'committee for popular struggle against counter-revolution'; other supplies of weapons were obtained through illicit channels. The soviet now under Bolshevik control, thereupon set about creating an infra-structure of para-military organizations. The Putilov works, which claimed two thousand militiamen at the time of Kornilov's 'revolt', raised that number to five thousand by October.[12] In Moscow a 'central staff' came into being at the beginning of September. Among its twenty-four members were representatives of various left-wing factions, but real power lay with its Bolshevik core. In vain did the moderate elements protest that such measures were illegal. The soviet pronounced in favour of the 'immediate arming of the workers'. In the Lefortovo district of the city benefit concerts were arranged to obtain money for the purchase of weapons; elsewhere arms and munitions were seized from soldiers on guard duty or acquired in exchange for goods. Militiamen at the Mikhelson factory, who for some months had been engaging in regular military training in open country outside the city, organized a raid on a weapon depot which yielded a haul of 120 rifles, 200 revolvers and 24 boxes of cartridges.[13]

In all this feverish political activity the modest original aims of the workers' militia units were forgotten. Established with the object of self-defence against instigators of *pogroms*, or in the hope of forcing employers' hands in industrial strife, they developed into the military arm of a single political party which made no secret of its intention to seize State power by insurrectionary means. Many ordinary Red guardsmen, and also members of the factory committees, will scarcely have been able to comprehend the import of this transformation. Driven to near-despair by the economic crisis, their nerves kept on edge by incessant propaganda, they responded uncritically to the appeals of a party that promised untold blessings once 'soviet power' had been achieved. They had acquired a taste for violence on a limited scale, and the insurrection seemed likely to be an easy affair. Small wonder that considerable numbers of working men – and even a few women too – committed themselves to the active or passive support of these bands. One recent analyst has estimated their total size on the eve of the October revolution at between 70,000 and 100,000. Of these, some 15–20,000 were in Petrograd or its environs, about 10–15,000 in Moscow and the Central Industrial region, and roughly the same number in the Ukraine.[14] Not all these men carried arms, and their discipline was poor. As a military force they were much less important than the mutinous soldiers. Yet together with the latter they were strong enough to overawe opponents who had lost the will to resist.

EIGHT *Trade Unions*

I N THE TURBULENT conditions of 1917 it was only to be expected that the factory committees, as primary organizations uniting workmen at the enterprise level, together with their para-military offshoots, should have grown more quickly and exercised greater influence than Russia's renascent trade unions. The latter were for a time destined to be the Cinderellas of the labour movement, overshadowed by more powerful bodies – notably, as we shall see, the soviets. However, their potential significance was not in doubt. Whatever differences might exist among socialist theoreticians about the relationship that should exist between trade unions and their own parties – a subject on which large literature by now existed – all of them were agreed that unions were essential. They were seen as the principal instruments through which industrial labour was to promote its sectional economic interests (in Marxist terms, 'the struggle against capital'). At this point no one cared to raise the awkward question as to the role which trade unions should play in the future socialist order.

Compared to the factory-committee movement, which had been fairly spontaneous in origin, the unions owed more to the influence of radical politicians. The major left-wing parties and factions had behind them a long and bitter struggle for control of such workers' associations as had been permitted to exist under the tsarist regime. Immediately after the February revolution they seized the opportunity to establish a foothold in the innumerable bodies that sprang up in the major industrial centres with astonishing speed. 'The unions began to sprout like mushrooms after a shower of warm rain', one of the men involved in this movement wrote later.[1] In Moscow the newspaper *Russkoye slovo* reported, in rapid succession, an inaugural meeting of postal and telegraph workers, a similar gathering of commercial and industrial employees, and the establishment of a provisional bureau of what was soon to become one of the country's most important unions : the All-Russian Union of Railwaymen (more familiarly known, after the abbreviated title of its executive, as *Vikzhel*).[2] Branches of the political parties, or the soviet executives which they controlled, gave the nascent unions assistance in a variety of ways : issuing appeals for members, advertising meetings in their press, finding accommodation, providing funds and facilitating personal contacts. Everyone was aware that timely action in the initial stages would bear fruit later as the movement gathered strength. In some cases the initiative was taken by members of previously existing legal or semi-clandestine unions, but the element of continuity was seldom very strong. It has been calculated that of 145 bodies formed during 1917 whose date of origin is known, fifty-one per cent were set up during the months of March and April and twenty-four per cent in May and July.[3] In Petrograd and Moscow alone 130 such associations came into being in March and April, and the corresponding figure for the whole country was over two thousand; seventy-four different trades and branches of production were involved.[4]

At the end of June, when the third All-Russian conference of trade unions met, it claimed to represent 976 unions with a combined membership of nearly a million and a half.[5] However, a number of organizations, especially those in the provinces, were represented indirectly or not at all. In October a contemporary source estimated that total union membership had reached the two million mark.[6] Materials collected later by the All-Russian Central Council of Trade Unions (ARCCTU), which apparently relate to the very end of the year, give a figure of two and three-quarter million union members, organized in 2,079 unions.[7] This figure excludes 399 unions for which no membership data are available, and on these grounds one recent student of the problem has claimed that the overall total may have been as high as three million.[8] However, it appears that many organizations simply reported as members all persons working at a particular enterprise, whose allegiance to the union was thus little more than a formality.

The two capital cities acted as pace-setters in this development. According to data reaching the ministry of Labour, in Petrograd alone there were by 1 October thirty-four unions with a combined membership of just over half a million; 432,000 of these belonged to the sixteen largest bodies.[9] This suggests that about half the associations extant in the capital five months earlier had since ceased to exist, presumably as a result of mergers. On the same date there were said to be at least sixty-seven unions in Moscow; excluding nine for which no membership data were available, they had a total of 486,000 members – almost as many as in Petrograd.[10] The degree of concentration here was less marked, as one might expect.

As these figures make clear, most trade-union organizations were at first extremely small and of local significance. The natural trend towards unification had two aspects, professional and territorial. On one hand various local groups of men engaged in identical or similar types of work came together under the leadership of an all-Russian body, usually set up at a meeting of representatives from organizations which thereupon turned themselves into its local branches, and the Central Committee of the new union was given (or assumed) directive powers. On the other hand local groups combined to set up city-wide or regional associations usually known as Central Bureaux (CBS),[11] superficially resembling trades councils in nineteenth-century England, which likewise attempted to coordinate the activities of their member organizations. Associations of the second type were more important, and were also more susceptible to political infiltration. There were no less than fifty-one such CBS by June, but many of them were ephemeral.

The most influential were those in Petrograd, Moscow and the major Ukrainian cities. The Moscow association developed out of a clandestine body that had led a nominal existence throughout the war years. As early as 2 March its organizers called a meeting of representatives of ten local unions, mostly of the craft type. When formally set up on 15 March it had twenty-two member bodies. It was at first under Bolshevik control but later in the year swung to the right. It refrained from endorsing a Bolshevik call for a one-day strike on 12 August, in protest at the convocation in Moscow of the State Conference, and shortly before the October insurrection issued a statement criticizing the slogan of 'soviet power';[12] by this time it seems to have forfeited much of its influence.

The factional battle was less acute in Moscow trade-union circles than it was in those of the capital. The Petrograd CB was formally constituted on 15 March at a meeting in Bolshevik party head-quarters arranged by V.V. Shmidt, an activist with experience among the metal-workers. It was attended by eleven men from seven trades and seven other persons whose occupation is not stated – and who were presumably intellectuals. Political arguments prevented the immediate election of an executive; and when such a body was eventually formed, on 30 March, it was evenly balanced between the two Social Democratic factions with four Bolsheviks, four Mensheviks and one Anarcho-Syndicalist. Shmidt was chosen as chairman; in May he was succeeded by D.B. Ryazanov, who although nominally a Bolshevik stood some way to the right of his colleague. It was not long before the leaders clashed over a symbolic issue : how member organizations should mark International Labour Day (which, owing to the lag in the Russian calendar, fell on 18 April). The Mensheviks and 'independents' in the CB wanted the celebrants to make up for the loss of production during the holiday by working on a normal rest day; the Bolsheviks considered this tantamount to 'appeasement of the bourgeoisie'. A vote showed eleven members in favour of the scheme and eleven against, so that no decision could be taken. The affair helped to strengthen the radicals, whose viewpoint was naturally more popular among rank-and-file trade unionists, and by May the CB was endorsing Bolshevik slogans. It even adopted a formal resolution condemning as 'slanderous' personal attacks on Lenin in the non-socialist press, at a time when such explicit support for the Bolshevik leader was still rare. The political tension impaired the organization's effectiveness. About two-thirds of the questions discussed between March and September dealt with political or organizational matters, making a total of fifty-nine items, whereas only fourteen discussions were held on industrial action against the employers and three on unemployment; the breakdown of the debates in the executive committee was similar.[13]

On the morrow of the July Days the CB's line became equivocal, probably reflecting the ambiguous attitude of its new chairman

Ryazanov, but after the Kornilov affair it once again moved to the left. It provided a thousand roubles for the so-called committee for popular struggle and three thousand roubles to secure Trotsky's release from prison on bail. Thereafter it actively backed preparations for the Bolshevik seizure of power.[14]

Most provincial CBS seem to have followed the lead of the Mensheviks, but little evidence has been published from which one could gauge the extent of their influence. Those in four major Ukrainian cities (Kiev, Kharkov, Odessa and Yekaterinoslav) were evidently quite influential, although in each place they were overshadowed by the local soviet. In the Donets the miners evinced little interest in trade-union affairs until the autumn of 1917 and even then had only a very rudimentary form of organization, since each pit committee acted virtually as its leaders thought fit. The spirit here was as much Anarcho-Syndicalist as Bolshevik. The latter party's influence prevailed in the textile towns of the Central Industrial region as well as in the Urals. Activists in the latter region complained of widespread ignorance about the functions of a trade union; in some places organizations came into being which comprised workers in a number of different and unrelated occupations.[15] Moreover, some men seem to have been forced to join such 'unions' under duress.

The CBS' statutes rendered them highly susceptible to external control. These were often patterned on the documents adopted in Petrograd or Moscow. The former, passed after intense debate on 1 May, specified eleven objectives: the first was 'to help develop the trade-union movement of the Petrograd proletariat and to articulate its class consciousness'; as for the task of 'assisting the working class in its economic struggle', this occupied a subordinate position in the list. The CB was pledged 'to ensure concerted action with ... the political party of the proletariat' (that is to say the Bolsheviks); the Menshevik draft, which was rejected, specified 'parties' in the plural. Its composition was weighted in such a way as to favour the larger unions, and only half the member organizations needed to be present to constitute a quorum. Each local organization of each socialist party was entitled to send one representative to sessions of the CB; but (perhaps to guard against the possibility that this provision might be used to the Bolsheviks' disadvantage) certain other persons (unspecified!) could be invited as well. By the end of this period plenary meetings of the Petrograd

CB were being attended by as many as eighty persons; the executive committee had swollen to twenty-three members, so that in practice much of its work fell to a directing bureau, consisting of Ryazanov, Shmidt and two secretaries (both wives of prominent activists). The funds were supplied by deductions from the budgets of member organizations. It was significant that nearly two-thirds of the CB's revenue should have been supplied by the metal-workers, who tended to treat the organization as an appendage to their own union. This influence helps to account for its militancy : on several occasions the CB intervened to prevent industrial disputes from being settled by peaceful arbitration.

It is worth noting that the statute of the Moscow CB, adopted on 12 June,[16] contained several provisions designed to safeguard a modicum of democracy. This reflected the views of V. Grinevich, a Menshevik and a leading authority on trade-union affairs. In this case each constituent union was allocated two seats irrespective of its size; the quorum required for decisions to be valid was fixed at two-thirds; and the election of officers and delegates was to be carried out in secret. It is not clear whether these juridical refinements made any difference to the manner in which business was actually transacted.

The state of the sources makes it hard to trace the fortunes of individual unions. Soviet writers generally focus attention on the organization formed by the metal-workers, in which the Bolsheviks soon won a commanding position, largely due to the influence of Shmidt and Shlyapnikov. In Petrograd workers were recruited *en masse* at gatherings in the factories at which the principal decisions were taken by a show of hands. Executives were established at city-district level in April, all but four of which were under Bolshevik control. By June the Petrograd organization had a 'fully formed apparatus' over a hundred strong, paid from union funds.[17] It soon forged links with other centres. By May the union's national membership was said to have reached 54,500, and by August 138,000. This was a sizeable fraction of the total number of workers employed in the metallurgical industry, which stood at 546,100 in January 1917[18] According to the rather suspect figures of ARCCTU, by the end of the year the metal-workers had 544,527 members in 236 organizations.

At their constituent conference on 23 April the Petrograd metal-workers drew up a statute in which the union's objectives were defined in economic and social terms. For the term 'class consciousness', on which the Bolsheviks laid such stress, it substituted '*mass self-awareness*', a nuance which may have reflected Anarcho-Syndicalist (or conceivably Menshevik) ideas.[19] However by May there was talk of 'strict centralism in administration from top to bottom and unconditional discipline among all members'. The existence of separate unions catering for men with particular skills was pronounced 'contrary to the interests of the labour movement', and an attempt to provide for their specialized needs by forming sections within the union was defeated.[20] Even gold- and silversmiths were to be incorporated. As the union's first historian puts it, 'the Petrograd metal-workers' union was obliged to launch a resolute organized offensive against a whole number of small [craft] unions which had managed to form during the March days and did not belong to the metal-workers' union, as they were obliged to do considering the type of work on which they were engaged.'[21] Such decisions were forced through at mass meetings which undercut the position of the sectional leaders. Among those included were not only men directly involved in the production of iron and steel but also support staff (electricians) and white-collar employees (engineers, foremen, draughtsmen). Unity and equality were the watchwords. Despite this emphasis on unity – and partly perhaps because of it – some months passed before the union could establish itself on a nation-wide scale. The formation of an All-Russian Union of Metallurgical Workers (*rabochikh metallistov*) was decided upon by thirty-seven delegates attending the third trade-union conference late in June, who thereupon chose a provisional central committee,[22] but it was not until January 1918 that the union could hold its constituent congress.

Despite the strong syndicalist current within the union its leaders pressed for the negotiated settlement of wage claims. In June they worked out a draft collective agreement which specified the qualifications and functions of men in each grade and even the amount of output for which they were to be responsible. Some employers objected, but after the men threatened to strike the government intervened and forced the agreement through. It was finally signed on 7 August.[23] In Moscow too the metal-workers' leaders attached much importance to solving disputes peacefully. Although they could not prevent a one-day strike by some 60,000 men early in

July, they were willing to submit their claims to a court of arbitration and then endeavoured to enforce its findings, which linked wage rises to promises of increased productivity.[24] However, in the provinces violent outbreaks became more frequent as the year wore on. A particularly long-drawn-out struggle occurred at Sormovo, near Nizhniy Novgorod, where some 25,000 men were employed, mainly in the manufacture of armaments. Efforts to have the Petrograd wage scales adopted throughout the country were thwarted by worsening inflation. And local unions were not always willing to heed the central leaders' instructions on negotiating procedures. Despite these setbacks the metal-workers' union deserves credit for attempting to maintain some semblance of order and sanity in industrial relations during this critical period.[25]

The next most important group of unions were those embracing textile-workers. These claimed a total membership of 240,000 by June, and probably numbered about 400,000 by October.[26] This was over half those employed in the industry (724,000 in January 1917). In view of the number of women in the labour force and the high incidence of unemployment during the summer, most members were more concerned with socio-economic than with political questions and looked to the union for practical aid in solving them. Union organizers made a point of trying to attract women members. At first most local nuclei were sympathetic to the Mensheviks or SRs – except in Petrograd, where the Bolsheviks, who had had a small group of partisans in one branch of the industry before the revolution, quickly secured a leading position. From this base they set out to undercut their rivals in the potentially more significant organizations of the Central Industrial region. In June they called a regional conference of textile-workers which the Menshevik-affiliated leaders considered irregular. Several of the resolutions passed reflected the Bolsheviks' demands (including workers' control of industry) and a new executive was elected in which they held positions of influence.[27] The background to this swing to the left was widespread discontent over the declining value of wages and the closure of factories short of fuel or raw materials.

At the end of September the textile-workers held their first nation-wide conference. It was attended by delegates from a number of enterprise-level organizations as well as trade unions in the proper sense. Doubtless the presence of these lower-echelon units helped to swell the vote in favour of a Bolshevik resolution on the political question of the hour : transfer of power to the soviets. Ya.E. Rudzutak, a Latvian who was to become a prominent Soviet politician and trade-union functionary in the 1920s, was elected chairman of the all-Bolshevik nine-man provisional executive.[28] Shortly before the October insurrection the textile-workers of the Central Industrial region came out on strike, so helping to undermine the Provisional Government's authority at the eleventh hour.

In many other branches of industry there existed a number of relatively small unions which were under strong pressure to merge. Their party affiliation often seems to have been determined by chance factors. Thus the glassmakers of Petrograd followed the Mensheviks, those of Moscow the Bolsheviks. By January 1918 they had joined those employed in making scent (Menshevik-led) and rubber products (Bolshevik-led), as well as several other groups, to form a union of chemical-industry workers which claimed over 100,000 members.[29] The general commitment to what was called the 'production principle' of organization (that is to say one union for each major branch of production) favoured the Bolsheviks. The small craft unions, along with those catering for the more highly skilled workers, tradespeople and 'white-collar' groups, were naturally anxious to preserve their own individuality and for this reason if for no other tended to sympathize with the Mensheviks or SRs. This was not a universal rule : among tailors, for example, there seems to have been a high proportion of Bolsheviks, and the same was true of pastry-cooks.

As compared with manufacturing industry, where concentration in large enterprises was the rule, the firms in which such people worked were usually small. This made it harder for union organizers to operate, and accordingly the proportion of members to the total number employed was lower. In the food industry less than one-third of the labour force (338,000 strong in January 1917) had been 'unionized' by the end of the year. In construction work, where seasonal labour was the rule and many workers regarded themselves first and foremost as peasants, there were only 76,000 trade unionists among a potential membership of about 1·25 million.[30] On the other hand the printers' union, which claimed 76,000 members at the end of the year, seems to have encompassed almost everyone qualified to join. It was a Menshevik stronghold and could boast a longer history than any other professional group.

A considerable number of unions catered for professional people and 'white-collar' workers. At one point there were said to be no less than 119 such bodies in Moscow alone.[31] Three of the most important groups may be singled out here. The first comprises the various associations of public and private employees, whose representatives met in congress in July and elected an all-Russian executive. By the end of the year its constituent associations claimed 386,540 members, which made them numerically the third largest group in the country. Although extreme left-wing sentiment gained ground in this quarter, the employees generally opposed the Bolsheviks' October *coup*.[32]

The All-Russian Postal and Telegraph (Workers') Union (*Potel'soyuz*) emerged at a mammoth congress held in May and June. The delegates elected a twenty-one-man executive on which the SRS had eleven seats and the Mensheviks four; the remaining six members had no party affiliation. The chairman, P.M. King, came from Vladikavkaz. From the start the union's Central Committee faced strong opposition from syndicalists, based chiefly in Petrograd, who sought to bring the nation's postal and telegraph services under union control. The left-wingers also succeeded in putting through the principle of the 'closed shop', adding a rule that members performing administrative functions should be excluded from executive posts in the union; but it does not seem that this latter provision was widely enforced, and the union's leaders retained control of its affairs. They set up a four-tier institutional hierarchy and ran as many as twenty-two newspapers. The communication workers included many skilled men and the union's influence was greater than the size of its membership might suggest : this stood at about sixty thousand by the year's end.[33]

Similar problems were encountered by the railwaymen's union. Unlike the foregoing, this was a federated body which allowed considerable latitude to its constituent organizations, the so-called 'line committees', based at the principal railway termini and junctions. It was relatively senior employees (engineers, clerks and such like) in privately owned lines who in March took the initiative in forming the nucleus of the future union. In April this body called a conference attended by several hundred delegates, most of them in the higher grades of the service,[34] which elected an All-Russian Executive Committee of Railway Workers (Vikzhel). Twelve of its fifteen members are said to have been 'white-collar' employees; politically they belonged in the main to the moderate socialist parties.

Wages on the railways had fallen behind those in industry, and it was in an atmosphere of growing tension that Vikzhel called the union's constituent congress, which opened in Moscow on 15 July and lasted for no less than forty days. All but two of the line committees (the Nikolayevsky line from Petrograd to Moscow and that from Moscow to Kursk) took a moderate position, and efforts to split the union won scarcely any support. The congress elected an enlarged executive of forty members, of whom fourteen could be characterized as right-wing, eleven as centrists and fifteen as left-wing.[35] A leading role in its affairs was played by two members of the SR party, Krushinsky and Malitsky. They sought to maintain solidarity among all railwaymen and to prevent the union from becoming a mere plaything in the political battle. On the left they faced opposition from a small but vocal 'labour group' on the executive, who according to P. Vompe were agreed 'that it was necessary to blow up Vikzhel, but disagreed fiercely whether to blow it up from without or to do so from within'.[36] The former viewpoint seems to have prevailed. This meant that the left-wingers recruited support for an alternate organization based upon the lowest-paid railwaymen (shunters, depot workers and so forth) and encouraged them to take strike action. One of the problems they encountered was that the union was demanding higher basic rates than were paid in industry, whereas the Bolsheviks, with their commitment to social egalitarianism, took the view that railwaymen should receive no more than industrial workers. Nevertheless they did have some success in winning over men on several lines, notably in the Petrograd area.[37]

The union leadership displayed considerable activity. In August it succeeded in settling peacefully, with the aid of the government, a threatened strike by the locomotive-drivers. Shortly afterwards railwaymen acting on the orders of their union and the Petrograd soviet played a vital part in halting the movement of General Kornilov's troops towards the capital. This action swung the mood of the union leaders sharply to the left and in mid-September the 'labour group' managed to put through a resolution endorsing a nation-wide strike. Called for 24 September, it was conceived as a demonstration of the union's strength rather than as a deliberate challenge to the Provisional Government, and when the latter made significant concessions the moderate leaders called off the strike with evident relief. An uneasy calm descended, broken by local strikes in the Petrograd repair shops and elsewhere in the north-west.[38]

As will be clear from the foregoing, all the trade unions were under heavy pressure to engage in political action, and especially to support the Bolsheviks in their campaign to depose the Provisional Government in favour of 'soviet power'. In this atmosphere it was scarcely possible for the unions to form a viable and effective national organization responsive to the will of their members. The idea of setting up such a body emerged early in the spring – characteristically, among the socialist politicians rather than within the trade-union movement itself. The All-Russian conference of soviets held in April resolved that a trade-union conference should be convoked as soon as possible, and that the labour department of the Petrograd soviet should participate in the arrangements along with the CBS of Petrograd and Moscow. The pre-eminence given to Petrograd and the insistence on haste were designed to ensure that the conference should have an acceptably radical political colouring. Those with democratic scruples[39] were without much difficulty overridden by the activists.

The nine-man organization committee, consisting of five Mensheviks and four Bolsheviks, at first planned to hold the meeting on 20 May, but under pressure from below was obliged to postpone it for one month. It overruled an attempt to make Moscow the venue for the conference rather than Petrograd, which would have eased the moderates' task, and adopted rules on representation which favoured the CBS and the larger unions. The 211 delegates who turned up were divided almost equally between the 'internationalists', as the radicals called themselves, and the 'advocates of trade-union unity'. The latter, who comprised Mensheviks, SRs, Bundists and politically unaffiliated deputies, had a slight margin of advantage. The atmosphere was less heated than some recent Soviet accounts suggest, for there was still a good deal of common ground between Bolsheviks and Mensheviks; however, the debates were conducted on factional lines. They were too arid and abstract to hold much interest for rank-and-file trade-unionists, who in any case were inadequately informed about the proceedings.[40]

There was, for instance, a long discussion on the tasks of trade unions, introduced by two *rapporteurs*, Grinevich for the Mensheviks and V.P. Milyutin for the Bolsheviks, which soon degenerated into a political wrangle. One provincial delegate endeavoured to inject a note of common sense. He complained that many unions were in a state of 'extreme disorder and anarchy', adding that even in Petrograd and Moscow their members did not always understand what these bodies were for. Despite the need for practical guidance, 'we've been debating for three hours and not a word has been said about what we want to hear.' In particular, should workers invariably be urged to press their demands by strike action? Ninety-eight per cent of the disputes with which he was familiar had ended in a negotiated settlement which had gone in the men's favour. 'Why use a sharp weapon when there are other means of solving conflicts?'[41] The resolution adopted on this point was, however, doctrinaire in the extreme. Strike action was proclaimed 'the principal and most powerful weapon of this [economic] struggle, which also helps to promote the growth of class consciousness and to fortify the spirit of solidarity among the working masses'. It was conceded that arbitration tribunals might also play a role, but only 'in certain circumstances' and as 'auxiliary methods of struggle' lest they impair the union's militant posture.[42] The definition of the trade unions' tasks stated that they could be fulfilled only if the unions remained 'militant class organizations' fighting 'in close organic collaboration with the political class movement of the proletariat'. The clumsy phrasing reflected a compromise between rival Bolshevik and Menshevik drafts. As in the debate in the Petrograd CB on 1 May the Bolsheviks had wanted the phrase to read 'the political party of the proletariat' (in the singular, which to initiates meant the Bolshevik party); the Mensheviks had wanted 'socialist parties' (in the plural); the agreed formula, by substituting the word *movement*, obscured the schism within the RSDLP and left room for either interpretation.[43] Such intellectual subtleties were beyond the grasp of many delegates to the conference, let alone their rank-and-file supporters.

The conference organizers agreed that the economic crisis could be solved only by measures of socialization in which the unions were 'to take a most active part'. For the Mensheviks F.A. Cherevanin submitted a complex plan which is of some interest in long-term perspective. It provided for public authorities at the central and local level, dominated by union and soviet representatives, which would issue instructions to the boards of the nationalized industries or to compulsorily syndicated private firms. On these boards the union and soviet spokesmen would constitute two out of five interest groups (the others being the entrepreneurs, government officials and technical personnel). A similar joint organ was to exist at enterprise level.

Characteristically, no one seems to have cared whether this intricate control system could be made to work in Russian conditions. The project was probably devised by its author as a means of countering attractive slogans of the factory-committee movement and to embarrass the Bolsheviks by exposing their ambiguous attitude towards it. Milyutin, the Bolshevik spokesman on this issue, was evidently in disagreement with Lenin about supporting direct actions from below such as seizure of factories. In calling for 'workers' control' he did not even deign to mention the factory committees, but instead pointed to the soviets and trade unions as the organs which should be entrusted with such functions.[44] He differed from Cherevanin only in wanting all the controlling bodies to have a majority of workers' representatives (however defined), whereas the Menshevik leader would have applied this provision solely to the top and bottom levels of his three-tier hierarchy. Thus there was clearly much common ground between them. As Social Democrats they were driven to collaborate against the threat of anarchosyndicalism, which Lenin seemed to be encouraging. Lenin did not speak at the conference (he addressed some of the Bolshevik delegates in private, but there is no surviving record of his remarks). The syndicalist view was eloquently expressed by Alexey Gastev of the Petrograd metal-workers' union, who denounced the Marxists for their doctrinaire attitudes, exclaiming that one had but 'to seize capital by the throat' for the problem of control to be settled.[45]

What then was the *raison d'être* of the factory committees, and how should they be related to the trade unions? The orthodox point of view, shared by both left-wing and right-wing Social Democrats, was that factory committees had no business to intervene in matters such as wages and working conditions, which were properly the sphere of the unions, and that in exercising their functions of control and regulation within the enterprise they should accept guidance and instructions from the latter. The resolution on this point, adopted by seventy-six votes to sixty-three,[46] provided that the unions should 'energetically help to form and consolidate factory committees, trying to turn them into *points d'appui* in the localities and getting them to carry out general union policy'. Thus they were to be allowed to check that collective agreements were enforced, but not to conclude such agreements themselves, for this was a union prerogative. Their members were to join the appropriate union themselves and in general do everything to raise its authority in the eyes of those who did not belong to it. Finally, elections to the committee were to be conducted by the union.[47] The last point meant in effect the elimination of the independent centralized apparatus which the factory committee movement was successfully building up. The CCFCP, established one month earlier, was pointedly ignored in the resolutions of the conference. However, syndicalism was to prove to be a tougher opponent than these advocates of State socialism expected, and in the months to come, actively fostered for tactical reasons by the Bolsheviks, it was to overshadow Russia's nascent trade-union movement.

The third trade-union conference completed its labours by electing a central executive and laying down rules to govern the organization of member bodies. The latter formally established the so-called 'production principle' of organization : all persons employed in the same type of enterprise were to belong to the same union branch, irrespective of any special skills they might possess. This was designed, of course, to promote centralized political control and to prevent splintering along craft lines. Each union was to be constructed on the principle of 'democratic centralism', a nebulous term here construed as meaning that executive bodies were to be elected by the members – directly in the case of small unions, in two stages in the case of large ones. Apart from election, no safeguards were laid down to prevent union leaders from abusing their power, presumably because it was tacitly assumed that they would automatically belong to one or other of the socialist parties and thus be amenable to their discipline. It was an article of faith among Social Democrats that if they exercised political guidance over a trade union, this could be only in the interest of its members. Other provisions restricted the right of local branches or sections of a union to take independent action without foreknowledge of headquarters and prohibited them from raising funds on their own behalf.[48] The principle of the 'closed shop' was not explicitly mentioned, although it was implied by the general spirit of this document. The representative of the Petrograd printers, Kammermakher, expressed opposition to it; so did the egregious Bolshevik Ryazanov, who went so far as to suggest that compulsory union membership would be equivalent to 'the restoration of serfdom'.[49] Another delegate, speaking for Rostov-on-Don workers, criticized the idea that union dues should be automatically deducted from members' pay by management.[50] In general, however, even the 'advocates of trade-union unity', as they euphemistically called themselves, did not show much overt concern for the preservation of democratic rights.

There is no record of any debate on the powers to be exercised by the Central Committee. This body (ARCCTU) had thirty-five members, clearly chosen to reflect the balance of power at the conference as much as from any other consideration. It comprised sixteen Bolsheviks, sixteen Mensheviks and three SRs. Some attempt was made to reproduce the geographical distribution of the trade-union movement: fifteen members were from Petrograd, five from Moscow and fifteen from the provinces. This arrangement gave an inordinate weight to the politically more 'advanced' capital cities. Nor did it represent fairly the distribution of membership between unions. Within ARCCTU there was an executive committee, also weighted on political lines, composed of five Mensheviks and four Bolsheviks, and within this again a five-man presidium. This latter included a chairman (Grinevich, Menshevik) a deputy chairman (Ryazanov) and a secretary (S. Lozovsky). Lozovsky was later to have a notable career as head of the Profintern (the Red Trade Union International). At this time he was nominally a Bolshevik, but his independence of mind excluded him from Lenin's inner circle and shortly after the October insurrection he was actually expelled for a time from the party.

It is customary in Soviet writings to deplore the 'weakness' and inefficiency of ARCCTU in the first months of its existence. Lozovsky himself supplied the material for such strictures by rendering an unusually self-critical report on its activities,[51] which however seems to have been coloured by a desire to ingratiate himself once again with the Bolshevik leaders. In this report he noted that ARCCTU lacked even permanent premises of its own and that it had been unable to hold plenary meetings owing to the disruption of the transport system; member unions had not paid their dues, so that ARCCTU had been obliged to survive on advances provided by the Petrograd metal-workers and printers. Lozovsky also gave the impression that the central executive had been paralysed by differences of opinion between the advocates and opponents of 'soviet power'.

This was no doubt the case; still more important will have been the fact that its leaders' attention was deflected from their proper task by various political assignments. Thus ARCCTU had not only to provide representatives to sit on the Economic Council (the chief economic planning body, set up by the Provisional Government in June) and on the Special Labour Committee of the ministry of Labour but also to ensure that the unions' voice was heard at the State Conference (August) and Democratic Conference (September), the two major political deliberative assemblies of the period. When the trade-union delegates at the Democratic Conference voted heavily against a coalition government including representatives of the 'bourgeois' parties, Grinevich resigned as chairman of ARCCTU; he was succeeded by a left-wing Menshevik, V.G. Chirkin.[52] It is not surprising that its leaders had little energy left to help promote and guide new unions in the provinces or to coordinate the activities of those already in existence.

Nevertheless neither the conference nor ARCCTU should be written off as failures. They had in a sense set the pattern for the future: one of centralized direction from above, by men whose entire way of thinking was coloured by their political convictions. Moreover, a kind of informal alliance came into being between Social Democrats active in trade-union affairs, directed against syndicalist elements on the far left as well as against the government and the employers. This phenomenon was not apparent at the time because everyone was obsessed with the political struggle. If in trade-union affairs the Mensheviks half-unwittingly prepared the ground for their rivals, so they did also in the soviets, the main forum of political life in Russia during this period.

NINE *The Urban Soviets: Structure*

ROM THE FIRST days of the February revolution socialist intellectuals looked upon the soviets of workmen's and soldiers' deputies as the principal medium through which they could mobilize the mass of the population in preserving and extending the gains that had been won. Although everyone in the camp of 'revolutionary democracy' (the term employed at the time to characterize all those who stood to the left of the liberal Constitutional Democrats or Kadets) agreed upon the significance of these popular assemblies, differences soon emerged as to their proper role in the political process. For the Mensheviks and SRs they were temporary organs through which the people might express their aspirations for radical changes in every sphere. The assumption was that their role would come to an end once the Constituent Assembly had met and Russia had settled down in the ways of parliamentary democracy. For the Bolsheviks, on the other hand, the soviets were potential organs of state power, whose task it should be to implement the 'dictatorship of the proletariat' under the watchful eye of the Bolshevik party.

The contradictions within this theory were not readily apparent to Russian workers or soldiers in 1917. In his 'April Theses' Lenin said next to nothing about the party's vanguard role, one of the cardinal tenets of Bolshevik doctrine since 1902. During the months that followed he and his party did their utmost to suggest that transfer of power to the soviets would lead to a real devolution of authority: what remained of the centralized bureaucratic State would be swept away and for the first time in history ordinary people would be able to run their own affairs. It is scarcely surprising that to the politically untutored Russian masses this propaganda had a very strong appeal. Already by June the moderate leaders of the Petrograd soviet, the most important such organization in the country, were finding it hard to keep their followers in line. During the July Days Bolshevik hotheads made a premature bid to establish 'soviet power'. Although this abortive *coup* temporarily discredited the extremists, the Mensheviks and SRS were unable to consolidate their position. They were torn between their dual loyalties: to the coalition government, in which they now set the tone, and to the soviet movement, which had assumed a nation-wide scope. Their contradictions and vacillations were remorselessly exposed by the Bolsheviks, who after the Kornilov revolt late in August swiftly emerged as the heroes of the hour: they won control of the soviets in Petrograd, Moscow, and a number of provincial centres. From this base they could challenge the relatively ineffectual national leadership of the soviet movement, still composed of moderate socialists, and launch the insurrection which brought them to power in October.

One might have thought that the decisive role played by the soviets in Russia's political history during 1917 would have made it easy to trace their role as organs of mass mobilization – that is to say, as bodies which shaped the opinions and directed the actions of those workers and others who followed their lead. In fact the reverse is the case, for most historians have been dazzled by the conflicts at the summit of the soviet hierarchy and have paid little attention to the way in which these institutions functioned.[1] Moreover, reliable source material on such matters is scarce. Of the nine hundred or so soviets which are thought to have been in existence by October 1917,[2] not one has left a complete record of its deliberations. The best documented, rather surprisingly, is that of Saratov, on the lower Volga – an important commercial centre but not a major focus of revolutionary activity.[3] For Petrograd we have minutes of the soviet's executive organs for a few months of the year,[4] and the affairs of that body were reported in some detail in the capital's daily press.[5] One leader of the workers' soviet in Moscow has written an anecdotal account, based on documents, of its activities,[6] but a good deal of material remains in the archives. The same is true of many provincial centres. An added difficulty is the fact that the newspapers put out by a number of such soviets (or on their behalf) are today bibliographical rarities. The Petrograd and Moscow soviets' *Izvestiya* ('News') each published items of information about similar bodies in various parts of the country, but in an irregular and haphazard manner. These reports were also heavily edited. Emphasis was laid upon formal pronouncements whose historical importance cannot be evaluated properly unless one knows details of the preliminary discussions or the voting pattern, which as a rule were not thought suitable for inclusion. Rather less official in character were the reports sent back by agitators in the field, from which extracts were occasionally printed, although these of course were also vetted for political reliability, so that they tend to reflect the attitudes and prejudices of the central soviet leadership.

In the case of resolutions passed at meetings of base organizations such as factory committees or village assemblies, it is easy to detect the influence of the activist who drew up the document and submitted it to a vote, but difficult to say how faithfully the demands put forward (often in the most elaborate detail) reflected the actual views of those present at the meeting. It is therefore impossible to arrive at a precise analysis of the state of opinion at the lowest levels in the soviet organization. All historical argument based upon the evidence of such formal resolutions is therefore somewhat suspect.

Fortunately more reliable information is available about the intermediate and higher levels of the soviet hierarchy, at which the main policy decisions were made. We may consider first the operation of the principal urban soviets and then examine the functioning of the national leadership, which came into existence later in the year.

Two basic points need to be stressed at the outset. First, in many urban soviets the working-class members were overshadowed by soldiers. Sometimes the two constituent elements remained organizationally separate; elsewhere, notably in Petrograd, they merged. If in the early months the soldiers' influence was generally exercised in the direction of political restraint, later the roles were often reversed. As the army became demoralized, large numbers of men in uniform sought to bring an immediate end to the war by whatever means lay to hand, and the soviet machinery offered tempting opportunities. Second, although the soviet leaders were subject to continuous pressure from below, to which they had to adapt if they were to survive politically, it would be wrong to visualize these bodies simply as assemblies of irresponsible and anarchic individuals, swayed by each gust of the wind of fashion. Their activities were in practice largely determined by their executive organs, whose role was much more significant than that of the plenum (as the assembly may properly be termed). In these executives decisions were taken by persons whom one might best call 'cadre elements'. They were often intellectuals, in the Russian sense of the word – that is to say, men who had acquired at least a smattering of education which set them apart from their fellows and so fitted them for a leadership role. As a rule they identified themselves with one or other of the socialist parties; a few had experience of political activity under the *ancien régime* and of these some could be characterized as 'professional revolutionaries' in the Leninist sense of this term, that is to say as persons engaged in full-time work on behalf of their party. This political experience – which might well have included a period in prison – gave cadre elements an outlook quite different from that of ordinary working men drawn into public affairs for the first time, who were as a rule also their juniors in age.

Let us now look at these two points a little more closely. Relations between the soldiers' and workers' soviets depended upon the social geography of each area. Within the territory subject to the jurisdiction of General Headquarters (at Mogilev) there were large concentrations of troops but relatively few civilian workers. The port city of Riga (lost to the enemy on 21 August) was the only major industrial centre close to the front. There were, however, a number of civilian workers employed in service capacities at important strategic points and railway junctions in rear-echelon areas, such as Vitebsk, Smolensk and Odessa. In the Petrograd military district, which included the naval fortress of Kronstadt and other establishments of the Baltic fleet, the situation was broadly similar : the whole region had been turned into a vast military encampment, and Petrograd itself was an important base. Moreover, a number of towns in the deep interior of the country (e.g. Moscow, Kazan, Voronezh) had sizeable garrisons, whose duties included the guarding of defence plants and other military installations as well as training and supply work. In all these places, as at the front, the soldiers responded to news of the February overturn by forming committees in their units. An additional stimulus to this was provided by the celebrated 'Order Number One' issued on 1 March with the imprimatur of the Petrograd soviet.[7] The soldiers' soviets seem to have come into being as territorial adjuncts to these unit committees. They served to coordinate the various demands put forward and to influence the local balance of power. In view of the uncertainties of military service in war-time, when units were liable to be posted elsewhere at short notice, soldiers' soviets were usually weaker organizations than their civilian equivalents, whose members had more or less stable jobs in factories or other enterprises. Moreover, most service-men were of peasant origin, and although the experience of warfare in such distressing conditions had modified their outlook they had not yet acquired skill in the arts of political organization. As a rule the cadre elements in these soviets were NCOs, with the unit clerk often playing a prominent role. In some places there were bodies combining officers and other ranks, but such was the suspicion in which officers were now held that these mixed committees soon came under pressure to split into their constituent elements.

In these conditions it is not surprising to find soldiers' soviets uniting with those of workers. The fact that the prestigious Petrograd soviet had quickly converted itself into a joint body of this type provided an additional stimulus to such mergers. (By contrast, in Moscow the two bodies remained separate until after the October revolution.) There existed a curious but politically significant convention whereby such organizations were referred to as soviets of workers' and soldiers' deputies, the components being listed in that order, even where the soldier element was larger and more influential; where a peasant element was added, it occupied third place. The general practice in a joint soviet was for the constituent elements to preserve a relic of their former independence in the shape of separate 'sections' (*sektsii*) in which they could discuss matters of professional concern; the two sections would come together for general meetings whenever political topics were discussed. Each section had its own elected executive, whose members belonged *ex officio* to the executive committee of the soviet as a whole. Where separate workers' and soldiers' soviets coexisted without merging, joint meetings of the two executives would be held; moreover, members of one body were normally empowered to attend meetings of the other, where they would be granted a 'consultative voice', that is to say the right to speak but not to vote, or at least to have only a kind of second-class vote, registered separately.

The main impetus behind the mergers was a vague feeling that all the 'democratic' elements in Russian society had a common interest in working together against their presumed enemies to the right. Fear was widespread of a counter-revolution led by conservative elements in the officer corps, who were suspected even of willingness to collaborate with the national enemy against 'revolutionary democracy'. The popular mood in soviet circles was at first patriotic and 'defensist' (at least in words), and the charge of collusion with the Germans still carried considerable weight. It impaired the fortunes of the Bolsheviks, who not unreasonably were themselves suspected of collusion with enemy agents. The moderate socialist leaders played on those fears. In the hope of combating the 'defeatist' spirit that had infected some workers and soldiers in the rear, notably in Petrograd, they encouraged mergers between soldiers' and workers' soviets, since the former were at this stage likely to be less radical. With the same aim in view they facilitated exchanges of delegations between front and rear, arranged joint meetings at which soldiers and workers promised one another mutual support, and solicited money and gifts from civilians for the men in the trenches. The results of all this activity were short-lived. Sometimes the delegates from the front came under the influence of anti-war agitators. The Bolsheviks welcomed this opportunity to rehabilitate themselves in the eyes of the soldiers and to expound their powerful argument that an immediate peace would harm neither Russia nor the revolution, since it would be followed by an international proletarian upheaval; the argument that defeatism benefited the enemy was dismissed as a mere 'bourgeois' calumny.

Given the general war-weariness, this propaganda was bound to strike a responsive chord. In some places where soviets had merged the soldiers' role was inflammatory from the first. In Ivanovo-Voznesensk, the great textile centre north-east of Moscow, each company of soldiers (*circa* two hundred and fifty men) elected one delegate to the local soviet, whereas at least five hundred workers' votes were required for this purpose.[8] Yet this was a Bolshevik stronghold. The soldiers involved here were young conscripts of local origin who retained their civilian attitudes. The radicalizing role of men in uniform was felt with greatest effect at Kronstadt.

On 17 May the local joint soviet, in which for obvious reasons sailors were more prominent than workers, decided to assume power. For several days the island stronghold was a *de facto* independent republic, posing a direct challenge to the government's authority within a few miles of the capital. Leaders of the Petrograd soviet were called in to parley with the rebels and a precarious semblance of order was restored. The initiative in this rebellion lay with local leaders influenced by anarchist ideas and unaffiliated to any of the major socialist parties; the Bolsheviks are said to have had the allegiance of only a third of the deputies to the Kronstadt soviet. Lenin personally intervened to moderate the sailors' enthusiasm, which seemed likely to discredit the slogan of 'soviet power'. Nevertheless it was his party which succeeded in turning the men's militancy to its own account.[9]

Thus one may take with a grain of salt Bolshevik complaints, based upon their experiences in Petrograd,[10] that the weighting of soviets with 'non-proletarian' elements placed them at a disadvantage. Ideology notwithstanding, this professedly working-class party derived much of its revolutionary impetus from war-weary men in the armed forces whose motives for opposing the government (and the moderate socialists) had little to do with class struggle in the Marxist sense. The failure of the offensive launched on 18 June undermined the army's shaky morale, discredited the country's leaders, and sent a wave of deserters pouring into rear-echelon areas. Assaults, robberies and riots became commonplace, even in hitherto fairly peaceful garrison towns. In the rear as at the front 'democratic' soldiers' organizations expanded their influence apace. This dissolution accelerated the leftward drift of the urban soviets and prepared the way for the radical change of political allegiance which occurred at the end of August. One of General Kornilov's principal aims was to constrain, if not to suppress outright, all self-constituted bodies within the army. The failure of his enterprise could not but augment their prestige. The more senior elective committees, at divisional level or above, held out against the radicalizing trend, but their influence was waning rapidly. The mood of the army transmitted itself to the country as a whole.

Let us now turn to our second basic point : the dominant role played in the soviets by the cadre elements. This influence made itself felt in two ways. On one hand the executive organs of each soviet acquired greater authority over the plenum or deliberative assembly; on the other hand there came into existence senior soviet bodies, claiming authority to direct the activities of local soviets on a provincial, regional and even nation-wide (All-Russian) scale. These two processes interacted in such a way as to reduce considerably the opportunities for spontaneous self-expression that had existed in the early days of the soviet movement.

At first everything was chaotic and informal. The assembly consisted in the main of deputies (or more correctly, delegates) elected directly by workers in their enterprise or by soldiers in their unit according to a certain norm. These arrangements were either patterned directly on those practised in Petrograd or Moscow, or else were adapted to suit local conditions. In Ivanovo-Voznesensk, as we saw above, each body of five hundred workers chose one deputy; in larger enterprises each thousand workers were to send an additional representative, and at the other end of the scale small firms employing less than five hundred men were invited to combine for electoral purposes. Elsewhere the norm might be higher or lower, without any particular significance attached to the fact : the aim of the organizers at this stage was simply to ensure that workers in every sector should have an opportunity to be heard. Little or no control was exercised over the initial elections, so that persons often attended and spoke who had no formal right to be there; however, in most cases the deputies were no doubt local activists known personally to their electors. Fear of penetration by hostile elements led to a tightening of the rules governing electoral procedure. This trend was reinforced by the struggle between various factions for influence over the deputies.

In some places properly supervised elections (or re-elections) were held at which candidates were obliged to define their political orientation – or at least were exposed to the electors for their approbation. Cases are known where ballots were cast in secret (for instance at the Sestroretsk arms works on 3 May)[11] but all too often such electoral meetings had an *ad hoc* character. Not surprisingly, the tone would be set by the most militant elements and no special effort was made to ensure a full turnout of voters. In principle anyone might raise an objection to a particular candidate on the grounds that his character or record made him unfit to serve. This procedure was justifiable where it was discovered that a man had previously spied on his comrades for the Okhrana, but it easily lent itself to abuse. At least one case is known of a man being compelled to withdraw because he had formerly been a Kadet supporter;[12] this was enough to discredit him as 'bourgeois'. To voice dissenting opinions required courage, for the mood of soviet assemblies was such as to put a premium on conformity. Minorities were liable to be threatened into withdrawing or remaining silent; the easiest course for them to take was simply to opt out of the soviet's affairs altogether or, if they were strong enough, to form a rival organization of their own. As the process of politicization took hold, the electoral procedure came to consist of two distinct moments : first, nomination by local activists belonging to one of the socialist groups; second, approbation at a mass meeting. There might even be a third stage : verification of delegates' mandates by a 'credentials commission'.

A soviet plenum was attended not only by deputies elected in this way but also by representatives of various organizations active in the labour milieu such as trade unions, sickness-benefit funds, local cooperative societies and – last but not least – political parties. These men were simply nominated by the body to which they belonged and often exercised an influence disproportionate to their numerical strength. In some soviets the weight of the elected element was also reduced by the presence of coopted members.[13]

Regulation of electoral procedures was accompanied by measures to ensure that plenary assemblies transacted their business in more orderly fashion. In the early weeks the atmosphere in such bodies was akin to that of a mass meeting. Rank-and-file deputies were keen to make the most of their newly acquired freedom of speech and would deliver lengthy reports on the situation in their respective workplace, setting forth the past and present grievances of their electors and vouching for their loyalty to the libertarian ideals of the revolution. These reports were usually listened to with rapt attention and helped to forge a sense of comradeship. However, in the eyes of the cadre elements such exchanges of experience appeared relatively unimportant, and even harmful in so far as they prevented orderly debate and diverted attention from more urgent political matters. Accordingly they introduced procedural devices modelled upon those of clandestine political parties in the bygone era. The assembly was expected to elect a collective presidium, whose membership reflected the deputies' party-political alignment, to keep to an agreed agenda, to debate the draft resolutions put before them, to take formal votes and so on. These votes – usually by show of hands – were supposed to be binding, although this principle was difficult to enforce since deputies came and went as the mood took them. Increasingly they found it necessary to identify themselves with one or other of the political caucuses or 'fractions' (*fraktsii*). These held meetings to discuss tactics before those of the plenum, which inevitably deprived the latter of much of its interest. Before long cadre elements were complaining of 'apathy' and declining attendance. They appealed to deputies to report back regularly to their electors, to help publicize the soviet's decisions, and generally to display greater political activism. The deputies responded with charges of insufficient democracy : too many important matters were being decided elsewhere, in caucus meetings or in the executive organs.

A certain tension between rank-and-file deputies and cadres was only to be expected, especially once the soviet machinery became more complex and the number of deputies increased. Already before October 1917 one may note the beginnings of the process, familiar to students of post-revolutionary Soviet history, whereby inflation of the size of representative bodies led to a growing concentration of power in the hands of a small executive. In the period under discussion this development seems to have occurred spontaneously rather than from political calculation, but the latter factor was not wholly absent.

The explanation lies partly in the nature of revolutionary ideology. It was generally believed that the soviets, as proletarian organizations whose members were bound by ties of class solidarity, had virtues denied to 'bourgeois' parliamentary institutions with their supposed 'legal formalism'. The assumption was that the checks and balances devised by liberal constitutional theorists were irrelevant to the revolutionary milieu, where the moral climate was quite different. As organizations for waging class struggle, so the argument ran, soviets did not need elaborate safeguards against abuse of authority by their leaders : it was sufficient merely to provide for the recall and replacement of any individuals who from time to time might slacken in their combative zeal. The overwhelming majority of cadres were presumed to be united by indissoluble ties of comradeship with the People whence all their authority sprang. If one were to define too closely the relationship between different elements within a soviet, this could only arouse distrust and weaken its effectiveness. And one should not seek to emulate 'bourgeois' jurists by distinguishing between different attributes of its power (legislative, judicial, executive), since the power inhering in a soviet was *ex hypothesi* integral and indivisible : it expressed in concentrated form the integral and indivisible will of the 'revolutionary masses' themselves.

This theory – still implicit rather than explicit – had obvious weaknesses, among which we may note just one : neglect of that elementary principle of public administration whereby in any organization the need for rule-making increases in proportion to size. The reluctance to regulate power relationships within the soviet movement led not to mass democracy but to élitism and bureaucracy. Sooner or later the spirit of comradeship was bound to become little more than a fiction concealing the exercise of absolute power by leaders guided solely by their 'revolutionary conscience'. Unless checked in time, these men would become accustomed to their governing role; they would take decisions in secret and oblige their followers to accept them as *faits accomplis*; and the deliberative assembly would degenerate into a mere rubber stamp for policies handed down from on high.

On a more pragmatic level, the cadre elements in Russia's soviets in 1917 felt that their superior political experience entitled them to assume a directing role in bodies which had, after all, in most cases been founded on their own initiative. The average deputy, to say nothing of his electors, was unschooled in the arts of organization and management; it was therefore essential for those who had such skills to step into the breach, if only temporarily. Unless leadership were provided, these 'workers' parliaments' might be crushed by their numerous potential enemies. These arguments were more than mere rationalizations of the will to power of leaders drawn from the revolutionary intelligentsia; on the other hand their natural self-assertiveness, nourished by the traditions of clandestine struggle, encouraged these men to take advantage of their commanding position.

It was not long before the deputies in the plenary assembly of a soviet found themselves confronted by an imposing array of executive organs constructed upon a hierarchical pattern. In theory each of these 'core bodies' (as we may call them) was elected by the one immediately below it, the executive committee (*ispolkom*) being constituted proportionally to the strength of each political grouping in the plenum, and having within it a directing bureau. Proportional representation was regarded as irreproachably democratic; and it certainly did ensure that organized minorities could make themselves heard (although one might add that it was less than fair to the politically unaffiliated). The bureau, sometimes referred to as a presidium, might act as collective chairman during meetings of both executive and of plenum; it also coordinated and directed the activities of various operational commissions or departments (*otdely*). These latter agencies, which consisted partly of deputies and partly of persons coopted for their specialized knowledge, functioned in permanence. In principle all deputies were expected to serve in one or other of the executive organs. This might on occasion involve them in missions to other parts of the country, in which case their absence strengthened the hand of those executive members who stayed behind.

Some evidence is available to illustrate the growth of bureaucratic practices in individual soviets. In Moscow, we are told, in the first days of the revolution 'the executive committee consisted in part of comrades elected directly by the soviet plenum, but most members were coopted on the recommendation of the socialist parties';[14] within it there was an executive *commission,* and within that a presidium. The result was a four-tier hierarchy, not counting the several commissions performing operational tasks. The working-class members of the executive committee voiced 'strong distrust' of the executive commission because it had not been duly elected and called for its liquidation. To counter their pressure the body in question was expanded, but this did not meet their objections and on 16 March the matter was discussed in plenary session. A spokesman for the executive (the Bolshevik P.G. Smidovich, an electrical engineer as well as a professional revolutionary of long standing) put forward a scheme whereby the executive was to comprise sixty members elected by the plenum, eight representatives of the socialist parties and ten coopted members; after a lively discussion this plan was adopted. A factional struggle for places on the new body then ensued. On 11 April the seven-man presidium, whose members were nominated by the three major socialist parties, was endorsed by the plenum, which then voted separately on each candidate for election to the executive committee, the sixty persons receiving the most votes being elected. Presumably voting was by show of hands; the list of candidates seems to have been compiled by agreement among leaders of the political parties. 'The basic group of executive committee members did not undergo any essential changes during the entire period of the February revolution [that is to say until October].'[15] An investigation published in June 1917 yields some interesting information about the composition of this organ. Thirty-seven per cent of its members were described as 'members of the intellectual professions', whereas only 4 per cent of the deputies in the plenum fell into this category; for (manual) workers the corresponding figures were 52 per cent and 83 per cent. (The remainder were employees and 'privileged workers'.) Fifty-four per cent of the executive committee members, as against 11 per cent of the deputies, had had some secondary or higher education.[16]

In Saratov 62 per cent of the total membership are said to have had secondary or higher education,[17] and it would be fair to assume that these men were also heavily concentrated in leadership positions. From the published records it is clear that the executive committee underwent an expansion during the year which reduced the weight of its elected element. In March it comprised fifteen elected members and nine other members nominated by five organizations; by September the former had risen to thirty, but alongside them were an undisclosed number of representatives nominated by nine organizations; in addition the elected presidiums of the two sections of the soviet, each eleven strong, had seats on the executive *ex officio*.[18] In March the soviet met every second day and the executive committee on each preceding evening; but at the end of July it was decided that the soviet should meet only once every two weeks, its workers' section once a week, and the executive committee twice a week whereas its core organization, the bureau, was to convene daily.[19] The published records from Saratov (which as already

	executive	meetings of other executive organs	plenum
March	19	—	15
April	16	—	4
May	17	—	2
June	12	3*	2
July	15	—	—
August	10	1†	1
September	12	1†	—
October	6	4†	1

* executive commission of workers' section
† bureau

indicated are incomplete) give a rough idea of the relative frequency with which meetings were held, as the table on p. 125 shows. These data also suggest that the executive committee itself lost influence to its bureau, which was nominally subordinate to it. There were occasions when attendance was higher at meetings of the latter than of the former,[20] and since the same persons dominated proceedings of both bodies the difference between them will in practice have been slight. Nevertheless in the eyes of ordinary deputies excluded from either body this increasing centralization must have seemed significant. In any case their attention will have been drawn to the fact once it became a matter of factional controversy.

This was the case in Petrograd, where the Bolsheviks and Menshevik Internationalists complained loudly at the activities of a bureau set up within the executive by I.G. Tsereteli, the moderate Menshevik leader, and his friends. N.N. Sukhanov, the well-known diarist of left-wing Menshevik persuasion, ironically refers to it as the 'star chamber'.[21] This core body came into being on 14 March, when it was given the task of 'preparing all business for the plenary sessions [of the executive] and solving current questions'.[22] One month later, in the face of mounting pressure for reform, notably by left-wing members of the soldiers' section, it was decided that the bureau should consist of all chairmen of operational departments and 'a few' other members of the executive committee who had no such responsibilities. It had the right to act independently in emergencies, subject to retroactive confirmation by the executive committee, and could decide all matters on the latter's agenda. It was 'to be as politically homogeneous as possible' and to consist of persons committed to implementing the executive's line. The Bolsheviks, against whom this provision was above all aimed, won a concession whereby executive committee members were permitted to attend bureau meetings, but without the right to vote, and on condition that they did not reveal the information they obtained or abuse it for partisan ends. This concession in effect opened the door to unofficial leaks and nullified the bureau's purpose as a supreme policy-making body, responsible for its decisions to the executive and indirectly to the plenary assembly.[23] The bureau was to meet daily, the executive committee three times a week.[24] But in May, the month during which the affairs of the Petrograd soviet's leading organs are best documented, the bureau actually met twenty-three times as against seventeen times for the executive committee, so that the latter could not really complain that it was being intimidated. To the rank-and-file deputies the issue was presented in party-political terms, and their growing support for the Bolsheviks at this juncture in part reflected dissatisfaction at the centralizing tendencies within the soviet.

The executive committee, which had numbered fifteen on 28 February, increased to forty-two one month later and by the middle of April had more than doubled to reach a figure of ninety; meanwhile the bureau grew from seven members to twenty-four.[25] As early as 3 March eleven commissions, later renamed departments, had been set up on an *ad hoc* basis, and on 14 April the executive formally elected several of its members to serve on each of them.[26] Some outside 'experts' were coopted, and a staff of clerks, typists and so on engaged. These office-workers were among those who complained – perhaps from a combination of technical and political reasons – that executive members were becoming 'inaccessible' and that the soviet's business was being handled inefficiently.[27]

The most important group of departments comprised those which exercised quasi-governmental functions: for miltary affairs, supply and labour. The latter helped to promote the formation of trade unions and to settle industrial disputes. There was also a department engaged in the preparation of legislative proposals for transmission to the Provisional Government. To these may be added the international department, which sought to promote anti-war sentiment among foreign socialist parties. The next group of departments embraced those concerned with various forms of agitation and propaganda at home: sending out speakers, compiling leaflets and publishing the soviet's two newspapers: *Izvestiya* ('News') and *Golos soldata* ('Soldier's Voice'). Finally one may mention those departments which existed either to serve the soviet's own needs (finance, secretariat) or else to strengthen its ties with like-minded bodies in Petrograd itself (where each of the main city districts had its own soviet) and especially in the provinces. The last of these departments, that for 'inter-city affairs' (*Inogorodnyy otdel*), took a leading part in coordinating the soviet movement at the regional and national level. For in the provinces the local leaders looked to Petrograd and Moscow not only for ideological guidance but also for directives as to how they should run their affairs.

TEN *The Urban Soviets: Creation of a National Leadership*

THE EMERGENCE OF a hierarchy of soviet bodies at levels superior to that of the city was a major step towards greater centralization. If in an urban soviet the hundreds of deputies entitled to attend the plenum found it difficult to control the actions of the several dozen members of their executive or the handful of men who comprised its bureau, it was still harder for them to know what was afoot in the bureau of a provincial (*guberniya*) or regional (*oblast'*) soviet. Although these latter bodies did not as yet play any notable part in shaping events, and indeed led a shadowy existence, an important principle was involved. At these upper levels in the emerging hierarchy there was no equivalent to the plenum of an urban soviet, meeting on an average once a week and at least potentially capable of enforcing its sovereign rights. Instead these 'super-executives', as one might call them, were elected by and responsible to periodical conferences or congresses of deputies. What happened in practice was simply that a powerful urban soviet executive extended its influence over the surrounding area. It took the initiative in calling the provincial or regional assembly and provided the most important members of the new executive. Often the composition of a provincial or regional executive overlapped with that of the executive in its major centre, whose members thus, as the phrase goes, 'wore two hats'. Naturally enough these leaders were not too scrupulous about distinguishing between their several responsibilities; they looked upon the provincial or regional soviets simply as convenient means of transmitting the revolutionary impulse to the smaller towns, and ultimately to the villages, in their vicinity; it was of little concern to them whether the new organs had any genuine identity or were mere fictions. The principle of indirect election invited such abuse.

The process of unifying the soviet movement began already in March. At the end of that month two regional conferences of soviets were held, one in Moscow and the other in Saratov. The former was attended by representatives of seventy workers' and thirty-eight soldiers' soviets. It decided to set up a provisional regional bureau consisting of sixteen persons in each of these two categories.[1] The Saratov gathering was a less ambitious affair. Attended by men from eighteen soviets in the lower Volga and Urals, it resolved that it would be premature to establish a provincial (or regional?) bureau, but instead empowered the Saratov city soviet executive to act provisionally in this capacity.[2] Possibly the local leaders (who, incidentally, were lawyers by profession) harboured some doubts about the assembly's representative character; however this may be, on 6 May, under pressure from radical elements, they decided to go ahead and to set up such a bureau. In the debate on this move in the executive committee of the Saratov soviet one member suggested that the new bureau would have little credibility if it consisted wholly of persons from the province who lived in the town of Saratov, and urged that a congress be called at which the bureau could be elected in a more representative fashion; this course seems to have been followed.[3] In some other centres, such as Yaroslavl and Nizhniy Novgorod, similar scruples were evident. Elsewhere bureaux were set up which are said either not to have functioned at all (Tver) or to have been badly attended (Voronezh); in the case of the Moscow bureau, the best documented of these bodies, we are told that 'most of its members were deputies to the Moscow soviet who did responsible work in party organizations and looked on their work in the bureau (known as MOBYUS) as secondary.'[4]

In Petrograd some soviet leaders endeavoured to delay the rush toward unification until the various local organizations had been given time to consolidate their position. However, they were unable to impose their views. Already on 15 March its newly formed bureau, in one of its first acts, recommended to the executive committee that a congress be called for the 28th of the same month, to be attended by delegates of the leading organs of forty-two municipal soviets.[5] The scheme was at once approved and published. The response seems to have been greater than the organizers had anticipated, and it was with some difficulty that they brought the meeting under their control. The All-Russian conference of soviets (as it came to be called : the moderates succeeded in downgrading it from the rank of congress, which would have implied that it was fully representative) met from 29 March to 2 April. It was attended by some six hundred persons in all, the bulk of them from the capital and the north-western region. No less than 120 other towns with 138 soviets were represented; each of these bodies was allotted two delegates, one for its workers and the other for its soldiers. Forty-seven other organizations, comprising different types of military committee, were permitted to attend, so that the soldiers enjoyed a dominant position. This was to the taste of the SRs, who together with the Mensheviks were able to ensure the passage of resolutions endorsing the line taken by the Petrograd soviet.[6]

These resolutions were widely publicized, and local soviets were encouraged to issue statements couched in the same terms. More important, they were advised to implant soviets in centres where none as yet existed, to merge the separate organizations for workers and soldiers, and to set up provincial and regional executive committees; thirteen such regions were defined. On 8 April the Petrograd soviet executive laid it down that, in complying with the last point, the local soviets should be free to determine for themselves what the norm of representation should be.[7] The whole structure was to be crowned by a national (All-Russian) congress of soviets and a central executive committee. It was hoped to call such a gathering within less than a month. Ten representatives of provincial soviets and six representatives of army organizations were added to the executive committee of the Petrograd soviet; this expanded body was formally charged with the task of organizing the congress.[8] The addition of out-of-town representatives was something of a face-saving device to avert suspicion of domination by the capital. It is not certain whether these men actually attended meetings of the Petrograd executive.

The rules governing the dispatch of delegates to the congress were in principle designed to ensure that smaller centres were not put at a disadvantage. Two deputies were to be chosen from each soviet with 25,000 to 50,000 electors; an extra deputy was allowed for each 25,000 electors up to a ceiling of 200,000 (eight deputies); those with less than 25,000 electors were to combine forces and send a joint deputy according to the same norm.[9] There was, how-ever, a fly in the ointment – or rather, two of them. In the first place it was left to the individual soviets to determine how many electors they represented; naturally enough, they were tempted to claim that they had a mandate from the entire working population of the neighbourhood, including groups which were only marginally, if at all, represented in the soviet. The Saratov soviet plenum, at a poorly attended session on 20 May, elected five delegates on the grounds that it represented 100,000 soldiers and workers, which considerably overestimated its influence.[10] Secondly, it was left unclear how regional and provincial soviets would be represented at the congress. There was a possibility that these somewhat spurious senior bodies might elect enough deputies to overawe those who had a better claim to speak for the rank and file of the soviet movement. In the event, however, time was too short for this threat to materialize. When the first All-Russian congress of soviets opened on 3 June – practical as well as political difficulties forced a postponement of the date – a mere 53 organizations claiming authority over regions, provinces or other areas larger than the town were represented, as against 305 local soviets. Of these 173 were bipartite (that is to say united workers and soldiers) and 72 had some peasant representatives; the latter seem to have played a largely decorative role, and only four soviets could claim to have a properly constituted peasant section. There were 34 military organizations, an appreciable drop from the 47 represented at the All-Russian conference of soviets two months earlier. This helps to explain the increased strength of the extreme left. All in all there were no less than 1,090 delegates, including 822 with a full vote.[11]

Of these men the majority were committed to support the stand-point of the moderate socialist parties whose leaders had joined the first coalition ministry in May. A questionnaire was circulated among the delegates asking them to state their political affiliation. Of the 777 who replied, 285 designated themselves as SRs and 248 as Mensheviks; another 20 and 8 respectively declared themselves sympathetic to these two parties. The Bolsheviks constituted the next largest group, with 105 adherents, and there were several other smaller left-wing socialist factions.[12]

Such a vast concourse was likely to prove to be difficult to manage, especially at a time when the atmosphere in the capital was heated by Bolshevik calls for massive demonstrations against the government and so-called 'compromising elements' within the soviet movement. There was at least one moment when the turbulence in the streets spilled over into the chamber where the debates were held, and delegates were continually moving to and fro. The commotion gave the radicals (or 'maximalists', as they were coming to be called) a weight out of proportion to their numerical strength. The congress presidium, anxious to allow every speaker ample opportunity to express his views, let the proceedings drag on until 24 June, by which time many delegates had withdrawn in disgust at the tedious, acrimonious and interminable debates. Nevertheless the organizers did eventually win votes of approval for all the resolutions which they sponsored. These were phrased in such a manner as to appease the maximalists and to convey to the uninitiated the impression that 'revolutionary democracy' was united in its attitude towards the burning issues of the day. Thus the resolution on the war, which endorsed the government's efforts to convince the Allies of the need to conclude a general democratic peace, passed with only eight dissentients. On such questions as the convocation of the Constituent Assembly, the right of minorities to national self-determination and the need for state control of the economy complete unanimity was recorded. The only issue on which the maximalists made a strong stand for their own principles was the question of the attitude which the congress should adopt towards the Provisional Government. (It was during the debate on this matter that Lenin delivered his celebrated retort to Tsereteli that the Bolsheviks were prepared to take power at any time.) The vote was 543 to 126 with 52 abstentions.[13] This looked like an overwhelming victory for the moderates; but in fact the latter were prisoners of the extreme left, since the text of the resolution obliged the socialist ministers in the government to consider themselves responsible to the soviet movement.

For the congress considered itself in effect a sovereign body. In order to buttress its claims to leadership until the next such gathering three months hence, it resolved to elect an All-Russian Central Executive Committee (CEC). The first question to be decided was the relationship between this organ and the rival nation-wide executive established a few weeks earlier by the All-Russian Congress of *Peasant* Deputies (see below p. 234). The urban soviet leaders were convinced on ideological grounds that it was their right and duty to lead the peasants, who in their view were lacking in 'revolutionary consciousness'. At private talks they suggested that the central peasant executive should be simply absorbed into the new body, but this proposal was handsomely defeated by a vote of 128 to 31 with 5 abstentions.[14] The peasant leaders would only join in a united executive on condition that their own organ preserved its integrity. The spokesmen for the workers' and soldiers' soviets had to reconcile themselves to the coexistence of two national bodies, which were to hold joint sessions whenever expedient.

The next step was to ensure that at such meetings the CEC would be able to dominate the central peasant executive so that it would profess suitably radical sentiments. To this end the Menshevik leader I.A. Isuv (evidently with the tacit consent of the Bolsheviks) suggested that the CEC should consist of no less than 300 persons, 200 of whom were to be drawn from the Petrograd area and 100 from the provinces. (The figure of 300, subsequently reduced to 250, had first been put forward by A.V. Lunacharsky, who was associated with Trotsky's fraction of 'Inter-districtites'.) In addition it was to include either the whole of the Petrograd soviet executive or 50 men drawn from it (the accounts differ), as well as 13 representatives of the various socialist parties and a handful of trade unionists.[15]

The sole argument advanced in defence of this extraordinary proposition was that it was necessary to 'utilize the experience' gained in the Petrograd soviet in directing the entire soviet movement during the previous three months or so. It was obvious that the role of the provincial members of the new CEC was seen as purely decorative; indeed, it seems to have been expected that these men would not even be duly elected by provincial soviets or other local bodies, but would in fact be men from Petrograd who had been dispatched on missions to other centres. All in all it could be said that the statute establishing the CEC contravened the most elementary principles of democracy as ordinarily understood. Nevertheless, or perhaps for this very reason, the congress organizers did not table the issue for debate. On 16 June it was adopted without discussion by a unanimous vote. Characteristically, the aspect of the scheme which attracted most attention was the party-political affiliation of the future CEC. The solution adopted to this problem was to choose its 150 Petrograd-based members on the principle of proportionality. This meant perpetuating the factional line-up at the congress, which was of course to the advantage of the Mensheviks and SRS who controlled it. These politicians evidently realized that such a large and faction-ridden body could only be a deliberative organ, not an executive one; and therefore they set up within the CEC, or rather above it, the by now traditional 'core organs' : a bureau of fifty members and a presidium of nine. However, since these bodies were also constructed on the basis of proportionality, they could scarcely be expected to provide clear or effective leadership. In fact meetings of the CEC's plenum were attended as a rule by a mere forty to fifty persons instead of the hundreds qualified to do so and were virtually indistinguishable from sessions of its bureau.[16]

What had in effect happened was the formal conversion of the Petrograd soviet's executive committee into a body claiming nation-wide authority. The most active members of the CEC were familiar figures who had risen to leadership positions in the soviet of the capital. The CEC also inherited the unwieldy administrative apparatus of the body whence it had sprung. It acquired no less than eighteen departments, most of which had one or more subordinate commissions as well. Within a few weeks this mini-bureaucracy was employing several hundred persons. It formed a rudimentary alternative authority to the shaky Provisional Government. In the eyes of many ordinary folk it appeared as the true *vlast'*, the rightful successor to the autocracy, whose commands deserved to be obeyed without question or delay.

The quasi-governmental character of the CEC becomes apparent from a closer look at its departmental structure. In addition to agencies for military and international affairs, supply and labour – inherited from the Petrograd soviet – it possessed others covering the business of a whole range of ministries. One of the most important was the agrarian department. Headed by S.S. Saakyan, this took a line more radical even than that pursued by the central peasant executive (see p. 238). Whereas the latter belatedly sought to restrain the peasants from settling the land question by direct action, the CEC's agrarian department set itself the aim of 'extending the narrow limits imposed on the peasants in their struggle against the landowners by the law on land committees'; to this purpose its 'agitation and organization section' sent out emissaries to the countryside, who were kept supplied with appropriate propaganda by another agency; meanwhile a third section exerted pressure upon the central State and public institutions.[17]

Another vital sector of the economy came within the purview of the department for rail transport. This had a section for personnel matters ('democratization') and others for industrial disputes, trade unions, technical questions and the inevitable 'agitation and organization'. There was also a central secretariat which endeavoured (not very successfully, it appears) to coordinate all these multifarious activities. The leaders of this department were all SRs. Its sphere of competence naturally infringed that claimed by the All-Russian Union of Railwaymen's executive, and the two bodies coexisted uneasily for some time until the union emerged as the more powerful contender.[18]

As a curiosity with ponderous implications for the future one may note the existence of an embryonic department for economic planning headed by Cherevanin. This was the unofficial counterpart of the government's Economic Council. Neither body made much of a mark, largely for reasons outside their control.[19] Of more immediate benefit to the population were the activities of the CEC's department of medicine and hygiene. Managed by a socialist politician who was also a doctor, G.D. Lindov, and with many qualified medical men on its staff, it laboured to halt the deterioration of such health services as existed for industrial and commercial employees; a section performed similar functions on behalf of the soldiers. Some other welfare activities were carried on under the auspices of the military department (chairman : V.Z. Zavadye), but the latter's main concern, of course, was political agitation among the troops.[20]

Several other departments of the CEC were more overtly political in purpose. Two concerned themselves with the affairs of local government institutions in town and country. Rather more significant was the judicial department, which as well as providing cheap legal aid kept an eye on various bills under consideration by the government. Since the latter had few secrets, the leaders of this agency (chairman : Bulat) were well placed to influence the shaping of policy on important matters involving internal security. This department was especially subject to contradictory political strains. After the July Days it set up a commission to determine responsibility for the disorders and to investigate allegations that the Bolsheviks had received financial support from German sources. Its activities aroused the hostility both of the ministry of Justice, which had initiated its own inquiry, and of elements within the CEC who were sympathetic to the Bolsheviks. Partly as a result of these pressures nothing much came of these investigations, which were soon overtaken by events.[21]

Rather different in political complexion was another CEC agency, the 'department for struggle with counter-revolution'. Its leaders (who are not named in the sources) evidently found their colleagues in the judicial department too moderate and therefore claimed an independent status. This was in fact a relatively ineffectual (and hitherto neglected) forerunner of the Bolshevik secret police agency, the Cheka (see below p. 352). It concerned itself mainly with collecting information about the activities of individuals or organizations deemed potentially hostile, such as clergy or landowners.[22] It seems to have relied upon the services of local zealots rather than to have set up a regular network of agents, although one may suppose that this restraint was due as much to lack of material resources (and time) as to any inhibitions about the merits of such conduct. The department urged local soviets to set up similar bodies, in contact with the centre, but it is not known how frequently its advice was taken. The Nikolayev soviet was reported in August to have established both an investigation and a judicial department to take action against former policemen and *agents-provocateur*.[23] Some other soviets may have gone further than this.

Agitation, orally or by the printed word, remained a major concern of CEC activists even after their attention had come to be concentrated on administrative tasks. There were at least three separate agencies concerned in one form or another with propaganda, using this word in its general sense.[24] The principal one was the 'agitation and literary department', which employed a staff of paid cadres as well as part-time volunteers. Between 7 March and 1 August (during the first part of which period it was still formally an agency of the Petrograd soviet) the department claimed to have satisfied 1,020 requests for aid; 145 of these emissaries had been sent outside the Petrograd region.[25] Its activities were of major national importance during the violent disturbances which broke out in the capital on 20–21 April, 10 June and 3–4 July. Even more influential were those emissaries sent to the front, at least in the early months. Such men normally remained on assignment for two to four weeks, which gave them a chance to contact a number of military units.

In practice they acted as they saw fit, veering and tacking as the winds blew about them. Some of them regarded themselves as apostles for their political parties as well as for the soviet. This did not matter much so long as all socialist factions shared common ground, but the establishment of Bolshevism as a distinct current led to conflict and confusion. It was clearly in the interests of Lenin and his followers to present their message as though it enjoyed the sanction of the soviet movement as a whole, which they had yet to conquer. Later in the year, as the Bolshevik Central Committee developed its own independent apparatus, there came into being two contending corps of agitators, whose members carried on a war of words and poached one another's cadres. To those outside the revolutionary milieu it seemed that pandemonium had broken loose.

The CEC's agitators were supposed to seek guidance from editorials in *Izvestiya*, which on 1 August formally became the joint organ of CEC and the Petrograd soviet; their Bolshevik counterparts, of course, followed the line set by *Pravda*. A number of provincial soviets published their own official press organs. Many of these publications were ephemeral and had a limited circulation. Contributors were not expected to display much originality, many items being reproduced from one of the central organs. This made for economy and gave the propaganda greater coherence – although to modern readers its tone seems unduly shrill.

The Petrograd *Izvestiya* (together with its military counterpart, *Golos soldata*) was edited by a board headed by F.I. Dan, a leading Menshevik politician. It enjoyed a semi-autonomous status *vis-à-vis* the other propaganda agencies. Among the latter – in addition to the main one discussed above – was the 'inter-city' department, inherited from the Petrograd soviet, and one concerned with the electoral campaign for the prospective Constituent Assembly. The former was in charge of training agitators (the agitation and literary department being responsible for the *content* of the propaganda they retailed). The latter, headed by the Menshevik L.M. Bramson, published a number of brochures giving practical advice to voters and to officials in charge of the elections. A regular series of courses for such persons was held in Petrograd. The course lasted two weeks and was given four times. The first students were mainly SRs or Mensheviks, but Bolsheviks soon became more common. An element of political bias could hardly be avoided in such programmes,[26] but they spread an elementary knowledge of democratic principles and practices.

Of the departments whose purpose was to service the CEC itself the most important was that concerned with raising financial support. Unfortunately its accountancy practices were so idiosyncratic that a thorough analysis of its affairs is scarcely possible. The CEC took over some of the assets and liabilities of the Petrograd soviet; it also acted as disbursing agency for several welfare funds (such as that for 'victims of the revolution') which were not clearly distinguished from its own accounts. According to one set of figures the Petrograd soviet had an income of over 3·5 million roubles between March and June, of which 1·8 million roubles were disbursed. According to other data, during the same period its income amounted to only 820,000 roubles and its expenditure to 490,000 roubles. The largest items were for propaganda, especially to the soldiers; the sum of 51,000 roubles was transmitted to soviets and other organizations in the provinces.[27] This credit balance evidently evaporated during the months that followed.[28] On 16 July the CEC's finance department appealed to all soviets to alienate 20 per cent of their income in its favour. The response to this appeal was slow and uneven. The Orenburg soviet sent in the fair-sized sum of 2210 roubles, whereas that of Zhitomir contributed 150, Nakhichevan (an industrial suburb of Rostov-on-Don) 25, and Shlisselburg (near Petrograd) a mere 5·50 roubles;[29] these latter payments may, however, have been intended only as instalments. A perusal of the lists of acknowledgements published in *Izvestiya* suggests that much larger sums were often received from casual groups of sympathizers or such bodies as factory committees than through regular soviet channels: for example, the Petrograd Pipe Works made a gift of 15,000 roubles in July.[30] Some contributors chose to earmark their payments for one of the relief funds rather than to place them entirely at the disposal of the CEC. On 9 August the central body summoned a conference to discuss the problem of finance. It was decided to launch a fund-raising drive during the celebrations due to be held later that month to mark the lapse of half a year since the Petrograd soviet was established. However, the occasion was overshadowed by the Kornilov affair and little money seems to have been collected. Some local soviets, acting upon Bolshevik suggestions, refused outright to comply with the request.[31]

Financial stringency obliged the CEC to abandon the practice, initiated by the Petrograd soviet, of subsidizing local soviets.[32] This may well have been a factor in driving some of these bodies to the left. Several of them called on members to allocate one per cent of their wages to the soviet.[33] Where such 'self-taxation' yielded too little for their needs, two alternatives were open. They could either borrow money or else resort to more coercive methods. Factory committees and other base organizations sometimes imposed levies upon industrial or commercial firms. Such practices were generally deplored by the moderate socialists in charge of most soviets, but necessity proved a stern taskmaster. The Menshevik-led Irkutsk soviet is said to have threatened to seize funds from the local branch of the state treasury unless money were forthcoming from Petrograd.[34] Bolshevik-controlled soviets were likely to show even less scruple.

Coups of this kind encouraged centralism as well as militancy, since deputies were inhibited from claiming the right to control expenditure of funds that had not been provided by their constituents. In some soviets 'revision commissions' were set up as a safeguard against misappropriation of funds, but one may doubt whether they were effective. If local leaders showed themselves resourceful in obtaining money, few of their followers would question the means employed. It is probably fair to say that the Bolsheviks, inspired by greater revolutionary *élan* and with a powerful organization behind them, were more efficient fund-raisers than their rivals. However, here we are encroaching upon a larger and delicate question to which no final answer can yet be given.[35] Suffice it to say that, vital as the financial problem was, it cannot of itself explain the Bolsheviks' victory, the reasons for which were above all political.

ELEVEN *The Urban Soviets:*
the Political Battle Joined

THE NATIONAL SOVIET leadership was a prisoner of the cruel 'dilemma of power' which faced Russia's democratic socialists in 1917. The weakness of the Provisional Government obliged them to assume joint responsibility for direction of the nation's affairs, yet by doing so they inevitably became ever more isolated from their popular following. They were faced with a profound crisis of conscience. On the one hand, collaboration with 'bourgeois' parties in the ruling coalition meant supporting the cause of national defence, which in turn implied calling a truce in the class struggle; on the other hand, if they substituted their own power for that of the government they would be inviting civil war. Whichever course they adopted, some of their principles had to be sacrificed on the altar of expediency. Yet Russian socialist intellectuals had been brought up in a tradition that was ideological rather than pragmatic. In their scale of values 'opportunism', equated with betrayal of principle, was a major sin. By instinct they were hostile to governmental authority, even if the regime in question was one with which they themselves were associated. Experience had not fitted them to exercise power, and relatively few of them (exceptional in this regard were Kerensky, Gots and Tsereteli) could adapt themselves quickly to the new environment; most clung to the habits of the underground world with which they were familiar. The division was one between realists and ideologues. It ran within the soul of each individual, forcing him to make a succession of agonizing choices. For idealists like Chernov or Martov the dilemma was sheer mental torture. Nor were the Bolsheviks immune : it was much harder for Lunacharsky or Ryazanov, for example, to reconcile themselves to Lenin's self-confident identification of the interests of the revolution with those of his own party than it was for Trotsky; even such a loyal lieutenant as Zinoviev vacillated at crucial moments, although his motives were perhaps rather more mundane. The Bolshevik leaders of 1917 had yet to acquire the 'hardness' – one might say, the moral insensitivity and ideological zeal – that later became their salient characteristic. They were for the most part drawn from the same social and intellectual milieu as their rivals. It is therefore not surprising that they should have shared, if less intensively, the doubts and hesitations that beset 'revolutionary democracy' as a whole.

This is not the place for an account of Russia's political history in 1917. We may restrict our discussion of the struggle between the Bolsheviks (and their allies) and the Menshevik – SR advocates of coalition to those aspects directly relevant to the urban soviets as organs of mass mobilization. In this context the point to be emphasized is that the factional contest did much to undermine the utility of these bodies in the eyes of their actual or potential constituents – that is to say, of ordinary workers or employees who looked upon them as means of winning some immediate alleviation in their lot. During these crucial months the soviet electorate underwent a process of differentiation. An element crystallized that one might call 'junior cadres' : men and women of non-intellectual background who were now for the first time drawn into the closed milieu of the revolutionary intelligentsia. They learned to use its peculiar jargon and became acquainted, at least superficially, with the basic components of these intellectuals' world-view. These men were dedicated without being fanatical : they did not consciously regard themselves as an élite, but on the contrary stressed their devotion to egalitarian and democratic ideals; yet their status as activists set them apart from the still unpoliticized masses – who followed their lead out of a vague sense of solidarity, without any clear idea of the objectives pursued by those who aspired to direct them.

In the early months of the revolution, as we have noted, many deputies (and even some executive members) were reluctant to identify themselves with any of the several contending left-wing groups. As E. Ignatov puts it, writing of the Moscow soviet in March, 'the workers' mood was not particularly favourable to factional struggle'.[1] There was a general feeling that, with tsarism barely overthrown, the democratic forces needed to work together to consolidate the new order. The same sentiment manifested itself among left-wing intellectuals. The old controversy between Populists and Marxists had lost whatever significance it may once have possessed, and even within the Social Democratic party, whose whole history had been one of stormy factional conflict, members recognized that they shared a good deal of common ground. This was the 'honeymoon period' of the revolution, when the Petrograd soviet coexisted with the Provisional Government, supporting it – to use the well-known phrase – 'in so far as' (*poskol'ku, postol'ku*) it fulfilled the expectations of the soviet cadres. However embarrassing this 'dual power' was for Prince Lvov's first cabinet (which held office until the beginning of May), and whatever its contribution to the collapse of orderly government, it did help to reconcile the warring socialist factions. In the local committees of the resurgent RSDLP Mensheviks and Bolsheviks cooperated in presenting joint lists of candidates for leading positions in soviets and other public bodies. This accounts for the predominance of Bolsheviks in some soviets where they had no mass following – as in Saratov, where three out of five presidium members belonged to that party although it had only 28 out of 248 deputies in the plenum.[2] Such Bolsheviks did not necessarily seek at once to exploit their position for factional ends: at this juncture the political situation was still very fluid and party discipline lax, even among those who laid most emphasis upon the virtues of efficient organization.

The situation changed after Lenin's return to Petrograd on 3 April. This event had an immediate impact on political life in the capital which was soon felt in other centres as well. The Bolshevik leader castigated his followers for their vacillating attitude on the principal questions of the day and urged them to break completely with the Mensheviks and SRS, whom he characterized as dupes of the bourgeoisie.[3] He denied that he sought to replace the present government by one consisting of workers, for this would have been to fall into the heresy of conspiratorial 'Blanquism'; what was needed was 'to struggle for influence within the soviets' and to 'explain' the

Bolshevik programme to the masses; the latter would then press the soviets (which would sooner or later come under Bolshevik control) to assume power.

Lenin's arrival, and the speedy adoption of his views by most of his followers, led to a polarization of opinion within the soviets, and in the first instance within their executive committees. Their Bolshevik members were called to order and persuaded to view their fellow socialists as actual or potential enemies whose influence had to be undermined by agitation and the use of manipulative skills. The Mensheviks' and SRs' response was weaker than the original challenge. This was partly because they were preoccupied with something that seemed far more important – extending the soviets' influence and so 'deepening the revolution' – and partly because they were embarrassed by any criticism fired at them from the left. The same psychological reflex was at work that had prevented the Mensheviks from offering sustained resistance to Bolshevik campaigns of detraction before 1917. The soviets now became the principal battle-ground in a power struggle between moderates and extremists, and were exposed to much the same treatment as had been meted out, in the revolutionary underground, to any Social Democratic organization in which Lenin or his followers had been present. That is to say, a nucleus of self-proclaimed loyalists would be established who would claim the right to speak on behalf of the organization as a whole and endeavour to split their opponents, winning some of them over and silencing or expelling the remainder.[4]

The intensity of the factional struggle varied greatly. It was at its peak in Petrograd and its environs, less acute in Moscow, and of slight importance in the Ukraine; in the Central Industrial region and the Urals the Bolsheviks faced little organized opposition in any case, and in the smaller provincial towns (especially in the south-centre) they had yet to make an impression; at the front the battle was fought almost wholly over the issue of war or peace. Under the impact of this offensive the soviets' structure and procedure, as we have seen, became more overtly politicized. Every action which the local leadership took (or might have taken), especially if it involved support for the government, was liable to be made the pretext for debate, with the opposition presenting its alternative 'platform' and tabling critical resolutions. The chief issues were the so-called 'freedom loan', Milyukov's note to the Allies and the ensuing crisis which led to the formation of the first coalition government, the impending offensive at the front, industrial relations and the problem of inadequate food supplies.

The Bolsheviks and their allies pressed for partial or general re-election of deputies, since they hoped to capitalize on their growing influence in such base organizations as the factory committees. Where they expected to increase their representation in the executive organs, they often urged that these be reconstituted according to the principle of proportionality (i.e. in proportion to the strength of factions in the plenum) rather than on the basis of parity for each political group; but the latter arrangement suited them better in places where they were weak, since it would at least give them a foothold in these bodies and thus a chance to propagate their views.

In Petrograd a Bolshevik 'fraction' (caucus) came into being in the soviet executive on the morrow of Lenin's return : an informal grouping had existed since early in March, but it had been relatively ineffectual. Alexandra Kollontay, the fiery feminist leader, was the most prominent personality in its six-member directing nucleus; interestingly enough, only one of the six (A.N. Paderin) was actually an elected member of the soviet's executive, but this was evidently no obstacle to efforts to win influence in this body.[5] The campaign for re-election of soviet deputies got under way during the latter half of April, assisted by the crisis developing at this time between the Petrograd soviet and the Provisional Government over Milyukov's note to the Allies. On 7 May, one day after the coalition cabinet took office, the Bolsheviks published in *Pravda* a model 'instruction' which their candidates were invited to present for endorsement to their electors. This was a simple restatement of the party's line on the major issues of the day. It undoubtedly helped to systematize their candidates' efforts, and before long *Pravda* was in a position to publish reports of ballots in which Bolsheviks had been successful. Thus at the Pipe Works, where Lenin himself took part in the electoral campaign, the Bolsheviks sent seven out of eight deputies to the soviet (13 May); at the Treugolnik plant the figures were thirteen out of seventeen.[6]

On 23 May the moderate-controlled Petrograd soviet executive resolved to issue procedural rules for such re-elections. They were to be held only once a quarter of the voters had demanded them and their wish had been reported to the soviet through regular channels; an electoral commission would then be set up; the elections would not be held until seven days had elapsed, to allow all parties sufficient opportunity to campaign; the sitting deputy must be present at the poll; finally, the results were to be approved by the soviet's 'credentials commission'.[7] All this was little more than an attempt to close the stable door after the horse had bolted. The new regulations contained no provision for a secret ballot, and, whatever the intentions of those who framed them, could plausibly be attributed to partisan considerations. In any case the soviet electorate in Petrograd was in no mood to engage in such formalities, and the rules do not appear to have been applied systematically.

On 31 May the Bolsheviks were able to chalk up their first major success in the Petrograd soviet : the adoption in the workers' section, by 173 votes to 144, of a resolution they had tabled condemning the government for its plans to evacuate certain defence establishments from the capital to safer areas in the interior of the country.[8] This was interpreted as a political move deliberately designed to disperse the most militant elements of the proletariat. The protest was linked with a call for 'soviet power'. At this time half the members of the workers' section were said to be pro-Bolshevik, as against only a quarter of the deputies enrolled in the soldiers' section.[9]

In Moscow the moderate socialist leaders made a more serious attempt than in Petrograd to regulate the procedure governing re-election of deputies to the local soviet. Predictably, the legitimacy of the lengthy and detailed instruction which they devised was contested by opposition spokesmen, who claimed that they were being victimized. About a quarter of the deputies were re-elected. The new men included a number of left-wingers.[10]

In both capital cities the Bolsheviks made skilful use of the lower-tier soviets in working-class districts, where it was easier for them to win support. In Petrograd these efforts were coordinated by a standing conference which (along with the CCFCP) served as a rival centre of authority to the Petrograd soviet executive.[11]

At the other end of the scale, that is to say in the upper reaches of the nascent soviet hierarchy, the Bolsheviks also made headway, not least because they were the most insistent on the formation of such regional and provincial executives. In this way the urban soviets, which had most claim to be considered representative and regular bodies, could be crushed between the upper and nether millstone.

The table on page 146, adapted from a recent study by a Soviet historian, gives a rough idea of the party affiliation of certain major soviets and executives at various dates between March and May.

city and type of soviet	plenary assembly			executive committee			G F as % of C
	A total number of deputies	B number of Bolsheviks	C B as % of A	D total number of members	E number of Bolshevik members	F E as % of D	
Petrograd (SWSD)	2800	65*	2·4%	90	15	16·5%	14·5%
Moscow (SWD)	625	143†	22·8%	75	23	30·6%	74·5%
Saratov (SWSD)	248‡	28‡	11·3%	14	7	50·0%	22·6%
Samara (SWSD: workers' section)	85	22	25·9%	15	10	75·0%	34·5%
Kiev (SWD)	444	62	14·0%	37	6	16·2%	86·4%
Kharkov (SWSD)	320	41	12·8%	29	2	7·0%	(183%)

Source of columns A–F: Andreyev (1967), pp. 77, 80; (English ed., pp. 52, 55)

* In March; by 25 May the Bolsheviks are said to have had 205 deputies (Andreyev [1967], p. 203), or according to another source (Freydlin [1967], p. 287), 230 (33–7 per cent)

† In March; by 1 June the Bolsheviks are said to have had 182 deputies (29·1 per cent) (*Dokumenty i materialy*, III, p. 216)

‡ On 25 March; by May the number of deputies is said to have risen to 532, of whom 53 (10 per cent) were Bolsheviks (Mints [1967–73], p. 116)

The data are selective and have no strong claim to accuracy, but column G does suggest that the Bolsheviks were more successful in winning control of levers of power within the soviets than they were at increasing their hold upon the deputies : in only one of these six towns did they have less than their due share of executive posts. In a number of soviets, especially in the Central Industrial and Ural regions, they were solidly ensconced by mid-summer. At Ivanovo-Voznesensk, for example, they claimed ninety per cent of the deputies and made a clean sweep of the executive committee.[12] Except in the Baltic area, only four major towns (Minsk, Tsaritsyn, Yekaterinburg and Krasnoyarsk) had soviets that were in Bolshevik hands; the remainder were under moderate socialist control, at least nominally.

One may well ask how much this mattered in practical terms at the time – as distinct from its potential significance for the future. No doubt it is broadly true that strong Bolshevik representation goaded the soviet leaders into taking radical measures they would otherwise have refrained from; on the other hand there may have been instances where such pressure caused the moderates to dig in their heels. In any case the term 'moderate' is hardly appropriate for the leaders of many of these non-Bolshevik soviets, who seem to have taken just as energetic a line in extending their power as did those under Bolshevik control. After all, the conduct of a soviet inevitably depended on a variety of factors rooted in the 'social geography' of the locality concerned, and was not simply a derivative of the political affiliation of its leaders. This point was recognized by one early Soviet historian of these bodies, Yugov, who could afford to approach the subject in a less partisan spirit than his successors. 'Often acting unconsciously', he writes, 'and still more often against their [leaders'] theories, if not against their will, the Menshevik [-controlled] soviets also interfered in the [state] administration. They regulated political and economic questions, sometimes infringed the rights of private property, issued orders and decrees, eliminated the "legitimate" authority and substituted their own.'[13] As an illustration he cites the example of the Tiflis soviet. Under the chairmanship of Noah Zhordaniya, one of the fathers of Georgian Menshevism, this body's leaders requisitioned a printing press, fixed the local bread ration, ordered employers to improve working conditions, and investigated suspect 'counter-revolutionaries'[14] – in short, engaged in measures of direct action such as were fashionable at this time. Those responsible were motivated less by party-political considerations than by their estimate of the local balance of power : they had to weigh up the relative risks of undue boldness, which might provoke reprisals, and excessive timidity, which would certainly lose them popular support.

These leaders are not wholly to be blamed for taking the law into their own hands. The general state of anarchy into which Russia was rapidly falling left them little alternative, and such practices were tolerated, if not actually encouraged, by the socialists within the coalition government, who looked to the soviets for support against the threat of reaction. The failure of the offensive in June and the ensuing political crisis led to a paralysis of will at the centre which naturally enhanced the influence of the CEC and of soviets throughout the country.

The Bolsheviks' involvement in the insurrectionary movement which culminated in the July Days, followed by official disclosures about their covert links with the Germans, caused them to lose influence in the principal soviet organs, at least for a brief spell. There were a few instances of Bolshevik deputies being arrested or forced to resign. It was now the majority socialists' turn to press for fresh elections. However, they did not do so with the same degree of determination as had been shown by the extremists, and the Bolsheviks were permitted to maintain their base organizations intact. Within six weeks or so their fortunes were once again in the ascendant.

In July differences emerged among the Bolshevik leaders as to the party's tactics toward the soviets. Some members of the Central Committee favoured a policy of conciliating the moderates. Others on the extreme left took the view that the soviets had now become hopelessly retrograde and that the Bolsheviks should boycott them, instead building up a counter-organization of their own. Lenin adopted an intermediate position. He agreed with the leftists that the soviets had fallen under the sway of 'petty-bourgeois' elements (here painting the picture unduly black) and recommended that the slogan 'all power to the soviets' be temporarily withdrawn; instead the party was to concentrate its efforts on the 'revolutionary masses' – but at the same time the Bolsheviks were to maintain their position in the soviets in the expectation that sooner or later the situation would change in their favour and permit a new offensive, as a result of which they would capture these vital organizations and overthrow the government. This policy was endorsed after some discussion at the party's sixth congress, held from 26 July to 3 August, and was put into practice – although its finer subtleties were beyond the understanding of many Bolshevik activists. The latter were more sincerely attached to the soviet idea than their leader; or at any rate they were less willing than he to subordinate these genuinely mass bodies to the party's insurrectionary purpose.[15]

Events moved too fast for these divergent tendencies within Bolshevism to become clearly formulated. During August extremists and moderates were drawn together by what appeared to be a major threat to the whole of 'revolutionary democracy' from army leaders, backed by centre and right-wing politicians who looked for leadership to the new commander-in-chief, General Kornilov. The Kadets, alarmed by the cabinet's leftward drift, exacted a high price for joining the second coalition, formed under Kerensky as premier on 24 July. The State Conference, called on 12 August to rally public opinion behind the new government, served merely to dramatize the divisions between left and right. In Moscow, three days before the conference met there, the plenum of the city soviet debated a Bolshevik motion to stage a general strike. The motion failed, but the result showed a significant increase in support for the extreme left : the voting was 342 against, 310 in favour. This may be compared with a poll held on 25 July to decide the soviet's attitude toward the new government, when the moderates had scored 363 votes against a mere 192 for the left (with 25 abstentions).[16] Characteristically, the strike call went out none the less – and was widely followed.

In Kharkov the moderates who controlled the soviet had first resisted a Bolshevik demand for fresh elections, on somewhat specious grounds; in August, however, they were obliged to yield. The poll led to a tripling of Bolshevik strength, although this was not enough to give that party a majority.[17] In the Urals Lenin's followers consolidated their relatively strong position by holding a regional congress of soviets, which elected a kind of 'supra-executive' consisting of seven Bolsheviks and three SRs; the moderates, in a gesture soon to be widely emulated, responded by walking out of the new assembly, so abandoning it to their rivals.[18]

The extreme left also did well in soviet elections held at this time in the Baltic area. In Petrograd itself the moderate leaders of the soviet for some time after the July Days refrained from calling meetings of the workers' section, where a vociferous pro-Bolshevik element had been responsible for some ugly scenes during the turbulence in the capital. This was not a very serious embarrassment, for these men simply withdrew to base organizations such as the district soviets and factory committees. They were also able to offset this apparent reverse by making gains in the soldiers' section.[19] In plenary sessions of the soviet held on 10 and 23 July Bolshevik resolutions were soundly defeated,[20] but it was not long before the pendulum began to swing back in their favour. They were helped by Martov's group of left-wing (Internationalist) Mensheviks, who shared their general attitude to the problem of the war. An emotive issue presented itself in the form of an order by the government reintroducing (with certain safeguards) the death penalty for front-line soldiers guilty of grave dereliction of duty. This was too much for the Petrograd garrison, which ever since 'Order Number One' had enjoyed a privileged position, and on 18 August Martov's resolution condemning this order was passed. By a wafer-thin margin (428 votes to 377, with 48 abstentions) the deputies defeated a Bolshevik amendement which would have censured the CEC for having associated itself with such unpopular policies.[21] Five days later the left-wingers scored a still more remarkable success. At a session of the workers' section called to discuss the apparent threat of counter-revolution the moderates chose to abstain, so making it appear that the Bolsheviks and their allies had the entire gathering behind them.[22] Thus the most prestigious urban soviet in the country was drifting rapidly into the Bolsheviks' hands even before the 'Kornilov affair' (26–30 August), which was to give them command of that assembly.

Meanwhile the moderates retained control of the CEC. With increasing frequency they resorted to the expedient of holding joint meetings with its peasant twin, the Executive Committee of the All-Russian Congress of Peasant Deputies, which could be expected to show some restraint on general political issues. At three such meetings held in July, attended by about three hundred persons, the maximalist elements usually managed to rally between forty and fifty votes.[23] However, this was not really a fair estimate of their strength. On the CEC, as in many urban soviets, the left improved its position, although it was far from able to impose its will: this opportunity would not come until after the October insurrection.

From this survey of the struggle for control of the soviet

machinery two general conclusions may be drawn. First, the fight seemed a good deal more important to the leaders than it did to rank-and-file deputies, to say nothing of their constituents in the factories and barracks. To many of the latter it will have appeared as an irrelevancy which diverted their organizations from their proper concern with vital practical issues. By September 1917, when the Kornilov affair shifted the centre of political gravity even further to the left, the hierarchy of soviet organizations had in effect become an extension of the socialist parties. This development was logical, perhaps inevitable: it could have been anticipated from an analysis of the events of February 1917, indeed even of those of 1905. Nevertheless this was not the purpose for which most ordinary working men and women had chosen their deputies. Here were the makings of a tragic paradox. For the soviets would soon give their name to a new revolutionary regime in which their role would be fictitious, since real decision-making power would lie with the chiefs of a single 'vanguard party'. This party would arrogate to itself all power in the new socialist order, on the grounds that only by doing so could it fulfil its ideological mission. The soviets, having carried out their function of mobilizing the masses, would soon be reduced to little more than ciphers.

Second, we need to refine the conventional image of the history of the soviets under the Provisional Government as one of life-and-death struggle between would-be democrats and would-be dictators (or, in Soviet terminology, between vacillating petty bourgeois and true proletarians). For much of this period, and over large tracts of the country, rank-and-file members of the rival socialist parties collaborated in extending the soviets' power. Their immediate policies, if not their ultimate ends, were broadly similar. All these men shared certain basic ideological assumptions about the need for unremitting class struggle; when forced to choose between 'deepening the revolution' and restraining it, they generally opted for the former. Both past habits and present necessities impelled them to adopt a radical posture. Thus the country slid ever further leftwards; the competition between moderates and extremists accelerated this shift as much as it impeded it.

The intellectual climate in Russia in the summer and autumn of 1917 was such as to facilitate the task of those who sought to establish a single-party regime based upon the soviets. Lenin's party had no hope of attaining its ends unless it could win the support, or at least the benevolent neutrality, of other political groups; and this in large measure it succeeded in doing. With few exceptions Menshevik and SR activists were not excessively perturbed by the fact that their Bolshevik comrades were establishing their hold over soviets or other mass organizations. Bolshevism was perceived as an aberration rather than as a major threat to ideals common to 'revolutionary democracy' as a whole. The moderate socialists played their part in building up a quasi-governmental authority with immense potential prestige, a machine which in other hands could serve as the infrastructure of a dictatorship strong enough to sweep them from the political scene. They had sown the wind and were to reap the whirlwind.

III The Countryside in Revolt
March—September 1917

TWELVE *Town and Country: the Social and Psychological Background*

Broadly speaking, the pattern of events in Russia's rural areas during the critical months between February and October 1917 was similar to that in the towns. The collapse of the old authorities, and the new government's inability to create a viable new administrative structure in their place, left a vacuum which the peasants themselves, or at least those who spoke in their name, made haste to fill. The rural population was suddenly granted an almost limitless freedom to seek its own solution to besetting problems, above all that of land reform. In this upsurge of activity the village was greatly stimulated by the example of the towns. There were, however, several important differences between the 'agrarian movement' (to use the customary euphemism) and the offensive in the urban areas considered above.

We may begin by identifying these differences, which were both sociological and psychological in character, and glance at the political context. Subsequently we shall examine in turn the two principal forms taken by the agrarian movement: first, the efforts of peasant producers to protect themselves against the harmful consequences that ensued from the collapse of the market; and second, the drive to achieve 'social justice' by seizing the land, stock and other goods belonging to individual proprietors (including peasant 'separators'). Finally we shall consider the growth of peasant organizations and the place they occupied in the country's political life.

As was pointed out above (p. 40) two and a half years of warfare had bred a mood of bitterness and frustration in the Russian village. There was a near-total lack of confidence in the empire's political and military leadership, but at the same time a feeling that peasants themselves could do little to bring about any improvement. Everything seemed to depend upon an end to the war, yet this basic question could be solved only from 'on high'. In some areas an undercurrent of violence made itself felt, but this was still a phenomenon of local and limited significance.

The collapse of the monarchy in February 1917 came to the rural population as a complete surprise. At first the peasants refrained from any overt response. With their natural caution they wanted to take stock of the novel situation in which they found themselves. Most were ready to give the new *vlast'* (central authority), whose nature they but dimly comprehended, time in which to meet their basic demands: for peace, better terms of trade, and above all an immediate start on a far-reaching land reform. A redistribution of wealth in favour of those who worked the land was seen by almost all peasants, especially in the Great Russian areas, as a self-evident necessity, an act of common justice. They were not concerned with the repercussions it would have upon the country's social fabric or its economic potential. If the reform led to the creation of a 'peasant Russia', in which the rural areas exercised hegemony over the towns, so much the better; they assumed that the elimination of ancient inequalities would automatically bring about an efflorescence of peasant farming from which the whole population would benefit. With such abundance in the offing townsfolk need suffer no more than a temporary dislocation in the supply of food.

The peasants' mood was thus initially one of self-confidence and optimism. A new age of human brotherhood seemed about to dawn. By and large they were willing to settle accounts peacefully even with their hereditary foes, the large landed proprietors, provided that the latter renounced all the privileges they had enjoyed in the past. The same was true of their attitude towards the independent farmers who had benefited by the Stolypin reforms: if they abandoned their separate plots and reintegrated themselves into the communal village society, they would be accepted as equals and would be allocated a fair share of the land. In the forthcoming 'black repartition' their needs, like those of every other household in the community, would stand the same chance of satisfaction. As the peasants envisaged it, equality was to be the guiding principle behind the reform. Each family farm (the basic unit of production) was to receive sufficient land, of varying quality, to support itself. The norm was to be established locally, by balancing the amount of land available against the number of persons to be fed ('eaters', as they were quaintly called), and then was to be revised at intervals as conditions changed to ensure that the principle of equality was maintained. Livestock and agricultural equipment were to be treated similarly. Provision would be made for landless agricultural wage-earners as well as for former members of the commune returning from the towns or from military service, in so far as they wished to claim their rights. The future social order was visualized as one in which all major decisions would be taken at the lowest possible level. The ideal was a kind of 'pan-Russian commune' embracing all those elements of the nation endowed with the plain virtues of the country-man – the peasant who earned his living by tilling the soil himself, or with the aid of his family, but without exploiting the labour of others.

We need not examine here how far this attitude reflected the theories of Socialist-Revolutionary intellectuals, which were themselves largely a refinement of ideas circulating at the turn of the century among peasants in those areas where communal ways of thought were still very much alive.[1] That communalism was indeed a living reality in 1917 is clear from the whole history of the agrarian movement, which culminated in a 'black repartition' such as had long been advocated by the more militant *narodniki*. This is not to say that the peasants themselves accepted, or even understood, the theoretical implications of Populist 'agrarian socialism', but they were closer to the PSR than to any other political party.[2] Nor is this the place to demonstrate that many of these ideas were naive and utopian, or that in economic terms the Populist programme threatened to perpetuate Russia's historic backwardness *vis-à-vis* more industrialized nations. What deserves emphasis here is that communalism served as a kind of talisman to distinguish the peasants from their urban cousins, whose experience in the industrial milieu gave them a different perspective.

Our understanding of these differences of outlook has not, alas, been much advanced by the vast corpus of Marxist (and specifically Leninist) writing that exists on the subject. These observers proceed from the assumption, which cannot be proved, that one is dealing here with two distinct social *classes,* one 'proletarian' and the other 'petty bourgeois', each distinguished from the other by its attitude to the ownership of property. Unfortunately there is no hard and fast evidence about the strength at this time of proprietorial instincts in either group. It is probably true that they were very weak among men whose entire lives had been spent at the factory bench (although some of these so-called 'hereditary proletarians' may well have aspired to possess a home of their own). At the other end of the spectrum were those peasants who could scarcely conceive of their existence except as owners of a family farm. It is reasonable to assume that such sentiments were more common among the more successful and prosperous villagers, with large families and holdings, but they were certainly not confined to such persons.

In the light of subsequent Soviet agrarian history it is clear that the Marxist approach, based on the concept of social class (determined by relationship to production), is an inadequate tool to comprehend the sociology of the Russian peasantry.[3] As was noted above (see p. 10), gradations of wealth and status followed a cyclical pattern determined as much by biological as by economic factors. The natural tendency towards material acquisitiveness was offset by a lingering respect for the values characteristic of an earlier age : loyalty to established authorities (especially those that were of peasant origin), family and group solidarity in the face of threats from without, and a sense of the dignity conferred by physical toil. Peasants had had less opportunity to acquire a formal education than their more fortunate kinsmen in the towns, but they displayed a more stable emotional attitude towards their environment, and their indifference or hostility towards certain aspects of modern secular culture was offset by their keener awareness of more basic human concerns.[4]

Reduced to essentials, the motive behind the agrarian movement of 1917 was a desire for greater economic security. It stood greater chances of success than its urban counterpart, for 'workers' control' was bound to create anarchy, mass unemployment and impoverishment – and ultimately the imposition of a new system of industrial discipline harsher in many respects than the old. On the other hand small peasant proprietors, tilling their newly acquired additional strips of land under the relatively benign tutelage of the village commune, could feel that they had indeed taken a great step towards controlling their own destiny. This was of course no final solution to the social problem, and disillusionment would come to the village just as it did to the town – but it would come later, and largely as a result of external action by urban activists jealous of the peasants' relative security.

Thus the townsman and the countryman each had a fundamentally dissimilar attitude towards social conflict, although in the short term their aims might seem to coincide. To this basic difference may be added another pertaining to political organization. Village politics were normally simple, in the sense that ideological considerations played scarcely any part. Many communities had no significant internal divisions. Where there was a struggle between rival groups, these were often described as 'the old' and 'the young': that is to say conservatives as distinct from innovators. Party labels counted for little. If confronted by urban agitators professing different political creeds, the peasants' natural instinct was to stay neutral. 'Some say one thing, some say another, but they are all chiefs (nachal'niki). We shall be for none of them but shall wait and see later who is right.'[5] This was how one peasant, when interviewed many years later, described the atmosphere in a village near Saratov. Hundreds of others were no different.

To be sure, proximity to a town or to a main railway line exposed many rural areas to external influences. Copies of newspapers were available in inns and similar places; they might be read out aloud, and in this way their message could reach even those who were illiterate. Numerous representatives were sent into the provinces by business firms, supply organizations, political parties, soviets and so on. In the late summer they were superseded by a stream of refugees from the hunger-stricken towns. Soldiers and sailors returned home on leave (sometimes without permission) and passed on their impressions of life in the trenches or in the barracks. Often they helped peasants to formulate their own aspirations and to give them concrete organizational shape.

The attitude taken towards deserters from the armed forces varied. Several cases are known where they were handed over to the authorities or even lynched. On the other hand their plight naturally won them a certain amount of sympathy from kinsmen and friends. Members of the armed forces on the run, especially if they had their weapons with them, were natural candidates for leadership in any conflict with the peasants' traditional foes. Soldiers were responsible for the first recorded instance of violence against a landed estate[6] and such behaviour became very frequent later on in the year. F.N. Novikov, a peasant from Borisov county (Minsk province), in the rear of positions occupied by the Third Army, later recalled : 'Six healthy young men dressed in soldiers' greatcoats came into our village on three carts. They called us all together and said : "Get ready, lads, harness your horses. Let's go and sack L ..." And the peasants went, some on horseback and others on foot. Some went to get rich on the lord's goods while others went to watch.'[7] In this way increasing contact with the outside world helped to worsen the social climate in the countryside.

Once violent action had become psychologically acceptable, the question arose of forming organizations able to sustain the dynamism of the movement. The traditional rural institution, the commune, now came into its own. It was the principal unit concerned in the redistribution of property, and in the course of this operation assumed powers that would have been inconceivable in more normal times. It was essentially a defensive rather than an offensive organization, serving to reconcile the interests of its members and to protect them against threats from without. It was an instrument of mediation rather than of combat. Another of its attributes was durability : it was rooted in the fabric of Russian agrarian society and could be eliminated only by the destruction of an entire way of life.

This strength was also a source of weakness. One effect of the communal tradition was to encourage among Russian peasants in 1917 the belief that any organization worthy of the name should aspire to a similar durability and fulfil broadly similar functions. Ordinary folk were sceptical of the merits of the numerous committees and councils that sprang up, modelled on those in the towns, which seemed to serve a merely ephemeral purpose. Such overtly political bodies, they reasoned, were no substitute for duly constituted authorities responsible to an assembly of all 'toiling' householders. These democratic instincts did the peasants credit. However, the corollary was that such political organizations were bound to come under the control of outsiders who had no intimate connection with the life of the countryside. Ultimately they would serve as a means of subjugating the village to the will of the town.

It was hard for peasants to organize themselves effectively at any level higher than that of the rural district. Communications were still so primitive that men living in different rural districts (*volosti*) within the same county (*uyezd*) could not easily make contact with one another, and at the provincial (*guberniya*) level the problems were correspondingly multiplied. When meetings were held and organizations formed, the decisions they took could only be enforced so long as their spirit coincided with the mood of the villagers. There was a chronic shortage of literate and energetic individuals able to serve as rural cadres. The tasks of coordination and decision-making inevitably passed into the hands of persons who could not easily be held to account for their actions and who took their cue from the urban political parties or soviets. The rural (peasants') soviets were less sophisticated than their counterparts in the towns and were even less rigidly structured. Where their leaders sympathized with the moderate wing of the PSR, some effort might be made to preserve their autonomy, but as the year drew to a close there was increasing pressure for mergers with urban soviets in a common organization directed by the latter's executive personnel. The establishment of centralized control over the countryside by the urban-based Bolshevik regime was to prove to be a lengthy and difficult operation, but the groundwork for later developments was laid during the winter of 1917–18.

THIRTEEN *The Provisional Government and the Agrarian Question*

THE LEADERS OF the new democratic Russia were unable to devise measures, particularly in regard to land reform, that might have prevented the agrarian movement from taking the anarchic form it did. The most obvious explanation for this lies in the sharp divisions between the so-called 'bourgeois' parties (the Kadets and all those to their right) and the socialists; to these must be added the equally acute differences within the PSR, which was split between several factions or 'tendencies'. Party-political bickering made it all but impossible for the Provisional Government to pursue a consistent line on any of the vital issues confronting the country. A second reason, which in a sense may be considered a product of the first, was the bureaucratic rivalry between the ministries of Agriculture and Supply. The boundaries of administrative responsibility between these two organs were far from clear; much authority also inhered in the ministry of Interior, whose staff generally backed the more cautious line of their colleagues in Supply. (These latter differences have been less adequately explored than the first.) A third factor was the basic commitment of all the moderate leaders to democratic principles, which they were prone to construe in a rigid and legalistic sense : they were unwilling to anticipate the popular will as expressed by a Constituent Assembly elected by the entire nation, since this body alone was entitled to pronounce on a matter so crucial as the fate of the land, Russia's principal resource. However praiseworthy such an attitude might be from a moral standpoint, in terms of practical politics it was a recipe for disaster, since it inhibited ministers from acting firmly to uphold public order. It need hardly be added that this restraint was not solely due to high-mindedness and that respect for the Constituent Assembly's rights could serve as a pretext for postponing awkward or controversial decisions.

In Prince Lvov's cabinet the portfolio of Agriculture was assumed by A.I. Shingarev, a Kadet physician and respected zemstvo leader. On 19 March the government, which had ignored agrarian matters in its initial policy statement, issued a general declaration to the effect that the land question must be settled by legal means and not by violence. It expressly condemned illicit seizures of property and announced that a land-reform committee would be set up under the auspices of the ministry of Agriculture.[1] As an earnest of good intentions the so-called apanage and cabinet lands, the property of the former imperial family, were declared state property (16, 27 March). These were mostly situated in the northern forest zone or in Asiatic Russia; although this was not explicitly mentioned, it was clearly intended that they should be distributed to peasant settlers. Meanwhile military detachments were sent to keep the peace in areas afflicted by agrarian unrest. On 11 April the government announced that all land sown to crops was under protection of the civil authorities and that any losses incurred by proprietors as a result of 'popular disturbances' would be reimbursed from public funds. If for some reason agricultural land were left unsown, this was to fall within the jurisdiction of the local supply committee, which might lease it for the season at a just rent; the latter was to be collected by agents of the committee on behalf of the owner. This decree, designed to maintain agricultural production, may be adjudged a reasonable measure, although there was a risk that the supply committees, which were now undergoing a process of 'democratiza- tion' (see below, p. 175), might interpret their prerogatives too broadly.

A few days later the government took another step which could not but impair its chances of maintaining control of the situation in the countryside. An act of 21 April[2] regulated the composition and powers of the land-reform agency projected on 19 March. Its prime purpose was to 'prepare' the land reform by collecting all relevant information. This necessitated creation of a bureaucratic apparatus headed by a Main Land Committee and extending downwards at least to county, and in some areas to district level. That some such structure was necessary if the land reform were to be effected in an orderly manner can hardly be doubted; nevertheless the measure is open to serious criticism on several grounds.

In the first place, there was no real need for a *separate* hierarchy of organs devoted wholly to the land-reform problem since there already existed a network of supply committees. Their responsibilities were bound to overlap, and it was already proving to be difficult to fill existing vacancies. It would have been logical at least to subordinate the new bodies to those concerned with supply, since the latter could be expected to display greater economic realism. As it was, their interrelationship was not even defined. Evidently the minister, or more probably some of his officials, wanted to weaken the supply authorities, which in soviet circles were already suspected of 'reactionary' tendencies. However this may be, the establishment of two parallel bureaucratic hierarchies was a prescription for administrative chaos.

In the second place, the decree made no provision whereby land-committees' decisions could be challenged in the courts. This oversight was belatedly remedied on 7 September[3] – by which time, however, the country's judicial apparatus had virtually broken down. The statute allowed aggrieved parties to appeal only from junior to senior land committees. In practice the sole way in which one could hope for a redress of grievances was to write directly to a minister or other highly placed personality. The optimistic belief that the liberated peasant masses could be trusted to govern themselves with a minimum of official interference led the country's new leaders to underestimate the need for checks and balances to prevent abuses of power.

In the third place, the composition of the new organs, especially at lower levels in the hierarchy, gave excessive weight to the popular (elected) *vis-à-vis* the official (nominated) element. The Main Land Committee had sixty-five members (not counting local representatives), among them men appointed from a wide variety of governmental and non-governmental bodies (including the Petrograd soviet). Its size inevitably made it a deliberative body, a forum for acrimonious political debate. It was also unfortunate that over three-quarters of its members had a Populist orientation, although this was due less to political manipulation than to the fact that so much of Russia's expertise on agrarian matters was concentrated in this quarter. Actual policy-making was in the hands of a council, initially of twenty-two and ultimately of fifty members, who worked on papers prepared in several commissions. These functional organs did some useful work during their brief spell of existence. In general the Main Land Committee deserves more credit than it is usually given. It was not its fault that its schemes were so quickly overtaken by events.[4]

The Main Land Committee could at least claim the services of a number of highly qualified experts; its local organs, however, were dominated by popular representatives whose views were inevitably coloured by prejudice. At the provincial level the official element consisted of ten men, but each county organ had the right to send one representative. Since there were normally about twelve counties to a province, these men could hope to secure a majority in the committee, even if they did not win over any of the official nominees. Characteristically, any agricultural experts invited to attend meetings of the provincial land committee were allotted only an advisory vote.

The provision that lower organs should be represented on higher ones seems to have been taken over from the practice of the urban soviets. Whatever its merits in an overtly revolutionary body, as a means of ensuring that the voice of the masses be heard, it was quite inappropriate in a governmental agency purporting to investigate social problems in an objective manner. This was bound to blur the lines of authority. The provincial committees had no effective means of controlling those at the county or district level.

The county committees included one representative from each district; since there were as a rule about two dozen districts to a county, these men could easily crowd out their nominated colleagues. The district committees were from the start envisaged as wholly peasant bodies. For this reason their establishment was made optional rather than obligatory. No provision was made for confirmation by senior bodies of their members' credentials. Soon complaints poured in that the district land committees were being penetrated by 'unsuitable elements', whereupon half-hearted efforts were made to enforce such controls retroactively. Not surprisingly they encountered stiff resistance.

Finally, it was ordained that, whereas the Main Land Committee was to make recommendations to the government, its ostensible subordinates at the provincial and county level could issue *obligatory* regulations. They were authorized to prevent private individuals – nothing was said about peasant communities! – from taking any action liable to diminish or depreciate the national land fund. Such persons could be removed physically from their property. Perhaps the framers of the decree were naive enough to believe that this provision would be invoked only against a handful of deliberate saboteurs. In practice, naturally enough, it could easily be invoked to justify confiscations of property motivated by partisan considerations.

In sum, the decree of 21 April created something of a Frankenstein's monster. There was clearly no prospect that land committees would confine their activities to collecting information on local needs, as they were supposed to do. On the contrary, they were invested with far-reaching authority to interfere in relationships between different categories of land users. It is hardly surprising that peasant activists soon became accustomed to look upon the land committees, particularly those at the district level, simply as extensions of their own self-constituted organs. Can one blame them? If the country's new leaders were unclear as to where the dividing-line ran between the State and society, why should such a distinction be apparent to the politically untutored populace?

The implementation of this decree – that is to say the 'preparation' of the impending land reform – fell not to the liberal Shingarev but to V.M. Chernov, the veteran PSR leader, who succeeded him on 4 May as minister of Agriculture in the first coalition cabinet. Chernov had been the architect of his party's agrarian programme and enjoyed great prestige among the population at large. His appointment was widely interpreted as a sign that the new government would press forward with radical measures in the agrarian domain. However, Chernov proved to be a great disappointment as minister. He neglected the work of his department in favour of general political and propagandistic activities. When faced with difficulties he vacillated. After leaving the government at the end of August Chernov launched a vigorous press campaign against his former colleagues, in particular Kerensky, whom he accused of having sabotaged his policies. This further weakened the government's prestige without offering any constructive alternative. By

October the 'village minister', as Chernov had been known, was a spent force in Russian political life.[5]

Throughout the summer and early autumn of 1917 the Provisional Government battled desperately to resist pressure from below for action to be taken on land reform at once, before the Constituent Assembly met. There was no administrative machinery available to restrain peasant activists from taking the law into their own hands and using violence to attain their ends. The creation of an elected district zemstvo, decreed on 21 May,[6] was a step in the right direction but inevitably took time to produce results. On the immediate issue of preserving rural order the government gave an impression of inconsistency, calling for calm yet taking measures that could but whet the appetite for radical changes.

Appeals for moderation, such as that issued by the Main Land Committee at its first meeting on 20 May, were undermined by the resolution adopted five days later at the All-Russian Congress of Peasant Deputies (see below p. 237), which virtually endorsed violent action by the land committees. This was not a governmental decision, to be sure – but the distinction was not readily apparent, especially since Chernov, who addressed the congress, did not dissociate himself publicly from its inflammatory resolution. On the contrary, he leaned heavily upon the CEC and the central peasant executive for support against his more moderate cabinet colleagues. Peasant activists were quick to sense that the government had no firm policy and to exploit their opportunity. It was common knowledge that the minister of Agriculture favoured granting the land committees (not the supply committees) full rights to decide the way in which *all* the land (not merely that left unsown) should be utilized. This meant allowing them to interfere in property rights as they thought fit, and was precisely the line taken in the peasant congress's resolution of 25 May.[7]

Chernov first tried to persuade his cabinet colleagues to endorse such a measure. When they baulked at it he turned to the Main Land Committee, which held its second general meeting from 1 to 6 July. In his address he openly criticized his fellow ministers and the committee passed a resolution in the sense he desired.[8] Chernov was also instrumental in persuading the Main Land Committee to admit twelve representatives of the executive set up by the peasant congress. This move led to the resignation of several moderate members. Both actions were unwise and contributed to the collapse of the first coalition.

Although Chernov's colleagues in the new cabinet did not yield to his pressure to enlarge the rights of the land committees, he made some headway. On 12 July his ministry was able to issue an edict prohibiting all commercial transactions (sales, exchanges, mortgages) in landed property,[9] ostensibly to prevent proprietors from concluding fictitious deals in the hope of escaping eventual confiscation. Encouraged by this success, Chernov attempted another *coup de main*. On 16 July he signed, on his personal authority and without his colleagues' consent, an instruction to local land committees empowering them to do some of the things that they were already doing in practice. In particular they could : (a) fix rents where the parties could not reach agreement directly; (b) lease to the needy draught animals and agricultural machinery deemed to be under-utilized; and (c) take over the management of model estates which became non-viable owing to action either by the peasants or by their owners.[10] This instruction was hedged about with qualifications and fell short of giving the land committees total control over land utilization. Nevertheless it did significantly enlarge their jurisdiction, and in existing circumstances gave peasant activists a green light to sequester property coveted by the local population. By mid-summer many land committees, especially at the district level, were behaving as if they did indeed have the right to supervise the way in which all land was managed. The government was losing control of the situation and some rural areas (notably in the overcrowded south-central provinces) fell into a state of near-anarchy.

Late in August the Main Land Committee held its third (and last) session, in an atmosphere already made tense by the confrontation between Kerensky and General Kornilov. S.L. Maslov, who was soon to succeed Chernov in fact (although his appointment was not confirmed until 3 October), reported on the progress being made in the commissions on drafting the land-reform bill. But the governmental spokesmen were unable to make much impression upon the angry delegates from the local land committees. Commissioners (commissars) were sent out by the government to stem the tide of unrest and strengthen the hand of the senior bodies in the land-committee hierarchy. In Kazan province commissioner Chernyshev took firm action to free persons who had been illegally detained and to apprehend the culprits, who included the chairman of a district land committee.[11] In Tula province a representative of the Main Land Committee purged the local land committees, several of whose members were among the sixty peasants arrested for infractions of public order.[12] However in other areas (Mogilev, Ryazan, Simbirsk) the government commissioners seem to have swum with the tide; cases were reported where they sanctioned illegal acts.[13]

The harassed government now looked to the new district zemstvo as a possible last bulwark of authority in the countryside. From August 1917 onwards elections were held throughout the country on universal suffrage to set up such bodies, simultaneously with elections to the reformed municipalities in the towns.[14] As a rule the poll went in favour of the PSR, but the turnout was generally low. In some places voters elected more candidates than there were posts available; in others there was a shortage of candidates and supplementary elections had to be held. In Minsk, Smolensk and Volhynia provinces, which had a high incidence of unrest, there was a certain amount of interference in the elections by left-wing extremists, who feared that the district zemstvo might act as a counterweight to the rural soviet. However, in more placid parts of the country such as the north-east (which had a democratic tradition on which to build) the district zemstvo seems to have struck root. In the winter and spring of 1918 these bodies resisted forcible dissolution in favour of the rural soviets.[15]

The Provisional Government had hoped that the district zemstvo would absorb or replace bodies that had been constituted spontaneously and irregularly; instead the reverse happened. The reform came too late to halt the rapid dissolution of the administrative structure, in which the land committees played such a fatal part. A few days before the Bolshevik *coup* Maslov published the draft of a bill which would have allowed these committees to manage a 'leasing fund', comprising land left unsown and a certain proportion of the land normally leased by proprietors; rents were to be fixed by the appropriate committee and collected by it on the owner's behalf.[16] The scheme is of interest only in so far as it shows that the Provisional Government was still unwilling to grant the land committees the comprehensive rights demanded by Chernov and those who stood to his left.

It has been argued or implied by Chernov himself and others (including the leading western authority on the PSR),[17] that if the land committees had been allowed to control all the land the Provisional Government might have brought the agrarian unrest under control and averted defeat at the hands of the Bolsheviks and their allies. In other words, the moderates ought to have attempted to outbid the extremists in the race for popular support. Attractive as this proposition may seem at first glance, it does not stand up to close examination. It fails to take sufficient account of the elemental force of the agrarian movement and the radicals' success in giving it organizational cohesion – matters that will be examined in later chapters.

Here, in an equally speculative vein, we may offer an estimate of the measures which, in the light of the evidence presented below, would seem to have been essential if rural disorder were to be contained. Four steps in particular were vital : first, the creation of a firm, orderly and coherent structure of authority extending downwards to the district level; second, timely action by such official agencies to eliminate the worst abuses in those regions where social tensions were most acute (for instance fixing minimum wage rates and rent ceilings according to a geographically differentiated tariff); third, an explicit commitment to pay fair compensation from state funds to those who could prove in court that they had been seriously harmed by these measures; fourth, a sizeable injection of capital into agricultural development.

One has only to list such desiderata to appreciate how remote they are from the realities of Russian life in 1917. To take the most obvious point first : so long as the war continued the nation's economy was bound to deteriorate further, so that no resources could be spared for development projects, however desirable. This meant that the government had no resources with which to wean the peasants away from their obsession with redistribution of the land – a process that was in any case likely to be lengthy, if the experience of the Stolypin reform was any guide. Nor were there sufficient educated persons available (if one rules out the army) to staff an effective administrative system covering the rural areas. Such educated persons as there were in rural areas had fallen under the spell of egalitarian doctrines; they were in any case unused to the exercise of power. Most of them were strongly opposed to the very notion of paying compensation to individual proprietors (even if the latter were peasants !). On the other hand, the few elements in the countryside who took a contrary view tended to make a fetish of private property rights and were reluctant to make concessions in favour of the disadvantaged sections of the community. The roots of these attitudes lay deep in the past. The outlook of the Russian intelligentsia (which Chernov in a sense embodied so well) had been shaped by the notion of an inherent conflict between 'society' and the absolutist – bureaucratic power. The idea that 'class struggle' was, or ought to be, the motive force in social development, ostensibly Marxist in origin, was an outgrowth of the deep schism left by centuries of serfdom.

It follows from this pessimistic analysis that the democratic politicians who succeeded to power in March 1917 did not possess the wherewithal to cope with the phenomenon of widespread agrarian unrest. To be sure, they can be faulted for their procrastination and for their internecine conflicts – the helmsman entering treacherous waters does not drive his craft upon the rocks – but these errors were not necessarily decisive in bringing about their downfall. This was caused essentially by long-term factors outside their control. Whether this was also true of the urban situation is open to debate; but civil war in the village was virtually inevitable once the tsarist regime had collapsed.

FOURTEEN *Passive Resistance: the Peasant and the Market*

THE LITERATURE ON the agrarian movement in 1917 is overwhelmingly concerned with the peasants' successful campaign to eliminate private landed property. Relatively little attention has been paid to other aspects of the rural scene, and in particular to the reaction by agricultural producers to the collapse of the national market. Yet this was as important in the short term as expropriation of the landowners was in the long term. Agrarian violence changed the social structure of the countryside; the peasants' refusal to hand over their produce to official purchasing organizations helped to disrupt the economy. By curtailing food supplies to the towns and to the army it aggravated the social crisis and indirectly helped to bring down the Provisional Government.

Study of this question is hindered by the dearth of source material. The archives of the various supply organs have yet to be explored systematically, so that we are still very much in the dark about the operations of the local commodity exchanges, banks or private firms that were involved in marketing agricultural produce. In any case their records may not have much to reveal about the motives and actions of the producers themselves, especially those that were peasants.

Already in 1916 farmers had begun to withhold part of their produce from the market in order to evade governmental controls (see above p. 34). The fall of the monarchy greatly increased these temptations. On one hand the Provisional Government maintained and intensified the 'tough' policy towards suppliers embarked upon in the last months of the tsarist regime; on the other hand it weakened the institutional machinery that had been set up to extract and distribute surpluses, in the hope that 'democratization' would make it more popular. It reduced incentives for farmers to part voluntarily with their grain or livestock but at the same time abandoned such instruments as it inherited for coercing them into doing so.

In the first days of the revolution the new government shared its authority in matters of food supply with the executive committee of the Petrograd soviet. A joint commission was established, which understandably enough concentrated its attention on increasing the flow of provisions to the capital and did not look much further afield. It was under the influence of this cooperation, and in order to satisfy the popular demand for more food supplies, that Prince Lvov's cabinet took its first independent decisions on this question.

On 9 March a State Supply Committee was set up under the minister of Agriculture (Shingarev). The latter extended the validity of the arrangements made by his predecessor whereby the government undertook to pay premiums and bonuses for timely fulfilment of allotted quotas under the levy scheme.[1] The principle underlying the levy was not questioned. On the following day he was authorized by his cabinet colleagues to draft a law making the buying and selling of grain a state monopoly. A decree to this effect was promulgated on 25 March. Little is known about the discussions that preceded its promulgation inside or outside the ministry, but its authors were clearly concerned above all with the interests of consumers in the army and the towns. They do not seem to have given serious consideration to the effect which such a measure would have upon producers.

The principle behind the decree of 25 March was the same as that which had inspired the levy: the agricultural population was expected to make further sacrifices in the cause of national defence. Henceforth farmers were obliged not merely to provide a fixed quota of grain but to hand over their *entire* crop, minus a certain proportion deemed necessary for seed, fodder and 'the subsistence of the producer, his family, and persons employed on the farm who receive an allowance in grain'. The amount of this exemption was to be fixed in the light of local conditions by a newly constituted elective body, the provincial supply committee. The non-exempted grain was to be taken by the producers at their own expense to the collecting-point indicated, where it would be 'taken into account' (an obscure term) by agents of the local supply committee. For the amount supplied the producer would be paid in cash at the fixed price, which was now raised by an average of 60 per cent.[2]

Most peasants who had a marketable surplus normally sold it in the autumn, for only the wealthier among them could afford to hold out until the first months of the following calendar year. The immediate impact of the law was thus confined to those who had accumulated stocks from earlier harvests, since the law covered these reserves in addition to the prospective harvest of 1917. The rise in the fixed grain price brought producers little relief. It barely compensated for the increase in the cost of living and certainly did not outweigh the measure's more disagreeable features. For instance, the law did not make it clear how, when and by whom the crop could be purchased : if by the new supply organs, would they be able to pay suppliers promptly, or would the latter be expected to run themselves into debt? Would there be enough collecting-points (with adequate storage space) within easy reach of the farms? Had producers been of a legalistic turn of mind, they might also have queried the authorities' right to prescribe how they should dispose of their crop before it was brought to the collecting-point, for the grain did not actually become state property until it was 'taken into account'.

Thus the decree gave suppliers ample grounds for concern. Although its provisions extended only to grain, it seemed to herald similar measures in relation to other products as well. Two matters in particular caused anxiety. One was the rapid depreciation of the currency, which threatened to make the fixed prices out of date almost as soon as they had been prescribed; the second was the nature of the controlling organs and the spirit in which their members approached their task. The law provided for the establishment of a hierarchy of supply committees at the provincial, county and rural-district level. In addition there were supply committees in the municipalities, which in the nature of things could only be interested in obtaining and distributing grain, not in helping farmers to produce it. The central State Supply Committee was to preside over this complicated structure. Both this body and all its subordinate organs were to be elected according to a complicated formula designed to provide for the representation of various local interests. Yet only on the most junior committees could actual producers hope for a majority. The provincial supply committee, with thirty to thirty-five members, was heavily weighted in favour of townsmen – indeed, of persons who were bound to appear to peasants as representatives of the social élite. It could be expected to take a demanding, consumption-oriented approach and to be indifferent, if not actually hostile, towards the interests of those who provided the food the rest of the country needed. It also threatened to be expensive.[3]

As in the land-committee hierarchy, the practice was adopted of including on the provincial supply committee representatives of the organs junior to it. The effect of this provision was to dilute responsibility throughout the supply apparatus. The lower (county and district) bodies, which were likely to be the most active in trying to control the amount of grain stored and sold, were staffed by persons untrained to assume such onerous functions. Their orders could easily be circumvented by peasants accustomed to evading orders from on high. The very idea of compelling peasants to accept rationing of a commodity which they themselves produced was fanciful. The state authorities could have enforced this only by conducting house-to-house inspections. It is doubtful whether the framers of the monopoly law expected supply officials to engage in detailed investigations of this kind. There certainly did not exist in Russia even the rudiments of the vast bureaucratic apparatus that such an operation would have required.

The grain monopoly law was in large part a propagandist measure, designed to convince the hard-pressed consumer that the new regime would compel agricultural producers to disgorge the riches they had supposedly accumulated. In so far as it encouraged townsmen to apply pressure themselves, in their capacity as members of the supply committees, it might even be termed demagogic. Its importance was not so much economic as political. It irritated and alarmed the peasants without seriously inhibiting their freedom to decide how much of their produce they should market, and on what terms, while among the urban population it stimulated utopian ideas about the expediency of an even more comprehensive system of economic controls. The Provisional Government's radical critics took it for granted that the implementation of extensive price control would present no special problem. The alternative policy, of offering increased incentives to the farmers, was ruled out on the grounds that it would benefit the large landed proprietors, and would thus be 'reactionary'.

The government moved slowly in setting up the supply apparatus. Such organs were evidently formed quite rapidly in the major consuming areas, but were slower to appear in those southern provinces that produced grain for the market.[4] The State Supply Committee was presided over by the minister of Agriculture, but its most prominent figure was the Menshevik V.G. Groman, who was also active on the Petrograd soviet. It tried, sensibly enough, to supply agricultural producers with machinery, fertilizer and other items of equipment greatly in demand, but had to fight hard to divert industrial resources from armaments to the needs of the rural economy. Whether or not, as has been suggested,[5] it should have gone on to encourage barter deals of foodstuffs for 'the enormous amount of goods that had come into its possession', instead of clinging so tenaciously to the rapidly depreciating paper currency, it could have assumed powers over sectors of industry capable of producing cheap consumer goods, notably textiles and footwear, and given special inducements (such as higher wages) to increase the flow of products to the countryside. The sale of such goods could have been made contingent upon satisfactory delivery of produce. Only tentative steps were taken in this direction. In July the ministry of Supply was allocated 50–60 per cent of all textile output after satisfaction of the army's needs. Between 1 March and 1 October five million puds of metal and metal wares and 120 million arshins of textiles, along with smaller amounts of other goods, were dispatched to the countryside.[6] Manufacturers were also recommended to arrange direct exchanges. But on the whole the central supply authorities were lethargic and unimaginative in trying to cope with the food crisis.

A decree of 17 April forbade private commercial firms to buy or sell grain except as agents of the local supply committee, whose agents' instructions were to be obeyed 'without reservation'. The supply committees were actually recommended to discriminate *against* private merchants when drawing up contracts for the provision of grain; instead preference was to be given to cooperatives and other 'public organizations'.[7] The object of this was to eliminate the corrupt practices of which grain merchants were rightly or wrongly suspected. However praiseworthy the motive, it opened the way to the same evil in other forms, for the 'public organizations' mentioned were not proof against dishonesty; on the contrary, since any administrative unit, and in practice even any economic enterprise, was able to set up its own 'supply committee', there was bound to be a hectic competition for scarce resources in which each body would seek to outbid the other. Naturally enough these committees' agents disregarded the unrealistic official price and sometimes offered suppliers illicit 'bonuses'.

Reports soon appeared of clashes between members of different supply boards, which were in fact nothing more than purchasing teams. Trainloads of grain bought on behalf of one body might be commandeered by another, which would order them not to be moved out of its jurisdiction. Late in July the Tver provincial supply board sent one of its members to Nizhniy Novgorod, where the local authorities were holding a consignment of 110,000 puds of grain that had been purchased on its behalf in Samara.[8] One month later the Moscow supply organization was reported to have no less than seventy agents in various places searching for grain.[9] It was in vain that senior supply officials endeavoured to maintain some semblance of order in the chaos. Meanwhile merchants and millers complained loudly that the government had brought the evil upon its own head by refusing to work through normal commercial channels and ignoring their professional experience.[10]

These arguments were eagerly taken up by the government's conservative critics, who had a good point. To safeguard the public interest it would have sufficed to establish a system of selective controls over the activities of private traders, with exemplary penalties against those guilty of blatant profiteering, instead of attempting to check each and every abuse. Unfortunately in such matters the democratic politicians were blinded by ideological prejudice. Although the practice of the war-industries committees, to look no further afield, showed that in an emergency private enterprise could be persuaded to collaborate with government in pursuit of limited common objectives, the lessons of this experience were disregarded.

There were, however, some signs of second thoughts as early as 29 April, when the government instituted (or more correctly, restored) the office of 'commissioner'.[11] These men were sent out to the provinces as counterweights to the elected supply committees. In practice, however, the uneasy coexistence of the two forms of authority accentuated the general confusion. One major defect was that the commissioners had no independent means of enforcing their will, short of appealing to the local military. Some of them attempted to uphold the interests of the State and the consuming regions, while others swam with the tide, endorsing the flexible line taken by the local supply organs. Nevertheless the principle behind the commissioner system was commendable.

In line with this reform on 5 May the State Supply Committee was placed under the authority of a newly created ministry of Supply, headed by A.V. Peshekhonov.[12] The latter belonged to the most right-wing Populist group, the Popular Socialists. Shortly after succeeding to office he announced that he would continue his predecessor's policies.[13] The establishment of a new ministry was a logical move, in view of the increased responsibilities that the supply organs were now assuming; nevertheless it had the disadvantage of dividing authority in agrarian affairs between two departments, Supply and Agriculture, whose chiefs vied with one another for influence within the cabinet. Chernov's effort to appease the peasants by enlarging the land-committees' powers inevitably undermined his colleague's attempts to bring the supply committees under tighter control. The supply organs moved slowly in compiling inventories of grain stocks. When the Moscow soviet investigated the progress that had been made, it discovered that they had been taken in only six provinces, of which four had been carried out in a superficial manner.[14]

As the summer wore on deliveries of agricultural produce to major urban centres, and to the army, fell far behind schedule. The Moscow city supply committee, as a result of its ubiquitous agents' activities, received enough grain and flour for its needs in May, but in the following month the number of railway wagons reaching the city was about a sixth below requirements. The position was still worse in July. In order to maintain the bread ration the authorities drew upon their reserves, but these were exhausted by the beginning of August. On the eighteenth of that month the ration was reduced to $\frac{1}{2}$ funt per person per day.[15] Some other cities in the 'consuming' provinces had to make do with half the amount; in Baku, which was not too far from one of the main grain-producing areas, the daily rate was maintained at $\frac{3}{4}$ funt.[16] On 26 June the central supply authorities fixed a maximum monthly 'consumption norm' for urban residents of twenty-five funts of flour or flour products,[17] but this was regarded simply as a ceiling or target figure, not as an entitlement which the authorities were pledged to fulfil. This gap between promise and performance, along with the wide regional disparities, added to the general discontent. The idea of food rationing was still unfamiliar to the consuming public, and the system adopted had many loopholes which unscrupulous persons were quick to exploit.

In several places merchants and supply officials were roughly handled by the crowds. According to one (uncorroborated) press report, the villagers of Bolshiye Sundyri (Kozmodemyansk county, Kazan province), in the course of a protest against the grain monopoly, 'inflicted cruel torture upon the chairman of the district supply committee, Zapolsky, whom they roasted on a bonfire and then killed.'[18] Elsewhere angry villagers resorted to the ancient custom of publicly shaming persons deemed to have infringed the community's interests. At Yashevka (Tambov county and province) a supply official named Minayev was suspected of fraud when requisitioning millet from two peasants. The villagers thereupon 'dressed him in a woman's skirt, placed a bag over his head adorned with 30-rouble banknotes, and thrust a spade into his hands with the inscription "for 30 pieces of silver he sold our freedom"; in this grotesque attire he was paraded around the village and obliged to make public confession of his guilt'.[19] Such personal assaults were less frequent than acts of passive resistance to the collectors. At Novopavlovka (Samara province), when the district supply board officials arrived, 'the church bells were rung and a large crowd assembled. Placing their women and children in the front ranks, the peasants cried : "only over our dead bodies shall you have the grain!" The board members and the soldiers left without it.'[20] In Yekaterinoslav province landowners and peasants are said to have made common cause against the low prices fixed for grain under the monopoly law and to have decided that, pending its revision by the central authorities, they would raise the prices of their own accord, charging 4·60 roubles instead of 2·90 for a pud of wheat; rye would fetch 4·35 roubles instead of 2·24, and barley 3·70 roubles instead of 2·50. They added that in their estimation even these prices were too low – as indeed they were, since in neighbouring Kharkov province 'speculators' were charging purchasers on the free market 8 to 14 roubles per pud of grain; in Podolia it fetched 15 to 17 roubles; and in a consuming province such as Vladimir the black-market price was 25 to 35 roubles.[21]

A number of supply committees, especially at the lower level, sided with producers and implored the higher authorities to be more lenient. In Orenburg province at the beginning of August one of these junior bodies, in Verkhneuralsk county, reported that it could only hope to exact grain at the fixed price by employing armed force; since this would lead to 'undesirable phenomena', permission was requested to purchase at the free-market price.[22] In Nizhniy Novgorod province the local supply authorities reported that peasants were hiding grain under the eaves of buildings, behind stoves, beneath floor-boards, or digging it into the soil of their plots. The latter operation was usually performed at night to minimize the chance of detection. Soldiers had been sent to the affected area, but they had been met by large crowds of women and children and had refused to shoot.[23] The provincial supply committee joined with members of the local municipality, zemstvo and stock-exchange committee in petitioning the government either to permit free trade or to double the fixed prices.[24]

Here opposition to the monopoly was evidently led by middle-class elements who wanted a return to free enterprise, but this was not always the case. The movement might acquire an extreme left-wing flavour, as in one district in Vyatka province, where protesters linked this issue with resistance to efforts to round up deserters,[25] or else be associated with the extreme right, as in Chernigov province, where anti-Semitic feelings were latent among the rural population.[26] The evidence suggests that the movement was not political but socio-economic in inspiration : it had its roots in the tension between country folk and townsmen. The peasants' anger was directed chiefly against the officials, but it could extend to any section of the urban community. In Kharkov province agricultural labourers on a sugar-beet estate refused to allow consignments of grain to be sent for the relief of hungry workers in a processing plant that formed part of the same enterprise; some time later a similar incident was reported from Tambov province.[27] At another place, not identified in the source, factory workers threw stones at a group of peasants who offered them cucumbers at 5 roubles a measure, an astronomically high price.[28]

Such manifestations of narrow-minded egoism were a consequence of the disruption of normal market relationships. The village seemed to be losing whatever margin of advantage *vis-à-vis* the towns it had won during the first years of the war, and it sought to maintain its relatively favourable position by a campaign of passive resistance. The central authorities had not expected this reaction and were nonplussed by it. In some areas hesitant efforts were made to enforce the grain monopoly by using troops, but these often proved to be counter-productive. The only alternative was to yield to the pressure from below. This meant that the government had to eat its words in public, for on 4 August it had issued a strong statement denying rumours that grain prices would be raised again during the current year.[29] On 27 August, however, it capitulated: they were to be doubled as from 1 September. At the same time the financial penalties imposed on those who concealed grain were reduced: they were now to receive seventy per cent of the new fixed price, instead of fifty per cent as before.[30]

This confession of weakness, instead of appeasing agricultural producers, served only to whet their appetites. The peasants objected to the measure primarily because it would lead to a corresponding rise in industrial prices; they linked their protest with a demand for fixed prices for all essential commodities.[31] Partly under the influence of radical propaganda from the cities the mass of agricultural producers swung round to the naive but comforting belief that price levels could without difficulty be held down by administrative fiat. They blamed their plight upon the most obvious scapegoats and called for immediate radical changes in the nation's social and economic life. But they also assumed that this upheaval would incline the terms of trade in their favour and dramatically increase their purchasing power. Since such benefits were unlikely to flow from the 'proletarian revolution' advocated by the Bolsheviks and their allies, there was little doubt that stormy weather lay ahead.

In this connection one naturally asks oneself how far the peasants' actual situation had worsened during the lifetime of the Provisional Government. Unfortunately the evidence is even more sparse than in the case of the industrial workers, and only a few general indications can be given. No statistics are available for peasant incomes. Nor do we know how much money was actually paid to farmers by supply organs in return for their deliveries. In normal times the peasants' response to scarcity conditions was to seek work in the cities, in transport undertakings, or on the latifundia of the deep south; but these avenues were now closed, and instead the population drift was in the reverse direction, from the hungry towns back to the village. In these circumstances the most obvious alternative source of income was from the sale of produce on the free (black) market. Peasant producers could either bring their surplus to nearby towns or else wait until the city folk came to buy it from them. This trade was illegal in commodities whose price was fixed, but the problem of evading official controls seems hardly to have arisen, except perhaps in the two capital cities, and the main obstacles were distance and shortage of transport. In exchange for their foodstuffs the peasants sought to obtain precious metals (especially gold and silver coins from the pre-1914 era), articles of clothing, domestic hardware, and items of furniture such as clocks, mirrors, bedding and so on. More immediately useful were the manufactured goods which industrial employees sometimes brought from their place of work, with or without permission of the management. In Petrograd certain factory committees organized the production of nails from scrap metal for direct exchange with the peasants – an operation which in the eyes of some zealots was not just good business but a step towards the moneyless economy of the future. In Yekaterinoslav a similar enterprise came into being with the consent of local industrialists.[32] How far income from this trade offset the losses incurred through the breakdown of regular commerce cannot be determined.

If one could not sell one's produce one could at least eat it. Any farmer in Russia who reaped a reasonably good harvest would not starve. What he did not consume he could store; some grain could be turned (illegally) into home-brewed liquor (*samogon*); some might be fed to farm animals, for the low prices for cereals stimulated peasants to increase their stock of cattle and poultry. A great many of these animals and birds were slaughtered for consumption, especially to avoid requisitioning.[33] All these factors need to be taken into account when estimating the overall change in peasant well-being. This undoubtedly worsened in 1917, even though in some favoured areas farmers may have prospered.[34] This deterioration was less drastic than that of the urban workers, but it was none the less real.

Although we cannot measure the decline, a rough idea can be obtained of the amount of grain which remained in peasant hands (for the season, at least). This information comes from detailed estimates recently made available of the gross harvest in 1917 and the amount of grain procured by the State.[35] These show that the gross harvest of food and fodder grains in European Russia (fifty-one provinces including the North Caucasus) was 3,041 and in the whole country 3,777 million puds.[36] Confining ourselves to European Russia, the total amount of surpluses in those provinces that had them was put at 728 and the total deficiency at 319 million puds. On this basis – making the very large assumption that the supply organization and transport system could provide for the necessary exchange – there should have been more than enough for all consumers. If these figures can be believed, the gross harvest in 1917 was not much below that of the preceding year (see above, p. 34).

The picture becomes more meaningful if we compare individual provinces, since there were wide disparities in their performance. Tver may be taken as typical of the non-black-soil provinces of northern Russia. The first of the recently published tables (which has several gaps) estimates this area's output of the six principal grains at 16·7 million puds; the second table puts it at 23·1 million puds. This suggests a significant improvement, for over the five last pre-war years the grain yield had averaged 20·1, and in 1916 it had stood at 19·8 million puds. Increases were registered in Pskov, Petrograd and Novgorod provinces, whereas in Vyatka the harvest was down by more than a third. In quantitative terms, however, the amounts of grain produced in the non-black-soil zone were very modest, especially when compared with the provinces of the fertile south; on the other hand the difficulties experienced in transporting foodstuffs from the latter region to the 'consuming' provinces enhanced the importance of such progress as was made there, even if it could not hope to fill the gap.

Turning now to the black-soil provinces, we find a less auspicious situation. Voronezh, which may serve as our sample, produced less than two-thirds as much as in 1916, although output in that year had risen appreciably above the pre-war average. (The figures in million puds were as follows : 1909–13 – 121·5; 1916 – 129·9; 1917 – 84·5.) Matters were a little better in Tambov and Kursk, where the decline was of the order of ten per cent and eight per cent respectively, and better still in Orel, where output was within two per cent of the pre-war figure (although considerably less than in 1916). On the other hand the harvest was catastrophically bad in the mid-Volga provinces of Penza, Saratov and Simbirsk, where it fell by 38 per cent, 44 per cent and 54 per cent below the previous year's figures. Samara province was also hard hit. Although all these provinces were the scene of serious agrarian unrest, it would seem that climatic rather than social factors were chiefly responsible for the shortfall.

Finally we may turn our attention to the steppe region, the country's principal granary. Taking Yekaterinoslav as our sample, it transpires that its output was slightly above the pre-war average, compensating for an unusually poor harvest in 1916. (The figures in million puds were as follows: 1909–13 – 174·5; 1916 – 109·4; 1917 – 176·0.) In Tavrida province, where 1916 had been unusually good, 1917 was even better, yielding 163 million puds of grain. For the five provinces that comprised New Russia the figure was 767 million puds, which was close to the pre-war average (783 million) and a great deal better than in 1916 (646 million puds).

How much of all this grain did the central supply authorities succeed in procuring? The recently published table showing procurements is not dated precisely; moreover, it relates to 'the agricultural year 1916–17', whereas the statistics on output apply to the calendar year 1917. It was presumably compiled in July, since the total amount collected, 508·5 million puds, is not much below the figure of 540 million puds announced by Prokopovich in his speech of 16 October mentioned above.[37] This would have been about a sixth to a seventh of the gross harvest, and about two-thirds (65·9 per cent) – or according to Prokopovich, a half – of the target figure. Geographically, the results were very uneven: some provinces (notably Vologda in the north and Saratov in the south) provided much more than had been required of them, while at the other extreme Kostroma yielded a mere 3·5 per cent of its quota. The largest amounts, naturally enough, came from the steppe region (including the northern Caucasus) and Samara province.

For the year that had now begun (on 1 August) Prokopovich fixed a target of 1,120 million puds, which was roughly equivalent to the amount of grain that had been put into commercial circulation before the war.[38] He predicted that again only half this amount would actually be secured; but even this modest objective was to prove to be wildly over-optimistic. In September the official agencies are thought to have taken delivery of forty-three million puds, of which less than half could be loaded for dispatch to consuming areas. During the first eleven days of October only two-thirds of the government's orders were fulfilled. Yet September and October were normally peak months in the grain trade. The railways were sinking into a state of near-paralysis; and the overthrow of the Provisional Government soon led to a complete breakdown of the supply organization (see below, pp. 422–6). The anarchy in the cities meant that there was no effective way of persuading producers to hand over their supplies. The bodies of armed workers and soldiers or sailors sent out under the auspices of the new regime to requisition foodstuffs cannot have brought in very much. During the first six months of 1918 the Soviet authorities claimed to have procured a mere twenty-eight million puds by these methods. For the last two and a half months of 1917 an estimate of 5 to 10 million puds would be generous. According to one Soviet source the total collected in the agricultural year 1917–18 was 73·4 million puds.[39] To this one must add the amount of grain that was sold or bartered by producers on the free market. Unfortunately it is impossible to arrive at any meaningful estimate of its extent, but it was probably larger than the exchanges of which the authorities were officially aware. If one deducts this combined amount, which cannot be expressed in quantitative terms, from the gross harvest one obtains an indication of the scale of the peasants' success in their campaign of passive resistance.

To put the point crudely, for the first time in modern Russian history the overwhelming bulk of the harvest remained on the farm, where it provided sustenance not only for millions of country folk but also for a flood of returning townsmen and members of the armed forces. If in the pre-war years about one-quarter of the grain produced in the country had found its way to the market, in 1917 the proportion cannot have exceeded a sixth and may have been less than that.[40] Moreover, in most of the exchanges between town and country the price was determined by the producer rather than the purchaser. Such figures as are available on grain prices[41] understate the extent of the farmers' gain since they do not cover the unofficial exchanges that were such an important element in commercial relations between town and country. Nevertheless the peasants' victory was to prove to be a Pyrrhic one, as we shall see.

FIFTEEN *The Spread of Agrarian Violence: a Regional Analysis*

'A HARVEST IS for a season, the land is for ever.' The Russian peasants of 1917 were in no danger of forgetting this elementary precept. On the contrary, they displayed an almost obsessive concern with 'the land question'. It was the subject of continuous discussion at village assemblies and at mammoth meetings organized by the various peasant organizations that sprang up all over the country. From words it was but a step to action. If at first country folk were prepared to wait and see what the new authorities would do, it was not long before they decided to settle matters for themselves, ignoring appeals for restraint. Confident in their absolute right to the land, they set about taking it while they could. Instances of agrarian unrest multiplied with astonishing speed. Within a few months almost every newspaper carried reports of confiscations of property, assaults on individuals, and other acts of violence; yet these were but a fraction of the total. Official agencies were likewise overwhelmed. By October 1917 they could no longer keep abreast of the countless breaches of the law that were occurring in many areas of the country, let alone arrest and punish the malefactors.

Partly as a consequence of this breakdown of authority, historians have made little progress in systematizing and analysing the information that exists on the agrarian disorders. It is not yet possible to give an accurate answer, based on statistical evidence, to many of the questions that a modern investigator would naturally ask: how many incidents occurred each month in the various provinces or regions? In what proportion do they stand to the total number of individual properties?[1] What types of action were undertaken, for what reasons, and by which sections of the rural community? How much effect did the disorders have on agricultural output? In what ways did the various local authorities react, and did their response contain or stimulate violence? These and other legitimate questions could be settled definitively only on the basis of extensive archival research. Unfortunately the documents that have been published since 1917 have been 'filtered', with increasing thoroughness over the years, in such a way as to obscure the actual relationship between the factors that shaped the agrarian movement. For example, we do not have the complete set of reports submitted to the ministry of Interior by provincial commissars, but only selections from them chosen to highlight the most serious disturbances. It is quite possible that an analysis of all these reports and other relevant government papers would give a more balanced picture than emerges from those sources upon which all writers hitherto have been obliged to rely.

The first attempts to assess these incidents statistically were undertaken at the time. Late in August 1917 the Main Land Committee released figures covering the period 1 March to 15 August, which were commented upon in the press.[2] The number of incidents recorded by this body was appreciably lower than that known to the Main Administration of Militia Affairs, a department of the ministry of Interior. An extensive selection from the latter records was published in 1927.[3] The compilers of this work also reproduced in an appendix tables compiled for each month from March to September in an attempt to classify the incidents according to area and type of offence. These figures have been widely quoted since, both by Soviet and non-Soviet scholars, usually without due regard to the defects inherent in this type of source material. The militia administration's records were built up mainly from reports by local militia agencies and complaints by the victims of illegal acts. The devolution of authority to organs of local self-government (municipalities and zemstva) greatly weakened ties between the ministry and its agencies, so that submission of reports was neglected. Communication was physically difficult. Moreover, some militia units came under the influence of extreme revolutionary groups and were led to condone (and even to participate in) the very actions they were supposed to prevent. The offences that were supposed to be reported were vaguely defined, so that local militiamen, who had little or no training for such work, were left free to fit the facts to the rubrics given; to make matters still more difficult, these were altered several times during the year. Complaints by citizens could seldom be verified; many persons who had been wronged were unable or unwilling to file a complaint, since even if they could contact the authorities there seemed little likelihood of their achieving redress. For all these reasons the militia reports are neither comprehensive nor reliable.[4]

Nevertheless there is as yet no substitute for them. Their principal value lies in the fact that they contain much first-hand material which illustrates graphically the nature of rural disturbances during this period; they can also be used as a basis for statistical computations, provided due care is exercised. They cannot, however, give an accurate idea of the overall number of incidents, as many historians have assumed. For example, Ya.A. Yakovlev, a leading Soviet scholar of the 1920s, claimed on the basis of militia reports that the total increased by 233 per cent between April and October.[5] A colleague, I. Vermenichev, attempted some even more ambitious calculations. He produced a statistical table, with figures correct to one decimal point, showing the ratio of what he called 'sackings and terror' to the total number of incidents in each region.[6] Many writers have made free with figures purporting to show the number of counties affected by rural unrest, overlooking the fact that a county might contain several dozen villages, and that it is hardly enough that incidents should be reported from one or two of them for the whole county to be categorized as 'disturbed'. Vermenichev arrived at a total of 5,782 incidents which could properly be described as agrarian in nature. Another scholar, I.V. Igritsky, found 5,978. Not to be outdone, P.N. Pershin, the doyen of Soviet authorities on the peasant question (and himself active in the land-settlement agency before and after the revolution), has claimed 6,103.[7] S.M. Dubrovsky, and following him P.N. Sobolev, give the same total as Vermenichev. The most recent Soviet student of the question reduces the figure, for reasons that are not plain, to 5,416. Finally, academician I.I. Mints, in his monumental three-volume official history of the October revolution, provides a table of monthly figures which add up to a mere 4,285.[8] According to Pershin, who has studied materials in local archives, the total number of incidents was anything from three to eight times greater, depending upon the province concerned, than the figure reported by the militia. As against this, allowance must be made for a tendency among writers on the subject to inflate the importance of minor squabbles and to count as separate incidents what were really just different manifestations of the same conflict. One cannot but sympathize with Pershin's plea that his colleagues should develop common criteria for enumerating agrarian disorders.

Only if it were possible to examine each incident (or group of incidents) in the context of local socio-economic conditions could one build up an accurate picture of the scope, nature and impact of the peasant movement. In the absence of such evidence, obtainable only from unpublished sources, we shall first consider the main features of the situation in four provinces, each of which may be taken as typical of the region in which it was located, and then examine the various kinds of action taken.

All authorities agree that agrarian disturbances were most acute in what contemporary economic geographers called the Central Agricultural and Middle Volga regions – that is to say, in those provinces extending approximately from Poltava in the west to Kazan and Saratov in the east. This was pre-eminently an area whose natural advantages (especially the fertile black soil) were offset by the effects of over-population, and where there was a long tradition of agrarian unrest. The problems of Voronezh province, extending over some 22,265 square miles on either bank of the middle Don, were typical of this belt. It was an overwhelmingly rural province, for only five per cent of its 3·1 million inhabitants lived in towns. It was divided into twelve counties and 230 rural districts. By January 1917 nearly 79,000 households had consolidated their holdings under the Stolypin reform. These comprised 16·2 per cent of the total number of peasant farms, which numbered 485,000, and held 13·7 per cent of the allotment land (473,000 dessyatines), but only about 9 per cent of such householders had physically separated their land from that of the rest of the community. Nearly 1,800 farms (*khozyaystva*) are recorded in the 1916 census as being in private ownership. (This figure presumably excludes the properties owned by the peasants just mentioned.) According to a history of the area published in 1957, which does not cite the source, 'on the eve of 1917 there were in Voronezh province 1,115 owners with a land fund in excess of 800,000 dessyatines.'[9] The difference between this figure and that reported by the census-takers in 1916 (1,786 farms) is presumably explained by the fact that some properties did not have agricultural land. The total amount of peasant allotment land can be calculated from the data given in the 1957 publication as 3,674,000 dessyatines. Thus the individual peasant proprietors held rather more than half as much as the farming landlords, and both groups together about one-third as much as the communal peasants. Much of the proprietorial land was non-arable. This explains why the 1916 census, which registered the apportionment of the crop area (*posevnaya ploshchad'*), found that out of a total of 2,532,000 dessyatines of land only 199,000, or 7·8 per cent, were in private ownership (the rest being held by peasant communities). However, as mentioned above (p. 33), the census data understate the extent of private landowning since many informants rendered false returns.

Cereals accounted for eighty-six per cent of the sown area; sunflower seed, potatoes and grasses made up most of the remainder. Crop yields were low: for rye the average in 1914–17 is said to have been forty-five puds per dessyatine (*circa* 600 lbs an acre). Some two-thirds of the land was arable. In consequence there was an acute shortage of meadow and pasture, as well as of timber (most of the woodland being state-owned). Livestock-raising expanded considerably in the pre-war years, and in 1916 there were in the province (in round figures) 700,000 horses, 1,100,000 large horned cattle (including 400,000 cows), 2,500,000 sheep and 400,000 pigs. These animals were unequally divided between peasants and private proprietors. From the 1916 census data it can be calculated that the latter, who comprised less than 0·4 per cent of the rural population (by households), owned (in round figures) 4 per cent of the horses, 5 per cent of the large horned cattle (but less than 3 per cent of the cows), 4 per cent of the sheep and 8 per cent of the pigs. These figures may overstate the degree of inequality, since the method whereby a farm was classified as 'peasant' or 'private proprietorial' was somewhat arbitrary. Moreover, draught animals and milch cows in private hands (which were generally of higher quality) were often rented out to peasants, but no figures are available on the extent of this practice. Similarly, much of the land in private ownership was leased to them, either on an individual or a communal basis. This was a source of friction, especially where tenants were obliged to use their own implements. Wage rates for agricultural labourers varied greatly between one county and another.[10]

The concentration of property, at least in livestock, may not seem very extreme, but one has to bear in mind that living standards in rural Russia were so low that any inequality loomed large in the minds of a peasantry still wedded to communal ways, as of the intellectuals who aspired to lead them. It was only to be expected that the villagers of Voronezh province should cast envious eyes at landowners' estates (which were concentrated in five counties). They also looked forward to the prospect of ironing out inequalities among the peasants themselves, even though disparities of income or differences in life-style between richer and poorer villages do not seem to have been particularly marked. Soviet sources speak of 54,000 'kulaks', but the criterion used in distinguishing such households from the rest is not made clear. About two-thirds of the peasants in Voronezh province had no more than one horse and very small allotments of land (if indeed they had either); in Zadonsk county, in the north of the province, the proportion of such persons was as high as 78 per cent. Ownership of land and horses were the two main criteria used by contemporary statisticians (and the interested public generally) to determine the peasants' economic and social status. They were crude criteria, which did not take account of many other relevant factors (for example, some landless peasants earned their living as artisans and did not need land); however, in the last resort this bias in the statistics does not matter very much. Most of those who dwelt in the rural areas of Voronezh province, like their fellows in other parts of the black-soil zone, were poor and conscious of their disadvantages *vis-à-vis* other social groups. This was enough to unleash the storm.

The militia statisticians recorded a total of 125 incidents in the province between April and September inclusive.[11] A close study of the reports from Voronezh province received by the Main Administration for Militia Affairs and published in this volume yields a lower figure of approximately 100. (The difference may be explained partly by double counting, and partly by confusing threats with offences actually committed.) Evidence of a further thirty incidents is provided by a documentary collection published in 1957.[12] Most of the new information relates to the period April to June; the documents for the last three months largely corroborate the data given in the 1927 volume. It is no doubt possible, as Pershin suggests, that many more incidents took place than were officially recorded; nevertheless we may take these as a representative sample. Fortunately in almost every case we are given the name of the county (and even district) concerned, brief details of the nature of the offence(s), and the social status (often also the name) of the aggrieved party. When these data are arranged systematically, the following conclusions suggest themselves.

First, the intensity of the movement varied from month to month. No specific incidents are recorded in March.[13] In April the total was 11; in May it jumped to 26; for the next three months it remained close to that figure (24, 28, 20), sinking slightly to 17 in September. (For purposes of comparison we may give the militia totals : 5, 15, 25, 32, 31, 17.)

Second, disturbances were much more frequent in some counties than in others. High scores were registered in Bobrov (24), Ostrogozhsk (22) and Novokhopersk (20); moderate ones in Zemlyansk (14), Zadonsk (10), Nizhnedevitsk (10) and Biryuch (9); low ones in Pavlovsk (7), Boguchar (5), Voronezh (4), Valuyki (3) and Korotoyak (1). As one would expect all three counties with a high score were those with a good deal of private landowning, and the same factor accounts for the strength of the movement in Zadonsk and Biryuch.[14] Apart from this the pattern of distribution has no apparent geographical logic : in other words, the high-score and low-score counties do not form distinct territorial blocs.

Third, unrest seems to have occurred in bursts. The most striking evidence of this comes from Zadonsk county, where six incidents including four outright seizures of property are reported in April, but only one in May and none in June. Similarly, Novokhopersk was apparently quiet between early April and the middle of May, after which seven incidents are known to have taken place. Ostrogozhsk had a kind of 'digestive pause' of a month, in late April and early May, and a shorter one in the first half of July. Since incidents were not always reported promptly, it would be unwise to insist too strongly on this point. However, it is worth noting that Melgunov, who examined only the monthly figures for certain provinces, arrives at the same conclusion.[15]

Fourth, there were variations between counties as regards the type of illicit activity engaged in. The greatest amount of violence occurred in Novokhopersk, with five reported instances of total confiscations of property and six of serious offences against the person (arrest, assault, and – towards the end of the period – homicide). The corresponding figures for Bobrov were three and five, and for Ostrogozhsk five and one. Here too we are admittedly dealing with approximations. The reports often mention sequestrations of property without making it clear whether they were partial or total – that is to say whether the owner was merely deprived of, say, his arable land but left in possession of his house and other facilities, or whether his entire property was taken. Similarly a good many cases of personal assault will have gone unrecorded when they appeared to be simply incidental to more serious violations. One naturally also seeks to discover whether particular types of offence were 'bunched' in time. There is little evidence of this, apart from such seasonally induced phenomena as an increase in conflicts over meadowland in late May and June, at haymaking time, and the appearance of a new category of offence, crop-stealing, in mid-July. In general conflicts over arable land were much more frequent than those over other agricultural facilities. There were twenty-one instances of the former (excluding confiscation of property *in toto*) as against eleven over pasture or meadowland and four over live-stock. A further eleven conflicts are recorded concerning rented land (in the main probably arable) and the same number concerning labour matters (wage rates, forcible removal of personnel, employ-ment of prisoners of war and so forth).

Fifth, the wronged parties were overwhelmingly private land-owners, some of whom bore aristocratic titles or had held senior rank in the imperial bureaucracy. However, a strong element of bias enters into the statistics here, since precisely such persons were most likely to inform the authorities of their plight. Some land-owners sent in a succession of complaints. Countess Orlova-Davydova, who owned much land in Bobrov county, reported attacks on one of her tenants (5 May), seizure of hay (28 July), alienation of rent payments and arbitrary arrests (9 September) and finally homicides (13 September).[16] As for the clergy, it appears that the peasants at first felt some moral inhibition about depriving them of their land, for such cases are recorded only after the end of June. On the other hand the unpopular 'separators' soon experienced their neighbours' disapproval. One of the first cases of this kind occurred in Zadonsk county on 14 May, where 'the peasants of Gryaznov district, taking advantage of the absence of their fellow-villagers T.N. Abramov and his brother on military service, sold all their movable property and real estate and refused to give it back'.[17]

Does the foregoing mean that by the end of September the rural areas of Voronezh province were in a state of total anarchy? This is the impression given in much of the general literature on the subject, but it needs qualification. Violence was sporadic rather than endemic. The wholesale destruction of estates seems to have been fairly rare; and in those counties with a low incidence of unrest life must have gone on with at least some semblance of normality. We know that in 1916 there were 1,786 landowners in the province, of whom 1,115 were actively engaged in farming. Even if the militia figures understate the number of incidents, and one multiplies them threefold to make a generous allowance for this,[18] some properties had not as yet been affected by social unrest. But it was only a question of time before they too would be drawn into the maelstrom.

Conditions were a good deal calmer in the non-black-soil zone of the north, of which Tver province may be taken as a sample. This was approximately the same size as Voronezh, but a tenth of it was swamp land unfit for cultivation. Of the rest only about a quarter was arable; the remainder consisted of pasture, meadow or forest. Most of the timber was owned by the State, but some belonged to ecclesiastical and commercial institutions. The density of population was considerably less than in Voronezh province. Poor soil and low crop yields forced peasants to migrate in search of work. Some moved permanently to the cities, while others took up seasonal employment in industry, trade or transport. Since farming made only a relatively modest contribution to peasant budgets, it was natural that social tensions should be less acute here than in the fertile, overcrowded south-central region. Another factor was the relative infrequency of large estates. The number of farms classified by the 1916 census-takers as proprietorial (*vladel'cheskiye*) was 2,375 – a third more than in Voronezh – but they were generally quite small : the average area sown to crop on them was only 13 dessyatines, as against 111 in Voronezh. This was not much more than was held by many peasants as allotment land. Most peasants held their land on communal rather than individual tenure, although by January 1916 47,000 households, nearly 14 per cent of the total number, had separated their plots as the first step towards enclosure. It is unfortunately not possible to establish how much of the total agricultural land, or the sown area, was in their hands. The other proprietors accounted for a mere four per cent of the crop area (as against 7·8 per cent in Voronezh) and held correspondingly lower proportions of the livestock : three per cent of the horses, four per cent of the large horned cattle, one per cent of the sheep, and five per cent of the pigs (in round figures).[19]

The central militia authorities recorded a total of sixty-six incidents between April and September 1917 inclusive. This was about half as many as in Voronezh province. Once again we may supplement this information from later documentary compilations,[20] exclude irrelevant data, make allowance for different types of illicit activity, and tabulate the results according to the twelve counties of which the province was comprised. This gives us a total of fifty-six incidents. Again the peak was reached in July. As in Voronezh, some counties were worse afflicted by unrest than others. Bezhetsk and Zubtsov had nine incidents, four counties each had six, and the remaining six counties no more than one or two (five incidents could not be localized). It is curious that Kalyazin and Kashin counties, which had least land per head, should have been among the least disturbed. This suggests that land shortage was not, as in the south, a major grievance. Disputes over arable land came third in order of importance, with nine recorded incidents; there were sixteen disputes over pasture or meadowland and eleven over timber; horses and livestock accounted for only two conflicts. We have five instances of an action that was entirely unknown in Voronezh : the levying of taxes upon private landed property at rates fixed by the commune.[21] This was an indication of the seriousness with which these village authorities approached their tasks. Traditions of self-government were much alive in this area, and the committeemen acted in a spirit different from the militancy of the south. In only one case (Ostashkov county, 10 July) do we hear of peasants seizing an estate outright and compelling the manager to abandon his duties.[22] More characteristic were limited actions which deprived the proprietor of a part of his land – usually, as noted above, his pasture or timber – or denied him access to its usufruct. Where there was violence, the curt description given in the militia report suggests that the action might be linked only indirectly, if at all, with agrarian problems. Thus 'on the night of 5/6 September 12 armed robbers burst into Semenova's estate Markovo, Rzhev county, threatened the proprietress with revolvers, made her hand over the keys, and seized 1,000 roubles and her silver plate. While they were searching for valuables the robbers played the piano.'[23] The image conjured up is of a band of common offenders (uncommon, perhaps, in their musical tastes) or perhaps of mutinous troops. Rzhev was a key railway junction on the main line from Moscow to Riga; the soldiers in the garrison had come under extremist influence in July, and at the beginning of September they arrested a number of their officers.[24]

In Mogilev province, which we may take as characteristic of the western provinces in general, the presence in the area of large bodies of armed men was at least as important as the state of agriculture in determining the course of events. This was in many ways an intermediate area. Its soil was for the most part of poor to moderate quality, and only a quarter was arable land; there was a heavy concentration on grain production (83 per cent of the sown area); pasture was short, but the area was well wooded. As in Tver, the density of population was low; as in Voronezh, there was a large number (2,894) of private estates, although their average size was less than half that in the latter province (41 dessyatines). Unlike either, the Stolypin reform, building on a tradition of non-repartitional tenure, had been very successful. In 1916 separators accounted for 36 per cent of the total number of peasant households (90,000 out of 249,000). The remaining (non-peasant) proprietors owned 1·2 per cent of the total number of farms, but held 11·2 per cent of the sown area, 6 per cent of the horses, 7 per cent of the large horned cattle, 2 per cent of the sheep and 3 per cent of the pigs. Even without the soldiers there was likely to be trouble.[25]

The militia registered 149 incidents between March and September, which we may agree is an underestimate: on several occasions its corespondents referred vaguely to 'a massive number of cases', without providing particulars;[26] recent Soviet sources are no more precise. Applying the same correctives as were used above, we arrive at a figure of 109 incidents. Once again the peak is reached in July (74, including 8 complete sequestrations, according to the militia; 40 by our reckoning). On closer inspection one finds an unusually heavy 'bunching' of incidents in the period from

25 June to the first week of August. Of the 23 incidents recorded from Cherikov county (the worst afflicted) during the entire seven months, 16 occurred at this time. A connection with the abortive 'Kerensky offensive' suggests itself. Although the militia did not as a rule pin the blame on mutinous soldiers, it is a reasonable assumption that they encouraged civilians to press their own claims. This was certainly the view of a spokesman for the local proprietors, S.I. Kaganovich, who told a congress of landowners that 'the excesses began after the spring sowing, when soldiers and other persons started to go round the villages making propaganda for transfer of land to the peasants,' an idea to which the peasant separators offered most resistance.[27] Soldiers are identified as responsible for several acts of violence in August and September. For example, the provincial commissioner reported that in Orsha county 'the number of robberies committed predominantly by soldiers has increased' and that 'two armed robberies have occurred by men wearing army uniform, in one case resulting in the death of two persons.'[28] Such actions were however, not the most characteristic of the agrarian disorders in this area – at least until October. Far more numerous were disputes over pasture and timber, which are mentioned forty and twenty-two times respectively (as against eleven instances of violent assault). The peasants were evidently induced to commit these offences by their grievous lack of grazing land and the consequent shortage of fodder for their cattle. Similarly, the appropriation of timber stocks or the illicit felling of trees had as its immediate cause a dire need for firewood : such incidents were concentrated in the spring or autumn, as one would expect.

Yekaterinoslav, our fourth and last sample province, may be taken as typifying the rolling Ukrainian steppe. It covered a large area between the Dnieper and Donets rivers, and was grain-growing country *par excellence*. Although the low rainfall and dry summer winds made the size of the harvest uncertain, in 1916 no less than 92 per cent of the sown area was devoted to cereals, especially wheat. A mere 47,000 dessyatines were under grass; timber was present in almost negligible quantities. The relative prosperity of the province had attracted landed proprietors, many of whom ran their estates on modern business principles. The 1916 census identified 4,465 such properties, whose average area was 95 dessyatines – not much below that in Voronezh. In addition no less than 30·2 per cent of peasant households (146,000 out of 483,000) had embarked upon the road to individual farming. The non-peasant proprietors, comprising 0·9 per cent of the total number of rural households, worked 14·3 per cent of the sown area and owned roughly similar proportions of the horses, large horned cattle and pigs (12 per cent, 13 per cent and 10 per cent respectively); in the case of sheep their share rose to 26 per cent, for this was an area where high-grade sheep-raising was well established.[29]

Looking at the data on agrarian unrest in Yekaterinoslav province in 1917, one wonders whether these particulars are as important as the centuries-old traditions of cossackdom. For this differs from the other provinces we have considered in the high proportion of violent incidents, notably armed robberies, which reached their peak in August (one month later than in most other parts of the country). It seems that we are dealing here with the beginnings of the anarchic guerila movement that was to distinguish the Ukraine during the civil war, with Nestor Makhno its most celebrated protagonist. The militia authorities in Petrograd recorded forty-eight incidents between April and September.[30] Our method of calculation yields a figure of fifty-nine, of which twenty-two incidents represent acts of violence and nine the outright seizure of estates. This is appreciably higher than the figure for conflicts over arable (fifteen) and pasture or meadow land (five).[31] The most prominent victims were landowners, some of whom bore Ukrainian names : the unrest was rooted in social rather than national tensions, so that it was no protection to belong to one of the minority groups. German settlers were among those who suffered, while men from one southern Slav community are mentioned as among the aggressors. The violence of these attacks increased as the year wore on, until by September acts of homicide had become commonplace. Later that month three soldiers carried out a raid upon a farm in Verkhnedneprovsk county in the course of which the owner, his servants and a prisoner of war all met their death. The local militia was helpless to intervene and sometimes its members even joined forces with the malefactors.[32]

The main impression afforded by this survey is one of diversity. The 'agrarian movement', at first sight a monolithic phenomenon, resolves itself on closer inspection into a series of disparate engagements, each with its own physiognomy, usually but not invariably rooted in specific socio-economic conflicts. To be sure, the unrest follows a discernible chronological and geographical pattern : it generally reaches a peak in July and is concentrated in particular trouble-spots within each area. But beyond that it is unsafe to generalize without leaving the realm of historical fact for that of ideology, as a study of the different types of action will confirm.

SIXTEEN *The Spread of Agrarian Violence: a Typological Analysis*

IT IS NOT easy to categorize the different types of action undertaken by unruly peasants in pursuit of their basic objective, the transfer of all land, together with other natural resources, into the hands of those who worked it. Measures of various kinds were often taken simultaneously, and the sources generally lack precision in this regard. Unsatisfactory as these materials are, they contain a good deal of scattered information about the characteristics of agrarian unrest in 1917 which lends itself to typological classification. One may distinguish between different forms of protest, beginning with the least violent. As was only natural, the peasants generally sought to undermine their enemies' authority and self-confidence by exercising various kinds of pressure before proceeding to sequester their property or to assault their persons.

The easiest action to take was to deny the proprietors use of the labour force upon which many of them depended to work their land. This labour was of three kinds : prisoners of war, migrants from other districts (including refugees), and local men. The first group was the most obvious target. On 9 April the committee of Shipov district (Yefremov county, Tula province) issued the following peremptory command to Prince Golitsyn, a local squire. 'You are hereby informed that by 10 am on 10 April you are required to send to the district office all prisoners of war employed on agricultural work, since they are needed by the citizens of this district. In cases of non-compliance this order will be enforced by the militia with the utmost severity of the law. Send also their effects and the appropriate papers. Signed....'[1] A landowner named Tolmachev, resident in Nizhniy Novgorod province, reported that as a result of the prisoners' removal 'the field work which was going ahead rapidly has had to stop and the stables are without hands.'[2] In some places the peasants asked only that the captives be paid at the same rate as native agricultural labourers – a demand that was probably motivated less by humanitarian or internationalist sentiments than by a more prosaic concern to maintain current wage levels. In most cases, however, prisoners were prohibited from working for individual proprietors and were made to perform jobs on the peasants' own plots. How extensive this shift was cannot be ascertained. The ministry of Agriculture stated early in 1917 that 600,000 prisoners were engaged on agricultural work.[3] An unofficial survey of ten unspecified provinces made at this time showed that of 41,000 prisoners employed there 19,000 worked on peasant farms and 22,000 on those of individual proprietors.[4] By 1 October the total number of prisoners employed in agriculture had fallen to 431,690, but this figure is not broken down further.[5]

One would like to know more about the prisoners' reactions to this change in their fortunes, their relationship to the new authorities, and their role in spreading 'defeatist' ideas in the villages. According to the vivid but sketchy memoirs of a Swedish Red Cross worker, the February revolution led to a number of easements (including, in some places, the introduction of an eight-hour working day), but these were offset by the effects of rising prices and a reduction in the cash element of their remuneration.[6] The prisoners appreciated the muzhiks' kind and simple ways but found it hard to adjust themselves to their low cultural level. As for their peasant masters, they seem to have had no problem in reconciling the temporary employment of these unfortunates with their moral contempt for the principle of hiring labour. It is worth nothing that most prisoners were employed in the southern half of the country[7] where some of the inhabitants had forsaken communalist principles.

Whereas prisoners could be expected to fall in fairly readily with the local committees' suggestions, a certain amount of persuasion was sometimes necessary in the case of native agricultural labourers. This was particularly the case with seasonal workers from other provinces who were unsure whether they could expect a share of the sequestered land to offset their loss of wages. In Kirsanov county, Tambov province, in July it was said that 'the rye is ripening on the stalk' because local peasants were forcibly preventing migrant labourers from helping with the harvest.[8] In Ranenburg county, Ryazan province – a well-known trouble-spot – activists at first exempted from the employment ban those who looked after the landowners' cattle, but later took more drastic measures, so that the animals had to be slaughtered.[9] In the south-western provinces of Kiev and Podolia, the centre of the sugar-beet industry, and to a lesser extent in the steppe and Baltic provinces, agricultural labourers pressed for higher wages. They also insisted on payment at daily rates in lieu of those fixed in their seasonal contracts.

As a result of these pressures the larger farms, which depended most heavily on hired labour, soon found themselves in grave difficulties. Where the land could not be sown or the crops reaped local peasant activists were presented with a plausible pretext for sequestration, since it was government policy to ensure that not a single dessyatine remained uncultivated. Another consequence of the massive withdrawal of labour was to stimulate tension between different segments of the peasantry.

According to one contemporary analysis of the Main Land Committee's statistics on agrarian unrest between March and August, conflicts involving employment accounted for 268 out of the 2,367 incidents reported, or 11·3 per cent; another 155, or 6·5 per cent, had to do with disputes over rented land.[10] Not too much credence need be placed in these unwarrantedly precise figures, but the overall proportions are probably about right. These were both relatively mild forms of action; if one wonders at the low proportion of disputes over rented land in a rural economy where leasing was so widespread, the explanation is simply that as the year wore on peasants preferred to take more militant measures which made disputes about their contractual obligations obsolete. The effect of these earlier and more limited actions was none the less significant. Those proprietors, particularly in the south-central region, who engaged in such archaic practices as crop-sharing and rack-renting (short-term leases at extortionate rates) soon had to abandon them, and indeed to withdraw from the scene entirely. Many of these men were absentee landlords and their expulsion was no great loss to the economy – although it is only fair to add that some of them were absent only because they were performing military service. These estates were especially vulnerable to peasant action, since the proprietors' strips of arable, pasture or meadow were intermingled with those of the villagers to such an extent that the term estate is really a misnomer.

The simplest and most obvious step which tenants could take was to reduce rent payments, or to cease them altogether. Such unilateral breaches of contract are said to have been most characteristic of the Central Agricultural region.[11] In one instance peasants agreed to pay rent at a fixed percentage (5·5 per cent) of the value of the land, since they calculated that this would provide the owner with a fair return.[12] However, such sophistication and restraint were rare virtues, and even in this instance those concerned soon went on to annul all lease contracts.[13] A more usual practice was to take as the norm the rent charged at some earlier date, such as 1914; sometimes deductions would then be made to take account of 'the present needs of the country' or 'the high cost of living'. In Buguruslansk county, Samara province, the deduction was of the order of seventy-five per cent – a figure later taken over by a congress of peasants from the entire province.[14] In Tambov a committee claiming to speak for the peasants of Kirsanov county lowered rents by a quarter, whereupon some district committees reduced them by a further sixty per cent.[15] In Kharkov province peasants arranged to pay twelve to fifteen roubles in lieu of the forty to fifty roubles charged hitherto.[16]

Where purely nominal sums were paid, such as one to three roubles per dessyatine (when the state land tax alone amounted to three roubles – and this in prosperous Kherson province),[17] the intention was clearly punitive. As was suggested above (cf. p. 170), the Provisional Government might without difficulty have 'frozen' rents at the 1916 rate or fixed maximum levels in different regions of the country; this would at least have strengthened the hand of those who were trying to keep unrest within tolerable bounds. The evidence suggests that until mid-summer only a minority of peasants took the radical course of refusing to pay any rent at all or confiscating leased land; even those who did so were not necessarily opposed to the principle of leasing, since they frequently arranged for confiscated land to be rented out to their fellow-peasants. In these circumstances it appears that a firm policy by the government would have had a beneficial effect.

Encouraged by this weakness in high places, peasants proceeded more and more frequently to inventory and to sequester the property of those who did not belong to the village community. This property comprised various categories of land (forest, pasture and meadow, arable), livestock and agricultural implements, crops in the field or in the barn, farm and residential buildings (along with their gardens, orchards and so on), and finally all manner of household and personal possessions. Weakened by depredations of this kind, its residents frightened into acquiescence, a landed estate or individual peasant farm was ripe for complete confiscation, to be followed by the redistribution among the local inhabitants of such property as had not previously been taken.

During 1917, and still more so in the ensuing years, Russia's woods and forests were the scene of a peculiar kind of guerilla warfare that has yet to find its historian. The importance of the timber industry in the country's economic life, always great, was enhanced by the shortage of coal and oil. Wardens were employed to protect the forests against damage, theft or fires, but these guards could hardly be expected to put up effective resistance to massive assaults, especially when those responsible carried firearms and were backed by local sentiment.

The peasants' attitude was ambiguous. On the one hand they wanted to preserve the forests, along with land of other categories, for the people as a whole (which by definition excluded private ownership); on the other hand they looked to them as a means of satisfying their immediate urgent needs. The contradiction was a matter of theory rather than practice. In so far as the peasants appropriated state-owned timber as freely as that in private hands, it may be said that the second motive was more powerful than the first.[18] Their major concern was to prevent private owners from felling timber or removing stocks which they themselves coveted. This was easily done by refusing to let local men work in the forests and by barring the main exits. Sometimes violence was used against recalcitrant timber-workers: in July a crowd of peasants at Smerd-yach, Novgorod province, assaulted and injured men preparing timber for delivery to two local entrepreneurs.[19] Even fiercer resistance was offered to any move by owners of wooded property to sell it, for this was interpreted (in some cases no doubt correctly) as 'speculation' – that is to say as an attempt to avoid confiscation by exchanging it for cash or other movable assets.[20]

There were complaints by private proprietors that the peasants, while preventing them from exercising their rights, were felling timber extensively themselves. Vorogushinin, a landowner in Cherny county, Tula province, stated that timber worth 12,000 roubles had been felled on his estate, and in nearby Orel the Sharovsk district committee (Sevsk county) allegedly permitted no less than 150,000 roubles worth to be taken from the property of a certain Golynsky.[21] One wonders what was done with such extensive supplies. Some will have been used to repair dwellings, as well as for fuel, but no doubt much of it was put aside in the hope of exchanging it for industrial goods or for foodstuffs from the south. In some areas peasants engaged in a flourishing trade in firewood, which fetched eighty kopecks a pud, or a third as much as rye at the official price.[22]

The grazing of cattle on forest land did considerable damage. Lack of pasture and meadow land had for decades been one of the major weaknesses of Russian agriculture, for the three-field system of cultivation, which was still general, encouraged farmers of all classes to devote an excessive proportion of their land to arable.[23] In the south-central region some unscrupulous squires would lease their hayfields and meadows to the villagers at high rents, taking advantage of the fact that they had no alternative sources of fodder for their cattle. For many of these proprietors the first sign of trouble in 1917 was the appearance on their land of animals that had no right to be there. This step was followed by restrictions upon the landowners' livestock, which was sometimes 'exchanged' for beasts of inferior quality belonging to peasants.[24] Proprietors were often forbidden to sell their animals. Such measures were but the preliminaries to the wholesale confiscation of livestock and horses belonging to those outside the commune. Sometimes they were offered trivial sums in compensation. At Bolshoy Lomov (Morshchansk county, Tambov province) 'a delegate sent by the peasants of Sobinka village appeared at Gorbunov's estate and informed him that the village assembly had decided . . . to requisition his thoroughbreds, paying him one rouble apiece.'[25] Gorbunov also lost his woodland, but was apparently left with a portion of his arable.

Unfortunately, although understandably, the reports sent in to the militia about the confiscation of land and crops are seldom precise as to the quantity which was taken; where a figure is given, it is difficult to evaluate its significance without knowing its relationship to the total acreage of land in different categories owned by the individual concerned. This prevents one from assessing accurately the impact of the government's effort to restrict seizures to land left uncultivated. Reports poured in that peasants were appropriating not only uncultivated or fallow land but also arable which had been ploughed and sown. Although the measures adopted by the local land committees were supposed to be temporary, pending the definitive settlement to be authorized by the Constituent Assembly, everyone concerned realized that this was a fiction. It was an axiom of rural life that 'he who sowed shall reap'. But this axiom was interpreted in a one-sided manner; if peasants sowed privately owned land, the crop was theirs (and by implication the land also); but so too was land sown by the proprietors, whose rights were deemed to have fallen into abeyance. If such appropriations could be speciously represented as having been undertaken for patriotic reasons, to keep the land in cultivation, so much the better; if this pretext were lacking, it was not too difficult to find another. There was virtually nothing the proprietor could do. In some places peasants trooped into the fields, mowed the grass or reaped the corn, and promptly took it off to their own barns; elsewhere they might wait until the crop had been dried and stacked, or even stored, before appropriating it. The situation was well summed up in a report from Lebedyan county, Tambov province, in the latter half of July 'Throughout the county land is being seized. The private proprietors are first placed in a situation that makes it impossible for them to carry on farming, and then the land committees, referring to the general interests of the state, ordain that these lands should be transferred to the peasants.'[26]

Another matter on which one regrets the lack of precision in the sources is that of compensation. Some landowners were offered derisory sums for their land or crops, as for their livestock. A sum of two or three roubles per dessyatine was all that the peasants of Kamashkir district (Saratov province) were prepared to give the proprietress Motovilova when they confiscated her land in July – and she could count herself fortunate, since many others got nothing.[2] On the other hand, there were instances where proprietors were given a portion of the crop, evidently to tide them over until the general repartition, or were even allowed to retain a portion of the land. The assumption here was that the community could afford to tolerate in its midst a few ex-landowners who had been 'rendered harmless', as it were, by sequestration of most of their belongings. It is impossible to say how widespread this practice was. In the Volga provinces, where some areas had ample land, the peasants were inclined to be liberal, and figures of 80–100 dessyatines are encountered.[28] Normally fifty dessyatines seems to have been regarded as the maximum area permissible in this region. Such compromises did not, however, last long.

Violence had been in the air ever since the spring of 1917, and the restraint shown at first was soon abandoned as the temptations increased. Threats of assault were uttered against proprietors or their dependants, who could not fail to realize that it was only a question of time before they were put into effect. Among the victims, as we have seen, were local officials, even those who had been elected to their post and served without pay; merchants, priests and fellow-peasants deemed disloyal to the community were other likely targets. The group most exposed to popular wrath were the managers in charge of estates whose proprietors were either on active service or resident elsewhere. Some of these men had made enemies by excessive zeal on behalf of their employers, for example in the collection of rents, but even those who had given no such cause for hostility became objects of suspicion. Near Novgorod a farm manager named Kolpakov was expelled from the area for having said, in an address to a peasant meeting, that counter-revolution was a possibility, as after 1905; this remark, intended as a warning against extremism, was taken by his audience as a sign that he wanted a return to the old regime.[29] Elsewhere managers were accused of improperly evading military service and were handed over to the authorities for appropriate action to be taken.[30]

During the spring searches of landowners' homes were carried out on various pretexts in a number of areas. In Voronezh province 'the village committee at Gorozhanka, Zadonsk county, arbitrarily inspected the house of N. Mikhaylovskaya, took away some hunting rifles, and sealed up her effects'.[31] From this it was but a step to placing suspects under arrest. In July the wife of a serving officer named Ushkanov, who lived alone with two small children at Aleshanka in Orel province, reported that she had become embroiled in a dispute between communal and independent peasants in the locality; when she refused to sign a petition on behalf of the former, she was arrested by a soldier, V.S. Byvshikh, who entered her house along with a group of villagers, whereupon the provincial commissar had intervened to obtain her release.[32] The local activists did not yet control the penal institutions and had nowhere to detain those whom they arrested. This may help to explain why they did not resort more frequently to the practice of taking hostages.[33] The main object of such arrests was probably psychological : to create a climate of insecurity which would oblige landowners and others to surrender their land, and eventually to abandon their homes altogether.

How far the campaign succeeded in achieving this aim it is again difficult to say. There are no statistics on the movements of the 2·4 million or so persons who lived on individual farms. Most of the young men were away on war service; and most such farms were looked after by relatives – often mothers or wives. (This accounts for the high proportion of women among those who submitted complaints to the militia.) Although some persons will have sought sanctuary in the towns, it appears that the greater number remained at home, despite the unpleasantness and danger involved, and hoped for better times.

Until September at least most assaults seem to have taken place in the course of armed robberies. It is impossible to draw a clear line between incidents of agrarian protest and ordinary criminal acts. We have already noted that banditry was widespread in Yekaterinoslav province (and by extension throughout the steppe zone); for rather different reasons it was also frequent in areas close to the western front. The object of these attacks was twofold : to intimidate the victims and to obtain funds, goods or foodstuffs. Some proprietors hired guards to protect their homes. These men naturally became a prime target for raiders. Ordinary domestic employees were not exempt either, and some of them lost their lives. In Voronezh province two members of the Shkarin family, who may have been brother and sister, each owned an estate. On the former's land the victims included the manager and his daughter, a housemaid and a guard; on the latter no harm seems to have befallen the servants but the proprietress herself perished.[34]

One early western investigator of these events noted that the murder of managers was 'infrequent' and that only an infinitesimal number of proprietors were killed.[35] These homicides must, however, be seen against the background of other forms of violence. It is true that the aroused peasants generally shrank from taking men's lives, as distinct from their property. This may be attributed in part to a residual concern for religious or humanitarian values and in part, more prosaically, to a fear of reprisals. At a guess, the number of landowners or their dependants who lost their lives was probably less than the number of robbers, bandits and deserters who met a similar fate. The militia records abound in instances of the latter kind.[36] Most members of the élite who lost their lives were killed in the course of armed robberies in which some allowance may be made for the aggressors' desperation and anxiety; they were not shot down in cold blood – the fate meted out to countless thousands by Cheka executioners during the years that followed. In 1917 one of the few recorded cases of landowners being lynched occurred in Simbirsk as early as March, when a wealthy proprietor named Gelshert was put to death by a crowd which had been led to believe that he was a traitor.[37] Another source of fatalities in the agrarian context was inter-ethnic conflict, particularly in Perm province, where Russians and Bashkirs sometimes clashed over territorial rights.[38]

By September the rural activists' patience was wearing thin – or perhaps one should say that their appetites had been whetted by the successes they had won. With the harvest all but gathered in, the moment seemed to have come for a final reckoning with the relics of the old agrarian order. The *pogrom*, or violent sacking, of an estate by an irate mob, which had been a relative rarity during the previous months, or at least had been restricted to certain well-defined trouble-spots (notably Spassky county, Kazan province), now came into its own as a characteristic phenomenon. One must hasten to add that even so it was localized in the overcrowded black-soil provinces and had a distinct focus in Tambov. The remoter causes of this wave of destruction and vandalism must be sought in land hunger and other ancient grievances, but the immediate catalyst seems to have been a specific incident : the murder, on 24 August, of Prince Boris L. Vyazemsky, a distinguished local figure noted for his liberal views. A crowd of peasants, said to be five thousand strong, invested his estate at Lotarevo (Usman county), which was one of the most advanced in the region and for this reason had been placed under government protection. Having fortified their courage with alcohol from the prince's cellars, they arrested Vyazemsky and his wife. The former was taken under escort to the nearest railway station, where he was set upon and put to death by soldiers from a passing troop-train. The mob then went on to sack a neighbouring estate. The affair was thought sufficiently serious for a judicial investigation to be held, as a result of which four persons were arrested, but the authorities were forced to hand the men over to the peasants of a neighbouring village.[39]

Attacks followed on several other estates, especially in Kozlov district, in the course of which two of the aggressors were shot by a landowner named K.P. Romanov.[40] This incident added further fuel to the fire. On 12 September the Kozlov section of the land-owners' association stated that twenty-four estates had been burned within three days.[41] A correspondent added : 'a rumour is spreading among the peasants that unless they take the land by 20 September it will be too late.'[42] Another legend was that Kerensky himself (evidently seen as a personal embodiment of the state power) had authorized the seizures. Anonymous letters, evidently written by semi-literates, were said to have circulated in which prospective victims were indicated. When questioned, peasants would say : 'Some unknown persons descended upon us, a dozen or so of them on horseback, who fired rifle shots into the air [and said] "Hey, come out and rob the lords, set fire to the estates. Who is not with us is against us. Whoever does not join in the burning will have it hot from us." '[43] Among the first estates to be attacked was that of a zemstvo leader named Ushakov, who had contributed to the well-being of the local people by building a school. He had said publicly that the peasants might have his land provided they left him his house and garden. But the mob, 'rendered savage by some incompre-hensible malice, broke into the house, dragged the furniture into the garden, and while the men, to the sound of a harmonica, set light to the house, the women, in their red skirts and gaily coloured kerchiefs, sat with their feet on a divan, singing and cursing with gusto.' The incendiaries also burned stocks of rye, despite Ushakov's pleas that this was earmarked for supply to troops at the front.[44]

On 15 September a detachment of troops, including cossack cavalry and armoured cars, arrived in Kozlov county from Moscow. Martial law was declared and meetings forbidden. At the village of Saburovka the troops succeeded in preventing the destruction of an estate, but elsewhere the disorders flared up anew. The soldiers of the 204th infantry regiment, stationed at Tambov, who had been responsible for some of the trouble, were compelled to lay down their arms, and by 25 September the provincial commissar, K.

Shatov, could claim that 'order is being restored in all counties. The culprits are being arrested and the property they have seized is being taken from them.'[45] There was some substance to the commissar's claim. On 10 October, in his next official fortnightly survey, he could state that there had been no further mass violence. He attributed this to the fact that the local land committees had taken all estates in the province under their supervision for immediate transfer;[46] but it might be equally true to say that the peasant activists could now relax because they had achieved their immediate aim.

This victory had been achieved at a considerable cost. Commissar Shatov stated that in Kozlov county alone fifty-four farms had been sacked, wholly or in part, including sixteen that had been burned. About a third of the losses, it is worth stressing, were suffered by peasants, mostly 'separators' from the commune.[47] A more recent calculation for Tambov province as a whole puts the figure at 105 estates and 'several dozen' peasant farms.[48] These figures need to be set beside that given in the 1916 census for the total number of 'private-proprietorial' farms, which was 3,075.[49]

Tambov was not the only province to be so afflicted. News of the events in Kozlov county, transmitted through the press as well as by word of mouth, soon reached other areas with similar problems. From the village of Zykov in Ryazan province we have an eye-witness account of the destruction of an estate which bears reproduction in full, so vivid is the picture it gives of the way in which the mob proceeded.

At mid-day the village assembly met to decide the fate of our property, which was large and well equipped. The question to be decided was posed with stark simplicity: should they burn the house or not? At first they decided just to take all our belongings and to leave the building. But this decision did not satisfy some of those present, and another resolution was passed: to burn everything except the house, which was to be kept as a school. At once the whole crowd moved off to the estate, took the keys from the manager, and commandeered all the cattle, farm machinery, carriages, stores etc. For two days they carried off whatever they could. Then they split into groups of 20, divided up the loot into heaps, one for each group, and cast lots which group should get which. In the very middle of this redistribution a sailor appeared, a local lad who had been on active service. He insisted that they should burn down the house as well. The peasants got clever. They went off to inspect the house a second time. One of them said : 'What sort of a school would this make? Our children would get lost in it.' Thereupon they decided to burn it down [the next day]. They went home quietly leaving a guard of 20 men, who had a regular feast : they heated the oven, butchered a sheep, some geese, ducks and hens, and ate their fill until dawn. . . . Thus the night passed. The whole village assembled and once again the axes began to strike. . . . They chopped out the windows, doors and floors, smashed the mirrors and divided up the pieces, and so on. At three o'clock in the afternoon they set light to the house from all sides, using for the purpose eight *chetverti* of kerosene.

The account ends with an unsuccessful approach by the narrator – the daughter of the proprietor concerned – to the local militia chief, who said he had no men to spare. Other local authorities were no more sympathetic.[50]

The movement spread northwards into Nizhniy Novgorod province, eastwards to Penza, and westwards to Tula and Orel. Still further west, across the Dnieper, the provinces of Podolia and Volhynia were also the scene of disorders. These seem to have been generated locally, and not to have had any direct connection with those in the southern-central region. In numerical terms the greatest damage was done in Penza, where 164 estates were sacked in September and October (and 267 in the seven months May to November), or about a fifth of the total (1,280 in 1916). About two hundred estates are thought to have been destroyed in the right-bank Ukraine, and according to one authority half as many in Podolia alone. For Orel province we have a figure of 98 estates, along with 6 liquor distilleries and 1 sugar refinery (the total number of properties being 2,644). No estimate is available for Ryazan; in three counties of Nizhniy Novgorod 41 estates are known to have been sacked, and in Voronezh the number is put at 26.[51] In very approximate terms, about one thousand properties were sacked and looted during this period, of which approximately a third belonged to peasants. As one western historian has recently remarked,[52] this was only one per cent of the total number. However, it has to be remembered that of the remainder a considerable proportion (how large it is impossible to say) had lost all or part of their land, which had in effect become unworkable.

Whether these events amount to a 'peasant war' – the standard term used in Soviet historiography, derived from an expression used at the time by Lenin (who took it from Engels) – must remain a matter of opinion. On one hand violent destruction of estates was restricted to a fairly well-defined region of the country; on the other it represented a climax in the history of the 'agrarian movement' (the subsequent redistribution of property being another). For this reason some general remarks on the nature of the phenomenon are in order here.

So far as the motives for these attacks is concerned, one is tempted to say that fear and envy were mixed in equal proportions. Obviously the threat of famine was a potent spur to action, but this was far from a self-sufficient cause (as one recent western writer has argued)[53] – and in any case hunger pangs are not quenched by setting fire to a bulging barn. The fear may well have been enhanced by Kornilov's bid for power, news of which will have reached the peasants in garbled form; correspondingly, the self-evident weakness of the counter-revolutionaries will have helped to stimulate them to violent action. A feeling of 'now or never' was widespread. If the communally minded villagers let the opportunity slip, something like the old agrarian order might yet be re-established. One man explained in quaint language what this aim was: 'the *muzhiki* are destroying the squires' nests so that the little bird will never be able to return' – the 'bird' here being a euphemism for large-scale landed property in general. The era was past when gradual reform might have seemed a preferable alternative: the February overturn had encouraged the peasants to hope that they might at last become masters of their destiny. These feelings were further stimulated by the soldiers and other politically motivated persons who streamed into the villages during the summer. The peasants put their own construction on the information that reached them about events in the towns or at the front. The term *burzhuy* (bourgeois) was used wildly to denote any real or presumed foe of the *muzhik*.[54] Activists preached that it was lawful to make war on the bourgeoisie: so the peasants went into battle in the only way they knew. The individual proprietors bore the brunt of their attacks because they were the most vulnerable of all 'outsiders', excluded from the closed world of the commune. The agrarian movement was neither a product of external agitation, nor a manifestation of class struggle. It was a phenomenon *sui generis* – plebeian, anarchic and anti-centralist.

Its archaic features were most evident in the effort to avenge ancient wrongs, in the joy with which the common people destroyed the symbols of their former subjection. Only this can explain such wilful and malicious acts as chopping down fruit-trees, ploughing up parks, smashing greenhouses and diverting water from ornamental fish-ponds. When confronted with objects whose value was not understood – libraries, works of art and other cultural objects – the mob followed its instincts, which suggested that these fancies were of no use to ordinary folk and should therefore be destroyed. With its pronounced levelling tendencies the agrarian movement exemplified the dynamic force behind the Russian revolution itself.

Despite this egalitarianism, or perhaps even because of it, there were bound to be conflicts among the beneficiaries. Most obviously, one commune might stand against another when it came to dividing up the confiscated booty (cf. below, pp. 411–12). Less obviously, there were gradations of view within the same community, based partly on social position and partly on differences of age, sex and temperament. The activists – where they were local men – were recruited from among the village youth, especially adolescents who faced the disagreeable prospect of military service. The patriarchs and those who walked in their shadow felt threatened by the new spirit of lawlessness and disrespect for authority. A peasant from Putivl county, Kursk province, noted that those households consisting wholly of women did not join in the sacking of estates.[55] (On the other hand in Minsk province one peasant woman soundly abused her spouse for carelessly smashing his share of the loot when other raiders showed more skill.)[56] Conventional ideas on morality and religion, as we have noted, also acted as a restraining force. Sometimes the clergy intervened in an effort to persuade the peasants to reconsider their actions – which might lead to the priest being deprived of his land along with that of the intended victim.[57] Although priests are sometimes said to have participated in village committees, there is no evidence that they sanctioned violence.[58] Fifteen peasants refused to join the villagers of Milshino (Venev county, Tula province), in sacking the estate of Princess Volkonskaya, although they were threatened with reprisals. 'There were cases', our informant adds, 'where peasants were forcibly dragged to the assembly and given their share of the confiscated property and told "if anyone is to answer for this, we all shall do so".'[59]

Were these men kulaks? Unfortunately it is impossible, on the basis of the evidence presently available, to reach firm conclusions about the attitude taken by the more well-to-do peasants (inside and outside the commune) towards the seizure of squires' land. In some cases they identified with their fellow-proprietors; in others they stood aside; on occasion they took part, often under duress; in a very few cases they are said to have taken the initiative – presumably in order to deflect popular wrath from themselves.[60] One eye-witness (the landowner S.P. Rudnev in Simbirsk province) states that none of the wealthier peasants attended the auction of his property because they thought it wrong to enrich themselves at others' expense.[61] There is, however, ample evidence of such persons taking a less altruistic attitude.

As for the victims of the 'agrarian movement', these included persons of every social group. The position of the 'separators' was if anything even less enviable than that of the great proprietors, for if dispossessed they had no obvious alternative source of subsistence. In Simbirsk province the villagers of Kuranino and Ardatovo are reported to have beaten, arrested and humiliated the local *otrubshchiki*. (The very term, meaning 'those who had cut themselves off', was an affront to the commune's egalitarian conscience.) Not far away, at Andreyevo, the wives of three soldiers who owned enclosed farms (*khutora*) were beaten by the villagers and made to sign documents agreeing that their plots should revert to the collective domain.[62] Such instances were by no means rare. Soldiers, too, might have their property confiscated while absent on active service, which meant that their wives and families would be left without any means of sustenance other than their meagre government allowance.[63] It has often been stated, in general accounts of the revolution, that the high rate of desertion from the Russian army during the summer and autumn of 1917 was motivated by a concern among the soldiers that, unless they were present at home, they would suffer a disadvantage when the confiscated land was repartitioned. There is little evidence of such sentiments during this period, although it may well have been a factor after the October revolution, when it became clear that a general redistribution of the land was imminent and had the backing of the new government.

With this phase of the agrarian movement we shall be concerned later. Here we may conclude by noting that the unrest that spread through the rural areas during these months was both cause and consequence of the general state of anarchy in the country : the rebellious peasants took advantage of the government's weakness to press their sectional claims, and this offensive in turn undermined respect for the public authorities. The economic consequences, too, were little less than catastrophic, even though, as noted above (p. 184), the disturbances were not the *principal* cause of this decline, and were not perceived as such by most city folk. Not only did the peasants consume (or destroy) much of the commercial crop : they also, in their eagerness to sow the confiscated land, neglected their own allotments.[64] Even some of the confiscated land was left fallow, since seed grain was short and there were more exciting things to do. This reduction in the sown area led to a critical situation during the years of civil war. Ironically enough the agrarian movement, which was a *sine qua non* of the Bolsheviks' accession to power, also presented them with their most challenging domestic problem.

SEVENTEEN *Formation of Rural Primary Organizations and Soviets*

THE SEQUESTRATIONS OF property and acts of violence discussed above were in many cases inspired, if not directed, by one or other of the countless *ad hoc* bodies that sprang up among the peasantry during this period. Ephemeral as these organizations usually turned out to be, they nevertheless acquired a considerable importance at the time owing to the lack of any coherent structure of regular, legitimate authorities in the countryside. The vacuum was filled by self-constituted bodies. We still know relatively little about these village and district committees or soviets, partly because they were so soon bent to serve another purpose: to establish in the countryside a regime committed to proletarian dictatorship.

When news of the tsar's abdication reached a village community, the assembly (*skhod*) would forgather to consider the matter, as it was wont to do when any major event occurred. Such meetings were normally attended by all heads of households, but the war had disrupted the tenor of community life and in many villages all adults (women included) had won a tacit right to be present. The information at the disposal of the *skhod* was often garbled and contradictory, so that messengers (*khodoki*) were sometimes sent to the provincial capital, or even to Petrograd, to find out the truth.

Particularly in the capital these men came into contact with revolutionary activists and returned home convinced that the great problems of land and peace would soon be settled in accordance with popular wishes. Frequently village assemblies would adopt formal resolutions, addressed to members of the duma, the government or the Petrograd soviet. A few of these resolutions found their way into the press. They were universally favourable to the new order and often promised it their support; but they also made it clear that the peasants expected the new regime to meet their demands. These aspirations centred upon the land problem, but not to the exclusion of more general issues, notably establishment of a democratic republic, convocation of the Constituent Assembly, administrative decentralization and provision of free education.[1]

Simultaneously or later there often came into being a committee which spoke in the village's name. Unfortunately there is no evidence as to the way in which these spokesmen were chosen. It was probably just a matter of 'natural selection' : the new spirit in the air made the village's traditional chiefs feel uncomfortable, and they either withdrew from the scene or were effaced; their place was taken by younger men, most of whom had in the past been identified with progressive causes and had actively opposed the *status quo* inside or outside the community. Village politics in Russia had been largely an affair of 'ins' versus 'outs' – a contest between two leadership groups, standing respectively for and against change, and competing for the allegiance of the other householders. Now that the wind from above was blowing in a different direction, this silent majority quite naturally shifted its support to the new chiefs. Where there was conflict, it will often have been between the under-twenties and over-forties, since the intermediate generation of menfolk had been thinned by the war. Women do not appear to have been thought suitable for election to positions of responsibility on the new committees.

The term 'committee' should not be interpreted too legalistically. The word had a fashionable ring, and it may be significant that one of the first recorded instances of its use by villagers was in the immediate vicinity of Petrograd (at Ivanovo, Shlisselburg county), where a 'people's committee' appeared as early as 8 March.[2] Other villages which took such an initiative early in March were situated in Kaluga province, which had close ties with Moscow.[3] In the weeks and months that followed similar executive organs emerged all over the country. Formally they derived their authority from the village assembly, but in the revolutionary climate no one was inclined to look too closely into their credentials. Nor should one draw too hard and fast a line between village and district committees, whose membership and functions overlapped.

The normal course of events was that, once a number of neighbouring villages had formed such committees, their leaders would come together and set up a district committee; this might then regularize its existence by seeking the approval of the village assemblies concerned. Thus in Murikovsk district (Moscow province) on 9 April 'the peasants of the district met in a full district assembly, and having discussed the main issues, decided to establish a district committee, as an administrative-political [and] economic unit to manage all the affairs of the district; it was to comprise thirty-five members, one representative of each village (or two for those that had more than fifty households); and to appoint as executive board (*pravleniye*) of the committee five men elected by the latter.'[4] The influence of urban ways is particularly apparent here, and this example, with its two-tier structure, was probably not typical. The number of members varied according to the size of the district and the amount of support shown in the various villages. In Orel province there were said to be from fifteen to sixty-six persons in the district committees, but in Penza only three;[5] the latter was presumably an executive. There was nothing regular or systematic about these organs and their membership was notoriously unstable. In Kharkov province critics called them 'one-day wonders' (*odnodnevki*), alluding to the fact that they tended to appear and disappear with such disconcerting frequency.[6]

At first some of them took a conservative stand. At Semenovka (Khorol county, Poltava province) the village committee was reported in June to have defined its tasks as helping the Provisional Government to fight counter-revolution, to increase supplies of grain for the army, and to promote mutual aid, especially on behalf of the families of serving soldiers.[7] However, it was not long before these committees began to issue declarations threatening measures against the foes of the community and to follow up such menaces with actions of the type analysed above. As the agricultural season advanced, diverting men's attention to more immediate concerns, many committees lapsed into limbo. Sometimes the original peasant leaders might be superseded by, say, the local teacher : this was the case in Ponigov district (Toropets county, Pskov province), where the teacher is said to have closed down the local school and to have devoted himself entirely to political agitation.[8] Sometimes the activists, whether they were peasants or not, became engrossed in the political turmoil at a higher level and lost touch with their home district.

Where a committee met regularly, it did so on a Sunday, when its members were free from agricultural work. If it had enough money, its representatives might be allotted 100 to 150 roubles a month to cover expenses.[9] Such funds were obtained, both at the district and village level, from the sale of confiscated stock and produce or from the leasing of land. Another source was levies upon members of the community – with the proprietors, if any were left, naturally paying a higher share. Some of the more moderately inclined committees opened bank accounts, on the assumption that they would later be required to account for their management of sequestered property. Elsewhere less scrupulous methods were adopted, and inevitably there were accusations that members had engaged in corrupt practices.

In the early months of the revolution, at any rate, the village and district committees seem to have represented fairly accurately the attitudes of those peasants who had any opinion to express. Cases are known where priests, merchants, intellectuals and even landowners were elected to such bodies. At Semenovka the twenty-six-man committee included the priest, who was however in no position to exercise leadership. He is said to have denounced the new order from the pulpit and then to have undergone a political conversion which undermined whatever moral authority he may once have had; he was not chosen as a member of the four-man 'presidium' which directed the village's affairs.[10] In Kozlov county, Tambov province, the peasants of one district elected (or at any rate accepted) as a member of their committee Prince B.L. Vyazemsky, who, as we have seen (p. 209) was to suffer such a tragic fate during the agrarian riots later in the year.[11]

However, as a rule these were genuinely peasant institutions. They were staffed in the main by young peasants who had been brought up in the rural milieu and knew something of its problems, and whose outlook had been broadened by military service or by contact with the towns. They owed their positions of authority mainly to the fact that they were more articulate and enterprising than their fellows. They were in no sense of the word intellectuals. Some of them were even illiterate, as is evident from the fact that resolutions passed by the committee had to be signed on their behalf by their fellows. Occasionally the district clerk (*pisar'*) put his pen at the service of the new authority, as emerges from the use, in declarations issued on its behalf, of a kind of bastard bureaucratic jargon.[12] This practice was said to be widespread in Volhynia.[13] Apart from their native intuition these committee-men had no particular qualifications for political leadership. They shared a general commitment to 'democracy' as this term was popularly understood in the Russia of 1917 (that is to say as a synonym for social equality), but they rarely had any definite political affiliation.

Where district committees became more politicized, and particularly where they called themselves soviets, this was often the result of extraneous influence. As early as 6 March leaders of the Moscow soviet of workers' deputies conferred with sixteen emissaries from villages close to the city; at the conclusion of their talks a statement was issued to the effect that 'the toiling peasants should go hand in hand with the workers and the people's army in defending the freedom that has been won' and – in more practical terms – that when the peasants returned to their villages they should dismiss any local officials inherited from the old regime and replace them by elected authorities of their own.[14] A number of urban soviets set up 'peasant sections' or 'provincial departments' to maintain contact with the countryside. Particularly energetic in this respect was the so-called Moscow regional soviet bureau (MOBYUS), which had a staff of nine 'instructors', as these professional propagandists were euphemistically called.[15] The Moscow city soviet also received appeals from local peasant leaders, some of them couched in deferential terms, imploring it to send 'organizers to acquaint us with the new order'.[16]

In response to such invitations, and to further their own political aims, a wide variety of urban bodies dispatched emissaries, armed with appropriate mandates, to preach the new gospel. Prince Lvov (here acting in his capacity as minister of Interior) later reported to the cabinet that on 26 March the militia first became aware :

... that parties, trade unions and various hybrid organizations [i.e. soviets?] based on Petrograd and Moscow were sending agents to the villages to organize the peasant proprietors (*sic*) and to spread among them their programmes for agrarian reform (*sic*). Later information established beyond doubt that a similar 'movement to the people' occurred in most of the provincial capitals, as a result of which from 25 March to 10 April the village was subjected to systematic investigation and instruction.[17]

The comparison with the benign 'movement to the people' of the 1870s was inept. The main purpose of these emissaries was of course not to 'investigate and instruct' but to form rural soviets which, like those in the towns, would act as an alternative focus of power to the government. Indeed, it was partly to combat this subversion that on 20 March Lvov himself instructed the provincial commissars to set up district committees 'where necessary', based on any organizations (such as cooperatives) that already existed at this level, including the self-constituted district committees where these 'enjoyed the trust of the population'. Local intellectuals and landowners should be invited to participate in such officially sponsored district committees, which were to be entrusted with administrative tasks pending the establishment of a district zemstvo.[18] This policy was sensible enough, and in more normal times might have sufficed to bring the popular organs under a measure of control. How many such officially sponsored district committees came into being is not known. In Vologda province, a relatively calm area, a quarter of the district committees are said to have been of this kind.[19] They do not seem to have been particularly numerous or effective, and the government made no concerted effort to follow up its initiative in a systematic manner.

The way was thus open for a proliferation both of self-constituted district committees and rural soviets. The difference between these two kinds of organization was probably obscure to most persons involved in them. After all, a soviet was no more than a council, and the term had not yet acquired the peculiar mystique that later became attached to it. For the organizers themselves the distinction was twofold. First, a soviet was seen as inherently superior to a district committee; the most desirable course, in their view, was for the latter to merge with the former and to change its title accordingly; if the committee insisted on preserving its identity, then at least it should take orders from the soviet. Second, the soviet was seen as pre-eminently a political organization, linked to the whole nation-wide 'soviet movement'. The distinction between the two organs was epitomized by the presence on the soviet of intellectuals and other persons extraneous to rural society.

These intellectuals were Socialist-Revolutionaries by political affiliation, who looked upon the rural soviets as useful instruments for strengthening their own party's hold upon the countryside.[20] The SRs and Mensheviks still controlled nearly all urban soviets, and the organizational scheme proposed for the rural soviets was modelled upon that which already existed in the towns.

On 1 April an SR newspaper published a statute drawn up by the party's Moscow branch for the soviet of Moscow province which is worth looking at closely.[21] It began with a statement to the effect that the peasants, as 'the overwhelming majority of the population', needed to have 'an organ to express their ideas and aspirations as well as to defend their interests'. This catered to the prevalent sentiment that the urban workers had contrived to win an alleviation in their lot by organizing soviets and that it was highest time for their country cousins to do the same. The drafters passed over in silence the fact that such 'organs' already existed in the form of village and district committees. Their functions were specified in the broadest terms. Clause four outlined a quasi-hierarchical structure for soviets at the district, county and provincial level, 'with an All-Russian Soviet of Peasant Deputies at the apex'. For district soviets the rural population was to choose one representative for every two hundred inhabitants by universal direct suffrage, but thereafter elections were to be indirect; the provincial soviet was to consist of ten men chosen from each county soviet. At all levels these bodies were to elect executives, which on no account were to have less than five members. These executives were 'recommended to form bureaux of assistance, attracting useful and knowledgeable persons'.

Whatever the intentions of the framers of this document, it was clearly a recipe for bureaucracy rather than democracy. In 1917 Moscow province had a rural population of about 1·5 million, who resided in 13 counties with a total of 167 districts. Had this scheme been adopted, 7,500 men would have been required to serve on the district soviets, 1,500 on those at the county level and 130 on that of the province; 900 would have been needed for various executive posts, assuming that the five-man minimum was adhered to in every case. Had the statute been implemented, where would the men and money have been found? A great deal of power would be concentrated in the hands of the mysterious 'useful and knowledgeable persons' – by whom was presumably meant the local PSR leaders.

In practice the latter did not bother about holding elections according to this complicated scheme, but simply called a provincial congress, which met at the end of April.[22] Within a few weeks the Moscow provincial soviet found it necessary to set up within its executive committee a bureau of twelve members to do 'all the current work'; within this bureau there was a three-man presidium. The same process of centralization was taking place here as in the urban soviets. The Moscow provincial soviet acquired an executive apparatus in the form of five departments (organization, representation in other bodies, finance, editorial and consultation).[23] Its leaders, to their credit, did try to maintain connections with their political base. At the end of July it was decided that provincial congresses should be convened monthly, and that county representatives should report back to their constituents each month.[24] However, the force of these measures was undermined by a provision that each county was to supply two persons to sit constantly on the provincial executive – so inflating its membership by twenty-six and turning it into a deliberative body.

A fatal logic led these would-be democrats, neglectful as they were of elementary principles of public administration, to create a monstrous apparatus which, in other hands, would serve as an instrument for subjugating the peasantry.[25] What was done in Moscow province would later be repeated throughout the countryside. The constitution-makers regulated some matters in elaborate detail, yet left the most important points vague, such as the relationship between executive and plenum. As in the urban soviets, this could lead only to a loss of authority by the deliberative assemblies in favour of a coterie of activists taking decisions in secret.

It is difficult to say how far this process took place with the connivance of the leaders concerned. Certainly the latter lost no time in taking steps to safeguard their authority. In this respect developments in Samara province are illuminating. Late in March the local Populist leaders arranged what was called a provincial peasant congress attended by twenty-two persons, all counties being represented. How they were chosen is not made clear; but it is plain that the radical politicians were present in force. This gathering adopted a detailed resolution on abolishing private landed property, in conformity with the SR programme, and an 'instruction' (*nakaz*) on the formation of committees at no less than four levels. The provincial executive was to 'form part of the provisional committee of people's power of Samara province', that is to merge with a committee of urban intellectuals that had not been elected by anybody.[26] A twenty-one-man body soon came into being, calling itself the Samara soviet of peasant deputies, and an executive committee, both consisting of 'authentic peasants'. In the words of the chairman of the executive, Sokolov, 'they were faced with responsible work which required all kinds of knowledge, and this knowledge of course they did not have. [Therefore] on 3 May the executive committee [or rather Sokolov?] co-opted several Samara intellectuals and decided to call a congress for 20 May.'[27]

At this congress, which at its height was attended by some five hundred persons, a strong undercurrent of left-wing sentiment made itself felt. It took the form not only of demands for immediate expropriation of the land but of dissatisfaction at the arrogance of the intellectuals. One delegate exclaimed : 'once again learned and intelligent people are being foisted upon us, but we don't need such people.' From the floor came demands that representatives of the political parties should not be given full voting rights in peasant organizations.[28] Perhaps in response to this pressure, the leaders found it necessary to specify the composition of the provincial executive. It was to have ten representatives from each of the seven counties in the province (presumably delegated by their assemblies, although this was not stated) and one from each county committee. To these seventy-seven rustics were to be added twenty-three persons 'elected by the whole congress from among those comrades with the greatest capacity for work' – that is to say radical politicians. The latter comprised twenty-one Socialist-Revolutionaries and two Social Democrats.[29] Thereby was created a body with the prestigious and symbolic number of a hundred members. It does not take much imagination to see which of these centurions were likely to emerge as the real masters of the Samara provincial soviet. The organization remained formally loyal to the Provisional Government so long as the latter existed,[30] but whether its practical activity was of assistance to that government is another question. The agrarian unrest in Samara province derived a considerable fillip from the decisions taken at the May congress, which despite their relatively moderate wording were interpreted by the peasants as giving them *carte blanche* to confiscate private property.[31]

Similar congresses were held in many other places during the spring which led to the formation of provincial soviets, or at any rate executives. Since all the territorial organizations in the area concerned were invited to attend, they were termed 'congresses of peasant deputies' rather than congresses of soviets. The initiative in convoking them seems invariably to have sprung from the SRS, and it was they who set the tone of the proceedings. But what kind of SRS were they? Already by May 1917 a vocal left-wing element had appeared, which stood for an early end to the war and an immediate start on socializing the land. For these men the provincial congresses were a valuable sounding board : both B. Kamkov and A.L. Kolegayev, two prominent leaders of what became the Left SR party, first emerged at the Kazan congress (13 May), which resolved that all that province's land resources should be put at the disposition of the district committees without delay.[32] This was one of the most radical of such congresses; so too was the one held in Penza on the following two days.[33] In both cases some Bolshevik activists were also involved, but the positions of leadership were in SR hands.

Most of these congresses, especially those which took the most radical decisions, were in the turbulent provinces of the black-soil zone. In the north the peasants were in less excitable mood, while the local SRS were often preoccupied with other matters; in the west the army authorities generally seem to have prevented such assemblies from being held until later in the year (although one was held in Minsk in April which took a left-wing stance). The most important provincial congress outside the black-soil zone seems to have been that in Petrograd province, held on 11–12 May. Its resolution on the land question was relatively moderate, by the standards of the time, since it specified that stock and buildings should remain in private ownership.[34] Restraint was also a keynote of the resolution passed at the congress in Moscow province referred to above.[35] However, one has to be careful not to read too much into paper statements of this kind, which had a purely formal significance. Rank-and-file activists did not consider themselves bound by the letter of their provisions. With ordinary peasants what counted was their general tone; the qualifying phrases and subtle shades of meaning were ignored. In practice it mattered little whether a congress was 'moderate' or 'radical' : the important thing was that it was held and the fact publicized.[36]

Precisely because the rural milieu was less politicized, the struggle between the rival socialist parties was more muted than in the towns. It was not necessary – at least in this period – for maximalist elements to engage in elaborate stratagems to undercut moderate-controlled provincial soviets or executives, since ordinary folk took little interest in their proceedings. Indeed, it is a fair guess that few peasants would have been able to identify any of the individuals who occupied posts of authority within the rural soviet hierarchy. Matters were not made any easier for them by the fact that the composition of these bodies was continually changing. Moreover, the left-wing parties had inherited a tradition of anonymity and de-emphasized the role played by individuals. This attitude contrasted starkly with that of the peasants, who were used to personal authority, as exercised by private proprietors, land captains and district elders under the old regime. The proliferation of organizations of every kind, often referred to by weird abbreviations, was bound to leave them confused. In general they responded sympathetically to the efforts undertaken on their behalf by organizers from the cities, but there was bound to be friction from time to time. We have already noted an instance of this in Samara province. In Voronezh, where the SRs had formed a combined soviet representing workers, soldiers and peasants, a motion was submitted at the second provincial peasant congress, held at the end of July, to withdraw the peasant 'section' and to form an independent peasant soviet similar to those that existed elsewhere. The leading personality among the local SRs, K.S. Burevoy, argued that it was essential for the three social groups to remain united, and the motion was handsomely defeated.[37] This clash was, however, symptomatic of a problem that was to loom large after the October revolution, when the peasants found themselves condemned to a position of permanent inferiority within the soviet hierarchy.

On the other hand, there is evidence from Pskov province of peasants pressing for their organization to merge with those of workers and soldiers.[38] No doubt this was to some extent a matter of class, the 'have-nots' hoping to get the better of the 'haves' with the aid of the soldiers; nevertheless it may also have reflected a genuine difference of opinion as to whether the peasantry constituted a specific social group with interests that could best be advanced by means of organizations solidly rooted in the rural milieu.

Several efforts were made at the time to count the number of soviets that existed at various levels. One estimate for 20 July yielded a total of 52 provincial and 388 county soviets.[39] Another writer claimed 100 per cent and 95 per cent coverage for provincial and county soviets respectively in the Great Russian provinces of European Russia, 90 per cent and 58 per cent in Ukraine, 59 per cent and 39 per cent in the Caucasus, and 17 per cent and 8 per cent in Siberia.[40] A recent investigator states that by October such organs existed in 67 of the former empire's 82 provinces and in 437 out of 650 counties (excluding Finland and enemy-occupied territory). District soviets are said to have been formed in 787 out of a total number of 6,770 districts, or over 11 per cent. The regional distribution bears out the picture of a heavy concentration in Great Russia[41] – that is in the area where communal traditions were strongest. These figures evidently exclude district *committees*, although in practice, if not in principle, the distinction between them and soviets was slight. As for *land* committees, we have a contemporary estimate (for July) of 52 provincial and 422 county organizations,[42] but this is probably an underestimate – quite apart from the fact that no attempt was made to enumerate the all-important lowest tier of district land committees. In addition to all these bodies there were the specifically political 'peasant unions' formed by the PSR, which were in effect extensions of its local branches. No estimate of their number or strength is available.

If historians have found it hard to bring some order into this chaos, one can imagine how it seemed to contemporaries. Ordinary folk saw it simply as 'a mess' (*kasha*: the Russian word is more expressive) from which little good could come. The all-important distinction between official and unofficial (self-constituted) organs of authority had been blurred. As in the towns, the soviets played an ambiguous role – associated in the work of government, yet considered by their adherents as responsible solely to the 'revolutionary masses', by which was really meant the activists who spoke in their name. This confusion was to prove to be the peasant organizations' undoing. The problem was most obvious at the summit of the structure. The central peasant executive (as we shall refer to it) was a kind of rural counterpart to the CEC. Formed under the aegis of the PSR, it played an important role in the political mobilization of the peasantry. To its chequered fortunes we may now turn.

EIGHTEEN *Peasants in Politics: Emergence of the Central Peasant Organizations*

Tʜɪs ᴄᴇɴᴛʀᴀʟ ᴀᴜᴛʜᴏʀɪᴛʏ was the Soviet of Peasant Deputies – or such at least is the title given in contemporary sources, and by many historians since. But did any such body ever exist? On closer inspection it dissolves into thin air. There was indeed an All-Russian Congress of Peasant Deputies, held from 4 to 28 May in Petrograd, shortly before the better-known First All-Russian Congress of Workers' and Soldiers' Deputies, which set up the ᴄᴇᴄ (see above p. 132). In similar fashion the earlier gathering set up an Executive Committee, composed partly of persons elected from the floor of the congress and partly of provincial representatives, which functioned until shortly after the October revolution. However, the central peasant executive was more artificial than its 'proletarian' counterpart. There was no peasant equivalent to the Petrograd soviet, which acted as a semi-permanent political forum and (to use the cliché phrase) 'barometer of revolution'. Petrograd could not claim to speak for the countryside as it did for the towns (or the army). It was also harder for members of the central peasant executive to maintain contact with their constituents, scattered as they were across the length and breadth of Russia.

On the other hand, this body was a safe ᴘsʀ bailiwick. In the

CEC the Socialist-Revolutionaries had to share power with the Mensheviks, and in the Petrograd soviet (as in many others) both these parties rapidly lost ground to the Bolsheviks. In the central peasant executive, by contrast, the struggle was between different factions within the PSR. On the right stood those, notably the chairman N.D. Avksentyev, who endeavoured to rally support for the government (in which Avksentyev himself served as minister of Interior) and prosecution of the war. On the left stood the protagonists of immediate peace and radical land reform, who looked for leadership first to V.M. Chernov and then to those on the extreme left wing of the PSR (A.M. Natanson, B. Kamkov). This group allied itself with the Bolsheviks and on the morrow of their seizure of power set themselves up as a separate political party, the Left Socialist-Revolutionaries (see below p. 315).

In the first few weeks after the February revolution it was by no means a foregone conclusion that the body which claimed to speak for all Russia's peasants – no less than a hundred and twenty million of them, so the enthusiasts claimed – would adopt the soviet label, which had hitherto been associated almost exclusively with the urban working class. In 1905–6 an organization known as the All-Russian Peasant Union (ARPU) had emerged as a potential national coordinating centre. Led in the main by intellectuals of Populist sympathies, it was formally a non-partisan body, as befitted the term 'union' in its title. However, it had scarcely struck root before it was suppressed. Some of its principal figures subsequently entered political life as Popular Socialists or Trudoviks.

In March 1917 these leaders, prominent among whom were the brothers S.P. and V.P. Mazurenko, set about the task of reviving the union. They established a 'main organizing committee' in Moscow which on 12 March issued a proclamation calling for support of the Provisional Government and moderation in pressing sectional claims. Soon afterwards the ARPU leaders made it clear that, while they advocated transfer of land to the peasants, they wanted this reform to be carried out in orderly fashion; the Constituent Assembly was to determine the conditions in which compensation should be paid to those expropriated and the rights which the new land-holders should enjoy. The ARPU spokesmen went on to warn the peasants – prophetically, as it turned out – that if they failed to organize, 'anyone will be able to conquer them, and the tyranny which has been overthrown will be followed by another, perhaps even more onerous'. They should hold congresses at every level to elect deputies to a national congress which would formally reconstitute ARPU and elect its executive (known as the 'main committee').[1]

It soon became apparent that the path towards union would be more difficult than these leaders expected. Not only did the peasant congresses that were held, as we have seen, generally take a more radical line, but a rival 'organizing committee' came into being in Petrograd. On 20 March the latter group held a meeting with various 'public and political organizations' (which were not named, but evidently included the local PSR chiefs, who stood to the left of their national leaders) and decided 'to insist that the congress of peasant deputies be held in Petrograd, without prejudice to the duration of its work' – and immediately at that. This declaration represented a triple challenge : the locale of the congress was to be the 'citadel of revolution', rather than Moscow;[2] its labours might be interrupted if they failed to satisfy the radical leaders; and it was to be convoked in haste, without waiting for the verdict of local congresses. Last but not least, its object was to set up a soviet of peasant deputies.[3]

In this way the Petrograd 'organizers' sought in effect to strangle ARPU at birth. A soviet was by definition a very different kind of body from a union. It was essentially an organ of political struggle, whereas a union's purpose was to advance its members' professional interests. A union of peasants, as of any other group of working people, was designed to attract a broader membership than any political organization; even if it chose to affiliate to a certain political party, it would preserve a certain degree of autonomy. Moreover, soviets were still seen as temporary organizations, a product of the revolutionary ferment, whereas the term 'union' implied durability : it would be necessary so long as there were peasants to till the soil.

The difference was one of substance, not merely of words. One of the first congresses held under the auspices of the Moscow initiating group, in Yaroslavl, was nearly broken up by elements who evidently took their cue from Petrograd. This congress is said to have been attended by about a thousand persons, some of whom had been associated with ARPU in 1905. The moderates thwarted a move to repudiate as untimely the creation of a union branch,[4] but this was no more than a tactical success. The Mazurenko brothers seem to have hoped that the two kinds of organization could coexist, with the soviets occupying a subordinate position, but even this aim proved to be difficult to achieve. At the end of April the congress of peasant soviets in Moscow province paid tribute to ARPU's services in 1905, but implicitly condemned its present activities.[5] Meanwhile in Petrograd the original nucleus split, evidently due to a quarrel between civilians and soldiers from the mutinous Petrograd garrison. The latter set up an organization known as 'the soviet of peasant deputies of the Petrograd garrison', which became a Left SR stronghold and played a notable part in spreading radical ideas all over the country.[6] The Mazurenko brothers refused to dissolve their organization in favour of the garrison soviet, and went to the Don, where they hoped to find the cossacks more responsive to their ideas.

A number of *stanitsa* (cossack settlement) and village assemblies passed resolutions in support of ARPU. They hoped that the Constituent Assembly 'would legislate a *durable* and just land settlement in conformity with the will of the *whole* people' (our italics): the emphasis was unmistakable. The cossacks and peasants of the south-east, like everyone else, attributed their poverty to shortage of land (which in their particular circumstances was not very convincing) and wanted all land to become 'the common property of the whole people'; however, they added that the land of private proprietors and peasant allotment-holders should be expropriated 'partly with compensation and partly without' on terms to be elaborated by the Constituent Assembly.[7] A regional committee was set up in the Don, and branches of ARPU appeared in other parts of the south, such as Yekaterinoslav, Tavrida, Chernigov and Ufa provinces.[8] Support was also forthcoming in Vyatka province in the north-east, where the peasants refused an invitation to rename their 'unions', which were unusually firmly rooted in the life of the area, soviets.[9] It was characteristic that ARPU should have greatest success in outlying areas which either had an individualist tradition or where the levelling impulses of the revolution were less in evidence. The Mazurenkos themselves were of Ukrainian origin, and like many of their compatriots favoured the formation of a Ukrainian land fund, to be administered by a regional assembly (*sejm*).[10] Russian peasants were not to expect any favours from a redistribution of property in the Ukraine. These events marked the beginning of the Ukrainian SR party, which differed from its Russian counterpart solely in the emphasis which it laid upon regional autonomy.[11]

In Petrograd, however, ARPU was elbowed aside by radical PSR activists in the arrangements for calling the All-Russian Congress of Peasant Deputies.[12] Their strength lay in the soldiers' committees, which were somewhat speciously presented as peasant bodies – although the view that the soldiers were just '*muzhiki* in uniform' was simplistic in the extreme : experience of the trenches gave the Russian soldier of 1917 an outlook different from that of civilians in any social category. According to a contemporary statement by an SR leader from Saratov, nearly as many soldiers were present at the congress as there were peasants : the figures were 750 and 900 respectively.[13] According to another such account, the military component amounted to 558 out of a total number of 1,167 delegates.[14] At its peak the congress had 1,353 delegates in attendance. A disproportionate number came from the black-soil provinces, which were a PSR stronghold.[15]

The congress opened on 4 May with a discussion of the political issues of the day. Resolutions were adopted in support of the newly formed coalition government and 'revolutionary defencism' at the front. Other sessions were devoted to economic problems such as supply and transport. The organization question came up for debate on 14 and 15 May. Mazurenko announced that ARPU intended to hold its national congress one week thereafter, and that this body would fix the place which the soviets should occupy within the peasant movement as a whole. This provoked an angry retort from V.A. Kilchevsky, the *rapporteur* on these matters (and the individual chiefly responsible for organizing the congress), who claimed that the soviets already represented no less than 150,000 peasants and had an authentically 'mass' character. ARPU, he alleged, was seeking to split the movement by establishing itself as a political party.[16] The charge was not wholly without foundation. On the other hand, ARPU had as much right to exist as the PSR; was there to be room for only one of them? The PSR leaders, committed to the ideal of unity, were inclined to be intolerant of dissenters – especially those who, as they thought, had no mass following worthy of the name. They did not anticipate that their arguments would soon be used against them by the extreme left.

On 20 May the congress endorsed Kilchevsky's scheme for the organization of peasant soviets, which reasserted the principles with which we are familiar. Such bodies were to be formed at all levels, from the national down to the district (and even the village, where practicable); they were 'to undertake practical measures', including control over representatives of the State; they were to synchronize policies with the local urban (workers' and soldiers') soviets. There was a sting in the tail of this section of the document. Wherever ARPU organizations existed, they were invited to turn themselves into soviets. It was a case of the biter bit, for the same operation had previously been planned against the soviets by ARPU.

The second section of the scheme laid down the functions (but not the composition) of that semi-mythical body, the All-Russian Soviet of Peasant Deputies, the composition (but not the functions) of its Executive Committee, and then made equivalent provisions in regard to the local peasant soviets. Even though these rules were often disregarded in practice, two points are worth noting.

First, the (central) Executive Committee was to consist of fifteen to thirty members elected directly by the congress in plenary session, plus at least two to be chosen later from each province, five from each army, two from each military district (three from those at the front) and ten from the navy. This gave the military element a stronger representation than had originally been intended. The civilian members elected at the congress were chosen according to a complicated arrangement which gave an additional weighting and senior status to men from the black-soil zone.[17] By these somewhat dubious means the PSR leaders hoped to keep the radical elements in a minority.

Second, since this body of 250 men would be too large to wield real power, there was to be within it a presidium of fifteen members. Nothing was said about a bureau, but it was not long before such a core body appeared: its first meeting occurred on 1 June.[18] The degree of centralization may have been greater on the central peasant executive than on the CEC, since so many of its members were expected to be absent from Petrograd on various assignments. It was decided that two-thirds of those actually in the capital should suffice for a quorum.[19] The Executive Committee met almost continuously during the first month or so of its existence. The July Days crisis led to a temporary suspension of its sessions, since most members went off to consolidate their position in their 'constituencies'. In late August and September meetings were held weekly, but by this time the organization's importance had considerably lessened.

To the thousand or so delegates to the All-Russian Congress of Peasant Deputies the debates on political and especially organizational matters were but a tedious prelude to the issue that was closest to their hearts : the land. It featured prominently in the 'instructions' (*cahiers, nakazy*) which about one-quarter of them brought along. These documents were collated and subsequently published : they were fated to play an unexpectedly important role in October 1917.[20] It was no secret that the PSR leaders were divided on this problem; few of those present, however, were clear about the precise nature of these differences – or those that divided radical Populists from Bolsheviks. They were soon to be initiated into these doctrinal subtleties. On 20 May the small Bolshevik group[21] asked that the agenda be amended to allow the congress to be addressed by Lenin, who was said to be in the hall. The suggestion was turned down, and it seems that this preliminary skirmish merely whetted the delegates' appetites for the impending confrontation.

All sources are agreed that Lenin's speech two days later had a powerful effect. As one presidium member put it, 'we feared that the ground would slip away beneath our feet.'[22] Not for the last time, the Bolshevik leader stole Chernov's thunder. According to Lenin 'landowning by squires is the greatest injustice, and there is not a moment to be lost in eliminating it.'[23] Direct action from below, he contended, was not subversion but an assertion of popular rights; if violence occurred, the responsibility lay with those who vainly sought to restrain the peasants in their just endeavour to destroy the present agrarian system. In the future socialist order the mass of peasants would not be small-holding proprietors but would lease their land from the State. They would have to reckon with the existence of a well-organized class of agricultural labourers and poor peasants whose particular interests the Bolsheviks sought to promote. Elements drawn from this milieu would be put in charge of a number of former private estates, which they would run on communal lines – small islands of proletarian power, as it were, in the midst of the petty-bourgeois sea.[24]

Although Lenin was careful to avoid being too specific about the Bolsheviks' ulterior intentions, he made it quite plain that they envisaged the struggle against the landowners as nothing more than the opening round of a class war in the villages. This would be fought out in the main between the proletarian elements and the small-holders; its duration and intensity none could foretell. One may doubt whether many of his listeners looked forward to such a prospect.[25] However, their misgivings on this score were offset by the brilliant prospects which he unfolded for the immediate future.

Lenin's intervention in the debate had the effect of putting all the other leading speakers on the defensive. In setting out their views they had to make clear where they stood in relation to Bolshevism. Chernov, the official *rapporteur* on the agrarian question, returned to the rostrum on 24 May. He adopted a soft and condescending manner. Under the Bolshevik scheme, he argued, the confiscated land would pass into the hands of the wealthier peasants and accentuate conflict; only the PSR policy of equalization of holdings could ensure that the coming distribution would be just. This was a weak argument, and indeed unfair to Lenin, who had in fact dealt adequately with this point by stating that, if the wealthier element benefited, (a) this was inevitable to the extent that they had greater capital resources; (b) the poor's turn would come later; (c) this was better than a compromise with the landowners. Had the PSR leader been a more perspicacious politician, he would have harped on his listeners' natural fear of an interminable conflict with irresponsible village proletarians subsidized and organized from without.

Chernov also took up Lenin's call for 'organized seizure' of the land. A few days earlier, in an exchange with the Bolshevik I.T. Smilga in the Main Land Committee, he had suggested mildly that this was a contradiction in terms – as indeed it was. Instead of developing this point, and making it clear exactly in what circumstances confiscation of property was legally and politically defensible, he simply argued that such uncoordinated acts would lead to new injustices and rivalries, since one district was likely to do better than another.[26] This was to underestimate the peasants' willingness to accept such disparities as an unfortunate necessity, and their ability to iron them out by making local adjustments; moreover, there was no guarantee that even greater disparities would not result from the nation-wide redistribution which the SRs expected the Constituent Assembly to sanction.

A rather more adequate response to the extremists was made by S.L. Maslov, who in the inner circle of the PSR stood some way to the right of Chernov. Maslov shared the general Populist prejudice against the employment of hired labour (regarded as *ipso facto* exploitative), but he made a number of sensible if unremarkable points : to maintain the integrity of the land fund, it was enough to prohibit commercial transactions in property (as the government was attempting to do), instead of issuing an unenforceable declaration nationalizing the land; this ban should be supervised by the land committees, as official agencies, and not by the soviets as *ad hoc* bodies; the rights of these committees should be laid down by statute; disputes with landowners should be settled by negotiation, with the aid of higher instances where required; peaceful compromise was at all times preferable to coercion, which should be used only as a measure of last resort. A spokesman for the 'Siberian group' of deputies, a Buryat Mongol named Sanpilyon, drew attention to the more technical aspects of the agrarian problem : the need for improved communications, increased output of mineral fertilizer and machinery, better educational facilities and so on. This was a timely reminder that the redistribution of landed property was but a first step in the peasants' social advance, which in the final analysis depended on economic rather than political considerations.[27]

It was, however, the mass of delegates who did not speak that made the greatest impact. Under their pressure for the congress to sanction an immediate start on land reform – the most popular idea was for a solemn declaration that the land was public property – the Right SR leaders called a restricted meeting with regional representatives at which a compromise resolution was hammered out. Published on 26 May,[28] this in effect gave the radicals everything they could have hoped for. It invited the peasants to form land committees at all administrative levels, which, in preparing the reform, were to abide by the principle that all state, church and privately owned land was 'to pass into the possession of the entire people for equal use by the toiling population, without any compensation'. This was of course the familiar PSR formula.

Until the Constituent Assembly met, 'all land ... without exception should pass into the disposition (*vedeniye*) of the land committees, which are to have the right to determine the manner of cultivation, sowing, harvesting, haymaking etc.' According to Gurevich[29] the private conclave at which the compromise was reached had agreed on use of the word *uchot*, meaning control, as distinct from *vedeniye*, which implied outright management. But whatever the purists might intend, the effect of this provision was to give the committees *carte blanche* to interfere in property relationships at will. Other clauses permitted them to dispose of available labour resources, to requisition agricultural implements and livestock,[30] and to fix rents. Finally they were to enforce the ban on property transactions which the coalition government had just imposed. In the light of these sweeping provisions it was ironic, as one contemporary critic noted,[31] that the resolution should end by voicing mild disapproval of arbitrary confiscations of landed property – for the whole purport of this document was to render such acts superfluous by legitimizing them.

The resolution was adopted almost unanimously : only two votes were cast against it and one delegate abstained. The Bolsheviks asserted their individuality by presenting a resolution of their own but it attracted only two dozen votes. It is worth noting that the final text seems to have gone *further* than the demands put forward by the peasants themselves in their *cahiers*.[32] However this may be there can be no doubt that the resolution greatly aided the radicaliza-tion of opinion in the countryside. The delegates themselves, return-ing to their 'constituencies', acted as the spearhead in this process

Already by the middle of June some members of the central peasant executive were trying to get the genie back into the bottle Instructions were sent to activists in the field specifying which kinds of leases they might invalidate as exploitative. The executive's organization and propaganda department, headed by F.A Martyushin, arranged lectures on the proper function of soviets and land committees.[33] Emissaries from the villages were received by members of another department and given advice on their particular problems, some thirty to forty persons being seen each day.[34] Another channel of communication was the executive's press organ However, as time went on *Izvestiya* began to speak with two voices Leading articles called for restraint while news items, selected to reflect the peasants' growing radicalism, were published without any comment. The central peasant executive also sent out delegates to 'investigate' rural disorders. Such men found themselves in an invidious position. Their authority derived from an institution which had committed itself to radical measures of 'control' over private proprietors and local officials. When faced with poverty and injustice they naturally tended to back the peasant activists rather than the duly constituted authorities, even though the latter might be fellow srs.

The plain fact was that in disturbed areas neither the central peasant executive nor local government authorities had any means of enforcing their will. A vivid description of their predicament is given by the government commissar for Novoaleksandrov county

(Kovno province). On 4 June his superior had called a province-wide congress of peasants. This had been quite peaceful until

> speeches were delivered by orators of the extreme left parties
> (SRS) which aroused everyone : all the land is yours and now, by
> a decision of the [self-constituted] district committees, you are
> empowered to take everything you need – fields, meadows, wood-
> land, lakes, pastures and so on. . . . Prior to this congress I managed
> somehow, although with difficulty, to restrain the peasants of
> Novoaleksandrov district from major acts of confiscation . . . but
> now I can do so no longer, for the peasant deputies returning
> from the congress pay no heed to my injunctions, saying they have
> heard something quite different there.[35]

The rural soviet movement had given the local activists their head,
and it would take more strength than could be mustered by the
Provisional Government, half-heartedly aided by the central peasant
executive, to check their excesses.

NINETEEN *Peasants in Politics: The Leftward Tide*

THE CHALLENGE FROM the extreme left which faced those who sought to lead the Russian peasantry soon assumed an institutional form. The first non-peasant bodies to spread ultra-radical ideas in the countryside were the so-called *zemlyachestva*. In time of peace these were loose associations of persons from the same rural area temporarily resident in one of the larger industrial centres. During 1917 they became politicized and similar bodies also appeared at the front (where many military units were in any case recruited on the territorial principle). The most influential *zemlyachestva* were in Petrograd, which had always attracted a large number of seasonal workers from the countryside; others came into existence at the naval bases of Kronstadt and Helsingfors. It was from the Kronstadt 'sailors' republic' that in the spring of 1917 the first sizeable parties of 'maximalist' agitators were dispatched to various rural areas. They seem to have concentrated upon the middle Volga provinces of Kazan and Nizhniy Novgorod.[1] On 6 June the self-constituted district committee at Kinkur, Vyatka province, announced that it had arrested a Bolshevik sailor named Grigoriy Tselishchev and requested the government 'to take immediate steps to stop the dispatch of Leninists into the interior of

Russia, in order to prevent their harmful influence'.[2] These agitators bore 'mandates' which *inter alia* empowered them to carry arms and to exercise full voting rights on county, district and village committees.[3] By July, according to a recent Soviet calculation, no less than forty-four *zemlyachestva* existed at Kronstadt; there were another twenty in Petrograd, which claimed more than thirty thousand members. The impact of those formed in Moscow and other centres was less important.[4]

The Bolshevik leaders were quick to realize the political importance of these bodies, and notices of their meetings were printed in *Pravda*. For example, on 25 June a meeting was arranged at the Phoenix works, in the Vyborg quarter of Petrograd, for 'citizens of Smolensk province, from any county, to organize a *zemlyachestvo* and to choose delegates for dispatch to the country'.[5] These emissaries were furnished with suitable political literature and coached in the essentials of the party's thinking on current problems, especially the agrarian issue; when they returned they were encouraged to deliver reports on their impressions. On 23 August the Bolshevik Central Committee approved a plan to introduce greater conformity into the work of these associations, and a few days later a Central Bureau was established for this purpose. Ya.M. Sverdlov, the guiding spirit behind this venture, also worked out a statute to define their functions, but this was not published until shortly before the Bolsheviks took power.[6] The delay seems to have been due in part to a certain indifference or lukewarmness toward such centralizing measures among those immediately concerned and in part to the fact that the Bolshevik leaders attached greater significance to the soviets once they had begun to make headway in this latter forum.

The most important of these soviets, so far as the peasants were concerned, was that established in the Petrograd garrison for soldiers of rural origin (see above, p. 232). This was not a Bolshevik creation but was led by left-wing SRs. The differences between the two maximalist groups were at this stage of minor consequence and did not impair their collaboration. The Bolshevik element became more important in September, when its members formally constituted their own nucleus ('fraction') within the organization, which now began to call itself by the simpler title 'the Petrograd soviet of peasant deputies'.[7] The significance of this change was ideological. It enabled the Bolsheviks to present what was essentially a soldiers' organization (with some admixture of industrial workers) as one entitled to speak for the peasants, and to make it a focus of opposition to the moderate-controlled central peasant executive. Its principal activity was to propagandize soldiers returning to their native villages. It is thought to have sent back about four to five hundred such persons before the October insurrection.[8]

A number of urban soviets, as we have seen, set up 'peasant sections' to proselytize the villages in their vicinity and (in more practical vein) to help their supporters secure food supplies. Those soviets under strong Bolshevik influence seem to have been the most active and also the most eager to promote mergers with peasant soviets, in order to overwhelm the SRs. Thus in the textile town of Shuya, M.V. Frunze (whom we have already met as Bolshevik spokesman at the All-Russian Congress of Peasant Deputies) organized such a fusion on 20 October, when the Bolsheviks were already masters of the locality in all but name. In the new united soviet of workers, soldiers and peasants (in that order) he was to be assisted as chairman by three deputies and three secretaries, drawn in equal proportions from each of the three sections.[9] This tripartite arrangement ensured that the peasants would be under the control of more militant elements. At Bryansk (Orel province), where the social configuration was similar – an industrial island in the peasant sea – the local metallurgical workers set up such a united soviet as early as May; it was directed by an executive committee of twenty-eight members, only six of whom were drawn from the peasants, who thus did not even enjoy numerical equality with the workers or soldiers; each group was, however, allowed to have an executive of its own.[10]

United (tripartite) soviets were still a rare phenomenon before October 1917. Recent investigators have uncovered evidence of 99 of them, classified as follows: 1 regional, 11 provincial, 51 county and 36 others: Cossack settlement (*stanitsa*), district, urban or city-ward (*rayon*).[11] The united regional soviet was in the north-west, where tendencies toward coalition were most prominent. This phenomenon had little to do with sociology but much with the presence here of large numbers of rebellious soldiers. It is not recorded when this regional organization was set up, and it does not appear to have exercised any significant influence; nevertheless its existence was a pointer towards future trends. The peasants had but a modest place on this and other such bodies in the region. In

Novgorod, where the initiative in forming a united provincial soviet was taken by the soldiers' committee of an army brigade stationed in the town (14 April), it was reported two months later that a mere 12 of its 130 members were peasants.[12] Among the eleven united soviets at provincial level known to have been in existence in October, only two (Novgorod, Smolensk) were in the area of heaviest military concentration, whereas three were in SR black-soil strongholds (Penza, Tambov, Voronezh), two in the relatively prosperous south-east of European Russia (Don, Yekaterinodar), one in the Urals (Perm), and three in Asiatic Russia (Fergana, Yeniseysk, Irkutsk).[13] It would probably be no exaggeration to say that most of these were paper organizations, much less important than the urban (workers' and soldiers') soviets of which they were in effect an extension; on the other hand in a few provinces (Moscow, Vladimir, Ryazan) preliminary congresses had been held and bureaux set up whose function it was to call such united provincial soviets into being.

As for united soviets of more limited territorial scope, in particular those at county level, these were of prime significance in the north-west (Pskov, Olonets) and also in the Central Industrial region; in the latter case we may grant that workers were at least as important as soldiers in establishing them. Even so we are dealing here with exceptions to the general rule. We know that peasant soviets existed in 437 counties out of a total of 650 (excluding Finland and enemy-occupied territory).[14] Yet in only 51 counties were there united soviets, and according to a contemporary estimate of the central peasant executive only 26 peasant soviets were united with others. (The difference can be explained in part by the coexistence of united and independent bodies.) Thus on the eve of the October insurrection the peasant organizations had as yet felt only slightly the impact of those who insisted that the peasants could enter the promised land of socialism only under the tutelage of their proletarian cousins. Or to quote Moiseyeva, on whose study we have drawn extensively here, 'in the struggle to unite the soviets in town and country the Bolshevik party had to overcome the petty-bourgeois vacillations of the peasant masses themselves, which were utilized by the compromising parties, for these strove obstinately to maintain the separate existence of soviets of workers', soldiers' and peasants' deputies.'[15]

'Petty bourgeois' the PSR leaders may or may not have been; that they vacillated is beyond question. Indeed, it is as storm-battered weathercocks that they are known to history. Victims of the cruel 'dilemma of power', they were unable either to govern or to carry through the profound social revolution for which large segments of the population craved. As the crisis deepened, the central peasant executive, like the moderate socialist parties to which it was affiliated, found itself outbid by extremists on the left.

By September this body had forfeited much of the authority with which it had been invested only four months earlier. Most of its members took the view that the main enemy stood to the right rather than to the left. Their attitude prevented it from lending consistent support to the government, and such moves as it made in this direction merely provided grist for the propaganda mills of its radical critics. Had its leaders been endowed with qualities of statesmanship, they might have strengthened their own position by conciliating ARPU. Instead they decided that the moment was ripe to deal their wounded rival the *coup de grâce*.

A convenient pretext lay to hand. The ARPU leaders proceeded with plans to hold a congress of their own, designed to establish their union as a national body. Kilchevsky saw in this 'an attempt to divide the peasantry and sow confusion in its ranks'. At a session of the executive on 20 June one speaker (Rudolepov) alleged that ARPU 'could not be anything other than a league of squires and separators, since anyone who wanted to work on behalf of the peasantry would join the [All-Russian] Soviet'.[16] A few days later a resolution was published summoning all peasants to obstruct the forthcoming congress, which was said to be 'irregular' (*samochinnyy*) – the very term that was used by moderates generally in regard to all self-constituted bodies; only soviets, according to this view, were legally valid (*pravomochnye*), and others should cease their existence forthwith.[17] Mazurenko, who did not mince his words, retorted that the executive was acting like the rural police of tsarist times. In a letter published on 8 July in the Kadet newspaper *Rech'* (the socialist press being closed to him) he denied Kilchevsky's charge that plans for the forthcoming congress had been concealed from the soviet leaders and went on to boast of the support his organization had won in the Ukraine, Siberia and elsewhere; finally he voiced vague ideas about pan-Slav brotherhood and Russia's need for the Straits. These last points were gratuitous and showed the ARPU leader's lack of political realism : if there was anything more likely to discredit him in the eyes of ordinary peasants, it was a commitment to war aims now widely regarded as 'imperialistic'. It also showed that he was uncertain as to the basic purpose of his organization : if it was to be a union, as distinct from a party, there was no need to make such a political *profession de foi*. A more experienced leader would have concentrated on exposing the central peasant executive's doubtful credentials.

The latter body designated men to attend ARPU's forthcoming congress and to expose the errors of its ways. The calculation was that, as an artificial body, it would at once collapse. The congress opened in Moscow on 31 July – twelve years to the day since ARPU had been founded. Three hundred and sixteen delegates attended from thirty-two provinces, along with thirty-four representatives from the armed forces. It was therefore a less multitudinous assembly than the Congress of Peasant Deputies in May, and less over-shadowed by soldiers; indeed, even its critics were constrained to admit, with some surprise, that the overwhelming bulk of those present were authentic peasants.[18] Geographically there was a preponderance of men from the southern provinces, particularly Yekaterinoslav. At the first session, devoted to procedural problems, four men sent by the central peasant executive were denied access; this led to protests on their behalf and the atmosphere soon became tense. Angry exchanges took place over the dispatch of messages of support to the government and the commander-in-chief, as the symbol of 'our beloved army'.[19] Chernov was the target of con-siderable criticism. Speakers deplored the low level of political consciousness among the peasants, which allowed them to be duped by 'rogues' and 'subversive elements'.

One might be inclined to dismiss this gathering as one of ardent 'defensists' and frightened petty proprietors, accepting at face value the allegations of its left-wing critics. However, when the delegates turned to the land question, there was no mistaking their radicalism. The policy differences between the organizations (for example, over compensation) could have been bridged if the political will had been there. Yet so deep was the socialist intellectuals' fear of ARPU's potential mass appeal, so ideological their approach to agrarian problems, that they preferred to disrupt the congress.

The schism came about on 5 August, over the artificial, partisan and purely political issue of organizational subordination. Amidst 'noise, cries and absolute chaos' the soviet representatives staged a demonstrative walk-out. Before leaving they read a solemn declaration, couched in tones of extreme moral self-righteousness, in which the ARPU leaders were denounced for 'brazenly attempting to split the toiling peasantry into two hostile camps'.[20] The charge was hypocritical since the soviet bodies had themselves sought to bring about a schism – and succeeded. About half the simple peasant delegates followed the peasant executive leaders from the hall.

History did not give Mazurenko's organization a chance to prove itself. A mere three months lay between its formal constitution as a national body and the Bolshevik seizure of power – too brief a span to permit generalization about its ultimate prospects. What chances would a peasant organization of the trade-union type – an equivalent of the German *Bauernbund* – have had in a Russia spared the trials of proletarian dictatorship and civil war? It could be argued – and was argued by some Populist *émigrés* in the 1920s – that such a non-partisan body was ideally suited to the circumstances of a rural society in which, as a result of the agrarian revolution, family small-holdings were paramount. However, an examination of the evidence suggests that ARPU was evolving in a different direction. It aspired to be a union – 'the word party has become hateful to the peasants', observed one of its spokesmen[21] – yet a party is what it rapidly became. It issued a number of statements supporting the war. In several provinces, notably in the south, it put up its own list of candidates in the elections to the Constituent Assembly, in opposition to the PSR. One may doubt whether these developments accorded with Mazurenko's original intentions. Never a strong or clear-minded leader, he was dragged along in the wake of events. No organization in Russia could remain aloof from politics during the critical autumn of 1917.

The ultimate gainers, of course, were the Bolsheviks and their Left SR allies. As for the Executive Committee of the (so-called) Soviet of Peasant Deputies, it followed ARPU into limbo. The chairman, N.D. Avksentyev, was simultaneously minister of Interior in the second coalition cabinet, formed at the end of July. An ardent 'defensist', he called on the provincial commissars to be 'the executants of the united will and power of the Provisional Government'.[22] Meanwhile other members of the peasant executive, echoing the line taken by Chernov, were petitioning that government to entrust more power to the land committees.

These tensions were aggravated by the Kornilov affair. The discredit in which Kerensky's ministers were now generally held adversely affected Avksentyev's prestige. For some weeks he had been too preoccupied with his governmental duties to handle the executive's affairs, and the role of chairman had devolved upon four deputies (soon increased to six).[23] These men, acting as a kind of informal bureau, neglected regular procedures in their anxiety to keep their more radical colleagues in line. Each faction had its eyes fixed on national political issues. On 16 September, at the Democratic Conference, the split within the executive was proclaimed before the general public when its members voted 44 to 34 in favour of a resolution maintaining the present coalition. The narrow margin testified to the growing strength of the left wing. Even more indicative was the poll taken on the previous day among all peasant representatives attending the Democratic Conference, when the principle of coalition was accepted by only 66 votes to 57 (with 6 abstentions).[24] The final line-up of peasant votes gave the partisans of coalition a majority (102 to 70 with 12 abstentions), but this did not reflect fairly the state of rural opinion, since the peasant executive disposed of a bloc vote.[25]

Thus there was a two-fold split: between 'right' and 'left' on the peasant executive and between the former and the rank and file. The leftists' growing strength led them to press for the convocation of another congress of peasant deputies. This, they hoped, would reflect the radicalization of rural opinion since May and elect a new executive more amenable to their purpose. By the time the delegates to this gathering convened the political situation had been radically transformed by the October insurrection. Within a few months even the left-wing peasant leaders would face the problem of coexisting with a Bolshevik dictatorship which made no secret of its aim to subordinate the village to its exclusive control.

IV   The Transfer of Power
October 1917—March 1918

TWENTY *The Dissolution of the Proletariat*

T HE BOLSHEVIK SEIZURE of power plunged Russia into chaos and confusion. The *coup* of 24–25 October in Petrograd was soon emulated in other major centres. Within a few weeks most of the country's main cities, and the armies strung out along the western front, had come under the control of maximalist elements sympathetic to the new regime. This was also the case in villages situated close to major concentrations of industrial or military might, or along important lines of communication. Elsewhere, in the remoter country districts and certain outlying regions, the transfer of power took much longer; and in certain national-minority areas 'soviet power' was established only after years of conflict, in which foreign powers sometimes took a hand. Already in November 1917 centres of armed opposition to Bolshevik rule came into being in the cossack lands of south-eastern Russia. The fighting that ensued inaugurated a bitter civil war which flared up in earnest in the spring of 1918.

Even within the territory that passed rapidly under Bolshevik control there was resistance, both active and passive, violent and non-violent. A number of military and civilian organizations emerged which endeavoured to coordinate this opposition. For the most part these bodies operated in clandestine conditions and their practical achievements were slight. The chief problem was that there was no consensus of opinion among anti-Bolsheviks. The more conservative elements were sympathetic to the struggles of the Volunteer Army and looked forward to the restoration of a strong Russia able to resume the war against the Central Powers. Democrats and socialists were generally suspicious of such 'patriotic' sentiments, fearing that they would stimulate a monarchist reaction. Some of them approved of the ends being pursued by the Bolsheviks and differed from the latter mainly over the means employed to reach them. They put their trust in the Constituent Assembly, as a prestigious symbol of national unity, expecting that Lenin's government would be compelled to bow before the will of the people or at least that some kind of compromise could be achieved. It was almost universally assumed that the new regime could not last for long. Had not the Bolsheviks themselves acknowledged that Russia, a backward agrarian country, was not ripe for socialism? Was not the industrial working class too weak and too inexperienced to run the State? Such arguments, although based upon a fundamental misapprehension of the Bolsheviks' purposes, seemed plausible enough at the time. They led many people to take the view that it would be a waste of effort to try to subvert a government that was bound to collapse in any case. After a few months other counsels prevailed; but by then the Bolsheviks had managed to consolidate their hold upon the country, in the main by skilful use of their well-tried organizational techniques, and were strong enough to suppress their actual or potential 'counter-revolutionary' opponents.

In retrospect the Bolsheviks' actual seizure of power in October 1917 seems less significant than their success in retaining power during the months that followed.[1] In considering this period we shall begin, logically enough, with the towns, concentrating our attention on the emergence of the new institutional structure and dealing in turn with its various components : factory committees, Red guards, trade unions and – last but not least – the soviets, which were of course the principal organs through which the Bolsheviks (and their allies, the Left SRS) sought to legitimize their rule. The political battle at the centre will be discussed only in so far as it is relevant to our theme, the mobilization of the masses in support of the dictatorship. Before embarking upon these problems, however, it will be expedient to consider briefly socio-economic conditions in the urban milieu at this time. What was the fate of Russia's industrial workers (and

other town-dwellers) during the infancy of the world's first 'proletarian State'?

Two main characteristics of the situation during the winter of
1917–18 deserve to be singled out here : the lack of personal security
and the deteriorating conditions of employment. There is a third,
still more obvious factor – the lack of food – but this may be reserved
for examination in another context, that of agricultural production
and supply.

There are, not surprisingly, no statistics covering the incidence
of criminal offences during the revolutionary period.[2] It is self-
evident that standards of compliance with the law deteriorated
during 1917. The 'democratization' of the courts and police was
partly responsible for this state of affairs. More important perhaps
was the anarchic spirit of the times : the February revolution
unleashed, along with a wave of genuine idealism, an urge among
the deprived segments of the population to gratify their wants at
once, whatever the cost to society. The maximalist elements, the
Bolsheviks foremost among them, had encouraged, or at least
tolerated, such tendencies for political purposes of their own. Any
means was welcome that helped to undermine the existing social
and political institutions. Some anarchists or syndicalists imagined
that in the new socialist order common folk would be free to indulge
in such acts of licence. These zealots were due for a rude awakening
once the realities of 'proletarian dictatorship' became apparent.
Lenin and his closest colleagues – and probably most party activists
as well, although there is room for argument on this point – were
advocates of centralism, discipline and unity. In their view transfer
of power to the soviets made it imperative to check tendencies
towards anarchic excesses in so far as they tended to weaken or
discredit the new regime. The qualification was important : such
actions were still tolerated to the extent that they made life difficult
for partisans of the old order. They could be justified as manifestations of 'revolutionary consciousness'. Moreover, the Bolsheviks did
not yet have the means to contain anarchic tendencies among the
masses.

The ambiguous attitude of those in power encouraged what one
Populist intellectual called 'an elemental movement (*stikhiya*) of
degeneration and destruction . . . [which] leaps from one social group

to another and from one locality to another'. He likened the rebellious soldiers to fungus spores, which spread their contagion by mysterious invisible channels.[3] The soldiers were indeed the element most prone to violent excesses. In the autumn and winter of 1917 millions of front-line troops 'demobilized themselves' without waiting for orders. They streamed back into the interior, where they were joined by men from rear-echelon and garrison units, who from the beginning of the year had shown themselves most responsive to revolutionary impulses. No authority, military or civilian, whether of the old obedience or of the new, could hope to control effectively these masses of anxious and embittered men, whose relief at their escape from danger was often mixed with a desire to take revenge on those whom they saw as responsible for their misfortunes.[4] Seldom could adequate arrangements be made to care for them or to transport them home. Hundreds of thousands made their way back on foot. The lucky few took a train – which sometimes meant literally commandeering the engine and rolling-stock and then forcing the railway authorities to facilitate the train's movement. One prominent Bolshevik complained to the party's military organization late in December :

> the comrade soldiers seize a locomotive, attach some carriages to it, and then discard it after travelling for a few versts. There are a lot of casualties among those who make the journey on the roofs. At the Nikolayevsky station they took the trains by storm. The comrade soldiers speculate in seats on the trains, beat up engine-drivers . . . and the personnel, preventing them from servicing the heating, so that the carriages freeze up and are ruined.[5]

The military supply agencies could not distribute sufficient rations and some of the men did not receive any pay, either because the administration had broken down or because their status was irregular. It was not surprising if they used the force at their disposal to meet their basic needs. How frequently they did so (and, on the other hand, how many instances of self-denial or altruism there were) cannot be ascertained. But there is no doubt that over many parts of the country bands of returning soldiers were responsible for numerous acts of lawlessness. Since these men were likely to be better armed than anyone likely to oppose them, they had to be treated warily, with a mixture of blandishments and threats, until such time as the decomposition of the old army removed the source of the problem. In the meantime their example was bound to prove to be infectious to a segment of the civilian population, including some of those, such as Red guards, who were called upon to quell their excesses.

One consequence of the collapse of authority in 1917 was that it became much easier to evade the ban on the distilling and sale of alcoholic liquor. During the war many central and local authorities had accumulated sizeable stocks of spirits, partly for medicinal use, and these now became a likely target for looters. In Petrograd alone there were 570 such depots, whose stock was valued at fifty million pre-war gold roubles.[6] Alcohol was involved in about a third of the violent outbreaks reported during the last three months of the year by the independent socialist newspaper *Novaya zhizn'*. Almost invariably soldiers were to blame : in only one instance are (unidentified) civilians mentioned as the initiators of a liquor riot (*pogrom*),[7] and it may be significant that this concerned a privately owned establishment. Rioters probably had less inhibition about expropriating State property, since the spirit monopoly had never been popular. In rural areas, where illicit distilling was rife, the product often found its way into the hands of speculators, and violence against the latter could be rationalized as part of the struggle against 'capitalist exploitation'. There was a rash of liquor riots in the southern provinces of European Russia during the autumn. Their geographical and chronological distribution suggests that those to blame were returning troops. The central and northern provinces seem to have been afflicted later and to a lesser extent.

The behaviour of the rioters followed a predictable pattern. They would threaten or bribe guards into admitting them into the premises; some of the men would stiffen their resolve by making an immediate start on the loot, while those with more self-restraint would try to remove it; the noise would usually bring neighbours hurrying to the scene, some of whom might join in the raid; when news of what was afoot reached the local authorities, they would send reliable troops or worker detachments to the scene; in some cases shooting broke out and there were casualties on both sides. One eye-witness of an incident in Odessa on 1–2 December, when a mob stormed a liquor store owned by a shipping company, put the number involved at about a thousand; on this occasion the rioters were dispersed by Ukrainian irregulars (*haydamaki*) and machine-guns were brought into play.[8] Sometimes the local authorities were reluctant to take action. Near Samara a few days later a crowd of men (some of whom are said to have drunk printers' ink) smashed and looted shops, but the local Red guard chief, when asked to intervene, replied : 'The devil take you ! For me the life of one worker is dearer than a dozen of your shops.'[9] There were occasions when it was enough to impose a curfew and strengthen the guard to deter the rioters. Elsewhere it was found necessary to tackle the problem radically by destroying the stocks in question. In Petrograd, where serious outbreaks occurred early in December, the city was twice placed under martial law; an 'extraordinary commissar' was appointed (appropriately named Blagonravov, literally 'of good morals'); special units were set up to combat the problem by propaganda; finally, large quantities of alcohol were removed from the vaults and poured into the canals.[10] However, on at least one occasion when the authorities took such timely action, this provoked the riot they hoped to avert. At Bakhmut (Yekaterinoslav province), where a hundred thousand barrels of vodka were reportedly stored, the soviet executive's decision to destroy them was contested by a squadron of dragoons. Some of these resourceful men salvaged their prey from the water, and when ordered to move on attacked a depository; a general orgy ensued, although the massive destruction feared by the city fathers did not occur and within a few days order was restored by a fresh body of troops.[11] In the Yaroslavl area the contagion spread from one town to another as the rioters' appetites were fed by reports of success elsewhere.[12]

In their statements at the time the authorities (both before and after the transfer of power) often attributed the *pogroms* to counter-revolutionary agents, and this view has found reflection in historical works. In Orel in mid-September proclamations are said to have been distributed by a mysterious 'Brown Hand Society' and at Bendery (Bessarabia province) three men arrested for anti-Semitic violence were identified as former policemen.[13] It seems that these were simply manifestations of latent popular chauvinism. No evidence has yet been adduced of complicity on the part of any known political group. The crowds followed a logic all their own, in which instinct was more important than reason. They might be as hostile to the new authorities as to the old, if these displayed zeal in checking their excesses. In Petrograd on 19 December some soldiers apprehended three men suspected of murdering an inn-keeper's wife; when N. Kostrin, a workman in the militia, attempted to restrain them, both he and the three suspects were promptly thrown from a bridge into the river, where they drowned; the unfortunate Kostrin was finished off by a soldier with his bayonet.[14]

Such lynchings were an *ad hoc* response to the breakdown of legal order, an expression of the widespread feeling that all things were permitted. The wave of anarchy took a variety of forms and claimed a variety of victims. Officials and tradespeople were the most obvious targets, but even Bolshevik leaders were not immune: in January E.A. Preobrazhensky, a prominent economic planner, was robbed of his overcoat in a Moscow market-place by a group of unidentified armed men.[15] But many of those who suffered were ordinary folk who had no means of self-defence.

The growing insecurity in the cities bred a climate of fear. In Petrograd and Moscow it was no longer safe to venture out of doors in the evening, and during the night it was quite usual to hear shots fired, the purpose of which remained obscure. This state of affairs helped to swell a vast spontaneous movement of the urban population into the countryside, where conditions still seemed relatively peaceful. The main reason for this emigration, however, was the rapidly worsening economic situation of industrial and commercial employees, particularly in Petrograd. The shortage of fuel and raw materials, together with lack of money with which to meet the wages bill, compelled many enterprises to close down. Such action could hardly be attributed to ill will on the employers' part: the roots of the crisis lay deeper, in the collapse of economic life under the strains of war and revolution. It soon became clear to ordinary work-people that they would have to fend for themselves in order to survive, for measures of socialization could at best provide only a long-term solution to the problems of economic reconstruction.

It has been reckoned that the retail price of nine basic foodstuffs rose more than fivefold between September 1917 and January 1918.[16] Since it made little sense to press for higher wages to keep pace with the galloping inflation, workers turned more and more frequently to desperate substitutes. S.G. Strumilin, who investigated the budgets of 345 'typical' workers in Petrograd in the spring of 1918, noted that monetary earnings were contributing less and less to total income. 'Often one may observe men taking part of their earnings in products which they make themselves at the factory and send to the village to be exchanged for foodstuffs they need.' Relatives in the country helped with food parcels. One respondent said that he made do by sending his wife out to shoot (presumably birds or rabbits : he did not elaborate). Others sold their clothing, took in lodgers, or simply ran up debts. Strumilin reckoned that married men now spent 65 per cent of their income on food, as against 49 per cent before the war (1908); expenditure on clothing had fallen from 12 per cent to 7 per cent and on accommodation from 21 per cent to 3 per cent.[17] Some months later (October–November 1918) a more representative sample was taken in Moscow, covering 2,173 persons in 238 enterprises. Conditions had deteriorated further by this time, so that strictly speaking the two sets of figures are not comparable, but in view of the lack of other data it is worth quoting them here. This inquiry showed that monetary earnings accounted for 65·5 per cent of the total income of married workers; the deficit was made up chiefly by drawing on savings (17·8 per cent) and accumulating debts (9·3 per cent). The respondents will probably have understated the proportion of their income from trade (2·5 per cent) and selling their effects (2·2 per cent), since this might have been considered 'speculation'. Married men in Moscow spent 70 per cent of their (total) income on food, 8·5 per cent on clothing and 4·8 per cent on accommodation.[18] Food had to be bought on the free market to supplement the meagre ration (factory canteens were still a rarity), but the additional expenditure this entailed was somewhat offset by the freezing of rents at artificially low levels. At Ivanovo-Voznesensk in June 1918 textile-workers reportedly earned an average of 10 to 12 roubles a day but paid only 5 to 7 roubles a month for a room with bed (10 roubles if they had children).[19] Some workers, especially in Petrograd, were able to improve their standard of accommodation by moving into expropriated housing, and the efflux to the countryside also eased the pressure on living-space.

One significant point revealed by these statistics was the reduction of income differentials between skilled and unskilled workers. This was largely a spontaneous development, but it was welcomed and promoted by the central Bolshevik authorities, who from time to time intervened in wage negotiations to ensure that contracts conformed to egalitarian principles – which at this time were still taken very seriously. The people's commissariat (PC) of Labour had a wage-tariff department which pronounced upon those agreements submitted to it by one or both the parties concerned. At first its officials were inclined to throw their weight behind the wage-earners.

Railwaymen and metal-workers both won settlements which seemed over-generous in view of the state of the economy. But from January 1918 the department preached the virtue of restraint and intervened more actively in the bargaining process. It drew up national wage scales which were to be applied in various branches of industry and endeavoured to link increases to improved productivity.[20] The agreements which it sanctioned generally specified that the maximum remuneration should be less than double the minimum; the latter was seen as a subsistence norm. Thus a collective agreement covering workers in the food industry, classified in three categories, fixed their maximum and minimum pay rates at 430 and 260 roubles a month. At the first congress of labour commissars (16–19 January) A. Shlyapnikov, the commissar, suggested that the maximum differential should be of the order of two to one; but some unions pushed through contracts which provided for a wider range.[21] The issue was soon overtaken by events. As money lost its value, virtually all segments of the working population were reduced to a state bordering upon penury; income differentials took a new form, determined mainly by the size and availability of the official food ration, allocated on a discriminatory basis.

To combat the scourge of unemployment, the PC of Labour, with the cooperation of the trade unions, extended the network of labour exchanges brought into being by previous governments. By June 1918 over 200 of them were said to be functioning, 73 in the region round Moscow and 22 in or near Petrograd.[22] However, they could not do much to satisfy the demand for jobs. At Ivanovo, it was reported, the office was besieged each day by about 750 persons but could find work for only about 50.[23] An official of the commissariat in Tver said that there was nothing his agents could do except clench their teeth and make speeches.[24] In some places officials and trade-union leaders set up local unemployment funds, in accordance with the decree of 23 December, which were financed by contributions from the employers, but the amount of benefits paid out was derisory: in Ivanovo, a total of 1,440 persons received such payments between February and June, the maximum sum (for a married man with family) amounting to 8 roubles.[25] This was unlikely to inspire confidence in the new regime's ability to honour the extravagant promises made in its decrees on labour protection, which were adopted partly with an eye to their demonstrative effect.[26]

For many employees it was thus a question of *sauve qui peut*.

In some enterprises arrangements were made to spread out the work available among everyone currently employed there. When this means was exhausted, factory committees and other organizations established priorities for dismissal. In the Ayvaz works in Petrograd, which ceased production on 20 December, it was decided that those with ties to the village should be the first to leave, since they could be expected to look after themselves.[27] At the Pipe Works it was a case of 'last in, first out'.[28] At Kozlov (Tambov province) there were complaints that women workers were treated unfairly by having to make way for returning soldiers.[29] At other places it was the refugees who were victimized, and Shlyapnikov had to appeal for more consideration to be shown to these unfortunates.[30] There was less sympathy, naturally enough, for those prisoners-of-war employed in industrial plants, who also were among the first to go.[31] The question then arose of compensation for those dismissed. The PC of Labour conceded the principle willingly enough and fixed the amount at the equivalent of four weeks' pay (later raised to six). This was reluctantly accepted by men in the Putilov works (who were granted a retrospective pay increase costing 10 million roubles), but at the Nevsky stearin works, also in Petrograd, their comrades won a scale rising to seven months' pay for those with over twenty years' service, plus a free ticket home and an undertaking that they would be re-employed as soon as conditions improved.[32] The authorities deplored such 'petty-bourgeois' tendencies – 'the workers' pursuit of an extra rouble', as G. Fedorov put it – and ruled that any severance pay above the norm should go into a common fund for the relief of all unemployed.[33]

Statisticians in the PC of Labour, valiantly trying to keep track of the developing crisis, estimated the total number of workless during the period January to April 1918 at 305,614 – a suspiciously precise figure obtained by adding up the figures reported by the local labour exchanges.[34] In Moscow 90,000 persons, or 9·6 per cent of those normally working, were said to be seeking jobs in April.[35] Both these figures are probably underestimates, since many unemployed did not bother to register with the authorities. In Petrograd, where the equivalent figure was 49,000, it was thought that only about a third of the cases came to official notice.[36] The total number of employees on 1 April was reckoned at 144,530, less than half as many as in January 1917 (365,777). Of those who had left, four-fifths had done so during the first three months of 1918. The decline was greatest among those working mineral products (49 per cent); among metal-workers and employees of the foodstuffs industry it amounted to 26 per cent. It was perhaps symptomatic that an increase (3·3 per cent) was recorded among large enterprises making paper.[37]

The great trek to the countryside was largely a spontaneous phenomenon. The authorities assisted it for a variety of reasons – because they feared a German attack, because these large agglomerations of humanity in the cities could not be fed, and because they hoped that at least some of the refugees would be emissaries of socialism among the peasants. Humanitarian considerations played some part as well. In the first six months of 1918 some 32,000 persons were evacuated from Petrograd with the aid of the labour exchanges, of whom 63 per cent were unskilled workers. One of the largest categories so expedited consisted of domestic servants. A curiously titled 'commission for the unburdening of Petrograd' was set up to organize the operation. In March 1918 64,000 workers, mostly in the metallurgical industry, were evacuated from Petrograd, along with much of their plant installations, since it was feared that these might fall victim to the German advance.[38] Similar measures were taken in other towns, but on a less extensive scale.

The story of this migration – one of many neglected aspects of the Russian revolution – cannot as yet be reconstructed satisfactorily from the sources available, but its importance is beyond all doubt. The population of Petrograd, which in 1917 had stood at 2·4 million, had fallen to less than 1·5 million by the spring of 1918. In Moscow, which in March became the new capital, the decline was less precipitous : from 2·0 million to 1·7 million. However, the exodus from both cities continued during the civil war years, until by 1920 Petrograd in particular bore the aspect of a 'ghost town', empty and desolate.[39] It could be said that as a result of the revolution the country underwent a process of 'rusticization' which left a deep imprint upon Russian culture and society. One consequence was to eat away the Bolshevik regime's social base in the industrial working class. This 'withering away of the proletariat' was a temporary phenomenon, to be sure, but it was nevertheless a sociological fact. The men who made the October revolution, in so far as they were civilians and not soldiers, were soon dissipated to the four winds – if not as evacuees, then as Red Army recruits or as political activists dispatched to one or other of the fronts in the civil war; their places would eventually be filled by men who came straight from the village and were cast in a different mould. During the period 1917–18, when this process was just beginning, the lower-echelon organizations served as the main channel of social and political mobilization. Through them large numbers of men became impregnated with the values of the new order and were elevated to positions of responsibility. Children of the revolution, functionaries of the future, they were bound to grow apart from ordinary working folk; proletarian by social origin, in their habits of mind and style of life they could not but differ from their former comrades who stayed behind at the factory bench.

TWENTY-ONE *The Factory Committees and 'Workers' Control'*

THE FACTORY COMMITTEES played only an auxiliary role in the struggle for power but came into their own during the weeks that followed the Bolshevik *coup*. Anarchist and syndicalist tendencies were strong among their members, most of whom expected that 'workers' control' would be interpreted in the most literal sense, that is to say that employees in each enterprise would determine what goods should be produced, how they should be marketed, and much else besides. Such sentiments were not alien to many of their leaders in the CCFCP and other organizations modelled upon it. However it soon became apparent that the Bolsheviks, as partisans of state socialism, intended the factory committees to occupy a modest place in the institutional hierarchy which took shape under the party's aegis. Moreover, as economic conditions worsened many ordinary working men and women realized that the factory committees could do little to protect them from unemployment or other ills, and in many enterprises opinion began to turn against them. In this situation their leaders, forced on to the defensive, had no choice but to abandon their aspirations for autonomy and to accept integration into the new State order on the best terms they could get.

In Petrograd, during the October uprising, the committees established in certain key enterprises, especially those geared to the war effort, were frequently called upon to supply men and material needed by the Bolshevik insurrectionary staff. For example, the Patronnyy zavod (Cartridge works) organization was told not to hand over any ammunition without permission of the MRC (see below, p. 350), and then to issue specified quantities to designated militia units. These orders were complied with, but characteristically this factory committee took simultaneous action to secure enough weapons for its own needs and went on to elect one of its own men as 'commissar', whom the MRC subsequently confirmed in his post. Thereafter the two bodies seem to have ignored one another for two weeks or so, until the commissar wrote to the MRC repudiating charges that the management was guilty of sabotage and pointing out that the factory was running dangerously short of fuel supplies.[1] A similar realism and independence of spirit are evident in a message sent to the MRC on 5 November by the factory committee in the Putilov plant, demanding somewhat peremptorily that the latter take more vigorous measures to obtain coal from the Donets; it then decided to send out emissaries of its own and elected a commissar.[2] At the other extreme, some committees in less important (or less militarized) enterprises addressed the new revolutionary authorities in deferential tones, imploring them 'not to leave us without a crust of bread' but to ensure that their wages would be paid promptly: there was a hint here of dissatisfaction at the new government's clumsy interference in the banking system, which had disrupted normal operations.[3] The MRC replied that it would take action and warned the men against trying to obtain cash by sequestering the plant.[4].

Factory committees sometimes adopted resolutions in support of measures taken or projected by the new government. For example, on 16 November the men of the Staryy Parviainen works called for fresh elections to the Petrograd municipal duma.[5] This move was evidently made in response to promptings from above, for on the same day the duma was indeed dissolved by the government, which was eager to present its action as taken in compliance with popular demand; however, there was no orchestrated campaign on this issue and the statement doubtless reflected the sentiments of those who drafted it. Other resolutions were more critical of Bolshevik policy. Some expressed support for a socialist coalition government.[6] The political situation was still very fluid, and the factory committees had to take account of rank-and-file opinion. Their natural bent towards radicalism did not necessarily mean that they identified themselves wholly with Bolsheviks. However, their ability to voice independent views was rapidly being eroded as sanctions were applied against individuals or press organs sympathetic to the moderate parties; simultaneously those factory committee members most sympathetic to the new regime were pressed to consider themselves as revolutionary cadres, whose duty it was to accept direction from agencies outside the enterprise. Almost without realizing it they came to regard their fellow workmen not as the ultimate source of their authority but as a force subject to their command. One indication of this change was the growing practice of utilizing factory committees as political shock troops to subvert soviets or other organizations under moderate control. The design was to swamp the regularly elected deputies in a crowd of persons who could be passed off as authentic proletarians, and to secure the adoption of pro-Bolshevik resolutions and the election of pro-Bolshevik executives. This manoeuvre was employed in Kiev on 29 November,[7] and on several other occasions to be discussed below.

There is some evidence that ordinary workers objected when their factory committees showed an undue concern with political rather than with practical matters, such as the struggle to maintain industrial production and employment, or treated these bread-and-butter issues in an excessively ideological spirit. In the nature of things measures of economic self-help were bound to loom large in their thinking. The most useful action the committees could take was to try to obtain fuel supplies. Delegations to the Donets were dispatched by men in a number of Petrograd factories, as well as by the CCFCP itself.[8] However, these agents got in one another's way and do not seem to have had much success. Occasionally they would obtain a firm promise of fuel supplies, only to learn later that the consignment had been intercepted *en route* by other needy claimants. Where enterprises had enough fuel but were short of raw materials, there might be a basis for a rudimentary barter deal. There were factory committees which, with more ingenuity than foresight, disposed of fixed plant (for instance machinery) as well as stocks of commodities. Some manufactured goods were also traded directly with peasants or others who had foodstuffs to sell.

Partly in pursuit of such practical ends, and partly as a matter of ideological principle, factory-committee activists forced managerial personnel to show them the firm's accounts and to permit them to verify every financial and commercial transaction. The 'control commissions' established for this purpose were nominally responsible to the work-people as a body through their elected representatives, but in practice their members did much as they pleased. There was thus ample scope for excesses and abuses. Supervision of accounts was often carried out with a pedantic thoroughness that sprang from the activists' suspicion of those whom they had been led to look upon as class enemies. It was inefficient and time-consuming, and often accompanied by acts of victimization. More serious were the acts of wanton destruction or damage to factory property, sometimes caused deliberately but more frequently brought about by neglect of proper servicing procedures.

The local militants tended to condone such incidents or to attribute them to negligence by the supervisory staff. Few of them were as yet reconciled to the idea, which was already in the air among the Bolshevik chiefs, that the prime functions of the factory committee were to impose industrial discipline and boost productivity; even if they accepted it, they usually lacked the means to put it into practice. The committee in the Putilov plant tried to set an example in this regard : early in 1918 it threatened with dismissal certain workers who went on strike for higher pay and forced them to abandon their demands.[9] But this was the exception which proves the rule. Not until the civil war began in earnest did factory committees, by this time subject to intensified political pressure from above, seek to act in this spirit. During the first six months after the Bolshevik *coup* irresponsible attitudes were general.

The ultimate sanction against recalcitrant employers, sequestration of the plant, does not seem to have been decided upon lightly. In many cases the men saw it as a measure of self-defence rather than as a weapon in the class struggle, a short-term expedient rather than a panacea. Nevertheless it was an unpleasant prospect for the industrialist concerned. Some of them sought to avert the blow by having their enterprise nationalized instead – that is to say by securing the protection of the central authorities against the local cadres. However, most nationalization orders issued during this period bore a punitive character, in that they simply sanctioned expropriation by the local factory committee or some other *ad hoc* body. It has been estimated that three-quarters of all the enterprises nationalized by June 1918 were taken over in this way. Most of them were located in outer regions such as the Urals or the Donets valley. In the two capital cities the authorities had more success in limiting the scope of this movement.[10]

For the same reason there was less industrial violence in those areas that were under relatively effective control by the central state organs. In Petrograd there were one or two cases of managerial personnel being arrested at the behest of enterprise-level bodies,[11] but the impact of such acts was slight when set against the arbitrary measures taken by such organs as the MRC (which gave birth to the Cheka). One factor here was that a high proportion of industrial plants in and around the capital, above all the metallurgical works, were already state-owned, so that the slogan of nationalization inevitably forfeited some of its appeal; moreover, where workers' control had already been implemented the results were scarcely encouraging. In the Central Industrial region textile-workers sometimes invited white-collar employees to serve on the control commissions, whose chief concern was clearly just to keep production going for as long as possible. As one of their leaders put it early in December, 'if the chaos in industry continues and we workers take no action, we shall be condemning our descendants to extinction by hunger'; such measures were therefore a matter of 'simple self-defence'.[12]

In the Donets valley, on the other hand, where there had been much social strife during the previous months, the situation was one of incipient civil war. The coal-miners, who had occupied many of the pits by force, accused their employers of collusion with ataman Kaledin's cossacks. (The latter occupied part of the area in November but were soon soon expelled by local para-military forces, with some aid from the centre.) A metal-workers' delegate from Yekaterinoslav reported on 15 October to colleagues in Petrograd that 'the workers have seized a whole number of factories and are maintaining output in the interests of the State and the revolution'; two days each week were allotted to the manufacture of commodities for sale to peasants in the vicinity.[13] In the Urals, where the factory-committee movement was perhaps more militant than anywhere else, most factories and mines sooner or later came under control of local workers' committees. An elaborate hierarchy of controlling organs emerged, headed by a Central Council of

Urals Factory Committees. Elected at a conference held early in December, this body had to contend not only with local counter-revolutionaries but also with the central authorities in Petrograd, who looked askance at its violent and self-willed behaviour.[14]

As is apparent from this brief survey, conditions varied greatly from one area to another, as well as between different branches of industry. Given the existing state of documentation, which has been tailored to produce a misleading picture of uniformity and political commitment, it is difficult to generalize about the factory-committees' achievements; still less easy is it to draw conclusions as to the merits and demerits of this type of industrial organization in more promising circumstances. Writers of syndicalist sympathies have hailed the Russian factory committees of 1917–18 as the embryo of a new system of industrial management based on freedom and self-government, and have deplored their absorption into a bureaucratic hierarchy which, although pledged to build socialism, reproduced many vices of the old order. This argument is attractive to some liberals as well as to libertarians. Without entering here into the ideological aspects of the question, one may point out that most activists at the enterprise level were not zealots inspired by a utopian vision but ordinary individuals brought close to desperation by the collapse of the economy and obliged to look after themselves as best they might. The reality of their day-to-day struggle was a far cry from the romantic ideas entertained by the theorists of syndicalism.

Most historians have been more critical, partly perhaps under the influence of the negative views expressed then and since by Bolsheviks and other advocates of state socialism. D.B. Ryazanov, who like most of his party colleagues expected industry to be managed largely by the trade unions, made no secret of his opposition to the factory committees. In January 1918, addressing the first All-Russian congress of trade unions, he accused them of ignoring the overall interests of the proletariat and the revolution, which the new government allegedly had at heart, and even insinuated that they had become covert agents of the employers (which to the Bolshevik mind made them counter-revolutionary and due for liquidation).[15] No doubt there were some instances of collaboration between managers and committee-men – as was only to be expected, since they had a common interest in maintaining production; there may also have been exceptional cases where such cooperation was induced by the promise of material rewards. But Ryazanov's argument is disingenuous: not only did factory committees generally take a more consistently hostile line towards 'capitalist' employers than the Bolsheviks (some of whom favoured a mixed economy), but they had also, as we know, established an organization of their own in order to coordinate their activities and suppress 'separatist' tendencies – yet it was precisely this independent body that the Bolsheviks now sought to destroy. They could not tolerate the continued existence of a body which could compete with their own party in rallying the industrial workers behind ultra-radical slogans.

Many years later, when the Soviet regime had become firmly established, communist historians began to take a more positive view of the factory-committees' achievements. The 'proletarian masses' were now held to have been actually or potentially loyal to the Bolsheviks throughout the revolutionary period; any leanings on their part to the left or right were simply discounted. The ideological and political struggle between the advocates of state socialism on one hand and the anarchists or syndicalists on the other, which revolved largely round the role the factory committees should play in industrial management, was side-stepped, and the latter were represented as path-breakers for the economic bureaucrats.

Although this interpretation distorts historical reality, it is not entirely invalid. For whatever the enterprise-level cadres may have desired, the ultimate *effect* of their activity was to increase the chaos that afflicted Russian industry. By harassing employers and other managerial personnel, and in the last resort by taking over factories which they could not run effectively, they created a situation in which the state power had to assert itself and impose its own nominees. The rapid pace at which nationalization of industry was pushed forward during 1918 was in part a response to the grass-roots radicalism of the factory committees. For initially the Bolshevik leaders had been willing to experiment with some form of 'state-capitalist' mixed economy, involving agreements with certain major private-enterprise concerns; but by the spring of 1918 these talks had to be abandoned, in part because of the opposition shown to them by the ultra-left cadres in the factories.[16] In this way the extremists themselves helped to bring on the excess of the so-called 'War Communism' period (1918–21), when what remained of Russian industry was militarized and subjected to rigid state control. Not for the first time in history, men who set out as libertarians turned into disciplinarians *par excellence.*

The integration of the factory committees into the new economic bureaucracy was a long drawn-out process, only the first phase of which can be examined here. It led to what one Soviet historian calls 'a fierce struggle' behind the scenes as the protagonists of differing viewpoints within the Bolshevik party vied for supremacy.[17] Largely on this account, the second congress of soviets was not presented with a draft decree on workers' control, analogous to those on peace and land. Instead, more than two weeks elapsed before such a decree was promulgated, on 14 November, and even this was little more than a temporary compromise.

Those prominent Bolsheviks, such as N.A. Skrypnik, who were most closely associated with the factory-committee movement in Petrograd took the slogan of workers' control seriously. They assumed that in a 'proletarian dictatorship' major economic decisions would be taken at enterprise level by the factory committees and that the superior organs in the factory-committee hierarchy would act in a coordinating capacity. Other Bolshevik leaders, such as Larin, Lozovsky or Ryazanov, whose experience had been in the trade unions, stressed the need for a central agency to direct the economy. They took it for granted that this agency would work hand in hand with the trade unions, who would nominate most if not all its members. Similar agencies would exist in the main provincial centres in the shape of the economic departments of the soviets. The factory committees were seen as occupying a subordinate but nevertheless important place, as agencies of control within the enterprise, for it was assumed that most of industry would remain for some time under private ownership, and such watchdogs would therefore be necessary. Only in exceptional cases would they displace management, and even then their decisions would be subject to confirmation from above, by the local (soviet) and central (state) economic agencies. These two points of view were at variance over the merits of spontaneous mass action and the likely pace of advance towards socialism; but they both sprang from a sincere, if naive, belief that the democratization of industry was a feasible goal. The former was closer to that of the anarchists and syndicalists, the latter to that of the Mensheviks, to which party many of these men had belonged before their conversion to Bolshevism.

Besides these two standpoints there was yet a third represented by Lenin himself – and probably shared by all those members of the Central Committee who, like their leader, thought primarily in terms of political strategy, not of immediate economic necessities (as did the 'right') or future social ideals (as did the 'left'). To these men what mattered most were the interests of the revolution, which they identified with those of their own party and the state order it was about to call into being. To the extent that workers' control was consonant with these interests, they endorsed it; to the extent that it was deemed actually or potentially harmful, they opposed it; its value was not intrinsic but relative. To be sure, Lenin was more than a cold calculating strategist and also had a romantic idealistic streak. Nowhere was this more apparent than on the issue of workers' control, for in Lenin's celebrated pamphlet *State and Revolution* he put forward some ideas on the subject which were quite utopian. Control of a modern industrial enterprise, he asserted, amounted to little more than the keeping of accounts and could therefore be performed by any literate person with an elementary knowledge of arithmetic.[18] In this doctrine there was a fanciful element which cannot be reconciled intellectually with the Bolshevik leader's life-long commitment to authoritarian principles of organization. E.H. Carr comments on 'Lenin's extraordinary skill in reconciling the obstinate pursuit of an ultimate objective which he recognized as necessary (i.e. state control) with the satisfaction of an immediate popular demand [that is to say workers' control] in apparent conflict with that objective.'[19] It might be objected that no such reconciliation of the two aims was achieved and that they coexisted as disparate entities. In August and September 1917 Lenin was inclined to idealize the masses' cravings for industrial democracy and to over-look the economic and political effects which would follow upon the satisfaction of these demands. By November, having been catapulted from obscurity into the seat of power, he quite naturally saw matters in a different light and his old instincts as a political realist came once more to the fore. By April 1918 he would be upbraiding Russia's workers for their lack of discipline and threatening draconian measures to boost labour productivity. If at first he had been to the left (in conventional terms) of most of his colleagues, he later swung sharply to the opposite extreme.[20]

In our context what matters is that Lenin was able to impose his flexible or 'dialectical' conception of workers' control. On 26 October he was confronted with a draft statute setting out the rights and duties of the controlling organs. This had been elaborated by the All-Russian Council of Factory Committees (ARCFC : the successor to the CCFCP, formed on the eve of the October insurrection) and envisaged the creation of a hierarchy of controlling bodies headed by a provisional All-Russian Council of Workers' Control. Evidently these leaders saw themselves as playing a major role in the new body, on which two-thirds of the seats were to be allotted to workers' representatives, chosen through soviets, trade unions and factory committees; the remainder were reserved for delegates of the employers, engineers and technical personnel.[21] Against this draft Lenin set one of his own which made no mention of any central body to regulate economic life, or of the ARCFC, and put the accent on sharpening the measures of control to be applied at enterprise level. Whereas the rival draft attempted to define closely the responsibilities of the controlling organs at every level, Lenin's left such matters vague in the extreme.[22] The most obvious explanation of his stand is that he expected the local soviets to take the initiative in directing economic life and wished to give them a free hand in devising methods of overcoming the stiff resistance to the new order which he expected would be offered by the employers. He had not yet shaken off his idealistic assumptions and looked askance at the notion of a central economic bureaucracy, particularly one staffed by individuals whose political loyalty was in some doubt. Another more subtle interpretation may also be advanced : namely, that Lenin wanted to erode the prestige of the ARCFC leadership by outbidding them, in the expectation that the workers would soon become sobered by the experience of anarchistic excesses and would accept more readily the restraints that would have to be imposed upon them from the centre. In support of this interpretation one may point to the many utopian and impracticable aspects of his plan. Controlling organs were to be introduced in *all* enterprises (agricultural, financial and commercial as well as industrial) employing more than five persons; in smaller firms the *entire* labour force was to participate in control operations; *all* the controllers' decisions were to be binding on management, no provision being made for appeal. Nothing was said about the relationship between the controlling organs and the political authorities at any level.[23]

The two drafts were then passed to a commission under Shlyapnikov, the PC of Labour, which tried to reconcile them. Lenin's draft was amended to make it more specific as to the projected institutional arrangements; simultaneously the ARCFC revised its draft by elaborating the provisions on control at enterprise level. To complicate matters, two further drafts were submitted, both of them fairly pragmatic in inspiration. Shlyapnikov predictably took Lenin's amended draft as the basis and a compromise text was elaborated which after further discussion was approved by the CEC on 14 November and published two days later.[24]

According to this compromise the ARCWC was to have about forty members appointed by various labour organizations, only five of whom would be drawn from the factory-committee movement. The idea of direct control from the shop floor in small enterprises was abandoned. The controlling organs were to include representatives of technical staff and white-collar employees as well as manual workers. The punitive provisions which had been prominent in Lenin's draft were toned down. Managers were still required to submit all their firm's documents for inspection, but they could challenge the controllers' decisions by appealing to higher instances in the hierarchy. Finally, the central organ was empowered to issue blanket exemptions from workers' control.[25]

All this suggested a victory for those who thought of workers' control as a basic and enduring principle of industrial organization. But appearances were deceptive, for the last word lay with the political strategists who took their cue from Lenin. The final paragraph of the decree stated that rules would be issued separately to govern relations between the workers' control organizations and other economic agencies. This indicated that the newly established ARCWC would not itself be the supreme body in the economic bureaucracy; it also suggested that opinion was shifting away from the idea of management through the soviets and towards the creation of a centralized apparatus. By the time these regulations had been devised in December, such an all-encompassing body had already been created : the Supreme Economic Council (SEC).[26] Its stated purpose was to coordinate the activities of all existing authorities, both central and local, with responsibility for economic affairs – a definition which clearly included the factory committees. The ARCWC was absorbed into SEC as one of its three constituent elements, the other two being government representatives (especially from the PC of Labour) and technical experts. Since ARCWC was itself a mixed organ, only a small fraction of its members being drawn from the factory-committee movement, it was clear that the latter's representation in SEC would be largely symbolic.

The life of ARCWC was ephemeral even by the unexacting standards of 1917 : created on 14 November, it held but two meetings, only one of them (on 28 November) before its incorporation into SEC some three weeks later.[27] On 7 December the syndicalist-minded leaders of ARCFC published draft instructions for the controlling organs which allocated them extensive rights. This document went further than a similar one published by a government commission six days later, which in January 1918 was duly sanctioned by the first congress of trade unions.[28] This 'war of regulations' was of little practical significance except in so far as it hardened opinion in the ruling spheres against ARCFC. The latter body, the sole remaining forum left to the syndicalists, followed ARCWC into limbo, being integrated into the economic council (*sovnarkhoz*) of the 'Northern region', which covered those provinces economically and administratively dependent on Petrograd.[29] A similar fate was meted out to other regional or provincial councils of workers' control.

Meanwhile the factory committees themselves were formally subordinated to the trade unions, of which they became the primary organizations or 'cells'. This development will be considered further below (see pp. 302–3). In practice, especially in the provinces, they continued to enjoy a good deal of autonomy until the enterprises concerned were caught up in the exigencies of the civil war.

The leaders of the factory-committee movement had expected to play an autonomous role in shaping the destinies of Russian labour. These ambitions were frustrated by a strange coalition of Bolshevik strategists and Menshevik (or ex-Menshevik) technocrats. If Lenin had initially harboured doubts about the need for a central body to direct the economy (which is plausible but by no means certain), he soon overcame his hesitations. Some time in November at the latest he seems to have decided that the syndicalists, whose ideas he himself had recently appeared to share, represented a greater danger to the security of the new regime than the Menshevik advocates of a mixed economy ('state capitalism') and a more moderate, reasonable form of workers' control. Both these tendencies had supporters within his own party, so that it needed only a slight touch on the tiller to adjust course. This tactical shift was followed by others which would enhance the bureaucratic features of the new industrial order and erode still further the real content of workers' control – without, however, endorsing the relatively pragmatic outlook of the Menshevik planners. If the latter, rejoicing at the defeat of syndicalism, imagined that they emerged from this contest as the victors, they were shortly to be disabused by the grim experiment of 'war communism', in which for some years economic rationality would yield place to ideological fanaticism.

TWENTY-TWO *From Workers' Militia to Red Army*

THE PARA-MILITARY FORMATIONS which had come into being during the spring and summer of 1917 played an auxiliary role in the transfer of power to the Bolshevik-dominated soviets. They were, however, generally less important than the soldiers' organizations. The autonomy they enjoyed during and immediately after the October insurrection was short-lived. In retrospect the historical significance of the 'Red guards' (as they now customarily called themselves) lies chiefly in the fact that they contributed much manpower to the Red Army, into which they were absorbed during 1918.[1] Just as the factory committees were integrated into the economic agencies of the dictatorship, so the Red guards became a constituent part of its formidable military apparatus. This process also had a social aspect. Before October 1917 the workers' militia, like the factory committees to which they had first been appended, served as an outlet for the accumulated energies of the most radicalized elements of the Russian working class; subsequently, in so far as this force became subordinate to the new State, it began to emancipate itself from its proletarian origins and even helped to militarize (or remilitarize) the milieu whence it had sprung.

As we have seen (cf. above p. 94) a new phase in the history of the workers' militia began early in September, when the left-wing parties mobilized their supporters in the factories in response to the threat of attack by General Kornilov's troops. In the Petrograd area, where these measures were most thorough, these para-military formations acquired a new respectability as defenders of 'democracy' against 'counter-revolution'. The moderate socialist leaders in the government and the soviets often took the view that these bands posed a less serious threat to civil peace than the cossacks or other army units deemed to be in sympathy with the extreme right. Subsequently many of them grew concerned at the extent of Bolshevik strength in the militia, but feared that any forcible measures would provoke further violent disorders and so preferred to do nothing. This situation suited the militia chiefs very well. They were more or less free to recruit new members, to improve the supply of arms, to hold regular training sessions, and to coordinate their plans by holding local conferences. In all this activity the central Bolshevik authorities seem to have played a relatively modest part. The party's Military Organization did little more than dispatch NCOs to the factories as instructors. For instance, twenty-one men were assigned to six enterprises in the Vyborg district of Petrograd.[2] Similar action had already been taken spontaneously. Some soldiers in the Petrograd garrison volunteered their services as part-time instructors; in other cases this role was assumed by workers who had previous military experience. At the Erikson electrical works three such men gave tuition in arms drill and military tactics for four hours a week on Thursday and Friday evenings to seventy-six men, two-thirds of those enrolled in the force.[3] Perhaps the most significant fact, in the light of later developments, was the assumption by these instructors of command functions; they would then be confirmed in their position by an 'election' in which the element of choice was minimal. Junior leaders (that is the chiefs of squads, as distinct from 'companies' or 'battalions') could still claim to be authentic representatives of their men.[4]

The morale of the Red guards in Petrograd on the eve of the October assault seems to have been rather uneven. Much depended on the availability of weapons. In the solidly proletarian Vyborg quarter, where the militia bands were more numerous and better organized than in any other district of the city, only one man in three had a rifle.[5] There is little evidence of aggressive spirit : the men were willing, indeed eager, to defend 'the gains of the revolution' from attack, but had no desire to be drawn into offensive action. It was for this reason that the Bolshevik leaders astutely presented their insurrectionary moves as wholly defensive in character. For ten days or so before the seizure of power in the city the militia forces were kept on the alert. On the evening of 24 October, when the seizure of strategic points within the city began, the initiative seems to have been taken by soldiers rather than Red guardsmen.[6] The latter were called upon to man several bridges across the Neva. This was an important mission, since these bridges controlled access to the centre of the city from the working-class suburbs (the river was not frozen, as it had been in February!) – but it was not likely to involve them in serious fighting. Although one squad surrendered to a force of military cadets and had to be replaced by fifteen soldiers of the Finnish regiment,[7] the militiamen performed this task successfully. They also patrolled the streets and provided about fifteen hundred men to guard the insurgents' headquarters.

In the actual combat operations, which were on a small scale, their role was subordinate to that of the revolutionary troops. N.P. Podvoysky, a leading member of the MRC, is explicit on this point. The assault on the Winter Palace, delayed for several hours by 'technical' difficulties, was carried out by soldiers of five infantry regiments and sailors of the Baltic fleet; militiamen were employed only in an auxiliary role on the right flank.[8] About 800 men at the most were involved. It is an interesting comment on the fallibility of human memory that in the 1930s, when surviving members of these bands were asked to complete a questionnaire giving details of their service experience, over 12 per cent of those replying claimed to have participated in the 'siege' of the Winter Palace; it has been calculated that this would have made for a besieging force some 46,000 strong![9]

Once the Provisional Government had been deposed, the militiamen's spirits improved significantly and there was an influx of recruits. A number of bands volunteered to help construct defences against the several hundred troops mustered outside the capital a few days later by Kerensky and General Krasnov, and some militiamen participated in the fighting which ensued. This was their first real experience of action. They also helped to suppress an ill-prepared uprising by military cadets in Petrograd on 29 October.

The large claims sometimes made on behalf of the Red guards' contribution to the success of this ostensibly 'proletarian' insurrection must therefore be dismissed. Podvoysky, for example, asserted that '[their] role in the uprising and in the preparations for it was exceptionally great', and speculated that in future upheavals such militia forces 'will be the core around which will be grouped the entire armed mass of the proletariat and all the soldiers loyal to the revolution'.[10] Modern Soviet historians are more cautious. Startsev writes: 'It is well known that in the October armed insurrection the Red guards were, together with units of the old army and sailors of the Baltic fleet, the leading military force'[11] – a formulation so ambiguous as to make the word 'leading' meaningless.

It is unfortunately not possible to enumerate accurately the total number of civilians and soldiers respectively who took part in the insurrection. Bolshevik writers are naturally prone to inflate the size of the former element. Trotsky speaks of having 'about 20,000 Red guardsmen' in a total force of 25–30,000, but little reliance may be placed in these figures.[12] Comparative data are available only for the Vyborg district, where the Red guards numbered 4,700 and two pro-Bolshevik military units 6,500;[13] in other districts the balance will have been still less favourable to them. Even if precise figures were available, they would tell us nothing about the morale or fighting capacity of the men concerned. In the Petrograd garrison, some 150,000 strong, only a few units were strongly committed either to the Provisional Government or to the Bolsheviks; the overwhelming majority preferred to remain neutral. This factor more than any other accounts for the ease with which power was transferred in the capital. The preponderant role played by the garrison (including the Baltic fleet) is evident from the records of the MRC, which have now been published in full. These abound in references to various military units, but contain little information about the Red guards.[14]

The predominance of soldiers vis-à-vis militiamen limits the value of Startsev's careful research into the social and political make-up of this latter force. His study of the representative sample mentioned above suggests that the Red guards were overwhelmingly (95·9 per cent) proletarian, and that some three-quarters of them were employed in the metallurgical industry; 43·7 per cent of Petrograd militiamen were Bolsheviks, 53·1 per cent had no party affiliation, and 1·9 per cent belonged to other left-wing parties (Left SRs, Mensheviks and Anarchists).[15] These data probably understate the importance of the Anarchist element. Early in January the strength of Anarchist influence in the Nevsky district became a matter of concern to the Bolshevik leaders of the Petrograd soviet, who considered the units there 'unreliable'; some of the men also seem to have sympathized with the moderate socialists.[16] Anarchist sentiments (in the general sense of this term) were widespread among rank-and-file militiamen. Once the fighting was over they gave vent to these destructive and violent instincts, posing a problem for the Bolsheviks as well as a threat to the security of ordinary citizens.

The new authorities were at first inclined to look leniently upon excesses committed by Red guards in the course of their quasi-police duties, such as carrying out unauthorized searches and 'confiscating' property. Another temptation to arbitrariness was the power they wielded as guards over persons arrested on such occasions; these unfortunates were often confined in makeshift prisons – one which became notorious was in the cellar of the Smolny Institute – and were badly treated.[17] Proceedings were instituted against the head of the Red guard 'staff' in the second city district of the capital (where a number of well-to-do persons lived) for 'rough treatment' of prisoners, but their outcome is not known.[18] On 11 January the chief authority overseeing the Petrograd Red guards issued a circular drawing attention to the penalty inflicted on one D.I. Mikhaylov, a rank-and-file militiaman in Kazansky district, who for 'drunkenness and riotous behaviour' was dismissed and sentenced to two years' prison with hard labour.[19] There seems little doubt that many militiamen became demoralized by duties which offered so many opportunities to abuse their power. Many offences were committed when drunk.

Lack of an assured income was another factor which encouraged arbitrary acts. The central authorities at first took the view that the Red guards should receive no pay (at least from public funds).[20] This seems to have brought them into conflict with their chiefs (notably I. Yurenev) in the Central Commandantura, who had a higher estimate of their morale and utility than the party leaders. Whether in response to pressure from below, or because of the worsening military situation, at the end of December the CPC relented and authorized the release of 2·5 million roubles to pay the Red guards. (A decision to this effect had been taken by the MRC as early as 12 November.)[21] Until that time they had virtually had to 'finance themselves'. Some money was obtained from local soviets and other labour organizations, but on several occasions they resorted to direct pressure on entrepreneurs.[22] In some cases the threat of arrest sufficed to extort funds from the employers, who offered only passive resistance to such strong-arm methods.

These material difficulties seem to have contributed to a decline of zeal. It was one thing to volunteer for service in an emergency, when it seemed that the whole future of the working class and the revolution was at stake; it was another to help maintain public order on a semi-permanent basis. Although some six thousand recruits are said to have joined the Red guards of the capital in November and December, this access of strength was more than offset by wastage. At the Staryy Lessner engineering plant the number of militiamen newly enrolled fell from 250 in early November to 34 in March; at the Rozenkrants copper and pipe works the figures were 266 and 10.[23] This was in part also a consequence of growing unemployment and the migration to the countryside.

The chief reason, however, why the younger men left was because they volunteered (or were mobilized) for service in one or other of the armed bands dispatched to fight on various fronts in the civil war. As many as nine to ten thousand militiamen are thought to have left the Petrograd area in this way (some of whom returned in the spring). A number of Finnish workers went to fight in their own homeland; two 'combined detachments' were sent to the southern provinces, one of which saw action against the Ukrainian autonomists while the other engaged Kaledin's forces on the Don.[24]

These postings presupposed the existence of a central agency able to issue orders to militia bands and expect them to be obeyed. Late in November the Central Commandantura of Red guards in the capital, which had led a somewhat shadowy existence, was turned into a staff headquarters (*glavnyy shtab*). The introduction of conventional military terminology was not fortuitous. The initiative in making this change lay with K. Yeremeyev, a young ensign who had been coopted to the government's Committee on Military and Naval Affairs and served as commander of the Petrograd military district.[25] In effect the latter organization absorbed the central headquarters of the Red guards into its own apparatus, which had survived the transfer of power.

This bureaucratization, or at least formalization, of the militia was not well received in the various city district headquarters. The local leaders felt that they had borne most of the responsibility for the militia's work during the revolutionary days and had acquired sufficient experience to continue to run their affairs without dictation from above. The men, too, seem to have set some store by the right to elect their own chiefs and sometimes made things difficult for the 'commissars' (as they were generally called) who were appointed to positions of command.

From the central government's standpoint, of course, this centralization seemed a logical and necessary step. The new regime faced a host of enemies; with the army in a state of collapse and politically unreliable, the militia had to be transformed into a proper fighting force, a bastion of the dictatorship. There were some idealists, such as E.A. Trifonov, who dreamed of converting the Red guards into a kind of 'people's police', in which all workers who were physically and morally up to the mark should be obliged to serve in rotation. This notion was in line with earlier Marxist and Bolshevik thinking, and fitted in with the idea of a general militia to replace the old standing army. However, it was soon shown to be utopian; although the plan was approved by the Petrograd municipal duma shortly before its demise, nothing more was heard of it.[26]

Political and military realities required that the Red guards should form a kind of *corps d'élite* within the new Red Army, plans for which were being drawn up from early December onwards in conjunction with certain 'military specialists' (as ex-imperial army officers were euphemistically called). At first it was intended that the Red Army should be a purely volunteer force of reliable proletarians. But this idea in turn had to be dropped when it became apparent that insufficient volunteers would be forthcoming and that the Soviet state might collapse under the weight of regular German divisions. On 18 February, after the breakdown of the Brest-Litovsk peace talks, Ludendorff launched an offensive which without difficulty put Petrograd itself within their reach. This threat forced the Bolsheviks to engage in a speedy build-up of their military forces. The size of the Red Army was rapidly increased. Among its regular formations were some that had grown directly out of militia bands; in others a leaven was provided by groups of individuals who had gained their first experience in the arts of war as members of these irregular units. The days of anarchy and experimentation were decidedly over.

The foregoing remarks relate mainly to Petrograd and its environs, where Red guard activities have been most fully studied. In the provinces, too, their role generally was less important than that of the soldiers, who bore the brunt of such fighting as took place. In Moscow the Bolshevik leaders were poorly prepared to rise in insurrection (see below, p. 354). There were groups of a few hundred militiamen in two industrial districts and among railwaymen; still others came into existence during the course of fighting; however, there was little coordination and they lacked popular support. No less than a hundred and forty thousand workers were employed in the Zamoskvorechye district, but of these only two hundred enrolled in combat squads (most of them in a single factory).[27] A photograph has survived of one of these bands. It shows a group of twenty-seven men posed in front of an armoured car and four pieces of light artillery; about half of them are carrying personal arms, and all but seven or eight are wearing uniform; one man (possibly the instructor?) has adopted a soldierly stance which contrasts with the nonchalant attitudes of his fellows, most of whom look as if they were in their twenties.[28] One leading Bolshevik complained shortly afterwards that 'only working youths joined the Red guards, and even they did not have enough weapons.'[29] The total number of troops available to the insurgents was put at fifteen thousand, as compared with three thousand armed workers.[30] The latter provided auxiliary services (such as digging trenches) but as the tide of battle began to turn in the insurgents' favour, militiamen from the outlying areas occupied various strategic points, incurring casualties in the process. The most important of these engagements was the seizure of a cadet college. This action involved ninety militiamen, who succeeded by a *ruse de guerre* : they pointed two captured cannons at the building, and although they had no shells to fire this produced the anticipated psychological effect.[31] The compromise settlement of 2 November, which provided for an honourable surrender by the anti-Bolshevik forces, was unpopular with some Red guards, who publicly protested against such leniency.[32] These zealots appear to have been Letts; on another occasion certain militiamen of more pacific disposition intervened to save the lives of prisoners from the wrath of the aroused soldiery.[33]

The Central Staff of Moscow Red guards, which scarcely made any mark during the fighting, came into evidence after the transfer of power. It reorganized itself on military lines, distributing among its seven members responsibilities for operations, training, supplies and intelligence;[34] it then endeavoured to assert its authority over the districts. This was made difficult by the lack of funds at its disposal, but the districts seem to have offered less resistance to centralization in Moscow than they did in Petrograd – partly because they had not yet had time to establish themselves institutionally, and partly because the Moscow leaders were more moderate in their pretensions than those in the capital. The draft statute which they prepared for adoption by Red guard units gave the latter the right to elect their own commander, and this made the proposed hierarchical pattern of organization more tolerable. The Moscow Bolsheviks had a not undeserved reputation for 'softness'; and this relative liberalism encouraged the Moscow Red guard staff to see itself as a provisional body whose principal task was to ease the birth-pangs of a 'people's militia'.

On 10 December these ideas were put to (and presumably endorsed by) a conference of representatives chosen by the 2,550 militiamen in the city. It was decided to hold another conference in the following month at which these organizational principles would be presented to delegates from the entire central region of the country. But by the time this gathering met, on 20 January, the situation had changed. The men were confronted with a new draft statute which provided that all militia units were to be immediately reorganized as units in the Red Army. The resolution adopted at this conference still spoke of a 'people's militia' and the election of commanders, but such ideas were now outdated. Several bands of militiamen from Moscow and elsewhere had already been dispatched for service on the south-eastern and western fronts. By the spring all such units had become integrated into the regular Red forces.[35]

In many provincial towns, as in Moscow, militia units appeared only a short while before the Bolshevik insurrection. This was the case in Kazan, for instance, where the workers' mood was much less militant than that of the returning front-line soldiers, who declared for Bolshevism already on 15 October and so came up against a certain opposition from the local workers' soviet. Matters were much the same in other towns in the central provinces which had sizeable garrisons, especially where the soviet was still controlled by the moderate socialist parties. Precisely because there was so little opposition, the industrial workers saw no great need to form armed units. No doubt the preponderance of female labour was an additional factor here.

In industrial centres in the Ukraine the situation was complicated for pro-Bolshevik militia units by the existence of other para-military formations which followed the lead of the autonomist Central Rada. In Kiev the latter emerged as the victors in the fighting which broke out late in October, and the local 'Red' forces were forced on the defensive. The establishment of Soviet power in the city two months later owed something to the activities of these bands, but much more to the intervention of the military forces dispatched into the Ukraine by the authorities in Petrograd.[36] These latter were accompanied by Red guard elements from Kharkov and the Donets valley, who also helped to effect the transfer of power in a number of other centres; some of them also saw service against Kaledin's cossacks. These units were relatively well armed but poorly disciplined, and their excesses did much to antagonize people of all classes. Later, when the Ukraine was occupied by the Central Powers, some of these men engaged in sporadic guerilla activity – of a kind that was to become endemic over much of the Ukraine during the next two years.

The region where workers' militia bands seem to have played a decisive role was the southern Urals. This was an area of technologically backward and lagging industry, where the mines and metallurgical works were as a rule located in isolated settlements some distance from major urban centres. Many of the powerful factory committees which had come into being during the spring and summer had militia formations attached to them. Flamboyantly calling themselves 'combat squads of the people in arms', they were organized on expressly para-military lines, with sections of sharpshooters, sappers, artillerymen, scouts and so forth, and provided a model for similar bands further to the north.[37] The socialist politicians in Ufa were afraid of the marked syndicalist tendencies displayed by the local partisan chiefs. Three brothers named Kadomtsev, who belonged to a family of impoverished gentlefolk, were in a position to provide leadership. They had all been involved in the violent 'expropriations' in the years after 1905, and paid for their activities with years of imprisonment or exile. (Other leaders, such as P.I. Zemstov, came from a skilled worker background.) The moderate socialists in Ufa rashly appointed one Erasmus Kadomtsev commander of the Ufa garrison, in which capacity he was able to supply the combat squads with a plentiful array of weapons.[38] This equipment raised the prestige of these bands and many younger men flocked to join them. Since the factories and mines were already under *de facto* workers' control by October, the transfer of power was little more than a formality in this region. One of the militiamen's first tasks was to impose their will upon the Bolshevik leaders in Ufa, who were inclined to favour a compromise with the moderate socialists; as an early memorialist put it, 'descending from their mountains into the valley, they straightened the line of conduct of the urban soviet and raised it to a revolutionary height'.[39] At the end of November an emergency congress of soviets in Ufa province decided that combat squads should be set up wherever feasible, and a central body was charged with coordinating their activities and meeting their requirements of arms and other supplies.

On 12 December a congress of combat squads was held, attended by delegates from no less than fifty such organizations, some of which were said to have several hundred members. More commonly they had only a few dozen; even so they were more militant and better organized than any militia bodies elsewhere. They distinguished themselves in local engagements against the forces of Colonel A.I. Dutov, ataman of the Ural cossacks. On the negative side they seriously disrupted the economy of the region by repressive measures against industrial managers and others deemed to belong to the 'bourgeoisie', and production soon came to a near-standstill. High-handed measures were taken against peasants of the surrounding areas, and by March 1918 some villages were in open revolt. There was also trouble with the Bashkirs, for whose religious beliefs and national aspirations these extremists had nothing but contempt.[40] These economic and political problems in the rear weakened the military effectiveness of the combat squads, which could not stand up against well-armed and disciplined troops.

Events in the southern Urals highlighted the dilemma that faced all such guerilla bands during the Russian civil war. In order to survive they had to provide at least the bare bones of a regular administration for the territories they controlled; yet to do so contradicted their essentially anarchistic world-view and surpassed their abilities. The Urals combat squads were an intermediate link in the chain that leads from the relatively inoffensive militiamen of 1917 to the desperate rural guerillas of 1918–20. What had begun as a movement to enforce workers' control in the factories, or simply to maintain order there, was soon induced to broaden its objectives, even to the point of helping to overthrow the feeble Provisional Government; but soon thereafter they either found themselves integrated into the regular armed forces of the Soviet State – as in the central districts, and above all in Petrograd – or else developed into independent partisan bands whose fortunes depended in the final instance upon the clash of forces beyond their control.

TWENTY-THREE *Harnessing the Trade Unions*

B Y THE AUTUMN of 1917 the Bolsheviks had managed to acquire a strong position in Russia's chief industrial trade unions and a significant following in those catering for craftsmen or white-collar workers. They had also won control of several CBS, notably that in Petrograd. However, on the national trade-union executive body, ARCCTU, the radical elements were in a minority and it could not therefore serve as a reliable tool in mobilizing the mass of union members in support of the insurrection. For Lenin and his party both the soviets and the factory committees were at this stage more important than the trade unions, whose *raison d'être* was to promote workers' sectional economic interests. Moreover, there was a feeling among many trade unionists that their leaders had become over-absorbed in politics to the neglect of their prime task, which was to consolidate the authority of these organizations among ordinary wage-earners by winning improvements in their conditions of employment. To the rank and file it was of secondary importance whether the employer was a private entrepreneur or a nationalized concern : in either case the object of union policy remained much the same.

The union leaders, however, were unable to take such a straight-forward view. The seizure of power by a party committed to socialist principles confronted them with a conflict of loyalties. On one hand they felt obliged to uphold a regime which claimed to represent the long-term, immanent interests of the proletariat; on the other hand they could not entirely ignore the immediate claims of those to whom they owed their positions of authority. In this early period of Soviet history trade-union officials were as a rule drawn directly from the working-class milieu; they knew industrial conditions at first hand; and they owed their election to their personal qualities as activists and organizers, rather than to their record for ideological rectitude. For these reasons they were responsive to pressure from below and self-reliant in their dealings with the new authorities. They were reluctant to accept the proposition, implicit in Bolshevism and soon proclaimed as a doctrinal tenet, that under the 'dictatorship of the proletariat' the trade-unions' functions ought to be the reverse of what they had been under capitalism, namely to help impose labour discipline and raise productivity. And these leaders were not willing to subordinate themselves unquestioningly to other agencies in the new official hierarchy. The struggle to preserve some vestige of trade-union independence against the drive for monolithic conformity was to continue, in one form or another, for many years to come. The first round, fought during 1917–18, forced the Bolshevik party and state authorities to accept a compromise. The trade unions were granted a greater say in the formulation of policy than had originally been intended; in exchange, however, they accepted a large measure of external control which reduced their freedom of manoeuvre.[1]

The situation varied greatly between one union and another. A key role fell to the All-Russian Union of Railwaymen. The leaders of its executive body, Vikzhel, sought to avoid a polarization of opinion along class lines, since this could lead to civil war – and to the collapse of their own organization. Sheer self-interest suggested a neutral stance in the political struggle between the Bolsheviks and the moderate socialists. Other considerations were involved as well. The Vikzhel leaders seem to have concluded that their union's role during the crisis late in August, when branches in several north-western centres had been mobilized to frustrate the movement of General Kornilov's troops towards Petrograd, could be repeated in future national emergencies. For Russia's telegraph system was dependent on the facilities provided by the railways, and it seemed that this could give the railwaymen themselves direct control over the most important means of communication. (Only the armed forces as yet used radio.) This technological advantage, coupled with their training as engineers, gave the Vikzhel leaders a self-assurance felt by few of their trade-union colleagues in other sectors of the economy; and this was probably as important as political loyalties in impelling them to try to mediate the crisis provoked by the Bolshevik assumption of power.

On the very day of the insurrection Malitsky and his non-partisan colleague Nestorenko travelled from Moscow to Petrograd in the hope of averting the takeover of the ministry of Transport. They rejected a suggestion by the newly appointed Bolshevik commissar, A.S. Bubnov, that they should help him run its affairs, and on the evening of 26 October issued a directive (*postanovleniye*) to all railway organizations and soviets to the effect that, pending the formation of a broadly representative socialist government, orders affecting the railways were to be obeyed only if they were sanctioned by Vikzhel. Special commissars were to be appointed where necessary to maintain order.[2] A union spokesman was present at the second congress of soviets; he had some difficulty in obtaining permission to speak, but then made a forthright appeal for conciliation.[3] After exchanges with the MRC, in which Ryazanov acted as intermediary, failed to bring any modification of the Bolsheviks' stand, on 28 October the Vikzhel leaders set out their position more clearly. 'All union branches should take every measure in their power to prevent troops from being moved against one another in a fratricidal struggle among socialists'; they were, however, to assist troop movements directed against 'counter-revolutionary' (that is non-socialist) forces. The objective was now defined as the creation of a 'homogeneous [that is coalition] socialist government' extending from the Popular Socialists on the right to the Bolsheviks on the left.[4]

During the next few days central and local union officials strove to implement this policy. Reports of the bloodshed in Moscow, received early on the twenty-ninth, inspired them with an even greater sense of urgency. Later that day an emotionally worded telegram was dispatched in which the union leaders repeated their demands in categorical fashion and ordered a general strike on the railways, to begin at midnight, unless fighting had by then ceased. This threat proved to be effective. The Moscow Bolsheviks agreed to a truce (which, however, did not last) and in Petrograd representatives of seventeen left-wing organizations met under Vikzhel's auspices to discuss 'the construction of [state] authority'. The strike order was revoked.[5]

The substance of these talks will be discussed below (pp. 317–19). Although they did not bring about the broadly based coalition government which Malitsky and his colleagues desired, the talks were not wholly unsuccessful. The division of opinion between the 'hard' and 'soft' Bolsheviks was advertised to the country at large, and indirectly at least the Vikzhel leaders could claim some of the credit for the political settlement formalized on 15 November. The Bolshevik *coup* had plunged the country into a state of latent civil war, and the railwaymen's union alone was not strong enough to impose a settlement upon the antagonists. Nevertheless the attempt was probably worth making, if only for its demonstrative effect.

Its failure naturally strengthened the position of the left-wingers within Vikzhel and among rank-and-file railwaymen, but despite these difficulties the union executive managed to retain its cohesion. From 13 to 15 November it held a conference of line-committee delegates in Moscow which generally endorsed its policies.[6] To the Bolshevik leaders this was a signal that they would need to exert all their political skill to bring the union under control. As a bait they could hold out the prospect that, if Vikzhel collaborated with the new regime, it would be allowed to control the nation's railway network. Bubnov's authority as commissar had not been formally confirmed and five men appointed by Vikzhel had been permitted to take charge *de facto* of the Transport ministry (where, however, their authority rested very lightly since most of the employees were on strike). As the new commissar Vikzhel proposed one of their chiefs, Krushinsky, whose political affiliation was to the Left SRS. However, his role in recent political wrangles made him unacceptable to the Bolsheviks; nor would they accept the candidate of the 'workers' group' on the union executive, who evidently had syndicalist sympathies.[7] The stalemate was provisionally ended by the appointment as deputy commissar of none other than Lenin's brother-in-law, M.T. Yelizarov. The latter was an engineer by profession and a member of the union who had kept out of the political battle. On accepting the post he stated publicly that he would exercise his authority exclusively in a non-political (*delovoy*) manner, acting as his union's delegate in the CPC. One of his first acts was to persuade the Petrograd MRC to lift its ban on rail travel outside the capital, as a gesture of liberalization.[8] Whatever Yelizarov's intentions, it was clearly impossible for him to keep to this independent line for long.

A race now ensued between the radical elements based in the Petrograd and Moscow networks on one hand and the Vikzhel leaders on the other to ensure that the forthcoming extraordinary congress of the union should be held under their own auspices. The former maintained that there was no longer any common ground between lower-grade employees and the more senior administrative, technical and clerical personnel, whom they roundly denounced as actual or potential 'saboteurs'. They also alleged that the existing union leadership was to blame for the current unsatisfactory pay scales.[9] The moderates countered by withdrawing their support from Yelizarov and demanding his recall.[10] On 12 December the radicals set up a rival deliberative body in advance of the congress. The Bolshevik leaders came to their aid by pushing through the CEC (in what some members charged was an irregular fashion) a highly egalitarian wage structure which fixed the differential between the most senior and most junior of the fourteen grades at 1 : 1·86.[11] Increases of pay costing 3·5 million roubles were also promised from which the lowest-paid men stood to benefit most. Lenin and Zinoviev addressed the radical gathering, which on 15 December passed by a large majority (154 to 5 with 10 abstentions) a resolution condemning Vikzhel's policy.[12] The executive body was not formally deposed, since this function belonged by rights to the full congress. The radicals expected this to follow their lead, but to make sure endeavoured to predetermine the composition of the latter's presidium.[13] This manoeuvre, however, seems to have backfired.

When the long-awaited extraordinary congress met, on 20 December, it soon became evident that a large number of delegates were alarmed at the drift towards dictatorship within their union, which reflected in microcosm, as it were, the general trend of events within the country. The proceedings were overshadowed by threats that the Constituent Assembly, due to meet in a matter of days, would be forcibly dissolved, and by other contentious political issues of national importance. The radicals continued from time to time to hold meetings of their own conclave, which they claimed represented over one million 'railway proletarians', using it as a kind of caucus.[14] Many rank-and-file delegates soon became exasperated at the all-too-obvious efforts to obstruct the work of the congress (for instance by raising procedural issues, challenging deputies' credentials and so on). When, on 27 December, the Bolsheviks insisted that they alone, as the largest faction, should have the right to choose the congress presidium, they were defeated by 216 votes to 192. It took more than a week for the congress to adopt its statute. Tempers were becoming frayed, and once the delegates passed on to politics the atmosphere grew still more heated. The symbolic debate on the rights of the Constituent Assembly ended on 3 January with another narrow defeat for the Bolsheviks and their allies (273 votes to 261 with 3 abstentions), whereupon they walked out again in high dudgeon.[15]

Drastic surgery now seemed imperative. On 6 January the radical caucus declared the vote 'coincidental' (*sluchaynyy*) and denied Vikzhel all right to exist. A commission was set up to take over its effects. A new executive, called Vikzhedor and designed to replace Vikzhel, emerged at the end of the month. Its party affiliation was as follows : twenty-four Bolsheviks, twelve Left SRs and three Menshevik Internationalists.[16] Meanwhile the line committees and local branches were purged of unreliable elements. The country's railways were now in utter chaos. Some months later, when their strategic importance had been vividly demonstrated, a new structure of authority began to take shape in which military agencies reigned supreme. The new railwaymen's union had marked syndicalist tendencies and was to give the Bolsheviks trouble throughout the civil war.

In several other unions in the communications sector developments took a broadly similar course. The Union of Employees and Workers on Inland Waterways, although it could not command the numerical strength of the railwaymen's organization, enjoyed a certain importance since the canals, so long as they remained navigable, could serve as an alternative artery for transporting supplies to the hard-pressed northern cities. On 7 November its executive committee, backed by union representatives from various regions of the country, threatened to join in the prospective general strike on the railways.[17] This move came too late, however, to have any practical results. The Bolsheviks mobilized the rank-and-file members of the union against their 'counter-revolutionary' leaders and by February 1918 could hold a congress in which they and their allies effectively called the tune.[18]

They met with greater resistance from the organization catering for employees and workers in the postal and telegraph service

(*Potel'soyuz*). On the morrow of the insurrection its central executive associated itself with the Petrograd 'salvation committee' (see below p. 318) and decided that, to preserve civil peace, use of the telegraph services should be denied to the insurgents. However its Central Committee was unwilling to take a strong stand, partly because its members were divided. The chairman, King, received only half-hearted support from his deputy, Semenov, who favoured a compromise with the Petrograd MRC. After several days of vacillation, no doubt impressed by Vikzhel's example, the executive presented the insurgents with an ultimatum, but within twenty-four hours its leaders had once again changed their minds. A bolder line was taken by civil servants in the central ministry, who refused to comply with the orders of the Bolshevik commissar (N.P. Avilov) and withdrew their labour. On 10 November this decision was formally endorsed by the union Central Committee, and then at a mass meeting. Avilov responded by ordering all the strikers to be dismissed as 'saboteurs'.[19]

The Moscow postal union leaders took a more intransigent stand than their Petrograd colleagues. They denounced the Bolsheviks for their 'mad adventure' and cut communications with other centres. They were unable to maintain this resolute stand for long. The union Central Committee sent technicians to reopen some telegraph lines, and several union leaders were arrested. A bargain was then struck whereby the union recognized the local commissar's authority in return for the right to continue in control of the communications network. Similar compromises were reached in a number of provincial centres.[20]

The union leadership began preparations for a nation-wide strike – a move which, if successful, would have seriously embarrassed the new regime. To this end an emergency congress of delegates from many parts of the country was summoned in the relative calm of Nizhniy Novgorod (18 November). After a week of rather aimless debate the delegates adopted a strongly worded statement reaffirming support for the Constituent Assembly. By 52 votes to 8 (with 4 abstentions) the delegates decided to set up a strike committee which was to take action if the Bolsheviks used force against the assembly.

Unfortunately for the postal leaders, Russia's national parliament was not to meet for another five weeks, and during this period the Bolsheviks could extend their influence within the union. The less resolute members began to ask themselves 'whether it was not fruit-less to reply to rifles with wordy protests and resolutions' and to question the merits of striking over a political issue on which members' opinions were so sharply divided. On 5 December the men were awarded another sixty-rouble monthly bonus (backdated to June), followed by a hundred roubles as the customary Christmas gift. From the New Year an egalitarian wage and salary structure went into force. This raised postmen's earnings to between nine and eleven times the pre-war level, whereas for senior administrators the increase was twofold to threefold.[21] Once the Constituent Assembly had been dissolved material incentives were superseded by crude political pressure.

On 5 February there opened a conference of union members who supported 'soviet power'. Only twenty-nine delegates attended, ten of whom (including Semenov) were from the capital. Although the provincial men present were worried about the legality of the pro-ceedings, it deposed the union's existing leadership and transferred its powers provisionally to an organ called *Sovdeppotel'*. The Central Committee had been forewarned and went underground, supported in this step by most local committees. On 14 March it called the union's third congress at Tambov, a provincial capital in PSR territory. Seventy-nine delegates appeared. This time the radicals were in no mood to be trifled with. On the first day chairman King was arrested and taken to Moscow under armed escort; the other delegates were given forty-eight hours to disperse. It remained for *Sovdeppotel'* to call a national congress of its own supporters. This met from 26 April to 25 May 1918, at a time when the Bolsheviks were quarrelling with the Left SRs. The latter had a strong following in the new union, and it was only by excluding some of their most vociferous supporters that the Bolsheviks managed to bring it under their control.[22]

Passive resistance to the Bolshevik takeover was also offered by the unions of public and private employees. In Petrograd the newly appointed people's commissars, on making their first appearance in the ministries over which they sought to exercise control, found them all but empty, for on 27 October the civil servants decided on strike action.[23] In taking such a step they were motivated by a mixture of political and practical considerations. The Bolsheviks' millenarian expectations and plebeian image could not but antagonize men who by instinct and professional training valued order and regularity in the conduct of public affairs. Sheer self-interest also dictated a cautious attitude to the new regime : if it were to fall, as seemed only too likely in these early days, its successor might well punish those who had collaborated with it. And the Bolsheviks were not prepared to honour pension rights and other advantages which officials enjoyed, or even to pay them a regular salary.

The problem of finance was crucial from several points of view. Non-cooperation by the staff of the state bank deprived the CPC of funds it urgently needed. By a mixture of threats and blandishments, however, the Bolshevik commissars succeeded in breaking this resistance. On 11 November a number of senior officials, including the former deputy minister of Finance, were dismissed without pension rights, and some of them were arrested.[24] Such measures were abetted not only by sympathizers among junior personnel but also by some senior officials, including M.K. Lemke and P.M. Trokhimsky.[25] When all the banks were merged on 14 December similar action was taken in regard to the bank-employees' unions, which were merged into a single organization, known as *Banktrud*; but it was not until 1919 that the Bolsheviks secured a firm foothold in it.[26] The dissolution of the Constituent Assembly deprived the strikes among public servants of much of their *raison d'être,* since they had been largely designed to demonstrate support for that body. The strike committee, led by the Menshevik S.M. Shvarts (at that time an official in the ministry of Labour, and subsequently a noted authority on Soviet labour problems), announced that it was suspending its activities and in a final gesture demanded reinstatement of all those who had been dismissed for following its call.[27] With unemployment growing at an alarming rate there was little prospect of such a demand being granted, even had the Bolsheviks wished to employ a large number of officials in Petrograd. The transfer of the capital to Moscow two months later gave them an opportunity to screen civil servants for their political reliability.

Among the craft unions that of the printers stood out for its opposition to the Bolshevik takeover, and in particular to the repressive measures taken against the independent press. By the nature of their trade the printers had a strong commitment to freedom of opinion; quite apart from the political implications, such closures threatened them with loss of their livelihood. As early as 30 October their Petrograd organization associated itself with protests against the MRC's suppression of several allegedly 'counter-revolutionary' newspapers, and also with the demand for a broadening of the government.[28] In December re-elections to the local executive gave this a Bolshevik majority, but the new leaders made themselves unpopular and were ejected a few months later.[29] In Moscow the suppression of the democratic organ *Russkoye slovo* gave rise to a conflict between the printers' union and the Moscow soviet and CB, both of which were now Bolshevik-controlled. At a discussion on 6 December one of the men's leaders, I. Buksin, declared defiantly that on the issue of liberty of the press 'the printers' union will fight the Bolsheviks as it had fought the tsar'. But it soon transpired that the new foe was a more formidable opponent than the old. By the end of the month the union found itself threatened with exclusion from the CB on the grounds that it was engaging in 'political sabotage'.[30] Similar conflicts took place in Samara, Kharkov and Odessa.[31] The union's second All-Russian conference met from 14 to 21 December. Of the ninety-six delegates only twenty-two were Bolsheviks or Left SRs. The two sides bridged their differences in matters of organization, agreeing to set up a new federated association,[32] but this body seems to have allowed its members a good deal of latitude. Menshevik influence continued to make itself felt in its affairs until 1920.

Most industrial unions took a different line from those discussed hitherto. Having come under Bolshevik control during the previous months or weeks, they naturally enough voiced strong support for the principle of 'soviet power'. Whether they were equally enthusiastic about single-party rule may be doubted. It does not seem either that these unions as such played a very significant part in the October events. Individual union chiefs and even whole executives associated themselves with the insurrection, but they did so by virtue of their position in the soviet or some other organization rather than as responsible officials of their union.

In mid-October the Bolshevik union chiefs in Petrograd adopted a militant attitude which was of some value to Lenin in his struggle against the moderate members of his party's Central Committee. At its 'expanded session' on 16 October these men were present along with the party's military experts, who advocated a more cautious policy.[33] On closer examination these ideas are less enthusiastic than they might appear, for they present the seizure of power as a course of action imposed upon the proletariat by economic necessity.[34] There can be little doubt that these union leaders viewed the impending insurrection in a different perspective from that of Central Committee members preoccupied with political and military strategy.

Once the chips were down, the Petrograd metallurgical-workers at least rose nobly to the occasion. On 25 October their executive appealed to all members 'to close ranks under the banner of the Petrograd soviet' and assigned 50,000 roubles to meet its needs.[35] Those unions which had formed militia units put them at the disposal of the insurrectionary staffs. The CB allowed the MRC to use its premises as its headquarters. But this was the extent of the practical aid which the trade unions gave the Bolshevik enterprise. Even verbal resolutions in support of the *coup* do not seem to have been readily forthcoming. A 1963 documentary collection cites a mere three statements by union bodies in the capital, only the first of which can be considered influential.[36] The absence of affirmative resolutions by the textile-workers' and chemical-workers' unions is striking. It is known from other sources that the metallurgical-workers' council, at its meeting of 5 November, came out in favour of a homogeneous socialist government, as did the Petrograd CB.[37] Evidently it was the vacillating stand taken by the latter organization that impelled Lenin to address it in person on 9 November. This meeting was an 'expanded session', which in practice meant that 'representative working men and women' could be introduced in order to swing the vote in the direction desired.[38] A resolution was adopted supporting 'soviet power' and condemning strike action as 'sabotage'.[39]

Subsequently the metallurgical-workers' union, dominated as it was by its militant Petrograd branch, became something of a Bolshevik bulwark. Although only 75 of the 161 fully qualified delegates at its inaugural congress, which opened on 15 January 1918, belonged to this party, they carried their non-affiliated colleagues with them. The union took the line that workers in this branch of industry (half of whom it claimed as members), should throw off their 'conservative psychology' and devote their energies to boosting productivity. It opposed demands for wage increases which the new proletarian State could not afford and tried to limit pressure for further reduction of differentials, which were fixed in the ratio of 1 : 3·9.[40]

Meanwhile in Moscow the pro-Bolshevik union leaders followed the somewhat vacillating line of the party's city committee. Their task was complicated by the fact that the local CB was lukewarm about the insurrection. Although its prestige was not high, and it did nothing to obstruct the rising, its political orientation did have a certain negative importance in that the local Bolsheviks, unlike their comrades in Petrograd, were for some time unable to include the CB among sponsoring organizations of the appeals and exhortations which they issued. On 26 October a nine-man 'revolutionary centre' was set up which was afterwards said to have rendered the insurgents 'great service'.[41] As for the CB, it issued a proclamation on its own account calling on workers to rally in support of the MRC, and was a co-signatory of two others. The first of these, issued on 28 October, appealed to the workers to leave the factories and to follow the MRC's instructions; the second, dated 3 November (after the fighting was over), called on them to resume normal working. The order of signatories made it clear that the CB's status was that of an auxiliary to the MRC, the soviet, and the Bolshevik party's Moscow committee.[42] In Moscow, even more so than in Petrograd, the Bolshevik union chiefs harboured 'conciliationist' tendencies. On 15 November it was decided to reorganize the Moscow CB, which 'after fierce debates' had rejected a Bolshevik resolution on the political situation. The new scheme provided for representation according to the size of the unions concerned and was clearly designed to favour the big battalions.[43] A Bolshevik commentator uttered dark hints against alleged 'saboteurs' in the CB and urged Bolshevik trade unionists to ensure that they were elected to leadership positions.[44]

In several provincial towns Bolshevik-controlled CBs acted in similar fashion, but by and large both they and the trade unions associated with them were overtaken by the rapid pace of events. Anarcho-syndicalist elements, carried away by the spirit of the times, viewed the trade unions as organizations which had outlived their usefulness now that capitalism was supposedly a thing of the past, for in a socialist order would not producers at last be free to determine their own destiny?[45] Faced with the challenge of these heady notions, Social Democrats of all persuasions tended to rally. This helped the Bolsheviks, who could play off their opponents on the left and on the right. Their victory was sealed at the first All-Russian congress of trade unions, held from 7 to 15 January 1918.

Like the Vikzhel congress, this gathering was overshadowed by the dissolution of the Constituent Assembly, which occurred the day before its inaugural session. This demonstration of force was bound to impress waverers. Such political factors apart, the Bolsheviks were aided by their usual skill in matters of organization. The congress was probably the most representative of its kind in the long annals of Russian labour. Nevertheless one cannot assume that its composition reflected accurately the political sentiments of the 2·5 million or so men and women whom it was said to represent. The haphazard way in which the delegates were chosen was bound to favour the more militant elements and those from the north and centre.[46] Many outlying regions were all but cut off from Soviet-held territory by the civil war and transport breakdown. The evidence suggests that most rank-and-file members gave their support to the Bolsheviks and their allies, whereas the moderates' strength lay in the higher reaches of the union bureaucracy. By political affiliation there were 281 Bolsheviks to 67 Mensheviks; the Left SRS had 21, the Right SRS 10, and the Maximalists and Anarcho-Syndicalists 6 each; 37 delegates were free of party ties. No less than a third of the Menshevik delegates represented all-Russian or regional organizations, whereas only 7 per cent of their Bolshevik counterparts fell into this category.[47] As at the third conference some six months earlier, the moderates set up an informal group under the label of 'trade-union unity and independence'.[48] This designation was calculated to appeal to Lozovsky, ARCCTU's secretary, and other waverers in the radical camp. For the politicians the interest of the proceedings centred upon a tug-of-war behind the scenes for the allegiance of these 'centrist' elements.

The debates got off to a stormy start, with eloquent protests against the shooting two days earlier of unarmed demonstrators defending the Constituent Assembly. Once this contentious issue had been set aside, Lozovsky rendered a self-critical report on ARCCTU's activities which naturally enough touched off further political recriminations. The resolution adopted on this item was phrased in such a way as to omit any expression of confidence in that body. Thereafter the delegates settled down to a discussion of 'the current moment' – a topic hallowed by tradition at congresses of the RSDRP. Zinoviev, who reported for the Bolsheviks, presented bluntly the by-now familiar thesis that under socialism the trade unions ought to be, and indeed already were, organs of proletarian dictatorship; their members were learning to manage the economy and to put the interests of the working class as a whole above their own narrow sectional interests : 'It stands to reason that we too are in favour of trade-union independence, but only from the bourgeoisie. . . . At a time when the working class and poorer peasants have succeeded in transferring power to the working class, and when the unions are part of that power, what is the real meaning of independence?'[49] For the Mensheviks Martov countered that for all the talk of socialism, there had as yet been no essential change in the situation of industrial labour; in his party's view Bolshevism was doomed to fail, and the prospect of imminent counter-revolution made it all the more imperative to strengthen the trade unions as the workers' surest weapon against the exploitation that lay ahead. Somewhat contradictorily, however, he was prepared for unions to play their part in controlling the economy 'in so far as elements of realism . . . and a consideration of the actual forces [available] permit the union, as an independent organization, to modify the plans of the [state] power.'[50] Such equivocations were characteristic of Martov. He refused to accept that the Bolshevik dictatorship could lead to socialism, yet he could not advise workers to stand aside from the grandiose experiment under way : they were to assist it, meanwhile correcting its faults. On practical grounds there was perhaps something to be said for such a policy, but in the long run it was hardly a feasible course of action, if only because the Bolsheviks had their own ideas about the unions' functions and would not tolerate the kind of sustained opposition which Martov had in mind.

The Mensheviks had a limited success at the congress, in so far as both Lozovsky and Ryazanov came out in favour of trade-union independence. It would be 'an immense loss', said the former, if the unions were to have decisions imposed upon them by coercion. Ultimately, once the international revolution had triumphed and the hour of socialism was at hand, they would doubtless become administrative organs, taking over duties from the State; but any immediate merger with the apparatus of government would be 'a colossal historical mistake'.[51] Zinoviev, heated by the polemic, took his argument to an extreme, retorting that independence for the unions was equivalent to counter-revolution, since the survival of the proletarian state depended upon the support of organized labour. The Bolshevik resolution received 182 votes, as against 84 cast in favour of the Menshevik-inspired alternative.[52]

This lengthy document laid down the guiding principles of Soviet trade unionism.[53] The principle of 'neutrality' was strongly condemned (the foreign word *neytral'nost'* being used in preference to independence (*nezavisimost'*), evidently in order to blur the issue, for the Mensheviks had always opposed the former, and would now find it embarrassing to vote against it). The unions were 'to assume the main work of organizing production and restoring the shattered productive forces of the country'. This meant 'taking an energetic part in all the centres (*tsentry*) regulating production' – a reference to the administrative organs being set up under the SEC to administer various branches of industry; supervising workers' control; registering and redistributing labour; arranging for an exchange of products between town and country; helping to convert industry to peace-time production; combating 'sabotage' (whether by 'bourgeois' elements or by their fellow-workers was not explicitly stated); and implementing the principle of general labour service.

All these tasks fell equally within the competence of state organs. What was to be the relationship between ARCCTU and its member unions on one hand and, on the other, the SEC, its subordinate organs, and the economic commissariats? This was to become one of the key questions in Soviet politics during the next years. The Bolshevik leaders had not yet thought the matter through; for tactical reasons, too, they sought to convey an impression of broad-mindedness. On this point the resolution was vague in the extreme: 'In their developed form the trade unions, in the process of the developing socialist revolution, should become organs of socialist power, as such working in joint subordination with other organizations in implementing the new principles governing the organization of economic life.' This wording was designed to reconcile those who, like Lozovsky, wanted to postpone such integration until a (presumably remote) socialist future with those who, like Zinoviev, wanted to make a start at once. The phrase about 'joint subordination' implied that the economic state organs would enjoy no greater degree of authority than the unions, since it was not stated to which body they were to be subordinate. The way was open for a prolonged struggle between various elements in the new power hierarchy, in which the mass of trade unionists were only indirectly concerned.

The other main issue before the congress was that of workers' control and the regulation of industry. On these matters relations between Bolsheviks and Mensheviks were less strained and a common approach was feasible. Lozovsky and G.V. Tsyperovich (a professional economist who was not yet a party member) put forward a moderate programme for the gradual extension of state control to certain basic industries, in the first instance coal-mining, and warned against over-hasty and ill-prepared attempts at wholesale national- ization. This soft approach won guarded support from the chief opposition spokesman, Cherevanin, who concentrated his attention on the need to ensure that the regulating organs were representative of all the interests concerned. He introduced a resolution calling for a struggle against both what he called 'factory separatism' (that is syndicalism) and 'the complete subordination of the controlling organs to the state organs for the regulation of industry'.[54] The Bolsheviks could scarcely ask for more, and their own resolution, which carried the day, met these points. The trade unions were promised a leading part in measures to ensure that the economy was run 'on strictly democratic lines', which would guard against extremism in either direction : the existence of workers' control would prevent 'the emergence of a new industrial bureaucracy'[55] and at the same time trade-union participation would help to ensure that the principle of workers' control was given a narrow interpreta- tion.

This compromise was spelled out in two other resolutions on this point. One of these, introduced by Ryazanov and adopted almost unanimously (over the protests of the six Anarcho-Syndicalists) placed the factory committees under the 'leadership' of the trade unions.[56] Its main virtue was its brevity : four articles as against thirty-eight in the other, entitled 'workers' control'.[57] In the latter it was plainly stated that there could be no question of 'giving the workers of an individual enterprise the right to take final decisions on matters affecting its very existence'.[58] Controlling authorities, made up of trade unionists and other officials, were given the right 'to close down a factory temporarily or to dismiss all or some of the persons employed there in the event of its workers disobeying its orders'.[59] These orders could be appealed to the local council of workers' control, but this body was unlikely to enjoy much vitality or autonomy.

These decisions set the tone for Bolshevik labour policy in 1918. The unions were given the power to deprive a man of his livelihood, which might mean sentencing him to death by starvation – or at least forcing him to return to his native village. The practical problems that loomed so large in the lives of ordinary working people at this time received much less attention at the congress than many dele- gates no doubt wished. The original agenda contained a number of items which could not be discussed because of the priority given to more explicitly political issues.[60] The leaders of all factions thought in ideological terms and evidently found these questions embarrassing. On unemployment, after a brief and inconclusive debate, the congress simply endorsed an appeal, drafted by the Petrograd CB, for voluntary limitation of working hours[61] – in the circumstances little more than a propagandist gesture and certainly no substitute for an effective programme of labour protection. The unspoken assumption was that such measures would be elaborated within the PC of Labour with the close collaboration of the central trade-union bureaucracy.

The final act of the congress was to elect a new executive to replace the ineffectual body appointed the previous June. Perhaps as a reward for the Mensheviks' willingness to compromise, the leaders of the victorious faction did not insist on making ARCCTU an all-Bolshevik body. The voting, by lists of nominees, produced an inner core consisting of seven Bolsheviks and four Mensheviks. The latter were thus somewhat over-represented proportionately to their numerical strength at the congress, although naturally enough they did not occupy the key posts. Zinoviev became chairman, while Shmidt and Lozovsky were to act as secretaries. Among the Mensheviks were I.M. Maysky, who many years later was to achieve world-wide prominence as a Soviet diplomat, and Chirkin, the former chairman. M.P. Tomsky, who was to play such a leading role in Soviet trade-union affairs over the next ten years, was one of five candidate members. However, it appears that in practice he deputized for Zinoviev, who was preoccupied with weightier matters, and he succeeded him a few weeks later, when the Soviet government moved to Moscow.

The record of these events does not bear out the contention advanced by Bolshevik historians – and for that matter by Menshevik ones also[62] – that Soviet trade unionism was born to the sound of unremitting factional conflict. To be sure, there was no lack of ideologically coloured exchanges at the congress. But in the final instance Bolsheviks and Mensheviks were driven together by their common fear of the anarchist and syndicalist tendencies rife among rank-and-file Russian trade unionists. As the socialist politicians saw it, these radical ideas threatened the basic assumptions of their creed and could be thwarted only by centralized control from above. Logic decreed that the trade unions, in the very process of bridling the rebellious factory committees, should find themselves harnessed to the economic bureaucracy – the whole top-heavy apparatus being driven forward by an omnicompetent party leadership.

TWENTY-FOUR *The Central Soviet Organs and the Establishment of Bolshevik Dictatorship*

THE MOST SENIOR organs in the nation-wide soviet hierarchy played a key role in legitimizing and consolidating Bolshevik rule. The second congress of soviets, which met on 25–26 October, gave formal endorsement to an all-Bolshevik government (Council of People's Commissars) hastily put together by the insurgent leaders at the moment of victory and also approved decrees containing the essentials of that government's policy. Before dispersing the delegates chose a new central soviet executive (CEC) to replace the one elected in June. This did not consist wholly of Bolsheviks but was under that party's effective control. The moderate socialists allowed themselves to be jockeyed out of the most prestigious leadership positions in the soviet movement, which made it much easier for Lenin's followers to claim that they had overwhelming popular support. In fact 'revolutionary democracy' was confused and divided. Most ordinary members of urban soviets, and even the political activists to whom they looked for guidance, expected the overthrow of the 'bourgeois' Provisional Government to lead to the creation of a coalition regime representing all those factions and tendencies that stood for immediate peace and radical social change. Hardly anyone wanted single-party rule. There were two main reasons for this. First, it was thought that such a regime would create a schism within the left from which counter-revolutionaries would profit. Second, safeguards were needed to prevent the abuses of power that would inevitably flow from minority dictatorship. Yet despite the 'democratic' (or rather, anti-centralist) traditions of the soviet movement, within a few months the basis had been laid for a regime in which all power was concentrated in the leadership of the Bolshevik party and the soviets were its pliant instruments.

Lenin's attitude to the soviets had throughout been governed by tactical considerations. Although his celebrated pamphlet *State and Revolution* (written in August–September 1917, but not published until the following year) seemed to foster anarchistic illusions of 'direct democracy', he nowhere modified the fundamental principle of his creed, that the 'vanguard party', as the embodiment of proletarian class consciousness, had the right and duty to direct the masses in carrying out the revolution and building the new socialist order. The ambiguities in his thought were left for the future to resolve. In his view 'soviet power' was inseparably linked to an insurrection led by the Bolsheviks. He criticized relentlessly those associates who sought to conciliate the moderate socialists and to concentrate on consolidating the party's mass base. He branded as treasonable the notion that the Bolsheviks should participate along with the rest of 'revolutionary democracy' in the so-called Democratic Conference, a deliberative organ set up by the Provisional Government in conjunction with the CEC to bolster its authority until the Constituent Assembly met. 'History,' he wrote, 'will not forgive us if we do not assume power now.'[1] His exhortations and threats won over most of the waverers on the Bolshevik Central Committee, and on 10 October that body, meeting in secret, took its historic decision to prepare for insurrection.[2]

The vague wording of this resolution reflected the hesitations of those present.[3] Two of Lenin's lieutenants, G.E. Zinoviev and L.B. Kamenev, voted against the decision and subsequently tried to have it reversed. Theirs were by no means isolated voices : the Moscow Bolshevik leaders took a similar line. These right-wingers held that an armed insurrection at the present time was uncalled for and might well end in defeat. A non-violent approach was both possible and desirable, for the party's chances in the Constituent Assembly elections were excellent; and the national legislature, if backed by soviets and other mass bodies, could keep the threat of counter-revolution at bay and enable the party to carry out the essentials of its programme.[4] These 'united front tactics', as they would one day be called, presupposed that the other left-wing parties and groups would accept Bolshevik hegemony within a new ruling coalition, each component of which would preserve its own identity.

This perspective overlooked some cherished principles of Lenin's operational theory. For twenty years the Bolshevik leader had held firmly to a narrow and cynical view of alliances between his own party and others. Such groups were to be treated not as equal partners but as forced accomplices; agreements with them were to be entered into solely for specified limited aims; the arrangements made must ensure Bolshevik 'hegemony', that is to say that the ally's influence did not percolate into the party's own ranks, whereas movement in the reverse direction was facilitated; a close watch was to be kept throughout upon the balance of forces between the contracting bodies; once this balance had shifted decisively to the Bolsheviks' own advantage and the alliance had lost its usefulness, it was to be denounced, the onus for the breach being placed squarely upon the other partner; 'utilization', not unity, was the watchword.[5] As Lenin saw it, the fluidity of the present revolutionary situation made such precautions doubly necessary, since party discipline had slackened and there was an added risk of penetration by elements of doubtful reliability. It was precisely for this reason that he was so insistent upon the need for insurrection. This was more than just a practical question : it would serve to distinguish the true 'vanguard' elements from the 'fellow-travellers', whose identity was at present far from clear. To those who argued that a superfluous act of violence would repel potential allies, Lenin could reply that it would impress those who wavered between the two sides : determined action would lead them to throw in their lot with the victors – on terms which the latter could dictate.

It cannot be denied that this 'hard' view of the situation showed acute psychological insight. Many would-be democrats had a secret yearning to be led by any body of men who seemed to know what needed to be done; they were willing to adjust their convictions to power-political realities and to give the new regime a measure of support however dubious its credentials might be. But it also involved a high degree of risk for the party and the cause it sought to promote, as indeed Lenin came close to acknowledging some years later, when in his defence he quoted Napoleon's adage : '*On s'engage et puis ... on voit*.'[6] Naturally he would not have conceded that a general who chooses to *avoid* giving battle might justify himself with similar arguments.

The right-wing Bolsheviks' proposal for a compromise between the Constituent Assembly and the congress of soviets, as a class organ, did at least reflect a due concern for the revolutionary regime's legitimacy. They sought to ensure that the new coalition government, unlike the four preceding cabinets, should be based upon deliberative assemblies in tune with popular opinion. Certainly they hoped that the soviet organ would eventually displace the national legislature, but for the time being 'bourgeois' constitutional forms would be respected and civil liberties would not be restricted more than was necessary to meet a genuine counter-revolutionary threat.

For Lenin, however, the civil war had already begun and conciliatory policies could but aid the enemy. He was content for the 'proletarian dictatorship' to derive legitimacy from its own actions in implementing the Marxian blueprint. He had always been contemptuous of 'bourgeois' parliamentary institutions, and the forthcoming Constituent Assembly was no exception. Moreover, he was at heart almost as opposed to soviet constitutionalism as he was to the 'bourgeois' variety, since he believed that concern for legal formalities should not be permitted to hinder his party's freedom of action. Not until 8 October did he expressly state that the new proletarian regime should be responsible to the soviets, and even so he did not specify how this responsibility should be exercised. It was clearly in the party's interests to keep this point vague; perhaps he was still uncertain how far the soviets could be trusted. His published writings reveal no interest in the workings of the soviet machinery as it existed at that time. Lenin ignored such concrete problems as the relationship between executive and deliberative bodies, or between organs at different levels in the hierarchy. His prime concern was to ensure that members of his party formed a disciplined 'fraction' in each soviet organ and exercised as much influence over its activities as possible. Indeed, between July and early October he seems to have been unduly obsessed by the problem of maintaining party control over the soviets and to have underestimated their serviceability as forums for agitation and mass mobilization.

This at any rate was Trotsky's view – at the time and later.[7] As chairman of the Petrograd soviet (see below, p. 347), his approach was bound to be less conspiratorial than that of Lenin, who led a clandestine existence until the evening of 24 October. There were also temperamental differences between the two men. By and large they were in agreement, and the nuances that separated them were of no practical account at the time. Both were strongly committed to armed insurrection and to a radical break with the moderate socialists; both wanted the insurrection to take place before the second All-Russian congress of soviets, so presenting the latter with a *fait accompli*; both believed in the necessity of a strong revolutionary government in Petrograd to be composed mainly or even wholly of Bolsheviks; both saw the soviets' role in the proletarian dictatorship as instrumental, that is as auxiliary to that of the party.[8] But Trotsky was more aware of the need to provide the new regime with an acceptable democratic image. He was less afraid than Lenin that such measures would erode the party activists' will to seize power or delay the insurrection beyond the point when it could succeed; on the contrary, he believed that by taking every opportunity to popularize the party's programme in the Petrograd soviet and elsewhere the Bolsheviks would strengthen their following while hypnotizing their opponents into inaction. As with Lenin's policy, and also that advocated by the right-wing Bolsheviks, an element of risk was involved, for the moderate socialists and the government were given ample warning of the party's insurrectionary intentions, and time in which to plan countermoves. But the underlying psychological calculation was sound : many of the Bolsheviks' enemies had lost the will to resist the insurgents, and the almost open preparations being made for their overthrow lulled them into a false sense of security.

The CEC leaders' handling of the insurgency threat was weak and pusillanimous. Divisions of opinion prevented them from pursuing a consistent line. The prevailing tendency was to conciliate the Bolsheviks by pressing the government to grant the substance of their demands. Faced with massive pressure from below, the CEC leaders played for time. They were unwilling or unable to wage a determined campaign to win back those soviets that had passed under Bolshevik control. Instead they concentrated on fighting a rearguard action over convocation of the second All-Russian congress of soviets, orginally due for mid-September.

Two alternative courses of action were conceivable on this matter. Either they could ensure that the congress met as soon as possible and was attended by every body qualified to send a representative – or they could delay the congress on various pretexts in the hope that the radical wave would eventually subside. One may doubt whether the merits and demerits of these options were carefully weighed. The moderates' political instincts led them to opt automatically for the second, although they would almost certainly have gained more by the first. It would at least have deprived the radicals of the powerful argument that they were being victimized for their views by men who had turned traitor to their class; the areas of relative Bolshevik strength and weakness would have been clearly exposed, so casting doubt upon their claim to speak on behalf of the soviet movement as a whole; finally, had the moderates formed a cohesive group at the congress, prepared to defend their position to the last, they could have obstructed the Bolsheviks' scheme to present their government as a soviet one. But all this was not to be.

The procrastination policy began in earnest shortly after the Bolsheviks had won control of the Petrograd and Moscow soviets. On 13 September the CEC Bureau decided to hold, in lieu of a full congress, a consultative meeting of those soviet (and army committee) representatives attending the Democratic Conference. This move was a counterpart to that carried out by the government on a national scale when it convoked this gathering as a substitute for the long-promised Constituent Assembly. It proved to be even less successful. The radical members demanded that the congress be called by mid-October at the latest, and that responsibility for the arrangements be taken away from the CEC's inter-city department and entrusted to the Bolshevik-controlled Petrograd and Moscow soviets. The CEC Bureau resisted the second point but was obliged to concede the first, fixing the date of convocation for 20 October.[9]

A few days later (26 September) the Bureau set up a commission to handle the procedural problems involved. It rejected a proposal (by the Menshevik leader F.I. Dan) to hold a preliminary poll of all local soviets to ascertain their wishes in the matter. It laid down norms of representation similar to those established for the first congress of soviets that had met in June. Mandates were to be strictly vetted. The armed forces' organizations were allotted 240 seats, but nothing was done to facilitate peasant representation. A number of bodies, responding to suggestions by the moderate leaders, passed resolutions condemning the forthcoming congress as untimely and dangerous to the democratic cause. Even more frequent, however, were resolutions inspired by sentiments quite the reverse. Particularly important in this regard was a message sent out on 13 October by radio-telegram to all soviets on behalf of the Northern regional congress of soviets. This was a gathering of delegates from various radical organizations (mainly military) in and round Petrograd, summoned by the local Bolsheviks. Written by Trotsky, this statement alleged that the CEC Bureau was attempting to sabotage the forthcoming All-Russian congress. It altered the agenda and called upon all like-thinking organizations to make certain they sent delegates.[10] The CEC Bureau thus faced the dilemma of either allowing their opponents to seize the initiative by force or else undertaking a last-minute campaign to ensure that all moderate organizations were duly represented. It decided on the latter course (17 October), and in order to win more time postponed by five days the date on which the congress was to convene.

Had the Bolsheviks indeed timed their *coup* to coincide with the congress, as is sometimes maintained,[11] this delay might have caused them serious embarrassment. But this was not the case, and postponement of the congress proved to be a mixed blessing from the standpoint of those who ordered it. It lent plausibility to Bolshevik accusations that the CEC was manoeuvring to avoid defeat. The delay was not long enough to make much material difference to the composition of the assembly, since most delegates had already been elected and dispatched. Only at a very late date, on 21 October, did the CEC Bureau fix a quorum for the congress. Two-thirds as many delegates as had been present in June were required to attend for the proceedings to be considered legal.[12] Significantly, the moderate leaders did not take as the criterion a certain proportion of *all the soviets in the country* – probably because they themselves did not know how many of them there were : a graphic indication of their poor organizing ability and lack of political *savoir faire*. Only such a ruling could have ensured that the congress represented the soviet movement as a whole.

When the appointed day dawned most of Petrograd was already in the insurgents' hands. This of course had been the Bolshevik leaders' intention from the start, although how far the insurrectionary events of 24–5 October were prompted by the imminence of the congress, and how far they were simply the product of a natural escalation of tension between the contending forces, it is difficult to say. The session was due to begin at 3 pm, but had to be postponed for several hours because the insurgents' plans went awry. They had failed as yet to take the Winter Palace, where the Provisional Government was still in session, and without this prize they could scarcely dare ask the delegates to endorse a new 'soviet' regime. To have acted precipitately would have been to invite a rebuff. Only about half those present were Bolsheviks (or at least called themselves such). In addition they had some seventy to eighty supporters in other groups.[13] An overwhelming majority of delegates were in favour of the slogan 'all power to the soviets'.[14] Yet, as we know, they read their own meaning into this phrase : a coalition of all the left-wing parties represented in the soviet movement. Thus the problem facing the Bolsheviks on 25 October was to secure from a body so constituted an unequivocal declaration of support both for their *coup* and for the formation of an all-Bolshevik government – something that was bound to shock as well as excite the average delegate, to whom both events came as a surprise.

The situation was accordingly one that still left opponents of the insurrection room for manoeuvre. They could hope to win a number of Bolshevik supporters, to say nothing of ordinary unsophisticated deputies, to the view that a socialist coalition government was essential if bloodshed between erstwhile comrades were to be averted. A proposal to discuss this crucial question first was made by Martov, leader of the left-wing (Internationalist) Mensheviks. It was welcomed by the right-wing Bolshevik A.V. Lunacharsky and adopted unanimously.[15] However, the non-Bolshevik leaders, taken aback by the *coup*, had not concerted their tactics beforehand and muffed their opportunity. Representatives of three socialist parties (SRS, Mensheviks and Jewish Bund) announced that they would have nothing to do with 'a military conspiracy organized and executed by the Bolshevik party ... behind the backs of all other parties and groups represented in the soviets', and strode from the hall. This gesture of moral indignation, however understandable, was politically short-sighted, since it split the opposition forces, leaving Martov and his radical followers isolated. Trotsky seized his chance. He pronounced an anathema against those who had departed, describing them as 'miserable cliques' devoid of popular support, traitors to the working class at its supreme moment of trial. It was now that (according to the chronicler Sukhanov) he uttered a phrase destined to become famous : 'you may go where you belong – to the garbage heap of history.'[16] The mood of the assembly now hardened. The very idea of a negotiated political settlement was discredited. The average deputy reasoned that in order to enjoy 'soviet power' he had no choice but to follow the Bolsheviks' lead. It was now the turn of the Menshevik Internationalists and some other small radical groups to leave the chamber. Finally, in the early hours of the morning of 26 October, by which time news had arrived of the fall of the Winter Palace, those delegates who were still present adopted quasi-unanimously a resolution stating that the congress was 'taking power' and appealing to the masses for support.[17] In the words of one historian

> It was an academic resolution, because power had already for some time been in the hands of the Bolshevik party and its organization. But its significance as a symbol was immense. As Trotsky all along intended, it set the seal of legality on an armed insurrection. Moreover, it enabled the Bolsheviks to claim the right to wield popular power by themselves, in view of the departure from the congress of the socialist parties other than the Left SRs.[18]

That same evening the delegates reassembled for the second (and last) session of the congress. This time Lenin appeared in person, to be greeted with rapturous applause by the throng. They endorsed by acclamation decrees embodying the two principal planks in the Bolshevik programme – an appeal to all belligerent peoples and their governments to conclude an armistice and begin immediate negotiations for a 'just, democratic peace', and the abolition of property rights in land for all non-'toilers' (see below, pp. 386–92). The first document was passed unanimously; one solitary delegate voted against the second, while eight men abstained.[19] Having thus cemented their hold upon the affections of the assembly, the Bolshevik leaders could proceed to the delicate matter of 'the construction of [state] power'. Kamenev tabled a decree listing the members of the new government, to be known as the Council of People's Commissars (CPC). This list had been drawn up in private by the insurgent leaders after talks with the Left SRs. All the proposed commissars were Bolsheviks. Lenin was to be chairman and Trotsky to manage foreign affairs; most of the other members were as yet relatively unknown.[20] The new government, like the old, was termed 'provisional'; it was 'to govern the country until the Constituent Assembly meets'.

In the debate that followed B.V. Avilov, on behalf of the few Social Democrats who had not withdrawn, put the by-now-familiar argument that in view of the danger of counter-revolution it was imperative 'to form at once a government drawing its support from the whole, or at least the majority, of revolutionary democracy'.[21] For the Left SRs, V.A. Karelin followed him to the rostrum to explain why, in the talks held earlier that day in Smolny, his group had refused to join the CPC. They objected to it mainly because it was a 'ready-made government' which was evidently designed to be permanent, whereas the Left SRs preferred rule by temporary committees. It is difficult to see how such a regime could provide the 'firm authority' they simultaneously desired, yet there was a certain logic in their stand. In their eyes the central Soviet government should live up to its title by being fully responsible for its actions to the soviet movement, of which the national congress was the supreme organ. Heirs to the anti-authoritarian Populist tradition, they believed in direct democracy. They knew, or at least suspected, that the Bolsheviks harboured different aims. Nevertheless they considered that this ought not to rule out collaboration between the two parties, provided that they could negotiate mutually acceptable terms. The Left SRs were not prepared to accept a Leninist *diktat*. On the other hand, they appreciated that the Bolsheviks had much mass support behind them, and for this reason held that a bargain with them was essential, for if they were spurned or isolated by other socialists this would play into the hands of 'reaction'. There was another aspect to this calculation: the Left SRs hoped that by cooperating with the Bolsheviks they could bend them to their own purposes. As they saw it, practical experience would lead their allies to moderate their dictatorial tendencies and bow to the will of the 'revolutionary masses', of whom the majority were of course not proletarian; in the optimal outcome, the Bolsheviks could be persuaded to take part, on an equal basis with other parties, in a broader socialist coalition such as the majority of the soviet movement clearly desired.[22]

It is painfully clear in retrospect that this attitude, for all its undoubted sincerity, was naive in the extreme. The Left SRs, like almost everyone else, underestimated Lenin's ideological drive, resourcefulness and tactical skill. The 'hard' Bolsheviks – and it was they who made that party's policy – were determined that in a 'pro-letarian dictatorship' they themselves should exercise a monopoly of power. A temporary alliance might be expedient with other political groups, especially one that represented (or was thought to represent) the poorer segment of the peasantry, but only so long as it strengthened 'the hegemony of the proletariat' (that is its Bol-shevik vanguard). The underlying assumption was that any such compromise could only be of limited scope and duration, and that it would serve primarily as a means of winning peasant recruits to Bolshevism.

A marriage in which one partner welcomed promiscuity and the other hoped to steal the spouse's property could not fail to be a stormy one. Since the Bolsheviks were vastly superior in organiza-tional strength and discipline, and had a much clearer idea of what they wanted, they were bound to be the dominant force. They could extract far more advantage from any such alliance than their idealistic but woolly-minded associates.

These considerations were still implicit on 26 October. Neither Lenin nor Trotsky was unduly perturbed at the Left SR leaders' unwillingness to join the CPC at once. Replying to Karelin, Trotsky pointed out that some members of that group had helped to bring about the insurrection by joining the Petrograd soviet's MRC. The implication was that their comrades would soon see the light and throw in their lot with the victors – and if they did not, this would be of no great consequence. He threw cold water upon the very idea of coalition and extolled the Bolsheviks' achievement : 'Political combinations come and go, but the fundamental interests of classes remain, and victory goes to the political party that understands and satisfies these fundamental interests. . . . If we need a coalition, it is one with our garrison. . . . Of such a coalition we can be proud. It has stood the test of fire.'[23] Impressed by this rhetoric, the delegates passed Kamenev's resolution by a 'crushing majority' (evidently voting by a show of hands).[24]

Thus one day after voting to take power, the congress had granted to an all-Bolshevik central government, formed independently of it, the right to consider itself the embodiment of that power. It had conferred upon it a certificate of legitimacy, as it were. This was indeed a historic moment – but one that left a great many questions unresolved. How precisely would that government exercise its res-ponsibilities to the soviet movement which it claimed to represent, and beyond it to the working people as a whole? What checks, if any, were to be placed upon its authority? How were its powers to be delimited from those of the CEC – and of the thousands of local soviets scattered across the length and breadth of Russia?

In the early morning of 27 October the delegates dispersed to their 'constituencies', there to spread the word and implement the decisions of the congress. In so doing they would provide a practical answer to the last of these questions, which we shall examine in the following chapters of this section. As for the problem of the relationship between the two central executive agencies, the new government and the CEC, this arose later on that very same day, when the latter body, as reconstituted by the congress, held its first meeting.

The election of a new executive, with just over a hundred[25] members, had been the final act of the congress, and its composition reflected party-political alignments there. Unlike the CPC, a nominated body consisting wholly of Bolsheviks, the CEC was politically mixed, consisting initially of sixty-two Bolsheviks, twenty-nine Left SRs and ten others. The chairman, Kamenev, appealed for 'concerted and amicable work'. As a moderate Bolshevik, he sought to strike a conciliatory note. Like most members of the CEC, he was keen to see the government broadened to include other socialist parties, and wanted to ensure harmonious collaboration between the two organs.[26] When, at the CEC's second session two days later, the railwaymen's union delegate delivered an ultimatum demanding such a coalition (see above, p. 291), Kamenev announced that the Bolsheviks would take part in talks to that end.[27] He himself attended this meeting. He pleaded with the moderate socialists to accept the programme endorsed by the soviet congress; in return, he suggested, the CEC would take steps to see that the government was reconstituted; after all, was it not responsible to the CEC? The implication, subsequently made explicit, was that the 'soft' Bolsheviks were willing to sacrifice their irreconcilable leaders, Lenin and Trotsky, in the interests of compromise with the socialists.

Here was an olive branch which, had there been no October insurrection, might have been welcomed by many 'official' Mensheviks and SRs, to say nothing of their left-wing factions. But the die had been cast. It was now too late to negotiate a compromise acceptable to the moderates, who initially took a strong line at the talks. M.Ya. Gendelman, for the PSR, declared that it was utterly opposed to any government that included Bolshevik representatives and spoke of 'securing a decision by force of arms'.[28] A scarcely less militant line was taken by the Mensheviks Dan and Vaynshteyn. The latter spoke for a body known as the Committee for Salvation of the Fatherland and the Revolution, set up on 26 October, which included representatives of several 'democratic' bodies, such as the Council of the Republic, the Petrograd municipal duma, the old CEC and the peasant Executive Committee, as well as the two major socialist parties (PSR, Mensheviks). At the time this had the appearance of a formidable coalition. Kerensky's forces had not yet been beaten off; fighting was still going on in Moscow; the fall of the infant Bolshevik regime, whose leaders were known to be at loggerheads, was expected hourly. But within a few days the balance of forces had tilted against the 'counter-revolutionaries' and the Bolsheviks could take heart. Lenin swiftly asserted his authority over his party. Addressing its Petrograd committee on 1 November, he accused the right-wingers of weakness and treachery. 'As for an agreement [with the socialists], I cannot even speak of that seriously ... Our present slogan is : "No compromise! A homogeneous Bolshevik government!" '[29] His object was to torpedo the negotiations, since they threatened to eventuate in concessions he considered unacceptable. Most members of his party's Central Committee fell into line.

When the CEC met later that day, the Bolshevik spokesman (V. Volodarsky) set forth stiff preconditions for an agreement. Potential allies were required to promise to accept the CPC's programme as endorsed at the soviet congress and to wage 'unrelenting war' against enemies of the revolution; in return it was conceded that the government should be responsible to the CEC and that the latter should be enlarged to include representatives of trade unions, peasant soviets and armed forces' organizations.[30] The idea of an enlargement on these lines seems to have originated with the moderate socialists, as part of several schemes that were being mooted to 'democratize' the government. To Lenin and the intransigent Bolsheviks, however, dilution of the CEC appeared in a very different light : by agreeing to it, they hoped to fob off the opposition with a shadow concession that would leave the CPC, as the more important decision-making body, untouched. Probably not all Bolshevik members of the CEC realized what was in their leader's mind; however that may be, the new terms for agreement were endorsed in that body by 38 votes to 29.[31]

The inter-party talks continued, for although the PSR refused to take any further part in them the Mensheviks decided otherwise. They had now put forward conditions of their own for collaboration with the Bolsheviks : immediate cessation of all military action, freeing of political prisoners and restoration of civil liberties.[32] They knew that such demands were acceptable to the right-wing Bolsheviks and hoped to wean these men away from the hard-line Leninists. This calculation was sound. On 4 November the Bolshevik delegation in the CEC split. Two interrelated issues were under discussion. One was freedom of the press, which had been infringed by a CPC decree; the other was the legality of such decrees signed by the CPC on its own authority, without previous discussion in the senior soviet organ – in clear breach of the principle of governmental responsibility decided upon at the soviet congress and promulgated on 30 October. Had the moderate socialists not boycotted the CEC, the Leninists would have been soundly defeated. As it was, they came within a hair's breadth of being outvoted. The Bolshevik motion, when first submitted, received 25 votes, 23 being cast against it. The final vote was 29 to 23 with 2 abstentions.[33] Promptly five of the fourteen people's commissars and six other officials resigned from the government. Three of them (A.I. Rykov, V.P. Nogin, V.P. Milyutin) also resigned from the party's Central Committee, a more serious step, and in this action were accompanied by Kamenev and Zinoviev (neither of whom held government appointments).[34]

Thus a mere ten days after the insurrection an open breach yawned in the Bolshevik leadership. Lenin responded sharply. The critics were charged with violating party discipline and threatened with expulsion from the Bolshevik ranks (5 November). Kamenev was replaced as chairman of CEC by the stalwart Ya.M. Sverdlov.[35] No concession was made to the viewpoint of those who had resigned. On the contrary, the negotiations with the moderate socialists were allowed to collapse. This tough policy paid dividends. The moderate socialists were too demoralized and disunited to exploit the Bolsheviks' embarrassment. It was impossible for them to rally the dissidents to their cause, not least because they had absented themselves from the CEC, the main political forum of the day. Instead they now put their hopes on the Constituent Assembly – although it was doubtful when, if at all, the Bolsheviks would allow this democratically elected parliament to meet.

In the meantime it fell to the Left SRs, who remained on the CEC, to resist as best they could the Bolsheviks' determination to exercise a monopoly of political power. Yet their resistance was bound to be weak and ineffective, since the leaders of this party shared many of the assumptions and attitudes of their Bolshevik rivals, and indeed were rapidly acquiring a taste for power. Lenin and his intimates found the Left SRs' public criticisms irritating, but were prepared to put up with them until they had consolidated their hold on the country. They were astute enough to realize that collaboration with them was to their advantage. In the first place, it would assuage the widespread demand for a broadening of the regime's popular base. In the second place, the Left SRs regarded themselves as the true voice of the peasant masses, the heirs to the allegedly 'bankrupt' and 'discredited' centre and right-wing factions of the once mighty PSR; and although this claim did not rest on very solid foundations it was plausible enough to make it worth while to concede them a share in power, since the new coalition could then be presented to the world as a 'workers' and peasants' government', enjoying the support of the bulk of the Russian people and not simply a proletarian élite. In practical terms this meant doing two things: first, offering their leaders several portfolios in the CPC; second, broadening the CEC to include peasant and other representatives. To be sure, such an arrangement involved an element of risk. Nevertheless it was much less dangerous than either alternative: an all-socialist coalition such as had been advocated by the dissident Bolsheviks (and which Lenin had consistently rejected), or continued isolation, which might lead the Left SRs to make common cause with the moderates. If the Left SRs were harnessed firmly to the Bolshevik chariot, there was less likelihood of them drifting to the right – or, expressed in class terms, of 'vacillating between the proletariat and the bourgeoisie'.[36]

Thus did Lenin reason, and his arguments testify to his political acumen. The Left SRs proved to be susceptible to Bolshevik blandishments, although final agreement took longer to bring about than had been expected. Negotiations were begun on 6 November, as soon as the previous talks with the majority socialists had ceased. Various formulae were canvassed for enlarging the CEC. That eventually formalized on 15 November more than tripled its size. To the 108 members elected at (or coopted since) the second congress of soviets were added an equal number of 'peasant' representatives chosen at an extraordinary congress of peasant soviets, which was under Left SR control. (The proceedings of this latter gathering are discussed below, pp. 438–41). A further hundred delegates were to be provided by revolutionary organizations in the armed forces, and half that number by the trade unions (including ten from Vikzhel and five from Potel'soyuz). This gave an assembly 366 strong, which was more than in the old CEC that had functioned between June and October.[37] The proletarian element was fairly evenly balanced against the mass of peasants and soldiers. In the reformed executive bureau the Bolsheviks held only a slight margin of advantage : 40, as compared with 34 Left SRs; within this there was a presidium which (as reconstituted on 12 December) had 12 Bolsheviks to 7 Left SRs and 1 United Social Democrat.[38] There were twelve administrative departments, but these swiftly lost importance as their functions passed to the people's commissariats as the official organs of government.[39]

Simultaneously the significance of the CEC as a quasi-legislative forum declined also. One indication of this is that sessions were called less frequently. In the first ten days of its existence the CEC met five times; the number of meetings then rose to six (excluding one of ceremonial character); thereafter the figures are respectively as follows : four, two, two (and one ceremonial), two; two more meetings were held in the last fifteen days of the session. Meanwhile the CPC met 'almost daily and sometimes twice a day'.[40] Attendance at CEC meetings seems to have dropped, too, although this is less certain since record-keeping standards were poor and this decline will have been due in part simply to the assignment of delegates to work in the provinces. Even more important, the proportion of legislative acts that passed through the CEC diminished. According to one recent Soviet scholar (whose work was published in remote Vladivostok) the CPC passed 480 decrees in the first year of its existence, only 68 of which were submitted to the CEC.[41] Both the Left SRs and the United Social Democrats questioned the Bolsheviks' dictatorial tendencies. These 'soviet constitutionalists', as one might call them, were anxious to make the CEC a real 'workers' parliament and an effective check upon the activities of the government.

As we have seen, this question was at issue in the crisis that broke on 4 November. The opposition groups (and also the right-wing Bolsheviks) had misgivings about the provisions of a CPC decree, published on 30 October, which defined the procedure whereby laws were to be promulgated. This gave the CPC the right to compile and to publish legislative acts (article 1) and the right 'to suspend, amend or repeal any governmental decision' (article 6); the final text of every decree was to be signed by the chairman of the CPC (that is Lenin) or a commissar designated to act on his behalf; it was to enter into force immediately it was published 'for general information' in the official bulletin (article 3).[42] The decree was evidently designed to give the CPC a veto power that would nullify the CEC's rights. When challenged on this point (4 November), the Bolsheviks had argued that such reserve powers were vitally necessary. 'Formal deficiencies' in particular decrees, said Lenin, were of minor account when the very survival of the revolution was at stake.[43] His followers now took one step further away from bourgeois precedents by insisting that the CPC should be authorized to issue, on its own responsibility and without previous debate in the CEC, legislative acts on urgent matters that fell within the scope of the general programme adopted by the second congress of soviets.[44] This formulation could of course be interpreted very broadly, as the 'hard' Bolsheviks intended – and it was this that passed the CEC and became law.

The 'soviet constitutionalists' had been defeated but they had not yet surrendered. Fortified by their accession of strength in the chamber, the result of the 15 November agreement, they redoubled their efforts to bring the CPC under its control. At the first session held of the enlarged CEC (17 November) the Left SRs, backed by the railwaymen's leaders, protested that the government had exceeded its powers by dissolving the Petrograd municipal duma, a democratically elected body under socialist control, without consulting the CEC.[45] Sverdlov, the chairman, quickly took the wind out of the opposition's sails by tabling a document curiously called a 'constitutional instruction' (nakaz-konstitutsiya)[46] to govern relations between the two bodies. This formally reiterated that the CPC was responsible to the CEC (article 1) and went on to rule that 'all legislative acts, and likewise ordinances (rasporyazheniya) of major political importance, are presented to the CEC for examination and confirmation' (article 2). However, it was not specified whether this was to be done before or after they were published – that is to say whether the CEC was to be presented with a draft bill or an enact-ment *already legally binding* upon the deputies. Since the resolu-tion of 4 November remained in force, the latter was evidently Sverdlov's intention. In any case the CPC could choose which pro-cedure it wished to adopt. Article 3 of the document gave the government the explicit right to take action to thwart counter-revolutionary activities 'immediately, conditional upon [the CPC's] responsibility before the CEC'. That this power was to be interpreted broadly became evident six days later, when the CPC passed a decree on its own responsibility establishing the first 'revolutionary tribunal', with the right to try suspects by extra-legal procedure. Two other provisions (articles 4, 5) were that each people's commissariat had to submit a weekly report to the CEC and that interpellations bearing a minimum of fifteen signatures had to be answered at once by a government spokesman. Neither obligation, needless to say, was taken very seriously. Thus although the so-called 'constitutional instruction' at first glance seemed to concede something to the desires of the 'soviet constitutionalists', in fact it merely confirmed the *status quo*. It was passed without debate, only a few dissentients voting against it.[47]

With this the carpet had been pulled from under the oppositionists' feet. On 24 November they returned to the charge. The govern-ment's dissolution of the Petrograd municipal duma, Karelin argued, might be expedient but it was nevertheless illegal. This phrasing was carefully contrived to win maximum support among 'soft' Bolsheviks. On the first ballot his resolution passed by a single vote (85 to 84); on a recount the decision was reversed (88 to 85).[48] Never again were the 'soviet constitutionalists' to come so close to success. Later challenges on this issue[49] had an air of *déjà vu* and failed to arouse as much passion as before, since the outcome was no longer in doubt. Moreover, the Left SRs were now (from 12 December) in the government, and shared responsibility for its acts, so that this issue seemed a mere institutional squabble rather than a struggle over the principle of legality. The battle still went on behind the scenes within the CPC, a leading part being played by the Left SR people's commissar for Justice, I.N. Shteynberg,[50] but graver matters were now at stake. For events were rapidly moving towards a showdown between the Soviet government and the democratic left, whose fate was closely bound up with that of the Constituent Assembly.

It will be recalled that the moderate socialists, after the breakdown of their talks with the Bolsheviks early in November, had turned to the task of securing their hold over the nation's electorate. The polls for the Constituent Assembly were due to be held from the 12th of that month (the election was 'staggered' for practical reasons, some of the remoter constituencies not voting until 26 November). Campaigning was vigorous, and there is every reason to suppose that those who took part in the election had a reasonably clear understanding of the main issues at stake.[51] There was a high poll, especially in rural areas; in the towns the number of participants was usually between 50 and 70 per cent. Urban absenteeism reflected the influence on voters of maximalists who spread distrust of the assembly as a 'bourgeois' institution. This agitation, together with the preponderance of rural electors, helps to explain the successes of the PSR. Its candidates received nearly sixteen million ballots, or 38 per cent of the total; another five million votes (12 per cent) were cast for the Ukrainian SRs, so that these two kindred parties won the support of about half those who went to the polls. The Bolsheviks were the next strongest party. They won nearly ten million ballots, or 24 per cent of the total, including about half the soldiers' vote. The Kadets captured most of the middle-class vote (approximately two million, or 5 per cent of the total); another million and a quarter ballots (3 per cent) went to other non-socialist parties. The Mensheviks came out badly, winning a mere 3 per cent of the total poll (1,365,000 votes). The rest of the electorate cast their ballots for one or other of the national minority parties, socialist splinter groups or for local coalitions; some were unclassified.[52]

These results promised the PSR an absolute majority in the chamber, with 419, or 60 per cent, of the seats. The Bolsheviks would have 168, or 24 per cent.[53] To be sure, the PSR was not united : thirty-nine places fell to its radical wing. With assistance from the Left SRs and other allies in the national minority parties, the advocates of 'soviet power' could hope to control about a third of the seats. There was certainly no chance of their winning a majority. This meant that in their eyes the assembly would be a 'counter-revolutionary' body.

There had of course never been any question of the Bolsheviks abiding by the will of the entire people as expressed through the ballot-box. Such an idea was foreign to their political philosophy, based as this was on the notion of unremitting class struggle, with the Bolshevik party itself cast in the role of 'proletarian vanguard'. It was not, however, expedient to proclaim these beliefs from the housetops. As one early Soviet historian put it, 'Lenin thought that if the Bolsheviks came out against the Constituent Assembly before or during [the insurrection], this would cause vacillations among sizeable strata of petty bourgeois, peasants and workers who had not yet shaken off their illusory trust in the assembly.'[54] Lenin's instincts were to postpone the elections (and probably to prevent the assembly from meeting at all); but in the interests of party unity he took a more flexible line which blended organizational measures with propaganda.[55] He reckoned that by the time the assembly convened the Bolsheviks would have gained sufficient strength in the mass organizations to deal with it, using force if necessary. Kamenev and other right-wingers, who hoped for a compromise whereby the assembly would be integrated into the soviet machinery, differed but slightly from the Left SRs, who wanted to allow the assembly to meet so that it might discredit itself in the eyes of the populace.[56]

Already before this matter had been decided there had been major infringements of the voters' democratic rights. The October insurrection led to siege-like conditions in Petrograd and other cities : individuals were arrested, newspapers closed down, and electoral meetings obstructed. The All-Russian Electoral Commission, which bore responsibility for overseeing the poll, had to suspend regular sittings; in some areas ballot papers failed to arrive. Nevertheless the poll was held in general accordance with the arrangements made by the Provisional Government, which on 27 October the CPC pledged itself to respect.[57]

The Bolsheviks were still too weak, and too busy with more urgent matters, to interfere systematically in the electoral campaign. It was only after the first results became known that they faced up in earnest to the challenge of the forthcoming Constituent Assembly. On 21 November Lenin put before the CEC a bill designed to give electors the right to revoke the rights of deputies to *any* representative organ (including the assembly as well as soviets); the scheme aroused misgivings, but it was enacted two days later.[58] This showed that the Bolshevik leaders were still expecting the assembly to meet for some length of time, during which they could coerce it into sacrificing its less pliant deputies and so gradually bring it into line. This tactic savoured more of Kamenev or Bukharin than of Lenin. But simultaneously (23 November) the members of the All-Russian Electoral Commission were arrested *en bloc* and taken to Bolshevik headquarters, where they were detained for five days and then discharged from their functions.[59] A commission of Bolsheviks, headed by M.S. Uritsky (later chairman of the Petrograd Cheka), was set up to take their place.

The immediate pretext for this show of force was that the leaders of the main democratic parties and institutions had set up an informal coordinating body called the Committee to Defend the Constituent Assembly. This was conceived as successor to the Committee for the Salvation of the Fatherland and the Revolution. These leaders made no secret of their plan to challenge the regime by opening the proceedings on 28 November, the date that had been set by the Provisional Government.[60] A proclamation issued by the committee called on citizens to defend the Constituent Assembly to the last and promised that it would grant the people satisfaction of their basic demands for peace, land and public control of industry. *Izvestiya* responded by denouncing the assembly as a 'new idol' of the populace and reiterating that power must continue to rest with the soviets.[61] To gain time it was ruled that the assembly might open only when a quorum of four hundred deputies (over half) had assembled.[62] Events were clearly moving towards a showdown.

In the afternoon of 28 November large crowds assembled before the Tauride Palace, where the assembly was to meet. Under their protection some fifty deputies, mainly from PSR, managed to enter the buildings, despite the presence of armed guards at the gates.[63] As a demonstration this must, however, be adjudged a fiasco. Those present were too few in number to hold a regular session or to pass any legislation that might have made a favourable impact on the broader public. The affair showed that the PSR leaders had yet to take the full measure of their opponents. The Bolsheviks, naturally enough, reacted to the challenge with dispatch. A CPC decree issued that same evening (28 November) declared the Kadets 'the party of enemies of the people' and ordered their leaders to be arrested. An accompanying proclamation accused 'the bourgeoisie, led by the Kadet party', of plotting a counter-revolutionary *coup* under the cloak of the Constituent Assembly, and attempted to link the alleged plotters with the White generals who had begun operations in the cossack territories of the south-east.[64] These charges, which blurred the distinction between passive and active resistance, were designed to discredit not just the Kadets but also the PSR, and indeed the assembly as such, in the eyes of the populace. The outlawing of the Kadets was also a test of the opposition leaders' solidarity – a test which, it may be said, they triumphantly survived, for the democratic parties remained united in their defence of constitutional government. Unfortunately for them, however, the initiative had now very definitely passed to the Bolsheviks.

As those delegates favourable to their point of view arrived in the capital, they were dispatched, under Sverdlov's direction, to factories and barracks to agitate in favour of suppression of the assembly. It seems that they often found the people (at any rate the civilians among them) less enthusiastically disposed towards such a step than they had been led to assume, and that this 'softness' began to percolate upward into the party's top echelons. The Bolshevik deputies were organized into a 'fraction' (caucus), as was the practice with representatives to any deliberative body, and it was placed under the authority of a bureau appointed by the Central Committee (2 December). Almost immediately this bureau (of which Kamenev and Stalin were both members) found itself charged with 'right-wing views'. Nine days later it was dissolved, and instead N.I. Bukharin and G.Ya. Sokolnikov were put in charge of the fraction. The new chiefs were to take as their guide a set of theses prepared by Lenin, in which the party leader let it be understood that the assembly would be broken up by force if it failed to do the new regime's bidding. 'Any attempt ... to consider the question of the Constituent Assembly from a formal legalistic point of view', he wrote, 'is a betrayal of the proletarian cause'.[65] A meeting of soldiers in the Petrograd garrison was held on 14 December to enlist their support for the task in hand. On the seventeenth the Right SR leader N.D. Avksentyev, a former minister who had been elected to the assembly, was arrested and incarcerated in the Peter and Paul fortress; the Cheka also seized the chiefs of the Committee to Defend the Constituent Assembly and issued orders for the arrest of several other prominent opposition spokesmen, including Chernov and Tsereteli.[66]

The PSR leaders were in two minds how they should respond to these threats. The majority devoted themselves to working out the legislative proposals they intended to submit to the assembly when it met. They were confident, or at least hopeful, that if it were forcibly dissolved the people would rise in defence of their elected representatives, especially if these men were clearly identified with a programme of peace and land reform. Others were less sanguine. A group of PSR activists with military contacts made plans to call out these troops in support of the assembly. But when the moment came their resolution failed and the enterprise fizzled out ineffectively.[67]

The Bolsheviks were afraid that the Left SRS, and even some members of their own party, might be swayed into collaborating with the democrats. The propaganda campaign which they now unleashed was in large part directed towards such elements. It was argued that the electoral results had not really given the PSR a popular mandate, since that party had presented a single list of candidates even though it was deeply divided; the peasant electors had therefore really cast their vote for the Left SRS, who backed the government's revolutionary land programme, and thus indirectly for the Bolsheviks.[68] This was a way of saying to the Left SRS that they should remain wedded to their allies and resist the embraces of Chernov. For the same reason the prospective assembly, although composed predominantly of socialists, was categorized as incorrigibly 'bourgeois' and 'counter-revolutionary', suggesting that there could be no common ground whatever between its deputies and supporters of the soviets. It appears that this propaganda had a certain amount of success.

Even so it was far from clear how much resistance dissolution might engender, and every precaution had to be taken against unpleasant surprises. On 22 December the Bolsheviks made the CEC privy to their plans. The date of convocation was fixed for 5 January. Zinoviev warned that 'the Constituent Assembly can be recognized only if it adopts the programme of the second congress of soviets of workers' and soldiers' deputies and recognizes the Soviet government. If it should not do that, it would be a stone on the path of social revolution and the Soviet government will have to remove it.' There was little doubt that the deputies would refuse to make such a declaration of submission. Therefore another national congress of workers' and soldiers' soviets – the third – was to be called for 8 January 'to pass sentence on the Constituent Assembly'.[69]

It remained to draft the programmatic statement to be put before the deputies. This was written by Lenin and bore an appropriately high-sounding label: 'declaration of the rights of the toiling and exploited masses'. Adopted by the CEC on 3 January with only three dissentients, it was a cross between a draft constitution for the Soviet State and a summary of Bolshevik and Left SR policy objectives. (With minor amendments, it was embodied in the RSFSR constitution as adopted in July 1918.) It declared Russia to be a Soviet republic and proclaimed the aim of 'crushing the exploiters mercilessly, reorganizing society on a socialist basis, and bringing about the triumph of socialism throughout the world'. The assembly was invited to endorse the chief measures so far undertaken or decreed by the Soviet government (including some which had *not* been foreshadowed at the second congress of soviets, such as the establishment of a Red Army) and in effect to sign its own death warrant : 'the Constituent Assembly admits that it has no power except to work out some of the fundamental problems of the socialist organization of society' (by which was evidently meant that it should debate the issue of federation as the Bolsheviks understood it).[70] The declaration was accompanied by a decree stating that 'any attempt by any person or institution to usurp governmental authority will be considered counter-revolutionary . . . and will be suppressed by every available means, including armed force.'

On the night of 3/4 January a state of siege was declared in the capital. Uritsky instructed all Tauride Palace employees to obey only orders given by the palace commandant. A guard was mounted which comprised mainly sailors from the Baltic fleet who, as one eye-witness recorded, 'had bandoleers of cartridges draped coquettishly across their shoulders and grenades hanging obtrusively from their belts; from every corner protruded the long barrels of machine-guns.'[71] Shortly after midday a column of several hundred unarmed demonstrators approached the building, to find their way barred by Red guards. When the men refused to turn back shots were fired, first in the air and then at the marchers. There were several casualties, among them a member of the deposed central peasant executive named G.I. Loginov. Another column of marchers, which included workers from the Obukhov munitions factory, was fired upon near the same spot, and a grenade was thrown at them from an adjoining building. Some of the demonstrators succeeded in disarming members of the attacking force, but there is no reliable evidence that they actually used these weapons. Several similar clashes took place elsewhere in the city centre. In all ten people were killed and many more wounded.[72] A statement issued by the

Petrograd soviet executive claimed that the facts were the reverse of those given here : the demonstrators had allegedly fired 'provocative shots' at the guardians of order. Little credence can be given to this interpretation; its authors themselves made no pretence of objectivity, announcing that an investigation would be held, and if anyone were found to have 'spilled the blood of revolutionary workers' they would be brought to trial; nothing was said about punishing those who had killed demonstrators.[73] The shootings did, however, embarrass those in government circles who took a less rigorous stand, notably the Left SRs.[74]

It was thus in an atmosphere of extreme tension that the Constituent Assembly began its deliberations. A packed audience of workers, soldiers and sailors filled the galleries 'like a greyish-black thunder-cloud, in which from time to time one saw the flashing of gun-barrels and bayonets';[75] they made no secret of their feelings, addressing hostile remarks to the deputies gathered below. When the most senior person present, as *doyen d'âge*, attempted to open the proceedings, he was greeted with uproar from the pro-government deputies. Sverdlov came up to the platform, pushed the old man aside and announced that he himself had been authorized by the CEC to perform this role. This brought from the right and centre cries of 'wash your bloody hands !', but Sverdlov was not easily shaken. He went on to read the 'declaration of the rights of the toiling and exploited masses', to which the left-wing deputies responded by singing the *Internationale*. Their erstwhile comrades on the right joined in this ritual act with evident reluctance.[76]

Having thus prepared the ground psychologically, Sverdlov could move the election of a chairman : there was no need for him to give additional offence by claiming this office for himself. There were two candidates : Chernov, on whom the right and centre SRs had settled, with some misgivings, and Maria A. Spiridonova, a fiery twenty-eight-year-old ex-terrorist and Left SR leader. The Bolsheviks joined in backing Spiridonova, but it was Chernov who won most votes : 244, as against 151 for his rival.[77] On taking the chair Chernov delivered a long rambling speech designed to reconcile all the warring left-wing groups. If they sank their differences, he said, the Constituent Assembly could bring the nation peace, land reform and socialism and so confer upon Russia 'a stable, vital moral and political unity'.[78] According to a hostile eye-witness 'he seemed intoxicated by his own oratory'.[79] The general reaction to his speech was one of disappointment. He made no reference to the shootings; it was almost as if the October insurrection had never occurred. Even granting that his tactical aim was to win over the Left SRs, his approach was misguided, since he did not exploit those issues (notably arbitrary government) which principally divided them from the Bolsheviks. It might be said that he was trying to do in reverse what the extremist parties had done to the PSR in October : to steal their programme while rejecting their system of government. But whereas in October Lenin had acted from a position of strength in the soviets and other mass organizations, Chernov was speaking from a position of weakness, since the democrats had lost their hold upon all institutions of consequence other than the Constituent Assembly, and this august body now resembled nothing so much as the last crumbling bastion of a beleaguered fortress.

After Bukharin and Shteynberg had spoken for the governmental parties, Tsereteli did something to salvage the democrats' reputation. The right-wing Menshevik leader did not share Chernov's inhibitions. He roundly accused the Bolsheviks of abusing their power and said there was no reason why the assembly should approve everything they had done. The present government had rendered no proper account of its actions in the CEC or anywhere else and its foreign policy amounted to a headlong retreat before German imperialism. These arguments struck at the heart of the ruling coalition. Tsereteli ended by calling on all authorities in the land to obey the will of the people as expressed by their democratically elected representatives.[80] His speech, although it could hardly topple the government, did at least clear the air by exposing the main issues at stake.

After some further debate the Bolsheviks and Left SRs brought matters to a head by tabling a resolution that the assembly should take, as the basis of its agenda, their programmatic declaration. The outcome of the vote was a foregone conclusion. Only 146 ballots were cast for the motion as against 237 for the agenda proposed by the PSR.[81]

The assembly went into a brief recess while the government leaders met privately to discuss the next move – or rather, since it was clear what this move would be, how best to put it into effect. Lenin, according to one memoirist, was in a cheerful and optimistic mood : 'as you can see, now the situation is clear and we can get rid of them.' The Left SRS, still concerned about a possible popular back-lash, wanted to delay dissolution until the deputies had voted on the question of concluding an immediate peace.[82] The Bolsheviks rejected this course, fearing perhaps that such a debate might present the opposition speakers in too favourable a light. When the session was resumed F.F. Raskolnikov read out, 'in the tones of a public prosecutor', and to a chorus of interjections from floor and gallery, a statement denouncing the 'counter-revolutionary majority ... [for] trying to block the progress of the workers' and peasants' movement'; the PSR, he claimed, had not only fallen under bourgeois influence but was actually *directing* the bourgeois forces in their onslaught upon the people.[83] Having delivered this philippic, the Bolshevik deputies withdrew, laughing and shouting. An ugly scene ensued. One hot-headed deputy, a Ukrainian SR named Feofilaktov, drew his revolver upon another member (Yefremov) and had to be restrained by his colleagues; 'the guards standing in the corridor carefully readied their rifles and the soldiers in the gallery took aim at the human targets below them.' The assembly seemed about to end in a bloodbath.[84]

Gradually, however, order was restored and the debate continued in a rather confused fashion. Eventually the Left SRS pronounced themselves dissatisfied with their former comrades' attitude on the peace issue and withdrew. At this the PSR leaders, realizing the fate that lay in store for them, decided to push through in rapid succession a number of fundamental measures; these, they hoped, would show the general public that the assembly had its interests at heart and give the lie to propaganda that it had sold out to the bourgeoisie. The tactical calculation behind this move was astute, for in the incipient civil war it was important for democrats to have a positive symbol round which they could unite, and this the Constituent Assembly did to some extent provide. It was true that these measures were voted without proper discussion, and that they were displeasing to conservative anti-Bolsheviks, but these were necessarily secondary considerations. The first of these acts abolished private landed property without compensation and declared all the land to be national property; the second expressed regret at the Brest-Litovsk negotiations with the Central Powers and urged the Allies to conclude 'a just and general peace'; the third proclaimed the Russian State a democratic federative republic.[85] At the time these were policies which had a broad popular appeal; indeed it was largely by exploiting these very sentiments that the Bolsheviks had come to power. Now that the adverse consequences of their dictatorship were making themselves felt, the opposition could hope to win sympathy for such a programme – although, of course, there was now less hope than ever of their being able to realize it.

These final acts, 'declarative' and impractical as they were, to some extent compensated for the poor showing which the democratic deputies had initially made. When the crunch came they stood their ground and refused to yield to force without asserting their constitutional rights. Placed in a situation of extreme weakness *vis-à-vis* an implacable foe, they displayed a sense of dignity and even statesmanship. It is equally true that the democratic leaders had themselves to blame for their defencelessness, for throughout 1917 they had persistently misjudged the nature and source of the principal threat to their ideals.

The civil war was to pose an even graver test of their abilities to respond to the challenge of Bolshevik dictatorship. For the dissolution of the Constituent Assembly marked the end of an era. Never again would there be a national political forum in which popularly elected deputies could express open opposition to the regime in power. Henceforward such sentiments, if they could be ventilated institutionally at all, had to seek an outlet in lower-echelon bodies of more limited scope such as soviets, trade unions or factory committees.

The Bolsheviks lost no time in consolidating their victory over the democratic opposition. The one and only session of the Constituent Assembly ended at 4.40 am on 6 January. When some deputies returned to the Tauride Palace later that day, they were denied entrance by the guards. A decree dissolving the assembly was published by the CEC. It rehearsed the familiar arguments : the deputies were no longer representative of popular opinion, which had shifted to the left; socialism could be built not by a 'bourgeois parliament' but only by soviets chosen by the working people.[86] Would there then be new elections, from which members of the 'bourgeois' classes would be excluded? Would measures now be taken to make the CEC more representative of public opinion?

Only political innocents could ask such questions : yet they were asked all the same. The Left SRs were anxious to avoid too sharp a breach with 'bourgeois' legality. In the CPC they apparently suggested that, if the assembly were not to be reconstituted by fresh elections, then at least a 'revolutionary convention' should be formed in which the left-wing deputies would combine with delegates to the forthcoming soviet congress. In this way an element of continuity would be maintained. The Bolsheviks, of course, opposed this suggestion and the dispute was referred to the CEC. Lenin delivered a two-hour speech and evidently won over the Left SRS to his point of view.[87] One delegate, who spoke for the United Social Democrats (a splinter group), pluckily stood up for the rights of the defunct Constituent Assembly – to which, as he pointed out, the entire soviet movement had formally committed itself only two months earlier – and added a reference to those who had been killed while demonstrating in its favour. He was shouted down and prevented from concluding his speech. The errant Bolsheviks Lozovsky and Ryazanov were among those who voted against the assembly's dissolution.

The next step was to present this decision for endorsement to the third All-Russian congress of workers' and soldiers' soviets. This body met in the same hall as the Constituent Assembly, from 10 to 18 January; from 13 January it sat jointly with the third congress of peasant soviet deputies. At its peak it had a theoretical maximum complement of no less than 1,866 persons[88] – a fact which in itself speaks volumes about the seriousness of its deliberations. Its proceedings, which resembled those of a mass meeting, took place in an atmosphere of euphoria (*Izvestiya* spoke of 'revolutionary ecstasy')[89] engendered by expectations of imminent peace and the spread of revolution to Germany, whence serious disturbances were reported. Despite the large claims made on its behalf by supporters of the regime, the congress can scarcely be considered properly representative of the soviet movement as a whole. The arrangements for its convocation were haphazard in the extreme. This was partly due to the chaotic conditions of the time, but an element of deliberate calculation enters into the picture as well.

Four points may be made in this regard. First, the congress (or congresses) contained a very large military element.[90] These soldiers, many of whom came straight from front-line positions (now almost abandoned by their defenders), had little interest in the political and legal questions raised by the dissolution of the Constituent Assembly, or in devising the institutions of the new Soviet State, but responded with understandable eagerness to the prospect of peace. Tired and angry, they were easily swayed by the inter-nationalist oratory of spokesmen for the two governing parties.

Second, there seems to have been a greater representation of what we may term 'cadre elements' than at previous such congresses. Of 565 deputies who answered affirmatively to the question whether they worked actively in soviets – there is no way of knowing how representative this sample was of the total membership – 239 gave their occupation as members of the executive, 226 as chairman, 74 as secretary and 42 as member of the presidium. (Some respondents indicated more than one post.) It is also interesting that, in replying to another question, twelve per cent of the respondents stated that they owed their presence on the soviet to their political party, as distinct from election by any segment of the population.[91] Also present at the congress with voting rights were 130 delegates whose contact with the soviet movement was tenuous at best : left-wing members of the late Constituent Assembly and of the railwaymen's congress, representatives of factory committees and so on.[92]

Third, the congress, like its predecessors, was for obvious reasons most representative of those regions of the country where extreme radical tendencies were most marked, such as the north-west and centre. Of course, in some areas there were as yet scarcely any soviets, so that it would be unfair to blame the organizers for ignoring them. To ascertain the importance of this factor one would need to examine the geographical distribution of the soviets whose delegates' mandates have been preserved in the archives.

Fourth, the organizers abandoned the practice (which had probably never been widely observed) whereby associate delegates were sent to represent the minority viewpoint in the dispatching organization. A Menshevik journalist in Minsk complained that the congress of soviets in this region, which sent seven delegates, was attended by only about fifteen persons, of whom all but one or two had been soldiers without the slightest understanding of what the proceedings were about; in the city of Minsk itself the delegates had been chosen by the executive 'as if it were a family affair' (po-semeynomu); the moderates present had been silenced, even though a large workers' meeting had backed the Constituent Assembly.[93] In Kursk province several county soviets were denied representation at the congress on the grounds that they were too sympathetic to the PSR.[94] Complaints against such malpractices cannot be accepted at face value. The soviets had never been conceived as organs reflecting the full range of their members' opinions; they were cadre organizations, whose purpose was to mobilize support for their leaders' policies. The Bolsheviks were simply more ruthless and systematic than their rivals in eliminating dissent by their long-familiar manipulative techniques.

Yet precisely the use of such techniques prevents the third congress of soviets from being regarded as a fitting successor to the Constituent Assembly, whose mantle it now solemnly donned. There was in fact nothing democratic about it, if this much-abused term is taken literally. Its role was above all symbolic. It served to demonstrate one of Bolshevism's basic precepts : the solidarity, under the hegemony of the proletariat, of all three elements in the triad of toiling groups (workers, soldiers and peasants). The 'declaration of rights' which the Constituent Assembly had refused to discuss was enthusiastically endorsed – twice over, for good measure : first on 12 January, by the congress of workers' and soldiers' soviets, and then six days later by the deputies to both congresses meeting jointly.[95] The delegates also heard formal reports delivered, on behalf of the CEC and the CPC, by Sverdlov and Lenin respectively. Both expatiated with considerable frankness on the problems which these two executive organs had faced : at this early date the 'resonating' role of a soviet congress was still taken relatively seriously. Opposition speakers were allowed to take part in the debates, although they were subjected to fierce heckling. One who was prevented from finishing his speech was Stroyev, of the United Social Democrats, who reiterated the arguments he had earlier advanced in the CEC, condemning the violence done to the people's elected representatives.[96] Among other vocal critics of the ruling parties' policies was Martov, the left-wing Menshevik leader, who delivered a spirited attack on terroristic methods of government. But these speeches could not of course influence the outcome of the debate. The oppositionists had only a few dozen adherents in the throng and their voices were drowned in the chorus of government supporters.[97]

The individual who made the greatest impact was probably Trotsky, who delivered an exaggeratedly optimistic report on the progress of the negotiations at Brest-Litovsk. The mood of revolutionary exaltation, the feeling that international capitalism's final hour had struck, was turned to good account by the congress organizers in securing approval for measures designed to consolidate the regime internally. A new CEC was elected which reflected the shift of opinion in favour of the Bolsheviks,[98] with even less ability to influence the policy-making process than had been enjoyed by its predecessor. It was now that the government dropped the term 'provisional' from its title (see above, p. 315) and ordained that no further reference should be made in official legislative documents to the ill-fated Constituent Assembly. Two awkward and important domestic issues (the new constitutional framework and the land socialization law), on which the Bolsheviks and their Left SR allies were divided, were shunted off for discussion elsewhere.[99] The congress closed with the government to all appearances solidly based upon the will of the 'toiling masses', as articulated through the soviet movement, yet freer than ever to act as it thought fit.

By January 1918 the dictatorship had consolidated its grip upon the country to such a degree that it could only have been overthrown by external force. This achievement was due in large measure to the astute use which Lenin and his followers made of the spurious legitimacy conferred upon their government by the soviets. Having seized power on behalf of those whose interests the soviets claimed to represent, the Bolsheviks won from the second soviet congress a mandate to govern in its name. The Council of People's Commissars, at first an all-Bolshevik body and then a coalition in which that party called the tune, imposed its will upon the soviets' own central executive (the CEC), overcoming the ineffectual resistance offered by the 'soviet constitutionalists' (who included some right-wing Bolsheviks as well as Left SRs). Using the broad powers invested in these two organs, the ruling parties worked together to eliminate from political life all their principal opponents, and in particular the moderate socialists. They deprived them (or helped them deprive themselves) of their institutional base in the mass organizations and then struck boldly at the Constituent Assembly – a democratically elected and broadly representative parliament which embodied Russia's last hopes for civil peace and a pluralistic political order. Finally they sealed their victory by a plebiscitary verdict upon their actions to date – for this in essence was the role of the third congress of soviets, as of many similar gatherings in the years to come.

By any standards it was a remarkable achievement, brought about less by physical coercion (although this was certainly not lacking) than by the exercise of age-old political skills. But this victory was won at the price of a civil war which would in turn impose its imperatives upon the dictatorship, accentuating its oppressive character and driving it ever further from its original ideals. The very completeness of the Bolsheviks' triumph contained the seeds of tragedy for Russia as for themselves.

TWENTY-FIVE *The Urban Soviets: Petrograd and Moscow*

I T IS NOT yet possible to give a definitive account of the way in which the Bolsheviks took power throughout European Russia. In each city or region the situation was determined by a multiplicity of factors, each of which needs to be weighed in coming to a final analysis : the social and ethnic make-up of the population, the strength of ties between town and country, the state of communications and food supplies, the disposition of military forces and much else besides.[1] Nor are the materials adequate for such a study, since the relevant primary sources, where they have survived, have been subjected to thorough political screening; we still lack a full record of the proceedings of even *one* of the thousand or so soviets active at this time.[2] Yet there is no doubt that these bodies played an important part. Along with other mass organizations, they enabled the Bolsheviks to popularize their ideas and to legitimize their eventual assumption of sole power. Broadly speaking, their role was akin to that of the central soviet organs in Petrograd, but on a smaller scale.

During this period the urban soviets underwent a number of significant changes. First, the balance of power tilted even further in favour of the cadre elements in executive positions and against the delegates to the plenary assembly, to say nothing of the humble folk who voted for them. Second, the social composition of many soviets was altered by the merger of hitherto autonomous bodies representing workers and soldiers, and in some cases peasants as well. Third, local soviets were subjected to increasing control by regional organizations and by the central government. For the present all these tendencies existed in embryo, so to speak, but they were to be taken much further during the civil war. They were in part spontaneous in origin and in part the deliberate outcome of official Bolshevik policy. Let us first look briefly at these three phenomena in turn.

The decline of the plenum was to some extent due to the very success of the soviets in attracting mass support. The consequent expansion in the number of persons with a right to attend such meetings made it inconvenient to hold them as frequently as before. They therefore tended to be reserved for ceremonial occasions or moments when the local leaders felt it particularly urgent to stimulate mass enthusiasm (for example, when there was an immediate danger of counter-revolutionary attack). The periodicity of meetings offers a rough-and-ready gauge of the importance of the organ concerned. In the case of urban soviet plenums it is unfortunately seldom possible to establish this with certainty, but where the evidence is available the attempt is worth making.

Plenary sessions came into their own during the immediate preinsurrectionary days as a forum for extensive mass mobilization. Even so the cardinal decisions were often taken elsewhere, by what we shall call 'initiative groups'. These core organizations were termed by their founders 'revolutionary committees' (RCS; *revkomy*) or 'military-revolutionary committees' (MRCS; *voyenrevkomy*), the distinction depending (in principle, at any rate) on whether they were staffed wholly or primarily by civilians or soldiers. As a rule they comprised some regular members of the soviet's bureau or presidium plus a few activists coopted for the purpose. These men might be of varied party-political affiliation. Some of the most energetic individuals, especially among the soldiers, were not Bolsheviks but Left SRs. The Bolsheviks usually tried to ensure for themselves a majority on these bodies, but this often eluded them; in any case the current of opinion was running so strongly in their party's favour that many activists felt such precautions to be superfluous. Later on many non-Bolshevik RC or MRC members threw in their lot with the victors, and in some cases claimed that they had in effect been Bolsheviks all along – so creating an additional problem for the historian.

Once the immediate revolutionary crisis was over, these initiative groups normally surrendered their powers, ostensibly to the soviet or to its executive, in practice to its regular inner core or directing body. These bureaux or presidiums (as they were called interchangeably) were then as a rule confirmed in office by the deputies, either directly by a vote of the plenum or indirectly through the executive. Re-elections were also held where the cadres had opposed the October *coup* as soon as the maximalists had won the support of sufficient rank-and-file members. These elections were as free as the traditions of the soviet movement allowed – and certainly freer than they were to become in later phases of 'soviet power'. Delegates who advocated moderate policies would be granted a hearing and allowed to stand as candidates for election; moreover, the core organizations continued to be constituted on the principle of proportionality, so that moderate strength in the plenum would normally be reflected on the executive. However, two points need to be borne in mind here. First, the 'constituencies' electing delegates to a soviet were not stable but shifting, particularly in this period of high unemployment and 'self-demobilization' of the troops. Such conditions made it difficult to maintain regular, continuous links between the electorate and their soviet delegates or executive officers. Second, tolerance of dissenting opinions during the election and within the soviet itself was likely to be short-lived. Wherever it seemed that the moderates would be strong enough to influence policy, let alone to capture control of the organization, the maximalist elements took timely counter-measures. Opposition spokesmen might be harassed and their meetings broken up, election returns falsified, or soviet organs which they controlled merged with others which they did not. Considerable ingenuity was displayed in devising manipulative techniques of this kind, which generally had the desired effect of intimidating opposition supporters and driving them from the soviets.

The second change which took place was a contributory cause of the first. The amalgamation of worker and soldier soviets was a goal actively pursued by the Bolsheviks and their allies during this period, since this reinforced the radical tendencies in the soviet concerned and made it a more effective fighting organization. After the merger, as a concession to the group interests of each element, it was usually permitted to retain an autonomous 'section' of its own; but the meetings of these sections carried less weight than joint sessions. The leadership laid great stress upon unity of action and did its best to frustrate any fissiparous tendencies. In ideological terms such mergers could be justified as manifestations of proletarian-peasant 'class solidarity'; for this purpose soldiers were simply equated with peasants. Where civilian peasants were also included, turning the soviet into a tripartite body, this equation was conveniently forgotten. In practice the presence of *both* workers and soldiers served the maximalists as an added insurance against the possibility – admittedly rather remote – of the soviet slipping under the control of its peasant element. Should this nevertheless happen, the course taken was to dissolve the fractious section, hold new elections and replace it by more reliable collaborators. The same course was taken if dissent became too pronounced in either of the other sections, or among the rank-and-file members of a non-amalgamated soviet. In such cases the lower-echelon mass organizations (e.g. factory committees) could serve as a convenient tool for whipping up grass-roots support and 'swamping' electoral gatherings or recalcitrant plenary assemblies. If this procedure failed to produce the required results, or for some reason could not be applied, external pressure was brought to bear : reliable stalwarts from some other centre would be brought in to purge the dissentient body and force it into line. These men would be coopted to its executive or core organization to prevent any recurrence of trouble. There was no limit to the possibilities which the flexible soviet structure offered the maximalists.

Theoretically, of course, the same options were open to moderates as well, but in practice they were unable to use them – not simply because they had lost mass support, as their opponents tirelessly pointed out, but more pertinently because they lacked sufficient self-confidence; or, to put it another way, they were held back from such action by democratic scruples, although whether their principles were simply a cloak for irresolution it is difficult to say. Characteristically, one of the few significant cases of such manipulative techniques being applied against the Bolsheviks occurred in the Ukraine, where the socialists were emboldened by the strength of national feeling (see below p. 377). The normal response of the SRS and Mensheviks to what they regarded as illegal acts of force was to stage a demonstrative walk-out from the body concerned – at once a form of passive resistance and a self-satisfying moral gesture. No doubt they were influenced to some extent by the behaviour of their party leaders at the second congress of soviets. At the local level such a move might prove to be temporarily embarrassing to the maximalists, but it condemned those who made it to sterility – unless they used their liberty to recruit popular support, form a rival organization, and challenge the legality of the body which their opponents had captured. However, such a course was seldom practicable, if only because the Bolsheviks and their allies controlled the information media and disposed of superior physical force. Thus the moderates, all too aware of their disadvantages and uncertain of their popularity, generally refrained from following up their initial protest by resolute political action. As one sympathetic observer later remarked :

> All over Russia the same phenomenon was repeated. Wherever the SRs and Mensheviks had a fairly significant majority in the soviets, instead of staying in them to fight the Bolsheviks ... they voted to withdraw, voluntarily abandoning the battlefield. The Bolsheviks did not fail to take advantage of this decision and very quickly replaced the right-wing socialists with their own supporters. Thanks to this the Communists and their Left SR sympathizers soon had a majority of votes in almost all soviets and executives. Within a few months the right-wing socialists realized their mistake, but by then it was too late to undo it.[3]

The third change probably owed more than the first two to the express will of the country's new rulers, who were as we know convinced centralists. Although Lenin, in one of his first messages after the *coup,* urged the Moscow soviet to take action independently without waiting for instructions from Petrograd, reminding its leaders that they were now sovereign,[4] it was not long before he and his colleagues adopted a different tone. Moreover, the hundreds of activists (referred to loosely at the time as 'commissars') dispatched from the Petrograd area to provincial centres were armed with explicit instructions for local soviets. Not only were they to implement resolutely all decrees promulgated by the central authority : they were also to impose their control over every 'bourgeois' institution within their territory and to close down any such body suspected of counter-revolutionary proclivities. In order to strengthen the inter-mediate strata of the soviet hierarchy, which were still pitifully weak, these agents were recommended to convoke congresses of soviet deputies on the regional or provincial level, which were to elect the appropriate executives. Needless to say, there is reason to doubt the representative character of such bodies; however, their members certainly gained added authority and prestige from their new designations, which to the uninitiated suggested that their power stretched further than it actually did. To initiates such fictions were all part of the political game.

By the end of the year soviet executives had been set up in thirty provinces. Such bodies, known as *gubispolkomy,* varied greatly in authenticity and practical significance. In the words of a recent Soviet historian, 'the formation of the provincial organs of power was preceded, *as a rule,* by congresses of soviets'[5] – a recognition that their organizers were not always too scrupulous about their credentials. The most important regional soviet organizations were those of Moscow, Petrograd and the Urals; two others (North-west, Western) emerged out of local networks of soldiers' committees, and there were two more in Asiatic Russia. The Moscow regional executive (*oblispolkom*) was established after a reasonably representative congress, held in December (see below p. 457), but no such congress was held for the region round Petrograd. In 1918, as these executives struck root and developed greater vitality, they began to manifest what the central government regarded as 'separatist' tendencies and had to be brought to heel. Simultaneously efforts to systematize the work of local soviets were undertaken by the CEC's inter-city department, which sent out 643 emissaries during the first month after the *coup* (263 of whom went to the northern and north-western provinces[6] while the rest ventured further afield), and then by the PC of Internal Affairs. Its head, appointed on 17 November, was G.I. Petrovsky, who lacked seniority in the Bolshevik party and whose commissariat was for some time overshadowed by other more powerful central institutions. The circulars it dispatched are interesting mainly as indications of the direction which the CPC wanted the soviets to take. On 25 November the provincial soviets were required to report to the centre, and four weeks later a similar ordinance was sent to *all* soviets. They were now formally instructed to dissolve all public institutions and dismiss all individuals appointed or elected under the previous regime and to replace them by organs and agents of their own. They were 'to coordinate their activities with the general decrees and instructions of the central power', so creating 'an organism homogeneous in all its parts'.[7] Shortly thereafter

Petrovsky's commissariat worked out an organizational blueprint which each soviet was to follow in regard to its administrative apparatus, to consist of eleven departments; some scope was, however, still left to local leaders to adapt this scheme to their own needs.[8] The pressure for systematization intensified after the constitution of the RSFSR was adopted in July 1918, at a time when the civil war imposed its own imperatives.

These then were the main changes that took place in the urban soviets during the post-revolutionary period : how, one may well ask, did the populace react to them? Unfortunately there is little hard information on this point and one is reduced to generalizations.

The 'hard' and 'soft' attitudes that coexisted among the socialist politicians in Petrograd were reproduced on a wider spectrum in the lower depths. Rank-and-file soviet supporters were guided by the mixed emotions and contradictory sentiments characteristic of ordinary folk. Wherever political tensions were less acute and external agitation less in evidence, they sought to bridge differences that did not seem insuperable or simply let things slide and postponed awkward decisions. The 'conciliationism' and vacillations which Lenin detected even among members of his party's Central Committee were the norm among its lower-echelon activists, who reasoned pragmatically rather than ideologically. If the threat of 'counter-revolution' was so serious, should not all socialists make common cause against it? Was comradeship to count for nothing?

This spirit of compromise was carried over into their thinking on institutional issues. We have seen that most deputies to the second congress of soviets wanted a socialist coalition government and sought to reconcile the 'soviet parliament' with its 'bourgeois' counterpart. In local affairs their attitude was similar. In many places soviet activists collaborated in setting up mixed representative committees to deal with urgent problems until, as they hoped, some accommodation had been reached at the national level. These committees often included delegates from the democratically elected authorities, such as the municipal duma, zemstvo board or food-supply committee, along with working-class organizations such as soviets, trade unions and factory committees. Elsewhere they might be more limited in scope, but still representative of a wide range of left-wing opinion. The soviet leadership usually set the tone in these mixed bodies, whose other elements were 'open towards the left' and prepared to collaborate on generous terms. Such arrangements could be particularly useful in solving practical problems such as maintaining communications, food supplies and public services. They seemed far preferable to hot-headed action designed to bring the entire local administration under outright soviet control, when this body lacked the men and the expertise to assume such functions. Revolution *à l'outrance* seemed likely only to antagonize the population and to discredit the very idea of 'soviet power'.

This 'soft' empirical approach had much to commend it, yet in the eyes of ideological zealots it was of course deeply suspect. Given the situation in the centre, where the Leninists had emerged triumphant, it was only a question of time before a similar state of affairs came into being in the provinces as well. This process was carried out by local cadres supported by the most militant elements in the local population, particularly soldiers. These fanatics were driven by emotions precisely the reverse of those just described. Ruthless action, in their view, was essential to keep the revolution's enemies at bay; any backsliding was dangerous, perhaps even treasonable; regard for legal or moral proprieties was sheer sentimentalism. This spirit, which encouraged deeds of wanton cruelty and every kind of excess, was fated to infect ever wider circles of soviet activists, driving out feelings of moderation and restraint, until it would become the hallmark of the movement as a whole. In the autumn of 1917 it was probably still a minority viewpoint even in the main revolutionary centres; a few months later it had spread throughout provincial Russia – not just to the larger cities but to small market towns as well, and even to the countryside, wherever soviets had come into existence.

In the popular imagination the Petrograd soviet has come to be identified with the October insurrection: 'the chief bastion of Bolshevism among the working masses', 'an exemplar of revolutionary fervour' – the phrases come readily to the lips. But precisely what organization is meant? In speaking loosely of 'the soviet' one generally has in mind an initiative group, the famous Military Revolutionary Committee (MRC). Set up on 12 October, with Trotsky as its most prominent leader, it directed the actual seizure of power in the capital less than a fortnight later. Neither this *ad hoc* body nor the soviet's 'regular' executive organs should be confused with the plenum, which underwent an eclipse soon after the insurrection. If its members can be held to have 'made revolution' at all, they did so as individual emissaries invested with the soviet's prestige, rather than as participants in the work of a corporate body.

We may therefore examine first the changing fortunes of the Petrograd soviet's plenary assembly before turning to the history of its executive organs, which did indeed serve as buttresses of the dictatorship, not least in the matter of internal security.

On 31 August, amidst the excitement engendered by the Kornilov affair, the Bolsheviks submitted to the plenum a declarative resolution demanding the formation of 'a government comprising representatives of the revolutionary proletariat and peasantry'. This was passed in the early hours of the following morning by the handsome majority of 279 votes to 115, with 51 abstentions.[9] Since less than half the deputies had been present, the moderate leaders of the soviet refused to recognize the ballot as an expression of non-confidence in themselves – particularly since their own position on the matter at issue differed only slightly from that of the Bolsheviks. When the plenum next met, on 9 September, the moderates demanded a roll-call vote. To their discomfiture the poll went against them, although the margin was narrower than before : 519 votes were cast for the Bolsheviks to 414 for their opponents, 67 members abstaining.[10] One of the factors which influenced the outcome was the news that the Moscow soviet had just passed a similar resolution. Jealous of its revolutionary prerogatives, the Petrograd body did not want to be outpaced. Yet there is of course no doubt that its members' mood had now shifted further to the left, and it was in recognition of this fact that the presidium, conscious of its democratic obligations, resigned.

The new team of seven (confirmed in office on 25 September) was led by Trotsky, recently freed from jail. As chairman he lost no time in consolidating his party's hold on the delegates' affections. Plenary sessions were held frequently. On 11 September the soviet endorsed his suggestion that the new cabinet be formed by the Democratic Conference (an idea popular among uncommitted deputies, although frowned upon by Lenin). Ten days later, after the conference had made itself ridiculous by contradicting itself on the composition of the government, the soviet presidium was quick to exploit the moderates' embarrassment. The deputies reaffirmed with greater force their commitment to 'soviet power'. Yet another debate on the crisis was held on 25 September. On this occasion Kerensky's last cabinet (which had just been formed after inter-party talks) was denounced as 'a government of bourgeois omnipotence and counter-revolutionary violence' – rhetoric that made excellent propaganda, whatever may be thought about its accuracy.[11]

Thus by the end of September the several hundred delegates attending meetings of the plenum could feel that they were shaping the country's destiny. Their aspirations seemed to accord so closely with the directives they received that they were scarcely conscious of being guided at all. The plenum of the Petrograd soviet became a genuine revolutionary assembly, a resonator automatically echoing the signals emitted from above.

This state of affairs, it is worth noting, can be explained in terms not merely of crowd psychology but also of institutional mechanics. The executive committee, which would normally have acted as an obstacle to easy communication between presidium and plenum, had been effectively neutralized.[12] Curiously enough, this seems to have come about by accident. Nevertheless its results were certainly significant. The breakdown in the Petrograd soviet's power structure not only enhanced Trotsky's personal authority but also enabled him and his colleagues to set up a near-omnipotent MRC, of which more will be said presently.

The plenum met frequently during the period of the insurrection. On 18 October it discussed arrangements for the forthcoming soviet congress – it was on this occasion that Trotsky denied publicly that an insurrection was planned[13] – and from 23 October until 1 November sessions were held almost daily. These meetings were mass-mobilization devices *par excellence*. They were attended by vast throngs of revolutionized elements, especially soldiers and sailors, as well as the regularly elected delegates. No record has been kept of those who participated and voting was by acclamation. On the 25th the assembly was addressed by Lenin, who was given a tumultuous welcome.[14] On the 29th Trotsky gave an account of the abortive rising in Petrograd by military cadets, appealing to his audience to spare the prisoners and remain sober.[15] Soon afterwards the delegates found themselves drawn into the controversy over the composition of the new government. First they voted in favour of coalition (3 November); the next day they heard Lenin, but the presidium cautiously did not put the matter to a vote; on the 6th they fell into line, dutifully denouncing the Mensheviks as allies of General Kaledin. Their role was already coming to resemble that of the chorus in a Greek tragedy : blind instruments of fate, they could scarcely follow the intricate manoeuvres of their leaders upon which they were called to pronounce.

Thereafter the frequency of plenary sessions declined. Seven such meetings were held in the twelve days ending on 10 November, the same number registered for the whole of December.[16] Attendance also seems to have fallen, partly because many delegates had either left on errands or had assumed administrative functions locally. Simultaneously the nature of proceedings in the plenum underwent a change. Formal reports were delivered, mainly on current economic questions, by persons in authority. This made for order at the expense of spontaneous vitality. Two sessions were purely ceremonial.

In February 1918 the plenum's importance revived dramatically during the crisis over the Brest-Litovsk peace talks. On the 15th it heard Trotsky report on the breakdown of the negotiations and endorsed his formula of 'neither war nor peace'. Six days later, after the German advance, it reversed itself and approved Lenin's stand in favour of accepting enemy terms. This vote helped to swing opinion in the Bolshevik Central Committee behind Lenin. The delegates also organized the capital's defences against the expected German attack,[17] and throughout the emergency found themselves once again the centre of national attention. However, soon afterwards the Soviet government moved to Moscow; with this the Petrograd soviet inevitably forfeited its earlier national role and turned into a body of local (or rather, regional) significance.

At the same time the plenum came to be overshadowed by the reconstituted executive organs[18] as well as by the rapidly proliferating functional departments. In March 1918 these were transformed into fully-fledged commissariats, and north-western Russia came under the rule of a curious regional government directed by Zinoviev, known as the 'Union of Communes of the northern Region', which enjoyed a certain *de facto* autonomy *vis-à-vis* the CPC in Moscow.[19]

If the birth-pangs of the 'regular' soviet apparatus in Petrograd were so agonizing, one reason was that the MRC – its stepfather, so to speak – was loath to die. We now know a good deal more about the operations of this celebrated body, thanks to the labours of Soviet historians during the Khrushchev 'thaw'.[20] It was in essence a *junta* whose powers were defined solely by the ambitions of its leaders. The MRC, having arrogated to itself the functions of the soviet's regular executive, expanded its authority in every direction until its ill-considered actions provoked such opposition that it was cut down to size. In part these 'empire-building' tendencies reflected the ebullient temperament of Leon Trotsky. But this is by no means the sole explanation : for the new material makes it clear that the MRC was in fact run by an informal collective on oligarchic lines, and that Trotsky played a smaller part than has generally been assumed.[21] Equally important was the Bolsheviks' unwillingness to think in concrete institutional terms at a moment when they were being carried along on the tide of 'revolutionary spontaneity' and had yet to decide on the demarcation line between the central and local soviet authorities.

Curiously enough, the initiative in establishing the MRC came not from the Bolsheviks but from their rivals. On 9 October the Menshevik leaders in the executive committee proposed that such a body be formed with the limited task of gathering data on the military situation in Petrograd and the Provisional Government's intentions : specifically, whether its plan to transfer troops from the capital was indeed motivated by counter-revolutionary purposes, as the Bolsheviks loudly alleged. The latter swiftly recognized the advantages which this scheme offered to further their own insurrectionary aims behind a convenient soviet façade. Their representatives in the Petrograd soviet's military department (who were presumably privy to the Bolshevik Central Committee's decision of 10 October) devised a statute for the new body which streamlined its organization and broadened its tasks. On 12 October this statute was approved at a closed session of the executive committee; the next day it was endorsed by the soldiers' section and on 16 October by the soviet plenum.[22] The first full meeting of the MRC was not held until 20 October. The delay was evidently due to divergences among its members, as well as to opposition from the Bolshevik party's own military organization, whose chiefs doubted whether a call to insurrection would arouse sufficient response. Their caution was not unfounded, but the MRC leaders' estimate of the balance of forces proved to be more realistic. They appreciated that morale in the garrison had crumbled and that it would not be too difficult to win over, or at least to neutralize, the vacillating elements by a show of strength at the decisive points. A good deal of bluff was involved on both sides in Petrograd before and during the uprising.[23]

Whatever one thinks of the MRC's achievements as an organ of insurrection, there is no doubt that it served as the hub of the dictatorship during the weeks that followed – yet this aspect of its activities has received little attention, at least in western literature. Its significance is evident from the relative frequency of its sessions : whereas the CPC, nominally the supreme governmental authority, convened only twice during the immediate post-revolutionary days (27 October, 3 November), and did not meet daily until the middle of November,[24] the MRC met at least once and usually twice each day throughout this period. It grew rapidly in size, until by the end of its life it had about eighty members, of whom fifty-three were Bolsheviks.[25] Their principal job was to maintain liaison with sympathizers in various military units, factories and public institutions. Thus the MRC functioned as a substitute for the soviet.

The MRC's arbitrary actions (searches, arrests, expropriations, closures of newspapers and so forth) not only antagonized and intimidated ordinary persons : they also trespassed upon the prerogatives of other revolutionary organs. Even the CPC was not immune from its importunities. When I.V. Stalin, the newly appointed PC of Nationality Affairs, wanted to contact Moscow by direct wire, he had to ask permission from the MRC,[26] which had assumed responsibility for communications between Petrograd and other centres. One may surmise that he did not take kindly to such niggling controls. The MRC also antagonized V.A. Antonov-Ovseyenko, now in charge of the Petrograd military district, and his staff by dismissing one of his appointees.[27] The soviet in the central district of the city protested on 1 December that its work was 'paralysed' by the MRC's activities[28] – or to be more precise, those of its dependency, the so-called Military Investigating Commission. This body was first heard of on 1 November, when it refused to allow the former Foreign Affairs minister, M.I. Tereshchenko, who was in prison, to receive a visit from his relatives; the latter appealed to the MRC as the higher instance, which upheld the original decision.[29] The commission had five members, some of whom were already notorious for their severity. No public or private organization, however apolitical, was safe from the MRC and its sinister subordinate. On 24 November, for example, the Society for the Struggle against Infant Mortality came under suspicion, and it was decided that all gambling and card-playing in the city should cease forthwith.[30]

Such measures seemed likely to discredit the new regime without bringing any significant improvement in security. An unidentified member of the CEC observed cautiously that 'one should not close one's eyes to the fact that the activity of the [Military] Investigating Commission, speaking concretely [sic], suffers from defects in regard to logical consistency and regular work.'[31] Meanwhile Lenin had turned to F.E. Dzerzhinsky as the man he thought best qualified to replace it by a more systematic nation-wide political security system. As a preliminary move a 'commission for struggle against counter-revolution' was appointed on 21 November, whose geographical coverage presumably coincided with that of the MRC.[32] The CPC could then safely proceed to rid itself of this meddlesome body.[33] On 25 November it decided that its personnel and functions should be distributed among various people's commissariats, the Military Investigation Commission coming under the PC of Justice. There seems to have been some opposition to the plan, since on 30 November the CPC had to repeat its order[34] and meetings of the MRC continued to be held, although with decreasing regularity, until 5 December, when the CPC finally dissolved it. The decision stated explicitly that its police functions were to pass to a nation-wide security organ, whose existence was formalized two days later.[35]

This body, 'the All-Russian Extraordinary Commission for Combating Counter-revolution, Sabotage and Speculation', is better known from its Russian initials as the *Cheka*. Its tasks were not made public at the time and were defined vaguely :

(a) to punish and liquidate all attempts or actions connected with counter-revolution or sabotage, whatever their source, throughout Russia;

(b) to hand over for trial by a revolutionary tribunal all saboteurs and counter-revolutionaries, and to elaborate measures to combat them;

(c) to carry out a preliminary investigation only in so far as was necessary for preventive purposes.[36]

The wording could be taken as implying that suspects would be handed over for trial by another body with a quasi-judicial character. On the other hand the first phrase gave the Cheka virtual *carte blanche* to act as it pleased, and a final sentence prescribed the punitive measures it was to take : 'confiscation [of property], expulsion from domicile, deprivation of ration cards, publication of lists of enemies of the people, etc.' Left SR and other doubters within the CPC could be expected not to quibble over the inconspicuous 'etc.'. There is no doubt that Lenin wanted the new security organ to have unrestricted powers. On the following day he wrote to two officials emphasizing that 'the arrests which are to be carried out on the orders of comrade Peters are of *exceptional* importance and must be effected with great energy.'[37] The measures he proposed were still fairly mild, but the tempo of repression was soon drastically speeded up. By 14 January Lenin was declaring to the presidium of the Petrograd soviet, in connection with the food shortage: 'we can achieve nothing unless we use terror and shoot speculators on the spot.'[38] In February 1918 the central Cheka had 120 employees.[39] By the end of the year the entire organization was said by Latsis to have a staff of no less than 31,000.[40] There is no doubt that it played a vital role in consolidating the new order.

In this way the MRC of the Petrograd soviet, which began its brief life modestly, as an *ad hoc* organ to direct the Bolshevik *coup* in Petrograd, became the progenitor of the world's most notorious secret police force. Of all transformations wrought by the October revolution, this was perhaps the strangest.

In Moscow the workers' and soldiers' soviets were not merged until after the seizure of power, which was accomplished only at the cost of considerable bloodshed. It is thought that there may have been as many as a thousand casualties.[41] It is customary in Soviet historical writing to lay part of the blame for the violence in Moscow upon the right-wing tendencies of the Bolshevik leaders in that city. The charge is not wholly without foundation, although a greater share of responsibility rests with their masters, who imposed upon them an insurrectionary course which they themselves sought to avoid or postpone.

The Moscow soviet of workers' deputies came under Bolshevik control on 5 September, a few days after the similar turn of events in Petrograd and for the same reasons. The vote in the plenum (355 : 254) gave them a large majority, but in the executive committee, which was re-elected on 19 September, they found themselves with only a slight advantage: the ratio of Bolsheviks to non-Bolsheviks was 32 : 27, and in the presidium 5 : 4.[42] This meant that when the two soviets' executive committees met in joint session, the SRS, who controlled the soldiers' soviet, could impose their will. This was precisely what happened on 18 October, when such a meeting was held to discuss the question of assuming power. The Mensheviks and SRS refused, on grounds of principle, to permit the soviets to issue decrees, and a resolution in this sense was adopted by 46 votes to 33.[43] The next day the Bolsheviks took the matter to a plenum of the workers' soviet, where they received the support they called for. The moral was clear : joint sessions of the two executives must be avoided until they had consolidated their influence in the workers' soviet, notably by holding new elections. However, no sooner had they decided to hold such a poll (21 October) than the storm burst about their heads. Nogin and his colleagues seem to have assumed that the insurrection was still weeks away. It was not just a matter of emulating Petrograd, but also of restraining their more headstrong supporters in the barracks and factories. The temptations to act rashly were overwhelming. On 23 October the Bolshevik-controlled executive committee of the workers' soviet, meeting separately, issued a decree regulating the hiring and firing of industrial employees – an open challenge to the tottering government. The next day this decree was enthusiastically endorsed at a joint session of the two plenums. On the evening of the 25th, after news had been received of the events in Petrograd, the deputies met again, with excitement now at fever pitch, and approved the formation of an MRC to seize power in the city.[44]

The position of the Moscow MRC was an unenviable one. Whereas its Petrograd counterpart could space out its blows, it was thrust into battle within moments of its creation. Nor was it so homogeneous politically. The Petrograd MRC was under *de facto* Bolshevik control (its Left SR members collaborating with them loyally), whereas on the Moscow body three of the seven members disapproved of the insurrection. They explained their presence on the MRC by a desire to minimize the adverse consequences which the Bolsheviks' 'adventure' would have upon the Russian working class.

This opposition from within was less of a political handicap than might at first sight appear, since the non-Bolsheviks resigned during the battle; however, their influence helps to explain why that body acted so indecisively. It was little more than an informal conclave, in which some of those who spoke loudest, such as the soldiers' leader Sablin, a Left SR, were not even regular members. Its policy fluctuated according to the balance of forces and also the leaders' transitory mood. On 26 October Nogin (who was not a member of the MRC)[45] entered into talks with Colonel K.I. Ryabtsev, commander of Moscow military district, as a result of which both sides agreed to desist from further war-like actions; as part of the deal the insurgent forces were to withdraw from the Kremlin, which they had occupied. This agreement was duly reported to the soviet executive later that evening and presumably endorsed by it.[46] However, fighting broke out again shortly afterwards, for which each side blamed the other. Although the insurgents made significant gains in this battle, their leaders were worried at the possibility that the loyalists might secure reinforcements from outside the city with the connivance of the railwaymen; this led them to sanction further talks, held in a railway station under the aegis of Vikzhel, on 30 October. These yielded the outlines of an accord with the Public Safety Committee (a coalition of democratic bodies similar to that formed in Petrograd). There was to be an armistice, followed by a compromise political settlement. The more radical insurgent leaders repudiated the agreement at the last moment;[47] nevertheless talks were resumed on 1 November, this time in the municipal offices, with the United Social Democrat leaders mediating. By this time the loyalists' morale was sagging badly and an agreement was drafted without much difficulty. It was approved by the MRC early on 2 November and formally endorsed by both sides later that day.

The victors' first move (4 November) was to dissolve the municipal duma, which had served as a rallying-point for the democratic forces during the struggle. Thereupon action was taken to merge the two soviets. During the fighting the old leaders of the soldiers' soviet had been deposed (and even arrested) by maximalist elements.[48] Elections were arranged for a new executive, which first met on 14 November. No less than fifty-five of its sixty members are said to have declared themselves to be 'Bolsheviks', which probably did not imply much more on their part than a general commitment to the idea of 'soviet power'.[49] In any case there was no doubting their radicalism, and when the two plenums met later that day the throng voted strongly in favour of the proposed merger.[50] The new joint executive committee was weighted in favour of workers' deputies at the expense of those of soldiers (in inverse proportion to their respective roles in the struggle for power): there were to be sixty places for the former as against thirty for the latter. This arrangement gave the Bolsheviks sixty-two seats to the Left SRs' thirteen; the moderate opposition was represented by ten Mensheviks, four United Internationalists and one other. The all-important presidium had eleven Bolsheviks, three Left SRs, one United Internationalist – but no Mensheviks, for this party's local leaders had characteristically decided to boycott the organ invested with real power, lest they blemish their democratic reputation, although they saw nothing wrong in serving on the relatively ineffectual executive committee. The chairman was M.N. Pokrovsky, a professor who soon won fame as the regime's leading historian.

The drift towards centralization within the soviet structure was less marked in Moscow than it was in Petrograd. Plenary meetings were held irregularly, but averaged one each week until the end of the year. Moscow seems to have suffered less than Petrograd during this period from arbitrary police measures,[51] and those who were arrested (for instance striking public servants) were treated relatively gently. In the plenary meetings deputies were at first able to debate issues such as workers' control (28 November) with a fair amount of freedom : the official Bolshevik line was opposed from both the Menshevik and the syndicalist viewpoint.[52] But already by 15 December complaints could be heard about poor attendance. Although only a fifth of the deputies were present, it was held that this comprised a quorum, and the assembly endorsed an order setting up an extra-legal revolutionary tribunal. As in Petrograd, security matters were coming to the fore. On 21 December the assembly reconvened to discuss the supply question, but so few deputies appeared that the meeting had to be given a consultative character.[53] The rapidly darkening economic situation strengthened the hand of those pressing for emergency measures enforced by a stern dictatorial authority.

The Moscow Bolshevik leaders, anxious not to isolate themselves from other currents of left-wing opinion, tolerated a limited freedom of expression. On 8 November the MRC ordained that newspapers which had been forced to suspend publication during the rising might reappear so long as they did not feature calls to counter-revolution.[54] Naturally complaints were immediately heard that this liberty was being abused, and it was not long before individual offenders were penalized.[55] These acts of repression evoked protests among journalists, printers and other sections of the public, and in December all the non-Bolshevik papers ceased publication for thir-teen days in protest at the imposition of censorship and martial law. Nevertheless, for some months it was much easier to print material critical of the government in Moscow than it was in Petrograd. A similar precarious freedom was enjoyed by certain public institutions inherited from the old order, such as the supply agencies (see below p. 426). However, these modest signs of liberalism were speedily eliminated after March 1918, when Moscow became the capital of the Soviet republic.

TWENTY-SIX *The Urban Soviets: the North-west, the Central Industrial Region and the Urals*

BOTH PETROGRAD AND MOSCOW were metropolitan centres whence revolutionizing influences radiated outwards to provincial towns over a large area of indeterminate scope. While the basic pattern of events here was broadly similar, local peculiarities were also important. Our treatment will necessarily be selective, and will emphasize the institutional process whereby the soviets were converted from means of mass mobilization into instruments of party dictatorship. Although the evidence is patchy, memoirs which appeared in the 1920s can often supplement the studies and documentary selections compiled by Soviet historians in recent years.

In the north-western provinces of European Russia activists sent out from Petrograd met a ready response among soldiers on the northern front and sailors of the Baltic fleet. There was a high density of population and communications were relatively good. Most soviets in the area had come under Bolshevik control by September. One of the few exceptions was Luga, where the moderates held on until 17 November.[1] The congress of the northern region, which met in Petrograd from 11 to 13 October (see above, p. 312), was primarily a military and naval occasion. It set up a regional executive, which probably existed only on paper, under a seven-man bureau led by F.F. Raskolnikov, one of the best-known activists in the fleet.[2] MRCs were formed in most local soviets, and as soon as news was received of the Bolshevik *coup* in Petrograd these seized power. Their support rested mainly on the troops, civilian workers playing a subordinate role. Little resistance was offered by the officers. In the eyes of senior commanders (notably General V.A. Cheremisov, commander-in-chief of the northern front, whose role in the early days of the October revolution was crucial) the chief objective was to maintain a military shield, however fragile, against the Germans; they did not want to see their men dragged into a civil war, and still less to become involved themselves in the political squabbles of Petrograd. Some generals even had a grudging admiration for the determination and relative efficiency of the Bolsheviks. The latter were quick to turn the apparatus of soldiers' committees to their party's advantage. Developments in the Twelfth Army may be taken as typical. On 31 October an *ad hoc* gathering of men from various units backed the new regime by a narrow majority (248 votes to 243) and set up a provisional executive, with parity representation, to prepare an extraordinary army congress. This met at Wenden on 14–15 November. It yielded a two-thirds majority for the Bolsheviks and their allies, who took three-quarters of the seats on the executive.[3]

Further to the rear the maximalists sometimes found the going tougher. In Novgorod the citizens seemed not to have forgotten that ancient city's medieval traditions. The local soviet executive, a tripartite body which claimed authority over the whole province, had a democratic majority. On 9 October it voted to recall its delegate from the northern regional congress and six days later summoned a provincial congress of its own, stiffened with men from the lower-echelon organizations – one of the rare instances when the moderates employed this technique.[4] When the Provisional Government fell, the soviet adopted a neutral stance. On 13 November the Bolsheviks and Left SRs, encouraged by the mood of the garrison, set up an MRC. This is said to have won a 'chance majority' in the soviet (that is its executive committee) owing to a split between opposing factions; thereupon it deposed the commissar appointed by the Provisional Government and chose two men to succeed him, one from each of the insurgent parties. Simultaneously the Bolsheviks and Left SRs on the soviet executive committee denounced the existing presidium for 'sabotage' and chose a new team, which presumably included themselves. They did so without consulting the soviet plenum, and in spite of the fact that the presidium had been elected as recently as the beginning of October. The majority leaders on the executive responded by abolishing the MRC and ordering its members to stand trial for the abuses they had committed. The returns in the Constituent Assembly elections made them confident of their strength (the Bolsheviks won only 400 out of over 7,000 civilian votes), and they evidently reckoned that they could also carry the provincial congress of soviets. However, this was called on a basis that favoured the maximalists: whereas peasants could send three deputies for every rural district, one deputy could attend for every two hundred soldiers or workers; moreover, those parties which 'accepted soviet power' were each allowed one representative from each county and three from the province as a whole. Thus when the congress met on 3 December it chose an executive heavily weighted in favour of the Bolsheviks (twenty-five, as against five Left SRs and six Mensheviks); this set up the customary bureau, of four men, the post of secretary being taken by the leading local Bolshevik, N.D. Alekseyev. The moderate elements refused to participate and hoped the tide would turn in their favour. The insurgent leaders were becoming increasingly unpopular among the civilians,[5] and the garrison was melting away as demobilization took its course. However, a demonstration on behalf of the Constituent Assembly was dispersed with some fatal casualties (4 January), which put the democrats on the defensive. They withdrew to the sanctuary of a local monastery. The Bolsheviks brought up artillery; the clergy intervened to prevent further bloodshed and damage to the building; and after a few days the opposition leaders left quietly. Passive resistance continued for some time to come.[6]

Nothing is said in these accounts of any plenum of the Novgorod soviet: the political battle seems to have been fought out between and within its executive bodies. One may speculate that one reason for the moderates' defeat was their failure to devise a deliberative organ that could challenge the authority of the self-styled provincial congress of soviets. Their eyes were fixed so firmly upon the Constituent Assembly that they neglected to consolidate their local political base. This attitude, common among democrats throughout Russia, was quite natural in a town so close to both metropolises.

The Moscow soviet leaders maintained contact with a number of organizations in the Central Industrial region and beyond, to the middle Volga in the east and Tambov and Kursk in the south. The body most immediately concerned in this task was the 'bureau of soviets of the Moscow region', better known as MOBYUS (see above, p. 129), which was under moderate control. On 30 September it convened a congress of affiliated organizations which manifested strong maximalist tendencies. Only by mustering the peasant vote did the organizers succeed in securing a majority for their resolutions. The chief practical result of the proceedings seems to have been to persuade the Mensheviks and SRs to allow MOBYUS to be reconstituted on the principle of proportional representation, instead of parity among the three socialist parties as hitherto.[7] This virtually gave the Bolsheviks charge of the organization, although in fact they made little immediate use of their opportunity: in making preparations for the transfer of power in the central region they preferred to use party channels. In any case the Moscow Bolsheviks were too busy with the affairs of the city and its immediate environs to devote much attention to the provinces until after they had won control of the metropolis. On 11–12 November MOBYUS held a plenary meeting to ascertain the situation. The delegates' reports showed that the maximalist current was running strongly almost everywhere. The moderates present were overawed, and when a motion was passed condemning their stand they obligingly walked out.[8] Two weeks later MOBYUS announced that a regional congress of soviets would be convened on 10 December.[9] This gathering was attended by men from 112 local soviets, which were, however, of very diverse size and status.[10] It passed a number of resolutions in support of the new regime's policies and goals, notably in the economic field, and set up a regional executive (*oblispolkom*). The latter regarded itself as entitled to give orders to all soviets within its sphere of operations, but in fact lack of personnel and funds prevented it from exercising much power. In practice each soviet tried to extend its influence as widely as it could.

In the Central Industrial region the transfer of power was effected fairly smoothly. The economic life of the area was naturally oriented towards Moscow, and the population was accustomed to look to that city for leadership. In its scattered towns and factory settlements the labour force was socially homogeneous and had a tradition of militancy. The Bolsheviks had made considerable headway among many groups of workers, including women employed in the textile industry. This swing to the extreme left was reflected in the results of the Constituent Assembly elections.[11] In the principal industrial centres the Bolsheviks controlled not only the soviet but the municipal duma as well. This was something of an embarrassment to a party that was so antagonistic to 'bourgeois' institutions. There was a risk that its 'class content' might become adulterated and that party members who assumed office in local government bodies might become unpopular, either because they were associated with the Provisional Government's policies or because their performance suggested that a Bolshevik administration would not bring much benefit to ordinary folk (for instance over food supply). Fortunately for the Bolsheviks, before this problem became acute it was rendered academic by the October revolution, which led to the liquidation of the municipal institutions concerned.

At Ivanovo-Voznesensk in August the Bolsheviks secured four-fifths of the seats in the municipal duma and its executive board. The latter 'became master of the town' and took over the work which had previously been done by the soviet, which was temporarily reduced to insignificance.[12] The news of the successful takeover in Petrograd was announced simultaneously to meetings of the duma and the soviet. The latter reacted by breaking into a tumult : shouts and curses mingled with the singing of the *Internationale* in 'a mighty incoherent roar'.[13] Subsequently it established an initiative group ('staff') of five members, which two days later, perhaps under the impact of the fighting in Moscow, was expanded into a seven-man body 'in order to give it more authority in the eyes of the population'. This contained two representatives of the soviet executive committee and one each of the Bolshevik and SR Maximalist parties, the municipal board, the railwaymen and the garrison.[14] Characteristically the Bolsheviks, uncertain as to the loyalties of this body, formed within it a presidium consisting wholly of members of their own party. On 4 November the 'defensist' elements were expelled on the grounds that their presence was no longer fitting, and one month later the 'staff' itself was disbanded as superfluous, its functions passing to the Bolshevik-controlled executive and duma board. Ivanovo now saw itself as the capital of a new *guberniya*, and the soviet executive broadened its powers accordingly.[15]

At the textile centre of Kineshma effective power lay with the soviet executive from 21 October, when the workers came out on strike. On hearing of events in the capital the executive called a plenary meeting of the soviet, which approved the establishment of an MRC. For once the moderates refrained from walking out of the assembly; however, they would not join the MRC either, but formed an organ of their own which claimed executive power. Faced with this situation the local Bolsheviks sought a compromise, which led to the establishment of a 'people's council' comprising representatives of the three soviets (which had not yet merged), local self-government organs and three trade unions. On this body maximalists and moderates were fairly evenly balanced. The arrangement was unpopular with many rank-and-file maximalists, especially soldiers, and sooner or later their leaders adopted a more resolute line.[16]

In some less heavily industrialized towns, such as Yaroslavl, there were anarchic outbreaks by drunken mobs which delayed the transfer of power for several days. Soldiers appear to have been mainly responsible; their misconduct added force to the Bolsheviks' campaign for a merger of the two soviets, which on 27 October met in a joint session attended also by 'representatives' of lower-echelon organizations (a typical example of the 'swamping' technique). The gathering voted in favour of establishing 'soviet power' and elected a provisional executive. This body then challenged the legitimacy of the two existing independent soviet executives[17] and the Committee of Public Safety called into being by the moderate leaders. The latter did not play their cards skilfully. They walked out of the hall when the motion was passed, yet a few days later permitted a duma representative to serve on the MRC. This gave the latter body an aura of legitimacy it by no means deserved and undercut the authority of the duma. Clearly the democratic politicians had not yet learned the rules of the game. The MRC proceeded to close down newspapers, punish striking municipal workers, and to arrest as 'counter-revolutionaries' local worthies with an unexceptionable anti-tsarist record. These measures led to protests at a soviet plenum held on 20 November, which apparently went unheeded: it is at this point that our primary sources fall silent. A recent Soviet study does not mention any soviet plenum held before 22 March 1918, when one was called to ratify the Brest-Litovsk peace.[18] Other meetings were probably held in the intervening period, but we do not know whether the discussions had much effect upon the policy of the executive organs. That the Bolsheviks faced a certain amount of passive opposition in Yaroslavl province is clear from the fact that no province-wide executive committee was formed until the end of February, whereas in Vladimir province such a body had existed since before the insurrection.[19] By and large, however, their problems were easily mastered, at least in the urban areas of the Central Industrial region.

In the Urals, too, the maximalists' message fell upon fertile soil. Industrial workers were even more prominent in the social make-up of the population than they were in the centre. Unemployment was probably less of a scourge, since many metallurgical factories were still fulfilling defence contracts, but in some of them production had been interrupted. Labour unrest focused upon the low level of wages, a long-standing problem which had its roots in the region's remoteness and technological backwardness rather than in the ill will of the employers; nevertheless the almost patriarchal character of industrial relations in the Urals, where cultural facilities lagged far behind those available in more developed regions, spurred demands for radical change.

Factory committees and militia bands overshadowed soviets, which were predominantly small enterprise-based organizations. Not surprisingly, recent investigators have arrived at differing estimates of their number and political allegiance. According to one authority, the Bolsheviks had a majority in 88 soviets out of a total of 145;[20] according to another, this was true of 'more than 100' out of some 160–70 for which data have been preserved.[21] Among the more important centres which stood out for a time against the drift towards extremism were Orenburg, Zlatoust, Perm and Nizhniy Tagil. On 13 October the Bolsheviks called a regional congress of soviets which was attended by a hundred and twenty representatives from fifty-six organizations; of these men eighty-six were classified as Bolsheviks, twenty-six as SRs, and six as non-aligned.[22] Its deputies to the second All-Russian congress of soviets brought with them a resolution in favour of coalition government, which they probably interpreted in the limited sense given to this term by the 'soft'

Bolsheviks.[23] The Urals soviet congress elected a regional executive committee,[24] but the extent of its authority in this period remains uncertain; it seems that most activists who belonged to it were preoccupied with securing their own local base.

This was certainly true of Yekaterinburg (now Sverdlovsk), the principal industrial and communications centre in the region. The Bolsheviks had captured the soviet late in July, and in October fresh elections were held which consolidated their hold. However, the differences between them and the other socialist parties were far less in evidence than they were in the central regions of the country. The local moderates, if that is the term for them, favoured 'soviet power', and this naturally encouraged conciliatory tendencies among the Bolsheviks.[25] On hearing of the insurrection in Petrograd, the executive committee declared itself the sole legitimate authority in the town and had this decision endorsed by the soviet (26 October).[26] However, tension soon developed once it became known that in the country as a whole the Bolsheviks' assumption of power was contested. On 28 October the SRs demanded the establishment of a coalition regime in Yekaterinburg similar to that being formed (as they thought) in Petrograd. The local Bolsheviks agreed to set up a 'committee of people's power' representing various local interests. This body, in which the Bolsheviks were in a minority of six to ten, ruled the town from 31 October until 22 November.[27] On that day the local Bolsheviks were addressed by a senior party official, F.I. Goloshchekin, and induced to take a tougher line. The existing chairman of the soviet (L. Sosnovsky) was replaced by P.M. Bykov, whose brief but informative memoir we have had occasion to quote. As he puts it frankly: 'the urban soviet was proclaimed the sole power in the town. [But] the new conditions facing the soviet executive called for a new organization and [so] out of it there was formed a bureau of five comrades who in practice did all the work.' Bykov mentions only one subsequent meeting of the soviet's plenum, on 13 December, when it approved the Bolshevik line on the impending Constituent Assembly. Local Right SR politicians who canvassed on behalf of the assembly were arrested and on 17 January tried by a drumhead tribunal, which branded them as traitors to the revolution. Stern measures were also taken against local employers, who were subjected to a 'contribution' of ten million roubles (of which only a fifth was collected). This militancy was unmatched by constructive measures of government, and the economic life of the region soon came to a virtual standstill. While the unemployed went off to fight ataman Dutov's cossacks with the partisans (see above, p. 286), 'the soviet devoted all its work to defending the conquests of October' :[28] it became in effect an instrument for military mobilization.

Yekaterinburg was situated for administrative purposes in the province of Perm. In the *guberniya* capital a curious situation prevailed : the Bolsheviks controlled the town duma, the Mensheviks the soviet. The latter came out in favour of a coalition government, whereupon the men of two large factories in the neighbourhood, with support from the pro-Bolshevik regional soviet executive, organized an RC to overthrow it. However, we are told, this 'soon turned against soviet power, transformed itself into a Committee of Public Safety, and then collapsed' – that is its members lost heart and became reconciled to the moderates, whose position on essentials was so close to their own. Such conduct was displeasing to the 'hard' Bolsheviks, who eventually succeeded in swamping the Perm urban soviet with their adherents from the nearby industrial settlements; by 15 December they were able to convoke a provincial congress of soviets at which their party had a comfortable majority.[29] In some isolated places, like the mining centre of Nizhniy Tagil, the Bolsheviks did not impose their power until the New Year, and then only by calling upon external assistance.[30] At Zlatoust, an even more important mining town and communications centre some two hundred miles to the south, the moderates held out until 18 March, when they were overcome by soldiers and militiamen with support from Chelyabinsk (the main town in the central Urals, which since October had been ruled by a Bolshevik-led coalition).[31]

Throughout the Urals the contending left-wing groups faced a common foe in the shape of cossack forces based on Orenburg. This was especially the case in Ufa, situated within striking range of the enemy, where the local leaders cooperated fairly well until their militancy brought them into conflict with the local peasantry as well as with Dutov's cossacks (and the Bashkirs).[32] So long as revolutionary measures were directed against 'bourgeois' groups, the latent differences between the Bolsheviks and the Left SRs could be held in check; but they were bound to develop as soon as the Bolsheviks extended their power into the villages and began to act in an arbitrary way against ordinary peasants. This problem loomed in the background wherever the towns were closely linked to the needs of the rural population, for here the dictatorship rested upon a weaker base and was tempted to use more drastic coercive methods.

TWENTY-SEVEN *The Urban Soviets: the Volga Cities, the Central Agricultural Region and the Ukraine*

BETWEEN THE TWO Bolshevik strongholds we have just examined, the Central Industrial region and the Urals, lay the river Volga, a major artery of commerce and communications. Along its banks were a number of important cities which had a distinctive social physiognomy. The labour force was more diversified; there was a substantial middle class with its own cultural and political traditions; and the population was swollen by an influx of workers employed in new war industries and of refugees from the war zone.[1] This influx intensified the pressure on scarce resources of food and accommodation and created, together with the garrison troops, a reservoir of frustration and disaffection. In these cities established citizens were ranged against rough subordinates who disposed of superior physical force. The former looked for guidance primarily to the organs of municipal self-government, the latter to the soviet and the soldiers' committees. On both sides one could detect a certain desire for local autonomy, a dissatisfaction with the ready-made formulas devised by party leaders in the metropolitan centres. More pragmatic in their thinking, the Volga politicians favoured conciliation rather than conflict. 'Great October' here took the form of a brief confrontation in which the antagonists exchanged more verbal salvoes than gunfire.

This was the case in Nizhniy Novgorod. The soviet represented workers in two suburban settlements, Kanavin and Sormovo, as well as in the city proper. Despite this it had only forty-eight Bolshevik deputies to fifty-five Mensheviks and sixty SRS; on the executive the seats were distributed proportionately. The local Bolsheviks reacted by reversing their usual tactic : they favoured separation of the soviets rather than a merger.[2] Already on 23 October the provincial commissar appointed by the Provisional Government set up a strong Committee of Public Safety.[3] Three days later the soviet adopted by a large majority (105 votes to 62, with 9 abstentions) a resolution condemning the Petrograd uprising. Faced with this strong opposition, the Bolsheviks had to form an initiative group on their own responsibility : the RC was appointed directly by the party's provincial committee.[4] Formed during the night of 27/8 October, it soon won for itself a strong position *vis-à-vis* the Committee of Public Safety. The two bodies entrenched themselves in different buildings and engaged in a war of nerves, while 'the man-in-the-street just scratched his head and did nothing.'[5] Emissaries went back and forth between the two camps bearing resolutions and appeals until 1 November, when a *coup de main* by the RC deprived the moderates of the support of the military cadets on whom they relied for their defence, whereupon their resistance collapsed. It is characteristic of the half-hearted attitude of the antagonists that when the soviet met on the following day it voted almost unanimously in favour of a socialist coalition regime and speedy convocation of the Constituent Assembly; on local issues the insurgents' resolution on 'soviet power' passed by a narrower margin.[6] The moderate leaders refused to join the soviet executive, which on 21 November went on to claim full control over the province and called in troops from Moscow to help it enforce its will. One memorialist remarks ironically : 'this military operation was brought off peacefully, without a shot being fired. Mandelshtam [a former general who had joined the Bolsheviks] turned out to be a greater conqueror than Julius Caesar.'[7]

In Saratov the confrontation was rather more violent. Although the soviet here was under Bolshevik control, that party's local cadres were divided over the merits of taking power. One of them even agreed to join his fellow officers on a mixed committee to preserve public order, for which he was reproved by his comrades.[8] Perhaps fearing a hostile vote in the soviet plenum, the Bolshevik caucus decided to hold an extraordinary session packed with representatives from the base organizations, over which they had more control. The moderates' resolution was defeated, whereupon they left the hall amidst emotional scenes, and the two sides prepared to do battle. The insurgents established their headquarters in the former governor's house, while their opponents fortified the municipal offices. The public was apathetic, and only a few hundred would-be combatants were enlisted on either side. The spirit of the affray is perhaps best rendered by the story that, when the insurgents eventually approached the barricades round the duma, they could nibble them away, since they were constructed in part of sacks of fruit. Despite these comic-opera aspects there was twenty-four hours' shooting which caused a number of casualties.[9] The new soviet executive, which is said to have been identical with the Bolshevik party's city committee, continued to proceed cautiously and refrained from dissolving the municipal duma until 25 November.[10] Early in December the Saratov soviet converted itself into a province-wide body by including in its membership persons who claimed to represent the peasantry.[11] The plenum seems to have displayed little activity, and had evidently been superseded by its executive bodies.

In other Volga towns the tale was more or less similar : hesitations among the Bolshevik leaders; formation by the 'hard' elements of an 'initiative group' with backing from lower-echelon bodies; and endorsement of its actions by the soviet. As a rule the RC or MRC was first broadened, to appeal to the vacillating elements, and then narrowed as these sympathizers were progressively eliminated. Finally it extended its power to the entire province.[12] Rather than follow these events in detail we may consider an instance where the Bolsheviks' victory owed more to military action than to political manipulation. In Kazan, which had a garrison 35,000 strong and important defence installations, the Bolsheviks' regional military committee was a more important organization than either the urban or the provincial soviet, which that party also controlled. On 19 October the army authorities tried to arrest a certain Lieutenant Drozdov, a Bolshevik on the run from prison who was popular with the men. This incident, coupled with the threat of dispatch to the front, led to protests and armed clashes. An MRC was set up in the headquarters of the 164th infantry regiment, and on 24 October an officer of this unit, Captain Mosalsky, aided by an artillery colonel and some young Bolshevik ensigns, took over the town without meeting any resistance. Only after this action had been completed did the soviet assemble to sanction it. A civilian authority was set up, which rather grandly called itself 'the Soviet government of the Kazan Republic', but real power continued to lie with the regional executive committee, resting upon the troops.[13]

Military intervention was also important in a number of smaller towns situated in the Central Agricultural region, comprising the relatively fertile provinces north of the Ukraine – an area of acute agrarian unrest. The peasants looked for leadership to the SRs, and the same attitude prevailed among the urban population, whose existence was closely bound up with the rural milieu. The only town where Bolsheviks controlled the local soviet was Belgorod, while in Orel they had 'an exact half-share';[14] both these places lay to the west, within the zone subject to military administration. Sometimes, however, the Bolsheviks were able to exert a disproportionate influence upon a soviet through their hold on its leading organs. Thus in Voronezh they had only 24 deputies out of some 120–140, and only 4 executive members out of 45, but on the presidium they occupied two posts out of six, including those of deputy chairman and secretary. This success was due partly to the zeal and ambition of the local cadres and partly to the benevolence shown towards them by their Left SR allies.[15]

The Voronezh soviet was under moderate control, and on 27 October it voted by fifty-one votes to forty-five to set up a Committee of Public Safety.[16] The extremists would have nothing to do with a mixed body such as this, yet were loath to overthrow it. From their indecision they were rescued by the soldiers, who feared that they were about to be disarmed by their officers. Leadership was provided by an energetic individual named Moyseyev (presumably a Left SR). At the cost of a few casualties the insurgents captured the main points in the town, including the regimental headquarters (30 October). As in Kazan, it was only after this military *coup* that the civilian RC showed any sign of life. It called a meeting of the soviet for 3 November, which endorsed the *fait accompli* and replaced its former executive by a bureau on which the Bolsheviks seem to have been more numerous, if not more active, than their Left SR partners.[17]

North-east of Voronezh lay the province of Tambov. In its sleepy capital there are said to have been no more than three Bolsheviks, who appeared there 'just before the October insurrection'; the local soviet was controlled by the SRs, but most delegates had no party affiliation.[18] Such strength as the Bolsheviks possessed was concentrated in nearby places that had undergone industrial development. Eleven miles from Tambov lay a defence establishment known mysteriously as 'Factory number 43'. It employed eight thousand men. Having won a following among them, the local Bolshevik cadres set about recruiting support in the town. It was not until 30 January 1918 that the soviet, run by a coalition of radical groups, formally 'recognized' the transfer of power in Petrograd, and even so the old local self-government organs were permitted to continue in being. This 'conciliationism' ended in March, when the Bolsheviks and Left SRs split and set up rival provincial executive organs. The former soon won supremacy, but remained a proletarian outpost amidst a sea of resentful or apathetic peasants.[19]

In Kursk, likewise, power lay at first with a Committee of Public Safety representing all the local institutions and parties, Bolsheviks not excluded.[20] By the end of November the soviet had dissolved this committee and established a provincial executive of its own, in which Left SRs were the most numerous group, but this body does not seem to have been very active. According to one early Bolshevik writer, 'the revolt in the capitals found no response here until February 1918, and even after that an anarchist-SR group long continued to make mischief.'[21] The strength of the SRs is evident from the composition of the provincial executive, which had as many rural as urban representatives.[22]

The general picture is one of the Bolsheviks and their allies relying on the garrisons and segments of the civilian labour force sympathetic to their cause, building up their strength until they could overawe the soviets and the mixed committees they set up. If the sources tell us next to nothing about soviet plenums, this is no doubt because, to an even greater extent than in larger centres, their character was primarily symbolic. From the standpoint of the insurgents they were unreliable instruments, likely at any moment to surrender to the 'petty-bourgeois vacillations' characteristic of the peasantry and those who spoke in their name.

If in the Central Agrarian region the Bolsheviks' task was made difficult by the relative weakness of the industrial working class, further to the south they faced another complicating factor : the Ukrainian national movement. This was strongest in Kiev and the middle Dnieper area. It was weaker to the east and south-east, in Kharkov and the Donets valley, which had a different ethnic composition, and also to the west and south-west, for a rather different reason : the overriding importance of the military factor. In these areas the chief element in the situation was the decomposition of the army, which cannot be examined here.[23]

Ukrainian nationalism had a strong social revolutionary content. Until November 1917 its protagonists did not see themselves as enemies of or rivals to the Bolsheviks. The main political divisions in the Ukraine reflected those in the rest of the country. Both the SRS and the Social Democrats had a common objective : an international federation of socialist nations, in which the Ukraine should enjoy full rights of self-determination. The Bolsheviks won much sympathy because they seemed to be the most consistent advocates of this idea. The universalist aspect of their ideology was less apparent at this time. However, shortly after the October insurrection in Petrograd it became clear that the CPC (and in particular Stalin, who held the post of PC for Nationality Affairs) interpreted the right of self-determination in a narrowly restrictive fashion. The interests of the international socialist revolution, he argued, had to be given priority. Behind this intransigence lay a very real fear for the security of the Soviet regime, which seemed to be gravely imperilled by the existence in Kiev of a government (the Central Rada) claiming authority over the whole Ukraine. Despite its socialist coloration and gestures of friendship towards Petrograd, the Soviet authorities could not take its 'separatism' lightly. They needed the grain and other supplies which the Ukraine could provide, and feared (or pretended to fear) collaboration between the Rada and the overtly 'counter-revolutionary' Volunteer Army and cossack forces that were mobilizing further to the east. It was not difficult to find pretexts for aggressive action. The Bolshevik commissars underestimated the strength of Ukrainian autonomist sentiment, and felt confident that swift military action would bring immediate results.[24]

We are concerned here less with the general course of Russo-Ukrainian relations than with the role of the urban soviets in the struggle for power, and shall therefore concentrate on the major centres, moving across the Ukraine from west to east. The city of Odessa lived in the shadow of the front. In times of peace a major entrepôt for Russia's foreign trade, its commerce had atrophied with the closing of the Straits; many businesses had shut down and unemployment was a serious problem. During 1917 a multiplicity of political groups had emerged, reflecting the ethnic diversity of the population. A large number of them were represented on a regional revolutionary committee, set up on 28 October, in which the tone was given by a military body, the rear section of *Rumcherod* (an acronym for 'executive committee of the soviets of workers' and soldiers' deputies of the Rumanian front, Black Sea fleet and Odessa military district'; its 'front section' was at headquarters, located near Jassy in Rumania). It was characteristic of the situation in Odessa that General Marks, commander of Odessa military district, should have served on this committee along with representatives of various armed forces organizations, the four soviets in the city, and the political parties. It saw its task as the preservation of order until such time as a socialist coalition government could be established.[25]

However, its authority was soon weakened by internal schism. On 15 November radical elements in the soldiers' and sailors' soviets made an unsuccessful bid for power. Their failure temporarily enhanced the prestige of the Ukrainian nationalists, whose claims were regarded by the Russian politicians with varying degrees of distaste. To the more extreme (Russian) soviet leaders the Ukrainians were highly suspect, and on 1 December – after the former had attempted a second unsuccessful rising – fighting broke out between the para-military forces which each had brought into being. These street clashes gave neither side a decisive advantage, but served to rally all the Russian elements behind the extremists. On 10 December the Bolsheviks and Left SRs had the support of the overwhelming majority of the delegates attending the second congress of the various organizations from which Rumcherod formally derived its power. This was an overwhelmingly military affair: over 850 of the approximately 1,100 delegates present were described as 'from the front'.[26] A resolution was passed by 509 votes to 320, with 38 abstentions, endorsing the Petrograd authorities' line towards the forthcoming Constituent Assembly, and a new executive was elected. Simultaneously the city's four soviets were induced to merge their presidiums (although not to abandon their separate identity). After a three-day battle (15–17 January) the left-wing forces led by the reformed Rumcherod won control of the city. Anarchy prevailed until early in March when Odessa was occupied by troops of the Central Powers.[27]

The fate of Odessa was shared, in rather less extreme form, by other cities on the right (western) bank of the Dnieper. In Nikolayev it was not until 4 January that the Bolsheviks became the largest faction in the local soviet. The official proclamation of 'soviet power' came ten days later, timed to coincide with the takeover in Odessa.[28] Both here and in Yekaterinoslav authority lay at first with a coalition of all left-wing forces. In the latter city the transfer of power was effected earlier, on 29 December, but at higher cost: there were three days of fighting between Russian and Ukrainian armed bands. After the fighting was over the soviet was induced to endorse the result by the use of the 'swamping' technique. A Bolshevik writer later admitted : 'Since meetings of the soviet were almost always held with the participation of factory committees, the Bolsheviks almost always secured a majority.'[29]

The nationalist challenge was for obvious reasons greatest in Kiev. The Central Rada's strength lay in the countryside rather than the towns. It had an inner core, the so-called Small (Mala) Rada. This twenty-seven-man council was dominated by Ukrainians (especially Ukrainian SRs) but included some representatives from the Russian and Jewish elements in the population. The Russian members were moderate socialists. The local Bolsheviks were divided in their attitude. The right-wingers, led by Yury L. Pyatakov, were willing to participate in the Small Rada, for they regarded the Ukrainian nationalists as potential allies. This point of view was contested by the left-wingers led by Yevgeniya B. Bosh, who viewed them as dangerous rivals. A fierce struggle broke out between the two groups.[30] There were two soviets in Kiev. In the one claiming to represent the workers the Mensheviks were the largest party, although the Bolsheviks ran them a close second, while the soldiers' soviet inclined towards Ukrainians; the joint executive committee seems to have been evenly balanced.

When news of the Petrograd insurrection was received, the workers' soviet passed a resolution of support but was soon forced on the defensive. The Small Rada set up an RC, which three leading Bolsheviks joined, as they did the Small Rada itself (25 October). The motive for this step was to insure themselves against an expected attack from the right. However, on the following day a dispute broke out over the interpretation to be given to this compact. When the Small Rada issued a statement condemning the Petrograd rising, the Bolsheviks walked out[31] and decided to act on their own. Their followers had already taken over the arsenal, but had been obliged to yield to Ukrainian troops. On 27 October the two soviets met in an 'expanded' plenary session and voted by 489 votes to 187, with 17 abstentions, in favour of 'soviet power' and set up a rival RC. Fighting broke out between the insurgents and cossacks loyal to the Provisional Government, which lasted for four days. The Ukrainians at first remained neutral but then intervened to bring about a compromise. The combatants exchanged prisoners; the loyalist forces withdrew or were demobilized; and authority within the city passed to the Rada, which thus emerged as *tertius gaudens*.[32]

The Russian socialists, faced with the problem of defining their attitude towards the new regional authority, were at first inclined to accept the Rada's pretensions. But was Ukraine's self-determination to be decided by the All-Russian Constituent Assembly or by some deliberative organ of soviets? For the Bolsheviks and left-wing SRs (whether Russian or Ukrainian) only the latter solution commended itself. Pyatakov and his friends hoped that the Rada would take the initiative in calling such a congress, at which they could hope to secure a majority. But the Rada, alarmed at the growth of extremist sentiments, now leaned toward the moderates. It took a number of measures which led to friction both with Petrograd and also with the local Bolsheviks, especially the hard-liners among them, who were inclined to put the worst construction on its motives. Once it became apparent that a congress of Ukrainian soviets would be unwelcome to the Rada, the Kievan Bolsheviks set about calling one themselves. This could not but strain the atmosphere still further, since the Rada was bound to view such a congress as a direct challenge to its own authority.

By 12 November the Bolsheviks, among whom the left-wingers were gaining ground, had pushed through a merger of the two soviets in the city. On its joint executive they had 23 places out of 58. This was an improvement on the 15 seats they had held previously in the two independent executives, but was not enough to give them a firm hold upon the new organization. At its first meeting on 15 November it rejected a Bolshevik draft resolution on the problem of state power and elected a presidium consisting of SRs and Mensheviks : two of the seven seats were offered to the Bolsheviks, but they preferred to go into opposition. For once the usual roles were reversed; but unlike their rivals, the Bolsheviks used their leisure to mobilize their supporters in the base organizations. Their determination soon brought dividends. On 16 November they called a meeting of the workers' section of the soviet, in which they disposed of a majority, and persuaded it to secede; a few days later they founded a joint soviet in the central district (*rayon*) of the city; they launched a propaganda campaign against the joint city soviet executive; and on 30 November they called a plenary assembly which carried their original resolution by 302 votes to 250 (some seven hundred persons being present, including peasants and factory committee representatives). It deposed the joint executive and elected a new one presented by the Bolshevik leader Ya.B. Gamarnik.[33]

By this time plans for an insurrection were nearing completion. The Rada forestalled the threat by disarming and expelling a number of pro-Bolshevik Russian troops (29–30 November). In response the soviet and other labour organizations declared a general strike. Meanwhile in Petrograd the news provoked the CPC into dispatching a strongly worded ultimatum to the Rada, threatening war unless its grievances were satisfied within forty-eight hours.[34]

Against this ominous background the Kievan Bolsheviks and their allies convened their All-Ukrainian congress of soviets (4 December). The Rada authorities rose to the challenge by inviting as many popular organizations as possible to send delegates. A large number of these were rustics representing agricultural cooperatives, peasants' committees and such like. The Bolsheviks, hoping to repeat their earlier manoeuvre, had prescribed norms of representation which would give the urban soviets a majority.[35] But it soon became apparent that their delegates would be lost amidst a throng of some two thousand persons, most of whom could be expected to favour the Rada.

Unable to prevent them from participating, the Kievan Bolsheviks hoped to attain their ends – the proclamation of Soviet rule in the Ukraine – by means of skilful direction of the congress, but the Bolshevik self-appointed directing committee had barely taken its seat and opened the meeting when a group of Ukrainian SR leaders, surrounded by an armed retinue, entered the assembly hall and ejected the Bolshevik chairman bodily from the podium.

The direction of the congress thus passed into the hands of Rada supporters.[36]

To nationalist cries of 'out with the Muscovites' the Bolsheviks left the meeting and decided to carry on the fight from Kharkov, 'the Ukraine's proletarian centre, where the workers had plenty of arms and could offer resistance to the Central Rada'.[37] In effect they now placed their hopes upon external aid.

At first it was still not clear whether the CPC's ultimatum would be followed by an actual offensive, if only because there were as yet few 'Red' troops willing to take part in such a campaign: to volunteer for action against Whites or the cossacks was one thing, to fight Ukrainian socialists quite another. It took the Red chiefs in Kharkov a month before they had a small force at their disposal.[38] During this period talks still went on between the CPC and the Rada both in Petrograd and in Kiev. In the latter city the Bolsheviks were very much on the defensive. Not until 15 January 1918 did they feel strong enough to issue a call to arms 'in aid of our brethren who are fighting'.[39] This step was taken despite orders to the contrary from the Kharkov Bolsheviks,[40] and was evidently a way of manifesting their independence. The Kievans wanted the Ukrainian capital to be 'liberated' by indigenous forces rather than by armed action from without. Although they welcomed the advance of the Red bands from Kharkov, they appreciated that to ordinary Ukrainians this offensive would appear as a foreign invasion. In effect this was a continuation of the old conflict between 'hard' and 'soft' Kievan Bolsheviks, which had now acquired a different focus. The former were less concerned about Ukrainian popular attitudes and readier to identify themselves with the Petrograd leadership.

The rising, staged before the advancing Red troops could bring relief, was ill prepared. Street fighting lasted for ten days (16–26 January) before the insurgents could claim a victory. There were several thousand casualties and considerable damage to property. Each side accused the other of committing atrocities. The battered city was then 'sovietized'. On 28 January the soviet plenum approved a Bolshevik proposal for an executive of sixty members, two-thirds of them drawn from their own party. This then elected a presidium of seven Bolsheviks and two Left SRs (one of whom belonged to the Ukrainian branch of that party); judging by their names, most of the Bolsheviks were Russians.[41] A general purge of non-soviet organizations was inaugurated; but this operation was still incomplete when the Central Powers' forces entered the city (3 March). Bolshevik rule had lasted but three weeks.

The transfer of power in Kiev seems to have been fraught with more bloodshed and turmoil than in any other city at this time. It was a grim augury of the struggles to come in many national minority regions during the civil war. There was much less violence in Kharkov, economic capital of the eastern Ukraine. This city had absorbed a much larger number of emigrants from the Great Russian provinces and Ukrainian national sentiment was correspondingly weaker. The joint workers' and soldiers' soviet had as its chairman a prominent Bolshevik activist, F. Sergeyev ('Artem'), but the SRS, Mensheviks and Ukrainian SDS each had a significant following;[42] in the elections to the Constituent Assembly the Bolsheviks won about 28 per cent of the total poll. In these circumstances their leaders felt it politic to court the other Russian parties, who shared their fears that Kharkov might be caught in a vice between Ukrainian forces and General Kaledin's cossacks.

On 21 November supplementary elections to the soviet produced an executive in which nineteen Bolshevik representatives faced an equal number of non-Bolsheviks (eleven Mensheviks, four SRS and four Ukrainians).[43] Disappointed at this result, the Bolsheviks turned to more forceful tactics. Having won over many of the Ukrainian armed bands in the city and obtained reinforcements from the Black Sea fleet, they occupied strategic points in the city (8 December).[44]

In this way a suitable climate was created for the establishment in Kharkov of a rival government to that of the Rada – a weighty matter which now took precedence over local concerns. Sergeyev had been present at the abortive congress of soviets in Kiev, and it was he who had proposed that the radical delegates should quit the city for his own. When they arrived there they found in session a congress of soviets from places in the eastern and central Ukraine. On 9 December its 77 delegates, who represented only 46 of the 140 soviets in that region, agreed to join the 124 men (from 49 soviets) who had come from Kiev in forming the first congress of workers' and soldiers' soviets of the Ukraine.[45] Formally inaugurated two days later, it adopted a declaration condemning the Rada and proclaimed the Ukraine a Soviet republic; a central executive committee (CECU) was established which would extend to Ukrainian territory all legislative acts issued by the CPC in Petrograd. In this way an aura of legitimacy was provided for the military operations against the Rada which had just begun.

The individual soviets in the territory controlled by pro-Bolshevik forces were now expected to recognize the new government as 'the supreme organ of soviet power on the territory of the Ukrainian republic', that is to submit to its dictates. Such a statement was duly made by leaders of the Kharkov soviet on 23 December.[46] The ten-day delay was evidently due to Sergeyev's misgivings at the turn which events were taking. He and his colleagues had assumed that Kharkov would become the capital of the new Soviet Ukraine.[47] This division between easterners and westerners reflected radically different appreciations of the Ukraine's socio-political make-up.

The most pressing reason for the easterners' reservations was the presence on their flank of hostile cossack forces. On 25 October General Kaledin announced that his army (voysko) government was assuming full power and sent troops to occupy many mining settlements in the Donets valley. After a few days they were obliged to withdraw, but in the latter half of November they took Rostov-on-Don.[48] In the face of these ominous events the various left-wing groups in the eastern Ukraine had to cooperate or perish.

The external threat played a role comparable to that of the Rada in the west. In the Donets, as in Kharkov, local coalitions came to power in which the leading role fell almost automatically to the Bolsheviks.[49] As one moved outwards from the metropolitan centres towards the periphery of European Russia, class and national hatreds became inextricably intertwined. In the Ukraine they were less acute than in the Caucasus and Central Asia[50] but they were nevertheless pregnant with significance for the future. The Ukrainian autonomists were socialists who had much in common with their Russian comrades; yet even they ultimately fell victim to the Bolshevik drive for total hegemony.

Provincial Russia generally went the way of Petrograd and Moscow. The stereotyped explanation of the Bolsheviks' success is that their ideas had an irresistible appeal. Like all grand simplifications, this has an element of truth: without popular support in the lower-echelon bodies, and particularly among the troops, the Bolsheviks could not have won control of so many soviets in such a short time. Yet the picture is incomplete and colourless unless one also takes account of the organizational devices they employed. For on the Russian left the Bolsheviks alone – or to be more precise, those cadres identified with the 'hard' Leninist position – possessed the will and experience necessary to turn vague and transient mass attitudes into firm political commitments; only they had a coherent theory of organization and the machinery to carry it into effect; only they were prepared to act ruthlessly and systematically in imposing their own conceptions upon the whole of the soviet movement; only they were willing to use coercion on a massive scale to suppress minority opinions, regardless of the democratic principles to which all left-wing groups paid lip service. The transfer of power, via the soviets, to the leading organs of the Bolshevik party was on the whole not a violent process, but one that owed much to the use of political arts as old as history.

V Neutralizing the Peasantry

October 1917—1918

TWENTY-EIGHT *Lenin's Land Decree*

THE TRANSFER OF power was above all an urban phenomenon. Only gradually did the new regime gain a foothold in the rural areas, and many years would elapse before it could feel secure against the threat of a 'counter-revolution' fuelled by the proprietorial instincts which, as Marxists assumed, came so naturally to the countryman. To the Bolsheviks, with their explicitly proletarian creed, the peasant was not only a necessary ally in the struggle for socialism but also a potential source of danger. To the peasants, with their traditional suspicion of outside authority, the leather-jacketed urban emissaries who symbolized the new power (the *tovarishchi*, as they sometimes called them, half in jest and half in fear) were a source of puzzlement. As the village was drawn against its will deeper into the maelstrom of civil war, misunderstandings increased on either side and the tension sometimes flared up into open violence. The 'black repartition', or general redistribution of property, that was carried out all over rural Russia during the winter and spring of 1917–18 brought its beneficiaries land but not liberty. The results were something of a disappointment to hundreds of thousands of ordinary country folk. Many peasant activists soon found themselves defending their conquests against encroachments by agents of 'soviet power'. A new menace had appeared, more awesome than the old.

In country districts, as in the smaller provincial towns, the news that Kerensky's regime had been overthrown and replaced by one of Bolshevik commissars engendered as much perplexity as satisfaction. Whatever faults could be laid at the door of the Provisional Government, it had at least arranged to call a Constituent Assembly from which the people expected to receive lasting benefits. What would be the attitude of its successor, which spoke in the name of the (primarily urban) soviets? What divided the Bolsheviks from other socialists? Who was Lenin and what did he propose to do about the land?

On the last point at least enlightenment was soon forthcoming. During the night of 26/7 October the second All-Russian congress of soviets endorsed the celebrated 'land decree', which at first glance seemed to give the peasants everything they could hope for. As a propagandist device the land decree could hardly be bettered; indeed, most historians would consider it the greatest single monument to Lenin's political skill. By a stroke of the pen the new regime won for itself the maximum possible credit among the land-hungry villagers, who were given grounds for belief that the 'proletarian dictatorship' had their fundamental interests at heart: had it not conceded at once what its democratic predecessor had long denied?

The significance of the land decree was so immense that we must explore briefly its immediate background, although such an exercise necessarily takes us into the arid world of ideological disputation. Only by doing so can we appreciate its shock effect – not only upon the peasants but upon most Bolsheviks as well – and also the ambiguous, contradictory situation it created.

Lenin had always fiercely combated as 'utopian' and 'petty bourgeois' the Populist notion that socialism could come about through an egalitarian redistribution of the land.[1] A week after his return to Russia in April 1917 he still scorned 'the petty-bourgeois political phrase-mongering which prevails among the SRs, especially their idle chatter about a "consumption" or "labour" norm, "socialization of the land", etc.'; he contrasted their romantic, idealistic approach with the scientific, materialist approach of the Bolsheviks, who held that small-scale farming was incompatible with market production – that is with the needs of a modern economy.[2] But at the same time he urged the Bolsheviks to support actively the incipient 'agrarian movement' among the peasantry. Was it not generally agreed that the peasants' purpose was precisely to establish a communal agrarian order in place of the confiscated estates, and would not the Bolsheviks thereby be bolstering reactionary tendencies in Russian economic life? Lenin's answer to this objection was to emphasize the importance of the class differences which he discerned among the peasants. The proprietorial tendencies, which in his view infected the more 'bourgeois' strata, were to be offset by mobilizing the 'proletarian' elements under the guidance of their urban counterparts. In organizational terms, alongside the peasant soviets, which could be expected to appeal to all segments of the rural population and to follow the SR line, the Bolsheviks were to encourage the formation of special soviets for landless labourers (*batraki*); the latter should take over the landlords' estates once they had been confiscated and manage them in the general interest, for 'it is particularly important to *increase* the production of foodstuffs for the soldiers at the front and for the towns – and to refuse absolutely to permit any loss of or damage to stock, tools, machinery, buildings etc.'[3]

The SR theorists might have countered that this scheme was just as utopian as anything of which they were accused : could these impoverished, ignorant and unruly men really be expected to run large estates effectively and produce a surplus? Would they not prove to be a destructive, anarchic force? But practical arguments of this kind, convincing as they seem, miss the mark. For Lenin's agrarian strategy was much more than a pragmatic policy proposal : it was an abstract theoretical construct, a compromise between doctrine and expediency. His scheme was designed to give the *maximum* amount of encouragement to peasant violence while doing the *minimum* amount of damage to the working class and its party. He knew that a 'black repartition' would exact a heavy economic and social cost but reckoned that this was part of the price that had to be paid for the socialist revolution. In the spring of 1917 it seemed clear that an offensive strategy in the countryside would pay handsome dividends.

On 28 April Bolshevik agrarian policy came up for discussion at the party's seventh conference. Some of Lenin's senior colleagues objected to what they regarded as 'adventurism' on his part. The critics did not, however, make their position plain or do anything concrete to frustrate their leader's policies. On this as on nearly every other matter under discussion Lenin had his way.[4] The upshot was that in 1917 the Bolsheviks went into battle with an agrarian programme that concealed their readiness in practice to make far-reaching concessions to elemental peasant revolutionism. Thus on paper they were pledged to support only those peasant committees that displayed collectivist tendencies by pooling confiscated property; again, land seizures were ostensibly recommended only in so far as they were 'organized' and did not involve damage or production losses. These qualifications could not but be disregarded in practice. This ambiguous document gave activists *carte blanche* to commit every kind of excess, while deluding the party leaders (Lenin included) as to the ease with which the agrarian movement could be directed into ideologically acceptable channels. What mattered in the programme was its 'spirit' – its relatively simple and straightforward message to practical workers in the field.

Lenin himself set an example by his fiery speech to the assembled peasant delegates on 22 May (see above p. 235). There is no evidence that during the summer or autumn he felt it necessary to apply the brake, or that he had any misgivings about the harmful economic effects of the agrarian disturbances. On the contrary, he viewed the unrest as a justified popular reaction against the Provisional Government's 'counter-revolutionary' tendencies.

It was almost casually that he commented, on 29 August, on the recently published digest of the 242 mandates (*nakazy*) submitted by delegates to the All-Russian peasant congress in May (see above p. 235). These demands, he argued, were unacceptable to the present regime, chained as it was to capital; 'only the revolutionary proletariat, only its unifying vanguard the Bolshevik party, can *in practice* carry out the programme of the poor peasants set forth in the 242 mandates'.[5] He gave no explicit undertaking to make this Populist-inspired document the first act in the agrarian policy of a Bolshevik government; but he probably already envisaged such a step, for he went on to strike a new note : 'The peasants want to keep their small farms, to establish egalitarian norms, and then level off their holdings periodically. Let them do so. On these grounds no sensible socialist will part company with the peasant poor.'[6]

Isolated in his Finnish retreat, and preoccupied with more immediate problems, Lenin does not seem to have initiated senior party colleagues into his plans. In any case they were willing to bow to their leader's authority in a sphere on which he was an acknowledged expert. The land decree, more than any other single legislative act, was Lenin's personal handiwork.[7] It had five articles.[8] The first stated that 'the squires' landed property (*pomeshchich'ya sobstvennost' na zemlyu*) is abolished immediately without any compensation.' The second placed the squires' estates, along with apanage and church land, together with their stock and equipment, at the disposition of the district land committees and county peasant soviets until the Constituent Assembly met. The third declared it 'a serious offence, punishable by a revolutionary court' to damage any confiscated property, since it now belonged to the whole people. The county peasant soviets were instructed to take 'all necessary steps to maintain the strictest order' when carrying out confiscations; they were to keep accounts of what was taken over and to guard it closely. Clause 4 provided that these authorities should be guided, pending final decision on the matter by the Constituent Assembly, by the digest of the peasant *cahiers*, the text of which was appended, followed by the fifth clause of the decree, which almost as an after-thought added that 'the lands of ordinary peasants and cossacks are not to be confiscated'.

Three points in particular need to be noted here. First, the decree did not make it clear who now owned the land. Logically, one would have expected in article 1 a second clause to the effect that the confiscated property now belonged to the 'workers' and peasants' state'. This omission was certainly deliberate. Although Lenin had maintained all along that the peasantry were sympathetic to national-ization of the land, this was less a certainty than a pious hope. In fact the peasants were wedded to the PSR concept of *social* ownership (*vsenarodnoye dostoyaniye*, as it was called in article 1 of the accompanying digest), which vested ultimate property rights in the *local* community, not the central State. According to this view only non-agricultural natural resources (minerals, forests, water) and ex-privately owned livestock and equipment (but *not* land) might be entrusted *either* to the State *or* to the local community, according to their size and significance (articles 2 and 5 of the digest). To be sure, the latter document was not free from ambiguities either, since the Populist intellectuals who had drawn it up were themselves in two minds about the future role of the State. But there was a considerable difference on this matter between them and the Bol-sheviks, who were committed to a strong 'proletarian dictatorship' and for whom socialism was inseparable from a fully planned and centrally directed economy. It was precisely this difference which

Lenin was at pains to obscure, and it was for this reason that the terms 'nationalization' or 'state ownership' were avoided in the decree.

Second, the decree contained only the merest hint of the Bolsheviks' commitment towards the unleashing of class war in the villages. Who were the 'ordinary' peasants and cossacks whose property, according to article 5, was exempt from confiscation? It did not take much imagination to see that this formulation could be stretched in such a way as to expose virtually any villager, even one who held only allotment land, to the risk of having it confiscated along with that of the 'squires' mentioned in article 1. The position of those numerous landed proprietors who were also 'toilers' was ambiguous, to say the least.

Third, the new government extended to the Populist document only a temporary and conditional validity, which would expire once the Constituent Assembly had pronounced final judgement. This was unexceptionable – provided that the Bolsheviks were indeed willing to allow the Assembly to meet and pronounce freely upon the ultimate disposition of the land, but as we know this was not the case. Lenin sought to convey a contrary impression:

> Even if the peasants follow the Socialist-Revolutionaries and even if they give this party a majority in the Constituent Assembly, then we shall say : let it be so. Life is the best teacher and it will show who is right. Let the question be settled by the peasants from one end and by us from the other. Life will compel us to approach one another in the common flood of revolutionary creativity, in the elaboration of new forms of state. We should follow life, we should allow the popular masses absolute creative freedom.[9]

Small wonder that Lenin's address was greeted with loud applause. Alas, there were limits to his tolerance of popular spontaneity. When he spoke of the peasants learning from experience that the Bolshevik solution to the agrarian problem was superior to that offered by the SRs, he did not exclude his party's right to influence their decision by every means at its disposal, including the might of the proletarian State. Nor did he envisage them taking a long time to make up their minds; on the contrary, he anticipated a speedy decision in the Bolsheviks' favour, induced as much by organizational coercion as by propaganda. This was evident – to look no further afield – from a revealing (but little regarded) phrase which he dropped at the time. The provisions of the digest, Lenin stated, were to be implemented 'as far as possible immediately, but in [regard to] certain of its parts with such necessary gradualness as the county peasant soviets shall determine'. In other words, these local authorities were to use their discretion. Where the PSR document conflicted too obviously with Bolshevik policy – for example, in its insistence on allocating land according to consumption norms, to ensure maximum equality – they should drag their feet. It was assumed that such soviets would soon come under the control of Bolshevik activists who would take their cue from the centre and squeeze out the local SRs.

It is only when one examines these subtleties that one can fully appreciate Lenin's political skill. The land decree was more than just clever tactics, a means of embarrassing the PSR by appearing to endorse a programme which had been devised under its aegis but which that party's leaders had hesitated to enact. It was also a strategic move, designed to neutralize the peasant masses at the critical moment when Russia's fate was being decided in the towns. It encouraged them, if not actually to support the new government, at least not to oppose it, since it seemed to be willing to let the peasants decide the agrarian problem for themselves. Ordinary folk would disregard the qualifications with which Lenin was careful to hedge his party's support for Populist goals.

In October 1917 the Bolsheviks had scarcely any means of directly influencing the situation in the countryside. But they could make a virtue out of necessity by extending their sanction to the peasants' acts of confiscation and redistribution of property, and claiming the credit for an agrarian revolution that was proceeding under its own momentum. They discredited their chief rivals, the PSR, aggravated the schism within that party's ranks and won the active collaboration of its maximalist elements, the Left SRs, during that crucial period when the fate of the dictatorship hung in the balance. Largely thanks to their aid, the Bolsheviks were soon able to establish a rudimentary new structure of authority in the countryside, based mainly on the rural soviets and district committees, but dominated by cadres from the towns. Once this had been done the way was clear for a new phase in the party's agrarian policy, one in which it could afford to break with the Left SRs and pass over to the offensive. The peasant could then be obliged to pay more heed to directives from above, to experiment with collective forms of agricultural production, and to furnish supplies to the urban masses at nominal (or even non-existent) prices. In this way the countryside would be reduced to a proper state of subordination to the towns, the bastions of proletarian dictatorship. For it was axiomatic that in the alliance between the industrial working class and the poorer segments of the peasantry the latter were to be very much the junior partner.[10]

In the short term Lenin's strategy may be accounted a brilliant success, but its long-term consequences were incalculable. For to some extent he was the victim of his own propaganda, or perhaps one should say of the ideological limitations of his thought. It is clear in retrospect that the Bolshevik leaders greatly overestimated the speed with which the Russian village could be brought to accept their ideas of socialism in general and collective farming in particular (even in its relatively non-coercive form). They also misjudged the impact which a deepening of the agrarian revolution would have upon agricultural production, and hence upon the supply of foodstuffs to the towns. The socio-economic cost of rural anarchy was bound to be immense. It was to prove to be more difficult than Lenin evidently expected (if his published writings are a true guide to his thoughts on the matter) to preserve 'cultured' estates from destruction or depredation; much more difficult to reorganize them on cooperative lines; and virtually impossible to manage them in such a way that they would both yield a large marketable surplus and provide the mass of villagers with a viable alternative to the traditional family farm.

Behind this miscalculation lay another error, of even greater magnitude. The entire Marxist perception of Russian peasant society was gravely distorted. There was little substance to the notion that the village was rent by acute class tensions which could be exploited to the advantage of the urban proletariat. All too often what urban zealots mistook for evidence of class struggle was inter-group conflict of a totally different kind (see below, pp. 409–12). The very success of the peasants' campaign to eliminate landowning by 'non-toilers' and to redistribute this property on egalitarian lines tended to level out such extremes of wealth and poverty as formerly existed within the village – although, as we shall see presently, the 'black repartition' did lead to friction for another reason, which may be summed up by the French expression 'l'appetit vient en mangeant'. The great social levelling operation which the peasants carried through at this time, coupled with the impact of civil war, also had the consequence of strengthening the traditional rural unit of organization, the commune, at the expense of that expressly revolutionary unit, the soviet.

For all these reasons the party soon found itself employing more coercion than had originally been anticipated in bringing the peasantry to heel. Town and country, which for a few months appeared to be marching in step, soon drifted even further apart than they had been in 1917. The conflict between them was to leave an enduring imprint upon Soviet social history.

TWENTY-NINE *'Black Repartition': The Village Triumphant*

T HE GREAT REDISTRIBUTION of property, dreamed of for centuries and accomplished in the main during the winter and spring of 1917–18, was carried out by the peasants themselves with only a minimum of guidance by the central authorities. Where the local people were slow to act they would be egged on by urban emissaries, but their role was only an auxiliary one. 'Instructors' and other agents of local soviets could put their expertise at the village community's disposal in settling technical matters, but it was the members of this community themselves who took the major decisions: what to do with the proprietors' estates and how to ensure that the share-out should be fair to all claimants.

In the most turbulent provinces the first effect of the October overturn was to give a fillip to the wave of looting and destruction that had begun there earlier in the autumn. A laconic news item in the Petrograd *Izvestiya*, reported from Buguruslan county (Samara province) in December, reads as follows: 'The peasants have not understood the land decree. They have begun to loot the livestock and equipment on the estates in this county. The soviet has sent armed detachments to restore order. The inventorying of estates is proceeding.'[1] Such violent acts were clearly contrary to the general interest, as well as to official Bolshevik policy, but it was often as hard for the new soviet authorities as it had been for those they replaced to suppress them. The military or para-military forces at their disposal were few in number and their morale was uncertain. The local leaders could not be sure that any action they took to restrain peasant mobs would be looked on with favour by their superiors. Morally, the central government was at least indirectly responsible for these excesses, since by usurping power it had encouraged everyone to do likewise; any deed of violence could be justified in terms of 'revolutionary spontaneity'. The Soviet historian Pershin notes that such acts of destruction were most frequent in the black-soil provinces, where the new regime's writ ran lightly, and that they ceased once the estates had been inventoried.[2] There is something to this argument, but it is not a self-sufficient explanation; it is a mere cliché to attribute pogroms to 'kulak greed' or to say that the Bolsheviks 'waged a systematic struggle against sacking and looting'.[3] From time to time soviet agencies did try to recover stolen property, ostensibly for redistribution to the poorest elements in the village, but in the prevailing anarchy these efforts could hardly produce the desired results. Some weeks after publication of the land decree the chairman of the soviet at Ostrogozhsk (Voronezh province) wrote to the government asking what should be done with valuables seized from ransacked estates. Lenin personally wired back : 'Compile exact list of valuables. Keep them in a safe place. You will answer for their survival. Estates are property of people. Institute proceedings for theft. Report to us court verdicts.'[4] No such reports, however, appear to have been submitted to him, and the revolutionary tribunals (where they existed) were not likely to take duties of this kind very seriously.

The number of estates destroyed at this time, and their ratio to the overall total, cannot be established with certainty. Early historians, working largely from newspaper material, probably painted the picture unduly dark. Recent Soviet studies enable one to take a more balanced view, although one has to allow for the current tendency to present the 'black repartition' as a smooth and orderly process. E.A. Lutsky has examined files now in the Ryazan *oblast'* archive, which contain responses to a questionnaire sent round to district land committees in 1918. Not all districts returned a reply, but those that did contained about half the estates in the province (766 out of 1,679). These documents show a total of 43 sackings in

October, 56 in November, 4 in December and 2 in January. There is a correlation between these figures and those for inventories carried out by the same authorities : 24 in October, 122 in November, 178 in December, 148 in January, 43 in February, and 62 between March and May (158 were undated).[5] As the landowners were formally dispossessed the local peasants had less reason – and less opportunity – to launch assaults upon their estates. In Tver province, in the non-black-soil zone, where data are available for 166 out of 261 districts, there were 33 sackings, whereas 810 estates were inventoried in May 1918.[6] That there should have been less violence here is only to be expected. In some places in this province peasants formed groups of volunteers to protect estates from destruction.[7]

It should not be imagined (as Soviet historians imply) that the process of inventorying an estate was necessarily non-violent. Not until 13 December did the PG of Agriculture issue instructions for the local authorities to follow, by which time a large number of properties had already been taken over in an 'irregular' manner. (Some provincial bodies issued regulations of their own.) These instructions were in any case 'not always observed in full'[8] and left ample scope for abuse. For example, an inventory was supposed to cover only property related to the running of the farm, but in practice this rule was interpreted broadly. On the estate of the brothers Shmelev at Melikhov (Kasimov county, Ryazan province) the inventory contained no less than 469 items, including mousetraps and cleaning brushes.[9] In the process, despite all the formalities, a good many domestic items changed hands as well, sometimes 'officially' and sometimes by stealth. In Tver province a proprietor named B.D. Veydeman complained to the local soviet's land department in April 1918 that the inventory-takers had deprived him of 'domestic furnishings, clothing, shoes, children's things and vegetables prepared for [his] own consumption'; the authorities duly forbade such practices, but it is not known whether the goods were restored.[10] It would have been strange if the peasant activists carrying out such operations had resisted the lure of easy gain at their moment of triumph. The law was vague – perhaps deliberately so. On 25 April the PG of Agriculture ruled that domestic effects could be taken only from those who had more than one residence – but then contradictorily permitted local organs to requisition 'just the surpluses', which they were left to determine themselves.[11] This was little more than an invitation to robbery.

The struggle was by no means a simple confrontation between victorious peasants on one hand and vanquished squires on the other. Quite frequently the county land committee – especially if it were still under moderate socialist control – would mediate between the two parties, and proprietors or farm managers would look to this body for protection against the villagers. In such cases the taking of an inventory seemed a preferable alternative to assault and destruction. They could even hope that, should the Bolshevik regime yield place to a legal order, such inventories might serve as a basis on which to claim compensation for losses suffered.[12] Where the county land committee had fallen into maximalist hands, landowners might turn to the *district* (peasant) committee for assistance against the local commune; for this committee had to concern itself with the interests of other villages in the district, whose leaders might also have some claim on the property concerned, and until these differences were settled one could hope to maintain the *status quo*. Interestingly enough, on this point emissaries from the new government saw matters in much the same way as the landowners : the district authorities were more likely to be convinced that the estate should be preserved in the interests of the national economy, whereas pressure for partition and redistribution was strongest at the lowest level, that of the village community.

The contest for the land thus often took the form of a three-cornered struggle between the local peasants, the landowner and the State. Each antagonist had something in common with the other. Peasants and landowners shared a distrust of the new rulers who sought to dictate to the village from above; landowners and state authorities shared a desire to keep the estates intact; and the plebeian elements in town and country shared a visceral hatred of social privilege. It was by no means a foregone conclusion that the last of these three alliances would prove to be the strongest.

We have seen above (p. 206) that landowners were sometimes left a portion of their land, tools and stock; they might also be allowed to go on living in their homes. Ya. Sadovsky, who owned a hundred dessyatines in Kursk province, was permitted to retain as much land as he could work without employing hired labour. One peasant told him : 'the comrades are all shouting about levelling, but here let's wait and see who'll come out best.'[13] Later the villagers helped him when he was late sowing his crop of millet.[14] It seems that some account was taken of the personal characteristics and situation of the individuals concerned : a measure of tolerance might be extended to families without breadwinners and others for whom expulsion would bring immediate distress. The activists had to reckon with the villagers' natural prudence and sense of fair play; for that matter even some of those most hostile to the squires as a social abstraction might temper their zeal when it came to using coercion against individuals long known to the local community. One formerly well-to-do observer of peasant life and attitudes in Tambov province was told by the villagers of Uvarov (Borisoglebsk county) : 'let our squire come to us and we shall share with him, give him land according to the number of eaters [in his household], as much as we have ourselves.'[15] Rudnev, living in Simbirsk, writes that 'I did not come across any special enmity or malice on the part of the resident villagers . . . ; they did not of course love their [former] masters but had a good-neighbourly and kindly attitude'; even two Kronstadt sailors, who returned in December laden with looted jewellery, soon adapted to the normal pattern of village life.[16]

Although some peasant committees fixed relatively generous norms for those willing to continue working the land, the rule was that estates of any size were confiscated, and generally it was not long before the proprietors' situation deteriorated. Instructions issued in June 1918 laid down that 'in order to consolidate the conquests of the working people, the soviet land departments should immediately expel from their estates . . . all former proprietors, their agents (*doverennye*) and non-toiling tenants.'[17] This blanket order was ambiguously worded and could not be enforced strictly : what, for example, was to be done with persons living as guests of their former tenants, or in farm buildings on their former estate? Later in 1918 the PC of Agriculture instructed the local authorities to allow them to stay on provided they were not 'counter-revolutionary' and did not employ hired labour; in each case a report was to be submitted.[18] Certificates of political reliability were made out by village authorities in favour of former members of the privileged classes.[19] However, as the civil war got into its stride such laxity became less and less frequent. Especially in or near the combat areas local activists, called upon to exercise constant vigilance, looked upon such persons with fear and hatred. A number was taken as hostages and put to death by the Cheka, once this organization had spread its tentacles into the countryside, or by some other para-military body armed with special powers; of those who survived the terror tens of thousands fell victim to starvation and disease; an unknown number somehow managed to live on in the countryside until the era of the New Economic Policy (NEP). Few of these, however, were able to record their experiences for posterity.[20] In Vyshniy Volochek county (Tver province), which had 348 private properties within its borders in 1917 (but not necessarily that many landowners), there were still 16 ex-owners resident in 1925 – when further action was taken against them.[21]

A similarly varied fate awaited the homes of these former proprietors. We have already discussed those that fell victim to the fury of the mob : what of the remainder? It is hard to reconstruct, from the dry records compiled by unsympathetic inventory-takers, what 'liquidation' of an estate entailed in practice. At Ramzaysk in Penza province the property of L.E. Protasova was disposed of as follows by the local land department : the residence was shared between the local soviet and a school; the distillery was ascribed to the local soviet's 'economic department'; the mill went to one commune and the orchard to another; the smaller farm buildings and furniture were sold at auction, realizing 5,591 roubles and 67 kopecks.[22] At Vazerki, in the same province, the commune resisted demands by a neighbouring village that the estate of Prince Shakhovskoy be partitioned, because this would frustrate their plans to use the manor as a school, the office as a hospital, and other buildings nearer the village as a cultural centre.[23] According to statistics compiled by the PC of Education in 1919, covering 210 counties, 1,490 cultural centres had been established, many of them in confiscated property, and in twenty provinces for which figures were available the total number of schools (most but not all in rural areas) rose by 3,011.[24] These data give a very misleading impression. The school system was in such chaos at this time, as a result of ill-conceived administrative reforms, shortage of teachers and equipment, and the general impoverishment of the population, that the new buildings put at its disposal could not be utilized to good effect.[25] More usual was the conversion of surviving residences to house the rapidly expanding rural administration (a role which might be combined with that of a 'model farm'). The majority, however, seem to have fallen into decay. Symbols of a vanished era, they no longer had any role to fulfil in the new society.

What the peasants really cared about, of course, was not the buildings on an estate but the livestock, equipment and the land itself – in that order, since for practical reasons the redistribution began with what could be alienated with least trouble. We may follow this order here.

A correspondent to a PSR newspaper, writing from Spassk county (Kazan province) in mid-November 1917, observed with rather naive astonishment that 'the peasants don't bother about the land – it's as if they don't need it at all – and concentrate all their interest on seizing someone else's cow, goat, pig or hens.'[26] A.V. Shabanov, a peasant from Saratov province, describes how 'the cattle, a flock of 500 sheep and [a number of] horses ... were herded into the village [to form] a common fund. We decided to divide the sheep equally among all the households but to auction the horses and cattle and to divide up the money likewise.' Those who refused to accept a share of the loot were forced to do so; the animals were to be slaughtered at once so that it would be harder to detect the culprits.[27] This was the normal course of events in the more turbulent provinces. Sometimes the communal authorities sold the confiscated livestock at nominal prices. In Kursk province horses were disbursed for a mere twenty to thirty roubles each, and in Kladovsk district for 5 roubles – whereas the market price at this time was over a thousand roubles. The practice of auctioneering confiscated livestock was regarded with some disfavour by egalitarian zealots on the grounds that it would benefit only the richer peasants. In one village near Moscow a peasant bid successfully for a fine mare, which he later sold for ten times the price he had paid; this was considered improper by his fellow-villagers, who obliged the offender to hand over the whole sum to the community.[28] Those who received an animal from the common pool were customarily forbidden to sell it.[29]

The Bolsheviks were unable to exercise much influence upon the redistribution process, not only because they had as yet only a modest organizational base in the countryside, but because their policy was contradictory. On one hand they held that larger shares of confiscated property should be given to the poorest elements in the village community, whom they regarded as their natural allies; on the other hand they were committed to the principle of keeping livestock herds intact, at least wherever these had some special agronomic merit (for instance pedigree cattle, breeding-stock). In practice expediency usually prevailed over principle. In 1919 the authorities in Tambov could locate only 4,000 head of cattle fit for breeding whereas in 1916 the private proprietors in that province had owned a total of 56,400 beasts. In twenty-seven provinces for which statistics are available for early 1919 the state-owned livestock-breeding farms had 4,000 horses, 16,000 cattle, 19,000 sheep and 1,500 pigs; these were trivial figures when set against the total privately owned livestock herd.[30]

The situation was broadly similar in regard to agricultural implements and other equipment – except in so far as large mechanical items were of less use to peasant smallholders, who were therefore more willing to engage in some cooperative method of utilizing them. Such machines were in any case relatively scarce, and many of them were idle through lack of fuel. During 1918 the PC of Agriculture, alert to the possibilities of mechanizing agriculture, and also perhaps to the leverage which this would give the State over the peasantry, tried to keep an eye on the places where this equipment was stored, to give instruction in its use, to develop repair facilities and so forth, but it does not appear that these *ad hoc* measures made much impact. In some areas efforts were made to take back material that had previously been confiscated and distributed among the peasants. This was done as early as March 1918 in Shadrinsk county (Perm province), where the future Soviet leader A.A. Zhdanov made his political début.[31]

As the snows melted, work began on partitioning the confiscated land, which until that time had remained formally under the control of some local authority (usually the district land committee). The first to be dealt with was arable that was under winter crops or due to be sown in the spring; then it was the turn of the pasture and meadow (as well as garden plots (*usad'by*), where these were involved); finally, in the summer months, the peasants proceeded to partition the fallow land and that earmarked for autumn sowing.[32] Forest land was generally excluded. The operation was very much a local one, decisions usually being taken at the village or district level, less frequently at that of the county; the provincial authorities summoned congresses and issued instructions, but the impact of all their labours was slight. Even critical observers were struck by the relative speed and skill with which peasant communities carried out this vast operation. One eye-witness later noted :

> I have no doubt that its painlessness was due not just to the fact that those who lost by it were in the minority, but also to the general and irreversible belief that it was right and proper to repartition the land. ... Left to their own devices, the peasants carried out [the repartition] within a few days, quite peaceably and fairly equitably, and then at once proceeded to plough and sow [their new plots].[33]

One reason for this was that the redistribution was generally regarded as a temporary measure, valid only for the current agricultural year. Thus many who were dissatisfied with their allocations put up with them for the time being in the hope that they would do better when the day of final reckoning came. They did not anticipate that, instead of a second and more perfect 'black repartition', there would be only local revisions, carried out in civil-war conditions and with loyalty to the regime as the chief criterion.

In the first phase of the redistribution, with which we are concerned here, social rather than political considerations were uppermost in the minds of those responsible. They faced three principal problems. First, should they include *all* land within their jurisdiction, including allotment (*nadel*) land held by ordinary members of the commune, or should the operation be restricted to land confiscated from private proprietors? Second, how large a territory was to be covered, and what was to be done about areas claimed by neighbouring communities or districts? Third, when making the allocation should one take account of differences in the beneficiaries' socioeconomic situation or simply go by the number of consumers ('eaters')? On all these points there were divisions of opinion, usually but not invariably based on economic self-interest; on occasion these might assume a political or ideological form, and it was as such that these controversies were perceived by political activists (and by most historians since). Broadly speaking, the egalitarians carried the day on the first and third of these three issues, but suffered a defeat on the second. Again we may examine them in turn.

Pressure to pool all the property in the village, including allotment land, was strongest in the black-soil provinces. In Zadonsk county (Voronezh province), a pace-setter in this regard as in the seizure of private property (see above, p. 192), no less than 84·3 per cent of the settlements redistributed all their land during 1918.

Occasionally one or two districts within a county would resist the levelling trend. In Karachev county (Orel province) general or 'black' repartitions were carried out in Khotynets and Shablynsk districts, whereas in Staroselsk and Dranov districts only the confiscated land was redistributed. Similarly, individual villages might follow the latter course within a district where their neighbours had opted for the former.[34] The reasons for such differences of conduct are not evident from the sources. The usual inference is that a reluctance to carry out a general repartition shows the strength of so-called 'kulak' elements. Unfortunately there is no way of telling how often this explanation fits the facts : the villagers kept no records, and the officials who attemped to keep track of their affairs were more interested in results than in motives.

The redistributions carried out in the non-black-soil provinces during the spring of 1918 appear to have been less egalitarian in the sense that peasant allotments were less frequently included – although it is difficult to be certain. Pershin suggests that this was due to politically motivated resistance by authorities under moderate socialist control, but it seems more likely that it can be explained by differences of a socio-economic nature. In this region tilling the soil had for decades accounted for only a fraction of peasant revenue; there were few large private estates (except in the north-west); agrarian relations, as we know, were less strained; and finally there was a vigorous democratic cooperative tradition. In some places the peasants adhered to the customary rule whereby the votes of two-thirds of the householders in a commune were required to effect a repartition; and they will have adopted the same procedure to determine its scope. In Totma county (Vologda province), where such a two-thirds majority rule obtained, it was decided that privately purchased land should be included only if there were insufficient land to satisfy everyone's needs. This was a reasonable solution in an area where there was plenty of land available and peasant poverty had other causes.

It is important not to lose sight of regional peculiarities and traditional peasant psychology. Egalitarian sentiment did not necessarily imply class conflict. The peasants' attitude was rooted in notions of moral and social justice : times were hard, and the interests of the community ought to prevail over those of individual members. The levelling tendency owed relatively little to the influence of ideas extrinsic to the rural milieu, or to orders from higher authority.

The truth of this proposition becomes clearer if we turn to our second question and examine the administrative level at which the decision was carried out. It is generally agreed that the provincial bodies (whether they were executive, for instance land departments, or deliberative, such as congresses of soviets) played relatively little part in implementing the land reform. It is harder to define the role of the county authorities. The archival material relating to this period (over two thousand documents covering thirty-seven provinces) used by Pershin, originates overwhelmingly from county organs or those at a higher level.[35] This may give a misleading impression of their importance *vis-à-vis* those at the district or village level, which in any case have left less documentary evidence of their activities. One may agree with Pershin that 'in redistributing land within a province, the county in most cases acts as an independent unit within its territorial boundaries',[36] adding the rider that this is even truer of the district. (The matter could be settled if the relevant materials concerning a single province were to be published in full.) Early Soviet writers were freer to discuss this matter. Knipovich, writing in 1920, recognized as self-evident that more redistributions were carried out by the peasants themselves at village or district level than under the control of superior administrative bodies.[37]

This point is of considerable importance since, the more successful the county authorities were in imposing their will, the greater the area included in the operation and the more egalitarian it was likely to be. Squires' estates and privately owned peasant lands tended to be grouped in certain areas of each county; consequently, these districts gained more than those that were less favoured if the redistribution were carried out at their *own* level. It was up to the county authorities to even out these differences wherever they were strong enough to do so. By and large, it was those in the black-soil zone that were most active in this regard : in particular certain counties in Ryazan, Orel, Kursk, Tambov, Penza, Simbirsk and Samara provinces.[38] In Zadonsk county (Voronezh province), where one would expect the county authorities to surpass all others in imposing their own county-wide programme, the record was uneven. To be sure, a county norm was worked out : one dessyatine and 131 cubic sazhens per 'eater'; some earnest rural mathematician then calculated that to achieve this blissful state of equality an area of precisely 16,936·7 dessyatines would have to be taken from twelve districts with a surplus and given to six that had a deficiency. Alas, 'in the course of a single season it was impossible to carry out land resettlement work on such a scale', and in the event only two districts were allocated some land at the expense of their neighbours. Elsewhere peasants were offered strips situated as much as thirty to forty versts (several days' journey) away from their homes, which they not surprisingly declined to accept. Only in 1919–20, after the defeat of the White armies, was a general redistribution carried through, the results of which are examined below.[39]

If this was the case in Zadonsk, one can appreciate the difficulties encountered in areas less given to egalitarian zeal. Only two counties, Shatsk (Tambov province) and Ranenburg (Ryazan province), carried out anything approximating a county-wide redistribution, and even these were incomplete.[40] Thus it was the districts which generally emerged triumphant from the fray : each district en· deavoured to secure for itself as much land as it could and to resist claims by its neighbours. This led to considerable inequities even within one and the same county (to say nothing of the same province), as we shall see in a moment.

The third problem, the mode of allocating confiscated property, was less difficult to resolve than the first two. According to one early Soviet statistical investigation, covering 1,103 villages, no less than 88 per cent distributed the land equally among all consumers; of the remainder three-quarters took as the criterion the number of adult workers.[41] If these figures are trustworthy, this was certainly an overwhelming victory for egalitarian principles. The alternative mode of distribution was popular in certain places in non-black-soil provinces (Novgorod, Kostroma, Yaroslavl, Smolensk) and also in parts of the south-east (Samara, Ufa),[42] where land was relatively plentiful. Once again it would appear that natural socio-economic differences were a more important reason for this than 'kulak pressure', the standard explanation advanced.

Where the so-called 'consumption norm' was applied, what happened in practice was simply this : the total amount of land (of various categories) available for distribution was divided by the number of 'eaters' or 'living souls' (an ancient term which expressed vividly the connection in the peasant mind between subsistence and possession of the land); each household (family) was then allotted its due share.

But what was understood by the term household? Should one treat each family as a unit, ignoring its size and composition, or should one take account of the sex and age of its members? The former method, more egalitarian than the latter, was adopted in parts of three non-black-soil provinces (Pskov, Novgorod, Kostroma).[43] In the rest of the country the peasants followed the Populist-inspired principles set out in the land socialization law of 19 February 1918 (see below, pp. 444–7), whereby the share of each household was fixed according to the number and category of dependants : adult women could claim 80 per cent, boys and girls aged sixteeen to eighteen respectively 75 and 60 per cent, and children aged twelve to sixteen 50 per cent as much as adult males.[44] These proportions were varied somewhat to suit local conditions.[45]

From this one may deduce that, although the *muzhik* might be a leveller in regard to the land, he was far from being one in regard to his family. The reasoning behind this age and sex discrimination was that women and children did less physical toil on the farm (which might not be true), and that accordingly households with a higher proportion of women and children were entitled to a smaller relative share of the land. Thus contrary to general assumptions then and since the 'consumption norm' differed in degree, rather than in principle, from the 'labour norm' : the former took account of division of labour within the family; the latter took account of it within society. With doubtful logic the communally minded Russian peasants (and their intellectual mentors) persisted in the belief that the former was in accordance with natural justice, but that the latter involved 'exploitation' and was morally and socially reprehensible.

The distributing authorities were also invited to draw up a list of priorities in meeting the needs of persons whose rights to a share might be in some doubt : men absent in the armed forces, refugees from other parts of the country, industrial workers who had returned to their native village, seasonal labourers and so on. Actual practice in this respect varied widely.[46] The determining factors seem to have been the strength of the claimant's connection with the community and the plentifulness of land available. Some villages and districts were as generous towards 'outsiders' as they were to 'non-toilers'; others took a narrow and egotistical stand, regarding them with fear and suspicion. One suspects that the second attitude became more prevalent as the year 1918 wore on, for the influx of such persons posed a threat to the community's well-being, and the growing pressures of civil war and economic scarcity made villagers increasingly look inwards, to the protection of their own immediate interests.

The black repartition itself had the same effect. The peasants' age-old land hunger had been appeased, at least for the time being : a digestive pause was now in order. But, to continue the metaphor, how nourishing was their fare?

THIRTY *'Black Repartition':*
Results and Prospects

I T IS NOT easy to arrive at a balanced judgement on the benefits conferred and the costs incurred as a result of the 'black repartition' of 1917–18, carried out as this was in the main by the peasants themselves – or more exactly, by the most subordinate units in the new structure of rural authority. In principle one may distinguish between the direct effects upon the village population and the indirect effects upon the economy as a whole, although this is admittedly a rather abstract and illusory distinction, and both sets of changes powerfully influenced the situation of the countryman *vis-à-vis* the new state power.

One problem is to assess how far the tensions which developed – tensions which grew still more acute during the years of increasing hardship soon to follow – may legitimately be regarded in terms of class conflict. This was of course how they were perceived by the country's new rulers and by tens of thousands of activists, not only Bolsheviks but Left SRS as well. Moreover, their view of the situation and their responses to it affected the way in which the peasants themselves thought and acted. But one should not lose sight of the elementary point that the pronounced egalitarianism inherent in Russia's agrarian revolution was bound to touch off a spate of petty jealousies among those who felt they had gained less than their fellows. Alas, equality does not necessarily make for harmony and contentment, especially if it is accompanied by violence.

That inequalities also occurred, in regard to allocations of livestock and land, stands to reason. We have noted above (p. 215) that those who had horses and carts with which to take away movables from a ransacked estate were likely to do better for themselves than those who lacked any such means of transport. It would, however, be misleading to suggest that this factor made any great contribution to social differentiation within the village. Rather more to the point, householders who were allocated a farm animal by the village authorities might find themselves unable to make use of it, for example because they lacked the necessary shelter or feeding-stuffs. This was one powerful reason why (if they did not slaughter their animal for food) they might consider selling it to one of their fellows – an action which, as we know, was considered unethical. So strong was the general feeling on such matters that operations of this kind can scarcely have led to any significant accumulation of wealth by the more prosperous elements in the village. Moreover, such tendencies were energetically combated by the urban activists.

Similarly, in regard to land there were cases where poorer beneficiaries, lacking seed corn, tools or draught animals, preferred to cede their allocations to others, perhaps in return for a share of the harvest or some other services. Such transactions were quite normal in pre-revolutionary times and might well be considered by both partners as a mutually advantageous bargain. However, in the present social climate they were likely to arouse criticism, and they were certain to be frowned upon by higher authority. Again one may doubt whether any great increase in social differentiation resulted.

Thus it may be said that much of the alleged inequality arising from the redistribution of confiscated property lay in the eye of the beholder. Moreover, many disparities of wealth which, seen from the outside, appeared to have a class basis were in fact differences of another kind, either 'inter-family' or 'inter-community', which we may examine in turn.

It will be recalled that when making an allocation the communal authorities took account of the composition of the recipient's household. A statistical study of the distribution of land and livestock in 1917 and in 1920 (to be discussed presently) reveals a correlation between the amount of land sown (one index of wealth) and family size. Those households sowing a minimal area (less than 0·1 dessyatines) or none at all had an average of 3·7 persons; those sowing up to two dessyatines had an average of 4·6 persons; the figures then rose proportionately until one arrives at those in the largest category of landholders (more than twenty-five dessyatines sown), which had an average of 10·2 persons.[1] Admittedly the correlation is not exact : larger households tended to have more land per member. One may also suppose (although no evidence of this has come to hand) that members of large families, whose superior economic potential naturally brought them political influence within the community, may have abused their power and prestige to ensure that their own norms were met, to the detriment of the claims of smaller and weaker families. At least, they may have been able to secure for themselves stock that was of better quality or land that was more fertile, better watered, more conveniently situated in relation to the village and so on. Yet this element of 'built-in corruption', as one might term it, would be less at this time, when the egalitarian spirit was at its height, than in any other period of Russia's rural history. Much more typical will have been instances where the traditional 'best families' in the community had to yield to new contenders from among the smaller and poorer households.

It is precisely the dual nature of the family farm, as at once a social and an economic unit, that generates confusion about the nature of intra-peasant conflict. Prosperity was a function of demographic accidents as well as of business proficiency. Tension between the well-to-do and the less well-to-do overlapped with tension between larger and smaller households. Often these might be divided by the ancient family feuds found in any self-sufficient rural milieu. At this moment, when all traditional institutions were being overturned and new ideas were percolating rapidly into the village, it was tempting for members of families that had hitherto been at a disadvantage to take their revenge for real or imagined slights suffered at the hands of the more fortunate. Thus a situation which, looked at from the outside, might appear to be a simple struggle of classes, was actually a much more complex social phenomenon.

At this point it must be noted that the revolution itself had the effect of decreasing average family size, particularly in the case of very large 'extended' families with eleven members or more (which by 1919 had fallen by twenty-eight per cent from the pre-war figure).[2] There was an eight per cent increase in the number of households by comparison with 1917, accounted for mainly by the fact that during the war the frequency of family divisions had diminished and the returning soldiers naturally wanted to set up homes of their own. Thus the 'black repartition' within the village community was accompanied, and to some extent offset, by greater individualism within the household.

Let us now turn to the disparities of wealth that had an 'inter-community' character, about which there is more precise information. Here, too, we are often dealing with age-old rivalries. Some years later a peasant living in Novgorod province wrote a letter to his former proprietor (then evidently an émigré) in which he described how he and his fellow-villagers had refused to allow men from neighbouring communities to share in the redistribution : 'they grumbled a bit but went away when our lads wouldn't let them in.'[3] In neighbouring Tver province the villagers of Loginov and Gorodno (Tver county) quarrelled over which of them had the right to confiscate the estate of a proprietor named Auzen; the men of Gorodno, who had formerly leased this land, 'unable to dispose of the estate because of the threats uttered by the peasants of Loginov district, asked the county land department to send troops to help them'.[4] It might be thought that the residents of Gorodno were poor peasants (*bednyaki*) tyrannized by well-to-do (*kulak*) neighbours. As it happens, we have another scrap of evidence about this community which seems to rule out such an interpretation. Early in May 1918 the representative of Gorodno district stated, at a conference of local land departments : 'when we distributed the squires' land we gave priority to those who had little land, but since they had neither seed nor stock we had to give it to everyone able to sow it.'[5] Thus whatever else the men of Gorodno lacked it was not land; we have a straightforward dispute between two communities, each of which threw up its own leaders. It was much the same story in Gaysin county (Podolia province), where Count Potocki owned an extensive estate of eight hundred dessyatines near the village of Bundury. When asked to share this land with the inhabitants of three neighbouring villages, the men of Bundury refused, on the grounds that none of their own peasants held more than eight dessyatines, whereas their neighbours had as much as ten, fifteen or even twenty dessyatines per household; they suggested that the claimants should expropriate these 'kulak surpluses' rather than covet the lands that now belonged to Bundury.[6]

These conflicts were thus as much territorial as social but the antagonists might seek to discredit one another by employing modish class war jargon. The term 'kulak', with its pejorative connotations, served them very well. Used by peasants in a moral sense, it acquired a sociological meaning when employed by urban activists. The latter failed to appreciate that in traditional village society the local leaders would normally be drawn from the more well-to-do families, and that in the event of a conflict between two communities each would naturally seek to portray the other as dominated by selfish 'bourgeois' elements and themselves as true commoners. Hence the allegation that whole villages consisted of kulaks. Although this was sociological nonsense, the charge gained wide currency in areas afflicted by famine, where conditions might vary markedly within a small geographical area. In Tver province the hungry peasants of Chembar district referred to their neighbours as 'well fed' or 'rich' because they refused to part with supplies on their behalf.[7]

In some places the tension broke out into violence. As early as November 1917 a PSR newspaper reported from Laishev county (Kazan province) that the villagers of Batka, who opposed the destruction of estates, had been set upon by men from other communities; fifteen persons had been killed or wounded in the fray.[8] A number of similar instances occurred later, as the civil war spread outwards into the rural areas, but it is difficult to distinguish such inter-community clashes from other acts of rural violence (see below, p. 431) which had little or nothing to do with the land question. What activists took to be evidence of growing class conflict in the countryside analogous to the urban phenomenon, with which they were familiar, was actually an instinctive anarchic response by a self-reliant and communally minded peasantry to the breakdown of orderly government and to the vast opportunities opened up by the long-awaited 'black repartition'.

In 1919 Soviet statisticians attempted to measure the extent to which the agrarian revolution had changed the distribution of property in the Russian village.[9] This investigation showed a withering of the two extremes and an inflation of the centre. Compared with 1916, those with more than 8 dessyatines of land had fallen from

7·9 per cent to 3·1 per cent of the total, while at the other end of the spectrum the proportion of landless peasants had fallen from 11·4 per cent to 6·5 per cent. Three-quarters of the households (74·0 per cent as against 59·1 per cent) held small plots of up to 4 dessyatines and 16·4 per cent (as against 21·6 per cent) had plots of modest extent (4–8 dessyatines).[10] These global figures are of course of limited value, and one has to take particular provinces to obtain a more realistic picture. In the south-central and mid-Volga provinces of Tula and Penza the proportion of landless households shrank from 6·5 to 1·8 per cent and from 7·7 to 3·8 per cent respectively; similarly, those with over 8 dessyatines fell from 13·2 to 5·3 per cent and from 14·4 to 5·2 per cent respectively. In two non-black-soil provinces, Yaroslavl and Vyatka, the reductions were as follows : landless households from 13·9 to 6·4 per cent and from 3·3 to 1·9 per cent; those with 8 dessyatines and upwards from 8·5 per cent to nil and from 19·4 to 8·6 per cent.[11]

One has to bear in mind that in a time of scarcity many peasants (and indeed ex-townsmen too !) who would not normally have taken the trouble to farm land of their own were now obliged to do so, a fact which artificially inflates the number of very small holdings. Nor will all those with such plots have had enough seed or tools to work them : the distinction between land held and land utilized must not be lost sight of. Thus these figures should not be taken as a reliable index of changes in the peasants' real income from the land (to say nothing of their overall income).

A better guide in this respect is offered by the data on distribution of livestock. The most important deduction to be drawn from them is that the typical family farm in 1919 was endeavouring to subsist with a horse and one or two cows. The number of those with no work horse had fallen slightly, from 28·7 to 25·1 per cent, as had those with four horses or more (from 1·2 to 0·7 per cent). The number of those with no cow shrank from 17·9 to 15·7 per cent, and those with four cows or more from 3·0 to 1·0 per cent. According to figures compiled by the military authorities, who were interested in the possibilities of requisitioning horses surplus to peasant needs (and therefore disregarded households with no horses at all), nearly four-fifths (79·3 per cent) of the remainder had but one animal. The regional breakdown gives a similar picture.[12]

The general conclusion suggested by these figures is that the long-awaited 'black repartition' did not bring the average peasant householder much additional wealth. If anything, it may be said to have simply spread the prevailing misery more widely than before. This conclusion does not necessarily mean that the agrarian revolution was wholly destructive, or that the old rural order should have been preserved : many other factors need to be taken into account. Certainly, however, the elimination of private landed property did not produce the immediate material benefits that many had anticipated.

Looking at the problem more closely, the first and most striking point is that the lion's share of the confiscated land went directly to the peasants : according to one authority, only 3·2 per cent was left for various kinds of state-sponsored cooperative farms (*sovkhozy, kolkhozy*).[13] The statistical information in regard to the latter is unreliable, but it is thought that by the end of 1918 there may have been nearly three thousand cooperatives of all types, embracing some 0·15 per cent of the rural population; they were as a rule ephemeral organizations, whose economic performance was disappointing despite the substantial aid they received from the state authorities.[14] Thus the peasants had as yet no grounds for complaint that the land they coveted had fallen into other hands : in this respect their victory was as complete as was practically possible. (The picture looks a little less favourable to them if one considers the distribution of *all* land, since the privately owned forests generally passed into the hands of the state authorities.)[15] In regard to livestock and equipment, the same situation may be observed. The overwhelming bulk of the confiscated movable goods remained in peasant hands.

How much difference did the additional allocations of land make to the average peasant household, when added to what it had previously held (and/or owned)? Data compiled by the PC of Agriculture, covering twenty-nine provinces, showed an average *per capita* increase of 0·39 dessyatines (from 1·87 to 2·26), or approximately 1 to 1·5 dessyatines per household.[16] The highest *per capita* increase was recorded in Petrograd province (0·77 dessyatines)[17] : this was an area which had a number of suburban estates, and a large decrease in the number of potential claimants. In Olonets, which had no such lands, the increase was a derisory 0·07 dessyatines. The averages in the Ukrainian provinces were generally a little higher than in the non-black-soil areas of the north and centre, as one would expect. However, it was precisely this region that suffered most from the ravages of civil war. The increase of claimants was also greater than in Great Russia, being estimated by one statistician at 15·5 per cent (to 1922).[18] The same source puts the average 'theoretical increase' per household over 1916 holdings at 41 per cent in Podolia, which benefited most, and at 6 per cent in Chernigov, which benefited least;[19] he adds the comment that 'the peasant households of these provinces, which received on the average additions of 1 to 1·5 dessyatines, have in fact remained in the same situation as they were in before the revolution.' Moreover, not all these lands could be utilized in practice – it was for this reason that he referred to the increase as a *theoretical* one. Kachinsky goes on to point out that some villages were actually worse off for land than they had been in 1916, not only because they now had more mouths to feed but also because they had been obliged to surrender to a neighbouring community land which they had traditionally leased.[20]

Can we not get down to the level of a particular village community? Fortunately detailed information is available for Zadonsk county (Voronezh province), where a county-wide redistribution was completed in 1919–20 and the results surveyed and published shortly afterwards.[21] This was a typical black-soil county, where before the revolution agricultural development had failed to keep pace with rapid population growth : in 1916 there were fifty-two inhabitants per square verst and land allotments were small : 58·5 per cent of households had less than 5 dessyatines. In 1917–18 no less than 91 per cent of the communities received additional land. The expropriated area amounted to 27,700 dessyatines, an addition of 16·8 per cent, but this increase must be halved to allow for land previously leased. The expulsion of Denikin's armies in 1919 was followed by a second redistribution involving all land except that on the few 'state farms' growing sugar beet. It was carried out on the same egalitarian principles as the first (but with closer involvement by the state authorities). The *per capita* norms set for various districts varied only slightly, from 0·95 to 1·20 dessyatines, and the differentials between villages within one and the same district were even narrower. Over the whole county these norms ranged from a minimum of 0·69 to a maximum of 1·77 dessyatines, but half the villages fell within a median band of 1 to 1·2 dessyatines and most were not far removed from it.

Asked what they thought of this almost quintessentially egalitarian reform (such polls were still possible in the early 1920s), 58 per cent of those questioned expressed satisfaction and 14·5 per cent dissatisfaction; 27·4 per cent were undecided. Interpreting these replies is a hazardous undertaking. Brutskus suggests that they reflected a fundamental disillusionment at the slight practical benefits that had ensued from realization of the Populist utopia rather than objections to the way in which the redistribution had been carried out. This judgement was not uninfluenced by party-political considerations; as a liberal he was more aware than the Populists that agrarian poverty could be overcome only by economic development, for which socialization of property could but set the scene. A truism today, this was by no means obvious to Russian intellectuals of the revolutionary epoch. In any case liberals and Populists were not all that far apart: Brutskus thought that differentials of landholding in Zadonsk county were rather wide, whereas the modern observer is more likely to be struck by their narrowness.

It can of course be argued that the peasants gained a great deal more from the agrarian revolution than simply a few additional strips of land. In attempting to assess the change in their overall socio-economic situation, one enters into still more speculative territory. They no longer had to pay rent to private proprietors or mortgage payments to banks : such 'capitalistic' relationships were taboo under the new regime (at least until the introduction of the NEP). Nor did they have to pay the land tax, zemstvo dues and so on. It is scarcely possible, however, to express these gains in quantitative terms.[22] Runaway inflation did as much as the redistribution of property to reduce the real value of these debts. New taxes (in kind) were levied in place of the old; although probably less burdensome physically, they were exacted in a more arbitrary manner. The elimination of large estates deprived some peasants of the income they had previously derived from them as wage-earners. The collapse of the economy led to a catastrophic decline in most forms of artisan activity, upon which peasants in the non-black-soil provinces were particularly dependent. Figures for five counties in Tambov province, in the Central Agricultural region, illustrate this graphically : in Kashira county, where 86 per cent of households had received such income in 1910/12, the proportion dropped to 53 per cent in 1917 and to 18 per cent in 1919; the corresponding figures for Yepifan county were 74, 18 and 3 per cent.[23] It could however be held that this decline was attributable to the general collapse of the economy (and more specifically, to the civil war which raged through this province in 1919) rather than to the impact of redistribution of the land. The same holds true of the reduction in income from the sale of surplus produce as private trade came to be seen as 'speculation' and the surpluses themselves disappeared. Against these material hardships must be set such imponderables as the psychological boost which ordinary country folk obtained from their triumph over their hereditary foes; for it need hardly be said that the agrarian revolution was seen by many of its participants, at least initially, as a mighty act of self-emancipation. Does this sense of liberation outweigh in historical significance all the disadvantages which flowed from the original revolutionary act? Here we are trespassing upon the realm of pure hypothesis.

Any attempt to pursue on this 'macro-historical' plane the analysis of the peasants' gains and losses from the agrarian revolution must take into account its effects upon the Russian economy – a subject that can be only touched upon here. It would seem that in the short term, and probably also in the long term, these effects were negative and retrograde. As has often been noted, not only by Communist writers, the dominant element in the Russian rural economy was now the peasant small-holder. The ancient evils of the three-field system of cultivation were perpetuated : each householder in the commune continued to farm his scattered strips – now more numerous than before, and often situated at an awkward distance from the village – in the time-honoured way. The revolution in property relationships did nothing of itself to improve agricultural techniques; indeed, the breakdown in social discipline associated with it had the opposite effect. Equipment fell into disrepair; livestock could not be properly cared for; essential maintenance work was neglected, and so on. This was by no means wholly the agriculturalist's fault. He no longer received supplies of essential manufactured goods from the towns, since normal market relations had all but ceased; consequently he had no alternative but to revert to a primitive natural economy, producing a minimum of foodstuffs to satisfy his family's immediate needs. The siege economy that was enforced until March 1921 gave the peasant producer no material incentive to improve his standards of husbandry, to raise yields or to cultivate more land. Moreover, the former separators and other well-to-do households were as a rule more enterprising and outward-looking than their fellows – men who had the education and drive, as well as the capital, to make innovations and to produce a marketable surplus. They could count themselves fortunate if they were simply reintegrated into the commune and not otherwise penalized; as noted above (p. 215), many of them suffered a worse fate than the former squires. As against this it should be pointed out that in some non-black-soil provinces the redistribution was carried out in a manner that left former 'separators' in a relatively favourable position whence they could stage a revival after 1921.[24]

In normal times these more prosperous and independent peasants, along with the squires, had contributed the bulk of the agricultural produce brought into commercial circulation. In the post-revolutionary era this source of supply dried up, presenting the Soviet government with its most persistent domestic problem. How was it to feed the urban population on whose support its existence primarily rested, and at the same time maintain the unbreakable alliance (smychka) between proletarians and peasants which Lenin proclaimed as the lynchpin of Communist social policy? How much coercion should be applied against recalcitrant peasant producers? This question had to be answered on the very morrow of the October insurrection. Famine was stalking Russia's cities, driving the dictatorship into a bitter confrontation not just with the 'kulaks' of revolutionary mythology but with the broad mass of villagers. Paradoxically the 'black repartition', by accelerating the decline of agricultural production, deepened the schism between town and country that was the leit-motif of the epoch.

THIRTY-ONE *The Food Crisis*

ALREADY DURING THE autumn of 1917 the spectre of mass starvation loomed over Russia's 'consuming' provinces, straining the meagre resources of the elected supply committees set up by the Provisional Government (see above, p. 179). Matters became much worse during the winter and spring of 1918. The Bolshevik *coup* stimululated anarchic actions of every kind. Measures of self-help could be legitimized in terms of revolutionary ideology. Simultaneously the number of supply organs grew unchecked, as did the size of their staffs. This development stemmed partly from a naive belief that the problem was predominantly one of organization which could be solved by administrative means, and partly from more mundane considerations : those employed in such bodies would stand a reasonable chance of being fed. While the bureaucratic organs, old and new, sought to define their mutual relationship the crisis grew ever more calamitous.

Censorship was still lax enough for truthful reports on economic conditions to be carried in the press. These dispatches convey a vivid and moving picture of human suffering on a scale hitherto without parallel in modern Russian history. Famine was no stranger to that country, but on previous occasions it had been restricted to more localized regions of the country and the public authorities, though far from efficient, could do more to provide relief.

In Petrograd the bread ration fluctuated almost from week to week. It may be taken as an indicator of changes in living standards generally. Three days before the Bolshevik *coup* it was lowered from three-quarters to half a funt per person; those engaged in heavy manual labour received fifty per cent more than other consumers. On 2 December the ration was increased to the former rate. This may have been in part a public relations exercise, but it was also due to a miscalculation by officials of the amount of supplies that could be obtained by requisitioning stocks in and round the city. In any case the relief was short-lived, for by 9 December the ration was back to half a funt. Thereafter the trend was downwards. On 20 December it fell to three eighths of a funt, and early in the New Year to one quarter. On 18 January came an announcement that it would be doubled, but this increase does not seem to have taken effect; at any rate by 2 March we hear that the ration was *raised* to a quarter of a funt. There were protests in the streets and in Spassky ward angry crowds besieged the office of the supply board. They were particularly incensed at alleged discrimination in favour of certain soldiers' and sailors' units, which were rumoured to be receiving as much as 1½ funt per head. The March increase was obtained only at the expense of adulterating the bread by mixing in various surrogates and raising the moisture content. By May the ration had fallen once again to ⅛ funt and on some days nothing was distributed at all.[1]

Rural areas in the vicinity of the capital experienced worse privation. 'Already in December 1917,' writes one Soviet historian, 'a significant part of the rural population of Petrograd, Pskov, Novgorod, Olonets and Cherepovets provinces were living off substitutes : cereals were mixed with oil-cake and wood bark, and some people had to eat moss or straw.'[2] According to a speaker at a regional conference of supply committees held in late April, Petrograd province required 250 wagons of grain in order to maintain the bread ration at ¼ funt per head. Actual arrivals amounted to 40 in January and 24 in (the half-month) February; in March they rose to 144, but by April had dropped once more to 35. Much of the shortfall was due to pilfering (mainly by soldiers withdrawing in disorder from the northern front); in January losses from this source were put at a hundred wagons.[3] Still worse was the plight of Pskov and Vitebsk provinces, which faced the menace of enemy occupation. It seems that on this account the central supply authorities cut down the amount of provisions sent lest they fall into enemy hands.[4] In Vitebsk the local authorities reckoned they had 150,000 consumers to feed, but grain deliveries in the period January to March 1918 totalled a derisory 16,661 puds. No doubt a little extra was available from army stocks and free-market trading, but one can readily understand why, as this informant reported, 'hunger riots have begun'.[5] The representative from Novgorod province at the regional supply conference in April reported that deliveries of seed grains amounted to 150,000 puds, as against a requirement of over two million; moreover, much of the seed had been eaten by the population. In Borovichi county no food at all was received from outside for twenty-three days.[6]

In the Central Industrial region, particularly in the rural areas, the situation was almost as catastrophic. The city supply authorities in Moscow estimated that 1,800 wagons of grain were required each month to maintain the ration at $\frac{1}{2}$ funt per head. Only 692 arrived in October; in the following month the figure rose to 1,079, but in December it fell to 546. Worse was yet to come: in January and February 1918 the number of wagons arriving was respectively 293 and 156, or 15 per cent and 9 per cent of monthly requirements.[7] Here the situation was alleviated somewhat by supplies of meat, fish, eggs and vegetables, which were much scarcer in the northwest. However, these soon tailed off.[8] At Koprino (Rybinsk county, Yaroslavl province), whence many residents normally went to work in the industrial establishments of the region,

> . . . columns of seasonal labourers poured back into the village to escape the famine, hoping to receive a hospitable welcome from their wives or parents, but in vain – for they were reduced to poverty and could not repay these guests for their previous generosity [in sending back part of their earnings]. There was no one who could help; hopes that food would be sent from Rybinsk were not realized; their native ingenuity was of no use, and they began to go hungry. The men of Koprino sent one cart after another across the Volga to Krasnyy Kholm, where they bartered clothing and household wares for flour. This was mixed with surrogates: husks of corn, dust from winnowing, oil-cake, moss,

hay, cabbage, stalks, nettles etc. A mixture of flour and potatoes, oatmeal and other leftovers was considered a luxury.[9]

At Serpukhov (Moscow province), where in December the number of wagon loads of produce had fallen to a tenth of what was required, workers and other poor people are said to have marched through the streets crying 'give us bread, we are dying of hunger.'[10] In Bogorodsk county (Moscow province), a leading centre of textile manufacture, the local supply committee decided to 'abolish' the grain monopoly and to petition the central authorities for a return to free trade.[11] At about the same time workers in nearby Ivanovo-Voznesensk sent telegrams of protest to the government. In one of these the signatories claimed that they supplied the rest of the country with textiles and therefore had a right to expect foodstuffs in exchange.[12]

These actions were not wholly spontaneous, for the Mensheviks still had a good deal of support in this region. However, it is absurd to assert, as Soviet historians occasionally do, that this agitation was artificially provoked for 'counter-revolutionary' ends. M.V. Frunze, who headed the Bolshevik apparatus in Ivanovo province, reported truthfully in May that 'the workers are worn out to the last degree'.[13] One must also bear in mind that there was still a great deal of common ground on practical matters among supply workers of various political tendencies. It might be said that the main difference was not between Mensheviks and Bolsheviks but between the few hard-core Leninists, who put political considerations first, and the rest – although this, too, is an over-simplification, as becomes apparent when one examines the structure of the supply machinery during this period.

The Bolsheviks took power without any well-defined policy to deal with the food crisis, whose seriousness they seem at first to have underestimated. Many activists took a conciliatory attitude towards the existing supply organs, on the grounds that these were demo-cratically elected bodies in whose inner circles pro-soviet elements were strongly represented. 'Soviet power' surely meant that these organizations should continue to function under control of the soviets, which would endeavour that they put first the interests of the broad masses of the population. The officials in the central ministry of Supply, like those in the local committees, were almost universally favourable to increased state regulation of economic life; scarcely any of them could be described as apostles of free enterprise. Moreover, there was as yet no alternative machinery to which the new government could turn in order to keep the urban population fed. For all these reasons, as one early Soviet historian put it, 'many leading workers in soviet organizations thought it inexpedient to take a high-handed tone, to destroy the old supply apparatus, or to split away from its experienced workers, who were prepared to compromise with us.'[14]

The first people's commissar of Supply, I.A. Teodorovich, was a moderate who advocated a socialist coalition government. He soon left Petrograd for Siberia in search of supplies.[15] In his absence two of his colleagues persuaded Lenin to appoint as deputy commissar a more forceful person, A.G. Shlikhter, a senior Bolshevik activist who could claim some expertise in agrarian matters.[16] He faced a movement of non-cooperation among officials in the supply apparatus. These men looked for leadership not only to their own trade union (and to the democratic parties) but also to a non-political national organization of supply workers, which was taking shape in Moscow. A congress of local representatives met on 18 November, without obstruction by the Bolshevik leaders in Moscow, who as we know were less intransigent than their colleagues in Petrograd. The delegates condemned the October *coup* and set up a ten-man provisional executive to manage the hierarchy of supply committees until such time as a legitimate government was restored.

This committee had better credentials than the shadowy people's commissariat in Petrograd; moreover, it commanded much support in the 'producing' provinces. Shlikhter was therefore obliged to play for time. He used a mixture of threats and blandishments. On 26 November a decree dismissed all alleged 'saboteurs' in the supply apparatus. The 'committee of ten' was dissolved and its members arrested. This was simply a gesture of intimidation, for they were immediately released and invited to take part in talks. V.G. Groman, the (Menshevik) economist and the most prominent member of the committee, offered a compromise: the Moscow-based organization would remain politically neutral and in exchange be allowed complete autonomy. Shlikhter countered with a proposal that it should coexist with his commissariat on a parity basis. The talks broke down, and on 5 December the CPC issued an edict branding the elected supply officials as 'saboteurs' and inviting the populace to take appropriate action against them. It was partly to meet this situation that three days later, as we have seen (p. 352), the Cheka was called into being and given powers to take action against alleged 'saboteurs' as well as counter-revolutionaries.[17]

Teodorovich, who had by now returned to Petrograd, disapproved of these tactics but was ousted by his rival, who succeeded him as commissar on 18 December. In Moscow, however, moderate views still prevailed. The Bolshevik leaders in the city permitted the 'council of ten' to call another congress of its supporters (28 December). This endorsed the line taken by the provisional executive body and gave this a more permanent character : henceforward it was to be known as the All-Russian Supply Council and was to have twenty-five members, most of them representatives of provincial and outlying areas (including the grain-rich Ukraine, North Caucasus and Siberia). The council could thus plausibly claim to be a genuinely national body and a worthy successor to the now virtually defunct Supply ministry in Petrograd. Two seats on the council were given to the Moscow Bolshevik leaders A.I. Rykov and V.P. Milyutin, who favoured a compromise solution.[18]

From this position of strength Groman and his allies confronted Shlikhter, who at first was obliged to yield. They suggested what was in effect a merger : a new body, to be called the Supreme Supply Council, was to be formed with its seat in Petrograd, as an integral part of SEC. When the question was debated in the CPC (11 January) Shlikhter found himself in a minority of one; seven members voted for the proposal and three abstained. It was at this point that Lenin began to devote serious attention to the question. He no doubt appreciated that the impending 'annexationist peace' of Brest-Litovsk would deprive Soviet Russia of access to its most important source of food supplies and that drastic measures would be required to cope with the resultant shortages. Addressing a joint meeting of supply workers and Petrograd soviet deputies on 14 January, the Bolshevik leader suggested the formation of several thousand supply detachments, each composed of ten to fifteen or more soldiers and civilian workers, empowered to shoot recalcitrants in cold blood.[19] This terroristic proposal – among the first of this nature to be put forward, but by no means the last – was rejected by his listeners.[20] Such measures went beyond those envisaged by most of his senior party colleagues, Shlikhter probably among them.

The latter was meanwhile building up an alternative organization to the All-Russian Supply Council, which rested mainly on the supply organizations set up within the armed forces.[21] When the third All-Russian congress of soviets met (10–18 January), certain delegates were invited to constitute themselves as a 'congress of soviet supply workers'; this then set up a thirty-five-man executive which was to be responsible directly to the CPC – and not to the SEC, as Rykov and his colleagues had suggested.[22] Lenin's hand is evident in the elaborate precautions taken to ensure that this body would have a solid Bolshevik core.[23] However, these precautions proved to be unnecessary, since the new executive never exercised any real power and became a mere decorative appendage of the commissariat. Orlov is most explicit about this : 'After the congress ended, the commissar's power did not fade but on the contrary acquired a force unusual at that time. This is understandable : the CPC [now] felt that it had a fairly firm base in the country's supply organization and could go straight ahead as it wanted, without having to waste time on diplomatic exchanges with representatives of vacillating [pro-] 'coalition' groups.'[24] On 15 February Trotsky was proclaimed 'supply dictator'[25] without the council even being consulted. It was not involved either in the decision to replace Shlikhter by another experienced Bolshevik activist, A.D. Tsurupa, who was destined to hold the post until 1921.[26] Shlikhter was sent off to Siberia, in the footsteps of his predecessor, to obtain grain from this quarter. This was an important assignment, for Siberia was soon the sole outlying region under Bolshevik control, but there is no doubt that political calculations entered into his departure from Petrograd. With his dictatorial ways he had made too many enemies among supply officials, and the Bolshevik leaders wanted to avoid unnecessary friction within their new apparatus at a time when it would be engaged in a life-and-death struggle with the peasant producers.[27]

From these complicated manoeuvres the hard-core Leninists emerged as the victors, although their triumph was not absolute. Groman and his friends had been outmanoeuvred : the senior positions in the supply hierarchy were held by men involved in the day-to-day formulation of party policy, who were in a position to give orders, if not always to enforce them. Yet the supply organizations at the regional and provincial level continued to be staffed by moderate socialists and politically neutral elements. The struggle went on behind the scenes between those officials who took an ideological approach and those more concerned with the economic rationality of the policies adopted.

It is difficult to evaluate the achievement of the realists. On one hand, by putting their expertise at the disposal of the regime they strengthened it and so prepared the way for their own eventual liquidation. On the other hand their activities helped to save human lives. Their presence was a constant thorn in the side of the hard-line Bolsheviks, who found their reasoned arguments embarrassing. Service in the supply organization was seen as a moral obligation by democratic intellectuals who had voluntarily relinquished, or had been forced to relinquish, their political role in the soviets. It was an arena in which they could hope to educate the country's new rulers in the responsibilities of power. Yet practical collaboration in this sphere was bound to involve compromises that many found difficult to justify.

There were two regional supply organizations, one centred in Petrograd and the other in Moscow. The former, known as the 'Northern Supply Committee', functioned from April to July and exercised authority over seven provinces. Its members used their contacts in commercial and cooperative circles to obtain food in exchange for a variety of industrial and consumer goods. The latter were mostly purchased on the free market, although some were requisitioned and others were supplied directly by workers in the factories.[28] A similar body, headed by T.A. Runov, performed analogous operations in the Central Industrial and Central Agricultural regions.[29]

How did their activities, and those of the urban (or provincial) supply committees nominally subordinate to them, impinge upon the life of the population, especially peasant producers? Much useful information may be gleaned from the bulletin put out by the Moscow city supply committee. This body may have been more liable than most to bureaucratic excesses. According to its statute it was supposed to consist of no less than 179 persons, of whom a mere 10 represented those who actually produced the food which the committee hoped to procure and distribute. This urban bias did not in practice matter very much, since the assembly was much less important than its executive. The latter's most prominent member was M.E. Shefler, a Menshevik who provided an element of continuity with the past, since he had been one of those appointed to the committee when it was first 'democratized' in March 1917;[30] many of his former colleagues had since resigned or been excluded. Its administrative apparatus, of impressive proportions, was modelled on that of the PC of Supply – which itself was evacuated to Moscow in March 1918, so making for duplication of authority.[31] The total number of employees must have reached several thousand.

Shefler and his colleagues were ardent believers in a fully planned economy. The aim was to distribute all consumer goods equally among the entire population – a utopian ideal in the best of circumstances, and a fantasy in an economy that was rapidly grinding to a standstill.[32] In practice the committee's agents performed two complementary tasks. The first was to extract food supplies from supply committees in the 'producing' provinces; the second was to obtain cash and goods with which to satisfy potential vendors. These transactions were supposed to be carried out at the official price, that is to say that set by the Provisional Government on 27 August. Unfortunately for the famished Muscovites, galloping inflation had made these prices totally unrealistic, and it was a problem even to obtain enough paper roubles to pay suppliers for the goods contracted for. The provincial agents sent back a stream of depressing reports. Typical was that from A.V. Barykov in Simferopol (Tavrida province). There was plenty of surplus grain available, he noted, but tens of thousands of puds earmarked for Moscow had been seized by agents from nearby towns such as Sevastopol; to obtain even a tenth of the amount commissioned, he declared, it was necessary at once to provide 10 million roubles worth of goods and 15 million roubles in cash 'of the old [tsarist] kind, for the new notes do not enjoy much confidence among the population'.[33]

Each issue of the bulletin contained details of contracts concluded and wagons loaded at various points – yet still the food did not arrive. The Moscow authorities complained that they had sent 20 million roubles' worth of goods to Voronezh but had not received a single pud of grain.[34] They surmised that the manufactures might not have reached the villages, or else that the trains had been intercepted *en route*; but the chief reason is more likely to have been that given by one such agent named Yesipov to a peasant congress in Petrograd province : at the fixed price of 4·86 roubles a pud no one in Voronezh would hand over grain, since on the free market they could get twenty-five roubles; enterprising operators were forming armed bands to escort consignments to the towns, where they could sell it for a hundred roubles a pud. When Yesipov offered them textiles, he was mocked by the local peasants, who said they needed other items instead.[35] It was impossible for supply committees to compete with these 'speculators' without betraying their belief in a centrally controlled economy. Yet the temptation was great to throw ideology to the winds if this would help to feed one's fellow citizens. When the Moscow committee's agent in Kazan stated on 13 April that in that province no grain whatever had been bought or sold at the official price for the past six months,[36] he was probably hinting that he had paid the free-market price demanded.

Where goods were bartered, this introduced imponderables that made central price-fixing an impossibility. The authorities extended their control over a wide range of items hitherto partly or wholly exempt from regulation (textiles, leather goods, china and glass and so on) but the official prices bore little or no relation to the actual value of such goods to those with produce to spare. Barter deals were seldom viewed as satisfactory by either party. They contributed to the mutual suspicions between town and country. We have seen above (p. 182) that already before October 1917 some factory committees and similar organizations had engaged in this 'products exchange', as barter trade euphemistically came to be known. Its scope now greatly expanded, and in some places it was organized on an elaborate basis. Workers in the metallurgical complex at Votkinsk (Perm province) published price lists giving grain equivalents for the equipment they produced. A plough fetched from 5 to 15 puds, a hay-making machine 29 puds, a cart 35 puds and so on.[37] In the eyes of supply officials these self-help operations were scarcely distinguishable from 'speculative' private trading by individuals.

All such practices come within the purview of the regulations which poured forth in a steady stream. To prevent malpractices by officials, on 10 April the PC of Supply instructed provincial committees to report every ten days what goods they had received and distributed and how this had affected the supply of grain; they were even supposed to confirm by telegraph the arrival of each consignment – but not, characteristically, the price at which the goods had actually changed hands. Any money received was to be banked on behalf of the central commissariat and could not be used to make local purchases.[38] Such regulations were bound to cramp the initiative of the men on the spot. What was worse, peasant suppliers were given no incentive to collaborate with the official agencies, for the transaction was to be carried out in such a way as to foment class conflict within the village. 'In no case whatever are goods to be handed over to individual farmers in exchange for their grain. Goods are to be distributed among the needy population ... in order to stimulate those who have no grain to force those that have to hand it over.'[39] In other words, those who were most likely to have a marketable surplus available were to be penalized; such commodities as the supply officials had at their disposal were to be given to those with least produce to offer.

This decree marks the threshold of 'war communism'. By the spring of 1918 functionaries at all levels were becoming disillusioned at the difficulties encountered in trying to obtain food by commercial methods, however unconventional, and were inclining further towards coercion. Certainly the results achieved to this point were unimpressive.[40] Whether they justified a sharp turn to 'hard line' policies must remain a matter of opinion. Let us first see what these policies entailed.

The alternative to trade was requisitioning. Strictly speaking, the two policies were not so much alternatives as interrelated, since an element of coercion is involved in any commercial deal concluded in conditions of scarcity. However, this academic point was unlikely to concern those in authority, who not unreasonably saw themselves as having a limited range of options between sanctioning extensive private trade and engaging in systematic confiscation.

For obvious reasons the toughest policies had a strong appeal for militants in Petrograd. The first 'supply detachments' (to use another current euphemism) were sent out by the Petrograd MRC as early as 27 October, when five hundred Kronstadt sailors were dispatched to various parts of the country; by 7 November the number of those who left on such missions is said to have reached seven thousand.[41] Most of them did not venture too far from the city. They managed to locate some supplies – mainly goods held up in transit or stocks whose whereabouts were already known to the regular authorities[42] – but their efforts could do no more than bring short-term relief, since they did not tap any new source of supply.

Dozens of men were also sent to the outlying regions. Some went to the Ukraine, where their activities helped to strain relations with the government in Kiev; it was not until after the Rada had fallen to the Red forces that significant amounts of produce were obtained from this quarter,[43] but almost immediately thereafter the flow was interrupted by the German occupation. Access to the Kuban and northern Caucasus was barred by cossacks loyal to General Kaledin, while Dutov's 'Orenburg cork' prevented shipments of grain from the Steppe region (modern Kazakhstan). This left Siberia, where (until the Czech rising in May 1918) transport difficulties were the main obstacle. This source is said to have yielded over 6·5 million puds of grain in the four months from December to March, of which half arrived in the latter month.[44] There were about thirty-three million persons resident in the 'consuming provinces',[45] so that these supplies could do little to ease the famine in the territory under Soviet control. The bulk of the resources needed would clearly have to come from this restricted area (roughly coextensive with Great Russia), which for generations had been an importer of cereals and where the 1917 harvest had been no better than average.

Awareness of these facts strengthened the hand of those who for ideological reasons favoured coercive measures against peasant producers. Lenin's suggestion of a massive recruitment of workers for the food detachments (see above, p. 424) was taken up in the Petrograd soviet, despite a warning by a local supply chief that such measures implied 'not the organization of supplies but the organization of hunger'.[46] It was decided that five thousand men should be mobilized into bands (*druzhiny*) for the purpose; they were given emergency powers, including the right of arrest. Within a few days four thousand men had been recruited.[47] They were equipped with political literature – some zealots carried as much as 5 funt of propaganda[48] – and, what was more important, weapons. Many of these detachments were in any case composed of soldiers and sailors : for example, a group calling itself the 'Northern Military Supply Band' was sent to the Urals.[49]

Unlike the emissaries of the supply organs, or even of the factory committees, these men did not as a rule take with them any goods with which to pay for the foodstuffs they appropriated. Some no doubt considered that inflammatory brochures were sufficient recompense; others had paper roubles advanced to them for the purpose; more commonly still, they simply issued promissory notes to the effect that the produce confiscated would be paid for at some later date at the official rate – by which time, of course, this would be even less realistic.

An impression of their conduct once they reached the villages can be gleaned from the memoirs of Okninsky, who lived among the peasants of Tambov. He describes the arrival of a supply detachment in his locality in May 1919 (by which time party policy towards the 'middle peasant' was supposed to have eased). Fifty soldiers appeared early in the morning, split up into groups of five or six, and made a thorough search of all homes, cellars, barns and outhouses – yet found nothing, because the villagers had been forewarned and had managed to conceal their reserves. As the soldiers could not leave empty-handed, they persuaded the district executive committee to share out the quota among the wealthier households, and enough grain materialized to fill several carts.[50]

Reports of clashes between requisitioning squads and peasants appeared as early as January 1918. A band led by G. Romanov from the Trekhgornaya mill in Moscow, which included some men from Ivanovo, suppressed what they termed a 'kulak insurrection' near Syzran (Simbirsk province).[51] It was at this time that Yesipov's detachment was active in Voronezh province (see above, p. 427). Firing broke out between it and another band of men described as 'speculators'. Casualties were suffered on both sides. Thereupon Yesipov recruited a group of 'poor peasants' from the locality and began to seize the alleged 'surpluses' in the peasants' barns. This tactic worked well in four villages but a fifth, informed of his approach, stood to arms. Yesipov returned to Voronezh for reinforcements and returned at the head of a party eighty strong, only to run into an ambush. The local peasants, led by some demobilized soldiers who had kept their weapons, put the attackers to flight.[52]

Despite these warning signs not only the Bolshevik chiefs but also most Menshevik officials in the supply organization, notably Groman,[53] stuck to orthodox principles. There were to be no deviations from the prices fixed by the central authorities and 'the most decisive measures' were threatened against any who ventured to disobey; there was to be a new central agency to administer the 'products exchange' programme; controls were to be extended to fish, and – a nice fairy-tale touch here! – the government would encourage fish-farmers on the shores of the Aral Sea.[54]

Tsurupa, the PC of Supply, with the backing of Trotsky and Lenin, wanted to go further. The idea of a ruthless 'supply dictatorship' had been in the air since January but had yet to become a reality (except perhaps in the Petrograd region); from May onwards it was to become the *leit-motif* of Bolshevik domestic policy throughout the country. This phase of events falls outside the chronological limits of our study and a few remarks must suffice.[55] By 10 May Lenin was talking of a 'reliable workers' army of 20,000 selected men' from the Petrograd area who were to launch 'a disciplined military campaign against the village bourgeoisie and the bribe-takers'.[56] He had evidently convinced himself and most if not all of his associates on the party's Central Committee[57] that the food shortage was due to 'kulak speculation' and that para-military measures would suffice to alleviate it. Both these assumptions were soon shown to be dubious, if not downright fallacious; nevertheless for the moment the Bolshevik leader had things his own way. On 13 May the CEC approved a remarkably demagogic decree which proclaimed it as a fact that 'the village bourgeoisie, satiated and well provided for ... remains stubbornly deaf and indifferent to the groans of the starving workers and poor peasants.' A 'merciless struggle' was to be unleashed against such persons; anyone who failed to hand over all his surplus grain was to be declared 'an enemy of the people', liable to a *minimum* sentence of ten years' imprisonment; those who denounced such miscreants would receive the equivalent of half their confiscated property.[58]

The supply machinery was now greatly expanded. To assist it in its task a new network of rural organizations was called into being, the so-called 'committees of village poor' (*kombedy*), which as their name indicates were conceived as organs of 'class struggle' with the peasantry. A total of about fifty to sixty thousand persons from outside the rural milieu descended upon the countryside, where they could turn for support to more than twice that number of *kombedy*.[59]

It is difficult to arrive at a satisfactory estimate of the achievements of the 'supply dictatorship' during 1918 in the absence of detailed monthly figures for procurements in each province where detachments operated. Unfortunately the statistical information available is disappointingly thin. Lenin, in support of his claim that the campaign had been a great success, cited PC of Supply data to the effect that, whereas only 28 million puds of grain had been collected between January and June, the figure rose to 67 million during the last six months of 1918; of this latter 37 million were procured in the three months August to October.[60] Such statements had an obvious propagandist intent : half-yearly totals were the least suited for comparison, since it was much easier to obtain supplies in the autumn, when the harvest had just been gathered in, than in the winter or spring, and the monthly curve of grain sales normally reached its peak in late September and October. A more meaningful comparison would be with procurement statistics for earlier years, but here we run into the difficulty that the area under Soviet control in 1918 was much smaller than that covered by statisticians under the preceding regimes, and excluded those 'producing' provinces that usually yielded the highest surpluses.

We have seen above (p. 184) that in the agricultural year 1916–17 the supply authorities procured 508·5 million puds of cereals from fifty-two provinces. This was more than five times as much as was obtained during the calendar year 1918, but without a regional breakdown this tells us little. According to one early Soviet statistical compilation state procurements, when calculated by agricultural years, amounted to 65 million puds in 1917–18 and 107 million puds in 1918–19.[61] Although these figures do not inspire great confidence, they suggest that the supply authorities did succeed in gaining control of such surpluses as were available in Soviet-held territory.[62] They also must have taken some grain that was *not* surplus but was needed by producers for their own subsistence. In another calculation it was claimed that 43·7 per cent of cereals consumed by inhabitants of Soviet-held territory was derived from trade through official channels (53·0 million puds as against 68·4 million for private trade), and that this represented 'a victory over capitalism'.[63] These figures could also be interpreted differently, as indicating the extent to which the population in the 'consuming' provinces owed its survival to the activities of these non-approved traders, for the grain monopoly yielded the equivalent of only one pud per person, or less than ⅛ funt per day. There is, unfortunately, no way of telling how much people might have consumed if a more flexible supply system had been adopted. At this point one encounters the argument that no such option existed, since any relaxation would have exposed the regime to an intolerable political risk.

Against this it may be held that the policies embarked upon in May 1918 entailed a high economic and social cost of which the leaders failed to take sufficient account until the damage had been done. No one paused to calculate the expense of maintaining the sixty thousand-strong army of supply agents. In principle these men were maintained from public funds, but in practice they lived off the land. In strictly economic terms they formed a class of parasites, for they contributed nothing to agricultural production or management. This was an immensely wasteful method of extracting farm produce, which required the services of myriads of functionaries to obtain relatively meagre accounts of grain. Figures for Tambov province show that the 4,816 persons belonging to supply detachments procured 12·3 million puds of grain during the last six months of 1918.[64] This is equivalent to 2,520 puds per head, and might be thought a satisfactory performance – until one considers that it was two and a half times greater than the national average.

The moral climate in which the supply detachments operated was one which encouraged every kind of licence and abuse. The regular authorities were unable to control their excesses,[65] although their complaints seem to have been instrumental in moderating official policy during the course of the campaign, and perhaps even in securing the liquidation of the *kombedy* in November 1918. Before that, however, the activists could disregard with impunity such modest limitations as had been placed upon their powers. It was, for example, quite easy for them to neglect the provision entitling producers to retain a fixed amount (twelve puds per head) for their own needs.[66] Preoccupied with political struggle, often knowing little of the rural milieu, they showed little understanding of the practical problems that might prevent agricultural producers from complying with their requirements. Much produce was allowed to spoil because those in charge lacked the necessary technical skills, and also because there was insufficient storage space; yet the central authorities were slow to respond to reports of such inadequacies. Bureaucratic rigidity at the centre went hand in hand with insensitivity and arbitrariness at the lowest level – a pattern that had many precedents in Russia's administrative history.

The requisitioning squads often arrived empty-handed. The PC of Supply reckoned that it could provide goods in exchange for only about a half (and in the Ukraine only a tenth) of the grain it procured, and the value of the commodities actually delivered cannot be ascertained.[67] Above all, the law deliberately refrained from laying down objective criteria to guide activists in assessing a peasant household's status, so that these angry and embittered men had to make their own judgements as to who was or was not a 'kulak'. No sociological expertise was required : it was enough to rely on one's intuition and one's bayonet. At Yurovo (Chernigov province), one inhabitant later recalled, 'a detachment came to the village assembly and commanded : "Poor to the right, rich to the left", and [the soldiers], led by comrade Garin, took up aim against the rich.' Within half an hour the 'rich' had surrendered.[68] According to one early Soviet investigator there were no fewer than fifty-four 'kulak uprisings' in four black-soil provinces (Voronezh, Tambov, Kursk, Orel) during the spring of 1918 alone.[69] Shortly afterwards the situation throughout the Central Agricultural region degenerated into one of latent civil war. Wherever possible revolts were suppressed with great severity, the ringleaders being shot and 'contributions' levied upon the communities deemed responsible.

Along with the 'supply dictatorship' came the levying of conscripts for the Red Army, onslaughts on religious belief by atheistic zealots, and the loss of the civil and political rights gained in 1917. But it was the regime's clumsy attempt to solve the food crisis which catalysed all the peasants' discontents. It ranged Russia's countryside against the towns in a struggle without precedent in modern times. In this contest the peasants had the advantage of numbers, but this did not compensate for their deficiencies in organization, which was bound to tell against them in the long run. Let us now consider what became of the embryonic institutions they had established during 1917.

THIRTY-TWO *Taming the Peasant Organizations: the Summit*

FOR MOST RUSSIAN peasants in 1918 Bolshevism was still an unknown quantity, and accordingly their attitudes towards 'proletarian dictatorship' were ambiguous. On one hand the revolutionary regime had sanctioned the long-awaited egalitarian land reform, destroyed the old state order and ended an unpopular war. On the other hand it had launched a new struggle in the Russian countryside whose purpose and scope were still obscure; moreover, the heavy burdens which it expected the peasants to bear were allocated according to principles that in their eyes contravened elementary notions of justice. It was far from clear whether the 'rights of the toilers', sanctified by generations of Populist rhetoric, would be respected by those who now wielded power in Petrograd.

The outcome of the civil war of 1918–20 was to show that, when the peasant millions were forced to choose between Reds and Whites, they generally preferred the former; the influence of the 'Greens', a rural third force, was confined to certain limited areas. Yet it is impossible to say how their vote would have gone if history had taken a less catastrophic course. One may envisage circumstances in which the peasants could have preserved more autonomy and exercised a greater political impact. Had the Soviet government faced fewer and less menacing external adversaries, and had its supply problems been less acute, it might have adopted more conciliatory policies towards the peasantry; this would have allowed a more harmonious relationship to develop between town and country generally, and more specifically a greater degree of cooperation between all the socialist parties, whether Marxist or Populist. But this is to day-dream : the harsh reality was that the October insurrection made civil war inevitable. There could be no turning back until the struggle had been settled by force of arms. One consequence of this was that already by the spring of 1918 the Communists ceased to collaborate on any significant scale with other organized political groups. Another was that, as the cities imposed their will upon the countryside, the peasants lost the ability to determine their own political future. The rural soviets and other bodies became subservient to a central government which made no secret of its urban bias. For this success, to an even greater extent than in the soviets of many provincial towns, the Bolsheviks were deeply indebted to their wayward allies, the Left Socialist-Revolutionaries. It was the support they received from this quarter which turned Lenin's party from a mere sect into a national organization and enabled it for the first time in its history to strike root in the countryside. Thus fortified, it could withstand all challengers.

This institutional process is easier to study at the national than at the local level. We have already discussed the consolidation of the dictatorship at the centre (see above, pp. 306–38) as it affected those soviet agencies which drew their support from the workers and soldiers, but have yet to see how this affected those that claimed to speak for a hundred and twenty million Russian peasants.

It will be recalled that in the autumn of 1917 the Executive Committee of the All-Russian Congress of Peasant Deputies was wrestling with the problem whether or not to convene a second congress of rural soviet organizations. In the eyes of the radical members of this body such a congress was long overdue. The peasants' mood, they argued, had shifted considerably to the left since May, when the first congress had been held, and the executive elected on that occasion had lost their confidence by its vacillating policies. The moderate members, most of whom belonged to the right and centre factions of the PSR, were embarrassed by this agitation. They sought to postpone the day of reckoning by pleading that the congress would be a costly affair and that the masses were tired of politics. Instead of such transparent subterfuges they might have done better to point out that the prospective gathering was likely to extinguish peasant soviets as independent organizations, since the radicals were intent on merging them with workers' and soldiers' soviets wherever expedient. However, the moderates' ideological preconceptions and political traditions inhibited them from making vigorous use of this argument. From the start rural soviets had been envisaged, not as authentic representative institutions, but as a channel whereby revolutionary intellectuals might extend their influence over the countryside. Ironically, the organizational weapon which the PSR leaders had forged with such difficulty was to be turned against them, and they themselves would fall victim to the exceptional laws they had previously devised against their foes on the right.

The central peasant executive's decision (23 September) to postpone convocation of the congress until after the Constituent Assembly elections did credit to its chiefs' sense of democratic proprieties but may be adjudged a tactical error. Had a national congress of peasant soviets been in session at the moment when the Bolsheviks struck, it would have been difficult for the latter to present their *coup* as enjoying the support of the soviet movement as a whole. As we know, the second congress of soviets which met on 25–6 October consisted almost wholly of worker and soldier delegates. It could be deemed representative of the peasantry only by invoking the cliché – at best a half-truth – that 'the lads in soldiers' greatcoats' were muzhiki at heart.[1] Naturally protagonists of the new regime were none too concerned about the under-representation of the peasantry, which served their purposes well : in terms of combative potential, a dozen front-line soldiers were worth more than a hundred ploughmen from some peaceful province in the interior.

Battle was joined immediately after the October *coup*. Maximalists and moderates alike realized that the decisions to be taken by the second congress of peasant deputies would prove to be crucial. Unwilling to wait three weeks or so for the outcome of the elections, they sought to predetermine the issue by engaging in political manoeuvres. The Left SRS, possibly at a hint from their Bolshevik allies, decided to convoke as soon as possible an extraordinary gathering of peasant deputies, which they hoped would endorse the land decree and present the regular congress with a *fait accompli*.[2] Not to be outdone, the right and centre SR leaders took up the idea.

They planned to give this gathering the status of a consultative conference, not a full congress, and to hold it either in Moscow or in Mogilev. In the latter city it would be under the influence of the moderate-controlled all-army committee at General Headquarters, with whose support Avksentyev and Gots hoped to form a new democratic government. These negotiations failed and nothing came of this scheme. Meanwhile a number of delegates had congregated in Petrograd, where they were courted by politicians from each camp. In the euphoric atmosphere that prevailed in the capital at this time it is not surprising that the maximalists should have had more success than their rivals, especially since most of the men were soldiers. By 10 November they decided that sufficient delegates were present to constitute a quorum and the congress was called into session.[3]

The exact number and affiliation of the delegates are not known for certain, for the proceedings were disorderly and men came and went as they pleased. One right-wing commentator claimed that only 202 persons were present, and compared this figure unfavourably with the 1,453 delegates said to have attended the first congress of peasant deputies in May.[4] This figure is probably too low (just as that given for the earlier gathering is too high). One source lists the party affiliation of 330 delegates on 18 November as follows: Left SRs 195, Bolsheviks 37, Maximalists 7, Anarchists 2, Menshevik Internationalists 3, United SDs 3, Popular Socialists 4, Right and Centre SRs 65, Trudoviks 4, non-party 14.[5] The balance of forces was probably more evenly matched than this breakdown suggests, since when the moderates finally walked out they took about 150 men with them, leaving about 175 in the hall.[6] No figures are available on the breakdown between soldiers and civilians, but Gaysinsky is probably correct in stating that 'the vast mass were from the trenches' – or at least wore army uniforms.[7]

What followed had its comic-opera aspects, although the game was being played for high stakes. The right-wing members of the central peasant executive challenged their opponents' credentials but were defeated, whereupon the left retaliated in kind. As one Bolshevik observer explained shortly afterwards, they feared that their foes might call upon 250–80 backwoodsmen to secure a majority; therefore it was 'the most elementary democratism' (sic) to prevent such an eventuality by formally depriving the existing executive members of the right to sit on the presidium.[8] This stratagem seems to have aroused some misgivings among the Left SRs, who were unwilling to make a clean break with their erstwhile party colleagues; however, precisely this was the consideration uppermost in the minds of the Bolshevik tacticians, who were anxious to provoke such a schism. As they saw it, it was in the nature of the 'petty-bourgeois' Left SRs to vacillate between the 'party of the proletariat' and the allegedly 'bourgeois' moderate socialists, and to keep them in line it was necessary to combine firmness on essentials with gestures of conciliation. In protest at their exclusion from the presidium the right-wing delegates left the hall, whereupon those who remained elected the popular firebrand Maria Spiridonova as their chairman; she was to be assisted by a fifteen-man presidium elected on factional as distinct from territorial lines (which favoured the left). As usual the tactics of demonstrative withdrawal proved to be self-defeating, and the maximalists could chalk up a success – although it was not long before the protesters felt that honour had been assuaged and returned to the fray.

The delegates then set about discussing the main political question of the day : how should power be distributed in the new soviet order? During the course of this debate (on 12 November) the Left SRs took three steps which alarmed their Bolshevik allies : first they voted not to hear an address by Lenin;[9] then they suggested that Chernov, who unexpectedly appeared in the hall, should be elected honorary chairman; finally they split over the question whether the sitting executive members should be given a full or consultative vote. Amidst scenes of hubbub, the delegates first ruled by 164 votes to 134 that the discussion of this point was inadmissible, and then divided 155 to 137 (with 6 abstentions) in favour of a formula which did indeed deprive their former leaders of full voting rights. These political pirouettes taxed some of the soldier deputies' patience. Under the impact of an announcement that the Entente Powers were threatening action if the Bolshevik regime concluded a separate armistice, they delivered an ultimatum of their own : they would not leave the hall until the question of power had been settled.

This forced the hands of the squabbling socialist politicians and led to the compromise formalized on 15 November (see above, p. 321). Under its terms a provisional executive hastily elected by the congress, 108 strong, was to join the 108 men who comprised the CEC; other representatives were to be added from the armed forces' organizations (100) and trade unions (50), so converting the CEC into a body comprising three unequal blocs, each representing one segment of the 'toiling' population; this assembly was to control the actions of the government (that is the CPC), which was itself to be broadened. At first glance this looked like a triumph for common sense and the principle of parity. This no doubt was how it was perceived by most of the delegates to the extraordinary peasant congress as they marched off to the Smolny Institute, to the strains of a military band, there to celebrate the merger with fitting ceremonies. In fact the settlement did not impose any restrictions upon the Bolsheviks' freedom of action but on the contrary gave them added prestige : thanks to the actual or imminent presence of the Left SRs in both main government organs, they no longer had to suffer the stigma of single-party rule and could appear as champions of the entire 'revolutionary masses'.

Although the compromise stated that the government should be a broad coalition 'from the Popular Socialists to the Bolsheviks inclusive',[10] it was a serious blow to the moderates, who had absented themselves from the congress (for the third time) while the decision was being taken. They were too weak to prevent the merger, but they could at least have kept up pressure upon the malleable mass of Left SR deputies. That all was not lost is evident from the fact that on 17 November one resolution went through by the margin of a single vote.[11]

The topic under discussion on this occasion was the date for the convocation of the second *regular* congress of peasant deputies. The scene was being set for the next round in the battle, which began on 26 November. It found the contestants less evenly matched than before. The right-wingers' morale had been sapped by their setback at the earlier congress and by other forceful measures taken to consolidate the dictatorship. According to a report submitted by the congress credentials commission on 1 December there were 796 authorized delegates, of whom 511 were entitled to vote; of these 305 were described as right-wing or centre SRs, 350 as Left SRs, and 91 as Bolsheviks; 44 had no party affiliation.[12] The balance between soldiers and civilians seems to have been rather more favourable to the latter than it had been at the previous gathering,[13] but there was no doubt which of the two groups would prove to be the stronger. This disproportion was deliberately contrived, since the delegates were elected on the basis of one for every 20–25,000 soldiers as against one for every 150,000 peasants. There was also a wide disparity in the representation of different regions of the country; the organizers had an interest in keeping down the number of delegates from the outlying regions, who were likely to be more conservative. (However, Saratov province, with 224 representatives, was over-represented.) In many cases, perhaps the majority, the delegates were chosen in *ad hoc* fashion rather than by duly constituted provincial or district assemblies.

These irregularities naturally aroused the indignation of the moderate leaders. The exchanges were very heated and at one moment the delegates came close to using their fists. The rights and wrongs of the argument are impossible to determine. On one hand, it was certain that this gathering had no good claim to be regarded as representative of the peasants as a whole, or even of those who had set up soviets (of which, as we have seen, there were about twelve hundred at the county and district level). On the other hand, those delegates could claim to speak for some of the most militant elements in the country, and there was no mistaking their support for the government's peace policy. This was the strongest card in the left-wing leaders' hand, and they naturally made the most of it.

After the usual battle over the composition of the presidium, which resulted in a narrow victory for Spiridonova over Chernov, the substantive debates began with a consideration of the outgoing executive's record. Martyushin and Chernov presented reasoned justifications of their conduct, as did a spokesman for its radical minority. The left-wingers wanted a resolution passed which explicitly condemned the old leadership for its 'compromising' policies. They would probably have had their way at once had it not been for the Bolsheviks' ill-considered decree of 28 November declaring the Kadets 'enemies of the people' and for the subsequent arrest of democratic politicians.[14] These body blows against the prospective Constituent Assembly were an affront to the middle-of-the-road deputies, and on 2 December the congress resolved, by 359 votes to 321, to protest against them and demand that the Assembly be allowed to meet without hindrance. In response to this unexpected challenge first Lenin and then Trotsky hurried to the rostrum in an effort to appease the throng. Lenin, adopting a defensive tone, assured his listeners that the government considered itself responsible to the soviets and would inform them of every move it made, but he refused to make any concessions over the Constituent Assembly and was interrupted by 'cries of distrust and indignation'. On the following day Trotsky was likewise greeted with shouts of 'down with the guillotiniste',[15] at which point the Bolshevik deputies, followed by the Left SRs, strode from the hall. On 4 December Spiridonova managed to reunite the two halves of the congress and had the debate on the Constituent Assembly reopened, with the object of reversing the vote taken two days earlier. The moderates asserted that the move was *ultra vires* and demanded that the congress presidium be reformed, in accordance with their original suggestions, in such a way as to reflect the deputies' territorial distribution rather than their factional affiliation. On this issue they once again found themselves in a minority and the schism became final.

The two sections of the congress continued to meet separately for several days, each claiming to be the sole legitimate body and endeavouring to wean away deputies from the other. The left-wing group could play this game more successfully than their rivals, since they were better organized, more confident of their popular support, and could appeal to the soldiers by invoking the armistice signed on 2 December. Nine days later those deputies were forcibly dispersed.[16]

The left-wing section of the congress had concluded its business the previous day. One of its last acts was to pass a strongly worded resolution condemning the old executive for its 'criminal' policy. Its successor, headed by Spiridonova,[17] was little more than a fiction and was destined to have a brief life, for at the same time arrangements were put in hand for the *next* congress of peasant deputies – the third in the line of 'regular' peasant congresses. The representatives to this gathering were not to be elected at mass meetings in the localities, as had been done before the November congresses, but were chosen from among those present at this meeting of the majority faction. In other words, the Bolshevik and Left SR delegates to the second congress simply extended their own mandate. This was a sign of growing contempt for constitutional formalities. The new congress was to be convoked with a minimum of delay. The date was first fixed for 1 February, but then advanced to 12 January. The haste was necessary to overcome grass-roots resistance to the proposed merger with the third congress of workers' and soldiers' soviets, which was to meet simultaneously and give blanket endorsement to the government's actions during the last two months.[18]

The dissolution of the Constituent Assembly on 6 January removed the last major obstacle to the realization of these plans. Four days later force was used to disperse a peasant congress called by moderate leaders as a counterweight to the impending third congress and some of its organizers were arrested.[19] This reduced the Left SRs' freedom of manoeuvre. When the third congress of peasant soviets eventually opened (on 13 January), it transpired that they had less deputies than. the Bolsheviks – the reverse of the situation at the second congress in November.[20] Spiridonova at once went off to pay homage to the peasants' 'proletarian' masters. Addressing the soldier and worker delegates (who had begun their session three days earlier), she confessed that 'we SRs are guilty of darkening the consciousness of the popular masses by compelling them to regard the Constituent Assembly as their saviour.' The peasants, she averred, were convinced that the soviet form of government was superior and desired nothing better than to merge with their comrades; they had but one demand : that the law on land socialization be passed at the current session.

The merger went through by a unanimous vote on the following day. The central peasant executive took on a new guise as the 'peasant section' of the united all-Russian executive of workers', soldiers' and peasants' soviets, that is the CEC. This 'peasant section' was constructed on the principle of parity for the two parties in the coalition, but modified by the principle of territorial representation. Its central core consisted of ten Left SRs, ten Bolsheviks and one SR Maximalist to hold the balance; to these were added three representatives from each province and one from each army.[21] The Left SRs still hoped that this arrangement would allow them a certain autonomy, especially in regard to agrarian matters, but within a few days it transpired that even this freedom was to be very narrowly circumscribed.

To all appearances, during the next few weeks the main bone of contention between the Left SRs and the Bolsheviks was the terms of the land socialization law – a document solemnly enshrining the rights accorded to the peasants by Lenin's impromptu land decree three months earlier. However, it may be argued that this issue, although of considerable theoretical interest, really served to camouflage a much more significant struggle for power behind the scenes. For the Soviet government's policy towards the peasantry would be determined less by the provisions of any legal monument than by a more prosaic factor : namely, who controlled the organs implementing that policy, the Bolsheviks or the Left SRs? Not surprisingly, the members of the latter party, idealistic revolutionaries that they were, failed to appreciate the political realities of their situation. While they concentrated on winning concessions from their allies on the phrasing of particular clauses in the land socialization law, they were being winkled out of the key positions they needed to control if that law were ever to be translated into practice.

To appreciate this point we have first to consider the theoretical implications. When Spiridonova demanded that the law be passed at once – for which she was loudly cheered by the assembled deputies to the third congress of workers' and soldiers' soviets – she was covertly inviting them to support the Populist programme of socialization against the Bolshevik programme of nationalization. One may doubt whether many of those present appreciated the subtle distinction between these terms, which was apparent only to those initiated into the intricacies of socialist doctrine. What was at stake here was the role of the State in the new agrarian order. The Left SRs thought that in a socialist society power should lie with the local communities (or at least with rural soviets acting in close liaison with them); the central authorities should issue guidelines to help these elected local organs redistribute the land, but thereafter should leave them more or less to their own devices. Any inequalities that resulted would be corrected by the peasants themselves as they saw fit, in accordance with their communal ways of thinking; even if the peasants decided to maintain individual proprietorship, the State should not intervene unless this infringed the rights of other communities. In short, 'rural toilers' were to enjoy the widest possible scope for independent development.

This vague libertarian ideology ran counter to the fundamental tenets of Bolshevism that the interests of the proletariat, as interpreted by its 'vanguard', must come first. The peasants were under an obligation to help the industrial workers in their forward march; they could not of themselves create socialism. The new economic order was to be established first in the towns, and then would spread outwards to the countryside as the class war within the peasantry got under way. For the proletarian State to legislate on behalf of the peasantry as a whole, or to attempt to regulate relations between the two antagonistic classes that were forming in the countryside, would be to renounce Marxism, to hold up the course of historical development, and to pander to the proprietorial instincts of the petty bourgeoisie. The law could, however, be amended in such a way as to incorporate provisions consonant with Bolshevism: in particular, the development of collective farms on former landlords' estates, which should serve as a model of socialism for the individualistic peasants of the vicinity. This meant coming to a compromise with the Left SRS. As in all such bargains, the Bolsheviks should strive to ensure that the least possible harm was done to the interests of the proletarian State and the prospects of Marxist-style revolution in the countryside. According to Krupskaya, Lenin said privately 'we must find a little handle which will enable us to sew up in our own fashion the Populist idea of socialization.'[22]

Thus the Bolsheviks were none too enthusiastic about implementing a land law whose main provisions they considered at best as utopian and at worst as likely to bolster the position of the 'kulaks'. They hoped that 'life itself', in the shape of the class struggle within the village, would provide its own corrective – and sought to assist this process in every way they could. The Left SR leaders, and in particular the PC of Agriculture, A.L. Kolegayev, took their legislative work seriously. They saw the measure as a major step forward to a socialist agrarian order. In more practical terms it would serve as a means of helping the peasants to carry out the 'black repartition' in an organized way. So far as possible the inequalities that were bound to arise from the actions of individual communities might be evened out by setting minimum norms of landholding per household.[23] This was why the Left SRS wanted the draft of the land socialization law to be discussed at length by the third congress of soviets, so that its provisions should become as widely known as possible; in this way the delegates, on returning to their constituencies, would then be able to guide the work of the local soviets (and their land departments) in implementing the law. It has been argued that they even schemed to achieve this by flooding the congress with persons sympathetic to their point of view,[24] but this overestimates their readiness to emulate the manipulative techniques that came so naturally to their Bolshevik allies, who had no desire for such a general debate.

Had the Left SRS really sought to outmanoeuvre the Bolsheviks, as Lutsky suggests, a convenient instrument lay close at hand. This was the congress of land committees, held in Petrograd simultaneously with the third congress of soviets, in which the Left SRS formed the strongest faction.[25] At its first session on 17 January they engineered a fusion with the peasant section of the third congress of soviets;[26] nevertheless they were unable to impose their views. The following evening, when the joint congress met to hear Kolegayev present the draft of the land socialization law, Sverdlov promptly proposed that it be shunted into a commission without further debate. This motion was defeated and a discussion ensued which highlighted the differences between the Populist and Marxist approaches. Bolsheviks praised the proposed state farms as a harbinger of the future collectivist agrarian order; SRS criticized them as urban outposts in the countryside, a latent threat to the communal way of life. Only the first nineteen articles were approved by the congress.

The remaining 'details' were then worked out behind closed doors. In such circumstances Lenin had little difficulty in persuading his Left SR interlocutors, Kolegayev and A.M. Ustinov, to make concessions.[27] The final text included an ambiguously worded provision which allowed the soviets (that is to say the state power) to expropriate land for non-agricultural purposes. Collective farms were to be given priority in the allocation of land and were mentioned in several other clauses as well.[28] These exchanges, which at one point nearly led to a breakdown of the talks, put a heavy strain on relations between the Bolsheviks and their allies. Within less than a month they had parted company for good. The final breach came over the Brest-Litovsk peace treaty, but the main point at issue lay closer to hand: the relation between the dictatorship and the peasant masses for whom the Populist leaders claimed to speak.

The defeat of the Left SRS, even more than that of the moderate socialists and democrats, was due less to political repression than to skilful manoeuvring. Their ideological misperceptions hastened their demise. True to their inherited beliefs, they continually inveighed against the 'counter-revolutionary menace', although in retrospect there is little doubt that their most dangerous foes were their Bolshevik partners, who sought a complete monopoly of power for their own party. The civil war was to drive the lesson home. Even in terms of casualties the Left SRS suffered as much at the hands of the Reds as of the Whites.[29] When open political action ceased to be possible they turned to conspiracy and terror. Such a course could have only two possible outcomes : execution by the Cheka or enforced conversion to the victors' cause.

During the immediate post-October period, when solid organizational work was still possible, the Left SRs devoted much less attention to such matters than did the Bolsheviks. This was partly because they were so convinced of the veracity of their revolutionary ideals that activities of this kind seemed humdrum and superfluous. They were united more by a common emotional state than by common ideological principles. Perhaps the Left SRs would in time have built up a ramified organizational structure, but time was short and before they could do so they had been outwitted and devoured.

THIRTY-THREE *Taming the Peasant Organizations: the Base*

IT IS MUCH harder to reconstruct the *Gleichschaltung* of peasant organizations in rural areas than it is to establish what happened to those at the centre. Contemporary publicists took relatively little interest in such matters, and the truth lies buried in countless local archives.[1] In general it may be said that five significant developments took place, the effect of which was complementary.

First, a large number of new base organizations came into existence at the village and district level, some of which were formed spontaneously while others owed their origin to activists from outside the rural milieu.

Second, the intermediate-level bodies, such as county soviet executives, passed under the control of maximalist elements favourable to the ruling coalition.

Third, these agencies sought, with varying degrees of zeal, to eliminate or bring under their wing all other organs of authority within their territory; they also set up new bodies, either regular (soviet departments, land committees) or irregular (Red guard bands, RCS, initiative groups and so on). In the process congresses of peasant deputies might be called, but their representative character was often doubtful.

Fourth, efforts were made to merge rural soviets at all levels but the lowest with their urban counterparts.

Fifth, there was increasing hierarchical subordination : the core organs of provincial soviets received directives from various central agencies (the CPC, the PCs of Supply, Internal Affairs and Agriculture) and themselves issued commands to county and district executives. By the spring of 1918 there existed a rudimentary but coherent structure of authority covering most rural areas then under Soviet control.

We may begin by examining the key role played in rural organization by the individual variously referred to in the sources as 'commissar', 'agitator' or 'instructor' – in short, an emissary from the towns, or more frequently from some military or naval unit. We have already met these men in other capacities, as instigators of radical land reform and as collectors of food supplies. It would be artificial to distinguish too narrowly between the different kinds of activity in which they engaged, although one should emphasize that the success of their mission depended very largely upon their ability as organizers.

During the winter of 1917–18 tens of thousands of individuals streamed back to the villages, partly on their own initiative and partly at the behest of one or other of the new authorities. According to incomplete data, between October 1917 and June 1918 4,700 'agitator-organizers' and 1,250 'commissars' left the two cities of Petrograd and Moscow alone on such tasks; the total for the whole country has been put at 47,550.[2] We may divide these emissaries into two principal categories. One, the most numerous and the least sophisticated, consisted of demobilized soldiers or unemployed workmen. To most such men 'soviet power' meant little more than peace and land reform. They operated mainly at the village or district level and had but intermittent contact with senior authorities. The other category comprised persons with more political experience – 'commissars' in the narrower sense of the term, who based themselves on the county town or provincial capital and kept in closer touch with developments at the national level. By and large their influence was likely to be greater than that of ordinary agitator–organizers, although the latter might well be in closer touch with popular aspirations.

In either case these men did much as they pleased, since the central authorities had not yet created any machinery for controlling them.

Some of them completed questionnaires from the CEC's agitation department with details of the actions they had taken. Others compiled written reports for the PC of Internal Affairs' confidential surveys of the political situation.[3] But only a few emissaries took such formalities seriously. Some of them were illiterate; many were suspicious of the centralizing tendencies manifested by the new regime; finally, communications were difficult and most emissaries were continually on the move. It was only in the spring of 1918 that they began to be assigned to a particular locality and to acquire a semi-permanent territorial base[4] – until they were mobilized into the Red Army and posted elsewhere.

Some idea of the mentality of emissaries of the first type and of the problems they faced can be gleaned from a so-called 'handbook-catechism' compiled early in 1918 for the use of soldiers returning to their villages.[5] Its message was simple: organization was the principal means of consolidating 'soviet power'.

> Each soldier comrade should understand that, on returning home from the trenches at the front, he and his fellows should occupy other trenches, as it were, in the districts of his own province. We say this for purposes of comparison.... A village is like a company at the front, a district is like a battalion, a county is like a regiment, a province is like a division, and so on. Just as the whole Russian army at the front and in the rear had its soldiers' organizations in which the men ran their own affairs, so [similar] organizations must be set up throughout the whole region.[6]

The military terminology was by no means inappropriate. These bands of returning soldiers often saw themselves, or were seen by their new chiefs, as an occupation force in potentially hostile territory.

On arriving at his destination, the neophyte activist was advised first 'to look around and ask your neighbours what is going on in the village, in the whole area.' For instance, had the population heard of the land socialization law? 'Find out what kind of people are working [politically] in the region and *whom they are for*, which party they belong to.' His second step should be 'to make a note of those peasants in the village who are more alert, more resourceful and more impoverished.'[7] Even if there were only two or three such persons, they should be taken aside and given rudimentary political instruction ('tell them ... about the Bolshevik party, how it stands firmly for the people, and about the other parties, how they deceive the people with promises. . . .'). This oral agitation was to be reinforced by pamphlets and newspapers, whereupon 'they will see the whole truth'.

The third step was to call a meeting of the village assembly. The agitator was advised to remain in the background, letting the villagers express their own views 'and just helping them when necessary'. But he should make certain that they chose a chairman and a secretary, 'so that everything is above board, as in the meetings of your unit', and that they passed 'a business-like resolution, so as to get on with the [land reform] right away'. Last but not least, he was to manage the elections. 'First and foremost, get the village assembly to decide that your own men, the bednyaks [poor peasants], occupy all elective positions and chase out (re-elect) all the kulaks who have got in.' The agitator himself and his 'resourceful comrades', it was suggested, might well figure among those elected. Thereupon the executive 'should proceed to administer the whole village, sweeping away all the old authorities'; one of its first functions was to recruit volunteers for the Red Army.[8]

The handbook-catechism is silent as to what the activist should do if the village assembly rejected his proposals, but it does not take much imagination to envisage the next step: to employ external force. He was advised to contact neighbouring activists, so that together they might perform at the district level the same operation that each had already carried out in his village. The object was to cover the whole region with a network of organizations loyal to the new regime. It is interesting that the writer did not expect such low-level emissaries to concern themselves with affairs on the provincial plane, still less to enter into any direct relationship with the central authorities: this was the business of the 'commissars'.

Many of those who followed this simple catechism, expecting that the village would readily submit to persuasion and manipulation in the manner suggested, found that the peasants did not automatically accept the new regime as the legitimate successor to the old. Their cautious and guarded attitude is plain from the formal resolutions adopted at village assemblies – even though these texts were drawn up on their behalf by activists. The inhabitants of Grudinin (Sychev county, Smolensk province) were typical in linking support for 'soviet power' with a favourable reference to the Constituent Assembly. Their resolution stated: 'we demand freedom of action for our socialist parties, in particular for the Bolsheviks.'[9] The phrasing was almost sibylline. The Bolsheviks could be pleased that they were singled out, yet the peasants of Grudinin clearly saw them only as one party among several; what they wanted was a coalition of all left-wing groups. It is of course possible that the resolution was simply dictated by an activist of Left SR sympathies, but it undoubtedly reflected a widespread sentiment.[10]

The misunderstandings between town and country are evident from some activists' reports. D.A. Alekseyev, a workman sent to Voronetsk district (Opochka county, Pskov province), where he became deputy chairman of the district committee, wrote that 'with the aid of front-line soldiers, of whom there are plenty, and the village poor' he had organized a number of meetings to explain the purposes of the new government, but that these had often gone on until late at night because 'many questions were not clear to the peasants'; for this he blamed the nefarious influence of merchants, priests and independent farmers.[11] V.I. Ganin, a soldier who had returned to his native village in Morshansk county, Tambov province (its very name, Staraya Gryaznaya or 'Old Dirty', proclaimed its backwardness) wrote to the Petrograd soviet that the population trusted the SRs and was hostile to the Bolsheviks. For him the whole question was one of publicity : 'we beg you to send some Bolshevik leaflets ... so that we may open the people's eyes and they may know who does them good and who does them harm.'[12] Here the central authorities could at least take comfort in the simple piety of the activist concerned. More discouraging was a report from an emissary operating in Vileyki county (Vilna province), published in *Izvestiya* on 4 January. 'The peasants regard the socialist parties, and especially the Bolsheviks unsympathetically. Dark forces are spreading among them rumours that the Bolsheviks want everyone to eat out of a common pot and similar absurdities. These rumours are to blame for the peasants' mistrust.'[13]

Rumour did indeed play a part in determining the attitudes of barely literate country folk, but this explanation was scarcely adequate. Much of the trouble stemmed from the excessive zeal these men often displayed. Dealing with peasants required tact, forbearance and sympathetic understanding – all qualities in short supply among these politicized workers, sailors and soldiers, who were inclined to see counter-revolutionaries at every turn and to ride roughshod over local opinion. To treat such elected bodies as the district zemstvo, supply organs, cooperatives and so forth (and even some allegedly kulak-dominated soviets) as 'bourgeois' and to dissolve them out of hand was to offend against elementary notions of right and wrong. The arbitrary actions undertaken by emissaries from outside the village community provoked resentment among ordinary peasants who were otherwise well disposed towards a regime which, as they saw it, had given them title to the confiscated land.

Naturally the situation varied greatly from area to area. Things were particularly bad in Petrograd province, since for geographical reasons it was the most exposed to the ministrations of these zealots. There was a fairly large number of district soviets here, most of which followed the lead of the Left SRs. This was not to the taste of the (Bolshevik-controlled) Petrograd soviet, which in mid-December launched a campaign to purge these organs of allegedly 'class-alien' elements by holding new elections, from which those whose credentials as 'toilers' were suspect were to be excluded. In those districts where such action was taken the Bolsheviks increased their share of the poll from 17 to 37 per cent, but were nevertheless unable to win control of the provincial congress of peasant soviets, which when it met on 24 February still had a Left SR majority.[14] It seems that this political battle did not improve the rural soviets' popular standing, if one may judge by a description of affairs in the province published in a Menshevik paper. 'The strenuous efforts to infuse the life of the whole region with soviets, right down to the district and village level, in practice means that any bunch of individuals, often mere boys or deserters, or else workers from outside and the like, can form themselves into a soviet and begin to administer the locality, without taking any account of the peasants who live there.' The re-elected soviets (or rather, executives), this informant continued, had no local roots and were looked upon as 'a new set of bosses' who interfered with everything but to no good effect; and in response to popular pressure they had been obliged to rescind some of their more obnoxious orders.[15]

In other provinces of the west and north-west, too, maximalist elements (mainly soldiers) often tried to 'sovietize' the rural adminis-tration in short order, not shrinking from the use of coercive methods. In Drissen county (Vitebsk province) it was reported on 17 February that soviets had been set up in all seventeen districts and that the zemstva, land committees and other elective bodies had been done away with – yet the account goes on to state that there was no food to be had and that the local population were starving.[16] It comes as no surprise to learn, from another source, that the revamped soviets in this county were elected 'at meetings attended by an insignificant number of participants'; in some districts only thirty out of the two to three thousand electors were considered fit to vote; some of the persons chosen were described as criminals who kept back money they received from the sale of timber and cattle; voting was by show of hands, which made a charade of the electoral process.[17]

In many non-black-soil provinces where the local peasant soviet leaders favoured the Left SRS rather than the Bolsheviks, they tried to postpone a direct confrontation with local non-soviet agencies (zemstva, supply committees, cooperatives) for as long as they could. In view of the famine this was no more than common sense, although to some zealots it smacked of subversion. In Tver province a congress was held on 4–8 January which had a characteristically broad composition. Called by moderate elements in the zemstva, it was attended by leaders of the district soviets and also by individuals chosen at village assemblies, about two hundred persons in all. The upshot was a decision to take over the zemstva gradually, as the soviet agencies developed their apparatus and learned to cope with administrative tasks.[18] Further information on the process of sovietization in Tver province is provided by recently published sources. The maximalists first 're-elected' the bureau of the provincial peasant executive and then called an extraordinary peasant congress (3 December), which resolved on a merger with the urban soviet. During the next month congresses were held in several counties (Korchev, Bezhetsk, Novotorzhok, Vyshniy Volochek); simultaneously a number of districts declared their allegiance to the new authorities. In some counties such congresses were evidently thought unnecessary. In others efforts to disperse the zemstvo provoked resistance. This was the case in Bezhetsk, where commissar F. Skvortsov was shot as he was in the very act of announcing dissolution of the local zemstvo board (20 January). In Vesegon county, in the relatively remote north-eastern part of the province, a revolt broke out five days later, which curiously enough was led by the local (joint) soviet. The Cheka at once took matters in hand. Latsis wired the garrison at Krasnyy Kholm: 'Send immediately all available troops to Vesegon to suppress the White Guardists and restore soviet power. Act with all severity.' Soon came the report : 'Order restored in Vesegon by Red guards and 299th reserve regiment. Soviet of deputies [re-]elected. Zemstvo liquidated. . . .'[19]

The situation was comparable in Perm province. Hundreds of activists streamed from the mines and metallurgical works of the Urals into the surrounding villages. Here they agitated for re-election of the rural soviets, which had in the main hitherto supported the PSR. At a province-wide congress which opened on 15 January only a fraction of the delegates joined the radical leaders when they seceded. In many areas the zemstva enjoyed strong local support, for in this overwhelmingly peasant province they had long been famous for their progressive policies. As a Soviet historian puts it, 'in a number of counties and districts it was only possible to establish soviet power and liquidate the zemstva by relying on armed detachments of Red guards.' On 24 January a three-hundred-man squad from the Lysven iron works and Kizelov mines occupied the building in which the Solikamsk county zemstvo was meeting and forced the deputies to disperse; the men then moved on northward to Cherdyn, where on 2 February they repeated their exploits. The last county zemstvo to hold out was that in Orshansk, which was suppressed by another Red guard unit on 20 February. Shortly afterwards the new-born district zemstva followed the county ones into limbo, to be superseded by several hundred district soviets in which maximalist elements called the tune.[20]

In the Central Industrial region matters were somewhat different, in that the rural areas had a more vigorous natural link with the factory settlements scattered in their midst. The town of Ivanovo-Voznesensk, for instance, now the proud capital of a new *guberniya,* had but recently developed out of a village of skilled artisans. Many peasants depended on the textile mills for their livelihood. Moreover, there seem to have been no significant differences in this region between the Bolsheviks and the Left SRs, who collaborated smoothly against the moderates.[21] The latter were squeezed between the upper and the nether millstone. In Moscow province the peasant executive, led by Ya.S. Oleynik, backed the right-wing SRs, but on 9–10 December the maximalist elements called a congress of worker and soldier soviets in the province, to which were invited, as a kind of rustic decoration, peasant representatives from ten counties. After an address by Inessa Armand, a leading Bolshevik feminist and party worker, this assembly decided to organize new elections to the local peasant soviets and to merge them with those in the towns. For this purpose it set up a core body (bureau) which called another congress, apparently more representative, for 17–18 December. The radicals, predictably enough, had a majority; equally predictably, the moderates walked out, and those who stayed behind elected a new executive which confirmed the decision to merge. Oleynik and his supporters made a last-ditch effort to reverse the trend of events. On 9 January they called a congress to protest at the dissolution of the Constituent Assembly, but their appeal received only lukewarm support, for by this time most of the county peasant soviets had passed under the control of the Bolsheviks and Left SRs.[22]

The Central Agricultural region differed in that it was a traditional PSR stronghold. Although many activists had swung sharply to the left they had not deserted the Populist camp, so that in the rural areas, to an even greater extent than in the towns, Bolshevism could establish itself only after a hard-fought struggle : as late as 1920–1 the peasants of Tambov province rose up in a major revolt. The first rounds in this conflict were fought already in November 1917. Especially in Saratov and Voronezh provinces there was some intricate manoeuvring by local politicians for control of the peasant soviet machinery. Since the district organs were solidly pro-SR, the Bolsheviks had to try to capture them from above rather than from below. In Saratov V.P. Antonov-Saratovsky and his colleagues organized a province-wide congress of soviets early in December which seems to have consisted mainly of soldiers quartered in the town.

> Through the military section and the local peasant soviet garrison were selected some 200 to 300 soldiers, with the calculation that each soldier [would represent] his own local district.... It was clear that the easiest way of getting Bolshevik-inclined delegates into the congress was to make use of such soldiers who were linked to their districts.[23]

This congress challenged the authority of the more genuinely representative body, which remained loyal to the PSR. It issued a declaration endorsing Bolshevik policy, proclaimed the local urban soviet the supreme organ within the province and chose a forty-man executive which promptly merged with that of the workers' and soldiers' soviet based in Saratov, 'thus acknowledging the hegemony of the revolutionary proletariat of the provincial capital'. However, a few months later, when the area passed under the authority of the democratic government based on Samara ('Komuch'), the peasant soviet re-emerged as a PSR bailiwick.[24]

In nearby Voronezh events took a rather similar course. On 4 December local right and centre SR leaders summoned their peasant supporters to a congress. Attended by 552 deputies, this took a line strongly critical of the Soviet government. A number of the delegates were treated roughly by soldiers from the garrison, who followed the Bolsheviks. Relying mainly on this military element, the maximalists then convoked a peasant congress of their own (28 December); this elected a twelve-man executive which duly merged with that of the urban (workers' and soldiers') soviet. The SRs countered by holding a rival assembly at Valuyki, a county town where their party was reputed to have twenty thousand members. The two gatherings coexisted uneasily for a few days during which the SR delegates were exposed to heavy pressure from the soldiers, who sealed their victory by electing a new provincial executive and then set up a network of county and district soviets.[25]

As these examples show, peasant organizations at district and village level were as a rule subjected to simultaneous pressure from two quarters. The low-level activists' propaganda was reinforced by administrative measures by county or provincial authorities whose claim to represent the rural population was dubious at best. Frequently these political manoeuvres were supervised by senior-level 'commissars' whose duties included the convocation of provincial and county soviet congresses.[26] The chief tasks of these gatherings were to proclaim formally the establishment of 'soviet power' and to push through the merger of local soviet organizations in such a way as to ensure the supremacy of the urban (and military) element.

The progress of these mergers would repay detailed study. The global figures show that of the soviets represented at the first three All-Russian congresses (June 1917, October 1917, January 1918) the number of bodies which claimed peasant representation rose from 76 to 119 and then to 162; this was respectively 25, 30 and 44 per cent of the total.[27] However, one has to bear in mind that at these congresses the more militant organizations were over-represented, and it was they that tended to be the most energetic in promoting mergers; moreover, some ostensibly 'peasant' organizations really consisted of soldiers (who might of course be of peasant extraction). These data need to be broken down according to geographical area and hierarchical status.

Unificatory tendencies were strongest in the west and in areas closest to the major industrial centres; they were also strongest in the upper levels of the hierarchy. The provincial soviets seem to have become joint (tripartite) organizations already in the autumn of 1917; however, this amounted to little more than a change of labels, designed to present these essentially urban bodies as more broadly based than they were. Mergers at county level had more substance. In Petrograd, Moscow, Tver, Vladimir and Nizhniy Novgorod provinces almost all county soviets had been fused by November 1917, and by the end of March 1918 this process had been virtually completed throughout Soviet-held territory.[28] At the district level matters were more difficult. Where the population consisted almost wholly of peasants, the merger could be no more than a formality. There were far fewer district soviets, relative to the total number of districts, than there were county soviets in relation to the total number of counties. By March 1918 the former are believed to have numbered 2,882.[29] This was nearly three times as many as in October 1917; they existed in about half the total number of districts in Soviet-held territory (between 28 and 33 provinces). These were in most cases feeble organizations, wielding much less authority than the village communes, whose prestige had been enhanced by their role in redistributing the land. Even where district soviets were elected by universal suffrage of 'toilers', as was still the general rule, they had yet to strike root in the rural milieu. For this reason it was relatively easy for the Bolsheviks to give them a 'worker-peasant' label as an outward symbol of identification with the new regime. This simply meant that the activists who ran them were committed to the principle of proletarian hegemony.

Precisely because the district (and village) soviets were such a weak reed to lean upon, the Bolsheviks were obliged to seek a substitute for them once the civil war intensified in the spring of 1918. The so-called 'committees of the village poor' (*kombedy* : see above, p. 432) were set up by an edict of 11 June 1918.[30] Their title was ambiguous and evidently reflected differences within the party leadership as to their durability, purpose and composition. Those who shared the concerns of the economic controllers were sceptical as to their value, whereas ideologically minded zealots regarded them with considerable enthusiasm; Lenin himself adopted a vacillating, 'centrist' position, veering to the right as the year progressed. At one extreme was the view that the committees were purely temporary organs designed to meet a specific emergency; they were to be auxilliaries to the regular supply apparatus with the explicit purpose of helping them extract surplus grain from their fellow-villagers; for this reason they should be open to anyone who was not a known 'kulak' or speculator. At the other extreme was the view that the committees had a permanent function to fulfil as organs of 'class struggle' among the peasantry; their economic role was accordingly seen as subordinate to their socio-political and ideological one as sword-bearers of Communism in the hostile 'petty-bourgeois' milieu; it followed that membership in them should be confined to those elements which possessed the proper proletarian class instincts, namely poor peasants (*bednyaki*) and landless labourers (*batraki*).

The text of the 11 June decree suggested that the right-wing line was the one which the party and government chiefs wished the committees to follow. However, in practice their activities naturally took a left-wing course. All too frequently they became political organizations *par excellence* which carried out a multiplicity of tasks, from purging the local soviet to recruiting soldiers for the Red Army. Their members saw themselves as scourges of the 'class enemy', whose identity they were themselves free to determine, and came to exercise an oppressive miniscule dictatorship within the village community. Forced to define its attitude towards this development, the leadership took the line that any 'excesses' or deviations from the proper path were due to the over-enthusiasm of local zealots. The problem was that it could not subject these committees to legal restraints without doing the same to other governmental agencies, including the Cheka. The only solution was to suppress them, and this step was duly taken at the end of 1918. Yet the erring members were not disowned, still less punished : they remained as a ginger group within the rural soviets. In fact they had performed an essential task in laying the basis of a permanent network of Communist party cells throughout rural Russia.

The number of such committees is difficult to discover with any degree of precision and estimates have varied considerably. In December 1918 a PC of Supply spokesman put it at 31,368; the figure has since gradually been raised as a result of detailed research, until one investigator reached a total of no less than 131,637 (in thirty-three provinces then under Soviet control).[31] This estimate is probably inflated by double counting, and it has to be remembered that many of these bodies were ephemeral. Their geographical density varied. They seem to have been most numerous in the Central Agricultural region (Orel, Tambov, Tula, Penza provinces), where the rural population was densely settled – and also in Vyatka, where it was not. The main reason was that they owed their existence to the initiative of urban emissaries, and these men were concentrated in regions thought to have a grain surplus available. Members of one supply detachment from Moscow operating in Orel province are said to have set up over fourteen hundred such committees; in Penza no fewer than four-fifths were organized 'with the help of Petrograd and Moscow workers'.[32]

Precisely because they were as a rule not genuinely indigenous institutions, they evoked a good deal of grass-roots opposition. Not just so-called 'kulaks' but many ordinary peasants regarded them as antagonistic to the interests of the community as a whole. Cases are recorded of village assemblies, and even district soviets, refusing to set up *kombedy*.[33] In other places the committees were set up, but instead of the elections to them being held on class lines, as the urban activists desired, all sections of the village community took part. This frustrated the main purpose behind the scheme, at least as these zealots saw it.[34] An investigation into approximately thirty-two hundred *kombedy* in five north-western provinces found that 17 per cent of them were irregular, in the sense that they did not represent the poorer peasants, while 21 per cent had been formed 'by appointment from above'.[35] One may assume that the proportion of irregular and externally imposed committees will have been higher in the black-soil zone, where Populist traditions were stronger and urban emissaries more numerous. It was here that these activists were most prone to take a left-wing line.[36]

Early in August Lenin offered a clarification of the vexed question 'who is a kulak?' It is arguable that he was seeking to limit excesses, under the impact of representations by senior supply officials; yet his action may have had the reverse effect. For what he did was to fix arbitrarily a global total of peasant households in each category : two million were declared to be 'kulaks' and therefore slated for liquidation ('merciless war against these kulaks! death to them!'); three million, reckoned as 'middle peasant' households were to be courted and not offended.[37] This was probably the first occasion when the leader of a modern State incited the populace to the social equivalent of genocide.[38] It is charitable to suppose that Lenin did not intend his words to be taken literally and was thinking in terms of selective killings designed to intimidate the survivors. (It was at this time that the Communist leaders, gripped by panic, launched what came to be called the 'Red terror'.)[39] A few days later, together with Supply commissar Tsurupa, he drafted a circular calling these committees 'revolutionary organs of *the whole* peasantry ... and not organs of the village proletarians alone'.[40] The committee-men were explicitly told not to dissolve rural soviets but only to purge them of 'counter-revolutionary' elements.

One suspects that activists were confused by these pronouncements and that the mass of peasants did not receive the message at all. Incidents of overt resistance multiplied throughout the summer and autumn of 1918, forcing the experiment to be brought to an end – or, to be more precise, directed into other channels. The reasons were various,[41] but probably the most important factor was the leaders' confidence that the Communist party and soviet agencies in the countryside had now been built up to a point where it was safe to rely on them. From the regime's point of view the *kombedy* could be said to have fufilled their purpose : they had stirred the disadvantaged elements from their lethargy and given them a stake in the new order. Whether for mundane reasons of self-interest (for instance fear of revenge by their victims) or for loftier motives, those who had been drawn into this struggle found it harder to turn back than to continue their careers as cadre members of the local soviet, if they could secure election to it, or as members of the district Communist party cell – and in many cases, of course, as both. 'We shall merge the *kombedy* with the soviets', Lenin explained to a gathering of these zealots; 'we shall turn the *kombedy* into soviets.'[42] The most energetic activists were put up as candidates in the soviet elections of February 1919, and with the party machine behind them the issue was seldom in doubt.[43]

At the end of 1917 the party's rural cadres had numbered a mere 2,400, grouped in 203 organizations; a year later the figures were 97,000 and 7,370 respectively.[44] This rapid growth meant that the county and district soviets could be kept under close party control. From July 1918 onwards they were purged of those professing allegiance to one or other of the non-Bolshevik parties, so that only the unaffiliated ('non-party') deputies remained. The latter were often pressed to declare themselves 'Communist sympathizers', which in practice meant accepting party discipline. The number of Communists and sympathizers in the soviets rose rapidly. Data collected in October 1918 showed that they had 81·4 per cent of the seats in 318 district soviets in the central provinces.[45] With a few exceptions executives were now staffed wholly by Communists (with a sprinkling of sympathizers). A new type of local leader was coming to the fore : men who had earned their spurs as Red Army soldiers in the civil war and who were accustomed to giving orders. If not as yet the 'iron-hard' Bolsheviks of popular legend, they were at least convinced centralizers. Their credo and value-system had much more in common with those of other Soviet functionaries than with those of the peasant population whence they had sprung. In Russia's rural administration, as in so much else, a new age had begun.

Epilogue

THE PARTY'S RURAL cadres gave the new *vlast'* a leverage over the countryside denied to any of the tsars. As Lenin explained at the eighth congress of the RCP(b) in March 1919, the policies adopted had been designed to neutralize a potentially hostile peasantry during the crucial months when the power struggle was being decided in the towns.[1] To use the military terminology now in vogue when discussing social relationships, the Communists had acquired a base in enemy territory whence they could launch fresh assaults as the occasion arose, and so gradually expand their influence until the whole multi-million peasant mass had been won over to the proletarian cause.

There was much evidence to support this sanguine view of the situation by the country's new leaders. The peasant organizations had lost their autonomy and had been brought under external control. The land reform gave the Soviet regime a trump card in its three-year struggle against the Whites. The latter came to be identified by many peasants with a restoration of the old order. The ambiguities and uncertainties in their agrarian policy lent themselves to exploitation by propagandists for the Reds, whose cause could plausibly be presented as that of the 'toiling masses' in town and country. In so far as the civil war was a contest for men's minds its outcome was seldom in doubt.

On the other hand this bitter struggle was accompanied on the Red side by violence on such a massive scale that many ordinary peasants were impelled to oppose the Bolshevik regime in defence of their vital interests. Having ejected the landed proprietors from their midst, the communally minded villagers had no desire to see their place taken by a new class of commissars appointed from above, who like their predecessors often treated rural folk with scornful arrogance and gave first priority to satisfying the demands of the state they served. The humble social origin of these men was no guarantee against such excesses : on the contrary, it was likely to heighten their ideological fervour and to lead them to take repressive action whenever they considered that peasant lethargy or obstruction threatened the interests of the proletarian dictatorship. Such measures naturally aroused feelings of resentment and bitterness, a reaction fortified by the peasant small-holders' natural anxiety about the future of the agrarian order established by the 'black repartition'. Would their gains be tolerated by a regime which made no secret of its fundamental opposition to private property and its determination to reshape society in accordance with Marxist principles?

During the civil war tens of thousands of peasants resisted the new order by force of arms. In the Ukraine guerilla warfare begun against the Central Powers in 1918 was later directed against the Russians, both Red and White. Many of these bands rallied to the leadership of the celebrated anarchist chieftain Nestor Makhno. The Soviet authorities also faced serious opposition in a number of other areas in the black-soil zone (notably Tambov province) as well as in western Siberia. Yet despite their genuinely popular character none of these peasant movements succeded in establishing a viable state order. Deprived of any external support and weakened by internal dissension, they all succumbed sooner or later to the assaults of the Red Army, reinforced by special Cheka units which gave no quarter to the defeated and demoralized rebels.[2]

Rather more successful was the passive resistance offered by a large number of peasant communities to 'soviet power' as it spread outwards to the periphery of the former empire. Already in 1917–18, as we have seen, the village had begun to turn inward upon itself. This tendency was accentuated as the civil war developed. Farmers cut down on the area they sowed to crop, partly from choice and partly from necessity, and reverted to a simple subsistence economy. They lacked any positive incentive to produce for the market, which scarcely existed. Money had lost all its value and private commercial exchanges were liable to be branded as 'speculative', with exemplary punishments being meted out to selected offenders. Fear of the heavy sanctions imposed upon defaulters led agricultural producers to comply with the demands of the supply authorities as best they could, but this did not mean that they accepted the basic assumptions that underlay their policy. The requisitioning of crops might be tolerated as an emergency measure, necessary to defeat the Whites, but there was no sympathy whatever for the view current among some urban zealots that strong-arm methods of this sort were desirable in themselves. As the civil war came to an end rural opinion turned decisively against the principles of 'war communism', which were widely regarded as unjust, irrational and counter-productive.

This resistance, both active and passive, was instrumental in persuading the party leadership to abandon forced requisitioning in March 1921 and to embark upon a series of concessions to peasant interests. The NEP was viewed by Lenin as an enforced strategic retreat. It was designed to give the regime time to consolidate its popularity in town and country before launching a new offensive against the capitalist influences that were deemed to prevail in the rural milieu. Many observers, both Communist and non-Communist, misconstrued the ambiguous and paradoxical situation created by the NEP. They believed that the party would be obliged to go even further along the road of compromise to the 'class enemy' until such time as it encompassed its own downfall. Émigrés with democratic (and especially Populist) sympathies hailed the policy shift as a victory for the individualistic small-holder, who had demonstrated plainly his aversion both to dictatorship and to state-imposed collectivism. This interpretation seemed plausible enough on one reading of the evidence. The peasants responded eagerly to the new system of material incentives; agricultural output rapidly recovered, reaching and then surpassing pre-war levels; most of the collective farms that had been set up during the civil war collapsed, whereas the cooperative movement went from strength to strength. Yet this was only one side of the coin. Simultaneously the ruling Communist party was tightening its hold upon the village. It maintained complete control over the information media, which were used to good propagandist effect. Although the peasantry had in fact become socially more homogeneous as a result of the revolution, regime spokesmen consistently proclaimed the opposite. The notion of an inexorable class conflict within the rural community appealed to some of the younger men, especially those who were disaffected and who sought to rise in the new Soviet hierarchy. The rural soviets were assiduously built up as a counterweight to the traditional peasant institutions, such as the *obshchina* and the Orthodox Church; as they expanded, they drew into their orbit a small but significant proportion of the rural population.

It was these cadres, aided by a new wave of emissaries from the towns, who from 1928 onwards would implement the policies associated with Stalin's 'great break': the imposition of harsh discriminatory measures against real or suspected kulaks, the enforcement of high delivery quotas for grain and other produce, and finally mass collectivization under duress.[3] During the period of the first Five-year Plan the peasants ceased to be an independent force in Soviet life and were ruthlessly subordinated to the interests of the socialist State. Collective farming, as it was interpreted under Stalin, became a means of extracting from the rural population most of the capital needed to finance rapid industrialization. Living standards in the countryside, although they improved in some respects, were deliberately kept well below urban levels. A pervasive system of police controls reached down to every farm, subjecting its members to intense psychological stress. During the so-called 'dekulakization' drive millions of innocents were arbitrarily seized and deported from their homes as potential enemies of the new order; many of them ended their days in the silent world of Gulag. Russia's traditional peasant culture died with them.

The fate of the proletariat was only slightly less tragic. After 1928 industrial workers were as liable as people in less favoured walks of life to suffer the penalties inflicted upon anyone who strayed from the accepted norms of Soviet public life. Yet under the NEP, and to some extent even after it had been abandoned, there was a psychological boost to be derived from belonging to the privileged group with which the proletarian State sought to identify itself. On the material side, by the last quarter of 1927 average real wages (including benefits) were officially said to have been 28·4 per cent higher than in 1913. The level was still low by international standards; moreover, there were wide differentials between workers in various branches of industry as well as between wage-earners and salaried employees. Nevertheless there was hope for further rapid improvement, and workers appreciated the various social services and educational facilities provided 'free' by the State. Unfortunately, with the advent of the planned economy urban incomes and living standards plummeted, and it was not until the early 1950s that 1928 wage levels were regained.[4] Furthermore, the Stalinist years witnessed the virtual elimination of such limited opportunities as had hitherto been available to the trade unions to defend their members' interests against those of the economic planners and managers. The propaganda organs emphasized that workers' highest obligation was to increase labour productivity and to help strengthen the socialist State, which allegedly embodied the general interest of the toiling masses and therefore should be given priority over the interests of any individual or group.

This argument was difficult to square with the existence of a new élite comprising party *apparatchiki*, army and police officers, economic managers and tame intellectuals – a social class or stratum defined, not by its relationship to the means of production, but by its access to the levers of power and influence. It would be an over-simplification to say that this group gained what the masses lost, for it suffered as much as any other during the bloody purges of the 1930s and its members never enjoyed freedom to pursue their sectional or professional interests. In the Stalinist political system the dictatorship made itself almost totally independent of social pressures from any quarter and could mould the nation's destiny as it thought fit.

Since this remarkable system still endures more than twenty years after the death of its architect, it may be regarded as the principal legacy of the Russian revolution of 1917. Any evaluation of this revolution's place in history must proceed from an awareness of the consequences to which it led : namely, the world's first experiment in totalitarian rule. The main features of such a regime, although familiar, are worth summarizing briefly here : the party in power suppresses all overt opposition from without or from within; it maintains strict control over all instruments of coercion and all information media; it mobilizes the entire populace in a continuous, infinite drive to attain certain goals of its own choosing; it prescribes both the pace of this advance and the means whereby it is to be attained; finally, it legitimizes its exercise of total power by reference to its ideological function, which is to provide authoritative guidance on every problem of the day.[5]

The question naturally arises whether this system of government emerged in Soviet Russia by chance or whether it was logically foreordained; and if the latter, at what point the course of events leading to it became irreversible. Since the evidence is inconclusive, every student of the question is entitled to hold his own views. Exponents of the role of free will in history may argue that there were numerous moments of crisis between 1914 and 1921 (and perhaps later still) when the apparently inexorable march towards ever greater centralism, élitism and moral cynicism might have been halted; and that the significance of fortuitous factors at many of these junctures should not be underrated. At the other extreme orthodox Soviet historians claim that every action taken by the Bolshevik leadership in carrying out the revolution and constructing socialism in the USSR has been in conformity with the objective laws of historical progress as defined by Marx and Lenin. The truth doubtless lies somewhere in the middle : the determinists' case cannot be proven, yet there does seem to be a certain logic in the unfolding of events. A dictatorial element was embedded in Leninism from its first appearance in 1902 (and arguably also in the radical tradition, both Russian and European, whence it sprang). The chances of an evolution towards dictatorship were augmented by Russia's entry into the First World War and then by the fall of the monarchy which plunged Russia into chaos and allowed Lenin's party to emerge as one of the principal contenders for power. They were enhanced immeasurably by the outcome of General Kornilov's attempt to reverse the leftward tide in August 1917 and then by the October insurrection itself, which led to the formation of a Bolshevik government resting on the soviets and other mass organizations. The relatively trouble-free extension of 'soviet power' to the rest of Russia enhanced the insurgent leaders' confidence that they were launched upon the correct course, and this view was hardened further by each victory in the civil war. In March 1921, when peace had returned, the ruling party had an opportunity to relax its exclusive hold on power, but instead it chose to move in the opposite direction and to make its dictatorship 'monolithic'. Finally, Stalin emerged – contrary to Lenin's wishes – as the leader best placed to succeed him on his death.

Each of these turning-points might be regarded as decisive; but perhaps the strongest claims can be made on behalf of the events of 1917–18 that have been the subject of this book. For it was in this period that the Bolshevik party first acquired a mass following. This meant that their intransigent, authoritarian style of thought and action communicated itself to large numbers of ordinary people, instead of being confined as heretofore to a small intellectual élite. This 'bolshevization of the masses' to some extent came about spontaneously : the soldiers' natural war-weariness fused with civilian demands for greater economic security, so creating a revolutionary climate favourable to the spread of apocalyptic expectations and a messianic sense of purpose. But it was also to some extent the product of conscious political action by a segment of the intelligentsia, which purveyed these ideas and emotions among the masses of the people. As early as March 1917 socialist politicians took charge of the mass organizations that sprang up and gave them a new direction; in many places these bodies actually owed their existence to intervention from above. The intellectual cadres who led such organs actively promoted their merger on a provincial, regional and ultimately nation-wide scale; simultaneously they sought to present them as the voice of the peasant millions as well. Although their representative character was often in doubt, these bodies were widely regarded as authentically 'democratic' and their popular appeal rivalled, indeed exceeded, that of the feeble Provisional Government. For a brief spell in the summer and autumn of 1917 the central soviet executives embodied the aspirations of hundreds of thousands of ordinary folk who for the most part had had no experience whatever of public affairs. They stood at the apex of a loosely organized structure of authority which had succeeded in its original function of mobilizing the masses – but for what?

No clear lead on this issue was forthcoming from the moderate socialist parties, whose leaders' attitude on all the burning questions of the day was ambiguous and contradictory. The Bolsheviks alone were schooled in the techniques of organizational manipulation and knew more or less what they wanted to achieve. In particular they were determined to bring all these mass bodies under the control of disciplined nuclei committed to the objectives of their own party. In the enthusiasm of the moment the differences between these objectives and those of the rank and file seemed trivial and evanescent. Yet they were fundamental. On the morrow of their *coup* the Bolsheviks used the soviets as a means of legitimating their party dictatorship. Those who sought to guard against arbitrary rule by keeping to constitutional practices within the soviet hierarchy were without difficulty outmanoeuvred, and all the other mass organizations – trade unions, factory committees, militia bands – were in their several ways obliged to serve the needs of the revolutionary regime. In this process the Bolsheviks (or more precisely, the Leninist Bolsheviks) acted resourcefully to silence or exclude dissidents, helped in many instances by the fact that most of their opponents preferred to yield rather than to fight and plunge the country into civil war. By the spring of 1918 the *Gleichschaltung* of the mass organizations was virtually complete except in some of the remoter rural areas and national minority regions. The Communists were masters of a ramified network of quasi-popular bodies which, although still poorly coordinated, rendered them valuable assistance in warding off the Whites and other opponents during the civil war. They could make use of this machinery for administrative, police or military tasks which bore only a formal resemblance to those for which it had been forged. Instead of being the architects of policy, the mass organizations became sounding-boards for decisions by the ruling oligarchy, an integral part of the new command structure.

This development, occurring as it were in the interstices of history, and scarcely regarded by contemporaries dazzled by events at the summit, goes far to explain the emergence of a political system which has been widely emulated or enforced in other lands and has yet to abandon its ambition to determine the destinies of mankind.

Notes

The full titles of books and journals appear in the Bibliography. Soviet historians are not obliged to specify the nature of the documents from which they quote and usually give only the archival reference. In such cases, when it seemed worth noting the fact, the abbreviation 'c.u.d.s.' (citing unidentified documentary source) has been added.

INTRODUCTION

1. The standard general work in English still remains W.H. Chamberlin, *The Russian Revolution, 1917–1921,* 2 vols, (New York 1935, repr. 1965).
2. The best history of the party is L.B. Schapiro, *The Communist Party of the Soviet Union* (London, New York 1960; rev. ed. 1970). A useful popular account of the Bolsheviks' fortunes up to their seizure of power is H. Shukman, *Lenin and the Russian Revolution* (London 1966). For the early history of the party see my *Rise of Social Democracy in Russia* (Oxford 1963), which may be supplemented by two Menshevik accounts now available in English: T. Dan, *The Origins of Bolshevism* (New York 1964; repr. 1970); S.M. Schwarz, *The Russian Revolution of 1905* (Chicago, London 1967). A. Rabinowitch provides a careful analysis of Bolshevik policy during the first months of 1917 in *Prelude to Revolution* (Bloomington, Ind., London 1968); a sequel is expected. Of the many biographies of Lenin now available in English, the most stimulating is A. Ulam, *The Bolsheviks* (New York, London, 1965).

3. For example, J.S. Curtiss, *The Russian Revolutions of 1917* (Princeton, NJ, London 1957) and, from a different standpoint, L. Trotsky, *Hist. Russ. Rev.* (London, New York 1932–3; several recent reprints). This tradition goes back to P.N. Milyukov, *Ist. vtoroy russ. revol.*, 3 pts (Sofia 1921–3).

4. 'State and Revolution in the Paris Commune, the Russian Revolution and the Spanish Civil War', *Sociol. Rev.*, 29 (1937), p. 67, cited by E. Kamenka, 'The Concept of a Political Revolution', in *Struggles in the State*, eds G.A. Kelly and C.W. Brown Jr (New York, London 1970), p. 118.

5. W.G. Rosenberg, *Liberals in the Russian Revolution* (Princeton, NJ 1974), pp. 3 f.

6. R.W. Pethybridge, *The Spread of the Russian Revolution* (London, New York 1972).

7. R. Pipes, *Formation* (Cambridge, Mass. 1954; rev. ed. New York 1968).

8. On the general problem of utilizing Soviet documentary collections, cf. G. Katkov, 'Soviet Historical Sources in the Post-Stalin Era', in *Contemporary History in the Soviet Mirror*, eds J. Keep and L. Brisby (London, New York 1964), pp. 130–44.

CHAPTER I   THE LEGACY OF BACKWARDNESS IN THE COUNTRYSIDE

1. A.G. Rashin, *Naseleniye Rossii* (Moscow 1956), pp. 46 f., 88.

2. T. Shanin, *The Awkward Class* (Oxford 1972), p. 103.

3. For a recent western analysis of the complex statistical evidence, see D. Atkinson, 'The Statistics on the Russian Land Commune', *SR*, 32 (1973), pp. 773–87. Cf. S.M. Dubrovsky, *Stolyp. zem. reforma* (Moscow 1963), pp. 574–6: a verified version of an official table first published in 1916. Another table (p. 577), which unfortunately covers only thirty-three provinces, gives figures corrected up to 1 January 1917 which are slightly higher for each province. Two other sets of data were compiled by former officials of the Land Resettlement Administration. P.N. Pershin gives a lower estimate of the number of consolidated holdings at the end of 1916 (1,596,625) but a higher estimate of the area of land involved (15,896,095 dessyatines); cf. 'Formy zemlepol'zovaniya', in *O zemle* (Moscow 1921–2), fasc. 1, p. 60. Pershin's data are reproduced in two English-language works: L.A. Owen, *The Russian Peasant Movement* (London 1937; repr. New York 1963), p. 87 and A.N. Antsiferov and others, *Russian Agriculture* (New Haven, Conn. 1930), pp. 386 f. However, both writers have for some reason chosen to reproduce the second rather than the first of two tables in *O zemle* (appx.), although this is confined to consolidations on allotment land and excludes those carried through on land belonging to the State or the state-supported Peasant Land Bank. For other western estimates, cf. G. Pavlovsky, *Agricultural Russia* (London 1930), p. 135 and G.T. Robinson, *Rural*

Russia under the Old Regime (New York 1932; repr. 1967), pp. 225 f.

4. G.L. Yaney, 'The Imperial Russian Government and the Stolypin Land Reform' (Ph.D. diss., Princeton 1961), f. 239, citing an earlier work by Dubrovsky. Dubrovsky himself, in *Stolyp. zem. ref.*, pp. 247–56, notes the difficulties involved in estimating the number of *khutora*.

5. I. Chernyshev, *Obshchina posle 9-go noyabrya 1906 g.* (Petrograd 1917), I, p. 165; II, p. 137, as cited by Owen, *The Russian Peasant Movement*, p. 82.

6. Pavlovsky, *Agricultural Russia*, pp. 135–9; *O zemle*, fasc. I, appx II; for more recent figures see Dubrovsky, p. 247.

7. Dubrovsky, *Stolyp. zem. ref.*, p. 420; cf. N.P. Oganovsky, *Russ. krest. i mir. khoz.*, 2nd ed. (Moscow 1924), p. 55.

8. Yaney, *Imperial Russian Gov., passim.*

CHAPTER 2   THE DISCONTENTS OF INDUSTRIAL LABOUR

1. A.G. Rashin, *Formir.* (Moscow 1958), pp. 171, 211.

2. P.A. Khromov, *Ocherki ekon. monop. kapit.* (Moscow 1960), p. 74. The best estimate of the empire's population in 1913 is 165·7 million: Rashin, *Naseleniye Rossii* (Moscow 1956), p. 49.

3. Based on R.S. Livshits, *Razmeshcheniye prom. v dorevol. Rossii* (Moscow 1955), esp. pp. 200, 221, 227, 253, 270; Rashin, *Formir.*, pp. 71, 190–204 and *passim*; Mln. Torg. i Prom., *Fab.-zav. prom. Yevrop. Rossii v 1910–12 gg.: obshchiye itogi* (Petrograd 1915), pp. ii–viii.

4. N.K. Druzhinin, *Usloviya byta* (Moscow 1958), p. 45.

5. I.M. Kozminykh-Lanin, *Gramotnost'* (Moscow 1912), pp. 26 f.

6. Yu. I. Kiryanov, *Rabochiye yuga Rossii* (Moscow 1971), p. 81.

7. Livshits, *Razmeshcheniye prom. v dorevol. Rossii*, p. 251.

8. L.S. Gaponenko, *Rab. klass Rossii* (Moscow 1970), p. 65. Allowance must be made for the fact that the inspectorate's responsibilities extended only to mechanized concerns employing more than fifteen workers.

9. P.A. Khromov, *Ekon. razv. Rossii* (Moscow 1967), pp. 74 ff.; M. Gordon, *Workers before and after Lenin* (New York 1942), p. 66.

10. P.A. Garvi, *Prof. v Rossii v pervye gody* (New York 1958), p. 12.

11. M.T. Florinsky, *The End of the Russian Empire* (New Haven, Conn. 1931; repr. New York 1961), p. 159; Gordon, *Workers before and after Lenin*, pp. 59–60.

12. Druzhinin, *Usloviya byta*, p. 23.

13. Khromov, *Ocherki ekon. monop. kapit.*, p. 74.

14. A. Gerschenkron, 'The Rate of Industrial Growth in Russia since 1885', *Jnl of Econ. Hist.*, 7 (1947), suppl., p. 154, referring to the period after 1908. He estimates that between 1900 and 1913 monetary wages and prices rose by an average of 28·0 and 28·7 per cent. Gordon's estimate

y
y

(p. 69) of a 15 per cent increase in real wages between 1900 and 1913 is too generous.

15. S.G. Strumilin, *Problemy, Izbr. proizved.*, III (Moscow 1964), p. 325. These figures apply to adults only and exclude Russian Poland.

16. Kozminykh-Lanin, *Gramotnost'*, pp. 34, 41, 47, 91.

17. Druzhinin, *Usloviya byta*, p. 8, citing an unnamed work by the pre-revolutionary statistician V. Varzar.

18. L.I. Frayman, *Indeksy stoimosti zhizni* (Moscow 1925), p. 126.

19. Druzhinin, *Usloviya byta*, pp. 35–9.

20. Druzhinin, *Usloviya byta*, p. 12.

21. Druzhinin, *Usloviya byta*, pp. 49–51.

22. Druzhinin, *Usloviya byta*, p. 46; Gordon, *Workers before and after Lenin*, pp. 184–5.

23. A. Lositsky and I. Chernyshev, *Alkogolizm peterb. rab.* (St Petersburg 1913), table 6, p. 58.

24. L.I. Dembo, *Ocherk deyat. kom. po vop. ob alkogolizme* (St Petersburg 1913), p. 119.

25. L.M. Ivanov, 'Samoderzhaviye, burzhuaziya i rabochiye', *VI*, 1 (1971), pp. 94–5.

26. Rashin, *Formir.*, pp. 579–83. In 1913 two-thirds of army recruits were described as literate: *Sb. stat.* (Moscow 1924), p. 53.

27. Rashin, *Formir.*, p. 601; *Sb. stat.*, p. 53.

28. Kozminykh-Lanin, *Gramotnost'*, p. 6.

29. Rashin, *Formir.*, p. 611.

30. Kozminykh-Lanin, *Gramotnost'*, p. 6. These figures relate to formal schooling only; about 10 per cent more had acquired this facility without attending any institution.

31. Min. Torg. i Prom., *Svod otchetov fab. insp. za 1913 (1914) g.* (St Petersburg 1914 [1915]), as cited by L. Haimson, 'The Problem of Social Stability in Urban Russia, 1905–1917', *SR*, 23 (1964), p. 627.

32. On the industrialists' relations with the government at this time, see K.A. Roosa, 'Russian Industrialists Look to the Future', in *Essays ... G.T. Robinson*, ed. J.S. Curtiss (Leiden 1963), pp. 198–218.

CHAPTER 3   RURAL RUSSIA AND THE WAR

1. Antsiferov and others, *Russian Agriculture*, p. 137; cf. P.B. Struve (ed.), *Food Supply in Russia during the World War* (New Haven, Conn. 1930), p. 342. The latter contains two important articles by K.I. Zaitsev and N.V. Dolinsky, 'Organization and Policy' (pp. 3–211) and by S.S. Demosthenov, 'Food Prices' (pp. 215–465).

2. A.M. Anfimov, *Ross. derevnya* (Moscow 1962). This capital work rests upon a richer foundation of statistical material than was available to writers in the Carnegie Endowment's valuable Economic and Social

History of the World War (Russian Series). It suffers, however, from an ideological bias which leads the author to distinguish at every turn between 'the landowning economy' and 'the peasant economy', although in the backward conditions of Russian agriculture the two were to a large extent interdependent.

3. Anfimov, *Ross. derevnya*, p. 246; cf. Demosthenov, 'Food Prices', p. 342.

4. Anfimov, *Ross. derevnya*, pp. 116, 196.

5. Anfimov argues (pp. 249–56) that the proportion of households with income from non-agricultural pursuits (*promysly*) decreased significantly; however, his figure for those in such employment is confined to male workers (2·4 million in 1917: p. 190), and he does not attempt to estimate the volume of their earnings in relation to pre-war income from this source.

6. Demosthenov, 'Food Prices', pp. 269–78.

7. Demosthenov, 'Food Prices', pp. 290–2.

8. Anfimov, *Ross. derevnya*, pp. 243, 292.

9. Demosthenov, 'Food Prices', p. 345.

10. Anfimov, *Ross. derevnya*, p. 211; G.S. Gordeyev, *Sel. khoz.* (Moscow, Leningrad 1925), p. 103; *Izv. TsVPK*, 18 August 1917.

11. Gordeyev, *Sel. khoz.*, p. 103.

12. Anfimov, *Ross. derevnya*, p. 115; Antsiferov, *Russian Agriculture*, p. 117; cf. Demosthenov, 'Food Prices', p. 304.

13. Anfimov, *Ross. derevnya*, p. 203.

14. Gordeyev, *Sel. khoz.*, p. 65.

15. Anfimov, *Ross. derevnya*, pp. 235, 237. The lack of accurate figures for the pre-war years makes it impossible to arrive at an estimate for the country as a whole.

16. Anfimov, *Ross. derevnya*, p. 192.

17. Anfimov, *Ross. derevnya*, pp. 95, 98, 195.

18. V.P. Milyutin, *Sel.-khoz. rab. i voyna* (Petrograd 1917), pp. 48, 125–31; Demosthenov, 'Food Prices', p. 343.

19. A.P. Pogrebinsky, 'Sel. khoz.', *IZ*, 31 (1950), p. 40.

20. Anfimov, *Ross. derevnya*, pp. 143, 280. We may give here three contemporary estimates, all of which indicate a less substantial decline:

	A	B	C
1909–13 (av.)	83·5	83·1	86·4 million dessyatines
1914	88·6	—	—
1915	85·1	—	—
1916	78·2	79·0	79·2

Sources: A: Gordeyev, *Sel. khoz.*, p. 88; B: *Sb. stat. sved.*, p. 123; C: N.P. Oganovsky, *Sel. khoz. Rossii v XX v.* (Moscow 1923; repr. The Hague 1968), p. 107.

The data in *Sb. stat.* (pp. 122–5) show that the largest decline occurred in the Central Industrial region and the south-east; considerable increases were registered in Siberia.

21. Anfimov, *Ross. derevnya*, p. 283.
22. Demosthenov, 'Food Prices', p. 311; Anfimov, *Ross. derevnya*, p. 293. Several other contemporary or near-contemporary sets of figures are available:

	A	B	C	D	E	
1909–13 (av.)	4350	—	3850	—	—	million puds
1914(–15)	4304	—	—	—	—	
1915(–16)	4659	—	—	—	—	
1916(–17)	3916	3791	3482	3336	3242	

Sources:

A: Yashnov, as cited in Pogrebinsky, 'Sel. khoz.', p. 44; A.N. Bakh and others (eds), *God russ. revol.* (Moscow 1918), p. 208.

B: A.M. Anfimov and others (eds), *Ekonomicheskoye polozheniye Rossii nakanune Velikoy Oktyabr'skoy sotsialisticheskoy revolyutsii: dok. i mat.*, III (Leningrad 1967) [cited as *EPR* III], pp. 158f. (a table drawn up in the Supply ministry in 1917: see below p. 500).

C: *Sb. stat.*, p. 131.

D: *Izvestiya TsVPK*, 22 March 1917.

E: S.N. Prokopovich, minister of Supply, to Council of Republic, 16 October 1917: R.P. Browder and A.F. Kerensky (eds), *The Russian Provisional Government: Documents* (Stanford, Calif. 1961) [cited as B&K], II, p. 647; cf. *NZ*, 24 October 1917.

A figure close to A (3955 million puds) is given in the League of Nations' *Report on Econ. Conditions in Russia* (1922), pp. 20 f., 27. A figure close to B is given by Gordeyev, *Sel. khoz.*, p. 91: 3780 million puds.

23. Anfimov and others, *Ekon. polozh.*, p. 296; cf. Demosthenov, 'Food Prices', p. 355.
24. Demosthenov, 'Food Prices', pp. 332, 364; Anfimov and others, *Ekon. polozh.*, p. 325.
25. According to Gordeyev, *Sel. khoz.*, p. 94, the number of horned cattle in fifty-one provinces of European Russia (but excluding the Volga provinces) actually rose from 32·0 to 33·4 million head between 1913 and 1916. Cf. Demosthenov, 'Food Prices', p. 317.
26. O.I. Averbakh (comp.), *Zakon. akty*, III (Petrograd 1916–18), pp. 727–30; Zaitsev and Dolinsky, 'Org. and Pol.', p. 51.
27. Zaitsev and Dolinsky, 'Org. and Pol.', p. 82; Demosthenov, 'Food Prices', pp. 312–3.
28. Demosthenov, 'Food Prices', p. 325; Pogrebinsky, 'Sel. khoz.', p. 44.
29. Demosthenov, 'Food Prices', pp. 374–5.
30. Zaitsev and Dolinsky, 'Org. and Pol.', pp. 135–7; Averbakh, *Zakon. akty*, V, pp. 82–93. Those guilty of collusion to raise prices were threatened with jail terms of up to two years, pp. 77–81.

31. Averbakh, *Zakon. akty*, v, pp. 537–41; Zaitsev and Dolinsky, 'Org. and Pol.', p. 96; Pogrebinsky, 'Sel. khoz.', p. 58, n. 91. T.A. Shishkov states that the amount collected fell short of the reduced target (522 million puds) by only 129 million puds, or 25 per cent: *Izv. TsVPK*, 22 March 1917.

32. Anfimov and others, *Ekon. polozh.*, p. 306; cf. tables for the whole empire in Demosthenov, 'Food Prices', pp. 388, 390.

33. Anfimov and others, *Ekon. polozh.*, pp. 307, 311; Demosthenov, 'Food Prices', p. 314, gives a lower figure of 740,000 puds of grain transported in 1915.

34. Anfimov and others, *Ekon. polozh.*, p. 322.

35. Demosthenov, 'Food Prices', p. 334.

36. Anfimov and others, *Ekon. polozh.*, pp. 347–8; A.B. Berkevich, 'Kr-vo i vseob. mobiliz. v yule 1914 g.', *IZ*, 23 (1947), pp. 3–43.

37. O. Chaadayeva, 'Sold. pis'ma v gody mir. voyny', *KA*, 65/6 (1934), pp. 142–3.

38. Unfortunately there is very little hard-and-fast information about peasant attitudes at this time. A volume of memoirs by peasants and former peasants, published many years later, contains a few general remarks about the pre-February period, but it is heavily coloured by hindsight. I.V. Igritsky (comp.), *1917 g. v derevne* (Moscow, Leningrad 1929; new ed., Moscow 1967). Some correspondence between under-privileged civilians was intercepted by the Okhrana; cf. E.N. Burdzhalov, *Vtoraya russkaya revolyutsiya* (Moscow 1967), pp. 35–6, but there is no means of ascertaining how representative this sample may be.

39. B.B. Grave, *Burzhuaziya nakanune fevral'skoy revolyutsii* (Moscow 1927), p. 134, cited by Burdzhalov, *Vtor. russ. rev.*, pp. 35–6.

40. 'Polit. polozh. v Rossii nak. fev. revol. v zhandarmskom osveshchenii', *KA*, 17 (1926), pp. 19–20.

41. Anfimov and others, *Ekon. polozh.*, p. 362.

42. 'Polit. polozh', p. 349.

43. Yu. I. Kiryanov, 'Kr-vo stepnoy Ukr. v gody I-oy mir. voyny', *Osob. agr. stroya Rossii* (Moscow 1962), p. 244.

CHAPTER 4   THE IMPACT OF THE WAR ON INDUSTRIAL LABOUR

1. L.S. Gaponenko, 'Rab. klass Rossii nak. Vel. Okt.', *IZ*, 73 (1963), p. 70, contests the lower estimates on which earlier historians have relied; cf. Gaponenko, *Rab. klass Rossii*, pp. 52–4.

2. Averbakh, *Zakon. akty*, I, p. 15.

3. Averbakh, *Zakon. akty*, p. 115 (*Voyenno-sud. ustav*, pt IV, para. 1278, n. 4).

4. Averbakh, *Zakon. akty*, p. 372.

5. Averbakh, *Zakon. akty*, III, pp. 47–50.

6. I. Menitsky, 'K ist. "Rab. gruppy" pri TsVPK', *KA*, 57 (1933), p. 79;

cf. B.B. Grave, *K ist. klass. bor'by v Rossii* (Moscow, Leningrad 1926), p. 134 and K. Sidorov, 'Rab. dvizh. v Rossii v gody imp. voyny', in *Ocherki po ist. Okt. revol.*, ed. M.N. Pokrovsky, II (Moscow, Leningrad 1927), pp. 221–2. For a similar case in Moscow in October 1915, cf. I. Menitsky, *Revol. d vizh. voyennykh godov* (Moscow 1924), II, p. 175.

7. Gaponenko, *Rab. klass Rossii*, pp. 55–6.

8. *Izv. TsVPK*, 16 May 1917.

9. Kiryanov, *Rab. yuga Rossii*, pp. 38–9.

10. Kiryanov, *Rab. yuga Rossii*, pp. 224, 227.

11. M.G. Fleer (comp.), *Rab. dvizh.* (Moscow 1925), p. 225.

12. Kiryanov, *Rab. yuga Rossii*, p. 241 n.; cf. Fleer, *Rab. dvizh.*, pp. 241, 299, for a higher contemporary estimate of the number involved. K.F. Shatsillo, 'Zabastovka Nikol. sudostr. zavoda "Naval"' v yanv. – fev. 1916 g.', *IZ*, 74 (1963), pp. 276–85, reproduces this figure of those mobilized (p. 284) but omits to mention that most of the men were later sent back.

13. Kiryanov, *Rab. yuga Rossii*, p. 69.

14. Sidorov, 'Rab. dvizh.', p. 246.

15. *Izv. TsVPK*, 2 May 1917.

16. S.G. Strumilin, *Zar. plata* (Moscow 1923), p. 17; cf. Grave, *K ist. klass. bor'by v Rossii*, p. 53.

17. Strumilin, *Zar. plata*, p. 22; cf. Strumilin, *Problemy, Izbr. proizved.*, III, p. 378.

18. Strumilin, *Zar. plata*, p. 9; Grave, *K ist. klass. bor'by v Rossii*, p. 56; the figures given in S. Zagorsky, *State Control* (New Haven, Conn. 1928), pp. 341–2, where the sources are not identified, differ slightly.

19. Strumilin, *Problemy*, pp. 333–5; table reproduced in Gaponenko, *Rab. klass Rossii*, p. 177; cf. B. Ward, 'Wild Socialism', *Calif. Sl. Stud.*, 3 (1964), p. 129.

20. Strumilin, *Problemy*, pp. 378, 382.

21. Kiryanov, *Rab. yuga Rossii*, p. 72.

22. Kiryanov, *Rab. yuga Rossii*, pp. 73–7.

23. 'Polit. polozh. v Rossii', *KA*, 17 (1926), pp. 11, 13; cf. Sidorov, 'Rab. dvizh.', pp. 241 f. for the data on which this survey was based.

24. D. Rozenblyum, 'Revol. i rab. dvizh.', in Bakh and others, *God russ. revol.*, p. 180.

25. Kiryanov, *Rab. yuga Rossii*, p. 94.

26. Fleer, *Rab. dvizh.*, pp. 6–7; Grave, *K ist. klass.*, pp. 65–73 and diagrams on pp. 401 ff.; Sidorov, 'Rab. dvizh.', p. 328.

27. Gaponenko, *Rab. klass Rossii*, p. 57.

28. Sidorov, 'Rab. dvizh.', p. 329.

29. Zagorsky, *State Control*, appx XXVI (facing p. 342).

30. Averbakh, *Zakon. akty*, II, pp. 255, 526; Gaponenko, *Rab. klass Rossii*, pp. 59–60.

31. Kiryanov, *Rab. yuga Rossii*, p. 42; cf. Grave, *K ist. klass.*, p. 52.

32. Gaponenko, *Rab. klass Rossii,* p. 67.

33. Gaponenko, *Rab. klass Rossii,* pp. 76–80. For earlier estimates A. Shlyapnikov, *Semnadtsatyy god,* 1 (Moscow 1925), p. 10; B. Kolokolnikov, in *Stat. truda,* 1–4, (1917), as cited in Pokrovsky, *Ocherki po ist. Okt. revol.,* 11, p. 148 n.

34. Kiryanov, *Rab. yuga Rossii*, p. 50.

35. Fleer, *Rab. dvizh.,* pp. 207–9; Grave, *K ist. klass.,* p. 110.

36. Grave, *K ist. klass.,* p. 120.

37. 'Iz ist. rab. dvizh. vo vremya mir. voyny: stach. dvizh. v Kostr. gub.', *KA*, 67 (1934), pp. 10 f.; Fleer, *Rab. dvizh.,* pp. 211–14; Grave, *K ist. klass.,* p. 123; Sidorov, 'Rab. dvizh.', pp. 283 f.

38. N.N. Markova and others, *Profsoyuz tekstil.* (Moscow 1963), p. 34; Sidorov, 'Rab. dvizh.', pp. 284–6; Grave, *K ist. klass.,* p. 124; Fleer, *Rab. dvizh.,* pp. 214–15.

39. Fleer, *Rab. dvizh.,* p. 7.

40. Shatsillo, p. 280, citing an unpublished diss. (Kiev 1951) by M.A. Svirid.

41. Grave, *K ist. klass.,* p. 158, c.u.d.s.

42. Grave, *K ist. klass.,* p. 161.

43. Fleer, *Rab. dvizh.,* pp. 236–40; Grave, *K ist. klass.,* p. 162; Sidorov, 'Rab. dvizh.', p. 264.

44. Fleer, *Rab. dvizh.,* pp. 136, 252–64; Grave, *K ist klass.,* pp. 164 f.

45. Sidorov, 'Rab. dvizh.', p. 254; Fleer, *Rab. dvizh.,* p. 139.

46. Kiryanov, *Rab. yuga Rossii*, p. 252; A. Shlyapnikov, *Nakanune 1917 g.* (Moscow 1920), pp. 275–81. The latter work is an important source on the period, which for ideological reasons Soviet historians treat with some caution.

47. Shlyapnikov, *Kanun,* pt 11, (Moscow 1922), p. 65.

48. Grave, *K ist. klass.,* pp. 173–4.

49. Grave, *K ist. klass.,* p. 186; Shlyapnikov, *Kanun,* pp. 222 ff.; Fleer, *Rab. dvizh.,* p. 192; Sidorov, 'Rab. dvizh.', pp. 265–8; Burdzhalov, *Vtoraya russ. revol.* (1967), p. 57.

50. Cf. police reports reproduced in B. Romanov, 'Kanun semnadts. g.', *KL*, 2: 11, (1924), pp. 202–12. Higher figures are sometimes encountered.

51. Grave, *K ist. klass.,* p. 190, citing a report to the ministry of the Interior dated 30 October 1916.

52. Some of his subordinates were more perspicacious. A report compiled early in October 1916 concluded gloomily that 'the internal structure of the Russian state is currently exposed to a very serious threat of grave perturbations'.

53. T. Sapronov, 'Mosk. Ts. Byuro v gody voyny', in *Mat. po ist. prof. dvizh. v Rossii* (Moscow 1924–7), IV (1925), pp. 77–104.

54. I. Menitsky, 'K ist.', pp. 49, 68; this document should be compared

with the original text published in *Izv. TsVPK*, 15, 18, 22, 29 April 1917, particularly the 'addendum' by E. Omelchenko. The latter explains that the report, written in February 1917 to mobilize public support for the Labour Group leaders after their arrest, played down the political work which they had accomplished under cover of their legitimate activities. Cf. also Fleer, *Rab. dvizh.*, pp. 272 f.; Grave, *K ist. klass.*, p. 144; G. Katkov, *Russia 1917* (London 1967), pp. 18–22, 441.

55. Zagorsky, *State Control*, pp. 92 f.

56. Grave, *K ist. klass.*, p. 146.

57. For their text, see I. Menitsky, 'K ist. gvozdevshchiny', *KA*, 67 (1934), pp. 34–92. Konovalov tried to control their content and prohibited distribution of two issues of the *Bulletin;* on the second occasion, however, its authors evaded this censorship by making their own arrangements (p. 35).

58. Menitsky, 'K ist. Rab.', p. 62.

59. Fleer, *Rab. dvizh.*, pp. 285–6.

60. Menitsky, 'K ist.', p. 67; text in Shlyapnikov, *Kanun*, pp. 123–32.

61. Menitsky, 'K ist.', pp. 70–72; Shlyapnikov, *Semnadtsatiy god*, I, pp. 27–30; cf. also Protopopov's evidence in *Padeniye tsarskogo rezhima* (Moscow, Leningrad 1924–7), I, pp. 142 f. Katkov, *Russia, 1917*, p. 234, argues that the government was really aiming at the liberal opposition, but offers little evidence in support of this view.

62. *Izv. TsVPK*, 16 February, 30 March 1917; it is this report which was later published by Menitsky.

63. Ward, 'Wild Socialism', p. 135, citing a history of the Putilov works published in the 1930s.

64. *Ist. arkhiv*, no. 5 (1961), p. 97, as cited by Burdzhalov, *Vtoraya russ. revol.*, p. 95.

65. The figures were in the region of 137,000 and 90,000 respectively: Fleer, *Rab. dvizh.*, p. 314; Burdzhalov, *Vtoraya russ. revol.*, p. 107 (cf. p. 90 n. for higher estimates for the former occasion). Not too much should be made of these figures.

66. Burdzhalov, *Vtoraya russ. revol.*, pp. 115 f.

67. On this point cf. Katkov, *Russia, 1917*, pp. 249–51, who remarks justly that 'some of the causes of the strikes still remain quite obscure'.

68. V. Kayurov, 'Shest' dney', *PR*, 13 (1923), p. 158, whose account is commendably frank, states that they had neither a fixed plan of action nor a clear idea of where this movement would lead. A similar impression is conveyed by Shlyapnikov, *Semnadtsatyy god*, I, pp. 61–3.

69. Burdzhalov, *Vtoraya russ. revol.*, p. 140.

70. For various estimates of the number involved: Burdzhalov, *Vtoraya russ. revol.*, pp. 109, 142. Of English-language accounts of the 'February Days' that by Katkov, *Russia, 1917*, pp. 262–84 is to be preferred to

that by Trotsky, *Hist. Russ. Rev.*, pp. 97–130. A good chronology is provided by N. Avdeyev in *PR*, 13 (1923), pp. 1–49.

71. Burdzhalov, *Vtoraya russ. revol.*, p. 176, c.u.d.s.; Trotsky, *Hist. Russ. Rev.*, who does not identify his sources, cites the same report (p. 109). Cf. also Shlyapnikov, *Semnadtsatyy god*, pp. 105–7.

72. Kayurov, 'Shest′ dney', p. 166; cf. Shlyapnikov, *Semnadtsatyy god*, p. 103.

73. This aspect of the revolution, neglected by earlier writers, has now been fully treated by Burdzhalov in his sequel volume *Vtoraya russ. revol.: Moskva*, (Moscow 1971).

74. *Izv.*, 22 August 1917 (also in B&K, I, p. 71); cf. Katkov, *Russia, 1917*, p. 359; Burdzhalov, *Vtoraya russ. revol.: Moskva*, p. 209.

75. S. Mstislavsky, *Pyat′ dney* (Berlin, Moscow, Petrograd 1922), p. 23; Shlyapnikov, *Semnadtsatyy god*, pp. 119–22; Burdzhalov, *Vtoraya russ. revol.: Moskva*, p. 212; Katkov, *Russia, 1917*, p. 360.

76. *Izv.*, 27 August 1917; Burdzhalov, *Vtoraya russ. revol.: Moskva*, p. 215; Katkov, *Russia, 1917*, p. 361; N.N. Sukhanov, *The Russian Revolution 1917* (London 1955; repr. New York 1962), I, pp. 57–73; O. Anweiler, *Die Rätebewegung* (Leyden 1958), pp. 127–31; English ed.: *The Soviets* (New York 1974), pp. 103–6.

CHAPTER 5   THE DRIFT TO INDUSTRIAL ANARCHY

1. M. Ferro, *La Révolution* (Paris 1967), pp. 174, 183.

2. It is, for example, apparently impossible even to mention such a central factor in the situation as wage-induced inflation. P.V. Volobuyev, one of the least doctrinaire historians, attributes price rises to 'the capitalists' deliberate policy of recouping by higher prices what they had to part with in paying labour under pressure of the workers': *Prol.* (Moscow 1964), p. 219. The implication is that inflation was a weapon used by the government and employers to browbeat the workers – a point much stressed in Bolshevik agitation at the time.

3. English text: B&K, II, pp. 712 f.; cf. B.M. Freydlin, *Ocherki ist. rab. dvizh. v Rossii v 1917 g.* (Moscow 1967), p. 80; P.V. Volobuyev, 'Politika burzh. i Vrem. Prav. v rab. vop., mart – avr. 1917 g.', *IZ*, 73 (1963), p. 132; B. Ya. Nalivaysky (comp.), *Petrogr. Sovet rab. i sold. dep.* (Moscow, Leningrad 1925), pp. 31, 75 f.

4. *Izv. TsVPK*, 22 March 1917.

5. *RS*, 19, 21 March 1917.

6. Volobuyev, *Prol.*, pp. 118–20; Freydlin, *Ocherki ist. rab. dvizh.*, p. 83; *RS*, 16 March; *Izv. TsVPK*, 11 April 1917.

7. Volobuyev, *Prol.*, pp. 121f.

8. On 10 May leaders of the metallurgical industry complained to the prime minister that eighteen Donets plants with total basic capital of 195 million roubles faced wage demands equivalent to 240 million

roubles, of which 64 million had already been paid (*Izv. TsVPK*, 16 May). These figures cannot be verified and take no account of the increased income that would accrue from higher prices.

9. Volobuyev, *Prol.*, p. 126, c.u.d.s.

10. Gaponenko, *Rab. klass Rossii*, p. 187, where these data are characterized as 'extremely tendentious'. They are, however, confirmed by recently published data relating to the Slyusarenko munition works, a small enterprise in Petrograd, where the wages bill rose from 30,000 roubles per month on the eve of the revolution to 34,000 roubles for the last two *weeks* in May: *EPR*, 1, p. 325. Cf. also *Izv. TsVPK*, 28 March for the case of a defence establishment which doubled wages as early as 20 March.

11. Volobuyev, *Prol.*, p. 128, c.u.d.s.; Gaponenko, *Rab. klass Rossii*, p. 190.

12. Gaponenko, *Rab. klass Rossii*, p. 353; according to *Izv.*, 30 July 1917, unskilled workers in the Putilov plant were then earning 6·20 roubles a day.

13. The monthly figures were 49·30 and 72·80 roubles respectively: Freydlin, *Ocherki ist. rab. dvizh.*, p. 212, citing N. Volens, *Zarabotnaya plata i rabocheye vremya Petrogradskikh tekstil'shchikov* (Petrograd 1919); cf. *Izv.*, 17 August. F. Bulkin, 'Ekon. polozh. rab. Petrogr. nak. Okt. 1917 g.', in *Prof. dvizh. v Petrograde* ed. A. Ansky (Leningrad 1928), p. 36, states that their average wage was only 6·78 roubles a day.

14. Gaponenko, *Rab. klass Rossii*, pp. 190 f. He mentions (pp. 359–63) what appears to be a different set of negotiations involving some of the same factories which resulted in 'substantial rises' amounting in one case to 300 per cent, but does not explain the connection between the two. Another account of the former episode by the same author (*IZ*, 83 [1967], p. 17) characteristically omits to state the amount of increase finally agreed.

15. *Izv. TsVKP*, 11 April, 13 May; Volobuyev, *Prol.*, pp. 130 f.

16. V.L. Meller and A.M. Pankratova (comps), *Rab. dvizh. v 1917 g.* (Moscow, Leningrad 1926) [cited as M&P], pp. 124 f.

17. *EPR*, 1, p. 342.

18. Volobuyev, *Prol.*, p. 136.

19. Volobuyev, *Prol.*, p. 219, citing M.P. Kokhn, *Russkiye indeksy tsen* (Moscow 1926), p. 160.

20. S.G. Strumilin, 'Dvizh. tsen i tarifnaya pol.', *Ekon. zhizn'* (18 December 1919).

21. V. Ya-y, 'Tseny na produkty i zar. plata mosk. rab.', *Stat. truda*, 1 (15 July 1918), p. 12.

22. V. Ya-y, 'Tseny na produkty', p. 10. In 1926 the Moscow Conjuncture Institute established the following index for average retail prices of nine categories of foodstuffs (1913 = 100): January 1917 – 3·36; May 1917 – 4·91; September 1917 – 7·44. A.L. Vaynshteyn, *Tseny i*

tsenoobraz. v SSSR (Moscow 1972), p. 157. I am indebted to Dr M. McCauley for this reference.

23. One such group were the workers in the Parviainen metal works in Petrograd, employed wholly on arms production. Strumilin, using his 'Leningrad price index', calculates that average real wages, which by February 1917 had fallen to 55 per cent of the June 1914 level, had more than doubled by April 1917 (to 134 per cent of the 1914 rate) and were still running at 126 per cent of that rate by September 1917. Unskilled labourers had more than doubled their real incomes, from 27·20 roubles in February to an estimated 60·30 roubles in September. (*Problemy*, pp. 370 f.).

24. Strumilin, *Problemy*, pp. 318, 382.

25. Volobuyev, *Prol.*, p. 221, citing *Fab.-zav. prom. 1917–18 gg.*, p. 57.

26. Strumilin, *Problemy*, p. 490.

27. Gaponenko, *Rab. klass Rossii*, p. 195.

28. Volobuyev, *Prol.*, p. 224.

29. *Stat. truda*, 4/5, 15 September/15 October 1918, pp. 9–17.

30. Gaponenko, *Rab. klass Rossii*, p. 436, citing an unpublished thesis by A.M. Lisetsky. Volobuyev, *Prol.*, p. 240, citing an article by Lisetsky in the *Uch. zap. Khar'kovskogo univ.*, 103 (1959) more cautiously puts the figure for September and October at 'well over a million'.

31. Gaponenko, *Rab. klass Rossii*, p. 385.

32. D. Rozenblyum, 'Revol. i rab. dvizh.', in Bakh and others, eds, *God russ. revol.*, p. 183.

33. *Torg.-prom. gaz.*, 1 October, cited in *EPR*, II, p. 353 and also by Volobuyev, *Prol.*, p. 218, P.H. Avrich, 'Russian Factory Committees', *JGOE*, 11 (1963), p. 170, and A.M. Pankratova, *Fabzavkomy v bor'be* (Moscow 1923), p. 218.

34. M.G. Fleer, 'K ist. rab. dvizh. 1917 g.', *KL*, 2: 13, (1925), p. 242. These statistics, based on complaints to the authorities by organizations and individuals affected, can give only a very rough impression of the general drift of events.

35. Volobuyev, 'Politika', *IZ* 73 (1963), p. 146.

36. Freydlin, *Ocherki ist. rab. dvizh.*, p. 117.

37. M&P, pp. 224 f.

38. *Izv. TsVPK*, 3 July, 3 August 1917.

39. Avrich, 'Factory Committees', p. 172.

40. B&K, II, pp. 720 f.; *RV*, 23 May 1917. The factory committee in question had recently come under Bolshevik control.

41. *Izv.*, 13 July 1917.

CHAPTER 6   THE FACTORY COMMITTEES

1. D.A. Kovalenko, 'Bor'ba fab.-zav.', *IZ*, 61 (1957), p. 72; on the follow-

ing cf. also F. Döring, *Organisationsprobleme* (Hanover 1970), pp. 45–70.

2. Kovalenko, 'Bor'ba fab.-zav.', p. 79.

3. Gaponenko, *Rab. klass Rossii*, p. 367, c.u.d.s.; cf. N. Dmitriyev, in Ansky, *Prof. dvizh. v Petrograde*, pp. 81 f.

4. Kovalenko, 'Bor'ba fab.-zav.', pp. 81 ff.

5. Ward, 'Wild Socialism', p. 138.

6. P.N. Amosov and others (eds), *Okt. revol. i fabzavkomy* (Moscow 1927), I, p. 28. A few days earlier the moderate leaders had called a similar conference, to which this was a counter-move.

7. Cited in Pankratova, *Fabzavkomy v bor'be*, p. 184; for the initial draft, see Amosov, *Okt. revol. i fabzavkomy*, I, pp. 32 ff. These ideas on the committees' powers went considerably beyond those of the Petrograd soviet leadership: cf. the latter's draft instruction of 20 March in P.O. Gorin and others (eds), *Org. i str. Sovetov* (Moscow 1928), pp. 98 f.

8. S. Volin, *Deyat. men.* (New York 1962), p. 7.

9. Amosov, *Okt. revol. i fabzavkomy*, I, pp. 46–56; cf. pp. 151 f. for later developments.

10. Kovalenko, 'Bor'ba fab.-zav.', p. 74.

11. *RS*, 17 March 1917.

12. Freydlin, *Ocherki ist. rab. dvizh.*, p. 130.

13. Kovalenko, 'Bor'ba fab.-zav.', p. 75.

14. B&K, II, pp. 718–20.

15. Pankratova, *Fabzavkomy v bor'be*, pp. 193 f. These statements have been toned down in the published minutes (Amosov, *Okt. revol. i fabzavkomy*, pp. 104–7).

16. V.I. Lenin, *Polnoye sobraniye sochineniy*, 5th ed. (Moscow 1959–65) [cited as *PSS*], XXXII, pp. 239 f.

17. Amosov, *Okt. revol. i fabzavkomy*, I, pp. 70, 107; Kovalenko, 'Bor'ba fab.-zav.', p. 82. The Anarcho-Syndicalists, who commanded about forty-five votes, followed the Bolshevik lead. Party alignments were still fluid and the Bolsheviks felt they could dispense with their normal practice of forming a 'fraction'. A vote on 'the current moment' indicated that, together with the Anarcho-Syndicalists, they commanded the allegiance of 72 per cent of those present. Amosov, *Okt. revol. i fabzavkomy*, p. 71.

18. Lenin, *PSS*, XXXII, pp. 195–7; *EPR*, II, pp. 11–12.

19. *EPR*, I, p. 410.

20. Pankratova, *Fabzavkomy v bor'be*, p. 187.

21. Ya. Milshteyn and V. Livshits (comps), *Ist. i praktika ross. prof. dvizh.* (Moscow 1925), p. 307.

22. Cf. documents in *EPR*, I, pp. 432–50, 185–7, one of which is transl. in B&K, II, pp. 764 f.

23. *EPR*, I, p. 189.

24. M&P, pp. 112–14.

25. *EPR*, I, pp. 196–201.
26. *Birzh. ved.*, 20 September 1917.
27. Volobuyev, *Prol.*, pp. 262 ff.
28. E.g. M&P, pp. 103, 112–14 (21, 22 August).
29. Cf. his private advice to industrialists' representatives on 15 August (*EPR*, I, pp. 412–3), the main point in which was a proposal for a consultative conference of the two sides in industry to work out basic rules to govern plant closures.
30. *EPR*, I, pp. 183–7, 437; English trsl.: B&K, II, pp. 721 f.
31. *Torg.-prom. gaz.*, 2 September, cited in B&K, II, p. 722.
32. According to data supplied by the activists concerned one year later, by October 1917 the proportion of enterprises in different branches of industry which had factory committees was as follows: railways 86 per cent, textiles 70 per cent, metallurgy and mining 61 per cent, printing 44 per cent, foodstuffs 28 per cent. The highest concentrations (circa 60 per cent) were in the north-west and Central Industrial regions. V.Z. Drobizhev, *Glavnyy shtab sots. prom.* (Moscow 1966), pp. 52 f. Allowance must, however, be made for the informants' eagerness to pre-date their organization's seniority.
33. Considerable confusion arises from the fact that the Bolshevik party could not keep check on those who flocked to its ranks during this stormy period, while those who joined after October sought to backdate their membership. Historians and others customarily call 'Bolsheviks' persons who ought more accurately to be referred to as 'maximalists' (or 'Bolshevik sympathizers'), but the normal usage will be followed here.
34. *Izv.*, 11–13 August 1917. Amosov, *Okt. revol. i fabzavkomy*, I, p. 254, confirms the existence of a fifteen-man nucleus within the CCFCP, but gives the total membership as twenty-five – the same number as had been appointed at the first conference. For the minutes see pp. 163–253.
35. Freydlin, *Ocherki ist. rab. dvizh.*, p. 159, citing *Sots.-dem.*, 23, 24 September.
36. Pankratova, *Fabzavkomy v bor'be*, p. 212.
37. Avrich, 'Factory Committees', p. 178.
38. *NZ*, 20 October. The low poll is curious: presumably many delegates regarded the vote as a mere formality.
39. *NZ*, 22 October.

CHAPTER 7   THE WORKERS' MILITIA

1. T. Hasegawa, 'Formation of Militia', *SR*, 32 (1973), p. 319 n. This excellent study, confined to Petrograd during the first weeks after the collapse of the monarchy, is the first western-language treatment of a neglected but all-important problem in the history of the Russian revolution. Cf. also Z. Kelson, 'Militsiya fev. revol.', *Byloye*, 29 (1925), pp. 161–78; 30, pp. 151–75; 33, pp. 220–35. The information on

internal security matters contained in the records of local government and judicial bodies has not been published.

2. Hasegawa, 'Formation of Militia', pp. 307–13, 316. Peshekhonov's memoirs, 'Pervye nedeli', appeared in *Na chuzhoy storone*, 1 (1923), pp. 253–319.

3. V.I. Startsev, *Petrogr. Kr. gvardii* (Moscow, Leningrad 1965), pp. 52, 101.

4. A. Shlyapnikov, *Semnadtsatyy god*, I, pp. 55 f., 103.

5. Cf. above, p. 91.

6. Hasegawa, 'Formation of Militia', p. 317.

7. Amosov, *Okt. revol. i fabzavkomy*, I, pp. 47, 50.

8. Startsev, *Petrogr. Kr. gvardii*, p. 55; Hasegawa, 'Formation of Militia', p. 316.

9. Text in V. Kayurov, 'Iz ist. Kr. gvardii Vyb. rayona v 1917 g.', *PR*, 69 (1927), pp. 228–30. Cf. Vl. Malakhovsky, 'Kak sozdalas' rab. Kr. gvardiya', *PR*, 93 (1929), pp. 55–9, where the factional differences are exaggerated. Rostov wanted to maintain close ties with the soviet, which the Bolsheviks suspected as potentially 'counter-revolutionary', and specifically allotted the guards the militia functions they already in practice exercised. In so far as there was any meaningful division of opinion among the organizers of the 'Red guards', it ran between those (both Bolsheviks and Mensheviks) who sought to subject them to external control and those (like Shlyapnikov) who emphasized their autonomy and 'democratic' (read: elective) character.

10. G.A. Tsypkin, *Kr. gvardiya v bor'be* (Moscow 1967), p. 57.

11. Ye. F. Yerykalov, *Kr. gvardiya v bor'be* (Moscow 1957), p. 25.

12. M.I. Mukhtar-Londarskoy, 'Boyevaya druzhina Kr. gvardii Putil. zav.', *Ist. arkhiv*, I, (1957), p. 207. See also below, p. 299.

13. Tsypkin, *Kr. gvardiya v bor'be*, pp. 53, 84.

14. D.N. Collins, 'A Note on the Numerical Strength of the Russian Red Guard in October 1917', *SS*, 24 (1972–3), pp. 270–80.

CHAPTER 8 TRADE UNIONS

1. E. Ignatov, 'Iz ist. Mosk. Ts. Byuro', in *Mat. po ist. prof. dvizh. v Rossii* (Moscow 1924–7), IV, p. 118.

2. *RS*, 9, 11, 12 March 1917.

3. M&P, p. 83, citing the 'jubilee issue' of *Prof. vestnik* (October 1918). This source puts at 16·5 per cent the proportion of unions formed during January and February 1917, which seems too high, but may simply include all bodies in existence before March 1917.

4. M&P, p. 83.

5. *Tret'ya vseross. konf. prof. soyuzov: stenogr. otchet* (Moscow 1927), [cited as III *konf.*], p. vii.

6. I.L. Borshchenko and others (comps), *Profsoyuzy v bor'be* (Moscow 1963), pp. 402–4.

7. Gaponenko, *Rab. klass Rossii*, p. 444, c.u.d.s.

8. Gaponenko, *Rab. klass Rossii*, p. 442.

9. *Torg.-prom. gaz.*, 5 October 1917, cited by M&P, pp. 83 f. and Borshchenko and others, *Profsoyuzy v bor'be*, pp. 402–4.

10. Gaponenko, *Rab. klass Rossii*, p. 443, c.u.d.s.

11. In Moscow the terms 'league of unions' or 'council of unions' were used. Later in the year both bodies came to be called 'trade union councils'. For simplicity's sake the original designation of the majority will be used here.

12. Ignatov, 'Iz ist. Ts. Byuro', pp. 109–16, 140; Borshchenko and others, *Profsoyuzy v bor'be*, p. 432; Gaponenko, *Rab. klass Rossii*, p. 445; Volin, *Deyat. men.*, pp. 16, 19; Garvi, *Prof. soyuzy v pervye gody*, p. 13.

13. A. Ansky, 'Petrogr. Sovet prof. soyuzov v 1917 g.', in Ansky, *Prof. dvizh. v Petrogr.*, pp. 45–77, esp. 58 f.

14. B. Freydlin, 'Petrogr. Sovet prof. soyuzov v 1917 g.', in *Mat. po ist. prof. dvizh. v Rossii*, II (1924), pp. 290–4; *Izv.*, 5 August; Volin, *Deyat. men.*, pp. 1, 19 f.; Borshchenko and others, *Profsoyuzy v bor'e*, pp. 414 f.

15. Freydlin, *Ocherki ist. rab. dvizh.*, p. 178.

16. Ignatov, 'Iz ist. Ts. Byuro', p. 126 – not May, as stated by Borshchenko and others, *Profsoyuzy*, pp. 368–71, c.u.d.s.

17. I. Lepse, 'Petrogr. Soyuz rab. metallistov', *Metallist*, 12 (1922), pp. 61–6; K. Bruk, 'Org. Soyuza metal.', in Ansky, *Prof. dvizh. v Petrogr.*, pp. 116–23.

18. Gaponenko, *Rab. klass Rossii*, p. 51; Freydlin, *Ocherki ist. rab. dvizh.*, p. 166; M&P, p. 83. The claim that 400,000 metal-workers' union members were represented at the third trade-union conference in June (M&P, p. 85) must be dismissed as rhetorical exaggeration.

19. Borshchenko and others, pp. 354 f.

20. Borshchenko and others, pp. 363 f.

21. Lepse, 'Petrogr. Soyuz rab. metallistov', p. 65.

22. *III konf.*, pp. 485–90.

23. S. Robinson, 'Iz ist. tarifnoy politiki', *Metallist*, 12 (1922), pp. 40–2; M&P, p. 204; Bruk, 'Org. Soyuza metal.', pp. 127 f.

24. B. Kozelev, 'Bor'ba za minimum', *Metallist*, 12 (1922), pp. 71–82.

25. *Izv.*, 25 July, 12 August; M&P, pp. 195–212; Gaponenko, *Rab. klass Rossii*, p. 354.

26. Markova and others, *Prof. tekstil.*, pp. 40, 47; ARCCTU's figure for the end of the year is 550,623, grouped in sixty-one unions (Gaponenko, *Rab. klass Rossii*, p. 444).

27. Markova, *Prof. tekstil.*, pp. 43 f.

28. Markova, *Prof. tekstil.*, p. 47; Borshchenko and others, pp. 480–2; Volin, *Deyat. men.*, p. 32.

29. Volin, *Deyat. men.*, pp. 29 f.

30. Gaponenko, *Rab. klass Rossii*, pp. 51, 444.

31. Freydlin, *Ocherki ist. rab. dvizh.*, p. 170.

32. Volin, *Deyat. men.*, p. 27; A. Miretsky, 'Dvizh. sredi gos. sluzhaschikh v 1917 g.', in Ansky, *Prof. dvizh. Petrograde*, pp. 231–42.

33. K.V. Bazilevich, *Prof. dvizh. rabotnikov svyazi* (Moscow 1927), pp. 81–5, 88 ff., 101–7.

34. A. Tanyaev, *Ocherki po istorii dvizheniya zhelezno-dorozhnikov v revolyutsii 1917 g. (fevral'oktyabr')* (Moscow 1925), cited by Pethybridge, *The Spread of the Russian Revolution*, p. 18. The latter work provides (pp. 1–56) the first general account in English of the Russian railways' role during this period, apart from an article by W.R. Augustine, 'Russia's Railwaymen, July-October 1917', *SR*, 24 (1965), pp. 666–79.

35. For their names and party affiliation, see P. Vompe, *Dni Okt.* (Moscow 1924), p. 10. This booklet, by an Inter-districtite member of the executive, is an invaluable source.

36. Vompe, *Dni Okt.*, p. 12.

37. *RV*, 24 August; [S. Lozovsky], *Otchet TsK VTsSPS* (Petrograd 1918), pp. 35–9.

38. Pethybridge, *The Spread of the Russian Revolution*, pp. 40–2, 46.

39. Ignatov, 'Iz ist. Ts. Byuro', p. 133.

40. Although the text of the resolutions was published shortly afterwards, the minutes did not see the light until ten years later, in the form of the publication referred to in n. 5.

41. *III konf.*, pp. 108 f. (Rozov, Yekaterinburg).

42. *III konf.*, pp. 448 f.

43. *III konf.*, pp. 445 f.

44. *III konf.*, pp. 301–3.

45. *III konf.*, pp. 326 f.

46. *III konf.*, p. 388.

47. *III konf.*, pp. 452 f.; cf. *Izv.*, 2 July 1917.

48. *III konf.*, pp. 446–8.

49. *III konf.*, pp. 217, 225 f.

50. *III konf.*, p. 216.

51. Lozovsky, *Otchet TsK VTsSPS*.

52. Volin, *Deyat. men.*, p. 3.

CHAPTER 9   THE URBAN SOVIETS: STRUCTURE

1. The pioneering work in this field by a western scholar is Anweiler, *Die Rätebewegung*. This offers a perceptive analysis of the soviets' role in revolutionary theory and practice before and during the revolution. Cf. also, by the same author, 'The Political Ideology of the Leaders of the Petrograd Soviet in the Spring of 1917', in *Revolutionary Russia*, ed. R. Pipes (Cambridge, Mass. 1968), pp. 145–75.

2. For various estimates of their number, cf. A.M. Andreyev, *Sovety rab. i sold. dep.* (Moscow 1967), p. 351. This figure excludes those in which peasants alone were represented.

3. V.P. Antonov-Saratovsky (ed.), *Sarat. Sovet* (Moscow, Leningrad 1931). On p. viii the editor notes the deplorable laxity with which these records were treated in the early years of Soviet rule. Some were discovered in the home of an official who was using them as a pillow.

4. Nalivaysky, *Petrogr. Sovet rab. i sold. dep.* A recent Soviet student – G.I. Zlokazov, *Petrogr. Sovet* (Moscow 1969), p. 10 – points to omissions in this record made for technical reasons and gives information about relevant unpublished archival holdings. More recently the proceedings of the (Bolshevik-controlled) district soviets in Petrograd have appeared as *Rayon. sovety Petrogr. v 1917 g.*, 3 vols (Moscow, Leningrad 1964-6). On these bodies see now R.A. Wade, 'The Rayonnye Sovety of Petrograd', *JGOE*, 20 (1972), pp. 226-40.

5. In 1931 E.P. Krivosheina compiled a collection of secondary sources (mainly newspaper extracts) concerning the soviet, but this has remained inaccessible. Similar in nature but wider in scope is the collection by Gorin and others, *Org. i str. Sovetov.*

6. E. Ignatov, *Mosk. Sovet rab. dep.* (Moscow 1925).

7. An analysis of the revolution as it affected the Russian army lies outside our subject. Three useful recent studies in western languages are G. Wettig, 'Die Rolle der russ. Armee in revol. Machtkampf', *Forsch. zur osteurop. Gesch.*, 12 (1967), pp. 46-389 (on the period February-July 1917); M. Ferro, 'The Russian Soldier in 1917', *SR*, 30 (1971) pp. 483-512; and A. Wildman, 'The February Revolution in the Army', *SS*, 22 (1970-1), pp. 3-23.

8. M.S. Yugov, 'Sovety v I-y period revol.', in Pokrovsky, *Ocherki po ist. Okt. revol.*, II, p. 156.

9. On this episode see F.F. Raskolnikov, *Kronshtadt i Piter v 1917 g.* (Moscow 1925); I.G. Tsereteli, *Vospom. o fev. revol.*, 2 vols (Paris, The Hague 1963), I, pp. 413-27.

10. In mid-March the soldiers' section of the Petrograd soviet had two thousand members (as compared with only seven to eight hundred workers); by May, however, partly owing to postings from the garrison, its strength had declined to about nine hundred: Zlokazov, *Petrogr. Sovet*, pp. 138, 229.

11. Zlokazov, *Petrogr. Sovet*, p. 225.

12. Ignatov, *Mosk. Sovet rab. dep.*, p. 66; cf. *Izv.*, 5 August. In April it was reported that in eight places within the Moscow region, nineteen managerial personnel were serving as deputies. The local (Menshevik) leaders decided to force them out to maintain class purity. Gorin and others, *Org. i str. Sovetov*, p. 124.

13. Yugov, 'Sovety v I-y period revol.', p. 157 (Kazan, Archangel).

14. Ignatov, *Mosk. Sovet rab. dep.*, pp. 10, 18; cf. Gorin and others, *Org. i str. Sovetov*, pp. 15, 20.

15. Ignatov, *Mosk. Sovet rab. dep.*, pp. 59–68.

16. Ignatov, *Mosk. Sovet rab. dep.*, pp. 446–50.

17. A.I. Razgon, 'O sostave Sovetov Nizh. Povolzh'ya v mart – aprel' 1917 g.', in *Sovety i soyuz rab. klassa i kr-va*, eds I.I. Mints and others (Moscow 1964), p. 90.

18. Antonov-Saratovsky, *Sarat. Sovet*, pp. 74, 201.

19. Antonov-Saratovsky, *Sarat. Sovet*, pp. 34, 169; cf. p. 209.

20. E.g. Antonov-Saratovsky, *Sarat. Sovet*, pp. 206 f.

21. N.N. Sukhanov, *The Russian Revolution*, II, p. 359.

22. *Izv.*, 16 March.

23. Nalivaysky, *Petrogr. Sovet rab. i sold.*, pp. 47, 103–5; Zlokazov, *Petrogr. Sovet*, pp. 178–81; cf. Anweiler, *The Soviets*, p. 108.

24. Nalivaysky, *Petrogr. Sovet rab. i sold.*, p. 223. On 5 August it was decided that the latter should make do with two weekly meetings, in addition to one for each section (*Izv.*, 6 August). Another paragraph in this statute ordained that 'no question may be placed on the agenda without [preliminary] discussion in the presidium'.

25. *Izv.*, 29 March; Zlokazov, *Petrogr. Sovet*, pp. 142, 179, c.u.d.s.

26. Nalivaysky, *Petrogr. Sovet rab. i sold.*, pp. 10, 107–9.

27. Zlokazov, *Petrogr. Sovet*, p. 143, c.u.d.s.

CHAPTER 10   THE URBAN SOVIETS: CREATION OF A NATIONAL LEADERSHIP

1. Gorin and others, *Org. i str. Sovetov*, pp. 104, 153 f.; Z.L. Serebryakova, 'Mosk. obl.', in Mints and others, *Sovety i soyuz rab. klassa i kr – va*, pp. 39 f.; it was familiarly known as MOBYUS.

2. Antonov-Saratovsky, *Sarat. Sovet*, p. 68; cf. Gorin and others, *Org. i str. Sovetov*, pp. 41–5, 105 f., 163–6.

3. Antonov-Saratovsky, *Sarat. Sovet*, pp. 109, 143.

4. Serebryakova, 'Mosk. obl.', pp. 49 f., 59. The Voronezh bureau was set up at a congress to which the provincial capital supplied fifty delegates and other places only thirty-two. Gorin and others, *Org. i str. Sovetov*, p. 303.

5. Nalivaysky, *Petrogr. Sovet rab. i sold.*, p. 50.

6. On the composition cf. M.N. Tsapenko (comp.), *Vseross. soveshch. Sovetov* (Moscow, Leningrad 1927), p. 189; Yugov, 'Sovety v I-y period revol.', II, p. 149; Andreyev, *Sovety rab. i sold. dep.*, p. 130; English ed.: *The Soviets*, pp. 98 f; Zlokazov, *Petrogr. Sovet*, p. 146. Organization matters were discussed at the last two sessions: Tsapenko, *Vseross. soveshch. Sovetov*, pp. 212–79. For text of resolutions: Gorin and others, *Org. i str. Sovetov*, pp. 176–91.

7. Gorin and others, *Org. i str. Sovetov*, p. 190; Nalivaysky, *Petrogr. Sovet rab. i sold.*, p. 95; *Izv.*, 6 April 1917.

8. Tsapenko, *Vseross. soveshch. Sovetov*, pp. 294–6.

9. Tsapenko, *Vseross. soveshch. Sovetov*, pp. 294–6; Gorin and others, *Org. i str. Sovetov*, p. 191.

10. Antonov-Saratovsky, *Sarat. Sovet*, p. 121.

11. *I-y Vseross. s'yezd Sovetov*, 2 vols (Moscow, Leningrad 1930) [cited as *I s'yezd*], I, p. xxvii; II, p. 10; Zlokazov, *Petrogr. Sovet*, p. 238.

12. *I s'yezd*, II, p. 10.

13. *I s'yezd*, II, p. 291.

14. *I s'yezd*, II, p. 61.

15. *I s'yezd*, II, pp. 62–7, 422–6; Sukhanov, *Zap. o revol.*, IV, pp. 275–81; cf. Gorin and others, *Org. i str. Sovetov*, pp. 280–3; Nalivaysky, *Petrogr. Sovet rab. i sold.*, p. 203.

16. Sukhanov, *Zap. o revol.*, IV, pp. 275–81 (where the interpretation of these events is, however, highly debatable).

17. *Izv.*, 30 July, 27 August.

18. *Izv.*, 25, 29, 30 July, 11, 27 August.

19. *Izv.*, 19 August. Rather more influential was the corresponding department of the Petrograd soviet, directed by V.G. Groman, another Menshevik who rose to prominence as a Soviet planner: cf. N. Jasny, *Soviet Economists of the Twenties* (London 1972), pp. 97–102.

20. *Izv.*, 15, 28, 29 July; 27 August; cf. also Gorin and others, *Org. i str. Sovetov*, p. 286.

21. *Izv.*, 7, 14, 15, 22, 26 July.

22. *Izv.*, 27 August.

23. Gorin and others, *Org. i str. Sovetov*, p. 215.

24. Russian revolutionary jargon distinguished carefully between progaganda and agitation, the former being more concerned with ultimate ends, and generally less militant, than the latter; organization was also treated as a qualitatively different kind of activity.

25. *Izv.*, 27 August.

26. Similar courses were held in Kharkov. *Izv.*, 16, 25 July; 5, 20, 27 August.

27. *I s'yezd*, II, pp. 433 f.; Anweiler, *The Soviets*, p. 108; Gorin and others, *Org. i str. Sovetov*, pp. 128 f.

28. In March and April executive committee members received a salary of 400 roubles a month, and thereafter were paid 'at the established rate' (not specified). With an average of ninety members, this would have cost 36,000 roubles, and a sum of this order duly appears in the accounts. There is no mention of any payment to the twenty-seven hundred or so rank-and-file deputies, although in Moscow they received 10 roubles for each day that they attended, meetings being held once a week. In Moscow and Saratov executive committee members received

300 roubles a month; in the more proletarian centre of Ivanovo-Voznesensk the rate was only 150 roubles. E. Ignatov, *Mosk. Sovet rab. dep.*, p. 62; Gorin and others, p. 127; Antonov-Saratovsky, *Sarat. Sovet,* p. 206; D. Furmanov, *Put' k bol'shevizmu* (Moscow, Leningrad 1928), p. 126.

29. *Izv.*, 16, 27 July; 11 August.
30. *Izv.*, 27 July.
31. Gorin and others, *Org. i str. Sovetov*, pp. 204–7.
32. *Izv.*, 27 July.
33. Ignatov, *Mosk. Sovet rab. dep.*, p. 73; *Izv.*, 21 July, 5 August.
34. Yugov, 'Sovety v I-y period revol.', p. 208. This incident took place in April, before regular fund-raising activities had begun in earnest.
35. On the vexed question of German–Bolshevik financial connections see Z.A.B. Zeman (ed.), *Germany and the Revolution in Russia* (London 1958), esp. pp. 94 f.; Z.A.B. Zeman and W. Scharlau, *The Merchant of Revolution: the Life of A.I. Helphand (Parvus)* (London 1965), pp. 206–34. The information gleaned from German archives is inconclusive. Foreign subsidies received by Russian political parties need to be evaluated in the context of their overall revenue.

CHAPTER 11   THE URBAN SOVIETS: THE POLITICAL BATTLE JOINED

1. Ignatov, *Mosk. Sovet rab. dep.*, p. 35.
2. Antonov-Saratovsky, *Sarat. Sovet,* pp. 3, 76; Razgon, 'O sostave', in Mints and others, *Sovety i soyuz rab. klassa i kr-va*, eds I.I. Mints and others, pp. 114–16.
3. Lenin, *PSS*, XXXI, pp. 134–8.
4. For a general analysis of Leninist organizational techniques, see P. Selznick, *The Organizational Weapon: a Study of Bolshevik Tactics* (New York 1952), and for the party's tactics towards the soviets before October: Anweiler, *The Soviets*, pp. 144–92.
5. Zlokazov, *Petrogr. Sovet*, p. 182.
6. Zlokazov, *Petrogr. Sovet*, p. 226; Andreyev, *Sovety rab. i sold. dep.*, p. 201; (English ed., p. 161).
7. *Izv.*, 25 May; Zlokazov, *Petrogr. Sovet*, pp. 227 f.
8. *Izv.*, 2 June; cf. Andreyev, *Sovety rab. i sold. dep.*, pp. 198–202; (English ed., pp. 154–9); Zlokazov, *Petrogr. Sovet*, pp. 230 f.
9. Andreyev, *Sovety rab. i sold. dep.*, p. 202 (English ed., p. 162), citing *Prot. VI s'yezd RSDRP(b), avg. 1917 g.* (Moscow 1958), p. 14, but omitting to note that Stalin was the speaker; cf. also L.F. Karamysheva, *Bor'ba bol'sh. za Petrogr. Sovet* (Leningrad 1964), pp. 78–110. Zlokazov, *Petrogr. Sovet*, p. 229, cites calculations by A.D. Sadovsky which show the party alignment in the soldiers' section as follows: SRs 306, Men-

sheviks 298, Bolsheviks 105 (and *circa* 200 deputies unaffiliated!). There are no corresponding data for the workers' section.

10. Andreyev, *Sovety rab. i sold. dep.*, pp. 198–203 (English ed., pp. 154–60); Yugov, 'Sovety v I-y period revol.', Pokrovsky, *Ocherki po ist. Okt. revol.*, II, p. 159; for the text of the instruction, Ignatov, *Mosk. Sovet rab. dep.*, p. 71. Cf. also Gorin and others, *Org. i str. Sovetov*, p. 350. In Kharkov the Menshevik leaders made a still more determined effort to ensure observance of democratic electoral procedures and provided that balloting should be in secret (pp. 351 f.).

11. Freydlin, *Ocherki ist. rab. dvizh.*, p. 300.

12. *PR*, 63 (1927), p. 268.

13. Yugov, 'Sovety v I-y period revol.', p. 206.

14. Yugov, 'Sovety v I-y period revol.', pp. 208 f. Yugov was able to consult the minutes of this and other Georgian soviets for 1917, published three years later when Georgia was an independent socialist republic with a Menshevik-led government.

15. On this important tactical shift, see Anweiler, *The Soviets*, pp. 171–4; Schapiro, *The Communist Party*, p. 169; Lenin, *PSS*, XXXIV, pp. 1–5; *Prot. VI s'yezd*, pp. 247–9.

16. *Izv.*, 27 July, 13 August (where the second vote is given as 364:304); Ignatov, *Mosk. Sovet rab. dep.*, pp. 293, 301.

17. *Izv.*, 23 July; Andreyev, *Sovety rab. i sold. dep.*, p. 261 (English ed., p. 217).

18. Andreyev, *Sovety rab. i sold. dep.*, p. 264 (English ed., p. 218).

19. Andreyev, *Sovety rab. i sold. dep.*, pp. 256–9 (English ed., pp. 214–16).

20. *Izv.*, 12, 25 July 1917.

21. *Izv.*, 20 August.

22. *Izv.*, 24 August.

23. *Izv.*, 6, 11, 23 July.

CHAPTER 12   TOWN AND COUNTRY: THE SOCIAL AND PSYCHOLOGICAL BACK-
GROUND

1. A perceptive critique of PSR ideology is offered by O.H. Radkey in ch. 1 of his *Agrarian Foes* (New York, London 1958). This work and its sequel, *The Sickle under the Hammer* (New York 1963), represent a major contribution to our understanding of the events of 1917–18 in so far as they affected that party. The author is, however, unduly critical of the stand taken by the moderate (pro-Allied) elements in the PSR leadership. Cf. the reviews by M. Vishnyak in *Novyy zhurnal*, 54 (1958), pp. 200–15, and by the present writer in *SS*, 16 (1964–5), pp. 63–68.

2. Ferro, *La Révolution*, p. 194, argues that the peasants' ideology was remote from that of the PSR intellectuals, and in support of this contention adduces the fact that, of a hundred resolutions submitted by

peasants to various central bodies in March and April 1917, a mere 2 per cent mentioned the desirability of a return to communal owner-ship. It is, however, misleading to take these petitions as a comprehensive or self-sufficient statement of peasant attitudes.

3. For a stimulating recent study of this question, see T. Shanin, *The Awkward Class* (Oxford 1972). Of the valuable early studies by A.V. Chayanov, a leading Populist authority on peasant society, two have now been translated into English: *The Theory of Peasant Economy* (South Holland, Ill. 1966); *Peasant Co-operation: Basic Concepts and Organizational Forms* (London 1973).

4. Cf. P.A. Sorokin, 'Gorod i derevnya: bio-sotsiologicheskaya kharak-teristika', *KR*, IV (1923), pp. 3–25: a stimulating essay by a Populist who subsequently won world-wide fame as a sociologist.

5. Igritsky, *1917 g. v derevne*, p. 124. The scarcity of first-hand contemporary documentary evidence from peasant sources – as distinct from petitions, resolutions and similar statements of a formal character whose authenticity is in some doubt – adds to the value of this compilation, for all its obvious political bias.

6. At Aleksandrovka, Fatezh county, Kursk province, in March 1917: K.G. Kotelnikov and V.L. Meller (comps), *Krest. dvizh. v 1917 g.* (Moscow, Leningrad 1927) [cited as K&M], p. 3; P.N. Pershin, *Agr. revol.* (Moscow 1966), I, p. 286.

7. Igritsky, *1917 g. v derevne*, p. 134.

CHAPTER 13   THE PROVISIONAL GOVERNMENT AND THE AGRARIAN QUESTION

1. *VVP*, 21 March 1917; English text: B&K, II, pp. 524 f. This statement was made in response to pressure by the Moscow Agricultural Society, which was already alarmed at the extent of the disorders: D.A. Lutokhin, 'Zem. vop.', *ZIIR*, II (1925), p. 347; cf. N.K. Figurovskaya, 'Bankrotstvo', *IZ*, 81 (1968), p. 28; Pershin, *Agr. revol.*, I, p. 292.

2. *VVP*, 23 April; draft text in A.V. Shestakov (comp.), *Sovety krest. dep. i drug.* (Moscow 1929), II, pp. 295–8. The English version (B&K, II, pp. 528–32), either by accident or design, omits articles 5 and 7, although these account for a mere four to five lines of text in a document running to more than three pages; article 7 is particularly important.

3. B&K, II, p. 644.

4. The negative view conventionally taken by both Soviet and western writers of the committee's activities is due in part to a lack of detailed information. This lacuna has now been filled by Pershin (who was himself associated with its work) in the monograph cited above, n. 6; cf. esp. I, pp. 294–7, 305–25 and also (for the political aspects) Figurovskaya, 'Bankrotstvo', pp. 30–7.

5. For a sympathetic but not uncritical study of his career, see O.H.

Radkey, *Agrarian Foes* (New York 1958), *passim*. Chernov's own auto-biographical account has been translated into English by P.E. Mosely as *The Great Russian Revolution* (New Haven, Conn. 1936).

6. B&K, I, pp. 284–90; D.G. Levin, *Novyy zakon o vol. zem. upravlenii* (Moscow 1917).

7. See below p. 237. Such a measure had previously been advocated by the Main Land Committee, after a fiercely contested vote. The PSR was the driving force behind both resolutions. Chernov repeated his ideas before the first All-Russian Congress of Workers' and Soldiers' Soviets on 23 June: cf. Gorin and others, *Org.*, pp. 254 f.

8. *Izvestiya Vseross. Soveta Krest. Deputatov* [cited as *Izv. VSKD*], 8 July; *Izv.*, 20 July; Figurovskaya, 'Bankrotstvo', pp. 45–49; Lutokhin, 'Zem. vop.', pp. 355 f.; Pershin, *Agr. revol.*, I, p. 297.

9. B&K, II, pp. 556 f. The ban was made retroactive to 1 March. Soon after taking office Chernov had prevailed upon P.N. Pereverzev, the minister of Justice, to instruct public notaries not to register such deeds (17 May), but on 13 June, after protests by banks and landowners, that ministry had repealed the ban (Lutokhin, 'Zem. vop.', p. 354; Pershin, *Agr. revol.*, I, pp. 302 f.).

10. Text in B&K, II, pp. 558–62. The first of these rights was limited to *county* land committees.

11. In Laishev county. Cf. D.S. Gutman and G.G. Derkach (comps), *Krest. dvizh. v Kaz. gub.*, I, (Kazan 1950), pp. 43, 48, 51, 53, 74, 90.

12. *Izv. VSKD*, 18 June; Pershin, *Agr. revol.*, I, p. 371; O.N. Moiseyeva, *Sovety krest. dep.* (Moscow 1967), p. 100; N.A. Kravchuk, *Mass. krest. dvizh.* (Moscow 1971), p. 177. Proceedings were instituted aga inst fourteen of the seventeen land committees in Yelna county, Smolensk province, involving a total of seventy persons (*NZ*, 13 October). Much was made in contemporary radical propaganda of these 'acts of repression', but it appears that in the whole country a mere seventeen or eighteen disobedient land committee members were actually sentenced to jail terms. Radkey, *Agrarian Foes*, p. 328.

13. *Izv. VSKD*, 15 August; K&M, pp. 148 f., 153; *EPR*, III, p. 322.

14. These latter are the object of a valuable recent study by W.G. Rosenberg, 'The Russian Municipal Duma Elections of 1917: a Preliminary Computation of Returns', *SS*, 21 (1969–70), pp. 131–63. No comparable work has yet been done on their rural counterparts.

15. Based on reports in various issues of *Izv. VSKD*, *NZ* and *RS* for September and October 1917; cf. also S.P. Rudnev, *Pri vechernikh ognyakh* (Harbin 1928), p. 82.

16. Text (originally published in *DN*, 18 October) reproduced in Shestakov, *Sovety krest. dep. i drug.*, II, pp. 322–32 and (in excerpt) in B&K, II, pp. 577–9; cf. Figurovskaya, 'Bankrotstvo', p. 64; Lutokhin, 'Zem. vop.', p. 362.

17. Chernov, *Dukh revolyutsionnoy Rossii: fevral'skaya revolyutsiya* (Paris, Prague, New York 1934), pp. 320–8; cf. Radkey, *Agrarian Foes*, pp. 446–9.

CHAPTER 14   PASSIVE RESISTANCE: THE PEASANT AND THE MARKET

1. Zaitsev and Dolinsky, 'Org. and Pol.', p. 97.
2. For the old and new rates, see *Stat. yezheg.*, *Trudy TsSU*, VIII, fasc. 1, pt 1, section 1 (Moscow 1921), pp. 94 f. Zaitsev and Dolinsky, who criticize the decree's provisions ('Org. and Pol.', pp. 98–100), omit to mention the price rise. The English text of the decree as given in B&K, II, pp. 618–21 is abbreviated. Cf. also Z. Lozinsky, *Ekon. pol. Vrem. Prav.* (Leningrad 1929), p. 137.
3. In September a critic complained that the wages bill for the Penza privincial supply committee was 32,000 roubles a month – four times what it had been before the February revolution, when only one man had been required to do the work now performed by seven (*RS*, 6 September). Such complaints were a little unfair in that the responsibilities of these organs had broadened considerably; moreover, most members served on an expenses-only basis, which helped to keep costs down.
4. It would be useful to have detailed information on the process whereby these new institutions came into being, and to know whether they appeared in response to central or local initiative, how far their composition accorded with the provisions of the law, and what the relationship was between senior and junior organs. Unfortunately the State Supply Committee's official journal, *Izv. po prod. delu*, has not been available.
5. Zaitsev and Dolinsky, 'Org. and Pol.', p. 122.
6. V.M. Ustinov, *Evol. vnutr. torg.* (Moscow 1925), p. 20; *RS*, 3 September.
7. B&K, II, p. 626.
8. *RS*, 3 August.
9. *RS*, 29 August.
10. Lozinsky, *Ekon. pol. Vrem. Prav.*, pp. 130 f.; *EPR*, II, pp. 339–42.
11. Zaitsev and Dolinsky, 'Org. and Pol.', p. 28 n.
12. B&K, II, pp. 629 f. To add to the confusion, until 1 June the food-supply administration was placed under the ministry of Finance 'to enable it to complete organization of the grain monopoly' – or rather, to keep it in the hands of Shingarev, who was transferred to this post, and out of the hands of Chernov, the new minister of Agriculture. This involved no less than three systems of subordination in as many months, a striking example of administrative muddle.
13. *RS*, 11 May.

14. Zaitsev and Dolinsky, 'Org. and Pol.', pp. 104 f. The authors do not give the source of this information, which seems a little suspect.

15. *RV*, 24 August; *RS*, 18 August.

16. *RS*, 22, 29 August.

17. *Novoye vremya*, 1 July.

18. *RV*, 16 September.

19. *RS*, 25 August. Cf. *Izv.*, 29 July, for a similar case of public 'shaming', resorted to by some soldiers in Yaroslavl against a comrade who had stolen a pair of boots: the offender was made to hold them by his teeth; a label reading 'I am a thief' was attached to his forehead, and a makeshift tin drum thrust into his hands, which he was obliged to strike in order to attract spectators, who beat him as he walked by.

20. *RS*, 13 September.

21. *RS*, 5, 18 August; *Den'*, 10 August; *Izv.*, 18 July, 8 August; *EPR*, III, p. 377.

22. *RS*, 5 August.

23. *RV*, 24 August.

24. *RS*, 21, 22 August.

25. *RS*, 2 August.

26. *RS*, 6 August.

27. *RS*, 21 August, 21 September.

28. *Den'*, 10 August; cf. *Izv.*, 8 August.

29. *RS*, 6 August; B&K, 11, p. 641.

30. B&K, 11, pp. 641 f.; *Sist. sb. dek. po prod. delu*, bk 1, (Nizhniy Novgorod 1919), pp. 213 f.; Zaitsev and Dolinsky, 'Org. and Pol.', p. 107; *RS*, 29 August.

31. E.g. in Tambov and Rostov-on-Don: *RS*, 21 September; *Birzh. ved.*, 22 September; cf. also *EPR*, III, pp. 198–203.

32. *Novoye vremya*, 1 July; Shestakov, *Sovety krest. dep. i drug.*, 11, p. 252; *EPR*, III, pp. 87–9; cf. also above p. 74.

33. Cattle continued to be requisitioned by the supply authorities, but were not subject to state monopoly as was grain, and the free market therefore continued to flourish. Prices evidently rose steeply. In July some peasants in Voronezh province protested that the State paid them only 9·60 roubles a pud, whereas they could get 35–40 roubles on the free market (*EPR*, III, p. 119). Unfortunately the livestock trade has received even less attention from historians than that in grain, despite its significance in the northern and central provinces.

34. The Chukhari people of Markovo (Belozersk county, Cherepovets province) later remembered the years 1915–17 as a time of unparalleled prosperity 'when they never drank tea without having white cakes as well': V.G. Tan-Bogoraz (ed.), *Revol. v derevne* (Moscow, Leningrad 1924), p. 25.

35. *EPR*, III, pp. 158 f., 204 f., 451–5 (the last table was first published in

Nar. khoz., 3, 1918, with some arithmetical errors that have here been corrected). All of them originate from the statistical services of the ministry of Supply. Two tables contain estimates of the gross harvest. One (pp. 158 f.) is dated 4 October 1917. The other (pp. 451–5) is not dated but was evidently compiled later, since the figures are generally higher and it is also more comprehensive in coverage; it is, however, clearly also only a *provisional* estimate. The figures for procurement (pp. 204 f.) relate to the agricultural year 1916–17 and were compiled at some unspecified time during 1917.

36. S.N. Prokopovich, last minister of Supply in the Provisional Government, addressing the Council of the Republic on 16 October, put the 1917 harvest in European Russia and northern Caucasus at 2954 million puds (B&K, II, p. 647; cf. *NZ*, 24 October 1917). A.E. Lositsky, a ministry of Supply official, later put the gross harvest of all cereals at 3812 million puds, and of the six principal grains at 3620 million puds; he estimated the net harvest (after deduction for seed) at 3100 million puds: *Urozhay khlebov v Rossii v 1917 g.* (Moscow 1917), as cited by N. [A.] Orlov, *Prod. rabota Sov. vlasti* (Moscow 1919, p. 284). The first of Lositsky's figures was reproduced without comment by the Soviet supply chief A. Svidersky, writing in *Ekon. zhizn'*, 23 March 1919; but subsequently lower figures were often quoted. Thus in *Sb. stat. sved. po SSSR, 1918–1923 gg.* (Moscow 1924), p. 131, the gross figure is given as 3350 million puds; and V.P. Milyutin, in his *Agr. pol. SSSR* (Moscow 1926), p. 140, reduces it further to a mere 2646 million puds (for the whole country less Transcaucasia and Central Asia). On the other hand the unofficial writer Gordeyev gives a higher figure than any of the above: 4843 million puds. (*Sel. khoz. v voyne*, p. 91). This is doubtless much too high, and there is no indication of the source.

37. *EPR*, III, pp. 158 f.; *Stat. yezheg.*, pt II, section I, p. 2.

38. Ustinov, *Evol. vnutr. torg.*, p. 12; cf. Orlov, *Prod. rabota Sov. vlasti*, pp. 8 f.

39. *Stat. yezheg.*, pt II, section I, p. 2.

40. V.I. Shal't, 'Razvitiye khlebooborota v SSSR', in *Khlebooborot*, ed. V.T. Tevosyan (Moscow 1957), p. 14.

41. Demosthenov, 'Food Prices', pp. 269, 271, reproduces (without revealing his source) ministry of Agriculture figures on grain prices in April and November 1917. Those for the black-soil region (the selling price in producers' markets) show an increase from 333·3 to 1087·2 (1909–13: 100) for rye and 331·3 to 1071·5 for wheat. Those for the non-black-soil region (the purchase price in consumers' markets) are much higher: from 456·7 to 1626·9 for rye and from 559·5 to 1731·9 for wheat. These figures must, however, be treated with caution: if they were derived from local commodity exchanges, it must be noted that the latter were no longer functioning normally by November. It is difficult to explain why prices in the Central Industrial region should be shown as 50 to

100 per cent higher than those in the Lakes region (which included Petrograd), where the supply problem was more acute.

CHAPTER 15   THE SPREAD OF AGRARIAN VIOLENCE: A REGIONAL ANALYSIS

1. The 1916 census, which covered forty-seven provinces of European Russia, recorded a total of 110,031 farms in the 'privately owned' category, with a total population (that is including families and resident employees) of 2,358,000. These farms had 7,687,000 dessyatines of land sown to crop, an average of 69·8 dessyatines per farm. Ya. S. Artyukhov and A.V. Chayanov (comps), *Sel.-khoz.* (Moscow 1918), pp. 6, 13. These figures, for all their defects, are more reliable than those contained in the agricultural census carried out in a more limited area (thirty-eight provinces) during the summer of 1917, when the disturbed conditions prevented the statisticians from carrying out their investigations properly. Where the 1917 data are relevant, they will be given in the notes to this chapter. *Pogub. itogi* (Moscow 1922?), pp. 42 ff.

2. E.g., in *Izv.*, 27 August; cf. Shestakov, *Sovety krest. dep. i drug.*, I, pp. 254–6. These data are conveniently reproduced in the form of a map by M. Martynov, 'Agr. dvizh. v 1917 g. po dok. Glav. Zem. Kom.', *KA*, 14 (1926), p. 225.

3. K&M.

4. The first to question the validity of this source was S.P. Melgunov, in an appendix to *Kak bol'sheviki zakhvatili vlast'* (Paris 1953); this has been included in the abridged English version of this valuable work, *The Bolshevik Seizure of Power*, ed. S.G. Pushkarev (Santa Barbara, Calif., Oxford 1972), pp. 198–204. It is, however difficult to accept his argument that one should ignore the figures for *pogroms* and seizures, and take into account only those for landed property offences (*zemel'niye pravonarusheniya*), in estimating the intensity of the agrarian movement. On the basis of this evidence he argues that the number of incidents fell decisively in September and remained at approximately the same level in October (English ed., pp. 201 f.). In our view this conclusion is too sweeping.

5. Ya. A. Yakovlev, 'Krest. voyna 1917 g.', in *Agr. revol. v 4 tt.*, II: *Krest. dvizh. v 1917 g.*, ed. V.P. Milyutin (Moscow 1928), p. 92.

6. I. Vermenichev, 'Krest. dvizh. mezhdu fev. i Okt. revol.', in Milyutin, *Agr. revol.*, II: *Krest. dvizh.*, p. 205.

7. Pershin, *Agr. revol.*, I, pp. 407 f.

8. Kravchuk, *Mass. krest. dvizh.*, pp. 15, 88, 107 (based partly on recent local studies); I.I. Mints, *Ist. Vel. Okt.*, II (Moscow 1968), pp. 838, 1120 f.

9. E.G. Shulyakovsky (ed.), *Ocherk ist. Voron. kraya*, (Voronezh 1961), p. 384.

10. According to the 1917 figures, the population was 3·3 million; no data were collected for private property; the number of sheep registered had fallen to 2·2 million and of pigs to 600,000: *Pogub. itogi*, pp. 2 ff. Data on Voronezh province are derived from (Brokgauz and Efron), *Entsik. slovar'*, (St Petersburg 1893–1904), VII, pp. 205–9; N.P. Oganovsky and A.V. Chayanov (comps), *Zemlevlad. i zemlepol'z.* (Moscow 1917), pp. 10 f., 26 f.; Artyukhov and Chayanov, *Sel.-khoz.*, pp. 6–23; A.N. Chelintsev, *Sb. stat. mat. Ukrainy* (Odessa 1922), pp. 1 f., 5, 8 f., 49; P.G. Morev, 'Mezhdu dvumya rev.', in Shulyakovsky, *Ocherk ist. Voron. kraya*, pp. 379–91.

11. K&M, pp. 363–99; Mints, *Ist. Vel. Okt.*, pp. 1120–5, gives figures for October as well, but these are best ignored.

12. E.G. Shulyakovsky and others (eds), *Bor'ba za Sov. vlast' v Voron. gub.* (Voronezh 1957).

13. We may disregard a single communication dated 15 March reporting 'disturbances among peasants in Novokhopersk': K&M, p. 3.

14. Morev, 'Mezhdu dvumya revol.', p. 385. These differences between counties could probably be explained by an analysis of property distribution as recorded in local cadastral surveys and such like.

15. Melgunov, *Bolshevik Seizure*, p. 201.

16. K&M, pp. 46, 152, 271.

17. K&M, p. 46.

18. Pershin, citing a study by Morev, gives a figure of 722 incidents in Voronezh province during this period: *Agr. revol.*, I, p. 408.

19. Principal sources as in n. 10. L. Kritsman (ed.), *Mat. po ist. agr. revol.* (Moscow 1928–9), II, pp. 124 ff., gives some details of peasant farming in four selected districts of Kalyazin county. According to the 1917 census the proprietors' sown area had shrunk to 4·8 dessyatines and of other peasants to over 2 dessyatines; horses owned by private proprietors amounted to 2 per cent of the whole; the figures for cattle were 3 per cent and for pigs 4 per cent.

20. Since neither of the two regional 'chronicles of events' compiled in 1941 and 1960 has been available, we have drawn on the material in two documentary publications with a nation-wide coverage: A.L. Sidorov and others (eds), *Vel. Okt. sots. revol.: dok. i mat.*, 9 vols. (Moscow 1957–63); *Vel. Okt. sots. revol.: khron. sob.*, 5 vols. (Moscow 1957–62) [cited as *DiM, KhS.*] These mention nine incidents not recorded in K&M; of these four occurred in March and early April, when the militia was being formed, and three in September, when its work was seriously obstructed. This strengthens the credibility of the earlier source.

21. K&M, p. 119; cf. *KhS*, II, p. 71.

22. K&M, p. 184.
23. K&M, p. 299.
24. *KhS*, II, pp. 485, 557; III, p. 491.
25. Artyukhov and Chayanov, *Sel.-khoz.*, pp. 6–23; other sources as in n. 10. According to the 1917 census private proprietors owned 5 per cent of the horses and 3 per cent of the cattle; they held 10·5 per cent of the sown area.
26. K&M, pp. 67, 120, 186.
27. *DiM*, IV, p. 478.
28. K&M, pp. 242, 300 (reports of 28 August, 7 September).
29. Principal sources as in n. 10. According to the 1917 census there were 5831 properties with 14·4 per cent of the sown area, 11 per cent of the horses, 10 per cent of the cattle, 8 per cent of the pigs and 26 per cent of the sheep. *Pogub. itogi*, pp. 42 ff.
30. K&M, pp. 363–403 *passim*.
31. The compilation by S.P. Khvostenko, *Oktyabr' v Yekaterinoslave: sbornik dokumentov i materialov* (Dnepropetrovsk 1957), is disappointing: apart from one incident, it merely reproduces material from K&M. A little fresh material is to be found in *KhS*. Both these recent publications take pains to omit all reference to armed robberies, so conveying a quite misleading impression of the nature of the 'agrarian movement' in this province.
32. K&M, pp. 228, 285 f.

CHAPTER 16   THE SPREAD OF AGRARIAN VIOLENCE: A TYPOLOGICAL ANALYSIS

1. I. Vermenichev, 'Krest. dvizh. mezhdu fev. i Okt. revol.', in Milyutin, *Agr. revol. v4*, II: *Krest. dvizh.*, p. 187. From K&M, p. 12, it is clear that similar messages were sent to all landowners in the county.
2. *RS*, 11 May.
3. *Izv. Min. Zemledeliya*, I (1917), cited by S.P. Trapeznikov, *Agr. vop. i leninskaya agr. programma* (Moscow 1963), p. 294. An official report of January 1917 gives a figure of 545,000: *EPR*, III, p. 61.
4. *Sev. zap.*, I (1917), cited by Trapeznikov, *Agr. vop. i leninskaya agr. programma*, p. 294. This survey is reproduced as a table in Ferro, *La Révolution*, p. 536, with no indication of its limited coverage.
5. *Vestnik NKT*, I (January 1918), p. 95.
6. E. Brändström, *Unter den Kriegsgefangenen* (Berlin 1922), pp. 106–8; for the pre-February period, pp. 53–61.
7. *EPR*, III, p. 65.
8. K&M, p. 149.
9. *EPR*, III, p. 322; K&M, pp. 88, 149, 266.
10. Moiseyeva, *Sovety krest. dep.*, p. 84.
11. Pershin, *Agr. revol.*, I, p. 364.

12. *EPR*, III, p. 322.
13. K&M, p. 148.
14. *Izv. VSKD*, 10 May (Nikolayev, Samara province) ; *EPR*, III, pp. 328 f. ; *DiM*, I, p. 694. Ferro (*La R volution*, p. 412) incorrectly states that the peasants *raised* the rent by this amount; cf. Shestakov, *Sovety krest. dep. i drug.*, I, pp. 51, 94.
15. Martynov, 'Agr. dvizh.', p. 193.
16. *RS*, 4 May.
17. Martynov, 'Agr. dvizh', p. 220; a similar figure is quoted from Samara: Shestakov, *Sovety krest. dep. i drug.*, I, p. 102.
18. There is some evidence of peasants seeking to protect state-owned forest land from private lessors (for instance in Tver province: *KhS*, I, p. 281 ; IV, p. 82), but whether their motive was altruistic or egoistic is difficult to say.
19. K&M, p. 198.
20. *RS*, 4 May; for similar incidents in Smolensk province, K&M, p. 127.
21. K&M, pp. 144 f.
22. *EPR*, III, p. 376.
23. In 1916, in forty-seven provinces of European Russia, 1·9 million dessyatines were sown to various grasses out of a total sown area of 71·4 million dessyatines (Artyukhov and Chayanov, *Sel.-khoz.*, p. 13). According to Oganovsky, *Sel. khoz. Rossii v XX veke*, pp. 200 f., the figure was only 1·6 million dessyatines. Small as this amount was, it represented an improvement on the 1901 figure of a mere 518,000 dessyatines.
24. E.g. M.R. (contrib.), 'Bor'ba za zemlyu v 1917 g. po Kaz. gub.', *KA*, 78 (1936), p. 91.
25. *RS*, 4 October.
26. *RS*, 2 August ; summary reference in K&M, p. 151.
27. K&M, pp. 150, 154.
28. K&M, pp. 16, 103.
29. *EPR*, III, p. 341.
30. *EPR*, III, p. 357 ; K&M, p. 154.
31. K&M, p. 128.
32. *DiM*, V, p. 462.
33. Extortion may have been the purpose behind the arrest, in Tambov province in July, of the wife of an estate manager, as reported in K&M, p. 150.
34. K&M, p. 271.
35. Owen, *The Russian Peasant Movement*, pp. 146 f.
36. K&M, pp. 62, 199 ; cf. also pp. 103, 168, 297, 356.
37. K&M, p. 4. This and certain other assaults were laid at the door of a local peasant activist named Druzhitsky: cf. p. 153.
38. E.g. K&M, pp. 199 f ; cf. *DiM*, II, p. 634.

39. *RS*, 25, 26 August, 20 September; *RV*, 26 August; K&M, p. 212 (the latter source incorrectly rendered in Owen, *The Russian Peasant Movement*, p. 209, where it is said that 'the whole party' was killed by the troops).

40. Igritsky, *1917 g. v derevne*, pp. 70 f. A teacher named K.P. Romanov, who rented land in Kozlov country, was among those killed by peasant action at this time (*RS*, 13 September). It is not certain whether the two men were identical or whether their prestigious but unfortunate surname had anything to do with the affair.

41. K&M, pp. 268 f.

42. *RS*, 14 September; cf. Pershin, *Agr. revol.*, I, p. 420; also A.E. Lutsky, 'Krest. vosst. v Tamb. gub. v sent. 1917 g.', *IZ*, 2 (1938), pp. 49–78.

43. 'Kto ne stanet podzhigat', tot sami podpalim.'

44. *RS*, 13, 21–3 September. The initiating group is said to have consisted of peasants from Sychenki (Yaroslavl province), many hundreds of miles away.

45. K&M, pp. 269 f.

46. This step was decided on by the Tambov provincial supply committee in the first days of October and then sanctioned by the soviet (*RS*, 7 October).

47. *DiM*, VII, p. 442.

48. Lutsky, 'Krest. vosst. v. Tamb.', p. 70.

49. Artyukhov and Chayanov, *Sel.-khoz.*, p. 6.

50. *RS*, 8 October.

51. Pershin, *Agr. revol.*, I, pp. 420–5. The records of the central militia authorities (K&M, pp. 385–99), quoted by some earlier writers, are clearly far from complete.

52. S.G. Pushkarev, in his edition of S.P. Melgunov, *The Bolshevik Seizure of Power*, pp. 203 f.

53. P. Sorlin, 'Lénine et le problème paysan en 1917', *Annales*, 19 (1964), p. 265.

54. A.L. Okninsky, *Dva goda sredi krest'yan* (Riga 1936?), p. 93, notes that the term was applied to wealthier peasants. The term *kulak* was used by urban intellectuals as a group classification at the time but did not penetrate widely into the village until later.

55. Igritsky, *1917 g. v derevne*, p. 45.

56. Igritsky, *1917 g. v derevne*, p. 134.

57. Igritsky, *1917 g. v derevne*, p. 121.

58. Owen, *The Russian Peasant Movement*, pp. 146, 201, gives a contrary impression, but his sources (K&M, pp. 3, 152) do not bear him out.

59. 'Otvechat', tak vsem.' *RS*, 10 October.

60. For an example of the latter, cf. Igritsky, *1917 g. v derevne*, pp. 106–9: A. Makarov of Kazan province states that the richer peasants had

horses to remove the lords' timber, and worked on this task intensively by night and day, whereas the poor peasants 'drooled but could not touch it'. However, Makarov is an unreliable witness and his remarks probably are but a reflection of official thinking in 1929, on the eve of forced collectivization and 'de-kulakization'. Ferro, *La Révolution*, p. 193, echoes uncritically the stereotyped view that poor peasants were at all times the most radical element in the village.

61. Rudnev, *Pri vechernikh ognyakh*, p. 103.
62. K&M, p. 93.
63. Cf. the case of I. Smilov and I. Penzin, of Penza province, in K&M, p. 156.
64. For evidence of this, see K&M, pp. 208 (Orel), 210 (Ryazan), 280 (Nizhniy Novgorod), 281 (Samara); also *RS*, 10 August (Saratov), 27 September (Chernigov).

CHAPTER 17   FORMATION OF RURAL PRIMARY ORGANIZATIONS AND SOVIETS

1. Cf. table in Ferro, *La Révolution*, p. 187.
2. Kravchuk, *Mass. krest. dvizh.*, p. 95.
3. Moiseyeva, *Sovety krest. dep.*, p. 34.
4. *Zemlya i volya*, 18 April, reproduced in Shestakov, *Sovety krest. dep.*, 1, p. 48.
5. Kravchuk, *Mass. krest. dvizh.*, p. 97.
6. *Birzh. ved.*, 9 July.
7. *Izv. VSKD*, 11 June.
8. E. Kononova in *Izv. VSKD*, 31 August, 2 September.
9. *Izv. VSKD*, 11 June, 31 August; Kravchuk, *Mass. krest. dvizh.*, p. 97.
10. *Izv. VSKD*, 11 June; cf. 'Obzor polozh. Rossii', *KA*, 15 (1926), p. 41.
11. Kravchuk, *Mass. krest. dvizh.*, p. 98; Moiseyeva, *Sovety krest. dep.*, p. 36, notes a similar case at Glazov (Mozhaisk county, Moscow province); cf. also Igritsky, *1917 g. v derevne*, pp. 111, 325.
12. For example, when the committee of Surkov village, Kursk province, decided to confiscate all privately owned land in the vicinity, its resolution was formally confirmed by the self-constituted district authorities in the following terms: 'the executive committee of Troitsa district hereby certifies the correctness of the aforementioned decision by its signature and by the affixture of the State seal'. For these villagers appropriation of the land was tantamount to a declaration of independence. *DiM*, v, p. 449.
13. *Izv.*, 18 August. As it happens, independent evidence is available about the composition of seventy-five peasant soviets in this province. According to a news item published in the Kadet organ *Rech'* (19 July), these comprised 21 officials, 23 medical personnel, 50 clergymen, 62 teachers, 92 landowners, 174 Jews (*sic*) – and 3807 peasants. The accuracy of

these figures cannot be vouched for, but the general proportion of peasants to non-peasants may well be about right.

14. Shestakov, *Sovety krest. dep. i drug.*, I, pp. 43 f.; cited by Kravchuk, *Mass. krest. dvizh.*, p. 94, c.u.d.s. – conceivably from the file of the paper concerned, since modern Soviet historians are less free than their predecessors in the 1920s to cite non-Bolshevik socialist sources.

15. Moiseyeva, *Sovety krest. dep.*, p. 26; Serebryakova, 'Mosk. obl.', pp. 57 f.; cf. also below p. 367.

16. Kravchuk, *Mass. krest. dvizh.*, p. 95.

17. Report of 3 June, partially cited by Vermenichev, 'Krest. dvizh. mezhdu fev. i Okt. revol.', p. 186.

18. K&M, pp. 403 f. Pages 403–27 of this compilation contain a selection from the circulars issued to provincial commissars by the Main Administration for Militia Affairs in the ministry of Interior.

19. Moiseyeva, *Sovety krest. dep.*, p. 36.

20. PSR rural organizations were generally weak, members sometimes being recruited *en masse*: cf. Radkey, *Agrarian Foes*, p. 234.

21. Shestakov, *Sovety krest. dep. i drug.*, I, pp. 45 f.

22. Shestakov, *Sovety krest. dep. i drug.*, I, p. 55; *RS*, 2, 3 May.

23. Shestakov, *Sovety krest. dep. i drug.*, II, pp. 28–30. It was as chief of the second of these departments that a future nominal head of the Soviet State, M.I. Kalinin, first played a significant role.

24. Shestakov, *Sovety krest. dep. i drug.*, II, p. 33.

25. There is much truth in the subsequent criticism of their approach by K. Kachorovsky, an expert on the peasant commune, who wrote that in 1917 'the intellectuals in fact tried to bureaucratize the communal (*vechevoy*) peasant democracy, transferring all power from the village assembly to special elected committees, whose significance the peasants did not understand': 'Kr-vo i intelligentsiya', *Sov. zap.*, 5 (1921), p. 221 – although whether they could have managed without such expressly political organizations is open to question.

26. Shestakov, *Sovety krest. dep. i drug.*, I, pp. 97 f.

27. Shestakov, *Sovety krest. dep. i drug.*, I, p. 102.

28. Shestakov, *Sovety krest. dep. i drug.*, I, p. 106. The remark quoted was uttered during a debate on the appointment of magistrates, and its extreme tone is said to have provoked cries of dissent. The radicals' mood was one of anarchic distrust of all authority, that of revolutionary intellectuals not excepted.

29. Shestakov, *Sovety krest. dep. i drug.*, I, p. 108.

30. Shestakov, *Sovety krest. dep. i drug.*, II, pp. 97–104.

31. Pershin, *Agr. revol.*, I, p. 360.

32. M.R. (contrib.), 'Bor'ba za zemlyu v 1917 g. po Kaz. gub.', p. 87; A.S. Smirnov, 'Petrogr. Sovet krest. dep. v 1917 g.', *IZ*, 73 (1963),

p. 102; Moiseyeva, *Sovety krest. dep.*, p. 63; Owen, *The Russian Peasant Movement*, p. 188.

33. Martynov, 'Agr. dvizh. v 1917 g. po dok. Glav. zem. Kom.', p. 205; Pershin, *Agr. revol.*, I, p. 359; Kravchuk, *Mass. krest. dvizh.*, p. 136.

34. Shestakov, *Sovety krest. dep. i drug.*, I, pp. 41-3.

35. *Izv. VSKD*, 22 May.

36. Despite this caveat, a detailed analysis of the proceedings of these congresses might prove to be rewarding. Since the SRs were in charge of them, Soviet historians are inhibited from discussing them systematically and it is difficult even to establish their precise chronology – let alone to ascertain the degree to which they were representative, the composition of their leading bodies, the text of their resolutions and so on.

37. Shestakov, *Sovety krest. dep. i drug.*, II, p. 68.

38. Moiseyeva, *Sovety krest. dep.*, p. 85.

39. *Izv. VSKD*, 25 July, as cited in Shestakov, *Sovety krest. dep. i drug.*, I, p. 231. A few days earlier *DN* gave a figure of 371 county soviets (out of a possible total of 813), but another source put the number of provincial ones at only 33: Moiseyeva, *Sovety krest. dep.*, pp. 27 f.; cf. Kravchuk, *Mass. krest. dvizh.*, p. 101.

40. *Trud*, 4 October (referring to July), as cited in Shestakov, *Sovety krest. dep. i drug.*, II, p. 9.

41. Moiseyeva, *Sovety krest. dep.*, pp. 168-73.

42. *Izv. VSKD*, 27 August, as cited in Shestakov, *Sovety krest. dep. i drug.*, I, p. 256. Moiseyeva, *Sovety krest. dep.*, p. 47, c.u.d.s., reproduces a figure for 1 July of 28 provincial, 209 county and 650 district land committees. A prominent peasant leader, speaking on 11 July, said there were 34 provincial land committees (*Izv. VSKD*, 13 July).

CHAPTER 18   PEASANTS IN POLITICS: EMERGENCE OF THE CENTRAL PEASANT ORGANIZATIONS

1. *VVP*, 12 April; A.V. Shestakov, 'Vseross. krest. soyuz: ist. ocherk', *Ist.-marksist*, 5 (1927), pp. 94-123, is unrewarding.

2. Already before 15 March ARPU leaders had approached both the government and the Petrograd soviet for support in holding a national congress of peasant *soviets* (Shestakov, *Sovety krest. dep. i drug.*, I, pp. 122-4). However, they evidently conceived this gathering as distinct from and subordinate to the proposed founding congress of their own union.

3. *Izv.*, 23 March, as cited in Shestakov, *Sovety krest. dep. i drug.*, I, p. 165.

4. Shestakov, *Sovety krest. dep. i drug.*, I, pp. 170 f.

5. *RS*, 2 May.

6. A historical sketch of this organization was published early in 1918 by

its Left SR leaders, entitled *Petrogradskiy Sovet krest'yanskikh rabochikh dep.: ocherk vozniknoveniya i deyatel'nosti, 1917–1918 gg.* This was based on archives that were subsequently destroyed. Excerpts are published in Shestakov, *Sovety krest. dep. i drug.*, I, pp. 292–302. The subject became a delicate one for Soviet historians not only because they were anxious to play down the role of the Left SRs but more particularly because Stalin passed a judgement on this organization which remained un-challengeable so long as the 'cult of the individual' lasted. An informa-tive and fairly objective account of its activities was given by Smirnov, 'Petrogr. Sovet krest. dep. v 1917 g.', pp. 90–110, where, however, there is no mention of the conflict within ARPU which led to its emergence. Apparently the latter organization is still deemed unfit for historical study.

7. Shestakov, *Sovety krest. dep. i drug.*, I, pp. 180–2.
8. Shestakov, *Sovety krest. dep. i drug.*, I, pp. 183–6; *Izv. VSKD*, 16 June.
9. Shestakov, *Sovety krest. dep. i drug.*, I, p. 117; *Izv. VSKD*, 12 July.
10. *Izv. VSKD*, 28 May.
11. Radkey, *Agrarian Foes*, pp. 261–78.
12. V.[Ya.] Gurevich, 'Vseross. krest. s'yezd i I-aya koalitsiya', *LR(B)*, 1 (1923), p. 177; M. Gaysinsky, *Vseross. s'yezdy* (Moscow 1933), p. 45.
13. Shestakov, *Sovety krest. dep. i drug.*, I, p. 102.
14. *Zemlya i volya*, 1 June, as cited by Gaysinsky, *Vseross. s'yezdy*, p. 49.
15. Data are available on the province of origin of 1091 deputies (*Izv. VSKD*, 31 May; excerpted in Shestakov, *Sovety krest. dep. i drug.*, I, p. 132). Of the fifteen provinces with most delegates (29 to 59 per province) only two (Tver, Moscow) were not in the south. The poll put the political affiliation of the delegates as follows: PSR 537, RSDLP 103, Popular Socialists 4, Trudoviks 6, non-party 136; the remainder presumably did not reply.
16. *Izv. VSKD*, 17 May; Gurevich ('Vseross. krest.') does not mention this debate.
17. *Izv. VSKD*, 20 May; Shestakov, *Sovety krest. dep. i drug.*, I, pp. 141 f.; Gaysinsky, *Vseross. s'yezdy*, 81–84.
18. *Izv. VSKD*, 2 June. The bureau was to consist of members of the presidium at the late congress plus the heads of the departments or commissions. Gurevich ('Vseross. krest.', p. 196) states that the bureau was elected at the congress itself, but may be mistaken on this point.
19. *Izv. VSKD*, 31 May.
20. E.A. Lutsky, 'Krest. nakazy 1917 g. o zemle', in *Istochnikoved. ist. Sovet. obshch.*, eds D.A. Chugayev and others, fasc II (Moscow 1968), pp. 113–61; cf. below p. 389.
21. The Bolsheviks controlled a small group of fourteen non-party soldier delegates from the western front, led by M.V. Frunze (the later civil

war military leader) and an even smaller group of civilians under
G. Razzhivin. Gaysinsky, *Vseross. s'yezdy*, p. 64.

22. Gurevich, 'Vseross. krest.', p. 186. The author also states, contradictorily, that Lenin's speech 'was listened to with curiosity and attention, but evoked no immediate response'.

23. Lenin, *PSS*, XXXII, p. 176.

24. For the text of Lenin's speech, first published in *Izv. VSKD*, 25 May, see *PSS*, XXXII, pp. 168–89. On Bolshevik agrarian policy in general, see below pp. 386–93.

25. This point is put pungently by Chamberlin in his classic *Russian Revolution*, I, p. 249:

> [Lenin's] demand that all power should pass to the soviets, the call for the special organization of farm-hands and of the poorest peasants, the suggestion that a model farm should be set up on every large landlord's estate, must have inspired headshaking and muttered disagreement. For what the average peasant really envisaged as a result of the agrarian upheaval was freedom from the burden of the landlord's rent, a slice of the landlord's rich fields and a cow or a horse from the landlord's stock. The idea that the state should step into the landlord's boots was far indeed from the desire of the insurgent peasantry.

26. *Izv. VSKD*, 27 May.

27. *Izv. VSKD*, 28 May.

28. *Izv. VSKD*, 26 May. The text in B&K, II, p. 597, reproduced from another source, is unfortunately marred by excisions and mistranslations. The most important excision is of the paragraph discountenancing arbitrary confiscations.

29. Gurevich, 'Vseross. krest.', p. 194.

30. The vague drafting of the latter provision was probably deliberate: the motivating clause referred to the lack of *horses* on peasant farms, but the operative clause spoke of livestock in general, and so could be interpreted as applying to *all* kinds of cattle and not just draught animals.

31. *RV*, 28 May, as cited in B&K, II, p. 601.

32. According to the digest of these instructions published on 19–20 August, the land committees were to manage only those areas which proprietors were unable to work themselves, not *all* the land within their jurisdiction; they were to requisition only stock which was 'idle' (a phrasing that could apply only to draught animals); they were to receive the rent for confiscated land regularly (not just 'in disputed cases') and to keep it intact on behalf of the central authorities; finally, a much stronger condemnation was made of illegal seizures of property. (*Izv. VSKD*, 19 August; for complete text cf. Shestakov, *Sovety krest. dep. i drug.*, I, pp. 151–60.) These are admittedly fine shadings of meaning.

One cannot be absolutely certain of the peasants' actual demands without undertaking a thorough analysis of the 242 mandates upon which the digest is based – and these have not been published (see Lutsky's study referred to in n. 20).

33. *Izv. VSKD*, 4, 11 June. Similar courses were also given in provincial centres, sometimes with an excess of zeal: in August D.N. Zabolotsky of the Executive Committee lectured a meeting of forty to sixty teachers from Kresty county (Novgorod province) for no less than ten hours but found the response 'weak': *Izv. VSKD*, 15 August.

34. *Izv. VSKD*, 10 June, 12 July.

35. *EPR*, III, pp. 365 f. (previously published in *KA*, 14 (1926), p. 225).

CHAPTER 19   PEASANTS IN POLITICS: THE LEFTWARD TIDE

1. *RV*, 16, 22 June; M.R. (contrib.), 'Bor'ba za zemlyu v 1917 g. po Kaz. gub.', pp. 85–97.

2. Kravchuk, *Mass. krest. dvizh.*, p. 66.

3. Shestakov, *Sovety krest. dep. i drug.*, II, p. 227; a similar mandate was published in *RV*, 16 June.

4. Kravchuk, *Mass. krest. dvizh.*, p. 71, citing a dissertation by V.A. Demidov (1959).

5. Shestakov, *Sovety krest. dep. i drug.*, II, p. 236 (*Pr.*, 25 June).

6. Kravchuk, *Mass. krest. dvizh.*, p. 71 f.; Pershin, *Agr. revol.*, I, p. 337.

7. Smirnov, 'Petrogr. Sovet krest. dep. v 1917 g.', p. 106.

8. Smirnov, 'Petrogr. Sovet krest. dep. v 1917 g.', p. 108, where it is pointed out that the figure of 1395 agitators dispatched, given in the sketch of this organization's history published in 1918, covers the period up to January of that year, and that some two-thirds of these men left after the October *coup*. Higher figures are sometimes found which give an inflated impression of the organization's role. Cf. Kravchuk, *Mass. krest. dvizh.*, p. 71, who does not, however, refer to Smirnov's work.

9. Moiseyeva, *Sovety krest. dep.*, p. 176.

10. Moiseyeva, *Sovety krest. dep.*, p. 87, c.u.d.s.

11. Moiseyeva, *Sovety krest. dep.*, p. 183, c.u.d.s.

12. Moiseyeva, *Sovety krest. dep.*, p. 88.

13. Moiseyeva, *Sovety krest. dep.*, p. 183.

14. Moiseyeva, *Sovety krest. dep.*, p. 172; cf. above p. 228.

15. Moiseyeva, *Sovety krest. dep.*, p. 183.

16. *Izv. VSKD*, 23 June; incomplete text in Shestakov, I, pp. 189–91.

17. *Izv. VSKD*, 28 June.

18. Shestakov, *Sovety krest. dep. i drug.*, I, p. 195; *RS*, 1 August.

19. *RS*, 2 August; *RV*, 2 August (repr. in Shestakov, *Sovety krest. dep. i drug.*, I, pp. 196 f).

20. Shestakov, *Sovety krest. dep. i drug.*, I, pp. 200–2; cf. *Izv. VSKD*, 22 August; *RS*, 6 August.

21. Shestakov, *Sovety krest. dep. i drug.*, I, p. 205.

22. *Den'*, 9 August.

23. *Izv. VSKD*, 25 August.

24. *Izv. VSKD*, 16, 22 September; Shestakov, *Sovety krest. dep. i drug.*, I, pp. 279 f. The peasant delegates echoed faithfully the contradictions within 'revolutionary democracy' as a whole. Only 28 votes were cast in favour of coalition with the Kadets, the only 'bourgeois' party of consequence.

25. Shestakov, *Sovety krest. dep. i drug.*, I, p. 284; Moiseyeva, *Sovety krest. dep.*, pp. 131–6 (who gives a more detailed geographical breakdown of the vote); Radkey, *Agrarian Foes*, pp. 435–8.

CHAPTER 20   THE DISSOLUTION OF THE PROLETARIAT

1. There is as yet no comprehensive survey in any western language of the Russian civil war of 1918–21 or even of any of its three main phases, apart from the general history of the revolution by Chamberlin, although there is a considerable literature on particular aspects. On the Bolsheviks' treatment of their opponents on the left, see especially the pioneering study by L.B. Schapiro, *The Origin of the Communist Autocracy* (London, Cambridge, Mass. 1955; repr. New York, Washington 1965); this may be supplemented by O.H. Radkey's very thorough account of the PSR's fortunes in this period (to spring 1918), *The Sickle under the Hammer* (New York, London 1963). On the Kadets see Rosenberg, *Liberals in the Russian Revolution*.

2. The number of males sentenced by regional (*okrug*) courts in 1913, 1915 and 1916 was respectively 62,167, 39,380 and 39,945. The drop in the number of offenders sentenced by lower courts was even greater. (There were very few female offenders.) *Sb. stat.*, pp. 67, 70.

3. A.A. Minin, 'Dukh razrusheniya v russ. revol.: sots.-psikholog. ocherk', in Bakh and others, *God russ. revol.*, pp. 33 f.

4. The dissolution of the Russian army after July, when mass desertion first occurred, has yet to be studied by western scholars. A. Wildman, 'The Front Soldiers' October: the Revolution in the Committees' (Ms., 1974) gives a foretaste of the monograph on which he is presently engaged. Cf. also J. Erickson, 'The Origins of the Red Army', in Pipes, *Revolutionary Russia*, pp. 224–56.

5. V.I. Nevsky, cited in *Grazhd. voyna: mat. po ist. Krasnoy Armii* (Moscow 1923), I, p. 121.

6. A.L. Frayman and others (eds), *Okt. vooruzh.* (Leningrad 1967), II p. 422.

7. *NZ*, 15 November (Durdin brewery, Petrograd) and *passim*; cf. Frayman,

Okt. vooruzh., p. 423; these sources disagree as to the conduct of the Red guardsmen on this occasion.

8. *NZ*, 13 December.

9. S. Polshkov (the author of these remarks), 'Okt. perevorot v Buzuluke', *PR*, 40 (1925), p. 237.

10. On the night of 3/4 December 69 such incidents and 611 other criminal offences were reported. V.D. Bonch-Bruyevich, *Na boyevykh postakh* (Moscow 1931), pp. 180–5; cf. *Izv.*, 6 December; Frayman, *Okt. vooruzh.*, p. 425. The militiamen of the Pipe Works alone claimed to have destroyed no less than fifteen hundred barrels and several hundred thousand bottles of wine and spirits: P.F. Kudelli (ed.), *Leningr. rab. v bor'be* (Leningrad 1924), p. 111. E. Sisson, *One Hundred Red Days* (New Haven, Conn. 1931), p. 135, describes a scene where '*izvozchiki* came running from the neighbouring cab-stands and, heedless of the booting they got from the [Red] guards, threw themselves full length on the snow to drink from the rivulet'.

11. *NZ*, 18 October.

12. *NZ*, 27 October, 9 November; N. Yevreynov, 'Iz vosp. o podgotovke Okt. v Kineshme', *PR*, 70 (1927), p. 192.

13. A. Popov (comp.), *Okt. perevorot* (Petrograd 1918), pp. 73 f.

14. *NZ*, 20 December. This may be the N.P. Kostrin who some weeks earlier worked as a driver for the Petrograd MRC: D.A. Chugayev and others (eds), *Petrogr. VRK: dok. i mat.*, 3 vols (Moscow 1966–7) [cited as *PVRK*], I, p. 183.

15. *Izv.*, 19 January 1918.

16. From 7·44 to 39·70 (1913 = 1). Vaynshteyn, *Tseny i tsenoobraz. v SSSR*, p. 157.

17. S.[G.] Strumilin, 'Prozhit. minimum i zarab. chernorab. v Petrogr.', *Stat. truda*, 2–3 (15 August–1 September 1918), p. 7.

18. A. St[opani], 'Byudzhet mosk. rabochego', *Stat. truda*, 10–13 (January–February 1919), pp. 1–5. These statistics, of which the arithmetic is not beyond reproach, are also cited in the useful early study by S. Zagorsky, *La République des Soviets* (Paris 1921), pp. 212 ff., but with an erroneous indication of the source.

19. *Stat. truda*, 4–5 (15 September–15 October 1918), pp. 25 f.

20. Cf. Avilov's first report on the work of his department in *Vestnik NKT*, 1 (January 1918), pp. 29–42. On Bolshevik labour policy in general during this period see E.H. Carr, *The Bolshevik Revolution* (London 1952; repr. Harmondsworth 1966), II, pp. 105–20.

21. For the proceedings; *Vestnik NKT*, 2–3 (February–March 1918), pp. 213–40. The debate anticipated the great struggles to come over the trade unions' role in a socialist economy: see below pp. 302–4.

22. M. Kh[esi]n, 'Rynok truda za I-uyu tret' 1918 g.', *Stat. truda*, 1 (15

July 1918), p. 7; for earlier figures, *Vestnik NKT*, 2–3, pp. 75, 121, 276; 4–5 (April–May 1918), p. 245.

23. *Stat. truda*, 4–5 (15 September–15 October 1918), pp. 25 f.; cf. *NZ*, 19 February 1918 and *Vestnik NKT*, 2–3, p. 277 for similar reports from Voronezh and Nizhniy Novgorod.

24. *Vestnik NKT*, 2–3, p. 200.

25. *Stat. truda*, 4–5 (15 September–15 October 1918), pp. 333 ff.

26. The decree promised that all unemployed persons would receive benefits amounting to half the average pay of an unskilled labourer. Text: B&F, pp. 304–8. The same criticism may be made of the decree of 29 October instituting the eight-hour working day. Lenin later acknowledged that these measures had been partly propagandist ('declarative') in character: Lenin, *PSS*, xxxviii, p. 198. The social insurance legislation was based on previous Menshevik drafts prepared under the auspices of the Provisional Government: see the detailed study by one of its authors, S.M. Shvarts, *Sots. strakh. v Rossii v 1917–1919 gg.* (New York 1968).

27. *NL*, 4 January 1918.

28. *NZ*, 19 February.

29. *NL*, 20 January; *Sev. zarya* (Vologda), 23 March.

30. *Izv.*, 22 February.

31. *Stat. truda*, 4–5 (15 September–15 October 1918), pp. 25 f.

32. Frayman, *Okt. vooruzh.*, ii, p. 514; *NZ*, 13, 20 December 1917; *Nachalo*, 15 February 1918; *NL*, 19 January, 14 February.

33. *Vestnik NKT*, 2–3 (February–March 1918), p. 100.

34. Kh[esi]n, 'Rynok truda', p. 7. A PC of Labour report published subsequently in D.A. Chugayev (ed.), *Rab. klass Sov. Rossii v I-y god dikt. prol.* (Moscow 1964), pp. 244 ff., gives a total of 308,000 registered unemployed, of whom 120,000 and 70,000 were in the Moscow and Petrograd regions respectively. Unskilled workers (70 per cent of the total) and women were particularly hard hit.

35. *Stat. truda*, 1 (15 July 1918), p. 24.

36. *Vestnik NKT*, 4–5 (April–5 May 1918), p. 238.

37. *Vestnik NKT*, 4–5 (April–5 May 1918), p. 242; for figures relating to 1 December 1918, see S. Kol[okolnik]ov, 'Izmeneniya v rab. armii Petrogr.', *Stat. truda*, 10–13 (January–February 1919), pp. 5–7.

38. A.V. Venediktov, *Organizatsiya gosudarstvennoy promyshlennosti v SSSR, 1917–1930*, I (Leningrad 1957), p. 118.

39. By August 1920 the population of Petrograd had sunk to 706,000: *Stat. yezheg.*, pt 1, section 1, p. 30. In 1918 the excess of deaths over births in Petrograd was 28·3 per 1000, as against 7·4 per 1000 in 1917. N.P. Oganovsky, *Russ. krest. i mir. khoz.*, 2nd ed. (Moscow 1924), p. 10.

CHAPTER 21   THE FACTORY COMMITTEES AND 'WORKERS' CONTROL'

1. *PVRK*, I, pp. 58, 64, 76, 101, 126, 216, 393; III, p. 32.

2. *PVRK*, I, p. 357; II, pp. 137, 199.

3. *PVRK*, III, p. 218; cf. I, p. 529; III, p. 136.

4. *PVRK*, III, p. 252.

5. *PVRK*, III, p. 106.

6. *NZ*, 31 October, 15 December (Reykhel and Anchar machine works).

7. E.B. Bosh, *God bor'by* (Moscow, Leningrad 1925), p. 60.

8. Döring, *Organisationsprobleme*, p. 60; Venediktov, *Org. gosud. prom.*, I, p. 125.

9. *Vestnik NKT*, 2–3 (February–March 1918), p. 239; cf. Venediktov, *Natsionalizatsiya promyshlennosti i organizatsiya sotsialisticheskogo proizvodstva v Petrograde, 1917–1920*, p. 121; L.B. Genkin, 'Rozhd. sots. distsipliny truda', *Ist. SSSR*, 1 (1965), pp. 3–27.

10. R. Lorenz, 'Wirtsch. Alternativen der Sowjetmacht im Frühjahr und Sommer 1918', *JGOE*, 15 (1967), pp. 228 ff.: on p. 230 the author reproduces a table from V.P. Milyutin, *Istoriya ekonomicheskogo razvitiya SSSR, 1917–1927* (Moscow, Leningrad 1928), p. 110, showing that of 521 enterprises nationalized by June 1918 150 were sequestered, mostly by local councils of national economy (*sovnarkhozy*). However, the terms sequestration and nationalization were used loosely at this time and the list cannot be regarded as complete; nor does it take account of the economic significance of the enterprises concerned. Cf. *Vestnik NKT*, 2–3 (February–March 1918), pp. 259 f.; Drobizhev, *Glavnyy shtab sots. prom.*, pp. 93–8.

11. Frayman and others, *Okt. vooruzh. vosst. v Petrogr.*, II, p. 539.

12. G. Safonov, in *Rab. kontrol' i nats. prom. v Kostr. gub.*, ed. M.A. Shpindler (Kostroma 1960), pp. 61 f., 72. A selection of documents on workers' control in the Central Industrial region is: V.A. Babichev and others (comps), *Rab. kontrol' i nats. krupnoy prom. v Iv.-Voz. gub.*, *Mat. po ist. SSSR*, III (Moscow 1956).

13. *NZ*, 21 October.

14. A.F. Danilevsky and others (eds), *Profsoyuzy v bor'be* (Moscow 1957), p. 110; see also below pp. 285 ff.

15. *I Vseross. s'yezd prof. soyuozv, 7–14 yanv. 1918 g.: polnyy stenogr. otchet* (Moscow 1918) [cited as *I s'yezd*], pp. 236 f. Similar complaints were voiced by other activists. I. Stepanov, writing in the Moscow *Sots.-dem.* on 30 December 1917, said that the factory committees 'are beginning ... to look upon all industrial enterprises through the eyes of their own factory. Their first object is to enable their own workers to survive this difficult period.' Cf. also G.V. Tsyperovich, *Sindikaty i tresty v Rossii* (Moscow 1919), pp. 158 f.

16. Lorenz, 'Wirtsch. Alternativen', pp. 218–21.

17. A.V. Lazarev, 'Iz ist. razrabotki leninskogo dek. o rab. kontrole', *VI*

KPSS, 3 (1960), p. 135. The treatment of this subject in English by P.H. Avrich, 'The Bolshevik Revolution and Workers' Control', *SR*, 22 (1963), pp. 47–63, largely supersedes Carr, *The Bolshevik Revolution*, II, pp. 72–9.

18. Lenin, *PSS*, XXXIII, p. 101 and *passim*.

19. Carr, *The Bolshevik Revolution*, II, pp. 71 f.

20. A. Nove observes that Lenin 'spoke a great deal about workers' control, but his behaviour after the seizure of power suggests that he regarded it very largely as a means of disorganizing the enemy rather than as a serious form of socialist economic organization': 'Lenin as Economist', in *Lenin: a Reappraisal*, eds L.B. Schapiro and P. Reddaway (London 1967), pp. 203 f.

21. Lazarev, 'Iz ist.', p. 134; Venediktov, *Org. gosud. prom.*, p. 82.

22. Lenin, *PSS*, XXXV, pp. 30 f.

23. To Lozovsky, who objected that this would mean allowing any group of workers to do as they pleased, Lenin replied: 'The main thing now is to get control going . . . We should not put any obstacles in the way of the masses' initiative. After a certain time experience will show what forms workers' control will assume on the national level.' Cited by Drobizhev, *Glavnyy shtab sots. prom.*, p. 33.

24. *Prot. zas. Vseross. Ts. Ispol. Kom. Sovetov* (Moscow 1918) [cited as *Prot. VTsIK*], pp. 44, 62; Venediktov, *Org. gosud. prom.*, p. 87.

25. *DSV*, I (Moscow 1957), pp. 77–85; English trsl. B&F, pp. 308–10.

26. The SEC was formally constituted by a decree of 1 December published four days later. Its chief architect was N.I. Bukharin. Carr, *The Bolshevik Revolution*, II, p. 80; A.A. Voronetskaya, 'Org. VSNKh i yego rol' v nats. prom.', *IZ*, 43 (1957), pp. 7 f. and more recently S.F. Cohen, *Bukharin and the Bolshevik Revolution* (New York 1973), pp. 61 f.

27. *Izv.*, 30 November.

28. *Izv.*, 13 December; Venediktov, *Org. gosud. prom.*, p. 92.

29. Döring, *Organisationsprobleme*, p. 69. The ARCFC, although ostensibly national in scope, had in fact been a regional body.

CHAPTER 22   FROM WORKERS' MILITIA TO RED ARMY

1. Cf. Erickson, 'The Origins of the Red Army', pp. 286–328, with a full bibliography.

2. Startsev, *Petrogr. Kr. gvardii*, p. 165.

3. Startsev, *Petrogr. Kr. gvardii*, p. 166.

4. Startsev, *Petrogr. Kr. gvardii*, p. 182; cf. N. Podvoysky, *Kr. gvardiya v Okt. dni* (Moscow, Leningrad 1927), pp. 5, 47. Startsev does not cite this important early Soviet source.

5. Startsev, *Petrogr. Kr. gvardii*, p. 192.

6. This is not the place for a detailed account of the actual course of the

insurrection. The English-speaking reader may be referred to the classic study by Melgunov, now transl. as *The Bolshevik Seizure of Power*, pp. 3–96 and to the perceptive (but poorly documented) work by R.V. Daniels, *Red October* (New York 1967; London 1968), esp. pp. 107–99; cf. also D. Geyer, 'The Bolshevik Insurrection in Petrograd', in Pipes, *Revolutionary Russia*, pp. 164–79.

7. P. Nikolayevsky, 'Na Trubochnom zavode', in Kudelli, *Leningr. rab. v bor'be*, p. 111.

8. Podvoysky, *Kr. gvardiya v Okt. dni*, p. 33.

9. Startsev, *Petrogr. Kr. gvardii*, p. 275. Startsev is justifiably cautious in his handling of these records, which he has subjected to rigorous statistical analysis (pp. 249–87).

10. Podvoysky, *Kr. gvardiya v Okt. dni*, p. 45.

11. Startsev, *Petrogr. Kr. gvardii*, pp. 273 f.

12. Trotsky, *Hist. Rus. Rev.*, pp. 325, 429.

13. Startsev, *Petrogr. Kr. gvardii*, p. 192. This estimate was made 'shortly after 15 October'. Startsev does not refer to Trotsky's estimates.

14. In two months twenty-four written communications were exchanged with the Vyborg district militia, twenty-six with forces in other districts, and sixteen with enterprise-level units: *PVRK*, III, p. 720.

15. Startsev, *Petrogr. Kr. gvardii*, pp. 260–3. Another 1·2 per cent belonged to the Bolshevik youth organization. Allowance is made here for the survivors' tendency to misrepresent their social origin and political allegiance at the time.

16. G.L. Shidlovsky (comp.), 'Pervye shagi bol'sh. Petrogr. Soveta v 1917 g.', *KL*, 24 (1927), p. 81.

17. Two descriptions of prison life in the Petropavlovka at this time are: F. Vinberg, *V plenu u 'obez'yan'* (Kiev 1918), *passim* and P.D. Dolgorukov, *Velikaya razrukha* (Madrid 1964), pp. 57–94 (the latter written in the 1920s).

18. Startsev, *Petrogr. Kr. gvardii*, p. 241.

19. Startsev, *Petrogr. Kr. gvardii*, pp. 242, 207 n.

20. D.A. Chugayev (ed.), *Triumf. shestviye* (Moscow 1963), I, p. 99.

21. Startsev, *Petrogr. Kr. gvardii*, pp. 202, 208; *PVRK*, II, p. 432.

22. V. Ya. Gessen, 'Petrogr. Kr. gvardiya i prom-ki v 1917 g.', *KL*, 27 (1928), pp. 81 f.

23. Startsev, *Petrogr. Kr. gvardii*, p. 233. In the Putilov works the number had declined to 800 by late November from a peak of 4000 in September (p. 209).

24. Startsev, *Petrogr. Kr. gvardii*, pp. 219–33.

25. Podvoysky, *Kr. gvardiya v Okt. dni*, p. 49; V. Antonov-Ovseyenko, *Der Aufbau der Roten Armee* (Hamburg 1923), p. 18; Erickson, 'The Origins of the Red Army', p. 293.

26. V. Malakhovsky, 'Perekhod ot Kr. gvardii k Kr. Armii', *KL*, 27 (1928), pp. 6–11; cf. *Grazhd. voyna* (Moscow 1923), I, pp. 99–102.

27. Podvoysky, *Kr. gvardiya v Okt. dni*, p. 68.

28. Tsypkin, *Kr. gvard. v bor'be*, pp. 136 f. In Petrograd 52·8 per cent were under twenty-five years of age: Startsev, *Petrogr. Kr. gvardii*, p. 265.

29. M. Olminsky, 'Khod sobitiy', in *Moskva v Okt.*, ed. N. Ovsyannikov (Moscow 1919), p. 34.

30. N. Muralov, 'Okt.-noyabr''', in Ovsyannikov, *Moskva v Okt.*, p. 56. Their opponents are credited with ten thousand men (mainly cossacks and military cadets). The rest of the garrison was neutral. Tsypkin (*Kr. gvard. v bor'be*, p. 117, c.u.d.s.: the 1919 volume is no longer ideologically respectable) accepts the fifteen thousand figure but offers no estimate of the number of Red guardsmen, for whom he claims without substantiation the role of 'principal strike force.'

31. Peche, 'Kr.gvardiya', in *Okt. dni v Moskve i rayonakh*, ed. S. Chernomordik (Moscow 1922), pp. 34 f. Tsypkin (*Kr. gvard. v bor'be*, p. 127) portrays this affair in a more heroic light.

32. Olminsky, 'Khod sobitiy', p. 37; Tsypkin, *Kr. gvard. v bor'be*, pp. 137 f.

33. Podvoysky, *Kr. gvardiya v Okt. dni*, pp. 72, 103.

34. Tsypkin, *Kr. gvard. v bor'be*, p. 164. The latter task fell to P.K. Shternberg, whose professional qualifications were unusual: he was an astronomer. Chernomordik, *Okt. dni v Moskve i rayonakh*, p. 148.

35. Tsypkin, *Kr. gvard. v bor'be*, pp. 162–96.

36. Bosh, *God bor'by*, pp. 121–36; see also below p. 378.

37. I. Podshivalov, *Grazhd. bor'ba na Urale* (Moscow 1925), pp. 54 f.; N.K. Lisovsky, *1917 g. na Urale* (Chelyabinsk 1967), pp. 354–6.

38. F. Vdovin, 'Man'yartsy', in *Okt. na Yuzhnom Urale*, ed. S. Shapurin (Zlatoust 1927), p. 80.

39. B. El'tsin, 'Dni Okt. perevorota na Yuzhnom Urale i v Ufe', *PR*, 10 (1922), p. 355; Lisovsky, *1917 g. na Urale*, p. 475 (who does not give his sources).

40. Podshivalov, *Grazhd. bor'ba na Urale*, pp. 107 f.

CHAPTER 23   HARNESSING THE TRADE UNIONS

1. Useful introductions to this subject in English include M. Dewar, *Labour Policy in the USSR, 1917–1928* (London 1956); S.M. Schwarz, *Labor in the Soviet Union* (New York, London 1952); Carr, *The Bolshevik Revolution*, II, pp. 105–20; more recent (but not entirely satisfactory) is J. Sorenson, *The Life and Death of Soviet Trade Unionism, 1917–1928* (New York 1969). The latest study by U. Brügmann, *Die russ. Gewerkschaften in Revol. und Bürgerkrieg, 1917–1919* (Frankfurt 1972), could not be taken into consideration here.

2. Popov, *Okt. perevorot*, p. 402; Vompe, *Dni Okt.*, pp. 16 f.

3. K.G. Kotelnikov (comp.), Ya. A. Yakovlev (ed.), *Vtoroy s'yezd Sovetov* (Moscow, Leningrad 1928) [cited as *II s'yezd*], pp. 87 ff.; cf. B&F. p. 137.

4. Vompe, *Dni Okt.*, pp. 19 f.

5. Popov, *Okt. perevorot*, p. 404; Vompe, *Dni Okt.*, pp. 21–6.

6. The proceedings, published as *Protokoly Moskovskogo soveshchaniya Glavnykh dorozhnykh komitetov Yevropeyskoy Rossii 13–15 noyabrya 1917 g.* (Petrograd 1918), are a bibliographical rarity.

7. Vompe, *Dni Okt.*, p. 51.

8. *Izv.*, 12, 14 November.

9. *Izv.*, 3 December.

10. *Izv.*, 10 December.

11. In the Petrograd region, where rates were highest: *Izv.*, 14 December; *Prot. VTsIK* (Moscow 1918), p. 110.

12. *Izv.*, 17 December.

13. *Izv.*, 21 December.

14. *Izv.*, 30 December.

15. *Izv.*, 7 January 1918; *Pr.*, 6 January; *NZ*, 9 January; *NL*, 12, 13 January; B&F, p. 652; Volin, *Deyat. men.*, p. 22: if the latter's data on the political affiliation of delegates to this congress are to be believed, about three-quarters of the delegates were non-partisan, which seems rather high.

16. *Izv.*, 28, 30 January, 21 February; *NL*, 14 February.

17. Popov, *Okt. perevorot*, p. 398.

18. T. Krylova, 'K ist. Soyuza vodnikov', in Ansky, *Prof. dvizh. v Petrogr.*, pp. 205–24; *Izv.*, 20 February. Of the 168 delegates to the congress 70 were Bolsheviks, 52 Left SRs and 12 Menshevik Internationalists; there were 4 Anarchists, 7 centre SRs and (curiously enough) 6 Kadets; 17 men had no party affiliation.

19. Bazilevich, *Prof. dvizh. rab. svyazi*, pp. 120–32; Popov, *Okt. perevorot*, pp. 399 f.; M.P. Iroshnikov, *Sozdaniye Sov. tsentr. gosud. apparata* (Moscow, Leningrad 1966), p. 199.

20. Bazilevich, *Prof. dvizh. rab. svyazi*, pp. 133–44.

21. Bazilevich, *Prof. dvizh. rab. svyazi*, pp. 162, 169–74.

22. Bazilevich, *Prof. dvizh. rab. svyazi*, pp. 185–225.

23. Iroshnikov, *Sozdaniye Sov.*, p. 162.

24. *Izv.*, 12 November; Iroshnikov, *Sozdaniye Sov.*, p. 194; B.M. Morozov, *Partiya i Sovety* (Moscow 1966), pp. 139–41.

25. Iroshnikov, *Sozdaniye Sov.*, pp. 247–50; the names are given here of some prominent 'collaborators' in other ministries. The party committee in the state bank had twenty-nine members by the end of November. Cf. *Ekon. zhizn'*, 1 (6 November 1918), p. 2 f. for a lively account by N. Osinsky, 'Kak my ovladeli Gos. Bankom'; there is a recent Soviet study of this subject: I.F. Gindin, *Kak bol'sheviki zakhvatili Gos. Bank*

(Moscow 1961). On the general problem of intellectuals' collaboration with the Bolshevik regime, see S.A. Fedyukin, *Sovetskaya vlast' i burzhuaznye spetsialisty* (Moscow 1965).

26. Volin, *Deyat. men.*, p. 28, citing A. Antoshkin, *Professional'noye dvizheniye sluzhashchikh, 1917–1924* (Moscow 1927), pp. 109 f.

27. Volin, *Deyat. men.*, p. 28.

28. *Izv.*, 9 November ; M&P, p. 302.

29. Volin, *Deyat. men.*, p. 24.

30. *Izv.*, 21 December ; Volin, *Deyat. men.*, pp. 25 f. citing *Moskovskiy Sovet professional'nykh soyuzov v 1917 g.* (Moscow 1927), pp. 175 f., 207–9.

31. V. Degot, 'Odesskiye pechatniki v revol. dvizh.', *Mat. po ist. prof. dvizh. v Rossii*, III (1925), p. 344.

32. Volin, *Deyat. men.*, p. 24, citing *NL*, 28 December.

33. Lenin, *PSS*, XXXIV, p. 396; *Prot. TsK RSDRP(b)* (Moscow 1958), pp. 93–104 ; English ed.: *The Bolsheviks and the October Revolution* (London 1974), pp. 95–110.

34. Garvi, *Prof. soyuzy v Rossii*, p. 26.

35. I.L. Borshchenko and others (eds), *Profsoyuzy SSSR* (Moscow 1963), pp. 536 f. This gift was approved *ex post facto* by the union's council on 5 November: A. Gurevich, 'Pyat' let bor'by', *Metallist*, 12 (1922), p. 23.

36. These were the Central Committee of the Union of Municipal Workers and Employees of Petrograd (which, however, said nothing about the insurrection and confined itself to endorsing the programme of 'revolutionary democracy' as a whole), a general meeting of members of the Petrograd Union of Chauffeurs and Automobile Technicians, and the executive of the Petrograd Union of Architectural Building Workers: Borshchenko and others, *Profsoyuzy SSSR*, pp. 536, 538, 541.

37. M&P, pp. 299, 319, citing *Tkach*, 1 (9 November 1917) and *Metallist*, 6 (30 November 1917).

38. Lenin, *PSS*, XXXV, p. 552.

39. Danilevsky and others, *Profsoyuzy v bor'be*, p. 61. Despite Lenin's address the CB decided on 13 November that strikes were permissible under the new regime: A. Ansky, 'Petrogr. Sovet prof. soyuzov', in Ansky, *Prof. dvizh. v Petrogr.*, p. 55.

40. *Izv.*, 21 January ; Gurevich, 'Pyat' let', p. 35 ; Robinson, 'Iz ist. tarif. pol.', pp. 45, 49. Evidence of syndicalist opposition to this line was reported in the Menshevik paper *Nachalo*, 2 (15 February 1918).

41. *KA*, 65–6 (1934), p. 184, n. 11 to E. Rozhen (contrib.), 'Mosk. voyenno-revol. kom.'. Danilevsky and others, *Profsoyuzy v bor'be*, p. 85, citing the same source, give the date as 25 October, as do Borshchenko and others, *Profsoyuzy SSSR*, pp. 539 f., but this seems unlikely. The announcement of the meeting was not published in the Moscow *Izv.* until the 27th and the MRC itself was not set up until the evening of the 25th. The announcement speaks of 'all' the Moscow trade unions as present and

as 'in a mood to give all possible aid to the MRC'. This is probably an exaggeration: were the printers, for instance, included? Danilevsky and others, *Profsoyuzy v bor'be*, claim that seventeen unions were present, but this information does not appear in the published source. For the latter claim: Usievich to Moscow soviet, 9 November, in S.A. Piontkovsky (ed.), *Sovety v Okt.* (Moscow 1928), p. 52.

42. Borshchenko and others, *Profsoyuzy SSSR*, pp. 544–7, 553.

43. *Sots.-dem.*, 18, 28 November.

44. *Sots.-dem.*, 30 November.

45. For the Anarchists' views on trade unions see P.H. Avrich, *The Russian Anarchists* (Princeton, NJ 1967), pp. 144 f., 207 f., and for the English text of a statement of the syndicalist credo Avrich (ed.), *The Anarchists in the Russian Revolution* (London 1973), pp. 74–6.

46. The official figures are as follows:

type of organization	number of unions represented	members claimed (round figures)	number of delegates with full vote
I All-Russian unions	18 (19)	2·5 million	37 (38)
II regional organizations	20	0·7 million	20
III local organizations (CBs)	48 (49)	1·8 million	68 (69)
IV local unions	156 (162)	2·4 million	289 (296)
		total	416 (428)

The figure of 2·5 million members is an estimate which allows for double counting. The higher numbers given (in brackets) for organizations and delegates include late arrivals. Sources: *I s'yezd*, pp. 132 f.; *Vestnik NKT*, 2–3 (1918), pp. 128 f.; *Izv.*, 13 January. Cf. also International Labour Office, *Le Mouvement syndical dans la Russie des soviets* (Geneva 1927), p. 20 n. Sorenson, *Soviet Trade Unionism*, pp. 25–32, summarizes the conference proceedings.

47. *I s'yezd*, p. 133. The difference would have been still more marked had the congress been attended by delegates of ten All-Russian unions which either were excluded or voluntarily absented themselves.

48. Garvi, *Prof. soyuzy v Rossii*, p. 34; Volin, *Deyat. men.*, p. 37.

49. *I s'yezd*, pp. 69–75.

50. *I s'yezd*, pp. 76 ff.

51. *I s'yezd*, p. 96.

52. Twenty votes were cast for the Left SR motion, which closely resembled that of the Bolsheviks, and forty-two delegates abstained. Some others were probably attending the third congress of soviets, held contemporaneously, or else have manifested in this way their disinterest in the proceedings: Volin, *Deyat. men.*, p. 41.

53. *Vestnik NKT*, 2–3 (1918), pp. 129 ff.; text in T.V. Batayeva (ed.), *Profsoyuzy v period postr. sots. v SSSR* (Moscow 1963), pp. 88–90; English translation in B&F, p. 639. Recent Soviet writers suppress Zinoviev's prominent role in the proceedings. The Menshevik resolution is reproduced by Garvi, *Prof. soyuzy v Rossii*, p. 122.

54. *I s'yezd*, pp. 190–206.

55. *Vestnik NKT*, 2–3 (1918), p. 133 (para. 14). Curiously the paragraph containing this phrase is *not* among the extracts from this document reprinted by Batayeva, *Profsoyuzy v period postr. sots. v SSSR*, pp. 96 f., who gives the unconvincing excuse that the omitted portions merely 'give a general characteristic of capitalism'.

56. Borshchenko and others, *Profsoyuzy SSSR*, p. 101; *I s'yezd*, p. 374; *Vestnik NKT*, 2–3 (1918), p. 141 f.; English trsl. in B&F, p. 642.

57. Borshchenko and others, *Profsoyuzy SSSR*, pp. 91–96; *I s'yezd*, pp. 369–72; *Vestnik NKT*, 2–3 (1918), pp. 134–9.

58. Borshchenko and others, *Profsoyuzy SSSR*, p. 91, section I, para. 5.

59. Borshchenko and others, *Profsoyuzy SSSR*, section IV, para. 16.

60. *Sots.-dem.*, 28 November.

61. *Vestnik NKT*, 2–3 (1918), pp. 145 ff.

62. Volin, *Deyat. men., passim;* Garvi, *Prof. soyuzy v Rossii, passim.*

CHAPTER 24   THE CENTRAL SOVIET ORGANS AND THE ESTABLISHMENT OF BOLSHEVIK DICTATORSHIP

1. Lenin, *PSS*, XXXIV, pp. 240 f., 246 f.

2. Lenin, *PSS*, XXXIV, pp. 342–6; for text of resolution: L.D. Trotsky, *Soch.*, 2nd ed. (Moscow 1926–32), XXI, pp. 490 f.; cf. Sukhanov, *Zap. o revol.*, VI, pp. 247–51. For an English version of Trotsky's speech: J. Reed, *Ten Days* (London 1926; repr. Harmondsworth 1966), pp. 279–81; cf. Trotsky, *Soch.* [1924], III, pt I, pp. 321–3.

3. 'Recognizing . . . that an armed insurrection is inevitable and the time perfectly ripe, the Central Committee proposes that all party organizations act accordingly and discuss and decide all practical questions from this point of view. . . .' Lenin, *PSS*, XXXIV, p. 393; Sukhanov, *Zap. o revol.*, VI, pp. 347–51 (English trsl. slightly abridged, in *The Russian Revolution 1917*, pp. 537–40). Geyer, 'The Bolshevik Insurrection in Petrograd', p. 173, notes that 'upon closer inspection . . . it appears that on October 10 the Bolshevik Central Committee still avoided making a clear commitment'.

4. B&F, pp. 60 f.; Lenin, *PSS*, 2nd ed., XXI, pp. 494–8; *Prot. TsK RSDRP(b)* (Moscow 1958), pp. 87–92 (English ed.: pp. 89–95). For a fair summary of their views: Anweiler, *The Soviets*, pp. 186–7.

5. For an exposition and critical analysis of Bolshevik doctrine on tactical

compromise, with essential texts, see W. Grottian, *Das sowjetische Regierungssystem* (Cologne 1965), II, pp. 390–413.

6. Lenin, *PSS*, XLV, p. 381.

7. Trotsky, *Soch.*, III, pt I, p. xlviii ; pt II, pp. 81–6, 96. The significance of the differences between Trotsky and Lenin were much exaggerated in later years by party historians anxious to discredit the former. Trotsky himself erred in the opposite direction, but less seriously ; he also over-emphasized his own personal role in organizing the insurrection and presented this as a more deliberately prepared operation than it was. This latter distortion was subsequently taken to an extreme in Stalinist historiography, while Trotsky's role was omitted from the record altogether. The rights and wrongs of this dispute need not detain us here.

8. An analysis of Trotsky's speeches and articles in this period, republished in his *Soch.*, III, pt I, pp. 219–327 ; pt II, pp. 3–78, shows that only once before 25 October did he refer to the forthcoming 'Soviet government' (on 12 October: pp. 11–13), but at other times remained studiously vague, as did Lenin, as to the nature of the 'soviet power' which the Bolsheviks so vociferously advocated. In later works, especially those written with the current struggle for power in mind, he was at pains to stress that he (and Lenin) 'did not fetishize the soviet form [of organization]' (cf., e.g., his 'Uroki Oktyabrya' (1923) in *Soch.*, III, pt I, p. lii) – but this is disingenuous.

9. *II s'yezd*, pp. xlvii f.

10. *II s'yezd*, p. li ; Sukhanov, *Zap. o revol.*, VII, pp. 29–32, 72–5 ; Trotsky, *Soch.*, III, pt II, pp. 13 f.

11. This view is based in part on Trotsky's subsequent mystifications, which led him to claim that the insurrection had been purposely 'timed' to coincide with the congress – as it eventually did. There is no independent evidence that plans had actually been laid for action on 20 October or on any other particular date. Therefore Trotsky was, formally speaking, quite truthful when he denied this before the Petrograd soviet on 18 October (*Soch.*, III, pt II, pp. 31 ff.). The Central Committee's decision of 10 October left the organizers free to strike as and when they thought expedient. It was not until 24 October that the party's Petrograd committee crossed the Rubicon by deciding 'to pass to the attack without the slightest delay'. Schapiro, *The Origin of the Communist Autocracy*, p. 64. On the MRC's tactics, see below p. 350.

12. *II s'yezd*, p. lii.

13. Schapiro, *The Origin of the Communist Autocracy*, p. 66 ; for various estimates of the figures, see B&F, p. 110 n.; *II s'yezd*, pp. 105–12. About a quarter of the delegates were from military organizations. The total number attending, about 670, was considerably less than in June – which was testimony to the strength of opposition or indifference to the congress.

14. Several questionnaires were circulated and the number of signatories varied. According to one such questionnaire the formula 'all power to the soviets' received 505 affirmative votes; 86 votes were cast for 'all power to democracy', to which 21 persons added 'with propertied elements but excluding Kadets'; and 55 respondents agreed that 'the government should be a coalition'. In another questionnaire the figures were respectively 491, 82, 21 and 54. *II s'yezd*, pp. 105–12.

15. *II s'yezd*, pp. 34 f.; B&F, pp. 110 f.

16. Sukhanov, *Zap. o revol.*, VII, p. 203 (English ed., p. 640); Trotsky, *Soch.*, III, pt I, pp. 61 f., 390 f.; Schapiro, *The Origin of the Communist Autocracy*, pp. 67 f.; for a vivid but impressionistic account of the scene, Reed, *Ten Days*, pp. 98–101.

17. *II s'yezd*, p. 55. Two votes were cast against the resolution (which had been substituted by the right-wing Bolshevik leader Kamenev for the more intransigent one tabled by Trotsky) and there were twelve abstentions.

18. Schapiro, *The Origin of the Communist Autocracy*, p. 68; some other splinter groups and individuals also decided to remain.

19. *II s'yezd*, pp. 56–77; B&F, pp. 124–32; for accounts by participants: Sukhanov, *Zap. o revol.*, VII, pp. 245–67 (English ed., pp. 656–66) and (less reliable) Reed, *Ten Days*, pp. 128–43.

20. *II s'yezd*, pp. 79 f.; B&F, p. 133.

21. *II s'yezd*, pp. 80–2; the last point is omitted from Bunyan and Fisher's otherwise thorough compilation (pp. 134 f.).

22. *II s'yezd*, p. 83. The Left SRs' political philosophy was not formulated until they held their first party congress, which opened on 17 November. Sukhanov speaks of them scornfully as 'harmless youngsters lacking anything resembling solidity, who could easily be twisted around one's finger' (*Zap. o revol.*, VII, p. 240; English ed., p. 654). For a more sympathetic analysis of their ideas: Radkey, *The Sickle under the Hammer*, pp. 99–101, 136–42.

23. *II s'yezd*, pp. 84–7; B&F, pp. 135–7.

24. *II s'yezd*, p. 90.

25. At the first meeting 101 members were named. With the admission of trade-union and factory-committee representatives this soon rose to 110 and then settled at 108 (until the compromise agreement of 15 November). The organization was only tentative at this stage, since it was unclear whether the other socialist parties would involve themselves in its work. Cf. *II s'yezd*, p. 174; *Prot. VTsIK*, pp. 8 and appx; B&F, p. 138; E.N. Gorodetsky, *Rozhd. Sov. gosud.* (Moscow 1965), pp. 169–87.

   Why 101 members? Two explanations may be advanced: (a) that the sponsors of the election were attracted by the symbolic value of the figure a hundred, but did not think it needed to be kept to precisely; (b) that they wanted the new CEC to be more viable than the old, whose membership had been grossly inflated. If the latter motive is correct, they were soon to be disappointed.

26. *Prot. VTsIK*, pp. 3–8; Sukhanov, *Zap. o revol.*, VII, pp. 270–3.

27. *Prot. VTsIK*, pp. 9 f.; B&F, pp. 156 f.

28. Vompe, *Dni Okt.*, p. 28; Radkey, *The Sickle under the Hammer*, pp. 65 f.

29. B&F, pp. 194–6; Schapiro, *The Origin of the Communist Autocracy*, pp. 73 f.; R.H. McNeal (ed.), *Resolutions and Decisions of the CPSU* (Toronto 1974), II, pp. 41–6. Lenin's statements to the Central Committee are in *PSS*, XXXV, p. 43.

30. *Prot. VTsIK*, p. 12; B&F, p. 197.

31. *Prot. VTsIK*, p. 14.

32. B&F, pp. 198–200.

33. *Prot. VTsIK*, p. 32. For an English text of the press decree: Reed, *Ten Days*, pp. 311 f.; cf. also *DSV*, I, pp. 24 f., 539.

34. B&F, pp. 202–4; M.P. Iroshnikov, *Sozdaniye Sov.*, p. 52. A similar stand was taken by Lozovsky, the Bolshevik trade-union leader: see above p. 111.

35. B&F, pp. 206 f. Zinoviev recanted within a few days; the other 'renegades' returned to the fold somewhat later.

36. Lenin, *PSS*, XXXV, pp. 58 f., 72 f., 75, 100 f. For a fair (and rare!) modern Soviet treatment, see R.M. Ilyukhina, 'K vop. o sogl. bol'sh. s levymi SRami, okt. 1917 – fev. 1918', *IZ*, 73 (1963), pp. 3–34.

37. *Prot. VTsIK*, pp. 65, 106 f.; *DSV*, I, p. 88.

38. *Izv.*, 21 November, 13 December.

39. *Prot. VTsIK*, p. 106; Morozov, *Partiya i Sovety*, p. 97.

40. Morozov, *Partiya i Sovety*, pp. 93–5. The CPC held seventy-seven sittings before the seat of government was transferred to Moscow in the first week of March 1918. According to the CEC's statute, adopted on 2 November, a quarter of the members had to be present for a 'restricted' meeting and a half for a full one: *DSV*, I, pp. 36–8. These rules do not seem to have been adhered to.

41. Morozov, *Partiya i Sovety*, p. 96, citing an unidentified author in the *Uchenye zapiski Dal'nevostochnogo Gosudarstvennogo Universiteta* (1958), fasc. 2, p. 105.

42. *DSV*, I, p. 21; Popov, *Okt. perevorot*, pp. 262 f.; Iroshnikov, *Sozdaniye Sov.*, pp. 108–10; English text: Reed, *Ten Days*, p. 321.

43. Lenin, *PSS*, XXXV, p. 56; Iroshnikov, *Sozdaniye Sov.*, p. 112.

44. *Prot. VTsIK*, p. 31; *DSV*, I, p. 33.

45. *Prot. VTsIK*, p. 72.

46. Text in *DSV*, I, p. 70; *Prot. VTsIK*, p. 72; cf. Iroshnikov, *Sozdaniye Sov.*, pp. 112 f. The clumsy term was evidently an attempt to satisfy the 'soviet constitutionalists' without upsetting Lenin, always on his guard against concessions to 'bourgeois' ways of thought.

47. *NZ*, 19 November.

48. *Prot. VTsIK*, p. 85.

49. Notably over the issue of an increase in railwaymen's pay (12 December : see above p. 292), when the CPC 'confirmed' the CEC's decision to establish new wage scales, although from a constitutional standpoint the latter's enactment was itself legally valid and needed no such endorsement: *Prot. VTsIK*, p. 141.

50. Cf. his memoirs *Volkskomissar* (Munich 1929). The author's later English version, *In the Workshop of the Revolution*, (New York, London 1953), is less reliable.

51. A perceptive and careful study of this question is O.H. Radkey, *Election* (Cambridge, Mass. 1950), esp. pp. 51–69. The chief Soviet source is I.S. Malchevsky (comp.), *Vseross. Uchred. Sobr.* (Moscow, Leningrad 1930) which reproduces (pp. 3–111) the minutes of that short-lived assembly and lists the deputies (pp. 116–38). Cf. also M. Vishnyak, *Vseross. Uchred. Sobr.* (Paris 1932).

52. Radkey, *Election*, pp. 16 f.

53. Radkey, *Election*, p. 21 ; useful discussion in Anweiler, *Die Rätebewegung*, pp. 260–73 (English ed., pp. 211–18).

54. Ya. A. Yakovlev, foreword to *II s'yezd*, p. xxxviii ; or, as a recent Soviet historian puts it : 'the Soviet government could not discard the slogan of the Constituent Assembly because of the danger of a split (*otryv*) between Soviet power and the masses': D.A. Kovalenko and others (eds), *Sovety v pervyy god prol. dikt.* (Moscow 1967), p. 125.

55. In the 1920s Trotsky and Stalin presented conflicting interpretations of Lenin's attitude. The former's *Lenin: Notes for a Biographer* (New York 1971), pp. 110–13 is to be preferred to the latter's *Works*, VI (Moscow 1953), pp. 411 ff.; *Soch.*, VI (Moscow 1954), p. 392, in which Stalin took pains to obscure the fact that he himself at one point took a more flexible line than his leader. Cf. Schapiro, *The Origin of the Communist Autocracy*, pp. 80 f., 84 f.; B&F, p. 339. For Trotsky's own views, see his *Soch.*, III, pt II, pp. 103 ff.

56. For their views see B&F, pp. 366 f.; for the vote of 6 November, *Prot. VTsIK*, p. 35.

57. Radkey, *Election*, pp. 46–50 ; B&F, pp. 341–4.

58. B&F, pp. 348 f. (abbrev. text) ; *Prot. VTsIK*, p. 74 ; *Izv.*, 23 November. The Left SRs wanted this right to be exercised by means of a referendum, but this was too 'democratic' for the Bolsheviks. The 'right to recall' was hailed by Communists then and since as one of the chief features distinguishing the Soviet political system from 'bourgeois constitutionalism'. It soon became simply a means whereby the ruling party could purge soviets and other bodies 'from within' of elements deemed undesirable.

59. B&F, pp. 349 f.; *Narod*, 24 November ; Radkey, *Election*, p. 49, fails to mention their dismissal.

60. Malchevsky, *Vseross. Uchred. Sobr.*, p. 140 ; B&F (p. 350) state erroneously that the date was fixed by the 'underground' Provisional Government on 16 November, but this body, which carried on a shadowy clandestine existence, merely endorsed the earlier decision of 9 August.

61. B&F, p. 351 ; *Izv.*, 25 November.

62. *Izv.*, 27 November ; this was not endorsed by the CEC until 1 December: *Prot. VTsIK*, p. 121.

63. *NZ*, 29 November; *Izv.*, 29 November ; P.A. Sorokin, *Leaves from a Russian Diary* (Boston 1950), pp. 109 f. (where the event is wrongly dated).

64. B&F, p. 357–9. Seven men were arrested, two of whom, A.I. Shingarev and F.F. Kokoshkin, were murdered just over a month later.

65. Schapiro, *The Origin of the Communist Autocracy*, pp. 84 f.; Lenin, *PSS*, XXXV, p. 166.

66. B&F, p. 366 ; *NZ*, 17 December. Avksentyev was released on 4 March : Vinberg, *V plenu u 'obez'yan'*, p. 132.

67. The best first-hand account of this episode is B. Sokolov, 'Zashchita Vseross. Uchred. Sobr.', *ARR* XIII (1924), pp. 36–70. A more detailed analysis is provided by Radkey, *The Sickle under the Hammer*, pp. 332–49, 368–75.

68. *Pr.*, 20 December; cf. Lenin, *PSS*, XXXV, pp. 162–6 ; XL, pp. 1–24, esp. 5 f.

69. B&F, pp. 367 f.; *Prot. VTsIK*, pp. 175–7 ; Malchevsky, *Vseross. Uchred. Sobr.*, pp. 144 f.

70. B&F, pp. 372–4 ; Lenin, *PSS*, XXXV, pp. 221–3. First published in *Izv.*, 4 January.

71. Shteynberg, *Volkskomissar*, p. 70.

72. *Vech. slovo* 1 (8 January 1918). This informative source was not available to Radkey, whose treatment (*The Sickle under the Hammer*, pp. 416–29) is otherwise admirably full.

73. *Izv., Pr.*, 7 January.

74. Shteynberg, the PC of Justice, claims in his memoirs that he did everything possible to prevent the shooting, which he attributes to panic (*Volkskomissar*, pp. 71–3). This explanation is too simple and obscures his party's share of the responsibility for the excessive 'security measures' which made the clashes all but inevitable.

75. Mstislavsky, *Pyat' dney*, p. 142.

76. *Izv.*, 6 January ; Malchevsky, *Vseross. Uchred. Sobr.*, pp. 3 ff. (English summary: B&F, pp. 371 f.); Radkey, *The Sickle under the Hammer*, pp. 386–90 ; Mstislavsky, *Pyat' dney*, pp. 144–6 ; Shteynberg, *Volkskomissar*, pp. 73–6.

77. *Izv.*, 6 January ; B&F, p. 372 ; Radkey, *The Sickle under the Hammer*, pp. 390 f.

78. *Izv.*, 6 January; Malchevsky, *Vseross. Uchred. Sobr.*, pp. 9–23; Radkey, *The Sickle under the Hammer*, pp. 391–5.

79. Shteynberg, *Volkskomissar*, p. 78; cf. N.P. Oganovsky, 'Dnevnik chlena Uch. Sobr.', *Golos minuvshego*, 4–6 (1918), p. 157.

80. *Izv.*, 7 January; Mstislavsky, *Pyat' dney*, p. 152.

81. *Izv.*, 7 January; *NL*, 12 January; Shteynberg, *Volkskomissar*, p. 83, B&F, p. 375, give the former figure as 136, which is evidently a misprint, but it has been repeated by Anweiler, *Die Rätebewegung*, p. 272 (217).

82. Shteynberg, *Volkskomissar*, p. 85; Bonch-Bruyevich, *Na boyevykh postakh*, p. 250; Radkey, *The Sickle under the Hammer*, p. 411.

83. B&F, pp. 376 f.

84. *NL*, 12 January; Mstislavsky, *Pyat' dney*, p. 154.

85. It is worth noting that the second and third of these measures were passed *after* the celebrated incident involving the anarchist sailor A.G. Zheleznyakov, commander of the Tauride Palace guards, who asked Chernov to end the debates because 'the guard are tired'. Many general accounts of the Russian revolution, both western and Soviet, give the impression that the chairman yielded meekly to this crude pressure, which was not the case. For details of the assembly's last moments, see Radkey, *Sickle*, pp. 413–16, where tribute is justly paid to Chernov's courage.

86. B&F, pp. 384–6.

87. *NZ*, 7 January, cited by B&F, pp. 380–4; curiously enough the published minutes contain no record of this session.

88. This total was made up as follows:

third congress of workers' and soldiers' soviet deputies:		
fully accredited delegates	942	
delegates with consultative notes	104	1046
third congress of peasants' soviet deputies:		
fully accredited delegates	705	
delegates with consultative votes	115	820
total		1866

Izv., 20 January; E.G. Gimpelson, 'Nek. novye dannye o sost. III Vseross. s'yezda', *VI*, 9 (1960), pp. 214–17. Gimpelson studied (unpublished) mandates in addition to the delegates' replies to questionnaires – the evidence on which previous figures were based. His total does, however, exaggerate the attendance by about forty of the number of deputies who elected to serve in *both* national congresses.

89. *Izv.*, 13 January.

90. A contemporary Menshevik report put the number of those from the front alone at 500: *NL*, 19 January. My calculations, based on Gimpelson's data and Chugayev, *Triumf. shestviye*, II, pp. 356–71, give a total of 685.

91. Chugayev, *Triumf. shestviye,* p. 365. There was no marked difference in this regard between the total of respondents and those who identified themselves as Bolsheviks.

92. Gimpelson, 'Nek. novye dannye', p. 216, n. 17.

93. *NL,* 18 January.

94. G.S. Gurvich, 'Vsya vlast' sovetam', *Prol. revol. i pravo,* 1 (1918), p. 11. This article is based on an informal inquiry among deputies to the congress.

95. *Izv.,* 13, 20 January; *UR,* 14, 20 January; *III Vseross. s'yezd* (Petrograd 1918), pp. 43 f., 87, as cited by Kovalenko and others, *Sovety v pervyy god prol. dikt.,* p. 134. Some extracts from the congress debates are reprinted in B&F, pp. 389–99.

96. *Izv.,* 13 January.

97. At the congress of workers' and soldiers' soviets, of 708 deputies who responded to questions on their party allegiance, there were 35 right or centre SRS, 22 Mensheviks and 18 Internationalist Social Democrats; 56 men indicated no party affiliation: Chugayev, *Triumf. shestviye,* II, p. 360. At the congress of peasant soviets there were a maximum of 77 right or centre SRS; 41 men were unaffiliated: Ilyukhina, 'K vos.', p. 31. For other figures, Chugayev, *Triumf. shestviye,* II, p. 370; Radkey, *The Sickle under the Hammer,* p. 446.

98. This had 160 Bolshevik and 125 Left SRS; another 10 members were sympathetic to the ruling coalition, while 11 members belonged to the opposition (7 SRS, 2 Mensheviks, 2 Internationalists). *Izv., UR,* 20 January; Kovalenko and others, *Sovety v pervyy god prol. dikt.,* p. 135. With 306 members it was a little smaller than the preceding expanded body formed in mid-November. The peasant members had their own 'section' to remind them of their former independence. A 12-member presidium (7 Bolsheviks and 5 Left SRS) was announced on 26 January. Sverdlov remained chairman.

99. The congress formally established the fundamentals of this constitution. The Russian Socialist Soviet Republic was to be a federation of Soviet republics of the peoples of Russia, with the congress as its supreme organ of authority. The elaboration of these provisions was left to the CEC. Chugayev, *Triumf. shestviye,* II, pp. 377 f.

CHAPTER 25   THE URBAN SOVIETS: PETROGRAD AND MOSCOW

1. For a preliminary evaluation, see my 'October in the Provinces', in Pipes, *Revolutionary Russia,* pp. 180–216.

2. A beginning was made on this task in 1928 by S.A. Piontkovsky, who edited a volume of documents entitled *Sovety v Oktyabre* containing minutes of the Yaroslavl soviet plenum and of the Odessa and Moscow soviet executives; that of the Petrograd soviet executive for 29 November-

16 December was published a little earlier by Shidlovsky ('Pervye shagi bol'shev. Peterb. Soveta v 1917 g.', pp. 65–82). Unfortunately the principles governing the selection of historical documents on the revolutionary era for publication soon changed for the worse; Piontkovsky himself perished in 1937.

3. N. Voronovich, 'Mezh dvukh ogney: zap. zelenogo', *ARR*, VII (1922), p. 57.

4. Lenin, *PSS*, XLIX, p. 8.

5. Kovalenko and others, *Sovety v pervyy god prol. dikt.*, p. 171 (our italics).

6. I.G. Dykov, 'Pomoshch' Petrogr. VRK v ustan. Sov. vlasti na mestakh', in *Ustan. Sov. vlasti*, eds A.M. Pankratova and others (Moscow 1953), p. 158.

7. *Izv.*, 25 November, 22 December; Chugayev, *Triumf. shestviye*, I, pp. 134–7.

8. *Izv.*, 17 January 1918; Kovalenko and others, *Sovety v pervyy god prol. dikt.*, p. 172, where, however, the bureaucratic tendencies implicit in the commissariat's policy are minimized. A more detailed scheme was drawn up by I. Ulyanov (presumably no relative of the Bolshevik leader) and published in *Izv.*, 25 January, 14 February.

9. Frayman and others, *Okt. vooruzh.*, II, p. 176; Andreyev, *Sovety rab. i sold. dep.*, p. 344.

10. Frayman and others, *Okt. vooruzh.*, II, p. 192.

11. Trotsky, *Soch.*, III, pt I, pp. 276–307.

12. The soldiers' section executive had 10 SRs, 9 Bolsheviks and 3 Mensheviks; that of the workers' section 13 Bolsheviks, 6 SRs and 7 Mensheviks; the combined executive was thus evenly balanced, with 22 Bolsheviks and 22 non-Bolsheviks. On 21 October the Bolsheviks, now more confident of their strength, added 10 leading members of their party. M.N. Potekhin, *Pervyy Sovet prol. dikt.* (Leningrad 1966), pp. 47–9.

13. *NZ*, 19 October; Trotsky, *Soch.*, III, pt II, pp. 31 f.

14. Lenin, *PSS*, XXXV, pp. 2–5.

15. *NZ*, 30 October; Trotsky, *Soch.*, III, pt II, pp. 69–72.

16. Frayman and others, *Okt. vooruzh.*, II, pp. 470, 472; not all of these seem to have been reported in *Izv.*

17. *Izv.*, 17, 23, 27, 28 February.

18. The executive committee, revived on 25 November, consisted of 34 Bolsheviks and 10 Left SRs, but seems to have been something of a fiction; the presidium, elected on 13 December, had 5 Bolsheviks and 2 Left SRs. Zinoviev became chairman – a post he was to hold until 1926. *Izv.*, 14 December; Kovalenko and others, *Sovety v pervyy god prol. dikt.*, p. 166.

19. Potekhin, *Pervyy Sovet prol. dikt.*, pp. 50–62.

20. *PVRK*. Unlike other recent documentary collections, this was *not*

compiled according to the 'illustrative method' normally used (see above p. xvi), but reproduces the relevant archive more or less *in toto*. For a review which raises some important historiographical questions, cf. J.J. Marie, 'Le Comité', *CMRS*, 8 (1967), pp. 189–204.

21. Its orders were often signed by men who were not members of the five-man Bureau. Moreover, on such documents almost any senior member was permitted to write his name against the title of 'chairman' or 'secretary' – offices which therefore had no real independent existence and were in effect fictitious (*PVRK*, i, pp. 14 f.; Marie, 'Le Comité', pp. 199–202). This may be explained in part by a desire to prevent a 'counter-revolutionary' government, should one come to power, from pinning responsibility for the committee's actions on one or two individuals; in part by Trotsky's romanticism and fondness for mystifying ruses; and in part by a sincere commitment to the principle of collective leadership. It may be objected that Chugayev's editorial *kollektiv* seeks deliberately to de-emphasize Trotsky's role, in conformity with official Stalinist and post-Stalinist policy, and that only independent archival research could establish the precise truth. Nevertheless the weighty evidence adduced in these volumes should in our judgement lead to a revision of the conventional western view.

22. *PVRK*, i, p. 41; Sadovsky, in *PR*, 10 (1922), p. 74.

23. We have already noted (p. 278) that soldiers (rather than Red guardsmen) played the key role in the insurrection. For the events of 24–25 October in the capital, see the sources listed on p. 517, n. 6.

24. Iroshnikov, *Sozdaniye Sov.*, p. 95.

25. *PVRK*, iii, pp. 662 f. lists 82 known and 15 possible members. The figure is reduced to 80 by E.D. Orekhova, 'O sostave Petrogr. VRK', *Ist. SSSR*, 2 (1971), pp. 118–30, who succeeds in omitting Trotsky altogether – a striking example of neo-Stalinist falsification.

26. *PVRK*, ii, p. 275; cf. p. 245 (I.A. Teodorovich).

27. *PVRK*, iii, p. 232.

28. *PVRK*, iii, p. 523.

29. *PVRK*, i, p. 481.

30. *PVRK*, iii, pp. 318, 320.

31. *PVRK*, iii, p. 249.

32. *PVRK*, iii, p. 232; Bonch-Bruyevich, *Na boyevykh postakh*, pp. 190 f.

33. Lenin's decision seems to have been taken under Dzerzhinsky's influence: R. Gul, *Dzerzhinsky – Menzhinsky* (Paris 1936), p. 67; cf. M. [Ya.] Latsis, 'Tov. Dzerzhinsky i VChK', *PR*, 56 (1926), pp. 81 f.; E.J. Scott, 'The Cheka', *St Antony's Papers*, i (1956), p. 2; *PVRK*, iii, p. 349; Iroshnikov, *Sozdaniye Sov.*, p. 210.

34. *PVRK*, iii, p. 479.

35. *Izv.*, 7 December; Iroshnikov, *Sozdaniye Sov.*, p. 214, citing unpublished minutes of the CPC for 6 December.

36. Latsis, 'Dzerzhinsky', pp. 82 f. This was the first occasion on which the document saw the light. The decree establishing the Cheka was not published in the press or in the official collection of laws at that time: Scott, 'The Cheka', pp. 3, 6; B&F, pp. 297 f.

37. Lenin, *PSS*, L, p. 18 (first pub. in 1960; italics in original). Ya. Kh. Peters was one of the ten officials appointed to head the Cheka. On the composition of its leadership see now Iroshnikov, *Sozdaniye Sov.*, p. 214; the lists of names given by Latsis, 'Dzershinsky', p. 83 and *Chrezvych. kom. po bor'be s kontr-revol.* (Moscow 1921), p. 7 are incomplete.

38. Lenin, *PSS*, XXXV, p. 311; cf. also my 'Lenin's Letters as a Historical Source', in *Lenin and Leninism,* ed. B.W. Eissenstat (Lexington, Mass., London 1971), pp. 258 f.

39. Iroshnikov, *Sozdaniye Sov.*, p. 215; Latsis, 'Dzerzhinsky', p. 90.

40. Latsis, *Chrezvych. kom.*, p. 13. Scott, 'The Cheka', p. 14, citing this source, attributes this information to 1921, but in the preface to Latsis's pamphlet, dated December 1920, it is stated that it was written 'nearly two years ago'.

41. An excellent study of the events in Moscow is given by Melgunov, *Kak bol'sheviki zakhvatili vlast'*, pp. 277–382 (unfortunately omitted from the abridged English translation). This is based on a critical examination of the abundant (but often inaccurate and tendentious) memoir literature as well as such contemporary sources as the minutes of the Moscow MRC, published in *KA*, 23 (1927), pp. 64–148, 44–5 (1931), pp. 80–161, 65–6 (1934), pp. 164–92, 71 (1935), pp. 60–115. Excerpts from the minutes of three soviet executive sessions were published by Piontkovsky in *Sovety v Oktyabre*, pp. 31–86.

42. Ignatov, *Mosk. Sovet rab. dep.*, pp. 333, 335.

43. Ignatov, *Mosk. Sovet rab. dep.*, p. 345.

44. Ignatov, *Mosk. Sovet rab. dep.*, p. 361; K. Ryabinsky (ed.), *Revol. 1917 g.: khr. sob., V: oktyabr'* (Moscow, Leningrad 1926), pp. 193 ff.; Kovalenko and others, *Sovety v pervyy god prol. dikt.*, p. 48; the voting was 394:106 with 23 abstentions. The Bolshevik majority was about twice as large as usual because the SRs refused to take part in the vote.

45. The four Bolsheviks were V.M. Smirnov (later one of Trotsky's most loyal supporters), N.I. Muralov, G.A. Usievich and A. Lomov (G.I. Oppokov). According to a recent Soviet secondary source there were four more Bolsheviks, including A.I. Rykov, and two USDI members, not one; but 'the MRC's personal composition later changed' (Kovalenko and others, *Sovety v pervyy god prol. dikt.*, p. 47). These circumlocutions are necessitated by an inability to mention N.I. Bukharin's prominent part in the Moscow party organization, on which see now Cohen, *Bukharin and the Bolshevik Revolution*, pp. 49–52. For the MRC's activities see Melgunov, pp. 307, 314, 321, 334–6, 350 f., 356–8, 365.

46. Melgunov, *Kak bol'sheviki zakhvatili vlast'*, p. 307 ; Piontkovsky, *Oktyabr' 1917 g.*, pp. 31–35.

47. Vompe, *Dni Okt.*, pp. 62 f.

48. Piontkovsky, *Oktyabr' 1917 g.*, pp. 50–52.

49. *Sots.-dem.*, 14, 17 November. In the plenum the ratio was somewhat less favourable to the Bolsheviks, who had 202 followers and 8 sympathizers among the 296 delegates (12 November).

50. 'Unanimously', according to the Bolshevik *Sots.-dem.*; by 'an overwhelming majority' according to the independent *UR* (15 November).

51. *Sots.-dem.*, 21 November.

52. *UR*, 29 November ; *Sots.-dem.*, 30 November.

53. *UR*, 22 December.

54. *Sots.-dem.*, 8 November.

55. *Sots.-dem.*, 9, 28 November.

CHAPTER 26   THE URBAN SOVIETS: THE NORTH-WEST, THE CENTRAL INDUSTRIAL REGION AND THE URALS

1. Ryabinsky, *Revol. 1917 g.: khr. sob.*, V: *oktyabr'*, p. 99 ; V. Leykina, 'Okt. po Rossii', *PR*, 49 (1926), p. 197.

2. Ryabinsky, *Revol. 1917 g.: khr. sob. V: oktyabr'*, pp. 63, 71, 86; cf. also Ignatov, *Mosk. Sovet rab. dep.*, p. 341.

3. *Izv.*, 21 November ; Leykina, 'Okt. po Rossii', pp. 186 f.; I.N. Lyubimov (ed.), *Revol. 1917 g.: khr. sob.*, VI: *noyabr' – dekabr'* (Moscow, Leningrad 1930), pp. 152, 159 ; L.M. Gavrilov and others (comps), *Bor'ba za ustan.* (Moscow 1962), pp. 55, 225. A detailed Soviet study is M.I. Kapustin, *Soldaty Sev. fronta za vlast' Sov.* (Moscow 1957).

4. Ryabinsky, *Revol. 1917 g.: khr. sob. V: oktyabr'*, pp. 53, 97.

5. One early Bolshevik memoirist conceded that the democrats 'enjoyed the moral support of almost the entire population of the town, not excluding part of the workers': A.P.I.[vanov], 'K ist. org. Sov. vlasti v Novg. gub.', *KL*, 24 (1927), p. 42.

6. Ivanov, 'K ist. org. Sov. vlasti v Novg. gub.', pp. 37–51 ; G. Likhachev, 'Okt. revol. v g. Novgorode', *PR*, 21 (1923), pp. 162–7 ; A.[P.] Ivanov, 'Vlast' Vrem. Prav. v Novg. gub.', *KL*, 17 (1926), pp. 16–28. Recent Soviet accounts are less illuminating and sometimes misleading: Gavrilov and others, *Bor'ba za ustan.*, pp. 286, 378, 468, 615 f., 638.

7. G.A. Trukan, 'Bol'shevizatsiya Sovetov tsentr. Rossii nak. Okt.', in *Okt. i grazhd. voyna v SSSR*, eds I.M. Maysky and others (Moscow 1966), pp. 72 f.

8. *Sots.-dem.*, 12 November ; *Izv.* (Moscow), 13 November, cited by Yu. P. Aksenov, in *Ustan. Sov. vlasti na mestakh*, II, ed. D.A. Chugayev (Moscow 1959), p. 87.

9. *Sots.-dem.*, 25 November.

10. Kovalenko and others, *Sovety v pervyy god prol. dikt.*, p. 180; *Sots.-dem.*, 14, 16, 21 December.

11. The Bolsheviks won 64 per cent of the vote in Ivanovo-Voznesensk – more than in Moscow, where the corresponding figure was 48 per cent. Cf. Radkey, *Election*, pp. 24 f., 53; P.I. Kozlov and N.I. Reszvyy, 'Rozhd. Sov. vlasti v Yarosl. gub', in Chugayev, *Ustan. Sov. vlasti na mestakh*, II, p. 249.

12. I. Firger, 'Okt. revol. v Iv.-Voznesenske: iz vosp.', *KL*, 6 (1923), pp. 279 f. The duma lingered on at least until December: F.N. Samoylov, 'Okt. v Iv.-Voznesenske', *PR*, 71 (1927), p. 106. A similar state of affairs is reported from Yekaterinoslav: cf. E. Kviring, 'Yek-slavskiy Sovet i Okt. revol.', *LR*, 1 (1922), p. 64. It anticipates a problem that French and Italian communists have faced since the Second World War.

13. D. Furmanov, 'Nezabv. dni', *PR*, 10 (1922), p. 229; cf. Furmanov, *Put'*, pp. 95 f. Furmanov, who died in 1926, became a noted Soviet novelist; at this time he defined himself politically as a SR Maximalist. Cf. also F.[N.] Samoylov, 'Okt. revol. v Iv.-Voznesenske', *PR*, 33 (1924), p. 196.

14. *Izv.*, 7 November; Furmanov, 'Nezabv. dni', p. 232 and *Put'*, p. 99; Chugayev, *Triumf. shestviye*, I, p. 319 (an account of these events given shortly afterwards to MOBYUS).

15. Lyubimov, *Khr. sob.*, pp. 6, 77; Samoylov, 'Okt.', pp. 105 f.; Gavrilov and others, *Bor'ba za ustan.*, pp. 143, 404.

16. Chugayev, *Triumf. shestviye*, I, p. 318; Leykina, 'Okt. po Rossii', p. 203; N. Yevreynov, 'Iz vosp. o podg. Okt. v Kineshme', *PR*, 70 (1927), p. 189–90, where the author stresses his own contribution to the change of course. There is a ring of truth in his account of the local garrison's role in these events, which is more suggestive of 1825 than of 1917:

> The official transfer of power into the hands of the soviet took place some days after the Moscow rising. What happened was this: we called out the reliable units of soldiers on to the square before the *Realschule*, formed them into a square and said a few words to them in the soviet's name.... After that the soldiers shouted 'hurrah' several times, which signified that they had come over.... It was something in the nature of a loyalty oath.

The men are described as 'stony-faced and tense'.

17. Leykina, 'Okt. po Rossii', p. 203, citing a rare local 1st part source. The minutes of this meeting (and two subsequent plenums) have since been published: Piontkovsky, *Oktyabr' 1917 g.*, pp. 116–23. These add the significant detail that the new executive was given *carte blanche* to coopt anyone it wished. The vote on 'soviet power' was 88 to 46, with 9 abstentions, but on the question whether the soviet should join the Committee of Public Safety set up under the aegis of the municipal

duma, opinions were more evenly divided: 80 votes were cast in favour, 84 against, and 12 men abstained.

18. Kozlov and Rezvyy, 'Rozhd. Sov. vlasti', p. 256, c.u.d.s. This work makes no mention of the soviet's minutes published in 1928, presumably since Piontkovsky's volume is no longer considered ideologically reliable.

19. Kozlov and Rezvyy, 'Rochd. Sov. vlasti', p. 251; Leykina, 'Okt. po Rossii', p. 204; Chugayev, *Triumf. shestviye*, I, pp. 348 f.

20. F.P. Bystrykh, 'Bol'sh. Urala vo glave mass', *VI KPSS*, 4 (1967), p. 54.

21. Lisovsky, *1917 g. na Urale*, p. 423 n.

22. Ryabinsky, *Revol. 1917 g.: khr. sob. V: oktyabr'*, p. 79.

23. A.F. Butenko and D.A. Chugayev (eds), *II s'yezd Sovetov* (Moscow 1957), p. 396.

24. Lyubimov, *Khr. sob.*, p. 8.

25. [P.M. Bykov], 'Yek-burgskiy Sovet', in *Rab. revol. na Urale*, comps P.M. Bykov and N.G. Niporkin (Yekaterinburg 1921), pp. 92 f.

26. Bykov, 'Yek-burgskiy Sovet', p. 94; Lisovsky, *1917 g. na Urale*, pp. 445 ff.

27. Bykov, 'Yek-burgskiy Sovet', p. 95 (23 November); Lyubimov, *Khr. sob.*, p. 194; Lisovsky, *1917 g. na Urale*, pp. 449 f.

28. Bykov, 'Yek-burgskiy Sovet', p. 100.

29. Leykina, 'Okt. po Rossii', pp. 221 f.; Lisovsky, *1917 g. na Urale*, pp. 462–5; Butenko and Chugayev, *II s'yezd Sovetov*, p. 293; Lyubimov, *Khr. sob.*, p. 55.

30. Lisovsky, *1917 g. na Urale*, p. 455; Butenko and Chugayev, *II s'yezd Sovetov*, pp. 312 f.

31. Lisovsky, *1917 g. na Urale*, p. 479; Butenko and Chugayev, *II s'yezd Sovetov*, p. 272; Shapurin, *Okt. na Yuzh. Urale*, p. 61.

32. B. El'tsin, 'Dni Okt. perevorota na Yuzh. Urale i v Ufe', *PR*, 10 (1922), pp. 354–6; Lyubimov, *Khr. sob.*, pp. 8, 22 f.; Leykina, 'Okt. po Rossii', p. 204; Gavrilov and others, *Bor'ba za ustan.*, p. 329.

CHAPTER 27   THE URBAN SOVIETS: THE VOLGA CITIES, THE CENTRAL AGRI-CULTURAL REGION AND THE UKRAINE

1. According to the census of June 1917 the urban population of Saratov province was 678,500 and of Nizhniy Novgorod province 393,600, whereas normal growth projections would have yielded figures of 442,000 and 198,000 respectively. L.S. Gaponenko and V.M. Kabuzan, 'Mat. sel.-khoz. perepisey 1916–1917 gg. kak ist. istochnik', *Ist. SSSR*, 6 (1961), p. 114.

2. Z.L. Serebryakova, 'Perevybory kak odin iz putey bol'shevizatsii Sovetov', in *Bor'ba za pobedu i ukrepl. Sov. vlasti*, ed. S.S. Khesin (Moscow 1966), pp. 25 f.

3. V. Illarionov, 'Okt. revol. v Nizheg. gub.', *PR*, 53 (1925), p. 142.

4. L.M. Kaganovich, 'Partiya kom.', in *1917–1918: god prol. dikt.* (Nizhniy

Novgorod), 1918, p. 5; cf. A. Pisarev in *1917–18: god prol. dikt.*, p. 14.

5. Pisarev, p. 17.

6. Pisarev, pp. 19 f.; Lyubimov, *Khr. sob.*, p. 62; *RG*, 9 November; Gavrilov and others, *Bor'ba za ustan.*, p. 128 gives the vote as 57 to 52, but a contemporary report to MOBYUS records it as 136 to 83 with 4 abstentions (Chugayev, *Triumf. shestviye*, I, pp. 316 f.). The more recent source is less reliable; characteristically, it omits to mention the deputies' expression of support for the Constituent Assembly.

7. [N.I.] Muralov, 'Otryvki vospom.', in Chernomordik, *Okt. dni v Moskve*, p. 30; Lyubimov, *Khr. sob.*, p. 189.

8. V.P. Antonov-Saratovsky, *Pod styagom prol. bor'by* (Moscow, Leningrad 1925), I, pp. 148 f.; cf. P. Lebedev, 'Fev.-Okt. v Saratove', *PR*, 10 (1922), pp. 252 f.; Kovalenko and others, *Sovety v pervyy god prol. dikt.*, p. 59.

9. Antonov-Saratovsky, *Pod styagom prol. bor'by*, pp. 147–75, 188; Lebedev, 'Fev.-Okt. v Saratove', pp. 252–61; Leykina, 'Okt. po Rossii', pp. 217 f. For an account in English based on reports in two local newspapers, see W.E. Mosse, 'Revolution in Saratov', *SEER*, 49 (1971), pp. 586–602.

10. Antonov-Saratovsky, *Pod styagom prol. bor'by*, pp. 195, 205–9, 214; Lebedev, 'Fev. Okt. v Saratove', p. 270.

11. *Izv.*, 7 January; Chugayev, *Triumf. shestviye*, I, pp. 376–8; Gavrilov and others, *Bor'ba za ustan.*, p. 373.

12. Such was the general picture in Samara: cf. Lyubimov, *Khr. sob.*, pp. 8, 120; I. Kolychevsky, 'Lit. ob Okt. revol.', *PR*, 33 (1924), p. 218; Leykina, 'Okt. po Rossii', p. 214; Chugayev, *Triumf. shestviye*, I, p. 393. Cf. also E.I. Medvedev, 'Zavoyev. i uproch. vlasti v Sam. gub.', in Chugayev, *Ustan. Sov. vlasti na mestakh*, II, pp. 309–72.

13. *Izv.*, 8 November; K. Grasis, 'Okt. v Kazani', *PR*, 33 (1924), pp. 124, 133 f.; V. Povolzhsky, 'Pered Okt.', *PR*, 10 (1922), pp. 343 f., 347; Leykina, 'Okt. po Rossii', p. 212; Kolychevsky, 'Lit. ob Okt. revol.', pp. 216 f.; Gavrilov and others, *Bor'ba za ustan.*, p. 137.

14. From data in Butenko and Chugayev, *II s'yezd Sovetov*, pp. 239, 326; Kovalenko and others, *Sovety v pervyy god prol. dikt.*, p. 60.

15. I.[Ya]. Vrachev, 'Okt. revol. v Voronezhe', *PR*, 33 (1924), p. 162.

16. Vrachev, 'Okt. revol. v Voronezhe', p. 168; figures corrected following Gavrilov and others, *Bor'ba za ustan.*, p. 42.

17. Vrachev, 'Okt. revol. v Voronezhe', pp. 169–81, 187–9; Lyubimov, *Khr. sob.*, pp. 7, 16, 26, 62, 86; *NZ*, 9 November; *Sots.-dem.*, 23 November; Piontkovsky, *Sovety v Oktyabre*, pp. 87–90 (soviet plenum minutes). Gavrilov and others, *Bor'ba za ustan.*, p. 135, do not mention the latter source.

18. Kolychevsky, 'Lit. ob Okt. revol.', p. 223, citing local 1st part sources.

19. Kolychevsky, 'Lit. ob Okt. revol.', p. 223; Leykina, 'Okt. po Rossii',

pp. 207 f.; Butenko and Chugayev, *II s'yezd Sovetov*, p. 395; Gavrilov and others, *Bor'ba za ustan.*, pp. 42, 113, 336; *Izv.*, 17 February 1918.

20. *NZ*, 11 November. The local Bolsheviks, who as late as September are estimated to have numbered only thirty, did not split from their Menshevik comrades until 2 November: Kolychevsky, 'Lit. ob Okt. revol.', p. 222; Gavrilov and others, *Bor'ba za ustan.*, p. 124.

21. Kolychevsky, 'Lit. ob Okt. revol.', p. 222.

22. Gavrilov and others, *Bor'ba za ustan.*, p. 320. Recent Soviet sources do not state its party composition, which in itself suggests that the non-Bolsheviks were in the ascendant.

23. For a brief survey see my 'October in the Provinces', pp. 202–7.

24. For further accounts of these developments see Pipes, *Formation*, pp. 114–26; J.S. Reshetar, Jr, *The Ukrainian Revolution* (Princeton, NJ 1952), pp. 89–97; O.S. Pidhainy, *Ukrainian Republic* (Toronto, New York 1966), pp. 166–238, 401–55.

25. Leykina, 'Okt. po Rossii', pt 2, *PR*, 58 (1926), pp. 249 f.; Gavrilov and others, *Bor'ba za ustan.*, p. 45; *NZ*, 9 November; *RG*, 5 November.

26. For the party composition cf. Leykina, 'Okt. po Rossii', p. 251. The list given in Gavrilov and others, *Bor'ba za ustan.*, p. 442, characteristically omits those groups whose existence present-day Soviet historians would prefer to overlook: the Ukrainians (80) and the non-party delegates (76) – to say nothing of such smaller groups as the Anarchists (8), whose influence in this region was soon to grow appreciably.

27. Leykina, 'Okt. po Rossii', pt 2, pp. 251–5; Chugayev, *Triumf. shestviye*, II, pp. 84 f., 431.

28. Ya. Rappo, 'Bor'ba sil v Okt. revol v Nikolayeve', *LR*, I (1922), pp. 81–103; Kolychevsky, 'Lit. ob Okt. revol.', p. 231; Gavrilov and others, *Bor'ba za ustan.*, pp. 25, 62, 78, 304, 602; Chugayev, *Triumf. shestviye*, II, p. 118.

29. Gavrilov and others, *Bor'ba za ustan.*, p. 641; V. Averin, in *PR*, 70 (1927), p. 163.

30. A detailed account of this conflict is given by Bosh in her memoirs: *God bor'by*. Although highly partisan and sometimes inaccurate, it is an important source; cf. also the early works cited by Pipes, *Formation*, p. 313. More recent is P.T. Tronko (ed.), *Kievshchine* (Kiev 1957).

31. An excellent account of these manoeuvres is given by Pipes, *Formation*, pp. 70–72; cf. also Gavrilov and others, *Bor'ba za ustan.*, pp. 22 f.

32. Pipes, *Formation*, p. 72; I. Kulik, 'Okt. dni v Kieve', *LR*, I (1922), pp. 39–43; Gavrilov and others, *Bor'ba za ustan.*, pp. 44, 61, 77, 90, 102; Tronko, *Kievshchine*, pp. 360, 367.

33. Bosh, *God bor'by*, pp. 59 f.; Chugayev, *Triumf. shestviye*, II, p. 80; Gavrilov and others, *Bor'ba za ustan.*, pp. 237, 243, 258, 280, 352; Tronko, *Kievshchine*, pp. 413 f., 420, 425, 433, 442, 447, 460.

34. *DSV*, I, pp. 174–80; Tronko, *Kievshchine*, pp. 473–5 (first published in *Pr.*, 18 December). Cf. Pidhainy, *Ukrainian Republic*, pp. 415 f.

35. Tronko, *Kievshchine*, pp. 440–2.

36. Pipes, *Formation*, p. 121, citing P. Khristiuk, *Zamitki i materialy do istorii ukrainskoi revoliutsii, 1917–1920* (Vienna 1921–2), I, pp. 130 f.; cf. Bosh, *God bor'by*, pp. 75–80; Leykina, 'Okt. po Rossii', pt 3, *PR*, 59 (1926), pp. 244 f.; Gavrilov and others, *Bor'ba za ustan.*, p. 390.

37. Bosh, *God bor'by*, p. 80; Tronko, *Kievshchine*, pp. 487–9.

38. For the organization and strategy of the campaign, see V. Antonov-Ovseyenko, *Zap. o grazhd. voyne*, I (Moscow 1924), pp. 47–62.

39. Tronko, *Kievshchine*, pp. 519 f.

40. Pipes, *Formation*, p. 125, citing *Ist. KP(b) U*, II (Kiev 1933), p. 126.

41. Tronko, *Kievshchine*, pp. 549–51, 556.

42. A contemporary Bolshevik source (Butenko and Chugayev, *II s'yezd Sovetov*, p. 360) gives the alignment of the deputies as 120 each for the SRs and Bolsheviks, 40 each for the Ukrainians and Mensheviks. This may understate the strength of the latter groups, for when the leaders set up a coalition RC on 26 October they gave each of these four factions two seats on the presidium and reserved a ninth place for the Menshevik Internationalists. *NZ*, 7 November; Gavrilov and others, *Bor'ba za ustan.*, p. 23.

43. *NZ*, 12 November; Gavrilov and others, *Bor'ba za ustan.*, pp. 136, 266, 304.

44. Antonov-Ovseyenko, *Zap. o grazhd. voyne*, pp. 27 f.; Gavrilov and others, *Bor'ba za ustan.*, p. 425.

45. Gavrilov and others, *Bor'ba za ustan.*, p. 433; Leshchenko, in Pankratova, *Ustan. Sov. vlasti*, p. 446.

46. Gavrilov and others, *Bor'ba za ustan.*, p. 530; cf. Chugayev, *Triumf. shestviye*, II, p. 132.

47. N. Aleksandrova, *Artem: biograficheskiy ocherk* (Moscow 1922), pp. 130–2.

48. Gavrilov and others, *Bor'ba za ustan.*, pp. 274, 281, 322, 329, 346; P.N. Sobolev and others, *Ist. Vel. Okt. sots. revol.* (Moscow 1967), pp. 310–21.

49. P. Kenez, *Civil War in South Russia* (Berkeley, Calif. 1971), pp. 85–95; Butenko and Chugayev, *II s'yezd*, p. 368; Ryabinsky, *Revol. 1917 g.: khr. sob. V: oktyabr'*, p. 174; Lyubimov, *Revol. 1917 g.: khr. sob. V: oktyabr'*, pp. 43, 178.

50. See Pipes, *Formation*, ch. IV, V and bibliography, pp. 316–27; and, more recent, R.G. Suny, *The Baku Commune, 1917–1918* (Princeton, NJ 1972).

CHAPTER 28   LENIN'S LAND DECREE

1. For the earlier stages of this controversy, see my *Rise of Social Democracy in Russia*, pp. 79–84, 194 f., 294–6.

2. Lenin, *PSS*, xxxi, p. 167.

3. Lenin, *PSS*, p. 167.

4. For text of the decision, see McNeal, *Resolutions and Decisions of the CPSU*, I, pp. 224 f.; cf. also I.I. Varzho (comp.), *Agr. pol. Sov. vlasti* (Moscow 1954), pp. 107–9, and for a recent Soviet analysis E.V. Illeritskaya, 'V.I. Lenin i razresheniye agr. vop. v Rossii', in Maysky and others, *Okt. i grazhd. voyna v SSSR*, pp. 192–210.

5. Lenin, *PSS*, xxxiv, p. 114.

6. Lenin, *PSS*, xxxiv, p. 115.

7. Cf. the careful analyses by E.A. Lutsky, 'Podg. proyekta Dek. o zemle', in Maysky and others, *Okt. i grazhd. voyna v SSSR*, pp. 233–48, esp. p. 239 and M.I. Iroshnikov, 'O tekste leninskogo dek. "O zemle"', in *Issled. po otech. istochnikoved.*, eds N.E. Nosov and others (Moscow, Leningrad 1964), pp. 90–99; Bonch-Bruyevich, *Na boyevykh postakh*, pp. 117–21.

8. Text: Lenin, *PSS*, xxxv, pp. 24–6; the English tr. in B&F, p. 129 is somewhat inexact.

9. Lenin, *PSS*, xxxv, p. 27.

10. The best recent Soviet treatment of Bolshevik agrarian policy is Pershin, *Agr. revol.*, II, pp. 11–78. The account by V. Zaytsev, *Politika partii bol'shevikov* (Moscow 1953), pp. 21–35, is more didactic but does have the merit of emphasizing power-political considerations which Pershin and others now tend to play down – as does Sorlin, 'Lénine et le problème paysan en 1917', pp. 250–80.

CHAPTER 29   'BLACK REPARTITION': THE VILLAGE TRIUMPHANT

1. *Izv.*, 9 December (full text).

2. Pershin, *Agr. revol.*, II, p. 178.

3. Pershin, *Agr. revol.*, II, pp. 179, 184.

4. Lenin, *PSS*, L, p. 17.

5. E.A. Lutsky, 'K ist. konf. pomeshch. imeniy v 1917–1918 gg.', *Izv. Ak. Nauk SSSR, ser. ist. i filos.*, 5 (1948), pp. 510 f. This gives a total 31 short of 766. Although Lutsky does not account for the gap, it may be that 31 estates had not yet been inventoried by October 1918, when the last reply was submitted.

6. N.S. Zhuravleva, 'Konfiskatsiya', *IZ*, 29 (1949), pp. 52, 55 f.

7. *NZ*, 19 February 1918.

8. Pershin, *Agr. revol.*, II, p. 192.

9. E.A. Lutsky, 'Peredel zemli vesnoy 1918 g.', *Izv. Ak. Nauk SSSR, ser. ist. i filos.*, 6 (1949), p. 511.

10. Zhuravleva, 'Konfiskatsiya', p. 54.

11. *Sb. dekretov – po nar. khoz.* (Moscow 1918), p. 487.

12. Pershin, *Agr. revol.*, II, p. 196.

13. 'Tovarishchi vse shumyat – uravnyat', a tam, mol, posmotrim, kto bogatey budet.' Ya. D. Sadovsky, 'Kak ya delil zemlyu', *RM*, 10–12 (1923–4), pp. 324 f. The term *tovarishch* was used by country folk in a sense directly contrary to that which it customarily conveyed in the towns: not 'one of us' but 'one of them'.

14. V.M. Chernov, ' "Chernyy peredel" 1918 g.', *ZIIR*, 2 (1925), p. 156.

15. Okninsky, *Dva goda sredi krest'yan*, p. 61.

16. Rudnev, *Pri vechernikh ognyakh*, pp. 86–89.

17. *Sb. dek.*, p. 488.

18. *Sb. dek.*, p. 962 (circular of 6 September 1918); B.[N.] Knipovich, 'Naprav. i itogi agr. pol. 1917–1920 gg.', in *O zemle*, fasc. I, p. 23.

19. Zhuravleva, 'Konfiskatsiya', p. 57.

20. S.P. Rudnev, who farmed 5000 dessyatines in Simbirsk province, accepted confiscation of his estate with equanimity and sowed the 8 dessyatines left him; in August the area became the scene of fighting between Red and White (Czechoslovak) forces, whereupon he left with the latter. His memoirs, from which we have cited (n. 16), are a useful source; so too are those of A.L. Okninsky, written in 1924. Before the revolution Okninsky was an official in the judiciary; during the civil-war years he worked as an accountant in a district soviet office in Tambov province. He states (p. 62 n.) that most local landowners (of which he was not one) entered the public service under the new regime. Cf. also Uchitel'nitsa, 'Tri gg. v derevne', *KR*, 4–6 (1923), p. 188.

21. Zhuravleva, 'Konfiskatsiya', p. 59. They farmed 190 dessyatines, or an average of 11·9 dessyatines each – more than in 1917, when the average land-holding had measured only 7·8 dessyatines.

22. Pershin, *Agr. revol.*, II, p. 214.

23. Pershin, *Agr. revol.*, II, p. 385.

24. Pershin, *Agr. revol.*, II, p. 387, citing *Kratkiy otchet Narodnogo Komissariata Prosveshcheniya, 1917 – oktyabr' 1920* (Moscow 1920), p. 33.

25. On the state of primary education at this time, cf. S. Fitzpatrick, *The Commissariat of Enlightenment* (Cambridge 1970), pp. 26–58, esp. pp. 44, 52–7. The ethnographer Tan-Bogoraz, who studied conditions in Kursk province in 1923, notes that the village school could readily be identified by its neglected and dilapidated appearance: *Revol. v derevne*, p. 7.

26. *Narod*, 24 November 1917.

27. Igritsky, *1917 g. v derevne*, p. 126.

28. Z, 'K poznaniyu proisshedshego', *RM*, 3–5 (1923), p. 251.

29. Pershin, *Agr. revol.*, II, pp. 355, 374.

30. In 1916 (in forty-nine provinces of European Russia) the private proprietors owned 1·4 million horses, 2·2 million cattle, 3·4 million sheep and 800,000 pigs (in round figures): Artyukhov and Chayanov, *Sel. khoz.*, pp. 15 ff.; cf. A.N. Chelintsev, 'Pomeshch. khoz. v Rossii

pered revol.', *ZIIR*, 2 (1925), p. 49. The figures recorded (for thirty-eight provinces) by the very defective 1917 agricultural census were as follows: 800,000 horses, 1 million cattle, 1·6 million sheep and 500,000 pigs (in round figures). *Pogub. itogi Vseross. sel. khoz. i pozem. perepisi 1917 g.*, pp. 42 ff. Cf. also Pershin, *Agr. revol.*, II, pp. 364, 369.

31. Lutsky, 'Peredel', p. 232.
32. Lutsky, 'Peredel', p. 239 ; Pershin, *Agr. revol.*, II, p. 225.
33. Z, 'K poznaniyu', p. 242.
34. Pershin, *Agr. revol.*, II, pp. 323 ff.; cf. Lutsky, 'Peredel', p. 233 (Kasimov county, Ryazan province).
35. Cf. Pershin, *Agr. revol.*, II, pp. 539–72 for a list of the several hundred cited in his work. This list is particularly praiseworthy in that it gives a description of the nature of each document.
36. Pershin, *Agr. revol.*, II, p. 289.
37. Knipovich, 'Naprav.', p. 25.
38. Pershin, *Agr. revol.*, II, pp. 295 f.
39. Pershin, *Agr. revol.*, II, pp. 296 f.; cf. pp. 415–16.
40. Pershin, *Agr. revol.*, II, pp. 298–302.
41. G.V. Sharapov, *Nachalo sots. preobraz.* (Moscow 1960), p. 14, citing *Vestnik stat.*, 13 (1923), p. 142.
42. Pershin, *Agr. revol.*, II, p. 261.
43. Pershin, *Agr. revol.*, II, p. 263.
44. *DSV*, I, pp. 413 f.; Knipovich, 'Naprav.', p. 25.
45. Pershin, *Agr. revol.*, II, pp. 261–3.
46. Pershin, *Agr. revol.*, II, pp. 255–7.

CHAPTER 30   'BLACK REPARTITION': RESULTS AND PROSPECTS

1. A.V. Peshekhonov, 'Dinamika', *ZIIR*, 2 (1925), p. 21 ; Yu. A. Polyakov, 'Sots.-ekon. itogi', in *Ist. Sov. kr-va*, eds M.P. Kim and others (Moscow 1963), p. 39.
2. Peshekhonov, 'Dinamika', pp. 13 ff.; A.I. Khryashcheva, *Kr-vo v voyne* (Moscow 1921), p. 19, gives detailed figures for household size in five counties in Tula province for 1911–12 and 1917 which corroborate this trend.
3. Chernov, ' "Chernyy peredel" 1918 g.', p. 116 ; the letter was originally published in the *émigré* newspaper *Rul'* in 1922.
4. Zhuravleva, 'Konfiskatsiya', p. 54.
5. Pershin, *Agr. revol.*, II, p. 329. Pershin does not connect the two items of information.
6. M.A. Rubach, *Ocherki po ist. revol. preobraz. agr. otnosh. na Ukr.* (Kiev 1957), pp. 351 f.
7. V.M. Selunskaya, *Rab. klass* (Moscow 1968), p. 133.
8. *Narod*, 20 November; cf. *NZ*, 30 November (Morshansk county, Tambov province).

9. These data, first published in full as *Ekon. rassloyeniye krest'yanstva v 1917 i 1919 gg.*, were based on a sample of 5 to 10 per cent of the peasant households in 229 counties in 25 of the provinces then under Soviet control. (Cf. Pershin, *Agr. revol.*, II, p. 534 and Peshekhonov, 'Dinamika', p. 13). The main findings were also given in *Izv.*, 7 November 1920; Khryashcheva, *Kr-o v voyne*, p. 34; and in Knipovich, 'Naprav.', fasc. I, pp. 24–8; they have also been reproduced in a number of more recent Soviet and western works. It is important to bear in mind the relatively small sample on which these figures were based. A recent investigation into the extent of social differentiation during the civil war period is Polyakov, 'Sots.-ekon. itogi', pp. 12–48, which reaches unsurprisingly orthodox conclusions. On the general problem of social differentiation among the Russian peasantry, see now Shanin, *The Awkward Class*, esp. pp. 52–55.

10. Knipovich, 'Naprav.', p. 25; in 1920, when Soviet territory had expanded, the PC of Agriculture carried out a 25 per cent sampling of peasant land-holding in forty-eight provinces (including some where the agrarian reform had yet to run its full course). The categories were slightly different, so that the results cannot be compared exactly with those for 1919; account should also be taken of the deficiencies of the 1917 census, which was used in 1920 for comparative purposes. Nevertheless the overall picture is similar to that recorded by the 1919 investigation, as the following table shows:

A   Sown area (dessyatines)

dessyatines	*1917* (%)*	*1920* (%)
nil	10·6	7·5
under 2	30·4	39·2
2–3·9	30·1	28·7
4–9·9	25·2	20·5
over 10 dess.	3·7	4·1
	100·0	100·0

* 10% sample

B   Horses

	1917 (%)	*1920* (%)
nil	29·0	26·6
1	49·2	51·0
2	17·0	13·6
3	3·4	4·3
4	0·9	} 4·5
5 or more	0·5	
	100·0	100·0

A.I. Khryashcheva, *Gruppy i klassy v kr-ve* (Moscow 1926), p. 84; cf. Peshekhonov, 'Dinamika', p. 21; Polyakov, 'Sots.-ekon. itogi', pp. 24ff.

11. Knipovich, 'Naprav.', pp. 26 f.

12. Knipovich, 'Naprav.', p. 25. In Tula and Penza the number of households with no horse declined from 30·1 to 19·8 per cent and from 36·8 to 29·7 per cent respectively. Those with four horses or more declined from 1·8 to 0·4 per cent and from 1·1 to 0·1 per cent respectively. In Yaroslavl and Vyatka, on the other hand, those with no horse declined marginally in the first case (from 40·2 to 37·6 per cent) and actually increased in the second (from 14·3 to 14·9 per cent); those with four horses or more declined from 0·2 per cent to nil and from 0·8 to 0·1 per cent.

13. Gordeyev, *Sel. khoz.*, p. 106.

14. The best analysis of the contradictory and frequently inflated data is provided by Pershin, *Agr. revol.*, II, pp. 510–24, who also offers a map showing their areas of geographical concentration.

15. Yu. Larin, *Ekon. dosov. derevni* (Moscow, Leningrad 1926), p. 196 (from a sketch prepared for a visiting delegation of British trade unionists).

16. [V.D.] Brutskus, 'Die russ. Agrarrevol.', *Ztschr. f. d. ges. Staatswiss.*, 78 (1924), p. 312, citing B.N. Knipovich, *Ocherk deyat. NK Zem. za tri goda, 1917–1920* (Moscow 1920), which has remained unavailable to me.

17. B&F, p. 679 n., citing Knipovich, *Ocherk deyat.*

18. V. Kachinsky, *Ocherki agr. revol. na Ukr.* (Kharkov 1922), fasc. I, p. 36.

19. The respective figures were: Podolia: 2·1+0·9 = 3·0 dessyatines; Chernigov: 3·5+0·2 = 3·7 dessyatines. Kachinsky, *Ocherki agr. revol. na Ukr.*, p. 37.

20. Kachinsky, *Ocherki agr. revol. na Ukr.*, p. 41.

21. V. Keller and I. Romanenko, *Pervye itogi agr. ref.* (Voronezh 1922). This work is summarized by Brutskus in 'Agr. revol. v chernozem. uyezde', *Ekon. vestnik*, 3 (1924), pp. 152–65; it is also discussed by V. Kilchinsky, 'K rezul'tatam agr. revol.', *KR*, 5–6 (1923), pp. 159–69.

22. Sharapov (*Nachalo sots. preobraz.*, p. 7) puts this at 2 milliard gold roubles. A similar figure is given in the official history of the civil war: *Ist. grazhd. voyny v SSSR*, III (Moscow 1958), p. 141.

23. Khryashcheva, *Kr-vo v voyne*, p. 40.

24. Vyatka led in this respect, followed by Perm, Yaroslavl and Novgorod: P.N. Pershin, 'Formy zemlepol'z.', in *O zemle*, fasc. I, pp. 70–2; cf. his *Agr. revol.*, II, pp. 234–7.

CHAPTER 31   THE FOOD CRISIS

1. *Izv.*, 4 November, 9, 18 December 1917, 18 January 1918, 2 March; *NZ*, 21 October, 1 December, 19 February; *NL*, 19 February; *Nov. Rossiya*, 21 April 1918; M.I. Davydov, *Bor'ba za khleb* (Moscow 1971),

pp. 21, 27, 29, 73; *Prot. zas. I-go s'yezda Prod. kom. Sev. obl.* (Moscow 1918), p. 27.

2. N. Sautin, *Vel. Okt.* (Leningrad 1959), pp. 130 f.

3. Shilov to first congress of Supply committee of northern region: *Prot. zas.*, p. 11. A wagon was reckoned to hold 1000 puds of grain.

4. *Prot. zas.*, pp. 15, 26.

5. Vladychkin in *Prot. zas.*, p. 26.

6. Vladychkin in *Prot. zas.*, p. 23; Sautin, *Vel. Okt.*, p. 132.

7. *God raboty Moskovskogo gorodskogo prodovol'stvennogo komiteta, mart 1917 – mart 1918* (Moscow 1918), pp. 42–5; different figures, compiled late in January, are given in *Byull. Mosk. gor. prod. kom.* (28 January 1918).

8. Figures of meat deliveries are given in *God raboty*, pp. 50 f. The egg ration, which stood at eight per person in October, sank to four in November and December; for the first six months of 1918 it averaged two. For fats the corresponding figures are $1\frac{1}{4}$, 1 and $\frac{1}{4}$ funt for the last three months of 1917; in February and March none was distributed at all: G.V. Shub, *Potrebl. gor. naseleniya* (Moscow 1918), p. ix.

9. A.F. Vinogradov, 'Ot burlaka do VUZa', in Tan-Bogoraz, *Revol. v derevne*, p. 93.

10. *NZ*, 20 December.

11. *Byull.*, 13 January.

12. *Byull.*, 12 January.

13. Davydov, *Bor'ba za khleb*, p. 73.

14. Orlov, *Prod. rabota Sov. vlasti*, p. 28.

15. Davydov, *Bor'ba za khleb*, p. 33.

16. Davydov, *Bor'ba za kleb*, p. 33. Shlikhter later described himself as 'ready to wage civil war in supply policy': *Ilyich kakim ya yego znal* (Kharkov 1924), p. 45. For his appointment: *Pr.*, 23 December.

17. Davydov, *Bor'ba za khleb*, pp. 34 f., where Stalin is identified as an advocate of compromise on this issue; *Narod*, 5 December 1917; Morozov, *Partiya i Sovety*, p. 115; Ya. D. Shchupak Papers (IISH Amsterdam), file 1, f. 28.

18. *Byull.*, 19 January; Davydov, *Bor'ba za khleb*, p. 36.

19. Lenin, *PSS*, xxxv, p. 312.

20. A resolution in this sense was, however, passed by the CPC: Lenin, *PSS*, xxxv, pp. 314, 483; cf. Davydov, *Bor'ba za khleb*, pp. 37 f. and below, p. 430.

21. *Byull.*, 19, 28 January; for details of the armed forces' supply organization see Orlov, *Prod. rabova Sov. vlasti*, p. 26. It is not evident whether the initiative in this move came from Shlikhter or the right-wing Bolsheviks in SEC.

22. *Izv.*, 16–19, 23 January; cf. B&F, pp. 657 f.

23. Of the 29 persons elected at the congress, less than half (15) were Bolsheviks; six party members were therefore coopted. (Orlov, *Prod.*

rabota Sov. vlasti, p. 36.) It was also provided with the usual 'core organizations': cf. Davydov, *Bor'ba za khleb*, p. 39.

24. Orlov, *Prod. rabota Sov. vlasti*, p. 40.

25. He headed an 'extraordinary commission on supply and transport' known from its Russian initials as Chokprod. For the text of decree: B&F, pp. 661 f.

26. A semi-fictionalized account of his appointment is given by V. Krasilchikov, *Intendant revolyutsii: povest' ob Aleksandre Tsurupe* (Moscow 1968), pp. 14–26. Trotsky's appointment is of course not mentioned by present-day Soviet writers.

27. Davydov, *Bor'ba za khleb*, pp. 40 f.; Lenin, *PSS*, xxxv, p. 314.

28. There is a brief description of its work in the Shchupak Papers, file 1, ff. 36–42.

29. Davydov, *Bor'ba za khleb*, p. 45.

30. *Byull.*, 11, 17 January; cf. V. Gendelman, 'Org. i struktura MGPK', *God raboty*, p. 24.

31. *Byull.*, 17 January.

32. *Byull.*, 28 January (report to All-Russian Supply Council).

33. *Byull.*, 25 January.

34. *Byull.*, 31 January.

35. E.S., 'Khlebnye bitvy v Vor. gub.', *NL*, 5 January.

36. *Byull.*, 14 April.

37. I.A. Gladkov, *Ocherki Sov. ekon.* (Moscow 1956), p. 191, citing *Nar. khoz.*, 1 (1918), p. 16; Selunskaya, *Rab. klass i Okt. v derevne*, pp. 123–7; *Izv.*, 23 January; *NZ*, 30 January.

38. Articles 12 and 14 in *Sb. dek. po nar. khoz.*, pp. 808 f. For the decree of 2 April on products exchange: B&F, pp. 665 f.

39. Article 5 in *Sb. dek. po nar.*

40. According to D.Z. Manuilsky, addressing the CEC on 28 April, the PC of Supply had sent 600 wagons of industrial goods and manufactures and had received only 400 wagons of grain in exchange: Davydov, *Bor'ba za khleb*, p. 69. These figures evidently refer only to the central organs' activities and do not cover all authorized trade.

41. Davydov, *Bor'ba za khleb*, pp. 25 f. There is some doubt about these figures, since in the prevailing anarchy it was impossible to distinguish between those who went at the behest of the new authorities and those who 'sent themselves'; nor is it practicable to differentiate between emissaries performing supply tasks and ordinary agitators, for in a sense the two roles were complementary.

42. *Izv.*, 27 January, reported that in Petrograd alone searches for food supplies had led to the discovery of 60,000 puds of beef, 11,000 of grain, 13,000 of potatoes and 26,000 of flour; but these claims do not inspire great confidence.

43. Gladkov, *Ocherki Sov. ekon.*, p. 193, c.u.d.s., states that 'prior to 1 March'

[i.e. in February alone?] 140 wagons of produce were dispatched daily, and that the figure rose to 300 wagons on 10 March and to 400 wagons on 1 April. Reckoning 1000 puds to the wagon, this would give about 14 million puds, which is almost certainly too high.

44. Davydov, *Bor'ba za khleb*, p. 49; Gladkov, *Ocherki Sov. ekon.*, p. 194; cf. Yu. P. Alekseyev, 'Ekspeditsiya A.G. Shlikhtera za khlebom', *Ist. SSSR*, 3 (1966), p. 137.

45. According to Gladkov, *Ocherki Sov. ekon.*, p. 360, although this seems an underestimate: according to the 1916 census, 35·8 million persons lived in the seventeen provinces contained in the Central Agricultural, Central Industrial and Lakes regions alone. Artyukhov and Chayanov, *Sel. khoz.*, pp. 6 ff.

46. *Izv.*, 18 January; *NL*, 18 January.

47. *Izv.*, 19, 21 January; Selunskaya, *Rab. klass*, pp. 56 f.

48. Selunskaya, *Rab. klass*, p. 61.

49. D.S. Baturin, 'Narkomprod v pervye gg. Sov. vlasti', *IZ*, 61 (1957), p. 342.

50. A.L. Okninsky, *Dva goda sredi krest'yan*, pp. 101 ff.; cf. below p. 460.

51. Selunskaya, *Rab. klass*, p. 58, c.u.d.s.

52. *NL*, 5 January 1918. A brief report from Voronezh dated 10 January (*Byull.*, 13 January) refers to a 'requisitioning commission of 43 front-line soldiers' operating in Voronezh province.

53. The late N. Jasny, who has recently provided a sympathetic portrait of Groman based on personal knowledge, speaks of him as 'obsessed' by the idea of a national economic plan and refers to his 'lack of practical sense': *Soviet Economists of the Twenties*, pp. 98 f. After 1921 Groman recognized his errors – as indeed did Lenin.

54. *Prot. zas.*, pp. 67 f.

55. For accounts in English of Bolshevik agrarian policy during the 'war communism' period see J. Bunyan, *Intervention* (Baltimore, Md 1936), pp. 456–99; Carr, *The Bolshevik Revolution*, II, pp. 151–76; and, for a spirited critique of conventional western views on economic policy-making in general during this period, P. Craig Roberts, ' "War Communism": a Re-examination', *SR*, 29 (1970), pp. 238–61.

56. Lenin, *PSS*, L, p. 72.

57. Zinoviev, *de facto* ruler of Petrograd and the northern region, is alleged by Stalinist and post-Stalinist writers to have delayed implementation of the new policy. If he did so, this was probably from a desire to preserve the former capital's proletarian cadres rather than from any consideration for economic rationality, still less for peasant interests. Rykov and others were sympathetic to the arguments advanced at the time by moderate socialists and had a greater sense of current realities. Cf. M.V. Pavlov, 'Bor'ba partii za osushch. leninskikh ukaz. po org.

pokhoda rab. v derevnyu, 1918 g.', in *Nekotorye voprosy sotsialisticheskoy revolyutsii* (Leningrad 1971), pp. 80–2.

58. English text: Bunyan, *Intervention*, pp. 460–2; summarized in Carr, *The Bolshevik Revolution*, II, p. 578 (where for some reason its provisions are called 'not very impressive'); Russian text: *Sb. dek.*, pp. 739–41. The decree is often dated 9 May, when it was passed by the CPC.

59. For the former figure see Pavlov, 'Bor'ba partii', p. 88, who corrects the higher estimate of 80,000 offered by Selunskaya, *Rab. klass*, p. 171; other authorities arrive at figures of approximately 70,000: A.S. Umnov, *Grazhd. voyna* (Moscow 1959), p. 45; Davydov, *Bor'ba za khleb*, p. 105. About half these men were civilians and the rest members of the armed forces. The latter comprised the so-called 'Supply Army' (*Prodarmiya*), which had a maximum operational strength of 33,000 men: cf. Yu. K. Strizhkov and V.D. Shmitkov, 'Novyy istochnik po ist. deyat. Prodarmii v 1918 g.', in Chugayev and others, *Istochnikoved. ist. Sovet. obshch.*, II, pp. 257, 260. One tends to think of the supply detachments as consisting of manual workers, yet this may not necessarily have been the case, at least in regard to those from Petrograd. Of 7171 such persons who responded to a questionnaire on this point, only 1218 (17·8 per cent) fell into this category, the rest comprising employees (5 per cent) or 'cadre workers'; 8 per cent described themselves as Communists and 13 per cent as Communist sympathizers, but over three-quarters of the detachment *leaders* belonged to the party. (Pavlov, 'Bor'ba partii', p. 86; cf. Sautin, *Vel. Okt.*, p. 140.) For statistics on the *kombedy*, see below p. 461.

60. Lenin, *PSS*, XXXVIII, p. 312; XXXIX, p. 274. He seems to have had in mind September and October, for the commissariat's figure for the five months August–December was 62·3 million puds: Umnov, *Grazhd. voyna*, p. 57, c.u.d.s.; cf. also *Nar. khoz.*, 8 (1919), p. 100, where monthly totals are given for August 1918 to January 1919.

61. Gordeyev, *Sel. khoz.*, p. 111, citing *Chetyre goda prodovol'stvennoy raboty*, an official publication of the PC of Supply. This source put the 1916–17 figure at 323 million puds, or only 64 per cent of the official figure as recently published by Anfimov; one suspects, therefore, that its statements on procurements in 1918–19 are liable to a high margin of error.

62. As calculated by the PC of Supply during the summer of 1918, these stood at about 75 million puds (excluding northern Caucasus, with which communications were sporadic): Orlov, *Prod. rabota Sov. vlasti*, p. 287.

63. Lenin, *PSS*, XXXIX, p. 275; XXXVIII, p. 362.

64. S.F. Tylik, 'Vedushch. rol' rab. Petrogr.', in *Iz ist. Vel. Okt. sots. revol.*, ed. V.A. Ovsyankin (Leningrad 1967), pp. 160, 175.

65. In Tambov the provincial supply 'collegium' lost track of the situation in the counties and was unable to maintain a regular statistical check

on the large amounts of grain collected. Orlov, *Prod. rabota Sov. vlasti*, p. 306.

66. Orlov, *Prod. rabota Sov. vlasti*, p. 316; on the behaviour of the requisitioning detachments see also Bunyan, *Intervention*, pp. 476–9.

67. Shlikhter, *Ilyich kakim ya yego znal*, p. 74. Umnov, *Grazhd. voyna*, p. 65, mentions an official claim of 1919 (*Vtoroy g. bor'by s golodom* [Moscow 1919], p. 36) to the effect that 159·4 million arshins (113 million metres) of fabrics and 1·7 milliard roubles' worth of other items were dispatched by the PC of Supply between March and December 1918. If one takes the average official price for grain at August 1918 rates as 14 roubles a pud, and reckons procurements for these nine months at 77 million puds, producers would have been entitled to 1078 million roubles' worth of goods. Had they in fact received *more* goods (to say nothing of cash payments) than they were entitled to, official propagandists would not have failed to stress the fact – and the regime would have had no problems with the peasantry. These figures are therefore best ignored – as are others in *Nar. khoz.*, 12 (1918) giving even higher figures for distribution of fabrics by Tsentrotkan'. Another source cited by Umnov (*Vestnik agit. i prop.*, 9–10, [1921], p. 20) claimed that 35,000 wagons of goods were sent to the countryside 'in 1917–18' – a figure which can be set alongside Lenin's data on grain procurements in 1918 of 95 million puds; on the loading criteria then in force the latter would have required 95,000 wagons. This proportion seems much more realistic, although the crudity of such a means of assessment is all too obvious.

68. Igritsky, *1917 g. v derevne*, pp. 182–5.

69. A.V. Shestakov, *Klassovaya bor'ba v derevne TsChO v epokhu voyennogo kommunizma* (Voronezh 1930), p. 69, cited by Davydov, *Bor'ba za khleb* p. 76 and Selunskaya, *Rab. klass*, p. 135.

CHAPTER 32   TAMING THE PEASANT ORGANIZATIONS : THE SUMMIT

1. Out of 777 delegates listed in *II Vseross. s'yezd*, pp. 113–40, 26 represented 16 peasant soviets. Of these men 17 were Left SRs, 6 Bolsheviks, 2 centre SRs and 1 a Ukrainian. Another 112 delegates, according to our calculations, represented merged soviets that had peasant components. Gorodetsky, *Rozhd. Sov. gosud.*, puts the total at 119.

2. The idea may have originated with V.P. Milyutin, the first (Bolshevik) PC of Agriculture: *Prot. VTsIK*, p. 3; Gaysinsky, *Vseross. s'yezdy*, p. 179; R.M. Ilyukhina, 'K vop. o sogl. bol'sh. s levymi SRami', *IZ*, 73 (1963), p. 15. Cf. also Radkey, *Sickle*, pp. 207 ff.; (Radkey did not use *Prot. VTsIK*.)

3. Radkey, *The Sickle under the Hammer*, pp. 73–91 (the Mogilev talks),

206–9; Gaysinsky, *Vseross. s'yezdy*, pp. 179 ff.; Gorodetsky, *Rozhd. Sov. gosud.*, p. 194.

4. B&F, p. 211 n., citing *DN*, 11 November.

5. Gaysinsky, *Vseross. s'yezdy*, p. 182; Ilyukhina, 'K vop. o sogl. bol'sh. s levymi SRami', p. 16; Gorodetsky, *Rozhd. Sov. gosud.*, p. 195; for other figures *DN*, 14 November.

6. Chernov's figures, as reported in *Izv.*, 15 November and *DN*, 15 November (the latter reproduced in B&F, pp. 216 f.); Radkey, *The Sickle under the Hammer*, p. 212.

7. Gaysinsky, *Vseross. s'yezdy*, p. 183. For a vivid (but inaccurate) account of the congress, see Reed, *Ten Days*, pp. 255–71. The analysis by Radkey, *The Sickle under the Hammer*, pp. 207–23, is to be preferred.

8. M. Kh[ayn], *Izv.*, 16 December 1917: a revealing survey of the intrigues at the congress.

9. The reason given for this was that such an invitation would be taken as evidence of partiality, but the chief motive was probably fear of the Bolshevik leader's oratorical powers. Later he addressed two sessions of the assembly, on 14 and 18 November: Lenin, *PSS*, xxxv, pp. 94 f., 100 f.

10. *DN*, 14, 15 November.

11. *Izv.*, 18 November. The vote was 41 to 40 with 5 abstentions. The poll was low because many left-wing deputies were absent at caucus meetings. B&F err in stating (p. 211) that the extraordinary peasant congress *ended* on 15 November, although certainly its main task had been completed by that date; it lingered on until the 25th.

12. *Izv.*, 3 December, as amended on 16 December; Ilyukhina, 'K vop. o sogl. bol'sh. s levymi SRami', p. 31.

13. According to the credentials commission, on 1 December there were 294 military to 489 civilians, or 37·5 per cent of the total. Later the ratio was put at 374 military to 491 civilians, or 43·2 per cent. Cf. Radkey, *The Sickle under the Hammer*, p. 226.

14. *DSV*, i, pp. 161 f.; see above p. 326.

15. *Narod*, 4 December; *Izv.*, 3, 7 December; Radkey, *The Sickle under the Hammer*, p. 241. This was an allusion to his threat that the guillotine could serve 'to shorten people by a head', to which Martov retorted that its use would 'lengthen the ears . . . of those who purported to solve social problems with its assistance'. *Iskra*, 4 December; I. Getzler, *Martov* (Melbourne, London, New York 1967), p. 176.

16. *NZ*, 13 December; Radkey, *The Sickle under the Hammer*, p. 251.

17. *Izv.*, 12, 13 December.

18. *Izv.*, 29 December.

19. *NL*, 12 January; N.P. Oganovsky, 'Dnevnik chlena Uch. Sobr.', *Golos minuvshego*, 4–6 (1918), p. 169; Radkey, *The Sickle under the Hammer*, p. 440. The moderates' executive, 89 strong, continued to exist

clandestinely for some time but exercised little influence: Gaysinsky, *Vseross. s'yezdy*, p. 259.

20. Ilyukhina, 'K vop. o sogl. bol'sh. s levymi SRami', p. 31; for other figures Radkey, *The Sickle under the Hammer*, p. 446.

21. Selunskaya, *Rab. klass*, p. 77, citing *Golos trud. kr-va*, 30 January. This important source on Left SR affairs has not been available.

22. N.K. Krupskaya, *Vosp. o Lenine* (Moscow 1957), p. 316 (citing M.V. Fofanova).

23. There is no truth in the assertion, often repeated by Soviet historians (also by Carr, *The Bolshevik Revolution*, II, p. 54) that the Left SRs were spokesmen for the 'kulaks' and less egalitarian than the Bolsheviks. If anything, the reverse may well have been the case, since as Populists they saw equality of income and status among peasants as a primary goal, and were more confident than the Bolsheviks that the state power could and should be used to encourage it, whereas their allies reasoned that differentiation was an inevitable evil so long as 'capitalist' private farming remained the norm; they looked rather toward spontaneous action by 'poor peasants', backed by 'soviet power', to keep it in check. In practice there was probably little to choose between the two parties. We are dealing here with a persistent myth which has its origin in the Bolshevik ideological assumptions that (a) the 'kulaks' formed an identifiable social class with interests of its own; and (b) that these interests must be articulated by some political group or other. With the defeat of the moderate socialists and the breakdown of the ruling coalition the Left SRs became the most obvious candidates for the role of 'spokesmen for the kulak' and the evidence was tailored accordingly in official Bolshevik pronouncements.

24. E.[A.] Lutsky, 'Vseross. s'yezd zem. kom. v yanv. 1918 g.', *Dok. i soobshch. Inst. ist.*, II (1956), p. 60.

25. The membership was as follows: 150 Left SRs, 125 right or centre SRs, 81 Bolsheviks, 17 Maximalists, 9 others, and 151 non-party delegates. They represented thirty-seven provinces. Lutsky, 'Vseross. s'yezd zem. kom. v yanv. 1918 g.', p. 60, citing *Golos trud. kr-va*, 30 January 1918.

26. Lutsky, 'Vseross. s'yezd zem. kom. v yanv. 1918 g.', p. 62. This arrangement, as elaborated on the following day, provided that the joint meetings should be attended not by the whole mass of deputies but by three representatives from each region of the country. This territorial (as distinct from political) basis of their selection was a concession to the right.

27. Pershin, *Agr. revol.*, II, p. 38.

28. Articles 22, 26, 35 of pt VII (*DSV*, I, pp. 407 ff.); the English text in B&F, pp. 673–6 is truncated; see also Pershin, *Agr. revol.*, II, pp. 43–52; Lutsky, 'Vseross s'yezd zem. kom. v yanv. 1918 g.', pp. 68 f. The decree was passed by the CEC on 27 January and published on 3/16 February.

Its appearance in *Izv.* was delayed another three days, but it is not certain whether (as is frequently stated) this was done so that it might coincide with the date of Alexander II's manifesto emancipating the serfs (19 February 1861). Both Soviet and western historians have attempted to evaluate which party gained most from the negotiations (cf. Pershin, *Agr. revol.*, II, p. 38; Sharapov, *Nachalo sots. preobraz.*, p. 13; Carr, *The Bolshevik Revolution*, II, pp. 50 f.), but these arguments miss the point, for what mattered most – and Carr comes close to recognizing this – was control of the levers of power, not verbal concessions.

29. 'Zhertvy bol'sh. i belogo terrora', *Znamya truda*, 15 March 1922, p. 17. For the later history of the party, see Schapiro, *The Origin of the Communist Autocracy*, pp. 121–9 and for a critical self-examination of its history A. Shreyder, 'Puti Okt. revol.', in *Puti revol.* (Berlin 1923), pp. 95–106.

CHAPTER 33   TAMING THE PEASANT ORGANIZATIONS: THE BASE

1. Some information appeared at the time in the Left SR daily *Golos trud. kr-va* as well as in local newspapers. The unpublished materials have been examined by several Soviet scholars, but none of them has yet dealt comprehensively with this theme. Selunskaya, whose work is most valuable, notes (*Rab. klass*, pp. 71, 137) that information on the composition of county soviets is to be found in TsGAOR, f. 393, op. 3, d. 2; she does not identify the documents in question, which may be activists' replies to questionnaires sent out by one or other of the central authorities.

2. Selunskaya, *Rab. klass*, p. 68.

3. Selunskaya, *Rab. klass*, pp. 66 f.

4. Selunskaya, *Rab. klass*, p. 65, c.u.d.s.

5. Ya. Burov, *Organizuyte derevnyu!* (Petrograd 1918).

6. Burov, *Organizuyte derevnyu!*, p. 34.

7. 'Zaprimet', kakiye est' na derevne krest'yane posmekalisteye, poboyche da pobedoveye.'

8. Ibid., pp. 37–41.

9. *Izv.*, 9 November.

10. E.g. Sadovsky commune, Bobrov district, Voronezh province (17 November), signed by fifty-one peasants, published in Shulyakovsky and others, *Bor'ba za Sov. vlast' v Voron. gub.*, pp. 223 f. Numerous such resolutions are reproduced in recent documentary collections, whereas those that were equivocal are, needless to say, omitted.

11. Sautin, *Vel. Okt.*, p. 16; cf. Selunskaya, *Rab. klass*, p. 82.

12. Kovalenko and others, *Sovety v pervyy god prol. dikt.*, p. 179, c.u.d.s.

13. *Izv.*, 4 January 1918.

14. V.M. Gubareva, *Razvertyvaniye sots. revol. v derevne* (Moscow 1957), pp. 9–39; cf. Sautin, *Vel. Okt.*, pp. 16 ff.

15. *NL*, 31 January.

16. *Izv.*, 17 February.

17. *NL*, 19 February. Cf. *NL*, 18 January, for a similar report on the Minsk provincial peasant soviets.

18. A.I. Moiseyev and others (eds), *Podg. i proved. Vel. Okt. sots. revol. v Tverskoy gub.* (Kalinin 1960), pp. 415 f., 475; *Izv.*, 28 January, 19 February.

19. Moiseyev and others, *Podg. i proved. Vel. Okt. sots. revol. v Tverskoy gub.*, pp. 348 f.; T.A. Ilyina, 'Ustan. Sov. vlasti v Tverskoy gub.', in *Tverskaya gub. v pervye gody Sov. vlasti*, eds M.A. Ilyin and A.M. Rumyantsev (Kalinin 1958), pp. 33–6; further details of the affair are to be found in A. Todorsky, *God s vintovkoy i plugom* (Moscow, Leningrad 1927; first published in 1918).

20. K. Ya. Voitinova, 'Bor'ba za pobedu Okt. revol. v Permskoy gub.', in Pankratova and others, *Ustan. Sovet.*, I, pp. 292–5.

21. See the table in Kovalenko and others, *Sovety v pervyy god prol. dikt.*, pp. 115 f., giving the composition of the executives, where known, in a number of county peasant soviets in this region.

22. Kovalenko and others, *Sovety v pervyy god prol. dikt.*, pp. 108 ff.

23. Antonov-Saratovsky, *Pod styagom prol. bor'by*, pp. 226–9.

24. Antonov-Saratovsky, *Pod styagom prol. bor'by*, p. 230; Pershin, *Agr. revol.*, I, p. 463; Radkey, *The Sickle under the Hammer*, pp. 450–2.

25. Pershin, *Agr. revol.*, I, p. 464; P.N. Sobolev, 'Ustan. Sov. vlasti v Vor. gub.', in Pankratova and others, *Ustan. Sovet.*, I, pp. 349–52; Radkey, *The Sickle under the Hammer*, pp. 270–5; Shulyakovsky and others, *Bor'ba za Sov. vlast' v Voron. gub.*, pp. 233 f.; less informative is the account by P.N. Abramov, 'K ist. pervogo etapa Okt. revol. v derevne', *IZ*, 81 (1968), pp. 11 f.

26. *Izv.*, 3 November. Modern editions of text: *DSV*, I, pp. 41 ff.; Varzho, *Agr. pol. Sov. vlasti.*, pp. 126 f.

27. Gorodetsky, *Rozhd. Sov. gosud.*, p. 469.

28. Kh. A. Yeritsyan, *Sovety krest. dep. v Okt. revol.* (Moscow 1960), p. 130; Pershin, *Agr. revol.*, I, p. 466; Selunskaya, *Rab. klass*, p. 76; N.S. Mutovkin, *Voyenno-polit. soyuz rab. klassa i trud. kr-va* (Moscow 1965), pp. 56 f.

29. V.R. Gerasimyuk, 'O kolichestve vol. i sel. Sovetov v 1917–1918 gg.', *VI*, 8 (1961), p. 207. The PC of Internal Affairs claimed in December 1917 that it knew of 6088 district *executive committees*: Kovalenko and others, *Sovety v pervyy god prol. dikt.*, p. 175. This figure is probably exaggerated – although there were no doubt more executives than there were soviets, for the simple reason that many such bodies did without the camouflage of a deliberative assembly.

30. Bunyan, *Intervention*, pp. 472 f.; *Sb. dek.*, pp. 741–3.

31. V.R. Gerasimyuk, 'Nek. novye stat. dannye o kombedakh RSFSR', *VI*, 6 (1963), pp. 208–11, correcting figures given in his 'Kom. bednoty Ross. fed. v tsifrakh', *Ist. SSSR*, 4 (1960), p. 125, where earlier estimates will also be found (pp. 120 f.); cf. also Umnov, *Grazhd. voyna*, p. 55; Sautin, *Vel. Okt.*, p. 148.

32. Kovalenko and others, *Sovety v pervyy god prol. dikt.*, p. 357, citing *Ist. arkhiv*, 10 (1930), p. 47 and *Izv. NK Prod.*, 24–5 (1918), p. 15; cf. Alekseyev, 'Ekspeditsiya A.G. Shlikhtera za khlebom', p. 141.

33. Kovalenko and others, *Sovety v pervyy god prol. dikt.*, p. 351, c.u.d.s.

34. V.S. Bronshteyn, 'Iz ist. org. kom. bednoty v Tul. gub.', *Ist. arkhiv*, 4 (1956), p. 183.

35. Sautin, *Vel. Okt.*, pp. 147 f.; Kovalenko and others, *Sovety v pervyy god prol. dikt.*, p. 352; Gaysinsky, *Vseross. s'yezdy*, p. 96.

36. For the social composition of *kombedy* in the middle Volga region see A.L. Litvin, *Kr-vo Sr. Povolzh'ya* (Kazan 1972), pp. 92 f. The global figures presented by N.S. Mutovkin, *Voyenno-politicheskiy soyuz* (Moscow 1965), p. 63, to the effect that four-fifths of *kombedy* members were 'poor' peasants and a fifth 'middle' peasants, are best ignored. Zinoviev exaggerated in implying a few months later, in an effort to discredit the committees, that *all* of them 'were nominated by representatives of the [soviet] executive committee or the party organization acting jointly': cited by Carr, *The Bolshevik Revolution*, 11, p. 60 n.

37. Lenin, *PSS*, XXXVII, pp. 41 f.

38. J. Monnerot notes that 'although we have no word equivalent to "genocide" the fact exists none the less': *Sociologie de la révolution* (Paris 1969), p. 334.

39. On 9 August, for example, he sent a curious telegram to a party chief in Nizhniy Novgorod directing him 'to introduce mass terror at once, to shoot and deport the hundreds of prostitutes who have made our soldiers drunk, ex-officers etc.' – once again that sinister 'etc.' (Lenin, *PSS*, L, p. 142). On Lenin's personal responsibility for the Red terror, and on its dating *before* the attempt on his life on 30 August 1918 (and not in response to it as has been generally assumed), see my 'Lenin's Letters as Historical Source', p. 259.

40. *DSV*, III, p. 223 (our italics).

41. *Inter alia* the fact that each committee could claim 300 roubles a month for expenses: Gerasimyuk, 'Kom. bednoty Ross. fed. v tsifrakh', p. 120, c.u.d.s. Presumably this right was not generally invoked, for even at the dizzy rate of inflation in 1918 this would have imposed an intolerable burden upon the treasury.

42. Lenin, *PSS*, XXXVII, p. 181; cf. S.S. Korkin, 'Iz. ist. part. rukovod. kombedami', *VI KPSS*, 6 (1959), p. 79.

43. A rather different view is given by a hostile eye-witness from Tambov

province, who states that the peasants now regarded the soviet as an alien organization and deliberately chose for political and administrative posts those least skilled at working the land, who naturally did what they were told by the more experienced activists. Okninsky, *Dva goda sredi krest'yan*, p. 46.

44. L.I. Klyuchnik and V.P. Nikolayeva, 'Nek. stat. sved. o sost. part. org. v 1918 g.', *VI KPSS*, 1 (1961), p. 125.

45. Kovalenko and others, *Sovety v pervyy god prol. dikt.*, p. 363. By the end of 1918 non-Bolsheviks comprised only 4 to 5 per cent of the delegates to provincial soviet *congresses*. A.M. Dedov, *Bor'ba Komm. partii za ukrepl. Sovetov v 1917–1920 gg.* (Moscow 1957), p. 14.

EPILOGUE

1. Lenin, *PSS*, xxxviii, p. 194; cf. xl, p. 11.

2. Cf. J.M. Meijer, 'Town and Country in the Civil War', in Pipes, *Revolutionary Russia*, pp. 259–77; S. Singleton, 'The Tambov Revolt, 1920–1921', *SR*, 25 (1966), pp. 497–512. Of Soviet studies the most useful is Yu. A. Polyakov, *Perekhod k NEP i Sovetskoye krest'yanstvo* (Moscow 1967).

3. M. Lewin, *Russian Peasants and Soviet Power*, trsl. I. Nove (London 1968).

4. J.G. Chapman, *Real Wages in Soviet Russia since 1928* (Cambridge, Mass. 1963), pp. 145, 164; M. Dewar, *Labour Policy in the USSR, 1917–1928* (London, New York 1956), pp. 138, 140.

5. For an excellent introduction to the subject, see L.B. Schapiro, *Totalitarianism* (London, New York 1972).

Chronological Table

This table emphasizes events of national significance which are related to the theme of this book. Dates are Old Style until 1/14 February 1918. The left hand column refers to General History, and the right to Mass Organizations.

General History	Mass Organizations
1861	
19 February Edict emancipating the serfs published	
1898	
March First congress of RSDLP	

1903

July–August Second congress of
RSDLP : Bolshevik-Menshevik
schism

1904–5 Russo-Japanese War ; revolutionary disturbances in Russia

1905

9 January 'Bloody Sunday'

13–19 October General strike

7–19 December Moscow insurrection

1906

February Fundamental Laws
provide for constitutional government

1906–11 Stolypin's agrarian legislation

1912

February Lena goldfields strike
and massacre

1905

Formation of trade unions and
soviets

31 July–1 August First congress
of All-Russian Peasant Union
(ARPU)

24 September–7 October First
All-Russian conference of trade
unions

13 October–3 December
St Petersburg soviet (chairman :
Trotsky)

6–10 November Second congress
of ARPU

1906

24–8 February Second
All-Russian conference of trade
unions

4 March 'Temporary rules' provide limited freedom of association
(in practice most mass organizations are suppressed as subversive)

1914

June–July General strikes in Baku and St Petersburg

1 August Russia declares war on Germany

1915 Military reverses

July–August Growing tension between government and duma; Progressive Bloc formed; Nicholas II takes command at General Headquarters

August–November Elections to Labour Groups on War Industries Committees

1916

February Second congress of War Industries Committees; strike at Putilov arms works

9 September Price of grain regulated

October Growing industrial unrest in Petrograd

1 November Fourth duma reconvenes for fifth session; Milyukov's speech suggesting that the court and government may be guilty of treason; tsarist regime generally discredited, begins to disintegrate

December Conference of regional War Industries Committees

December 16/17 Assassination of Rasputin

December 27 Prince N.D. Golitsyn appointed Chairman of Council of Ministers

1917

January
9 Strike in Petrograd to commemorate 'Bloody Sunday'
26/27 Members of Labour Group of Central War Industries Committee arrested
31 Wave of strikes and disturbances among industrial workers, especially in Petrograd

February
14 Duma reconvenes after Christmas recess
18 Strike begins at Putilov arms works
22 Men locked out by management
23 Workers demonstrate for first time in centre of Petrograd
24 Armed clashes with police and cossacks
25 General strike
26 Nicholas II dissolves Duma; mutiny in Pavlovsk guards regiment
27 Mutinies spread; certain Labour Group leaders released from prison Duma decides not to disperse; sets up Provisional Committee which assumes responsibility for public order; Golitsyn resigns
28 Provisional Committee sets up Military Commission to control troops and Joint Supply Commission with Petrograd soviet; commissars appointed to ministries General strike in Moscow

1917

February
27 Provisional executive committee of Petrograd soviet instituted; it calls first plenary meeting
28 Regular executive committee of Petrograd soviet established Soviet formed in Moscow

March

1/2 After talks with soviet, Provisional Government formed (Prime Min. and Min. of Interior; G.E. Lvov; Min. of Foreign Affairs: P.N. Milyukov; Min. of War: A.I. Guchkov; Min. of Agriculture: A.I. Shingarev; Min. of Justice: A.F. Kerensky

2 Nicholas II abdicates in favour of Grand Duke Michael, who declines to become head of state (3 March); Nicholas arrested (8 March)

6 General strike in Petrograd ends; amnesty declared

9 State Supply Committee established with soviet representation

10 Abolition of Police department

12 Abolition of death penalty
Stalin, Kamenev and other Bolshevik leaders reach Petrograd from exile; adopt a 'soft' line towards Provisional Government and soviet

12, 16, 27 Legislative acts taking into state possession former Crown properties

19 Government declaration on land reform

24 Bread rationing introduced in Petrograd

25 Decree on grain monopoly; local supply committees to be set up
Special Council set up to draft electoral law for Constituent Assembly (does not meet until 25 May)

27 Government declaration on war aims

27 to 4 April 'March conference' of Bolshevik party workers attending All-Russian conference of soviets; unification with Mensheviks discussed; joint session with Menshevik representatives (4 April) fails

March

1 Executive committee of Petrograd soviet decides not to participate in Provisional Government; soviet enlarged to include soldiers; 'Order Number One'
First factory committee set up in Petrograd, followed by nuclei of other mass organizations (trade unions, cooperatives etc.)

10 Agreement between Petrograd soviet and employers on introduction of eight-hour working day and factory committees

12 ARPU sets up Main Organizing Committee

14 Bureau formed within executive committee of Petrograd soviet
Petrograd soviet appeals to 'people of entire world' to support campaign for a democratic non-annexationist peace

15 Petrograd and Moscow Central Bureaux (CBS) of Trade Unions formed

19 ARPU holds congress at Yaroslavl

21 Eight-hour day introduced in Moscow by direct action; later emulated in many other centres

25–27 Regional congress of soviets in Moscow

25–28 All-Russian congress of co-operative organizations

before 28 Regional congress of soviets in Saratov

29 to 2 April All-Russian Conference of Soviets; resolution (1 April) on supporting Provisional Government 'in so far as' it implements programme of 'revolutionary democracy'

April

3 Lenin, Zinoviev and other Bolshevik émigrés return to Petrograd; Lenin announces 'April Theses' (4 April): no support for Provisional Government, but to work for a republic of soviets

11 Government decree placing crops under protection of authorities

12 Law on freedom of assembly; on freedom of press (27 April)

15 Law on elections to municipal and district dumas

17 Law on formation of militia

18 Milyukov's note: government will adhere to obligations towards Allies

20-1 'April Days': demonstrations in Petrograd and Moscow in support of the soviet's stand on war and peace; pressure by Kerensky and others on Milyukov to resign

21 Decree setting up Main Land Committee and provincial bodies to prepare land reform

24-9 Seventh All-Russian conference of RSDLP(b); agrarian programme adopted (28 April); Central Committee (CC) elected (9 members, 5 candidates)

30 Resignation of Guchkov

May

2 Resignation of Milyukov

3 Government forbids transactions in land

4 Trotsky returns to Russia

5 Formation of First Coalition with participation of socialists (Prime Minister and Min. of Interior: Lvov; Min. of Foreign Affairs: M.I. Tereshchenko; Min. of War and Navy: Kerensky; Min. of Finance: Shingarev; Min. of

April

Provincial peasant congresses in black-soil zone: Samara (25-29 March); Kherson (3-4 April); Tambov (6-7 April); Tula (5-? April); Penza (7-12 April); Voronezh (8-12 April); Saratov (?-11 April) etc.

7 Conference of railwaymen's delegates decides to set up All-Russian Union of Railwaymen; Vikzhel (executive committee) elected

15 Conference of factory committees in enterprises working for war effort in Petrograd

22 Petrograd soviet votes to support Liberty Loan

23 Delegate conference of metal-workers (Moscow)
Decree on factory committees and labour relations

29 Peasant congress in Moscow province

May

4-28 All-Russian Congress of Peasant Deputies (PSR in control): elects executive committee (20 May); addressed by Lenin (22 May), Chernov (24 May); calls for transfer of all land to peasants without compensation (25 May)

7 Union of Metallurgical-Workers holds delegate conference
Peasant congresses in several provinces: Petrograd (11-12 May);

Agriculture: V.M. Chernov; Min. of Labour: M.I. Skobelev; Min. of Supply: A.V. Peshekhonov; Min. of Posts and Telegraphs: I.G. Tsereteli

6 Coalition government issues policy declaration embodying most aims of 'revolutionary democracy'

7–12 All-Russian conference of Menshevik and United organizations of RSDLP; split over coalition issue

7 Conference of *Mezhrayontsy* ('Inter-districtites'), SD group led by Trotsky

11 Declaration on soldiers' rights

19–20 Main Land Committee holds first meeting

21 Laws on elections to provincial and district zemstva and on creation of a district zemstvo

25 to **4 June** Third congress of Party of Socialist-Revolutionaries (PSR); emergence of left-wing nucleus; election of CC (20 full, 5 candidate members) weighted towards right and centre

27–30 Elections to Petrograd district dumas: moderate socialists in lead

June

10 Bolsheviks call off demonstration in Petrograd under pressure from congress of Soviets Ukrainian Central Rada issues first Universal proclaiming autonomy as immediate goal

14 Provisional Government sets Constituent Assembly elections for 17 September; assembly to open 30 September

18 Military offensive begins; initial successes, then halted; serious reverses (28 June) lead to outbursts of anti-war sentiment at

Kazan (13 May); Penza (second, 14–15 May); Don region (14–25 May); Samara (second, 20 May); Yaroslavl (24–25 May)

14 to **22 June** Congress of postal workers sets up Union of Postal and Telegraph Workers (*Potelsoyuz*)

17–25 Kronstadt soviet defies Provisional Government; settlement mediated by Tsereteli, Skobelev of Petrograd soviet executive (and government ministers)

29 All-Ukrainian peasant congress

30 to **3 June** First conference of factory committees in Petrograd; addressed by Lenin (31 May); passes Bolshevik resolution on workers' control; sets up CCFCP (Central Committee)

31 Workers' section of Petrograd soviet passes Bolshevik resolution (first major success for that party in the soviet)

June

3–24 First All-Russian Congress of Workers' and Soldiers' Soviets: resolutions on attitude to government (8 June), to the war (12 June), to the offensive (19 June), and to convocation of Constituent Assembly (20 June) reflect views of moderate socialists; but radical pressure makes itself felt. Election of Central Executive Committee (CEC) (24 June) in which Petrograd elements predominate

16 First regional conference of textile-workers' delegates decides

front and in rear; breakdown of discipline in many units

25 Elections to Moscow city duma: PSR wins nearly half total vote

July

1–6 Main Land Committee holds second session

2 Provisional Government announces intention to grant autonomy to Ukraine; Kadet ministers resign in protest, also against general leftward tenor of government policy

3–4 'July Days': radicalized soldiers and workers, joined (on 4 July) by sailors from Kronstadt, demonstrate in Petrograd under the slogan 'all power to the soviets'; Bolshevik CC decides, in Lenin's absence, to back the movement, which peters out for lack of a practical objective; many casualties; Lenin goes into hiding

5 Bolshevik newspapers banned and offices sacked; government reveals information discrediting Lenin and others as 'German agents' and orders them arrested (6 July)

7 Lvov resigns; Kerensky becomes Prime Minister (8 July) and seeks to reconstitute the government

12 Ministry of Agriculture circular restricting commercial transactions in land
Provisional Government re-establishes death penalty at the front for serious offences

to set up a trade union

18 Moderate leaders of Congress of Soviets organize counter-demonstration to that planned by Bolsheviks for 10 June

21–28 Third All-Russian Conference of Trade Unions: slight margin of advantage for Mensheviks and allies; election of ARCCTU

29 Formation of provisional executive committee of All-Russian Union of Metallurgical-Workers

July

8 CEC and Executive Committee of Congress of Peasant Deputies give backing to government provided socialist ministers report frequently to them

15 to 24 August Constituent congress of All-Russian Union of Railwaymen; re-elects Vikzhel as regular executive

17 to 2 August Constituent congress of All-Russian Union of Water (Marine and River) Transport Workers

23–28 All-city conference of factory committees in Moscow

25 CEC calls on 'revolutionary democracy' to support new government

31 to 6 August Congress of All-Russian Peasant Union (ARPU) disrupted by radical elements loyal to Executive Committee of Congress of Peasant Deputies; schism (5 August)

16 Chernov's circular enlarging jurisdiction of land committees

17 Tsereteli's circular ordering firm measures against illicit land seizures and other disorders

18 Gen. L.G. Kornilov appointed commander-in-chief

20 Chernov resigns (temporarily) from the government; CEC demands his reinstatement

21 Meeting of party leaders gives Kerensky free hand to form new government

23 Arrest of Trotsky

24 Formation of Second Coalition (Prime Minister and Min. of War and Navy: Kerensky; Min. of Foreign Affairs: Tereshchenko; Min. of Finance and Deputy Prime Min.: N.V. Nekrasov; Min. of Agriculture: Chernov; Min. of Labour: Skobelev; Min. of Supply: Peshekhonov; Min. of Interior: N.D. Avksentyev; Min. of Posts and Telegraphs: A.M. Nikitin; Min. of Trade and Industry: S.N. Prokopovich

26 to 3 August   RSDLP(b), despite ineffective government 'repression', holds sixth party congress; 'Inter-districtites' join Bolshevik party; calls for defence of soviets against 'counter-revolution' even though slogan of transfer of power to soviets is no longer deemed apposite; elects new CC (21 full members, 10 candidates)

August

3-5 Second Congress of All-Russian Union of Trade & Industry

6-10 Seventh council of PSR: nominates candidates for Constituent Assembly elections

9 Government postpones Constituent Assembly elections from 17 September to 12 November, and convocation from 30 Sept-

August

Provincial peasant congresses held: Voronezh (?-4 August); Penza (third, 5-6 August); Tula (third, 5-6 August) etc.; these and other grass-roots bodies are often far to the left of the central soviet organizations

7-12 Second conference of factory committees in Petrograd

ember to 28 November

12–15 State Conference held in Moscow

12 One-day Bolshevik-inspired strike; Kornilov receives hero's welcome from conservatives; Kerensky fails to rally all 'healthy' forces of nation

19–26 Menshevik (RSDLP) 'unification' congress fails to reconcile warring factions; elects CC (25 full members, 18 candidates : 8 and 6 are left-wing Internationalists)

21 Riga occupied by Germans, threatening security of Petrograd; Petrograd mil. district placed under jurisdiction of C-in-C

22 Min. of Labour's circular reasserting employers' authority within enterprises

24 Min. of Supply assumes powers to dissolve disobedient land committees; and to regulate supply of textiles to population (25 August)

26–30 'Kornilov affair': Kerensky receives V.N. Lvov, who gives him distorted picture of Kornilov's demands for reconstitution of government along dictatorial lines (26 August); Kerensky suspects Kornilov of plotting and removes him from his post; Kornilov responds by ordering troops to march on Petrograd, as previously agreed with Kerensky, to crush subversion (27 August); troops are halted and disarmed by popular levies loyal to soviet; Kadet ministers resign from government (28 August); Kerensky assumes post of C-in-C (30 August); Kornilov and other generals arrested (from 1 September)

27 Provisional Government doubles grain prices

16 to **21 October** Strike of leatherworkers in Central Industrial region

17–21 Second regional congress of soviets of Urals

27 CEC, to whom Kerensky appeals, sets up Committee for Popular Struggle Against Counter-Revolution in which radical elements predominate; it helps to organize 'defence' of capital against Kornilov's troops and distributes weapons

29 Moscow soviet and labour organizations decide to set up 'Red guard'; their example is widely followed

31 to **1 September** Petrograd soviet plenum adopts Bolshevik resolution in favour of 'soviet power'

September

1 Russia proclaimed a republic; five-man Directory formed (Kerensky, Tereshchenko, Nikitin, Col. A.I. Verkhovsky, Adm. D.N. Verderevsky)

4 Trotsky released on bail

14–22 Democratic Conference (delegates of parties, soviets, unions, zemstva etc.), called to bolster government's authority and broaden its basis; contradictory vote on continuation of coalition with Kadets (19 September); resolves to set up from its members a Council of Republic ('Pre-parliament')

15 Bolshevik C C rejects Lenin's call for armed insurrection; decides not to walk out from Democratic Conference, but to recall party's deputies from its presidium (21 September)

23 Council of Republic holds first 'preparatory' session; approves agreement among democratic party leaders on composition of Third Coalition

24 Elections to Moscow municipal duma: Bolshevik successes

25 Third Coalition government officially formed (Prime Minister: Kerensky; Min. of Foreign Affairs: Tereshchenko; Min. of War: Verkhovsky; Min. of Finance: M.V. Bernatsky; Min. of Labour: K.A. Gvozdev; Min. of Supply: Prokopovich; Min. of Agriculture: S.L. Maslov)

October

7 Council of Republic holds first session; Bolsheviks led by Trotsky withdraw demonstratively

September

5 Moscow soviet plenum passes Bolshevik resolution; elects new executive committee which has slight Bolshevik majority (19 September)

8 Bolsheviks win control of presidium of workers' section of Petrograd soviet; plenum confirms its pro-Bolshevik allegiance; presidium resigns (9 September); new elections yield pro-Bolshevik presidium (chairman: Trotsky), which first meets on 25 September

10 Third conference of factory committees in Petrograd (according to some authorities (5–10 September)

21 Petrograd soviet opposes Council of Republic and calls for a second congress of Soviets, to meet on 20 October, to establish soviet power

23 C E C agrees to convoke second congress of Soviets for 20 October; Executive Committee of Congress of Peasant Deputies decides to postpone convocation of second congress of Peasant Deputies until after elections to Constituent Assembly

24 All-Russian Union of Railwaymen calls national railway strike; after wage increases are granted the strike is called off (26 September)

Strikes in textile and oil industry called by unions concerned

30 to **5 October** Moscow regional bureau of soviets (M O B Y U S) calls congress of soviets in central provinces

October

10–11 Fourth conference of factory committees in Petrograd; decides to call an All-Russian conference

7(?) Lenin returns to Petrograd in disguise

10 Bolshevik Central Committee votes 10:2 to prepare for armed insurrection

11 Zinoviev and Kamenev circulate privately a statement criticizing the cc's decision, which later (17 October) becomes public knowledge

16 Bolshevik Central Committee holds 'expanded' session confirming decision of 10 October (12 votes to 2 with 4 abstentions)

17 cec postpones convocation of second congress of Soviets from 20 to 25 October

24 Prov. Government declares Petrograd in state of insurrection and takes ineffectual countermeasures against mrc; calls troops from front

11 pm: Lenin arrives at Smolny Institute and gives a greater sense of direction to the insurgents

25 Kerensky leaves Winter Palace, seat of the government, to obtain reinforcements; cabinet remains in session and is arrested by troops under V.A. Antonov-Ovseyenko (night of 25/26 October), some ministers being taken to Peter and Paul Fortress

26 Council of People's Commissars (cpc) formed 'to govern the country until the Constituent Assembly' under the control of Congress of Soviets and cec (Chairman: Lenin; pc of Foreign Affairs: Trotsky; pc of Interior: A.I. Rykov; pc of Agriculture: V.P. Milyutin; pc of Labour: A.G. Shlyapnikov; pc of War and Navy: committee of Antonov-Ovseyenko, N.V. Krylenko, P.E. Dybenko; pc of Justice: G.I. Oppokov (Lomov); pc for Nationalities: I.V. Stalin)

11–13 Congress of soviets of northern region strongly backs campaign for transfer of all power to soviets

12 Petrograd soviet executive committee formally resolves to set up a Military Revolutionary Committee (mrc), as first proposed by Mensheviks on 9 October, and approves its statute; statute endorsed by plenum (16 October); mrc holds first meeting (20 October)

13 Urals regional congress of soviets; elects regional executive

15 Conferences of metallurgical-workers, textile-workers endorse 'soviet power'

15–16 Second all-city conference of factory committees in Moscow

17–22/23 First All-Russian conference of factory committees; elects arcfc

21 mrc tells mil. staff of Petrograd district that all its decisions must be controlled by mrc 'commissars'; on refusal instructs all units to disregard staff's orders unless countersigned (22 October) and appoints commissars to various units (23 October)

24 mrc places units on a war footing and makes military dispositions to guard against government's 'repressive' moves; (evening) troops loyal to mrc and other formations begin to take over other strategic points in Petrograd

25 Most of Petrograd under mrc control; Petrograd soviet plenum holds extraordinary session (2 pm); told by Trotsky that Provisional Government overthrown; second congress of Soviets opens (10.40 pm); moderates walk out in protest at Bolshevik *coup*
Moscow: soviet executive sets up mrc (evening)

26 Second congress of Soviets,

Committee to Save Fatherland and Revolution formed by moderate socialists and other democrats based on Petrograd municipal duma; the example is widely followed in the provinces

Kerensky and Krasnov's Third Cavalry corps advance toward Petrograd; troops occupy Gatchina (27 October) and Tsarskoye Selo (28 October) but receive little support and are defeated at Pulkovo (30 October); operations suspended (31 October); Kerensky goes into hiding (1 November)

Moscow: street fighting, punctuated by talks, until 2 November

Kiev: Bolsheviks leave Small Rada; street fighting (28–31 October) leaves Rada forces in strongest position

29 Petrograd: uprising by military cadets crushed

Eight-hour day decreed; other largely 'declarative' acts of social legislation follow (accident insurance 9 November; unemployment insurance 11 December; sickness insurance 22 December)

shortly after hearing of fall of Winter Palace (2 am), declares that it will 'take governmental power into its own hands' and that local authority shall be transferred to soviets; it appeals to the masses to support the revolution and to resist Kerensky's forces

MRC troops patrol Petrograd

26/27 Second session of second congress of Soviets opens (8 pm); abolishes capital punishment; endorses Lenin's proclamation proposing that all warring peoples and their governments begin immediate negotiations for a just, democratic peace; endorses land decree abolishing certain forms of private property and taking as the basis of agrarian policy the digest of peasant instructions compiled in August by certain PSR leaders; hears protest by Vikzhel representative on question of a socialist coalition government but approves all-Bolshevik CPC as submitted by Kamenev; elects a new CEC of Bolsheviks, Left SRs and other radical elements

27 Petrograd MRC sends out first emissaries to requisition food supplies

First meeting of new CEC; its legislative rights defined narrowly by CPC (30 October); it adopts a statute governing its procedure (2 November, revised 17 November)

28 Vikzhel urges union branches not to permit fratricidal strife among socialists; (29 October) threatens general railway strike unless fighting ceases

30 to **3 November** Inter-party talks held under Vikzhel's auspices to explore possibilities of all-socialist ('homogeneous') coalition government

November

1 Lenin insists on stiff terms for re-constitution of the government, causing the inter-party talks to break down

4 Zinoviev, Kamenev and other Bolshevik leaders resign from government and party CC

6 Talks begin with Left Socialist-Revolutionaries on terms for their participation in government

7 Central Rada proclaims Ukraine an independent republic ('Third Universal')

Gen. N.N. Dukhonin, C-in-C, ordered to propose an armistice; on his refusal he is dismissed and replaced by Krylenko (9 November), who urges direct nego-tiations by troops at the front; Krylenko arrives at General Head-quarters; Dukhonin murdered by troops (20 November)

9 State monopoly on press adver-tising

12 Elections to Constituent As-sembly begin

14 Central Powers agree to armis-tice negotiations; talks begin at Brest-Litovsk (19 November)

14 Decree on workers' control; establishment of All-Russian Council of Workers' Control (ARCWC)

18 First detachments sent from centre against 'White' Cossack forces of Gen. Kaledin

20–8 First Congress of Party of Left Socialist-Revolutionaries

22 Temporary truce signed at Brest-Litovsk

23 Arrest of All-Russian Commis-sion on Constituent Assembly elections (liquidated 29 Novem-ber) and decree published allow-

November

5 Many local soviets assume power, forming (Military) Revolutionary Committees, liquidating local Committees to Save the Father-land and the Revolution and other 'bourgeois' organizations, im-posing restrictions on press, and adopting policies in line with those of the CPC in Petrograd

10–25 Extraordinary Congress of Peasant Deputies held, with Left SR majority; leaders decide to elect delegates to the CEC in the number of 108 (equal to those elected by the second congress of Soviets); the new expanded CEC, which also includes trade union and armed forces delegates, holds its first (ceremonial) meeting (15 November)

11–12 Conference of soviets in central region called by MOBYUS

13–15 All-Russian Railwaymen's Union holds conference of line organizations in Moscow

16 Fifth conference of factory com-mittees in Petrograd

18–25 Extraordinary congress of Union of Postal and Telegraph Workers in Nizhniy Novgorod; declaration favouring coalition government (25 November); strike committee appointed to act if Constituent Assembly is threat-ened

26 to 11 December Second (reg-ular) Congress of Peasant Deputies held; Left SRs in strongest position; delegates protest at threats against Constituent Assembly (2 Decem-ber); are addressed by Lenin and Trotsky (3 December); schism (4 December); left-wing majority secedes

ing voters to recall deputies from any organization

25 First clash with troops of the future 'Volunteer Army' in southern Russia

26 to **5 December** Fourth congress of PSR

28 Deputies to Constituent Assembly try to open proceedings on the appointed day, but are charged with subversion; Kadet party outlawed

29/30 Kiev: Central Rada forces forestall planned Bolshevik *coup*

30 to **7 December** Extraordinary congress of RSDRP (Mensheviks); victory for left wing led by Martov

December

1 Supreme Economic Council (SEC) established; it absorbs ARCWC; holds first session (5 December)

2 Armistice signed at Brest-Litovsk

4 Soviet government issues ultimatum to Central Rada (rejected on 6 December); All-Ukrainian congress of Soviets in Kiev disrupted by Ukrainian nationalists (5 December); Bolshevik and Left SR delegates withdraw to Kharkov

7 Establishment of Extraordinary Commission to Combat Counter-Revolution and Sabotage (*Cheka*)

9 First session of Brest-Litovsk peace conference
Final agreement reached with Left SRs on terms of their entry into Soviet government (CPC); they participate in its work for first time (12 December)

13 Instructions to land committees on inventorying estates etc. published (adopted 4 December)

14 Decree nationalizing banks
Fighting breaks out between forces loyal to Central Rada and pro-Bolsheviks based on Kharkov

27 Vikzhel accepts political settlement whereby its candidate becomes PC of Transport and the union has representation on the CEC; radicals based on Moscow issue call for an extraordinary congress of the union, to meet on 10 December

29 Petrograd soviet executive committee resumes sessions as MRC is gradually phased out; presidium re-elected under Zinoviev (13 December)

December

4 All-Ukrainian congress of Soviets in Kiev opens

5 Abolition of MRC of Petrograd soviet

7 All-Russian Union of Employees' Unions begins strike in public institutions

10–16 Congress of soviets of central region, Moscow; regional executive established

11 First militiamen from Petrograd sent to fight in Ukraine

12 First All-Ukrainian congress of Soviets called at Kharkov under auspices of Bolsheviks; it elects Central Executive Committee (CECU), denounces Rada government and proclaims itself supreme authority in all Ukraine; its claims endorsed by Soviet government (16 December)

12 Congress of (radical) railwaymen opens; hears Lenin (13 December); denounces Vikzhel (15 December)

14–21 Second All-Russian conference of Union of Typographical Workers

(CECU)
18 I.A. Teodorovich, PC of Supply, succeeded by A.G. Shlikhter
CECU launches invasion of Rada-held territory; forces take Yekaterinoslav (28 December), Krivoy Rog (9 January), Chernigov (14 January)
23 Ukrainian Rada representatives return to Brest-Litovsk with mandate to seek separate peace
28 All-Russian Supply Council formed in Moscow as counterweight to PC of Supply in Petrograd

20 Congress of All-Russian Union of Railwaymen opens
22 PC of Interior issues circular to all soviets on reconciling autonomy with needs of central authorities; (27 December) issues instructions on local soviets' rights and duties
27 Radical railwaymen secede from congress of All-Russian Union of Railwaymen; depose Vikzhel (6 January 1918)

1918

January
5 Dispersal of demonstration in favour of Constituent Assembly
5/6 Constituent Assembly meets; refuses to take Bolshevik Declaration on Rights of Toiling and Exploited Peoples as next business; Bolsheviks withdraw, followed by Left SRs; under threat of dissolution the Assembly adopts an SR land law and declaration on peace; deputies disperse and are refused readmission; CEC decrees dissolution (6 January)
6/7 Murder of Shingarev and F.F. Kokoshkin in hospital by sailors
7 Lenin's '21 Theses' on immediate conclusion of a separate annexationist peace; Central Committee adopts by a vote of 9:7 Trotsky's formula of 'neither war nor peace' (11 January)
11 Krylenko issues order of the day calling for a socialist army based on Red guards; Lenin inspects

1918

January
3 CEC adopts Declaration on Rights of Toiling and Exploited Peoples
5-30 Railwaymen's congress held under Bolshevik auspices; elects as successor to Vikzhel an All-Russian Executive Committee of Railwaymen (*Vikzhedor*)
7-14 First All-Russian Congress of Trade Unions; Lozovsky reports on behalf of ARCCTU; debates on trade-unions' functions under socialism and on workers' control; election of new executive (11 full, 5 candidate members under Zinoviev)
10-18 Third congress of Soviets of Workers' and Soldiers' Deputies
13-18 Third congress of Peasant Deputies; sits jointly with congress of Soviets of Workers' and Soldiers' Deputies; the joint congress endorses fundamental principles of constitution of Russian Socialist Soviet Republic as a federation

first detachments of new force (13 January); CPC decrees organization of Workers' and Peasants' Red Army (15 January)

15/16 Abortive Bolshevik rising against Rada government in Kiev; fighting ensues (to 26 January), when Red forces under M.A. Muravev enter the city; Rada deposed, CECU proclaimed as sovereign authority; CECU moves from Kharkov to Kiev (30 January)

19 Statute provides that all Red guards (militia) units are to be reorganized as Red Army units

Formation of Economic Council of Northern Region

27 Rada government, in flight from Kiev, authorizes Ukrainian delegation at Brest-Litovsk to sign separate peace with Central Powers, so placing Soviet delegation at disadvantage

28 Soviet delegation announces it will demobilize forces

and charges CEC with drafting a constitution to be submitted at next congress (15 January); first nineteen articles of land socialization law approved (18 January), details to be worked out by a commission

15–19 First (constituent) congress of All-Russian Union of Metallurgical-Workers

15–20 First All-Russian Congress of Union of Textile-Workers

17–? Congress of land committee representatives

19 ARCFC absorbed by Economic Council of northern region

22–24 Sixth conference of factory committees in Petrograd

February

15 (N.S.) Trotsky appointed head of Extraordinary Commission on Supply and Transport; edict on suppression of 'bagmen' (19 February)

18 German troops advance, meeting scarcely any opposition; CC votes 7 : 6 to accept German terms

19 Publication of land-socialization law, final terms of which have been determined in private talks between Bolshevik and Left SR leaders

22 German peace terms announced; CEC votes for their acceptance; Left Communists leave CC of RSDLP (b)

February

14–27 First (Extraordinary) congress of Water Transport Workers

15 Trotsky addresses Petrograd soviet on breakdown of Brest-Litovsk peace talks

19–23 Congress of radical elements in Union of Postal and Telegraph Workers disbands the union (22 February) and sets up *Sovdeppotel'*

25 First congress of trade union of leather-workers

March

1 Central Rada re-establishes itself in Kiev with German military aid

3 Signature of Brest-Litovsk treaty: heavy territorial and other losses for the Soviet republic

5 Allied landing at Murmansk with consent of local Soviet authorities

6–8 Seventh congress of RSDLP (b): approves the treaty of Brest-Litovsk (8 March); changes party's title to RCP (b)

12 Seat of government moved from Petrograd to Moscow

15 Left SRS leave CPC in protest at Brest-Litovsk treaty

16 Publication of Trotsky's appointment as PC of War and Navy and Chairman of Supreme War Council

April

2 Decree on 'products exchange'

8 Central Powers' forces enter Kharkov; Rada government overthrown

28–29 Skoropadsky proclaimed Hetman of Ukraine

May

9 PC of Supply entrusted with emergency powers by CPC (confirmed by CEC 13 May); reorganized as organ of 'supply dictatorship' (27 May)

14 'Chelyabinsk incident' involving Czechoslovak troops leads to full-scale civil war and Allied intervention; Siberia passes under White control and a government led by SRS is formed at Samara

25 First congress of economic councils (*sovnarkhozy*) opens

June

11 Decree instituting committees of village poor (*kombedy*)

March

10 Constitution of 'Petrograd commune'

12–17 Fourth All-Russian trade union conference

14 Third congress of Potelsoyuz held at Tambov; dispersed by force

14–16 Fourth congress of Soviets; ratification of treaty of Brest-Litovsk

April

3 ARCCTU adopts resolution on labour discipline

26 to 25 May *Sovdeppotel'* holds national congress

June

14 Mensheviks and most SRS excluded from CEC and provincial

28 Decree nationalizing certain large enterprises

soviet apparatus

July
6 Left SRs assassinate German ambassador, Count Mirbach, and seize certain public buildings in Moscow; suppressed (8 July); uprisings at Yaroslavl, Murom etc. staged by elements sympathetic to Right SRs and Allies
16 Assassination of Nicholas II and members of his family at Yekaterinburg

July
4–10 Fifth Congress of Soviets adopts constitution of RSFSR

August
1 Allies land at Archangel; at Vladivostok (3 August)
27 Supplementary treaties with Central Powers
30 Assassination of M.S. Uritsky, head of Petrograd Cheka, and attempt on life of Lenin; (6 September) 'Red terror' formally introduced (in fact, extended)

August
3 Trade unions encouraged to form requisitioning detachments

November
11 Armistice ends First World War; Soviet government denounces Brest-Litovsk treaty (13 November)

November
Committees of village poor transformed into regular soviet agencies in the countryside; new elections held to soviets, yielding sizeable Communist majorities and virtually eliminating opposition

1918/19 During winter shift of emphasis in Bolshevik policy towards the 'middle peasant'

1919

January
16–25 Second All-Russian Congress of Trade Unions

1921

March Introduction of NEP (New Economic Policy): compromise with peasantry

NEP affords increased role for mass organizations as 'transmission belts' of Party policy, with limited autonomy

1929/30 Stalin begins forcible collectivization of agriculture; totalitarian revolution, intensified controls over intellectual life, including historiography of the revolution

1937 Climax of the 'great purge'

1956 Twentieth congress of CPSU; relaxation of controls over historiography

Glossary of Russian Terms

Note English terms have been used in the text wherever possible. For Russian weights and measures see p. xvii.

apparat	administrative staff
batrak	hired agricultural labourer
bednyak	poor peasant
cherespolositsa	fragmentation of land allotments in a number of territorially separate parcels or strips
dacha	section of timbered land
desyatok	squad, team of about ten persons
druzhina	squad, unit of workers' militia
duma	municipal self-government body (1870–1917/18)
dvor	(peasant) household
fabrichno-zavodskiy komitet	factory committee
fraktsiya	in a deliberative body, an organized group of persons having a common allegiance; caucus
frontovik	front-line soldier
glavk	board for administration of an industrial branch or sector

guberniya	province (principal territorial division in Russia before 1929/30)
gubispolkom	executive of provincial soviet
haydamak	(Ukraine) : guerilla fighter
ispolkom (ispolnitel'-nyy komitet)	executive (esp. of soviet)
khodok	elected (esp. peasant) emissary sent on errand or with petition
khutor	independent self-contained farm in private possession containing owner's homestead
khutoryanin	owner of *khutor*
kollektiv	group united by common actions or interests
kombed	committee of village poor
komissar	commissar (plenipotentiary emissary)
kulak	lit.: 'fist'; rich peasant; often used loosely as synonym for a peasant who exploits his fellows
miroyed	lit.: 'commune-eater'; peasant who exploits fellow members of a commune (*mir*)
nadel	allotment of land
nakaz	instruction, mandate
narodnik	Populist, agrarian socialist
oblast'	region (area embracing several provinces, esp. as economic unit)
oblispolkom	executive of regional soviet
obshchestvo	(educated) society
obshchina	(peasant) commune, *mir*
okrug	region, esp. in territorial-administrative sense
otdel	department (administrative organ of soviet)
otrub	parcel of land separated from that of commune as private property under the legislation of 1906–11
otrubshchik	owner of *otrub*
pogrom	riot accompanied by killing and/or destruction of property
posevnaya ploshchad'	sown area
prodkom	supply committee
prodotryad	squad, detachment to requisition (food) supplies
promysel	craft or other non-agricultural means of livelihood
rada	(Ukraine): soviet, council

rayon	city ward, borough
samochinnyy	of an institution, established by popular initiative without legal sanction
sektsiya	in a joint soviet, an element defined by class allegiance (e.g. peasants)
serednyak	'middle peasant'; intermediate group between *kulak* and *bednyak*
skhod	village assembly
sosloviye	social estate with rights and duties fixed by law
sotnya	squad, detachment, of about a hundred men, esp. in militia
sovet	soviet: council of workers', etc., elected deputies (or more correctly, delegates)
sovnarkhoz (sovet narodnogo khozyaystva)	(local) council for economic administration
stanitsa	Cossack settlement
Stavka	General (Army) Headquarters
tovarishch	comrade
tovaroobmen	barter, products exchange
troyka	commission; group of three men appointed for a special task; 'initiative group'
tsentr	board for administration of an industrial branch or sector
uchot	control, checking
usad'ba	homestead with garden plot
uyezd	county (administrative division of a province)
vlast'	(central) authority
volost'	district (administrative division of a county)
voysko	Cossack military formation, 'host'
vzvod	small military detachment, company of workers' militia
zemlyachestvo	association of persons from same area formed for mutual aid
zemstvo	rural local self-government body (1864–1917/18)

Abbreviated Organizations

ARCCTU	All-Russian Central Council of Trade Unions (*VTsSPS*)
ARCFC	All-Russian Council of Factory Committees
ARCWC	All-Russian Council of Workers' Control (*Vserossiyskiy sovet rabochego kontrolya*)
ARPU	All-Russian Peasant Union (*Vserossiyskiy krest'yanskiy soyuz*)
CB	Central Bureau (*Tsentral'noye byuro*): local trade-union council
CCFCP	Central Committee of Factory and Works Committees of Petrograd (*TsKF-ZKP*)
CEC	All-Russian Central Executive Committee of Soviets of Workers', Soldiers' and Peasants' Deputies (*VTsIK*)
CECU	Central Executive Committee of the Ukrainian Soviet Socialist Republic (*TsIK UkSSR*)
Cheka	All-Russian Extraordinary Commission for Combating Counter-Revolution, Sabotage and Speculation
CPC	Council of People's Commissars (*Sovnarkom: Sovet Narodnykh Komissarov*)

CPSU	*see* RCP(b)
CSA	Central Statistical Administration (*TsSU*)
CWIC	Central War Industries Committee (*TsVPK*)
Kadets	Constitutional-Democrats; members of the Party of People's Freedom (*Partiya narodnoy svobody (Konstitutsionno-demokraticheskaya)*)
MIC	Military Investigation Commission (of the Petrograd soviet)
MOBYUS	Bureau of Soviets of the Moscow Region (*Moskovskoye oblastnoye byuro sovetov*)
MRC	Military Revolutionary Committee (*VRK: voyenrevkom*)
PC	People's Commissariat (*Narodnyy Komissariat*)
PLSR	Party of Left Socialist-Revolutionaries
Potelsoyuz	All-Russian Union of Postal and Telegraph Workers
PSR (SRS)	Party of Socialist-Revolutionaries
RC	Revolutionary Committee (*revkom*)
RCP(b)	Russian Communist Party (Bolsheviks); formerly RSDLP(b); subsequently AUCP(b), All-Union Communist Party (Bolsheviks), and CPSU, Communist Party of the Soviet Union
RSDLP	Russian Social-Democratic Labour Party
RSFSR	Russian Soviet Federation of Socialist Republics
Rumcherod	Executive Committee of Soviets of Workers' and Soldiers' Deputies of the Rumanian Front, Black Sea Fleet and Odessa Military District
SDS	Social Democrats
SEC	Supreme Economic Council (*Verkhovnyy sovet narodnogo khnozyaystva; Vesenkha*)
SRS	*see* PSR
USDI	United Social-Democratic Internationalists
Vikzhel	Executive Committee of the All-Russian Union of Railwaymen

European Russia in 1917–18

Bibliography

This list is confined to the main works consulted and excludes journal articles. Wherever possible anonymous collaborative volumes have been entered under the name of their principal editor or compiler. Abbreviations in square brackets are those used in the Notes.

I Books and Pamphlets

ALEXANDROVA, N., *Artem: biograficheskiy ocherk* (Moscow 1922)

AMOSOV, P.N. and others (eds), *Oktyabr'skaya revolyutsiya i fabzavkomy: materialy po istorii fabrichno-zavodskikh komitetov*, 2 pts (Moscow 1927)

ANDREYEV, A.M., *Sovety rabochikh i soldatskikh deputatov nakanune Oktyabrya, mart – oktyabr' 1917 g.* (Moscow 1967); English ed.: *The Soviets of Workers' and Soldiers' Deputies on the Eve of the October Revolution, March–October 1917*, trsl. J. Langstone (Moscow 1971)

ANDREYEV, N.V., *Pobeda Velikoy Oktyabr'skoy sotsialisticheskoy revolyutsii v Smolenskoy gubernii* (Smolensk 1957)

ANFIMOV, A.M., *Rossiyskaya derevnya vo vremya Pervoy mirovoy voyny, 1914 – fevral' 1917 g.* (Moscow 1962)

ANIKEYEV, V.V. and others (eds), *Perepiska Sekretariata TsK RSDRP(b) s mestnymi partiynymi organizatsiyami: sbornik dokumentov*, I: *mart–oktyabr' 1917 g.* (Moscow 1957)

ANSKY, A. (ed.), *Professional'noye dvizheniye v Petrograde v 1917 g .: ocherki i materialy* (Leningrad 1928)

ANTONOV-OVSEYENKO, V. [A.], *Der Aufbau der Roten Armee in der Revolution* (Hamburg 1923)

ANTONOV-OVSEYENKO, V. [A.], *Zapiski o grazhdanskoy voyne*, I. (Moscow, Leningrad 1924)

ANTONOV-SARATOVSKY, V.P., *Pod styagom proletarskoy bor'by: otryvki iz vospominaniy o rabote v Saratove za vremya s 1915 g. do 1918 g.*, I (Moscow, Leningrad 1925)

ANTONOV-SARATOVSKY, V.P. (ed.), *Saratovskiy Sovet rabochikh deputatov, 1917–1918 gg.: sbornik dokumentov i materialov* (Moscow, Leningrad 1931)

ANTOSHKIN, D.V., *Kratkiy ocherk professional'nogo dvizheniya v Rossii*, 3rd ed. (Moscow 1928)

ANTSIFEROV, A.N. and others, *Russian Agriculture during the War* (New Haven, Conn. 1930)

ANWEILER, O., *Die Rätebewegung in Russland 1905–1921* (Leiden 1958); English ed.: *The Soviets: the Russian Workers, Peasants and Soldiers Councils, 1905–1921*, trsl. R. Hein (New York 1974)

ARONSON, G.YA., *Dvizheniye upolnomochennykh ot rabochikh fabrik i zavodov v 1918 g.* (New York 1960)

ARTYUKHOV, YA.S. and CHAYANOV, A.V. (comps), *Sel'sko-khozyaystvennaya perepis' 1916 g.;* Oganovsky N.P. and Chayanov, A.V. (comps), *Statisticheskiy spravochnik po agrarnomu voprosu*, fasc. II, pt I. (Moscow 1918)

AVDEYEV, N. (comp.), *Revolyutsiya 1917 g.: khronika sobytiy*, I, 2 (Moscow 1923)

AVERBAKH, O.I. (comp.), *Zakonodatel'nye akty, vyzvannye voynoy 1914–1915* [etc.] *gg.*, 5 vols (Petrograd 1916–18)

AVRICH, P.H. (ed.), *The Anarchists in the Russian Revolution* (Ithaca, NY, London 1973)

AVRICH, P.H. (ed.), *The Russian Anarchists* (Princeton, NJ, London 1967)

BABICHEV, V.A. and others (comps), *Rabochiy kontrol' i natsionalizatsiya krupnoy promyshlennosti v Ivanovo-Voznesenskoy gubernii, Materialy po istorii SSSR*, III (Moscow 1956)

BAKH, A.N. and others (eds), *God russkoy revolyutsii, 1917–1918 gg.: sbornik statey* (Moscow 1918)

BATAYEVA, T.V. (ed.), *Profsoyuzy v period postroyeniya sotsializma v SSSR, oktyabr' 1917 g.–1937 gg.* (Moscow 1963)

BAZILEVICH, K.V., *Professional'noye dvizheniye rabotnikov svyazi, 1917–1918* (Moscow 1927)

BOGDANOV, N.P. and others (eds), *Oktyabr' i profsoyuzy* (Moscow 1967)

BONCH-BRUYEVICH, V.D., *Na boyevykh postakh fevral'skoy i Oktyabr'skoy revolyutsii*, 2nd ed. (Moscow 1931)

Bor'ba bol'shevistskoy partii (cf. Yegorov, A.G.)

Bor'ba za pobedu i ukrepleniye Sovetskoy vlasti (cf. Khesin, S.S.)

Bor'ba za Sovetskuyu vlast' v Voronezhskoy gub. (cf. Shulyakovsky, E.G.)

Bor'ba za ustanovleniye Sovetskoy vlasti (cf. Gavrilov, L.M.)

Bor'ba za vlast' Sovetov na Kievshchine (cf. Tronko, P.T.)

BORSHCHENKO, I.L. and others (comps), *Profsoyuzy v bor'be za sverzheniye samoderzhaviya i ustanovleniye diktatury proletariata, 1905–1917 gg.* (Moscow 1963)

BOSH, E.B., *God bor'by: bor'ba za vlast' na Ukraine s aprelya 1917 g. do nemetskoy okkupatsii* (Moscow, Leningrad 1925)

BRÄNDSTRÖM, E., *Unter Kriegsgefangenen in Russland und Sibirien, 1914–1920* (Berlin 1922)

BROWDER, R.P. and KERENSKY, A.F. (eds), *The Russian Provisional Government, 1917: Documents*, 3 vols (Stanford, Calif. 1961) [B & K]

BRÜGMANN, U., *Die Geschichte der russischen Gewerkschaften in Revolution und Bürgerkrieg, 1917–1919* (Frankfurt 1972)

BRUTSKUS, B.D., *Agrarnyy vopros i agrarnaya politika* (Petrograd 1922)

BUBNOV, A.S. and others (eds), *Grazhdanskaya voyna 1918–1921*, 3 vols (Moscow 1928–30)

BUNYAN, J., *Intervention, Civil War and Communism in Russia, April–December 1918* (Baltimore, Md, 1936)

BUNYAN, J. and FISHER, H.H., *The Bolshevik Revolution 1917–1918: Documents and Materials* (Stanford, Calif. 1934; repr. 1965) [B & F]

BURDZHALOV, E.N., *Vtoraya russkaya revolyutsiya: vosstaniye v Petrograde* (Moscow 1967)

BURDZHALOV, E.N., *Vtoraya russkaya revolyutsiya: Moskva, front, periferiya* (Moscow 1971)

BUROV, YA., *Organizuyte derevnyu! Primernaya pamyatka-nastavleniye dlya ot'yezzhayushchikh v derevnyu tovarishchey-soldat i krest'yan-khodokov* (Petrograd 1918)

BUTENKO, A.F. and CHUGAYEV, D.A. (eds), *Vtoroy Vserossiyskiy s'yezd Sovetov rabochikh i soldatskikh deputatov: sbornik dokumentov* (Moscow 1957)

BYKOV, P.M. and NIPORKIN, N.G. (comps), *Rabochaya revolyutsiya na Urale: etyudy i fakty: sbornik* (Yekaterinburg 1921)

CARR, E.H., *The Bolshevik Revolution, 1917–1923, (A History of Soviet Russia)* 3 vols (London 1950–3; repr. 1966)

CHAMBERLIN, W.H., *The Russian Revolution, 1917–1921,* 2 vols (New York 1935; repr. 1965)

CHAYANOV, A.V., *The Theory of Peasant Economy,* trsl. R.E.F. Smith (South Holland, Ill. 1966)

CHELINTSEV, A.N., *Sbornik statisticheskikh materialov po voprosam organizatsii krest'yanskogo khozyaystva Ukrainy* (Odessa 1922)

CHERNOMORDIK, S. (ed.), *Oktyabr'skiye dni v Moskve i rayonakh: po vospominaniyam uchastnikov* (Moscow 1922)

CHERNOMORDIK, S. (ed.), *Put' k Oktyabryu: sbornik statey, vospominaniy i dokumentov* (Moscow 1923–6)

CHERNOV, V.M., *Dukh revolyutsionnoy Rossii: fevral'skaya revolyutsiya* (Paris, Prague, New York 1934)

CHUGAYEV, D.A. and others (eds), *Istochnikovedeniye istorii Sovetskogo obshchestva,* fasc. II (Moscow 1968)

CHUGAYEV, D.A. and others (eds), *Petrogradskiy Voyenno-revolyutsionnyy komitet: dokumenty i materialy,* 3 vols (Moscow 1966–7) [*PVRK*]

CHUGAYEV, D.A. (ed.), *Rabochiy klass Sovetskoy Rossii v pervyy god diktatury proletariata: sbornik dokumentov i materialov* (Moscow 1964)

CHUGAYEV, D.A. (ed.), *Triumfal'noye shestviye Sovetskoy vlasti,* 2 pts (vol. 9 of A.L. Sidorov and others (eds), *Velikaya Oktyabr'skaya sotsialisticheskaya revolyutsiya: dokumenty i materialy)* (Moscow 1963)

CHUGAYEV, D.A. (ed.), *Ustanovleniye Sovetskoy vlasti na mestakh v 1917–1918 gg.,* II (Moscow 1959)

COHEN, S.F., *Bukharin and the Russian Revolution: a Political Biography, 1888–1938* (New York 1973)

DANIELS, R.V., *Red October: the Bolshevik Revolution of 1917* (New York 1967; London 1968)

DANILEVSKY, A.F. and others (eds), *Profsoyuzy v bor'be za pobedu Oktyabr'skoy sotsialisticheskoy revolyutsii* (Moscow 1957)

DAVYDOV, M.I., *Bor'ba za khleb: prodovol'stvennaya politika Kom-*

munisticheskoy partii i Sovetskogo gosudarstva v gody grazhdanskoy voyny, 1917–1920 (Moscow 1971)

DEDOV, A.M., *Bor'ba Kommunisticheskoy partii za ukrepleniye Sovetov v 1917–1920 gg.* (Moscow 1957)

DEMBO, L.I., *Ocherk deyatel'nosti Komissii po voprosu ob alkogolizme za 15 let, 1898–1913* (St Petersburg 1913)

DEWAR, M., *Labour policy in the USSR, 1917–1928* (London 1956)

DOLGORUKOV, P.D., Prince, *Velikaya razrukha* (Madrid 1964)

DÖRING, F., *Organisationsprobleme der russischen Wirtschaft in Revolution und Bürgerkrieg, 1917–1920: dargestellt am Volkswirtschaftsrat für den Nordrayon (SNChSR)* (Hanover 1970)

DROBIZHEV, V.Z., *Glavnyy shtab sotsialisticheskoy promyshlennosti: ocherki istorii VSNKh, 1917–1932 gg.* (Moscow 1966)

DRUZHININ, N.K., *Usloviya byta rabochikh v dorevolyutsionnoy Rossii: po dannym byudzhetnykh osledovaniy* (Moscow 1958)

DSV, see Russia

DUBROVSKY, S.M. (ed.), *Osobennosti agrarnogo stroya Rossii v period imperializma: materialy sessii Nauchnogo Soveta po probleme 'Istoricheskiye predposylki Velikoy Oktyabr'skoy sotsialisticheskoy revolyutsii', may 1960 g.* (Moscow 1962)

DUBROVSKY, S.M. (ed.), *Stolypinskaya zemel'naya reforma* (Moscow 1963)

DUBROWSKI, S. [= DUBROVSKY, S.M.], *Die Bauernbewegung in der russichen Revolution 1917* (Berlin 1929)

EISSENSTAT, B.W. (ed.), *Lenin and Leninism: State, Law and Society* (Lexington, Mass. London 1971)

Ekonomicheskoye polozheniye Rossii nakanune Velikoy Oktyabr'skoy sotsialisticheskoy revolyutsii: dokumenty i materialy, 3 vols; vols 1, 2 (ed.) A.L. Sidorov and others, vol. 3 A.M. Anfimov and others (Moscow, Leningrad 1957–67) [*EPR*]

FAINSOD, M., *How Russia is Ruled*, rev. ed. (Cambridge, Mass., London 1963)

FEDOROV, K.G., *VTsIK v pervye gody Sovetskoy vlasti, 1917–1920 gg.* (Moscow 1957)

FERRO, M., *La Révolution de 1917: la chute de tsarisme et les origines d'Octobre* (Paris 1967)

FITZPATRICK, S., *The Commissariat of Enlightenment: Soviet Organization of Education and the Arts under Lunacharsky* (Cambridge 1970)

FLEER, M.G. (comp.), *Rabocheye dvizheniye v gody voyny* (Moscow 1925)

FLORINSKY, M.T., *The End of the Russian Empire* (New Haven, Conn. 1931; repr. New York 1961)

FRAYMAN, A.L. and others (eds), *Oktyabr'skoye vooruzhennoye vosstaniye v Petrograde*, 2 vols (Leningrad 1967)

FRAYMAN, L.I., *Indeksy stoimosti zhizni i metody ikh ischisleniya v raznykh stranakh, 1914–1924 gg.* (Moscow 1925)

FRENKIN, M.S., *Revolyutsionnoye dvizheniye na Rumynskom fronte, 1917 g.– mart 1918 g.: soldaty VIII armii Rumynskogo fronta v bor'be za mir i vlast' Sovetov* (Moscow 1965)

FREYDLIN, B.M., *Ocherki istorii rabochego dvizheniya v Rossii v 1917 g.* (Moscow 1967)

FURMANOV, D., *Put' k bol'shevizmu: stranitsy dnevnika* (Moscow, Leningrad 1928)

GAPONENKO, L.S., *Rabochiy klass Rossii v 1917 g.* (Moscow 1970)

GARVI, P.A., *Professional'nye soyuzy v Rossii v pervye gody revolyutsii, 1917–1921*, edited by G.Ya. Aronson (New York 1958)

GAVRILOV, L.M. and others (comps), *Bor'ba za ustanovleniye i uprocheniye Sovetskoy vlasti: khronika sobytiy, 26 oktyabrya 1917 g.–10 yanvarya 1918 g.*; Sequel to *Velikaya Oktyabr'skaya sotsialisticheskaya revolyutsiya: khronika sobytiy* (Moscow 1962)

GAYSINSKY, M., *Bor'ba bol'shevikov za krest'yanstvo v 1917 g.: Vserossiyskiye s'yezdy Sovetov krest'yanskikh deputatov* (Moscow 1933)

GERASIMYUK, V.R., *Nachalo sotsialisticheskoy revolyutsii v derevne, 1917–1918 gg.* (Moscow 1958)

GETZLER, I., *Martov: a Political Biography of a Russian Social Democrat* (Melbourne, London, New York 1967)

GEYER, D., *Die russische Revolution: historische Probleme und Perspektiven* (Stuttgart 1968)

GIMPELSON, E.G., *Sovety v gody inostrannoy interventsii i grazhdanskoy voyny* (Moscow 1968)

GINDIN, I.F., *Kak bol'sheviki zakhvatili Gosudarstvennyy Bank* (Moscow 1961)

GLADKOV, I.A., *Ocherki Sovetskoy ekonomiki 1917–1920 gg.* (Moscow 1956)

God russkoy revolyutsii (cf. Bakh, A.N.)

GOLDER, F.A. (ed.), *Documents on Russian History, 1914–1917;* trsl. E. Aronsberg (New York 1927; repr. Gloucester, Mass. 1964)

GORDEYEV, G.S., *Sel'skoye khozyaystvo v voyne i revolyutsii* (Moscow, Leningrad 1925)

GORDON, M., *Workers before and after Lenin* (New York 1942)

GORIN, P.O., *Organizatsiya i stroitel'stvo Sovetov rabochikh i soldatskikh deputatov v 1917 g.: sbornik dokumentov* (Moscow 1928)

GORODETSKY, E.N., *Rozhdeniye Sovetskogo gosudarstva, 1917–1918* (Moscow 1965)

GRAVE, B.B., *K istorii klassovoy bor'by v Rossii v gody imperialisticheskoy voyny, iyul' 1914 g.–fevral' 1917 g.: proletariat i burzhuaziya* (Moscow, Leningrad 1926)

GRENARD, F., *La Révolution russe* (Paris 1933)

GROTTIAN, W., *Das sowjetische Regierungssystem: die Grundlagen der Macht der kommunistischen Parteiführung*, 2 vols (Cologne 1965)

GRUNT, A.YA., *Pobeda Oktyabr'skoy revolyutsii v Moskve, fevral'– oktyabr' 1917 g.* (Moscow 1961)

GUBAREVA, V.M., *Razvertyvaniye sotsialisticheskoy revolyutsii v derevne v 1918 g.: po materialam Petrogradskoy gubernii* (Moscow 1957)

GUL, R., *Dzerzhinsky – Menzhinsky – Peters – Latsis – Yagoda* (Paris 1936)

GUSEV, K., *Krakh partii levykh Sotsialistov-Revolyutsionerov* (Moscow 1963)

GUTMAN, D.S. and DERKACH, G.G. (comps), *Krest'yanskoye dvizheniye v Kazanskoy gubernii nakanune Velikoy Oktyabr'skoy sotsialisticheskoy revolyutsii: sbornik dokumentov*, 1 (Kazan 1950)

IGNATOV, E., *Moskovskiy Sovet rabochikh deputatov v 1917 g.* (Moscow 1925)

IGRITSKY, I.V. (comp.), *1917 g. v derevne: vospominaniya krest'yan* (Moscow, Leningrad 1929; new ed. Moscow 1967)

ILYIN, M.A. and RUMYANTSEV, A.M. (eds), *Tverskaya guberniya v pervye gody Sovetskoy vlasti, 1917–1920 gg.: sbornik statey i dokumentov* (Kalinin 1958)

IROSHNIKOV, M.P., *Sozdaniye Sovetskogo tsentral'nogo gosudarstvennogo apparata: SNK i narodnye komissary, oktyabr' 1917 g.–yanvar' 1918 g.* (Moscow, Leningrad 1966; 2nd ed. Leningrad 1967)

Istochnikovedeniye istorii Sovetskogo obshchestva (cf. Chugayev, D.A.; Ivnitsky, N.A.)

Istoriya Sovetskogo krest'yanstva (cf. Kim, M.P.)

IVNITSKY, N.A. and others (eds), *Istochnikovedeniye istorii Sovetskogo obshchestva*, fasc. 1. (Moscow 1964)

Iz istorii Velikoy Oktyabr'skoy (cf. Stishov, M.I.)
Iz istorii Velikoy Oktyabr'skoy (cf. Ovsyankin, V.A.)

JASNY, N., *Soviet Economists of the Twenties: Names to be Remembered* (Cambridge 1972)

KACHINSKY, V., *Ocherki agrarnoy revolyutsii na Ukraine*, fasc. 1 (Kharkov 1922)

KAKURIN, N.E. (comp.), *Razlozheniye armii v 1917 g.* (Moscow, Leningrad 1925)

KAPLAN, F.I., *Bolshevik Ideology and the Ethics of Soviet Labor, 1917–1920: the Formative Years* (New York 1969)

KARAMYSHEVA, L.F., *Bor'ba bol'shevikov za Petrogradskiy Soviet, mart–oktyabr' 1917 g.* (Leningrad 1964)

KATKOV, G., *Russia, 1917: the February Revolution* (London 1967)

KEEP, J.L.H., *The Rise of Social Democracy in Russia* (Oxford 1963)

KELLY, G.A. and BROWN, C.W. Jr (eds), *Struggles in the State: Sources and Patterns of World Revolution* (New York, London 1970)

KENEZ, P., *Civil War in South Russia, 1918: the First Year of the Volunteer Army* (Berkeley, Calif., Los Angeles, London 1971)

KHESIN, S.S. (ed.), *Bor'ba za pobedu i ukrepleniye Sovetskoy vlasti, 1917–1918 gg.: sbornik statey* (Moscow 1966)

KHROMOV, P.A., *Ekonomicheskoye razvitiye Rossii: ocherki ekonomiki Rossii s drevneyshikh vremen do Velikoy Oktyabr'skoy revolyutsii* (Moscow 1967)

KHROMOV, P.A., *Ocherki ekonomiki Rossii perioda monopolisticheskogo kapitalizma* (Moscow 1960)

KHRYASHCHEVA, A.I., *Gruppy i klassy v krest'yanstve*, 2nd ed. (Moscow 1926)

KHRYASHCHEVA, A.I., *Krest'yanstvo v voyne i revolyutsii: statistiko-ekonomicheskiye ocherki* (Moscow 1921)

KIM, M.P. and others (eds), *Istoriya Sovetskogo krest'yanstva i kolkhoznogo stroitel'stva v SSSR: materialy nauchnoy sessii, sostoyavsheysya 18–21 aprelya 1961 g. v Moskve* (Moscow 1963)

KIRILLOV, I.A., *Ocherki zemleustroystva za tri goda revolyutsii, 1917–1920 gg.* (Petrograd 1922)

KIRYANOV, YU.I., *Rabochiye yuga Rossii, 1914–fevral' 1917 g.* (Moscow 1971)

KLEPIKOV, S.A. (comp.), *Atlas diagramm i kartogramm po agrarnomu voprosu* (Moscow 1917)

KLYATSKIN, S.M., *Na zashchite Oktyabrya: organizatsiya regulyarnoy armii i militsionnogo stroitel'stva v Sovetskoy respublike, 1917–1920 gg.* (Moscow 1965)

KONDRATEV, V.A. (comp.), *Moskovskiy voyenno-revolyutsionnyy komitet, oktyabr'–noyabr' 1917 g.* (Moscow 1968)

KOTELNIKOV, K.G. and MELLER, V.L. (comps), *Krest'yanskoye dvizheniye v 1917 g.* (Moscow, Leningrad 1927) [K & M]

KOVALENKO, D.A. and others (eds), *Sovety v pervyy god proletarskoy diktatury, oktyabr' 1917–noyabr' 1918 gg.* (Moscow 1967)

KOZMINYKH-LANIN, I.M., *Gramotnost' i zarabotki fabrichno-zavodskikh rabochikh Moskovskoy gubernii* (Moscow 1912)

KRAVCHUK, N.A., *Massovoye krest'yanskoye dvizheniye v Rossii nakanune Oktyabrya, mart–oktyabr' 1917* (Moscow 1971)

Krest'yanskaya Rossiya. Sbornik statey po voprosam obshchestvenno-politicheskim i ekonomicheskim, 9 vols (Prague 1922–4)

Krest'yanskoye dvizheniye v Kazanskoy gub. (cf. Gutman, D.S.)

Krest'yanskoye dvizheniye v 1917 g. (cf. Kotelnikov, K.G.)

KRITSMAN, L. (ed.), *Materialy po istorii agrarnoy revolyutsii v Rossii,* 2 vols (Moscow 1928–9)

KRUPSKAYA, N.K., *Vospominaniya o Lenine* (Moscow 1957)

KUDELLI, P.F. (ed.), *Leningradskiye rabochiye v bor'be za vlast' Sovetov, 1917: stat'i, vospominaniya i dokumenty* (Leningrad 1924)

KUDELLI, P.F. (ed.), *Pervyy legal'nyy Peterburgskiy komitet bol'shevikov v 1917 g.: sbornik materialov i protokolov zasedaniy PK RSDRP(b) i yego IK za 1917 g.* (Moscow, Leningrad 1927)

KUKUSHKIN, M.S., *Moskovskiy Sovet v 1917 g.* (Moscow 1957)

LARIN, YU., *Ekonomika dosovetskoy derevni* (Moscow, Leningrad 1926)

LATSIS, M.YA., *Dva goda bor'by na vnutrennem fronte* (Moscow 1920)

LATSIS, M.YA., *Chrezvychaynye komissii po bor'be s kontr-revolyutsiey* (Moscow 1921)

LEAGUE OF NATIONS, *Report on Economic Conditions in Russia with Special Reference to the Famine of 1921–1922 and the State of Agriculture,* C. 705 M. 451 (1922) II ([Paris] 1922)

LEITES, N., *A Study of Bolshevism* (Glencoe, Ill. 1953)

LENIN, V.I., *Polnoye sobraniye sochineniy* [5th ed.] 55 vols (Moscow 1959–65) [Lenin, *PSS*]

LEONHARD, W., *Die politischen Lehren, Sowjetideologie heute,* II (Frankfurt 1962)

592 BIBLIOGRAPHY

LEPESHKIN, A.I., *Mestnye organy vlasti Sovetskogo gosudarstva, 1917–1920 gg.* (Moscow 1957)

LERNER, E. (ed.), *Fabzavkomy i profsoyuzy: sbornik statey* (Moscow 1925)

LEVIN, D.G., *Novyy zakon o volostnom zemskom upravlenii: zakon 21 maya 1917 g.–nakaz 11 iyunya 1917 g.* (Moscow 1917)

LISOVSKY, N.K., *1917 god na Urale* (Chelyabinsk 1967)

LITVIN, A.L., *Krest'yanstvo Srednego Povolzh'ya v gody grazhdanskoy voyny* (Kazan 1972)

LIVSHITS, R.S., *Razmeshcheniye promyshlennosti v dorevolyutsionnoy Rossii* (Moscow 1955)

LORENZ, R., *Anfänge der bolschewistischen Industriepolitik* (Cologne 1965)

LOSITSKY, A. and CHERNYSHEV, I., *Alkogolizm peterburgskikh rabochikh* (St Petersburg 1913)

LOZINSKY, Z., *Ekonomicheskaya politika Vremennogo Pravitel'stva* (Leningrad 1929)

LOZOVSKY, [S.], *Otchet VTsSPS za iyul'–dekabr' 1917 g.* (Petrograd 1918)

LUKOMSKY, A.S., *Vospominaniya*, 2 vols (Berlin 1922)

LYUBIMOV, I.N. (comp.), *Revolyutsiya 1917 g.: khronika sobytiy*, 6 (Moscow 1930)

MAKINTSIAN, L. (ed.), *Krasnaya kniga VChK*, 1 (Moscow 1920)

MAKSAKOV, V. and NELIDOV, N., *Khronika revolyutsii*, fasc. 1: *1917 god.* (Moscow, Petrograd 1923)

MALCHEVSKY, I.S. (comp.), *Vserossiyskoye Uchreditel'noye Sobraniye* (Moscow, Leningrad 1930)

MALE, D.J., *Russian Peasant Organization before Collectivization: a Study of Commune and Gathering, 1925–1930* (Cambridge, New York 1971)

MARKOVA, N.N. and others, *Profsoyuz tekstil'shchikov: kratkiy istoricheskiy ocherk* (Moscow 1963)

MAYSKY, I.M. and others (eds), *Oktyabr' i grazhdanskaya voyna v SSSR: sbornik statey k 70-letiyu akademika I. I. Mintsa* (Moscow 1966)

McNEAL, R.H. (ed.), *Resolutions and Decisions of the Communist Party of the Soviet Union*, vol. 1: *The RSDLP, 1898–October 1917*, ed. R.C. Elwood; vol. 11: *The Early Soviet Period, 1917–1929*, ed. R.H. McNeal; 4 vols (Toronto 1974)

MEDVEDEV, YE.I., *Krest'yanstvo Srednego Povolzh'ya v Oktyabr'skoy revolyutsii* (Kuybyshev 1970)

MELGUNOV, S. [P.], *Kak bol'sheviki zakhvatili vlast'*: *Oktyabr'skiy perevorot 1917 g.* (Paris 1953); English trans.: *The Bolshevik Seizure of Power*, ed. and abridged by S.P. Pushkarev in collaboration with B.S. Pushkarev, transl. J.S. Beaver (Santa Barbara, Calif., Oxford 1972)

MELGUNOV, S. [P.], *Martovskiye dni 1917 g.* (Paris 1961)

MELGUNOV, S. [P.], '*Rossiyskaya kontr-revolyutsiya*': *metody i vyvody generala Golovina*: *doklad* (Paris 1938)

MELGUNOV, S. [P.], *Vospominaniya i dnevniki*, 2 fascs (Paris 1964)

MELLER, V.L. and PANKRATOVA, A.M. (comps) *Rabocheye dvizheniye v 1917 g.* (Moscow, Leningrad 1926) [M & P]

MENITSKY, I., *Revolyutsionnoye dvizheniye voyennykh godov (1914–1917)*: *ocherki i materialy*, 2 vols (Moscow 1924)

MEYER, A.G., *Leninism* (Cambridge, Mass., London 1957)

MILONOV, YU.K., *Kak voznikli profzoyuzy v Rossii* (Moscow, Leningrad 1926)

MILONOV, YU.K. (comp.), *Putevoditel' po rezolyutsiyam Vserossiyskikh s'yezdov i konferentsiy professional'nykh soyuzov* (Moscow 1924)

MILSHTEYN, YA. and LIVSHITS, V. (comps), *Istoriya i praktika rossiyskogo professional'nogo dvizheniya*: *khrestomatiya dlya profkruzhkov i profkursov* (Moscow 1925)

MILYUKOV, P.N., *Istoriya vtoroy russkoy revolyutsii*, 3 pts (Sofia 1921–3)

MILYUTIN, V.P., *Agrarnaya politika SSSR* (Moscow 1926)

MILYUTIN, V.P. (ed.), *Agrarnaya revolutsiya*, II: *Krest'yanskoye dvizheniye v 1917 g.* (Moscow 1928)

MILYUTIN, V.P., *Sel'ski-khozyaystvennye rabochiye i voyna* (Petrograd 1917)

MINTS, I.I., *Istoriya Velikogo Oktyabrya*, 3 vols (Moscow 1967–73)

MINTS, I.I. and others (eds), *Sovety i soyuz rabochego klassa i krest'yanstva v Oktyabr'skoy revolyutsii* (Moscow 1964)

MINTS, I.I. and others, *Sverzheniye samoderzhaviya*: *sbornik statey* (Moscow 1970)

MOISEYEV, A.I. and others (eds), *Podgotovka i provedeniye Velikoy Oktyabr'skoy sotsialisticheskoy revolyutsii v Tver'skoy gubernii*: *sbornik dokumentov i materialov* (Kalinin 1960)

MOISEYEVA, O.N., *Sovety krest'yanskikh deputatov v 1917 g.* (Moscow 1967)

MONNEROT, J., *Sociologie de la révolution*: *mythologies politiques du XXe siècle* (Paris 1969)

Morozov, B.M., *Partiya i Sovety v Oktyabr'skoy revolyutsii* (Moscow 1966)

Moscow: Sovet Rabochikh i Krasnoarmeyskikh Deputatov – Prodovol'stvennyy Otdel, *God raboty Moskovskogo gorodskogo prodovol'stvennogo komiteta, mart 1917–mart 1918* (Moscow 1918)

Mstislavsky, S., *Pyat' dney: nachalo i konets fevral'skoy revolyutsii*, 2nd ed. (Berlin, Moscow, Petrograd 1922)

Mutovkin, N.S., *Voyenno-politicheskiy soyuz rabochego klassa i trudovogo krest'yanstva v SSSR v period inostrannoy voyennoy interventsii i grazhdanskoy voyny, 1918–1920 gg.* (Moscow 1965)

Nalivaysky, B.Ya. (comp.), *Petrogradskiy Sovet rabochikh i soldatskikh deputatov: protokoly zasedaniy IK i byuro IK* ([Leningrad] 1925)

Narkiewicz, O.A., *The Making of the Soviet State Apparatus* (Manchester 1970)

Nikitin, B., *Rokovye gody: novye pokazaniya uchastnika* (Paris 1937?)

Nikolayevsky, B.I., *Men'sheviki v dni Oktyabr'skogo perevorota*, inter-university project on the History of the Menshevik Movement, Paper no. 8 (New York 1962)

Nosov, N.E. and others (eds), *Issledovaniya po otechestvennomu istochnikovedeniyu. Sbornik statey posvyashchennykh 75-letiyu prof. S.N. Valka* (Moscow, Leningrad 1964), (*Trudy Leningradskogo otdeleniya Instituta istorii*, fasc. 7)

O zemle: sbornik statey, 2 fascs (Moscow 1921–2)

Ocherki po istorii Oktyabr'skoy revolyutsii (cf. Pokrovsky, M.N.)

Oganovsky, N.P., *Russkiy krest'yanin i mirovoye khozyaystvo*, 2nd ed. (Moscow 1924)

Oganovsky, N.P. (ed.), *Sel'skoye khozyaystvo Rossii v XX veke: sbornik statistiko-ekonomicheskikh svedeniy za 1901–1922 gg.* (Moscow 1923; repr. The Hague 1968)

Oganovsky, N.P. and Chayanov, A.V. (comps), *Zemlevladeniye i zemlepol'zovaniye, Statisticheskiy spravochnik po agrarnomu voprosu*, fasc. 1 (Moscow 1917)

Okninsky, A., *Dva goda sredi krest'yan: vidennoye, slyshannoye, perezhitoye v Tambovskoy gubernii s noyabrya 1918 g. do noyabrya 1920 g.* (Riga 1936?)

Oktyabr' i grazhdanskaya voyna (cf. Maysky, I.M.)

Oktyabr'skaya revolyutsiya i fabzavkomy (cf. Amosov, P.N.)

Orlov, N.[A.], *Prodovol'stvennaya rabota Sovetskoy vlasti: k godovshchine Oktyabr'skoy revolyutsii* (Moscow 1919)

Osobennosti agrarnogo stroya Rossii (cf. Dubrovsky, S.M.)

OVSYANKIN, V.A. (ed.), *Iz istorii Velikoy Oktyabr'skoy sotsialisticheskoy revolyutsii i sotsialisticheskogo stroitel'stva v SSSR: sbornik statey* (Leningrad 1967)

OVSYANNIKOV, N. (ed.), *Moskva v Oktyabre: illyustrirovannyy sbornik zametok [i] vospominaniy uchastnikov dvizheniya* (Moscow 1919)

OVSYANNIKOV, N. (ed.), *Oktyabr'skoye vosstaniye 1917 g. v Moskve: sbornik dokumentov* (Moscow 1922)

OWEN, L.A., *The Russian Peasant Movement, 1906–1917* (London 1937 ; repr. New York 1963)

PANKRATOVA, A.M., *Fabzavkomy Rossii v bor'be za sotsialisticheskuyu fabriku* (Moscow 1923)

PANKRATOVA, A.M. and others (eds), *Ustanovleniye Sovetskoy vlasti na mestakh v 1917–1918 gg.* [I] (Moscow 1953)

PAVLOVSKY, G.[A.], *Agricultural Russia on the Eve of the Revolution* (London 1930 ; repr. New York 1968)

PERSHIN, P.N., *Agrarnaya revolyutsiya v Rossii: istoriko-ekonomicheskoye issledovaniye*, 2 vols (Moscow 1966)

Petrogradskiy Sovet (cf. Nalivaysky, B.Ya.)

PETHYBRIDGE, R.W., *The Spread of the Russian Revolution: Essays on 1917* (London, New York 1972)

PIDHAINY, O.S., *The Formation of the Ukrainian Republic* (Toronto, New York 1966)

PIONTKOVSKY, S.A., *Oktyabr' 1917 g.* (Moscow, Leningrad 1927)

PIONTKOVSKY, S.A. (ed.), *Sovety v Oktyabre: sbornik dokumentov* (Moscow 1928)

PIPES, R., *The Formation of the Soviet Union: Communism and Nationalism, 1917–1923*, rev. ed. (Cambridge, Mass., London, 1964 ; repr. New York 1968)

PIPES, R. (ed.), *Revolutionary Russia* (Cambridge, Mass., London 1968) ; repr. as *Revolutionary Russia: a Symposium* (Garden City 1969)

PODSHIVALOV, I., *Grazhdanskaya bor'ba na Urale, 1917–1918 gg.: opyt voyenno-istoricheskogo issledovaniya* (Moscow 1925)

PODVOYSKY, N., *Krasnaya gvardiya v Oktyabr'skiye dni: Leningrad i Moskva* (Moscow, Leningrad 1927)

PODVOYSKY, N., *God 1917* (Moscow 1958)

POKROVSKY, M.N. (ed.), *Ocherki po istorii Oktyabr'skoy revolyutsii: raboty istoricheskoy seminarii Instituta krasnoy professury*, 2 vols (Moscow, Leningrad 1927)

POLIKARPOV, V.D. (ed.), *Etapy bol'shogo puti: vospominaniya o grazhdanskoy voyne* (Moscow 1963)

POLOVTSOV, P.A., *Dni zatmeniya: zapiski glavnokomanduyushchego voyskami Petrogradskogo voyennogo okruga . . . v 1917 g.* (Paris 1927)

POPOV, A. (comp.), *Oktyabr'skiy perevorot: fakty i dokumenty* (Petrograd 1918)

POTEKHIN, M.N., *Pervyy Sovet proletarskoy diktatury: ocherki po istorii Petrogradskogo Soveta rabochikh i soldatskikh deputatov, 1917–1918 gg.* (Leningrad 1966)

Profsoyuz tekstil'shchikov (cf. Markova, N.N.)

Profsoyuzy SSSR: dokumenty (cf. Borshchenko, I.L. ; Batayeva, T.V.)

Profsoyuzy v bor'be (cf. Danilevsky, A.F.)

puti revolyutsii: stat'i, materialy, vospominaniya (Berlin 1923)

pVRK, see Chugayev, D.A.

RABINOWITCH, A., *Prelude to Revolution: the Petrograd Bolsheviks and the July 1917 Uprising* (Bloomington, Ind., London 1968)

Rabocheye dvizheniye v gody voyny (cf. Fleer, M.G.)

Rabocheye dvizheniye v 1917 g. (cf. Meller, V.L.)

Rabochiy klass Sovetskoy Rossii (cf. Chugayev, D.A.)

Rabochiy kontrol' i natsionalizatsiya (cf. Babishev, V.A.)

RADKEY, O.H., *The Agrarian Foes of Bolshevism: Promise and Default of the Russian Socialist Revolutionaries, February to October 1917* (New York, London 1958)

RADKEY, O.H., *The Election to the Russian Constituent Assembly of 1917* (Cambridge, Mass. 1950)

RADKEY, O.H., *The Sickle under the Hammer: the Russian Socialist Revolutionaries in the Early Months of Soviet Rule* (New York, London 1963)

RASHIN, A.G., *Formirovaniye rabochego klassa v Rossii* (Moscow 1958)

RASHIN, A.G., *Naseleniye Rossii za 100 let* (Moscow 1956)

RASKOLNIKOV, F.F., *Kronshtadt i Piter v 1917 g.* (Moscow, Leningrad 1925)

Rayonnye sovety Petrograda v 1917 g.: protokoly, rezolyutsii, postanovleniya obshchikh sobraniy i zasedaniy IK, 3 vols (Moscow, Leningrad 1964–6)

REED, J., *Ten Days that Shook the World* (London 1926; repr. Harmondsworth 1966)

RESHETAR, J.S., Jr, *The Ukrainian Revolution, 1917–1920: a Study in Nationalism* (Princeton, NJ 1952)

Revolyutsiya 1917 g.: khronika sobytiy (cf. Avdeyev, N. ; Ryabinsky, K. ; Lyubimov, I.N.)

RITTER, G., *Das Kommunemodell und die Begründung der Roten Armee im Jahre 1918* (Wiesbaden 1965)

ROBINSON, G.T., *Rural Russia under the Old Regime: a History of the Landlord – Peasant World and a Prologue to the Peasant Revolution of 1917* (New York, London 1932 ; repr. 1967)

ROSENBERG, W.G., *Liberals in the Russian Revolution: the Constitutional-Democratic Party, 1917–1921* (Princeton, NJ 1974)

RUBACH, M.A., *Ocherki po istorii revolyutsionnogo preobrazovaniya agrarnykh otnosheniy na Ukraine* (Kiev 1957)

RUDNEV, S.P., *Pri vechernikh ognakh: vospominaniya* (Harbin, China 1928)

Russia (RSFSR): Laws and Statutes, *Dekrety Sovetskoy vlasti*, 4 vols (Moscow 1957–68) [*DSV*]

Russia (RSFSR): Laws and Statutes, *Sbornik dekretov i postanovleniy po narodnomu khozyaystvu, 25 oktyabrya 1917 – 25 oktyabrya 1918 gg.* (Moscow 1918)

Russia (RSFSR): Komissiya po issledovaniyu . . . opyta . . . grazhdanskoy voyny, *Grazhdanskaya voyna: materialy po istorii Krasnoy Armii*, 2 vols (Moscow 1923)

Russia: Ministerstvo Torgovli i promyshlennosti, *Fabrichno-zavodskaya promyshlennost' Yevropeyskoy Rossii v 1910–1912 gg.: obshchiye itogi* (Petrograd 1915)

Russia (RSFSR): Narodnyy Komissariat Prodovol'stviya, *Protokoly zasedaniy I-go s'yezda prodovol'stvennogo komiteta Severnoy oblasti, 28–30 aprelya 1918* (Moscow 1918)

Russia (RSFSR): Narodnyy Komissariat Prodovol'stviya, *Sistematicheskiy sbornik dekretov i rasporyazheniy pravitel'stva po prodovol'stvennomu delu*, bk 1: *1 oktyabrya 1917 – 1 yanvarya 1919* (Nizhniy Novgorod 1919)

Russia (RSFSR): S'yezd Sovetov, *Pervyy Vserossiyskiy s'yezd Sovetov rabochikh i soldatskikh deputatov, 1917: protokoly*, V.N. Rakhmetov and N.P. Myamlin (comps), 2 vols (Moscow, Leningrad 1930–1) [*I s'yezd*]

Russia (RSFSR): S'yezd Sovetov, *Vtoroy Vserossiyskiy s'yezd Sovetov rabochikh i soldatskikh deputatov: protokoly*, K.G. Kotelnikov (comp.) (Moscow, Leningrad 1928) [*II s'yezd*]

Russia (RSFSR): Tsentral'noye Statisticheskoye Upravleniye, *Pogubernskiye itogi Vserossiyskogo sel'sko-khozyaystvennoy i pozemel'noy perepisi 1917 g. po 52 guberniyam i oblastyam, Trudy TsSU,* v, fasc. 1 (Moscow 1922?)

Russia (RSFSR): Tsentral'noye Statisticheskoye Upravleniye, *Sbornik statisticheskikh svedeniy po SSSR, 1918–1923: za 5 let raboty TsSU, Trudy TsSU,* XVIII (Moscow 1924)

Russia (RSFSR): Tsentral'noye Statisticheskoye Upravleniye, *Statisticheskiy yezhegodnik 1918–1920 gg., Trudy TsSU,* VIII, fasc. 1, 2 pts (Moscow 1921)

Russia (RSFSR): Vserossiyskiy Tsentral'nyy Ispolnitel'nyy Komitet Sovetov, *Protokoly zasedaniy Vserossiyskogo Tsentral'nogo Ispolnitel'nogo Komiteta Sovetov Rabochikh, Soldatskikh, Krest'yanskikh i Kazach'ikh Deputatov, II sozyv, 27 oktyabrya–29 dekabrya 1917* (Petrograd 1918) [*Prot. VTsIK*]

Russia (RSFSR): Vserossiyskiy Tsentral'nyy Sovet Professional'nykh Soyuzov, *Materialy po istorii professional'nogo dvizheniya v Rossii: sbornik,* 5 vols (Moscow 1924–7)

Russia (RSFSR): Vserossiyskiy Tsentral'nyy Sovet Professional'nykh Soyuzov, *Otchet . . . za iyul'-dekabr' 1917 g,* (cf. Lozovsky, A.L.)

Russia (RSFSR): Vserossiyskiy Tsentral'nyy Sovet Professional'nykh Soyuzov, *Pervyy Vserossiyskiy s'yezd professional'nykh soyuzov, 7–14 yanvarya 1918 g.: polnyy stenograficheskiy otchet* (Moscow 1918) [*I s'yezd*]

Russia (RSFSR): Vserossiyskiy Tsentral'nyy Sovet Professional'nykh Soyuzov, *Tret'ya Vserossiyskaya konferentsiya professional'nykh soyuzov, 3–11 iyulya (20–28 iyunya st. st.): stenograficheskiy otchet* (Moscow 1927) [*III konf.*]

Russia (RSFSR): Vserossiyskiy Tsentral'nyy Sovet Professional'nykh Soyuzov, *Chetvertaya Vserossiyskaya konferentsiya professional'nykh soyuzov, 12–17 marta 1918 g.: protokoly i materialy,* M. Zayats and Yu. Milonov (eds) (Moscow 1923)

Russian Social Democratic Labour Party (Bolsheviks) [later Russian (All-Union) Communist Party (Bolsheviks); Communist Party of the Soviet Union]: S'yezd, *Protokoly i stenograficheskiye otchety s'yezdov i konferentsiy KPSS: VI s'yezd RSDRP (b), avgust 1917 g.* (Moscow 1958)

Russian Social Democratic Labour Party: Tsentral'nyy Komitet, *Protokoly Tsentral'nogo Komiteta RSDRP (b), avgust 1917–fevral' 1918* (Moscow 1958); English transl.: *The Bolsheviks and the*

October Revolution. Minutes of the Central Committee of the RSDLP (B), August 1917–February 1918, trsl. A. Bone (London 1974)

Russian Social Democratic Labour Party: Sekretariat, *Perepiska Sekretariata* (cf. Anikeyev, V.V.)

Russian Social Democratic Labour Party: Nizhegorodskiy gubernskiy komitet, *1917–1918 gg.: god proletarskoy diktatury: yubileynyy sbornik* (Nizhniy Novgorod 1918)

RYABINSKY, K. (comp.), *Revolyutsiya 1917 g.: khronika sobytiy*, 5 (Moscow 1926)

SAUTIN, N., *Velikiy Oktyabr' v derevne na severo-zapade Rossii, oktyabr' 1917–1918 gg.* (Leningrad 1959)

SCHAPIRO, L.B., *The Communist Party of the Soviet Union*, 2nd ed., rev. and enlarged (London, New York 1970; repr. 1971)

SCHAPIRO, L.B., *The Origin of the Communist Autocracy: Political Opposition in the Soviet State: First Phase, 1917–1922* (London, Cambridge, Mass. 1955; repr. New York, Washington 1965)

SCHAPIRO, L.B., *Totalitarianism* (London, New York 1972)

SCHAPIRO, L.B. and REDDAWAY, P. (eds), *Lenin: the Man, the Theorist, the Leader: a Reappraisal* (London 1967)

SCHWARZ, S.M., *Labor in the Soviet Union* (New York, London 1952)

SELUNSKAYA, V.M., *Rabochiy klass i Oktyabr' v derevne* (Moscow 1968)

SELZNICK, P., *The Organizational Weapon: a Study of Bolshevik Tactics* (New York 1952)

SHANIN, T., *The Awkward Class: Political Sociology of Peasantry in a Developing Society: Russia, 1910–1925* (Oxford 1972)

SHAPURIN, S. (ed.), *Oktyabr' na Yuzhnom Urale: yubileynyy sbornik k 10-letiyu Oktyabr'skoy revolyutsii* (Zlatoust 1927)

SHARAPOV, G.V., *Nachalo sotsialisticheskikh preobrazovaniy v derevne v pervye gody Sovetskoy vlasti* (Moscow 1960)

SHESTAKOV, A.V. (comp.), *Sovety krest'yanskikh deputatov i drugiye krest'yanskiye organizatsii*, 2 vols (Moscow 1929)

SHLIKHTER, A.G., *Ilyich kakim ya yego znal* (Kharkov 1924)

SHLYAPNIKOV, A., *Kanun semnadtsatogo goda: vospominaniya i dokumenty o rabochem dvizhenii i revolyutsionnom podpol'e za 1914–1916 gg.* (Moscow 1922), 2nd edn (Moscow, Petrograd 1923)

SHLYAPNIKOV, A., *Nakanune 1917 g.: vospominaniya i dokumenty o rabochem dvizhenii i rabochem podpol'e za 1914–1917* (Moscow 1920)

SHLYAPNIKOV, A., *Semnadtsatyy god*, 1 (Moscow 1925)

SHPINDLER, M.A. (ed.), *Rabochiy kontrol' i natsionalizatsiya promyshlennosti v Kostromskoy gubernii, 1917–1919 gg.* (Kostroma 1960)

SHUB, G.[V.] (ed.), *Potrebleniye gorodskogo naseleniya v Rossii* [Moscow 1918]

SHULYAKOVSKY, E.G. (ed.), *Ocherk istorii Voronezhskogo kraya: s drevneyshikh vremen do Velikoy Oktyabr'skoy sotsialisticheskoy revolyutsii* (Voronezh 1961)

SHULYAKOVSKY, E.G. and others (eds), *Bor'ba za Sovetskuyu vlast' v Voronezhskoy gubernii 1917–1918 gg.: sbornik dokumentov i materialov* (Voronezh 1957)

SHVARTS [=SCHWARZ], S.M., *Sotsial'noye strakhovaniye v Rossii v 1917–1919 gg.* (New York 1968)

SIDOROV, A.L., *Finansovoye polozheniye Rossii v gody I-oy mirovoy voyny, 1914–1917* (Moscow 1960)

SIDOROV, A.L. and others (eds), *Velikaya Oktyabr'skaya sotsialisticheskaya revolyutsiya: dokumenty i materialy*, 9 vols, vol. 9 in 2 pts (Moscow 1957–63) [*DiM*]

SISSON, E., *One Hundred Red Days: a Personal Chronicle of the Russian Revolution* (New Haven, Conn. 1931)

SOBOLEV, P.N. and others (eds), *Istoriya Velikoy Oktyabr'skoy sotsialisticheskoy revolyutsii* (Moscow 1967)

SORENSON, J.B., *The Life and Death of Soviet Trade Unionism, 1917–1928* (New York 1969)

Sovety i soyuz rabochego klassa (cf. Mints, I.I.)

STANKEVICH, V.B., *Vospominaniya, 1914–1919* (Berlin 1920)

STARTSEV, V.I., *Ocherki po istorii Petrogradskoy Krasnoy gvardii i rabochey militsii, mart 1917–aprel' 1918 gg.* (Moscow, Leningrad 1965)

STEINBERG, J. [=SHTEYNBERG, I.N.], *Als ich Volkskommissar war: Episoden aus der russischen Oktoberrevolution* (Munich 1929)

STEINBERG [=SHTEYNBERG], I.N., *In the Workshop of the Revolution* (New York, London 1953)

STISHOV, M.I. and others (eds), *Iz istorii Velikoy Oktyabr'skoy sotsialisticheskoy revolyutsii: sbornik* (Moscow 1957)

STRUMILIN, S.G., *Izbrannye proizvedeniya*, 5 vols (Moscow 1963–4)

STRUMILIN, S.G., *Statistiko-ekonomicheckiye ocherki* (Moscow 1958)

STRUMILIN, S.G., *Zarabotnaya plata i proizvoditel'nost' truda v russkoy promyshlennosti za 1913–1922 gg.* (Moscow 1923)

STRUVE, P.B. (ed.), *Food Supply in Russia during the World War* (New Haven, Conn., London 1930)

SUKHANOV, N.N., *Zapiski o revolyutsii*, 7 vols (Berlin, Petrograd, Moscow 1922–3); English ed.: *The Russian Revolution, 1917: Eyewitness Account*, ed., abridged and transl. J. Carmichael (London 1955; repr. New York 1962)
Sverzheniye samoderzhaviya (cf. Mints, I.I.)

TALIN, V.I., *Po perepisi: iz zapisok Sovetskogo statistika* (Berlin 1922)
TAN-BOGORAZ, V.G. (ed.), *Revolyutsiya v derevne: ocherki*, 2 pts (Moscow, Leningrad 1924–5)
TEVOSYAN, V.T. (ed.), *Khlebooborot i elevatorno-skladskoye khozyaystvo SSSR za 40 let, 1917–1957* (Moscow 1957)
TOKAREV, Yu.S., *Narodnoye pravotvorchestvo nakanune Velikoy Oktyabr'-skoy sotsialisticheskoy revolyutsii, mart–oktyabr' 1917 g.* (Moscow 1965)
TRAPEZNIKOV, S.P., *Agrarnyy vopros i leninskaya agrarnaya programma v trekh russkikh revolyutsiyakh* (Moscow 1963)
TRONKO, P.T. (ed.), *Bor'ba za vlast' Sovetov na Kievshchine, mart 1917 g.–fevral' 1918 g.: sbornik dokumentov i materialov* (Kiev 1957)
TROTSKY, L.[D.], *The History of the Russian Revolution* (London, New York 1932–3; repr. London 1965); abridged ed. by F.W. Dupee, *The Russian Revolution* (Garden City 1959)
TROTSKY, L.[D.], *On Lenin: Notes towards a Biography*, ed. and transl. T. Deutscher; US ed.: *Lenin: Notes for a Biographer* (New York 1971)
TROTSKY, L.[D.], *Sochineniya*, 12 vols (Moscow 1924[?]–7); vol. III: *1917 g.*; vol. XVII(i): *Sovetskaya respublika i kapitalisticheskiy mir: pervonachal'nyy period* ... (*1918*).
TRUKAN, G.A., *Oktyabr' v tsentral'noy Rossii* (Moscow 1967)
TRUTOVSKY, V., *Kulaki, bednota i trudovoye krest'yanstvo* (Moscow 1918)
TSAPENKO, M.N. (comp.), *Vserossiyskoye soveshchaniye Sovetov rabochikh i soldatskikh deputatov: stenograficheskiy otchet* (Moscow 1927)
TSERETELI, I.G., *Vospominaniya o fevral'skoy revolyutsii*, 2 vols (Paris, The Hague 1963)
TSYPEROVICH, G.V., *Sindikaty i tresty v Rossii* (Moscow 1919; 2nd ed. Petrograd 1920)
TSYPKIN, G.A., *Krasnaya gvardiya v bor'be za vlast' Sovetov* (Moscow 1967)
Tverskaya guberniya v pervye gody (cf. Ilyin, M.A.)
1917 g. v derevne (cf. Igritsky, I.V.)

ULAM, A., *The Bolsheviks: the Intellectual and Political History of the Triumph of Communism in Russia* (New York, London 1965)

UMNOV, A.S., *Grazhdanskaya voyna i sredneye krest'yanstvo, 1918–1920 gg.* (Moscow 1959)

Ustanovleniye Sovetskoy vlasti ne mestakh (cf. Pankratova, A.M.; Chugayev, D.A.)

USTINOV, V.M., *Evolyutsiya vnutrenney torgovli SSSR, 1913–1924 gg.* (Moscow 1925)

VARLAMOV, K.I. and SLAMIKHIN, N.A., *Razoblacheniye V. I. Leninym teorii i taktiki 'levykh kommunistov', noyabr' 1917–1918 g.* (Moscow 1964)

VARZHO, I.I. (comp.), *Agrarnaya politika Sovetskoy vlasti, 1917–1918: dokumenty i materialy* (Moscow 1954)

VAYNSHTEYN, A.L., *Tseny i tsenoobrazovaniye v SSSR v vosstanovitel'nyy period, 1921–1928* (Moscow 1972)

Velikaya Oktyabr'skaya sotsialisticheskaya revolyutsiya: dokumenty i materialy (cf. Sidorov, A.L.)

Velikaya Oktyabr'skaya sotsialisticheskaya revolyutsiya: khronika sobytiy, 4 vols; compilers-in-chief: I (27 February–6 May) V.V. Kutuzov; II (7 May–25 July) G.P. Makarova; III (26 July–11 September) S.L. Dmitrenko; IV (12 September–25 October) S.S. Tarasova; for sequel *see* Gavrilov, L.M. (Moscow 1957–61) [*KhS*]

VELIKORECHIN, A.I. and SELEZNEV, K.G. (eds), *Pobeda Oktyabr'skoy revolyutsii v Nizhegorodskoy gubernii: sbornik dokumentov* (Gorky 1957)

VENEDIKTOV, A.V., *Natsionalizatsiya promyshlennosti i organizatsiya sotsialisticheskogo proizvodstva v Petrograde, 1917–1920: dokumenty i materialy,* 2 vols (Leningrad 1957–60)

VERKHOVSKY, A.I., *Na trudnom perevale* (Moscow 1959)

VERKHOVSKY, A.I., *Rossiya na Golgofe: iz pokhodnogo dnevnika, 1914–1918 gg.* (Petrograd 1918)

VINBERG, F.[V.], *V plenu u 'obez'yan': zapiski 'kontr-revolyutsionera'* (Kiev 1918)

VISHNYAK, M., *Vserossiyskoye Uchreditel'noye Sobraniye* (Paris 1932)

VOLIN, L., *A Century of Russian Agriculture: from Alexander II to Khrushchev* (Cambridge, Mass. 1970)

VOLIN, S., *Deyatel'nost' men'shevikov v profsoyuzakh pri Sovetskoy vlasti,* inter-university project on the History of the Menshevik Movement, Paper no. 13 (New York 1962)

VOLIN, S., *Men'sheviki na Ukraine, 1917–1921,* inter-university project, Paper no. 11 (New York 1962)

VOLINE [EYKHENBAUM, V.M.], *La révolution inconnue*, 3 vols (Paris 1972)

VOLOBUYEV, P.V., *Ekonomicheskaya politika Vremennogo Pravitel'stva* (Moscow 1962)

VOLOBUYEV, P.V., *Proletariat i burzhuaziya Rossii v 1917 g.* (Moscow 1964)

VOMPE, P., *Dni Oktyabr'skoy revolyutsii i zheleznodorozhniki: materialy po izucheniyu revolyutsionnogo dvizheniya na zheleznykh dorogakh* (Moscow 1924)

VOZNESENSKY, A.N., *Moskva v 1917 g.* (Moscow, Leningrad 1928)

Vserossiyskoye soveschchaniye Sovetov (cf. Tsapenko, M.N.)

Vtoroy Vserossiyskiy s'yezd Sovetov (cf. Butenko, A.F.)

WOYTINSKY, W.S., *Stormy Passage: a Personal History through Two Revolutions to Democracy and Freedom* (New York 1961)

YEGOROV, A.G. and others (eds), *Bor'ba bol'shevistskoy partii za sozdaniye politicheskoy armii sotsialisticheskoy revolyutsii, mart–oktyabr' 1917* (Moscow 1967)

YERITSYAN, Kh.A., *Sovety krest'yanskikh deputatov v Oktyabr'skoy revolyutsii* (Moscow 1960)

YERYKALOV, Ye.F., *Krasnaya gvardiya v bor'be za vlast' Sovetov* (Moscow 1957)

ZAGORSKY, S., *La République des Soviets: bilan économique* (Paris 1921)

ZAGORSKY, S., *State Control of Industry during the War* (New Haven, Conn. 1928)

Zakonodatel'nye akty (cf. Averbakh, O.I.)

ZAYTSEV, V., *Politika partii bol'shevikov po otnosheniyu k krest'yanstvu vo period ustanovleniya i uprocheniya Sovetskoy vlasti* (Moscow 1953)

ZEMAN, Z.A.B. (ed.), *Germany and the Revolution in Russia, 1915–1918: Documents from the Archives of the German Foreign Ministry* (London 1958)

ZEMAN, Z.A.B. and SCHARLAU, W., *The Merchant of Revolution: the Life of A.I. Helphand (Parvus), 1867–1924* (London 1965)

ZLOKAZOV, G.I., *Peterburgskiy Sovet rabochikh i soldatskikh deputatov v period mirnogo razvitiya revolyutsii (fevral'–iyun' 1917 g.)* (Moscow 1969)

Unpublished Material

ATKINSON, D.G.G., 'The Russian Land Commune and the Revolution' (Ph.D. diss., Stanford 1971)

SHCHUPAK, Ya.D., [Unpublished papers] (International Institute of Social History, Amsterdam)

YANEY, G.L., 'The Imperial Russian Government and the Stolypin Land Reform' (Ph.D. diss., Princeton 1961)

II Periodicals, Newspapers and Serials

(Place of publication Moscow unless otherwise stated)

Annales: économies, sociétés, civilisations (Paris)
Arkhiv russkoy revolyutsii (Berlin) [*ARR*]
Birzhevye vedomosti (Petrograd)
Byloye (Petrograd/Leningrad)
Byulleten' Moskovskogo gorodskogo prodovol'stvennogo komiteta
California Slavic Studies (Berkeley)
Cahiers du monde russe et slave (Paris) [*CMRS*]
Delo naroda (Petrograd) [*DN*]
Den': organ sotsialisticheskoy mysli (Petrograd)
Doklady i soobshcheniya Instituta istorii Akademii Nauk SSSR
Ekonomicheskaya zhizn'
Ekonomicheskiy vestnik (Berlin)
Golos minuvshego [Petrograd etc.]
Iskra (Petrograd)
Istoricheskiy arkhiv
Istoricheskiye zapiski [*IZ*]
Istorik-marksist
Istoriya SSSR
Izvestiya Adademii Nauk SSSR: seriya istorii i filosofii
Izvestiya (VTsIK i) Petrogradskogo Soveta rabochikh i soldatskikh deputatov (Petrograd) [*Izv.*]
Izvestiya Tsentral'nogo Voyenno-promyshlennogo komiteta (Petrograd) [*Izv. TsVPK*]
Izvestiya Vserossiyskogo Soveta krest'yanskikh deputatov (Petrograd) [*Izv. VSKD*]
Jahrbücher für Geschichte Osteuropas (Munich etc.) [*JGOE*]
Katorga i ssylka [*KiS*]
Krasnaya letopis' (Petrograd/Leningrad) [*KL*]

Krasnyy arkhiv [*KA*]

Letopis' revolyutsii (Berlin, Petrograd, Moscow) [*LR(B)*]

Letopis' revolyutsii (Kharkov) [*LR*]

Metallist: organ *TsK Moskovskogo oblastnogo komiteta i Moskovskogo otdeleniya Vserossiyskogo Soyuza rabochikh metallistov*

Na chuzhoy storone (Berlin, Prague)

Nachalo (Petrograd)

Narod (Petrograd)

Narodnoye khozyaystvo Petrograd (later Moscow)

Novaya zhizn' : *obshchestvenno-literaturnaya sotsial-demokraticheskaya gazeta* (Petrograd, later Moscow) [*NZ*]

Novyy luch (Petrograd) [*NL*]

Novoye vremya (Petrograd)

Pravda (Petrograd, later Moscow) [*Pr.*]

Pravo naroda (Petrograd)

Proletarskaya revolyutsiya (*PR*)

Proletarskaya revolyutsiya i pravo

Rech' (Petrograd)

Russkaya mysl' (Paris) [*RM*]

Russkaya volya (Petrograd)

Russkiye vedomosti [*RV*]

Russkoye slovo [*RS*]

St Antony's Papers (Oxford)

Severnyaya zarya (Vologda)

Slavic Review, formerly: *American Slavic and East European Review* (Seattle etc.) [*SR; ASEER*]

Slavonic and East European Review (London) [*SEER*]

Sotsial-demokrat: organ *Moskovskogo oblastnogo byuro Sovetov, Moskovskogo komiteta i Moskovskogo oblastnogo komiteta RSDRP* [*Sots.-dem.*]

Sovremennye zapiski (Paris)

Statistika truda (Petrograd, later Moscow)

Uchenye zapiski kafedr obshchestvennykh nauk VUZov Leningrada: istoriya KPSS (Leningrad)

Utro Rossii [*UR*]

Vestnik Narodnogo Komissariata Truda (Petrograd, later Moscow) [*Vestnik NKT*]

Vestnik Vremennogo Pravitel'stva (Petrograd) [*VVP*]

Volya naroda (Petrograd)

Voprosy istorii [*VI*]

Voprosy istorii KPSS [*VI KPSS*]

Yezhenedel'nik Chrezvychaynykh Komissiy po bor'be s kontr-revolyutsiey i spekulyatsiey

Zapiski Instituta izucheniya Rossii (Prague) [*ZIIR*]

Zeitschrift für die gesamte Staatswissenschaft (Berlin)

Znamya: vremennik literatury i politiki (Berlin)

Znamya truda (Petrograd)

Index

agrarian movement, xiv, 10, 40 ff., 186–216, 394–407

agricultural output, 14, 32–4, 36, 38, 183 f., 216, 392, 417 ff., 466; prices, 5, 30, 35–7, 185

Agriculture, ministry of, 35, 162 ff., 178, 201, 500 (n. 41); PC of, 396, 398, 401, 414, 446

alcohol, alcoholism, 23, 29 ff., 182; and violence, 41, 90, 255, 280, 363

All-Russian Central Council of Trade Unions, 97, 111 ff., 300, 304

All-Russian Central Executive Committee of Soviets: convocations: I, 132–4, 150, 310–12, 318; departments of, 134–8; II, 292, 306, 317–23, 328 ff., 333, 336 ff., 351 ff.; III, 337, 444

All-Russian Conference of Soviets, 107, 130

All-Russian Congress of Peasant Deputies: I, 167, 229, 233–8, 245; II (extraordinary), 321, 438–41, II (regular), 247, 437 ff., 441–3; III, 334, 443 ff.; *see also* Executive Committee

All-Russian Congress of Soviets: I, 130–2; II, 270, 290, 306, 310–17, 329; III, 328, 333–7

All-Russian Council of Factory Committees, 272

All-Russian Council of Workers' Control, 272–4

All-Russian Peasant Union, 230–4, 244–6

All-Russian Postal and Telegraph Workers' Union, 105, 293–5, 321

All-Russian Union of Metallurgical-Workers, 102 ff., 298

All-Russian Union of Railwaymen, 105–7, 135, 289–93; executive committee (Vikzhel), 97, 105 ff., 289, 292 ff., 321 ff., 355

anarchism: and Bolshevism, 307; and Constituent Assembly, 528 (n. 85); and factory committees, 83, 87, 89, 263, 268–70; and militia, 279 ff., 286; and soviets, 439, 537 (n. 26); and trade unions, 99 ff., 102, 299 ff., 519 (n. 18); and violence, 198, 253, 257

Avksentyev, N. D., 230, 246 f., 327, 439

'black repartition', 7, 157, 214, 236, 392, 394–418

Bolsheviks: Central Committee, 51, 137, 241, 307, 318, 327, 349; Military Organization, 92, 277, 350; Petrograd committee, 57, 318; VI congress, 149; VII conference, 387; and Constituent Assembly, 137, 324–33, 360; and factory committees, 80-4, 87-9, 263; and insurrections, 253, 256 ff., 307, 310; and mass organizations, ix–xi, 307 ff.; and Mensheviks, 142 ff., 317; and militia, 92, 95, 277; and peasants, 5, 226, 386–92, 400, 445 ff., 451–4, 462 ff.; and soldiers, 118; and soviet congresses, 130 ff., 313 f., 235 ff., 238, 439, 441, 443; and soviets, 113, 124, 126, 139, 141–52, 241, 243, 347, 353, 359–81; and trade unions, 98–101, 103 ff., 106, 107–